D1107347

THE ANCIENT SUN KINGDOMS
OF THE AMERICAS

AZTEC

THE ANCIENT

MAYA

INCA

Victor Wolfgang von Hagen

SUN KINGDOMS

of the

AMERICAS

ILLUSTRATED BY *Alberto Beltrán*

The World Publishing Company CLEVELAND & NEW YORK

ACKNOWLEDGMENTS

The author wishes to thank the following publishers for their kind permission to reprint from the books indicated below.

Farrar, Straus and Cudahy, Inc.: *The Discovery and Conquest of Mexico, 1517–1521,* by Bernal Díaz del Castillo, translated by A. P. Maudslay. Copyright 1956 by Farrar, Straus and Cudahy, Inc. Used by permission of the publishers, Farrar, Straus and Cudahy, Inc.

Harper and Bros.: *Beyond the Mexique Bay* by Aldous Huxley.

Routledge & Kegan Paul Ltd.: *The Discovery and Conquest of Mexico, 1517–1521,* by Bernal Díaz del Castillo, translated by A. P. Maudslay. *Five Letters, 1519–1526,* by Hernando Cortés, translated by J. Bayard Morris.

Grateful acknowledgment is made to Phaidon Press Ltd., publishers of *Pre-Columbian Art: Robert Woods Bliss Collection,* and to Mr. Nickolas Muray, the photographer, for permission to reprint the color plates in this book.

PUBLISHED BY *The World Publishing Company*

2231 *West* 110*th Street, Cleveland 2, Ohio*

PUBLISHED SIMULTANEOUSLY IN CANADA BY

Nelson, Foster & Scott Ltd.

Library of Congress Catalog Card Number: 60–6695

FIRST EDITION

CO
COPYRIGHT © 1957, 1958, 1960, 1961 *by Victor W. von Hagen.* All rights reserved. No part of this book may be reproduced in any form without written permission from the publisher, except for brief passages included in a review appearing in a newspaper or magazine.   PRINTED IN THE UNITED STATES OF AMERICA.

CONTENTS

THE ANCIENT SUN KINGDOMS

OF THE AMERICAS

"Is there such a thing as an impartial history? And what is history?
The written representation of past events. But what is an event . . . .
It is a notable fact. Now, how is the historian to discriminate whether
a fact is notable or no? He decides this arbitrarily, according to his
character and idiosyncrasy, at his own taste and fancy—in a word,
as an artist. . . ."

ANATOLE FRANCE, *The Garden of Epicurus.*

Wooden mask covered with mosaic of turquoise, mother-of-pearl, and pink shell from the Mixtec culture of Mexico. The mouth with large canine teeth indicates that the face is only partly human and represents an animal such as a jaguar. (Nikolas Murray)

INTRODUCTION

WHEN the news of Cortés's exploits in Mexico suddenly burst upon the world in 1519, man in Europe had almost forgotten the very existence of an America. This was understandable. During the years that had passed since its discovery America had provided only false hopes. It had been expected that new foodstuffs would pour out unrestrainedly from the "spiceries" to relieve the monotony of European diet. Broadsides affixed to walls had proclaimed the discovery and books had told of "Joyful Newes out of the Newe Founde Worlde" "of rare and singular vertues of divers Herbes, of Trees and Plantes of Oyles and stones . . ." Even the discoverer of it all, Cristóbal Colón, now Admiral of the Ocean Sea, had fed the illusions by talking without stint of gold, rubies, and silver, which were to be found there more abundantly than in King Solomon's mines.

In anticipation of such riches, a convention between Spain and Portugal early in the discovery had, with the Pope's blessing, divided the Americas; the New World was to be shared between them in exclusivity. The King of France, witty François I, asked to see ". . . that clause in Adam's will which allowed the kings of Castille and Portugal to divide the earth between them . . ." But his irony availed him nothing and these two kingdoms soon settled themselves into the New World. Europe had waited with a certain breathlessness, one gathers from reading the contemporary accounts, and people expected the floodgates of plenty to open up. But, at best, the opening was a timorous settling; the Portuguese merely touched Brazil, and the Spanish confined themselves for the first twenty years to a small piece of the Isthmus of Panama and to the islands of the Antilles. Here was found nothing of the riches so highly vaunted by the original discoverers. Europeans dismissed "America" as yet one more instance of Spanish braggadocio—until there arrived in Seville, on December 9, 1519, the first treasure ship from Mexico.

Its arrival caused a tremendous sensation. Cortés had sent four fantastically attired Totonacs from the Mexican coast to accompany the treasures, and in the golden cache there were bells and jewels, earrings and nose ornaments of exquisite workmanship, and feather ornaments mounted in jewels, and there were even "books such as the Indians use." But that which stirred most was a golden wheel seventy-nine inches in diameter, of a thickness of "four reales,"

13

an Aztec calendar swarming with strange designs hammered out *à la repoussé* of solid gold. From the documents now extant one can still feel the contagious excitement of those who saw these treasures for the first time.

They so impressed Charles I of Spain, who now, please God, was Emperor Charles V of the Holy Roman Empire, that he took them to Ghent, his birth-place in the Lowlands, to impress his vassals by this display of the new Spanish wealth. Albrecht Dürer saw these Mexican treasures in Brussels and wrote of them in his diary (August 27, 1520): ". . . I have never seen anything heretofore that has so rejoiced my heart . . ." Dürer came of a family of gold-smiths and knew the techniques of the craft; as a leading figure in the Renais-sance he had seen much of the art of Europe. "I have seen the things which were brought to the King from the new *golden land* . . . a sun entirely of gold a whole fathom broad; likewise a moon entirely of silver, equally large . . . also two chambers full of all sorts of weapons, armor, and other wondrous arms, *all of which is fairer to see than marvels* . . . these things are so precious that they are valued at 100,000 gulden, I saw among them amazing artistic objects that I have been astonished at the subtle *ingenia* of these people in these dis-tant lands. Indeed I cannot say enough about the things which were before me . . ."

The Italian humanist Pietro Martire D'Anghiera could not say enough about "the two books such as the indians use." He remained "wrapped in astonishment," for to him the "books" were a greater index to the quality this new civilization than the gold. "The Indians of the golden land write in books," he said in his letters to other humanists as he analyzed the tech-nique of the book and the hieroglyphics ". . . which almost resemble those of the Egyptians . . . among the figures of men and animals are those of kings and great lords . . . so it may be presumed that they made report of each one's deeds . . ."

Unfortunately, while the learned debated the Aztec civilization, speculating as to its origin, it was already being overwhelmed and destroyed. Thousands more of these golden Aztec objects, brought to the king as his royal fifth, were melted down and minted into coin to pay off his immense debts incurred by European wars. As for other Aztec "books," and exquisitely made golden orna-ments, these as well as other objects of Aztec culture perished in the Con-quest. In the process of being taken, Tenochtitlán, the Aztec capital was utterly destroyed. "One of the most beautiful cities in the world," wrote Cortés, his eyes brimming with simulated tears as he walked through the stench of the fires and singed flesh. In the end that which survived of Aztec architecture was torn down to build churches and mansions for the victor, and what was not destroyed by man was overwhelmed by the insults of time.

Six years later, in 1527, the Mayas found themselves on the agenda of con-quest: Francisco de Montejo, the would-be conqueror, promised much to

Charles V, his liege lord, more gold than he had received as his royal fifth from the rape of Mexico. At that time Charles V had full need of it; he was at war again, this time with France, and moreover, Sultan Solyman of the Turkish Empire had seized Budapest and was threatening Vienna. At that moment no one in the Spanish court could pay too much attention to the happenings in America.

The Maya conquest went off badly. There was little gold, since they had none. After conquest and pillage, slavery followed. Those chieftains and priests, "in whom all learning reposed," who were not killed took refuge either in flight or silence. No intellectual in Europe ever saw a Maya "book," and since there was little or no gold to act as stimulant, the learned of Europe never had any communication about those marvelously contrived stone cities which the Mayas had built. This was not the fault of the participators in conquest nor the priests nor the administrators who followed. They penned voluminous reports which went unpublished.

New Spanish cities were fashioned out of the rubble of Maya ruins; other unruined temples were torn down to supply building material for Spanish churches, mansions, and administration centers. Ancient Maya T'ho became Mérida, the Yucatán capital "on account of the singularity of its buildings," the size of which, said a Spaniard in 1550, "fills one with amazement." As mere building material Bishop Landa doubted that "it will ever come to be entirely exhausted." It was "exhausted" in two decades. Those Maya structures which survived man's destruction were slowly overrun by jungle verdure until, in time, all of these magnificent cities had vanished.

Peru the real Kingdom of Gold appeared on the horizon just as the Maya civilization was in its death throes. Its conqueror Francisco Pizarro, long in years, empty in learning, although large in human spirit and guile, promised the court a new golden age. Joanna the Mad, the addled-brained mother of Charles V, herself signed his contract for its discovery and conquest.

On May 16, 1532, Pizarro set out from the coast of Peru with his 130 foot soldiers and 40 mounted cavaliers following the Inca royal road to seek the capital of the golden kingdom. In the varied history of man, was this not the most quixotic of journeys—170 men against three million, 170 men dedicated to conquer what was then one of the largest empires on earth? The sequence is known to every schoolboy, how stout Pizarro seized by stratagem the person of the Inca in the midst of his thirty thousand armed warriors and within one half hour—certainly among the most famous thirty minutes in history—subdued his whole empire.

On January 9, 1534, the galleon *Santa Maria del Campo* wharfed in Seville. Officials there who believed they had seen almost everything to be seen in these last fabulous years could not take in with their eyes the treasures that lay there: gold and silver lay piled on the dock, ingot upon ingot, all stamped with the royal seal. In a separate inventory to the king was a list of objects so beautiful that not even the most hardened conquistador in Peru could commit them to the crucible—thirty-four jars of gold, a golden stalk simulating maize, two golden platters, an idol of a man, life-size, over one hundred silver objects, the largest piece weighing 167 pounds. The total was worth twenty million dollars in bullion, and equal twenty times that amount in terms of modern purchasing power. Never in history had so much bullion arrived at a single moment in Europe. It was enough to bring back gold and silver as a standard of coinage. The effect of that treasure ship on the human imagination never quite wore off; even now in Italy when one speaks of something of fantastic value it is a "Perú."

At this golden moment Charles V still had greater preoccupations. He was undertaking the conquest of Tunis, so that ships, men, and money were of supreme importance. This time he did not even stop to look at the fabulous golden ornaments. He did that which for instinctive aesthetic reasons even the most debased of his subjects had not done; he ordered the whole of the Incas' treasure to be melted down into ingots. Of the long ton of original golden ornaments from the Incas' ransom not a single example exists in Spain today.

With that conquest, the animus, the soul, of the Peruvian was forever lost. The physical remains of that immense civilization, the buildings and temples of varying forms and functions that spread over two thousand miles along the Andes and the coast went the way of the conquest. Those which were not destroyed then were later toppled by the civil wars fought between the conquistadors over the carcass of the Inca Empire. As with the Aztecs and Mayas, so with the Incas—churches were either built out of the rubble or were set over the temples; Inca buildings were torn down to provide the stone to build manorial dwellings, and administration buildings were set up among the ruins. The lands being depopulated, a road system nearly as fine as that of the Roman Empire went into decay. The *tampu* resthouses which had appeared along the entire length and breadth of the network were reclaimed by the earth, and the suspension bridges which had spanned the awesome canyons along the route rotted and fell. The ingenious *acequias*, which had conducted water for irrigation into the desert, were neglected. The land was reclaimed by sand.

There were many Spaniards who deplored the disappearance of these cultures. Reports and demihistories called *relaçiones* were penned and so numerous that they filled an entire section of the library at El Escorial. But a book to be printed then had to have *privilegio*—a license showing that it had been approved by the authorities, civil and ecclesiastical—and then had to run the gamut of the King's Council, the Holy Office of the Inquisition, the Council of the Indies, the Royal Board of Trade, and yet more. That is one of the reasons why these manuscripts were not published until the middle of the nineteenth century. So without a continuous literature to make known these cultures, the Aztec, Maya, and Inca civilizations were, so far as the greater part of mankind was concerned, effectively, blotted out from human memory.

It was the Age of Reason that brought about a renaissance of archaeological interest in the Americas. The lure of the antique began with nature worship and "nature worship," so Aldous Huxley once observed, "was a product of good communications. In the seventeenth century all sensible men disliked wild nature." The change came when the French began to overhaul the old Roman roads, and men of quality could travel and "look at wild nature in comfort, and without serious risk . . . Poets responded to the invitation of engineers . . . and the lure of the antique became poetic."

It was Pompeii that provided the means and a Bourbon who provided the spark; knowledge and interest in the archaic, that is, in archaeology, was born. On the night of August 24, A.D. 79 Vesuvius had erupted, split open its seams, and poured down streams of lava. Lava enveloped the countryside, burying, among other minor cities, the larger ones of Pompeii and Herculaneum. In 1748 Charles IV of Naples (his mother was a Farnese) ordered an Italian engineer in his employ to start Pompeii's excavation. Under the volcanic ash he found well-preserved houses and the petrified bodies of people lying in natural positions as if arrested in flight. A whole preserved city was coming to light out of the past. The reports of these activities, along with a display in the museum of Charles IV of the objects dug out of Pompeii, brought numerous literati to Naples. Piranesi, the great etcher of the antique, limned the first picture of excavated Pompeii, artists engraved its monuments, and Winckelmann, the "father of archaeology" was inspired to publish his *History of the Art of Antiquity*.

The search for the antique became a royal passion. The fashion and fervor for it lapped over to America, and after that same Charles of Naples became Charles III, King of Spain, he made his interest in science known by patronizing botanical and archaeological researches. In 1773 the Maya ruins of Palenque lying in the tangled tropical forests of Chiapis, Mexico, were discovered. Their discovery was brought to the king's personal attention. He ordered his officials to explore the ruins carefully, to make drawings and preserve all the artifacts found so that they could form the basis for an *Ancient History of America*. Italian scholars were sent from Spain to Mexico to seek out ancient documents in order to prepare such a history. In 1777, a Mexican, Antonio Alzate, found the ruins of Xochicalco, and few years later, in 1790, while excavations were going on to alter the foundations of the Cathedral of Mexico City, the workmen came across a gigantic monolith—the Aztec calendar stone. Carved out of a single piece of volcanic trachyte, it was eighteen feet in diameter with its center dominated by the figure of Tonatiuh, the sun god, sculpted in large dimensions; ringed about it were symbols of calendric day-signs. In a previous time the archbishop would have ordered it smashed and worked into church masonry; now it was brought intact to the museum.

Its discovery was still an item of conversation in Mexico when news of Napoleon's invasion of Egypt came in 1798. Accompanying the army of thirty thousand were 175 of France's greatest scholars, who were to undertake, after the military conquest, a survey of Egypt's art and history. In the course of this expedition, French engineers found, in 1799, near to the Nile city of Rosetta, a black slab of basalt on which were carved Egyptian texts in three different scripts—hieroglyphic, hieratic, and demotic. Even in the midst of the Napoleonic Wars, men speculated on that Rosetta stone. They believed, and rightly, as time proved, that this black basalt intaglio held the key to the decipherment of the major Egyptian texts.

In Mexico those whose vocation was the antique hopefully believed that the Aztec calendar stone might itself be a form of Rosetta stone; such a speculation was still current when Alexander von Humboldt arrived in Mexico City on April 18, 1803. Already well known—his letters to scientific associates in Paris had been published in various journals—Humboldt had, since 1799, traveled and explored in South America with his friend, Aimé Bonpland, botanist and physician. The Spanish viceroy, José de Iturrigaray, himself welcomed Humboldt and let it be known that since Humboldt carried the King of Spain's rubric whatever he wished to see in Mexico was to be placed at his disposal.

Humboldt has been fully and rightfully extolled for his immense contributions to botany, geography, geology, astronomy, geophysics, meteorology, oceanography, and zoology; yet there is more to him. It was he who brought the buried American cultures into focus. His years of exploration in the Americas gave him a high sense of selection; He collected widely and well, and savants in America confided their collections into his hands. Later when he returned to Europe he searched the libraries at the Vatican, Berlin, Paris, Vienna, and Dresden for additional material. Eventually he set up his residence in Paris and began to publish his famous *Voyage aux régions équinoxiales du nouveau continent,* in thirty volumes, illustrated with 1,425 copper plates— the results of his five years of explorations. The volume on American archaeology was contained in one large folio and published in Paris in 1810 with the title of *Vues des Cordillères et Monuments des Peuples Indigènes de L'Amérique.* This gave the world for the first time a panorama of ancient American history, displayed as never before in accurate scale drawings of Inca buildings, calendar stones from Colombia, bas-reliefs of Aztec sculptures, colored engravings of pages of the Maya *Dresden Codex;* and drawings of the Aztec calendar stone with detailed explanations and numerous illustrations of Aztec, Zapotec, and Mixtec manuscripts with learned commentaries. Under this immense authority America was seen as a civilization with its art placed on the high levels of culture. That volume went through four editions in eight years.

It was the Romantic agony that gave check to the renascence of interest in American archaeology. It was the time of the cult of the picturesque; artists studded their canvases with ruins, turbulent cataracts, and forests of thick-gloomed trees. Language was turgid, people surrounded themselves with gentle melancholy, and it was the time of frightfulness and swooning ladies. It was the age that produced Viscount Kingsborough.

With the writings of Viscount Kingsborough, archaeological literature took a pseudoscientific turn. Archaeology became mysticial, religious, and irrational. It took away from America what it had and gave to it what it had not. The American Indian, so ran the thesis, was not Indian and his culture was not his culture. It was Mediterranean. It was Jewish. And the buildings found throughout the Americas and described by Humboldt had in point of fact, been created by descendants of the wandering tribes of Israel. That the American Indians were Jews was in reality an old theme. It appears early in history. For centuries there had been speculations on the fate of the 27,290 Israelites whom Sargon of Assyria had deported in 722 B.C. When the New World was discovered the Church had to account for the "Indian's" presence, hence it fell back on this theory. There was much speculation and even one so level-headed as William Penn said upon looking at the natives for the first time, "I imagined myself in the Jewish quarter of London."

It was Kingsborough who hardened this arrant nonsense into anthropological fact. Kingsborough was already somewhat fey in 1795 and his later years as an undergraduate at Oxford did not dispel a mystical turn of mind, so that when he saw an example of Aztec pictograph writing, his imagination was aroused and he determined to devote his life to the proving of the "Theory." He eventually gave up his seat in the House of Lords, freely opened his purse, and spent his fortune in collecting Aztec and Maya material. The first volume of his *Antiquities of Mexico* was published in 1830, but by the time the last of the eight folios made its appearance, in 1848, it was a posthumous publication. Viscount Kingsborough, Third Earl Kingston, had died in a debtor's prison for failure to meet a papermaker's bill. As to the text of his work—a potpourri of Greek, Hebrew, Latin, and Sanskrit—its form may be logic but its essence is confusion. There were adjustments of facts to fit preconceived ideas and invocations of scientific accuracy to mask the lack of scientific method. In the *Antiquities of Mexico* the categorically absurd met the ineffably incongruous.

Such attitudes were still popular when, in 1840, William H. Prescott began to write the *History of the Conquest of Mexico.* Few then believed that the Aztecs had reared the buildings ascribed to them; few accepted the fact that the American Indian had ever been capable of producing the civilization described by the early Spaniards. So Prescott went to the original unpublished records that lay in Spanish archives. With the appearance of his *Conquest of Mexico* in 1843, the evidence he had amassed was so formidable and the style of his writing so impressive that Prescott in that one book succeeded in giving America back to the Indians. At the same time, his friend John Lloyd Stephens, a New York lawyer who had traveled "for his health" through Egypt, Arabia, Petraea, Poland, and Russia, was then exploring Central America and helped to provide factual evidence. Stephens himself had a mind sensitive to the nuance of things and a spirited style of writing. With these assets, to which was added extensive exploration in the Maya area, he laid down the broad base of study of prehistoric American culture. Frederick Catherwood, an architect, was his companion. Catherwood had taken part in some of the earliest English expeditions to Egypt and, being thoroughly immersed in the art of the Old World, he was prepared to evaluate what had been discovered in the new. His accurate drawings with the dramatic overtones of Piranesi, illustrated wonderfully well the text of Stephens; together they authored publications which were then avidly read and which time has made into classics of archaeology; *Incidents of Travel in Central America* (1841) and *Incidents of Travel in Yucatán* (1843) continue even now to be republished.

The scientific basis was established. The indigenous American was now known to have been the builder of the cities which had proliferated throughout the land. Prescott had detailed their history out of the records; Stephens had adumbrated a Maya civilization in its entirety. And much progress would have naturally followed—had "Manifest Destiny" not intervened. In rapid succession came the annexation of California, the occupation of Texas, the war with Mexico (". . . I have been carrying on the Conquest of Peru," said Prescott, "while my Government was carrying on the Conquest of Mexico . . ."). And following this came the fervor for new-found gold and the vast empty western lands, ready for the taking, the rise of rail empires and dreams of interoceanic canal—all this interrupted for years what would have been the natural development of archaeological interest. There followed the Civil War with its consequent effect on all that was not purely military, and, when Europe intervened politically in the ancient Aztec and Maya lands by establishing Maximilian as Emperor of Mexico, this brought on years of wars that made the lands of the ancient Sun Kingdoms a place scarcely fit for archaeologists.

As for the Incas, they were still buried in time's oblivion. Peru was in the evening lands, far from Europe and North America, and what was known of its history lay only in literature. But ever since William Prescott had published his *History of the Conquest of Peru,* that historical literature had taken on formidable proportions. Spanish scholars, shocked by the spectacle of a half-blind Boston lawyer, who had never visited Peru (or for that matter, Mexico), writing the epic of Spain in America which they themselves should have written, began after this to publish the mountainous piles of records that lay in their archives.

It was Alfred Maudslay who, in 1880, began the modern phase of American archaeology. A Frenchman met him when Maudslay was in the Chiapis jungle where he had just discovered the Maya ruins of Yaxchilán. The Frenchman was beside himself with anger at not being the first discoverer himself. Maudslay soothed him by saying, "My having had the start on you was mere chance . . . you need have no fear on my account, for I am only an amateur traveling for pleasure . . ." But it was Maudslay's explorations, excavations, and recording of all that was then known of Maya texts (on monuments and buildings) that gave scholars throughout the world a firm basis on which to assault the mystery of the Maya hieroglyphs. He was the spiritual successor of John Lloyd Stephens. Untainted with Anglo-Pecksniffian principles, he was modest to a fault; so little is known about him personally that writers have variously titled him "Sir," "Lord," or "Doctor," none of which he was. Such a dearth of biographical information suggests how reticent he really was. The magnificent plaster casts of Maya texts that he made in the jungles lay in obscurity for many years until they were fetched up to be made into a Maudslay Room at the British Museum. He was little honored, and it was not until 1925 that Cambridge belatedly conferred on him an honorary degree.

After Maudslay's publications, interest in the Aztec, Maya, and Inca civilizations quickened. If no man is an island, neither for that matter is a culture; archaeologists of many nations were drawn to these lost civilizations, and each in his own way, peculiar to the intellectual background of his native land, made his contribution. More and yet more lost cities were rediscovered; and the problems which each new discovery posed grew in number and profundity as the literature mounted.

Something had come out of something. That was immediately apparent to the archaeologists when they began to peel back the layers of accumulated earth; they found one civilization imposed on the other. It was not, of course always in the precise sequence given out by oral traditions, yet it was fully revealing. The civilizations that white man first came upon in the New World were the culmination of centuries of cultural evolution. Wherever the archaeologist worked, each discovery, such as the finding of the bones of man and extinct mammals mingling in fossilized death, pushed man further back into time's horizon. By the very nature of the material that the archaeologist handled, the studies grew complex and technical. Astronomers were brought in to determine how the Mayas without instruments had observed the incorruptible firmament, and how they had managed to calculate very accurately the movements of the planets. Agricultural experts studied the distribution of maize, which, in Middle America at least, was the gastronomic base for ancient cultures. Plant geographers traveled these verdured lands to learn in what manner botany had abetted the rise of proto-American cultures. Geologists were brought in to determine the way in which Maya jade differed from Chinese jade. Physical and social anthropologists measured and calculated, weighed and divided the indigene's soul, and gauged the Indian's physical capacity for hunger and love.

What, after all, is this search for ancient man in the Americas? It is basically a tremendous and fascinating mystery. With the absence of written records such as occur in the Old World what do we have to go on? We have a profusion of strange-sounding names—Toltec, Mixtec, Chibcha, Cupisnique. We have a scale—the vastness of the American milieu. We have an enigmatic plot; Who was this mysterious Plumed Serpent god that permeates the whole of Mexico? Why did the Mayas suddenly abandon hundreds of their cities? Why were the Incas and the Mayas unaware of each other's existence? We have sets of clues from which deductions can be made, clues which might well puzzle a Sherlock Holmes. And there is continual novelty: the finding of tombs, such as that of a warrior god in a beautifully wrought underground sanctuary at Palenque, where a tomb was not supposed to be; or the finding of barbarically beautiful murals, such as at Bonampak in the jungle, unseen by any other human eyes since their abandonment a millenium before. More than a mystery, the quest is also a dream . . . a dream of every archaeologist that someday in the hushed sanctity of the forest he will find a place, a city, a ruin which no other explorer has ever seen. This is a fundamental human instinct, for life exists for the sake of newness. So archaeology is endowed with suspense; it combines the excitement of treasure hunting with romance. Potsherds and mummies, liths and skeletons are all clues on the road of cultural history.

Every technique that objective science offers is used by the archaeologist. The work demands exacting excavations, the study of so unromantic a theme as the shapes of cooking pots, the interpretation of contradictory data about time sequences. These are the minutiae out of which archaeological history is often shaped. In itself it does not make fascinating reading. The high romance of research loses something of its mystery, and with it, its patina of suspense, as the archaeologist cleans, repairs, and catalogues his material. This is the dreary part of the business. "The archaeologist," as the late Dr. Ernest Hooton insisted, ". . . remains inwardly a romanticist."

Does it not ask too much of the researcher that he produce an archaeology without tears? Can one withstand the rigors of excavation, whether it be in the jungle, desert, or high Andes, and then later weave all the discovered clues, those little nothings which are everything, into a book so exciting that anyone can grasp the whole course of a history-less people without exercising the brain? It happens by the very nature of the material that the principal subject, *man,* tends to disappear as the researcher becomes more and more involved in the various forms of evidence that excavations reveal. Since pottery, for example, does reflect stylistically a passage of time, much labor is devoted to this.

Whatever appears in this book, this history of the people of three civilizations that formed the Sun Kingdoms of the Americas, has been generously drawn from this technical literature. The object here, however, is not archaeology, but the history of man as told through archaeology. Samuel Johnson's Rasselas, when he contemplated all the massed buildings of Egypt, said something which in essence sets the theme of this book: "My curiosity does not very strongly lead me to survey piles of stone, or mounds of earth; *my business is with man . . .*" It is with *man*, Aztec, Maya, and Inca, that this book is concerned—his way of life, the manner of social organization, his food, trade and communications, war and religion, and above all his foibles and achievements. Its concern is human. It is not always easy to write about prehistoric people in human terms, for all that is left us are the remains of their art; and though their art speaks to us directly, nothing much else about them does. That is the reason why art is given so large a place in archaeological history. It is much easier, said one knowing writer, to photograph a temple or a painting than to ravel out a people's moral creed or a political philosophy.

However, there exists, as one anthropologist explained, a sort of psychic unity that binds peoples together. Human beings faced with the same problems under the same climatic conditions will come up with similar solutions. These three great contemporaneous civilizations, Aztec, Maya, and Inca, were, more or less, at the culmination of their power when white man appeared on the horizon. And all three had more in common than the mere worship of the sun. They were all American and their social and individual patterns of behavior were based on similar patterns of tribal organization. The Incas were probably completely unaware of the existence of the other two civilizations; yet they often acted similarly.

That man remains man, and seldom changes in basic outlook, despite immense advances in technology, is a great puzzle to sociologists (after all these centuries man has not even added an eighth to the seven deadly sins); in trying to explain these three cultures in their own terms, it is not necessary to quit the domain of man or invent a new vocabulary. What is new is in reality as old as the world itself. A woman's painted lips are a survival of time when the whole face or body was painted with a blood symbol for protection against the unknown; virgin water as a purifier is common to numerous primitive religions, sacrificial wine is nothing else than a blood surrogate—and the eating of the Sacred Host is present in all primitive rituals involving ceremonial cannibalism.

Love and hunger are the axis of the world. They are the fundamental desires and all humanity, in whatever epoch, revolves about them. George Sand, the novelist, saw the world in terms of love and lovers, Honoré de Balzac saw it in terms of hunger—man's feeling for preservation and augmentation, avarice and cupidity, privation and fast, pomp and circumstance. The people of these Sun Kingdoms were motivated by these self-same emotions. Their emphasis on trade and expansion involved ambitions which we can well understand; and such ambitions dominated their politics. Marriage to them was political, the merging of two powerful tribes or families, and this aspect of their life is certainly clear to us. War was the primary weapon of their politics —the growth of one people's way of life at the expense of another; it is a form of politics which we, the living, can well appreciate. Religion was a series of rituals and observances to bend the gods' will to that of man, to make his life on earth an easier one. That his gods resembled himself only shows how very human the Aztecs, Mayas, and Incas were; our gods as well as theirs can be understood in terms of man projected against the infinite.

Those people regarded themselves as the hub of the universe; all else revolved about them. And why not? It is a delusion common to all mankind. Yet the American Indian had no unity; he scarcely ever regarded other Indians as brothers. When we gave all these natives the generic name of "Indians," we imposed a nominal unity upon them which they never felt. To them another Indian tribe, even from an adjacent territory, was just as much a foreigner as the white man; hence, contending tribes aided the Spaniard to pull down their own world. Such obvious human facts as these find an analogy in our own civilization.

The purpose of any work of art, whether it is fiction, history, comedy, or even archaeology, is to make us understand, feel, and even relish the flavor of the time in which the particular work takes place. To engender this "feel" I have tried to weigh the results of scholarly research in terms of my own experiences. I myself—if personal allusions may be permitted—have lived, often over long periods of time, with numerous Indian tribes on a personal and intimate basis. I saw them, studied them, judged them in strictly human terms; and the literature which I consulted, and which is used here, has always been weighed and measured in the light of that experience.

I have made a sincere attempt to remain objective, yet I know that to say this is to deceive; one cannot fail to leave the imprint of one's own prejudices and personality on any work, whatever its nature. So this book is tainted with subjectivity. How can a historian decide what is and what is not a fact? He does so according to his own character and idiosyncracy, his own taste and fancy; in a word, he does so as an artist. Still I have trod the jungles on and off for three decades, felt the persistent sting of the insects, have gone through the usual diseases, climbed the Andes wretched with mountain sickness, been tossed off mules, sat in jails because of understandings or misunderstandings. All this has had an effect on the sharp edges of my romantic agony; they have been smoothed off by plentiful rubbings in the stream of life. When I wanted to know about, let us say, the life habits of the quetzal, that fantastically beautiful bird which yielded its long plumes to Maya chieftains and its name to the Plumed Serpent, I climbed the rain forests and sat it out for six long months, time enough to know its life history, and even essayed its capture in order to gain some insight into how the Mayas were able to supply such fantastic amounts of its plumage without making it extinct. When the origins of Maya and Aztec paper were questioned, I did not contend myself with merely inhaling the dust of libraries but set off to the jungles to collect the paper-making plants and run the gamut of the usual physical inconveniences which one always encounters in research such as this. The microscope, history, and the library only confirmed what was found at the source. Since 1930, then, with occasional intervals for writing and the necessary parentheses for warring and romancing, I have journeyed on many expeditions, large and small, and have lived in all of the lands that formed a part of the Sun Kingdoms of the Americas. Neither the Noble Savage nor his antagonist has prejudiced these materials. There *are* prejudices here; yet my varied activities in the field of ethnography, which have carried me far and wide, have given me some knowledge of local geography—and my selection and interpretation of the material is, in a sense a qualified *praejudicium*.

Beyond the archaeological and historical literature, which is fully acknowledged in the Bibliography and Notes, I have called upon much else that is not technical to give me the phrases and apothegms to help me take these people out of the flow of the purely archaeological and put them back into the human stream of life. I have borrowed much from the original chroniclers to liven up and reshape that which would be understandably dull if I did not give it a covering of humanism to clothe its bare archaeological bones.

There are many persons whom I should like to thank for making this book possible, in particular Robert Woods Bliss, who kindly allowed me the use of his color plates from his Aztec, Maya, and Inca collection; Victor Weybright, Chairman and Editor of New American Library, who had the first impulse for this book and gave it its title; and the staff of The World Publishing Company.

Victor Wolfgang von Hagen

"Silvania"
Lima, Peru
1 April 1961

AZTEC

I. *Jadeite figure of a seated rabbit. It wears a broad belt adorned with skulls and crossbones; attached to the front of the belt is a warrior's head in an eagle helmet. The eyes were once inlaid.* (Nikolas Murray)

The Historical and Geographical Background of The Aztecs

 Of Archaeological Explorers—and Time 1

THE AZTECS, of course, did not call themselves "Aztecs." And very definitely they were not an empire. Moreover they arrived so late on the Mexican scene and were so unimportant when they did come to the lakes, which was Mexico, that not a single tribe recorded their arrival. Their "kings" were in reality elected "speakers" and there were no "halls of Montezuma" (except in song), so that the misconception of there being an "Aztec Empire" is actually a non sequitur of history just as was in fact the Holy Roman Empire (which was neither holy, Roman, nor an empire).

Still the Tenochas, called "Aztecs," were the first of the ancient Sun Kingdoms to be made known to the other world and the first to tumble into Europe's lap, and with this dramatic impact on man's imagination the first impressions cannot be undone; we remain stuck with the "Aztec Empire."

How and why this barbaric American Sun Kingdom fell into the hands of a relatively few *conquistadores* is a twice-told tale; still, no matter how often retold, it never loses its wonderment—how "stout Cortez" made his way into the heartland of Tenochtitlán, seized its "king" and forced it to accept a *pax hispaniensis.*[41]

The literature on the Aztecs is simply overwhelming. There seems not a phase of their life that has not been explored, analyzed and written up; their origins, history, and rebus writing, their religion and calendar, have been gone over again and again; that which remains of their glyph scripts has been published; excavations within and outside the traditional "Aztec Empire" territory are being carried out progressively; for more than two decades reports, well documented and learned, continue to be issued at a rate that is truly astounding. For almost two hundred years some of the great names in literature have written on the Aztecs and their neighbors—and when all of this is seen together in one library it is so formidable in quantity and quality that it would seem almost an impertinence for anyone to write another account of the Aztecs. And yet. . . .

And yet since the Aztecs arrived so very late on the Mexican scene (there were so many cultures before them), and since they were magicbound every moment of their lives—peopling their world with gods and symbols—there has remained in the literature much that is bewildering, so that it is pertinent for their story to be told in human terms. More: since the history of the Aztecs (which involves mythology, astronomy, ethnology, and search into all that went on thousands of years before them) is complicated, it is not always an easy subject to write on or to read about.

There is very little in this life that is definitive, and there is seldom a book that exhausts a subject, particularly one so involved as the Aztecs. The old Roman who said on his deathbed that "much remains to be done and much will still remain nor shall any man after the revolution of a thousand ages be denied the opportunity of contributing something" could well have been speaking of the Aztecs. A concise new account of them does not have to make any apology.

There is now no lack of literary ammunition for it. It was the plaint of William Prescott when he began to write his celebrated *History of the Conquest of Mexico* in 1839[147] that he had to cast his cannons before he fired them, meaning that he had to create his own holograph library by having all the unpublished manuscripts

copied in Spain before he could begin. Such is far from the situation now—the material at one's disposal is awesome.

The Spanish conquerors of the Aztecs were for the most part lettered and literate and they felt the historicity of the moment. Hernán Cortés, who reported history as he made it, was, for his time, considered to be a man of learning; he had attended the University of Salamanca. His famous *Five Letters*[43] to his King-Emperor, written between the intervals of battle, are as alive as if printed in blood. There were others, too, who wrote of the conquest while the flesh of history was still warm. An "Anonymous Conqueror"[7] wrote a *Narrative of Some Things of New Spain and of the Great City of Temestitan;* another, one Andres de Tapia, who involved himself as much with women as with conquest, left his literary impressions of the fall of the Aztecs, a book which pushed him up as it pulled his captain, Cortés, down.[189] The most literary of the chroniclers, Francisco López de Gómara, penned his *Chronicle of the Conquest of New Spain,*[109] and as he was the household chaplain to Cortés, then Marquis of the Valley and full of riches and renown, he blew the glorification of Cortés theme so one-sidedly that it set an old war horse of the conquest, Bernal Díaz del Castillo ("I am now an old man, over eighty-four years of age, and I have lost my sight and hearing . . ."), to dictating his wonderful and ageless *The Discovery and Conquest of Mexico.*[48]

The crusading padres continued the literature where the soldiers left off. In their efforts to effect the change within Mexico from one mythology to another, they perforce studied the languages, the myths, and the round of daily life of the peoples. The most indefatigable of these was Bernardino de Sahagún,[162] who arrived in Mexico in 1529 and who left, after decades of devoted study, a history of the life and times of a people that is invaluable to any who work on the Aztecs. And there were many others. The literature is deepened because of them as well as by such as Dr. Francisco Hernández, a physician sent out by the King of Spain to examine the new plants of the "newfound world"; his five-year plant exploration with the aid of numerous native scribes and artists is one of the great monuments of botanical science[78] and

from it we have a wonderful glimpse into Aztec earth-knowledge.

The seventeenth century belonged to the padres; it was the period of printed vocabularies, dictionaries of Indian languages, breviaries, and a sort of demi-history—a literature they termed *relaciones*. But the eighteenth century brought the Enlightenment and with it an interest in the past, the sort of romantic speculation that appears in Count Volney's rhapsodic elegy to *Les Ruines*.[202] The learned world made much over symbols; the romantic agony was at hand and intellectual interest was rekindled in the remains of the "Aztec Empire."

The youthful Alexander von Humboldt arrived in Mexico in 1803 after four years of strenuous exploration in South America,[216] and with him and *Les Ruines*, the whole of the then available Mexican archaeological material was recast in a modern scientific mold. In 1810 he published, in one handsome folio, the first good reproductions of "American" art.[83]

In England, Edward King, Viscount Kingsborough, who had never seen an American Indian in his life—nor wanted to (for he had already preconceived Indians as having originated out of the wandering tribes of Israel)—was publishing *nine* folio volumes of reproductions of all the known glyph writings of the Maya and Aztec to prove his "American Indians are Jews" theory.[95] It cost him his fortune and his life. But by 1843 William Prescott had given the Indians back to the Indians by the publication of his *History of the Conquest of Mexico*.

Since then no one nation has had a Mexican monopoly. The North Americans, beginning with John Lloyd Stephens and William Prescott, have continued on uninterruptedly for a century; the late George Vaillant, Samuel Lothrop, Matthew Stirling, and Gordon Ekholm, to mention only a few, continue the tradition. The British have never been far behind; they have maintained the line from Frederick Catherwood to A. P. Maudslay, from Zelia Nuttall to T. A. Joyce.[92] It continues with C. A. Burland of the British Museum who carries on the inheritance. The Swedes were also interested in Mexico long before the comparative studies of Baron Erland Nordenskiöld were published; now Sigvald Linné continues it.

The Germans have been active in the Mexican field ever since

Humboldt wrote his first book and brought back to Berlin its first glimpse of Mexican glyph writing; from Eduard Seler to Ernst Förstemann (who helped decipher the Maya glyphs) to Hermann Beyer (who gave much substance to the theoretical studies), the interest and quality of scholarship have been continuous; Paul Kirchhoff[96] maintains it at the present day. The French have been interested since back in 1529, when André Thévet, cosmographer to the King of France, studied the Mexican Tribute Charts which a pirate had pocketed as his part of the rape of the Spanish convoy off Vera Cruz. From the 1840s, when the gentle aristocratic scholar Comte Adolphe de Circourt gave William Prescott aid, until the present-day scholarly work of Jacques Soustelle[182] (mentioned often in this book), the French have been stimulated by *le Mexicain*.

These last archaeological years have belonged to the Mexican scholars. New ruins have been found, restored, and investigated; careful stratigraphical work with advanced techniques has been carried out. The names of the Mexicans who have shown this wonderful capacity to examine their past are so many that a mere recitation of them all would sound like a bibliography—Manuel Gamio, Alfonso Caso, José García Payón, Eduardo Noguera, Ignacio Marquina, to mention only a few—and books, pamphlets, papers, constantly flow out of all this archaeological activity. The result is that the date of emergence of early man in Mexico is continually being pushed back.

All this activity has given rise to a general interest in everything that has formed man's past (for the past is contained in the present just as the properties of a triangle are involved in its definition) and there has been much public interest in the literature. Unfortunately, to have a generous panorama requires lengthy and involved reading. And so while the general reader would like to know something of all this, still the sheer bulk of the material . . .

I have tried to determine, in my manner, the essential quality of the Aztec and put it down in such a literary form as to attract, and not to frighten off before it instructs, the general and curious reader. Throughout I have aimed at simplicity with the object of following the advice of Anatole France, who said to a young writer: "I begin to ask myself whether supreme talent may not consist of writing very simply about very complicated matters."

2

A$_{LL \ MEXICO}$ is divided into two parts: the mountainous and the flat.

The land is one of extremes: the contrasts of the volcanic wastes, the high *mesetas* of thin air, the aridity of deserts, the lush parts folding one upon another, exiling valley from valley, has made this land the love and despair of man ever since he took possession of this Mexican earth.

If a figure must be devised for it, Mexico is shaped like a cornucopia, from the broad open tablelands of its northern boundaries, where bison once roamed, down a thousand miles south to the narrow isthmus where the land tumbles into mountains and tropical verdure with all the luxuriant richness that is centered there, where the Indians found jade, coral, shells, chocolate, amber, rubber, quetzal plumes—the paradise lands to the mountainbound dweller.

Mexico has extremes in climate, and, even though half the land lies in the tropical zone, altitude is more important than latitude. The eastern coast is broader and fiercely rained on by the trade winds; it is more lush, and it was the ground for early civilizations —the land of the Olmecs, Totonacs, Huastecs. The western coast has a narrower fringe of coast line: nature here is not so prodigal and this is reflected in the early cultures; they are threadbare compared to those on the "other side."

The Mexican land rises up from these two shores, sometimes abruptly, sometimes gradually, to the high plateau which is the bulk of the geography of Mexico. Orizaba, a snow-topped mountain (the Aztecs called it "Citlal-tépetl": "Mountain of the Star"),

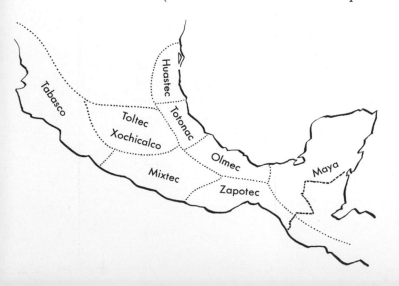

1. *The distribution of pre-Aztec tribes and cultures throughout Central Mexico and Guatemala-Yucatán. The Aztec came into cultural being in the part occupied by the Toltec.*

rises out of the verdured jungle to dominate at 18,000 feet the "cold lands." Here there is the naked misery of soil that the first Spaniards found: ". . . three days' march through a desert land uninhabitable on account of its barrenness, lack of water, and great cold. . . . Oh! the thirst and hunger suffered by the men assailed by whirlwinds of hailstones and rain." [43]

This high mesa land, varying between 3,000 and 10,000 feet, is classic Mexican soil. It has a troubled geology. Volcanoes in times past and continuing up into the present have belched out stone and pumice, tufa and obsidian, transforming much of what could have been fertile valleys into desert wastes. Nature has given Mexico some of the most spectacular scenery in the world, but it has extracted a heavy toll from man who has lived there. There are few navigable rivers; much of the land mass is made sterile by the volcanic outpourings; there are long, dry winters when dust storms carry off the loam and flash floods complete the ruin; there are high semidesert areas which are covered with the thickets of chaparral—cactus, mesquite, and sage. Then this direful aspect is replaced, in another region, with pine forests, and, when the land dips down into a watered zone, there are verdant, exuberant valleys.

Mexico had no Nile-like valley. It had no oases such as appear along the two-thousand-mile-long Peruvian coast to provide an eternal loam even in a rainless land; it had no burden animals—not even the llama. The wheel, had the Mexicans had it, would have done them no good as all is up and down, and high valley is walled from high valley almost throughout the length and breadth of the land; its heights are only passable to foot traffic.

Rain defines the seasons. On the high Mexican tableland it falls, the gods willing, between June and September; the rest of the months are dry except for a caprice of nature, and then it will fall out of season and may even snow in Mexico City, an event often recorded by the Aztec in their glyph history of unusual events.

The gifts of sun and rain not being equal, much of the land has been inhospitable to man. So while Mexico is vast, much of it in ancient times was empty of man and the empty places were where the soil was naked and sterile. The really fertile areas had been occupied since the earliest times, especially that incunabula of cultures, the valley of Anáhuac, the "land on the edge of the water," where Mexico City lies.

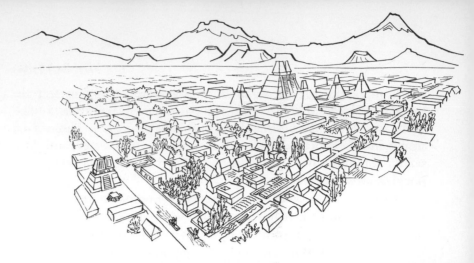

2. *Tenochtitlán as the Spaniards first saw it from the high road that crossed the volcanic ridges surrounding the plateau of Mexico. Today a dry plain, it was a lake at that time.*

Where the mountains rise high in the center of the high Mexican plateau, where the cone of Popocatépetl rears snow-crowned, and beside it the reclining white-woman mountain, Ixtaccihuatl, there is a series of intermontane basins. These begin many miles northward around the fish-filled lakes of Michoacán and form a series of lagoons and lakes culminating about these snow-covered mountains in the valley of Anáhuac. Great civilizations sprang out of this soil; the Toltec, who left behind their immense "Place of the Gods" at Teotihuacán, and the related culture of Tula, farther to the north. The land height being less than 8,000 feet, corn, the essential, grew here, as did much of the other needed things; maguey was plentiful for fibers and the sweetish syrup from which the pulque intoxicant is prepared; the saline lakes yielded salt, a primary basic need for cereal-eating peoples. The volcanoes erupting for untold centuries had piled up layer upon layer, forming inexhaustible rock quarries, source of the obsidian glass which when split became knives, weapons, and razors, and when polished, mirrors; and, for sculpture, a hard gray volcanic stone, capable of being chipped; and a peculiar porous stuff, *tezontli,* usable for building material.

Everything has its reasons—whether they are geographical or sociological. Imperialist cultures were born out of the harsh lands. In the tropic lands where man luxuriated in warmth and sensualism, the expansion mood was limited, but the man who came out of the high country, scoured by wind and hail, was the one with imperialistic ambitions—an effect of geography.

As the Incas in Peru, so the Aztecs of Mexico; they came from the raw, colder zones. By the time the Aztecs emerged as a tribe (circa A.D. 1200), the best lands were already occupied. They called themselves "Tenochas," descendants of northern tribes. In their search for land they had to run the gamut of numerous other peoples, already settled, who disputed passage with them. The hard necessity of war breeds men; peoples grow by and against other peoples to inward greatness, and the Aztecs were landless. They were, as others had been before them, far-ranging animals wandering from necessity—certainly in search of land but also perhaps just out of the "primary microcosmic urgency to move." [183]

So into the lakes of Anáhuac in their year Ome-Acatl, 2-Reed (1168), moved this god-tormented tribe, this "Aztec" people who were to systematize rapine and war into a tribute state and forever leave their impress on the Mexican land.

 The Year of the Spaniard   3

WHAT ARE the imponderables (called the genius) of a people that propel them forward and upward?

In 1168—a date fully accepted by historians—the Tenochas entered the lakes of Anáhuac from the northwest. Landless and friendless and already eyed with dismay by the other tribes settled about the lakes because of their readiness to offer human hearts to their gods, they had little of the outward trappings of human culture. A tribe small in numbers, composed of contending clans and forced out of one settled region after another, they finally selected several islets two miles out in Lake Texcoco and, carrying their god's image before them, they began in 1325 to build their city-state.

Within two centuries they were the overlords of Mexico, and Tenochtitlán, the "Place of the Tenocha," was the most sumptuous city ever raised by indigenous man in the Americas. The Spaniards, who had arrived to make its conquest and add its land titles to those of their Emperor-King, Charles V of Spain, entered "the great city of Tenochtitlán, Mexico, on the 8th of November . . . 1519."

"Gazing on such wonderful sights," wrote Bernal Díaz del

Castillo remembering it vividly after fifty years, "we did not know
what to say or what appeared before us was real." They proceeded
along a "Causeway . . . eight paces in width" which ran "two miles
from the mainland to the city . . . so crowded with people that there
was hardly room for them all . . . the towers were full of people . . .
canoes [came] from all parts of the lake."

Being close to the entrance of the city, they were met by the
"king's" entourage: the Great Moctezuma got down from his litter
and, supported by others, continued "beneath a marvellously rich
canopy of green coloured feathers with much gold and silver
embroidery and with pearls and [jade] suspended from a sort of
bordering, which was wonderful to look at. The Great Moctezuma
was richly attired . . . many other lords . . . walked before [him],
sweeping the ground where he would tread and spreading cloths
on it . . . "

As they entered the city they were hardly able to believe their
eyes. Bernal Díaz remembered that he "could [not] count the
multitude of men and women and boys who were in the streets . . .
in canoes on the canals, who had come out to see us. It was indeed
wonderful, and, now that I am writing about it"—he was then
eighty-four—"it all comes before my eyes as though it had happened but yesterday."

Put to rest in "great halls and chambers canopied with the cloth
of the country," they soon visited the Uei Tlatoani, the "Chief
Speaker," Moctezuma, in his own immense quarters. Moctezuma
lived in Lucullan luxury. "They prepared more than three hundred
plates of the food that Moctezuma was going to eat . . . such a
variety of dishes . . . so numerous that I cannot finish naming
them . . . Four very beautiful cleanly women brought water for his
hands . . . other women brought him tortilla bread . . . He was
served on Cholula earthenware . . . From time to time they brought
him, in cup-shaped vessels of pure gold, a certain drink made from
cacao . . ."

Later Bernal Díaz del Castillo accompanied Cortés and looked
at the stored treasures of this tribute-state and into where Moctezuma "kept the accounts of all the revenue . . . in his books which
were made of paper which they call *amatl,* and he had a great house
full of these books." And they saw the storehouses of cereals and
maize, beans and peppers, brought in as tribute, other storehouses

3. The valley of Anáhuac and the lakes of Mexico.

Although they have five names, the lakes were actually a continuous body of water. Since there was no outlet, the water was mostly saline except in the southern parts (lakes Chalco and Xochimilco) which received fresh streams of water from the snow-topped volcanoes. The system of dikes and causeways was later developed by the Aztec so as to control the salinity of the lakes.

Map labels: Zumpango; Xaltocán; Tlayomulco; LAKE XALTOCÁN; Teotihuacán; Ecatepec; Acolman; Tepexpan; Tlalnepantla; Tenayuca; Texcoco; Tepeyac; Azcapotzalco; Huexotla; Tlacopán; LAKE TEXCOCO; Coatlinchán; Chapultepec; TENOCHTITLAN; Chimalhuacán; Peñón; Ixtapalapa; Mexicalcingo; Coyoacán; Culhuacán; Ayotla; LAKE XOCHIMILCO; Zapotitlán; Xochimilco; Cuitlahuac; LAKE CHALCO; Chalco; Mixquic

full of war dress, "many of them richly adorned with gold and precious stones," and arms and shields and "a sort of broad-swords . . . like to hand-swords set with stone [obsidian] knives which cut much better than our very own swords," and bows and arrows stacked to the high ceiling and "artful shields . . . made so that they can be rolled up . . . and quilted cotton armour."

There was a royal aviary of which Bernal Díaz said: ". . . I am forced to abstain from enumerating every kind of bird that was there . . . from the Royal Eagle . . . down to tiny birds of many-coloured plumage . . . from which they take rich plumage which they use in their green feather work. All the birds . . . breed in these houses . . . each kind of bird has its proper food . . . and two hundred men and women to attend them. . . ."

There were the lapidaries, "the skilled workmen Moctezuma employed in every craft that was practised among them," and "workers in gold and silver" whose wares even the great goldsmiths in Spain were forced to admire (and Albrecht Dürer, also; see pages 12, 153). Then there were those who polished precious stones and jades and "the great craftsmen in feather work, and painters and sculptors . . . the Indian women who did the weaving . . . who made such an immense quantity of fine fabrics with wonderful feather work designs . . ."

The public markets, of which there were four in the city, were dominated by the great market place at Tlaltelolco, and "we were astounded at the number of people and the quantity of merchandise that it contained, and at the good order and control that was maintained . . . Each kind of merchandise was kept by itself and had its fixed place marked out. . . . [There were] dealers in gold, silver, and precious stones, feathers, mantles, and embroidered goods." Then "Indian slaves both men and women" which they brought into the "great market for sale as the Portuguese bring negroes from Guinea . . . tied to long poles, with collars round their necks . . . Next . . . traders who sold great pieces of cloth and cotton . . . and [those] who sold cacao." There was coarse cloth from the maguey fibers, sandals from the plant fiber. In another part "there were skins of tigers and lions, of otters and jackals, deer . . ."

And "those who sold beans . . . vegetables . . . fowls, cocks with wattles . . . hares, deer . . . young dogs—the eating variety— and every sort of pottery made in a thousand different forms . . . those who sold honey and honey paste . . . lumber, boards . . . beams, blocks . . . and the vendors of *ocote* firewood . . ."

"Truly, my Lord," wrote Hernán Cortés, continuing the description of this fabulous city when eloquence had failed Bernal Díaz "Truly, my Lord . . . the great city of Tenochtitlán . . . built in the midst of this salt lake, two leagues from any point in the mainland, is connected by four causeways . . . twelve feet wide . . . the city is as large as Seville or Cordova . . . as for the whole, it is so large I am unable to find out exactly the extent of Moctezuma's kingdom. . . ."

All this—to which, despite its rather Arabian Nights unreality, archaeology has now fully attested—was what the Spaniards found, a luxuriant form of life of a kind which no other people in the Americas had ever attained.

How had it all come about?

The answer—better the explanation—lies in the cultural history that had long preceded the Aztec.

No ONE knows precisely how early it was that man first migrated to the Americas. That man arrived as Man, that he did not grow out of any subhuman present in this continent (there was none), all are in agreement. But how did he arrive? Did he come socially matured, a cultural beast full-blown from the brows of Outer Asia—why, asked Herodotus in irritation, must the continents always be named after women?—casually wandering into the new land while following the spoor of mammals across that high bourn, the Aleutian land bridge from Outer Mongolia to the Americas; or did he come in a series of migrations over a long period of time from his Asiatic spawning grounds, sufficiently conscious of "something" out there, and continue these treks century upon century? Or did he come self-propelled in fragile open dugouts across these agitated seas and arrive fully accoutered in cultural panoply to impose himself on his dim-witted cousins earlier arrived?

No one really knows. And the controversy is as old as the discovery of the Americas. The omniscient Church collided at once with reality. If the flood as detailed in the Bible was true, if it destroyed all mankind except Noah and his chosen family to repopulate the earth, how did these Americans get to that continent, and, moreover, who were they? Where theologic logic failed, dialectics was triumphant: the Indians of course were Jews—one of the lost tribes of Israel. There are many labored tracts on this theme, written by the first padres in America.[64] One Fray Diego Durán— the rational part of whose pioneer work in Mexico is used often in this book—wrote that "the supposition is confirmed . . . these

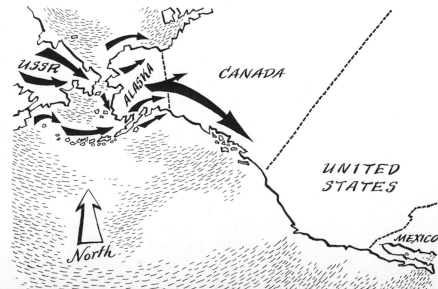

4. *The origin of man in America.*

natives are of the Ten Tribes of Israel that Salmanassar, King of the Assyrians, made prisoner and carried to Assyria in the time of Hoshea, King of Israel." The Church may have resolved God's anthropology but had not settled it among the philosophers; the famous Huig de Groot, pioneer of international law, believed in the seventeenth century that the North American Indians were Scandinavian, the Peruvians, Chinese, and the Brazilians, African. He was immediately answered by his countryman Johannes de Laet, who was stirred to great rage over so inept a deduction. Anyone, he wrote, except a dunderpate could see that the American savages were in reality—Scythians. By this time writers of Cromwellian England were involved in the controversy. Thomas Thoroughgood claimed that he had heard from a rabbi in Holland, who had been entertained by a community of Jews in Peru, that the Indians practiced circumcisional rites; that was all the evidence that he needed to compose his pamphlet *Jewes in America.* But he was soon challenged by another writer, whose tract was entitled *Americans no Jewes.*

So it has gone on through the centuries. Edward King, Viscount Kingsborough, was a victim of it. The Church of the Latter-day Saints, whose sacred Book of Mormon traces this genealogy, even today finances with "Golden Tablets of Moroni" highly equivocal research to support the theory that the American Indian is a descendant of one of the tribes of Israel.[178]

Anthropologists would be delighted to have so simple an explanation of the peopling of the Americas; instead of which . . .

Instead of which there are many theories and of sufficient variety to fit anyone's wishing. The theory that has long prevailed in anthropological circles is that man came out of Asia more than forty thousand years ago, abysmally primitive and in the early neolithic stage* of development, and his culture was arrived at by independent invention in the new American land. The wave of land migrations stopped after climatic change and after the Bering Strait "land bridge," subject then as now to constant earthquakes

---

* The Neolithic or New Stone Age is the period when men began to be food producers (after 5000 B.C.); before that was the Mesolithic, (10,000 B.C.) when he was a hunter and fisher; as Paleolithic man (15,000 B.C.) he was a food-gatherer and occasional hunter. All of the early cultures in the Fertile Crescent of the Near East, Sumerian, Egyptian, etc., were Neolithic.

with upheavals and subsidences, finally sank under Arctic waters.

This theory, upon which archaeological theories pyramided, is under siege from many quarters; archaeologists, botanists, geographers have attacked it as untenable. There are fifty "strikingly similar" features between Pacific island cultures and those of America, only to be explained by trans-Pacific diffusions. The "diffusionists" insist that crossings between the continents, by raft, ship, or outrigger, appear to have been numerous. Even though there is no proof, these theories have subsisted on the basis of faith, and now in the last years, of passionate feeling. But a feeling does not adduce its reasons. It has none; they must be lent to it. There is no positive proof on either side of the anthropological fence. Arguments, weighty and frivolous, are many. This has led one British scientist to conclude that "however, the cogency of such arguments, and there are [good ones] on both sides, is not generally accepted as convincing and it may be perhaps admitted that the position taken on either side is fortified by faith. . . ."

However, until someone comes along with facts that can be weighed in the balance, the American Indian had his cultural beginnings *here*. Early Neolithic man was a land wanderer, not a seafarer; he followed the spoor of animals and he came out of Asia over a land bridge which had been used for aeons of time by the mammals. So, in keeping with the opening leitmotif, which allows me to select "according to my character and idiosyncrasy, at my own taste and fancy—in a word, as an artist," it came about in this manner:

It was the end of the Ice Age and a new world was forming. The glacial ice that had held the world in eternal winter was melting and pouring brawling streams of frigid water into the agitated ocean. Plants that had survived pushed their pallid heads out of the tundra; spores of seeds, wafted on the streams of warmer air, found root, and, under the climatic change, rank luxuriance gradually usurped the place of ice. Over the face of this strange new green earth, after long periods of evolutionary progress, man, *real* man, appeared. He is not out of the pale of world memory; three hundred centuries ago he was making zoomorphic engravings on the walls of caves, creditable intaglios of bison, mammoths, deer, wolves. In body he was a completely formed type; he had wit, ornament, and a technique of living. The massive herds of mammals that roamed the earth soon made the acquaintance of this tool-using primate. He followed them, flowing around the Mediterranean and crossing it. He wandered through the wilderness of the Nile into the sylvan lands of India, Java, China, and throughout the whole of Eurasia. Finally he broke into that world-in-itself, Mongolia.

Slow century followed slow century and the metamorphoses of time were making changes in this primitive man—the descendants of the *pithecanthropi* were becoming distinct peoples. These Siberian dwellers had black, coarse hair and straight, flat, beardless faces with cheekbones in prominence and eyes indexed by the epicanthic fold. They were already, at this time, using stone celts for tools. Some of them then mutated out from their world and moved into an utterly new one: forty thousand years ago, these men with the Mongoloid eyes, following the northern paths of mammals, made the first invasion of the Americas.

Primitive man came to America over its roof. Westward from Alaska are twelve hundred miles of islands. The geologic residue of volcanic action, they stretch out in an endless chain across the Bering Sea within sight of outer Siberia. Once they were a land bridge, a connecting link between continents, and over them for countless ages had surged herds of proto-camels, proto-tapirs, and mammoth elephants crossing over from America.

It was the end of the Ice Age when this man came to America. We know of his presence, for he has left his bones commingled in fossilized death with extinct animals. Throughout the centuries following this migration these people moved down the unglaciated Alaskan corridor into the vast land theaters of America. Within five centuries they penetrated the most remote corners of the hemisphere, from icebound north to icebound south, covering eventually America's entire 135 degrees of latitude. Living here on the shores of frozen or tropical waters, at altitudes varying from sea level to several thousands of feet, living there in forests, grassy plains, or deserts; here starved, there in plenty; here with a night of six months' duration, there a night twelve hours long; here among health-giving winds, there cursed with disease—ancient man in America, greatly varying in his cultural milieu, was emerging into a new creature: *Homo Americanus.*

In 5000 B.C. this American did not much differ in his cultural accomplishments from primitive man elsewhere. At the time man in the Nile Valley was cultivating millet and barley and laying down the agricultural base upon which Egyptian civilization was to flower, the "American" was selecting the wild plants which would become his maize, potatoes, tomatoes, beans, and squash, on which he, too, would build his civilization.

In only one respect—and this is an important one for American cultural history—did he differ from the Eurasian. There was no Metal Age: man here never quit his Neolithic horizon, and his tool, although he did invent soft bronze, remained the tool of the *pithecanthropi*, the stone celt.

By the time the Egyptians had reached their cultural apogee and erected the Temple of Amon in 2100 B.C., the Babylonian civilization had come and gone; the legendary Cadmus had left the legacy of the alphabet, and the glory that was to be Greece was still contained in societies of Hellenic men abysmally primitive.

In America by that time, the period of great wandering had come to an end; vast spaces of the American earth were men-filled. Out of these cysts of geography cultures came into being. In the hyperborean regions, the Eskimo, flat of face and rotund of body, still lived in the environments of the Ice Age; on the North American plains, tall, keen-eyed tepee dwellers regulated their lives to the biology of the roving animal; farther south, where the caress of the sun was longer, the Indian, becoming partly sedentary, cultivated his plants and under the shelter of rock eaves erected crudely constructed pueblos. At the other extreme of America, the antipodal south, giant Fuegians, their naked bodies wrapped in guanaco skins, walked the frozen tundra, leaving the imprint of their widely spreading feet, "patagones," on the firebound land, Tierra del Fuego.

In the luxuriant jungles of that same South America, naked Indians with filed teeth hunted man and beast; while west of these dwelling places of the Amazon and the Orinoco was the evening land of the Andes. There in the high, cold, dun-colored valleys, a huge-lunged people were developing a great civilization. Around a frigid Andean lake called Titicaca, an Aymara-speaking race had, by the year 1000 B.C., laid down the agricultural patterns that would become Tiahuanaco, while around them and strewn over the rock-hard world there were many other tribes speaking Quechua, a related language. In time these "Incas" would form all the other Andean tribes into an empire. North of the Incas were the Quitus; north of the Quitus the territory of the Chibchas, whose strange custom of having their "king" wash off his gold-dust-smeared body in a mountain lake was to create the myth of El Dorado.

Between these geographic monsters, North and South America, lay Middle America and Mexico, their broken mountains studded with belching volcanoes. They were to be the scene of the great civilizations of ancient America.

Most of Mexico had a homogeneous culture. Whether it was Totonac, Toltec, Zapotec, Huastec, Maya, or Aztec, tribe was developed from family; animal diet was supplemented by crude agriculture—plots of ground were burned and seeds inserted in holes made by a fire-hardened stick. Agriculture revolved around corn as the staple, and society was then, as it has remained ever since, machineless. There were no draft animals; the denominator of speed was the foot. Dress was the breechclout; men walked on sandaled feet and women wore a short-petticoated cincture of woven cotton cloth; bare breasts matched bare feet.

In all these tribes society was organized on cognate kinship; the unit was the clan, and each clan had a totemic name. Together these clans became a tribe, bound not by the holding of land but by the ties of blood. Equally homogeneous was their religion. Belief was animistic: everything in their world, animate or inanimate, possessed "soul," everything was alive, sentient, willful. Gods, both good and evil, had to be propitiated; and art, when it evolved, became dedicated to the metaphysics of this theology. Stoneworking was universal among them. The tides of cultural inheritance ebbed back and forth among all tribes of Mexico and Middle America until that which had been the exclusive cultural property of one tribal kin became the cultural currency of all. There was no later cultural intrusion from either Europe or Asia—within itself and by itself, the Americas created their own world.

THE TENOCHAS, called "Aztecs," were the last to arrive at the valley of Anáhuac.

In point of historical fact they were so late in becoming the overlords of Mexico that other greater civilizations had come and gone and were only vague memories in mythology. The sole reason that "Aztec" is so deeply ingrained in history and man's knowing is that it was the dominant political tribute state at the time of the Spanish conquest in 1519, even though its domination was only over a portion of central Mexico. However, when "Aztec" burst upon Europe, it was etched deep in human memory. Today's Mexico had then no generic name, and so the name of the island tribute state "Mexico" was imposed upon and over the whole of the land.

It was only much later when the Spanish priest-chroniclers began to question the Indians in regard to their origins and beliefs that they were made aware of the pre-existence of civilizations far, far older and far greater than the Aztecs.

Decades of patient archaeological search have now revealed, all in all, a good deal about these pre-Aztec cultures; with each year scholars are pushing back time. "The earth became our archive," wrote George Vaillant, "the shovel, our reading glass, and in that which nature has eternally destroyed—scattering our materials all over the land," [198] they found and are continuing to find this new archaeological evidence.

By 1000 B.C. the great migrations were over. Peoples filled the fertile lands and were beginning to build temple-cities. In central highland Mexico, throughout the hotlands of Vera Cruz, and in the highlands of Guatemala, they laid down their city centers. Man became sedentary; he had developed agriculture and he knew leisure. During the same period in the "other lands," the Phoenicians were devising the alphabet, the Greek-Dorians were arriving in the Peloponnesus, and Europe, thinly populated, was coming out of raw savagery.

One tribe was already evident: the Olmecs (800 B.C.–A.D. 600?), who lived in the hotlands of Vera Cruz and Tabasco; 800 B.C. marks the beginning of the preclassic period in Mexico.

It was long suspected that the Olmec would prove to be one of the earlier cultures and now radiocarbon dating from the Olmec site at La Venta has confirmed the evidence that Olmec structures "appear to have been constructed and used during . . . four centuries . . . 800–400 B.C." [51]

In Aztec mythohistory, the Olmecs were known as "the people who live in the direction of the rising sun" [32] and a glyph history of them shows that their paradisiacal "wealth" consisted of rubber, pitch, jade, chocolate, and bird feathers. We do not know what they called themselves. "Olmec" derives from *olli* (rubber); their symbol, often seen, is that of the tree of life, the "weeping wood." They traded rubber and they presumably made the rubber balls used for the game called *tlachtli*. A talented and mysterious people, they appeared as early as 1000 B.C. along the Isthmus of Tehuantepec (where the waist of Mexico is slender and level between the two oceans), but they were particularly centered about the Coatzacoalcos River basin on the Gulf Coast. For untold centuries burial mounds and pyramids built by them lay covered by the jungle; here archaeologists have found carved jade, sensitively modeled clay figurines "of an unprecedented high artistic quality," [46] said Miguel Covarrubias.

Only in recent times have the great Olmec stone heads been unearthed, by Dr. Matthew Stirling. At Tres Zapotes he found one colossal head, seven feet high, flat-nosed and sensually thick-lipped. The carving is sensitive and realistic; the style is found among no other people and once seen will never be forgotten or confused with any other. Other colossal heads have been found; in similar style there are carved masks, heads in smaller scale, and votive axes, all exhibiting the same squat figures with perforated noses, pronounced Mongoloid features, and narrow slits for eyes. These have been found in widely scattered areas. The Olmec large-scale monuments, however, are found mostly between Vera Cruz, Tabasco, highland Guatemala, and Oaxaca—this is definite Olmec land. A stela found at Tres Zapotes and numbered by the bar and dot system, bears what is by far the earliest recorded "American" date: 31 B.C.

Only now are Olmec structural complexes coming into focus. They had temple-cities, erected stone stelae to mark the flight of time or to commemorate important events; the stepped pyramid, the courtyard, the *tlachtli* ball game, were all cultural features in general use. The Olmecs still occupied their traditional tropic land when the Spanish first arrived. There is no record of them beyond the observation that they tattooed their bodies, inlaid their teeth with jade, flattened their heads, plucked their face hair, hunted heads for trophies, flaying the skin and tanning them as the Jivaros in the Upper Amazon did the tsantsas, the shrunken human head trophies.

The art of the Olmecs is unique—simple, direct, forceful. There is nothing quite like it in all Mexico. Yet aside from this "art" they must have been possessed of certain social dynamics to stamp their pattern on Mexico's cultural history.

The Mayas (2000 B.C.–A.D. 1697), who appeared early, had a great influence over the development of culture in Mexico and were the longest-lived. For what length of time they built their temple-cities before their first calendar was set up is not known. The earliest stela, at Uaxactún, is dated A.D. 328.

From the earliest times there was much cultural interchange among all these peoples. A large trading area at Xicalango in Campeche was the Maya contact center for the outside world where, under terms of peace, things of their lands were exchanged with Central Mexico. Possessed of large and traditional tribal lands, the Mayas, free of any large-scale outside invasion until the

5. *Olmec culture, symbolized by the great stone heads with thick lips and broad nostrils, found in the hotlands of Vera Cruz and Tabasco. The Olmec culture dates back to and beyond 800 B.C.*

6. *Zapotec art, which centered about Monte Albán, is typified by this funeral ceramic.*

twelfth century, perfected their calendar, glyph writing, and stone carving, and evolved the complex temple-cities which can still be seen today. Their influence on the other cultures in the high Mexican plateaus was very marked.

Monte Albán (500 B.C.–A.D. 1469), a ceremonial center and temple-city, lies in Oaxaca atop high treeless hills overlooking the valley and the present-day Spanish city of the same name. One of the oldest in Mexico, its occupation continued from the earliest preclassic period, perhaps as early as 1000 B.C., until the coming of the Spaniard in 1522. This immense time period of twenty-five hundred years is divided into five archaeological horizons. Its beginnings are shrouded in mystery. Dr. Alfonso Caso, who first uncovered it and has worked on its problems continuously for twenty years, believes that its formal structures date as far back as 500 B.C. Even as early as this they had already developed glyph writing, a calendar, and a complete cosmogony.

Who were the early builders? From the beginning it seems it

was a city, although not habitable, of the gods, visited by men and women alike. Before the city (its original name is unknown) took on its Zapotec character, it had from the earliest times a temple with a frieze of dancing figures done in the Olmec style, a "powerful and mysterious archaism of expressive monsters." These Olmec-styled figures and stelae, with the still indecipherable glyphs, are the primary mystery of Monte Albán.

One will grasp how really early all this was if one remembers that in the same period of world history Nebuchadnezzar was destroying Jerusalem and carrying off the Jews to their first slavery; Cyrus, king of the Persians, was on the loose and the whole Middle East was in an expansion mood; by the time the people of Mexico were beginning to set up their temple-city states, Xerxes had conquered Egypt and was setting off to invade Greece. Although the American man had none of the stimulation of the Fertile Crescent of the Near East—which brought the wheel, iron, and the alphabet to the world—he was advanced in city planning, writing, and sculpture.

At about A.D. 300 Monte Albán moved into a transition period, threw off its Maya influence, and turned to its own sources—the Zapotec. For the four hundred years that followed, the great plaza was enlarged, and temples, pyramids, ball courts, and the frescoed tombs were constructed.

The Mixtecs (668*–1521), whose capital city was Cholula (the present-day Puebla), occupied a geographical buffer zone between the coast and the highland; they were subject to all the recurring waves of conquest, first from the coast (Olmec), then from the highlands (Toltec). Later they became conquerors; after 1350 they extended south into Monte Albán, only in turn to be overrun by the Aztecs after 1450.

The Mixtecs have wondrous tales to tell of themselves. The Indian noble Ixtililoxochitl, writing in the seventeenth century, told of giants and Olmecs and much about the pyramid to the Plumed Serpent, the greatest in all the Americas.[88] Quetzalcoatl was a mysterious figure through all Mexico and Yucatán. That he once

---

* This date was reached by Covarrubias by deducting the five hundred years of Olmec occupation of Mixtec land, mentioned by Juan de Torquemada in his *Monarquia Indiana* (Madrid, 1723), from the date of 1168, when the Olmecs were driven from Cholula.

7. *Mixtec art forms resemble the Aztec. Mixtec civilization, beginning as early as 700 B.C., was centered about Cholula. The illustration is taken from a part of a Mixtec codex, an origin myth.*

lived can be assumed (later rulers of the Toltec took his name as a patronymic just as Moslem rulers today carry the name of their prophet or the Romans called themselves "Caesar"). It is difficult to separate man from myth. Quetzalcoatl was a demiurge, priest, and ruler, conceived by virginal birth years after his father's death (his mother was made pregnant when she swallowed a piece of jade); he was ruler of the Toltecs for twenty years. He lived in Tula, lost a civil war,* fled with a good-sized Toltec force, reached the Coatzacoalcos River on the day of 1-Reed in Aztec reckoning (the sign under which he was born), and set sail into the open sea with the prophecy that he would again return on the recurrence of that date.

* What perhaps was a real political struggle for power between two concepts of government—the peace-loving "positive" Quetzalcoatl against the "negative" Tezcatlipoca, "Smoking Mirror," who brought the terror—was rationalized to "correlate historical events with an older mythus." [198]

He left his impress on the Mixtecs, who, like the others in this high cultural period, had writing and paper (some Mixtec codices survive). They were advanced in the arts of building and in agricultural and social planning, and, despite wars of rapine and conquest, their cultural influence lasted over thousands of years; they greatly influenced the Aztecs.

The Huastecs (500 B.C.–A.D. 1521), who occupied northern Vera Cruz and extended inland as well to include highland Mexico (now the states of Tamaulipas, San Luis Potosí, Hidalgo, and Querétaro), have also been determined to have been one of the earlier cultures,[26] enduring in more or less continued activity for two thousand years and silenced only by the arrival of the Spanish. The distinctive art forms of the Huastecs have been known for many decades, but it is only in the last fifteen years that Huastec architecture has been uncovered.[27]

The Totonacs, "discovered" by the collectors of modern art because of their nonobjective art styles, also appeared during the preclassic period. The Totonacs had, so far as it is known, an uninterrupted cultural continuity in central Vera Cruz from approximately 500 B.C. until the arrival in 1519 of Hernán Cortés. They formed a sort of linguistic "sandwich" between the Olmecs and the Huastecs, who were of Maya stock and speech. Totonac country has yielded for many decades some of the "finest and most sophisticated specimens of Indian art"[29]—the freehand clay figurines always in laughter; the "laughing heads" and life-sized stone heads attached to a tenon, meant to be placed in walls as an architectonic motif; the strange U-shaped objects as large as horse collars and resembling them in size and shape, carved from polished green or black stone, exquisitely decorated and made for an unknown

8. *One of the Totonac "laughing heads."*

9. *Totonac architecture is typified by the temple of Tajín at Papantla in Vera Cruz. The niches held small idols; the temple was atop the pyramid. The Totonacs began as far back as 500 B.C. They were a functional tribe in full flower when Cortés arrived in 1519.*

purpose. This art, gay, sybaritic, a contrast to the austere Maya or Aztec form, is a Totonac characteristic. They also left behind an impressive number of temple-cities which, although covered by jungle and eroded by the centuries, still retain their form, so that Mexican archaeologists are able to restore them. All this culture which had been nurtured for a thousand years was at the disposal of the Aztecs.

In the valley of Anáhuac, in the central Mexican plateau, after 200 B.C., the Toltecs learned better management of their agriculture and produced a social surplus. With that, Teotihuacán came into being.

Toltec-Teotihuacán (200 B.C.–A.D. 900), "Place of the Gods," thirty-two miles northeast of Mexico City, dwarfs in magnitude all else in Mexico and Middle America (save perhaps Tikal in Guatemala); the remains of the great ceremonial city alone cover an area of eight square miles. It challenges the imagination how the Toltecs at so early a period could have marshaled so many people—with enough leisure, unoccupied with their fight about the feeding trough—to build and maintain so enormous a religious center. So renowned was Teotihuacán that it served as model for all subsequent temple-cities, and the Toltecs remained—even when monuments were covered and were only a vague memory—the master builders, and thereafter all artisans who were masters, especially painters and *tlacuilo* writers, were called "Toltec" even down into Aztec times.

The history of these Toltecs, less vague when read in the light of recent archaeological findings, is found in the *Annals of Cuauhtitlan;* later, less speculative literature[107] and further exploration and excavation have filled in the gaps. The Toltecs spun in cotton, which means that they maintained contact with the hotlands, as cotton does not grow in the high plateau; men had thicker garments for cold weather and women dressed in loose-fitting *huipilli* and wrap-around skirts; warriors wore (as did the Aztecs one thousand years later) quilted cotton armor; their weapons were like those of the Aztecs; and their priests, as did the Aztecs, went about filthily in unwashed black tunics that swept the ground. Their chiefs dressed as did the common man, only more elaborately, and they were monogamous. In their houses the Toltecs constructed the *temascal* steam bath, a common feature among the Aztecs.

When Toltec history emerges through the myths that surround it, it follows a pattern. A priest-astrologer guided them through Mexico until they found a fertile valley. There they built their city of Tollan or Tula. The chronology of their kings, which must have been chanted for centuries, was etched into the memory pattern, so that when repeated to a double-languaged scribe and set down in

10. *Toltec-Teotihuacán was the classic culture of the valley of Mexico. It endured from 200 B.C. until A.D. 900. The symbol of Quetzalcoatl—a serpent's head wreathed in quetzal plumes—is Toltec.*

the sixteenth century, it gave the names of their rulers. It told of Toltec dominance under their eighth ruler, a rule which embraced all the land between Jalisco to the north and Cuernavaca to the south; it told of the elaborate ritual of their polytheistic religion and it mentioned in detail the woman known as *Xochitl* (pronounced "sho-chitl"), who made popular the beverage now called "pulque" by fermenting the juice of the maguey plant.

Like their rivals of the same period, the Toltecs of Teotihuacán had ideographic writing, tribal records, *amatl*-paper books which pictured their bewildering cosmogony; they also had the fifty-two-year cycle, magical *tonalpohualli* (the numeration of fate), a system of prognostication based on a period of 260-day count, and a lunar calendar for everyday use. And they built the awe-inspiring temple-city Teotihuacán.

Teotihuacán endured from 200 B.C., the approximate time of its shadowy and tenuous beginnings, until about A.D. 900. Its period of slow decline is revealed in its pottery. Here is reflected the gradual change that came over a tribe that lost its political power but kept its respect among others. Another tribe, the Chichimecs, moved into the Toltec domain and took up the remains of "empire" but found themselves swallowed up in the chaos between the years 1100 and 1300 that followed the breakup of the "age of cultural unity." [198] Meanwhile the Toltecs, now migratory, developed two other cultural areas, Tula and Xochicalco.

Tula (A.D. 900–1156) is of the greatest important. Tula, which was once regarded as pure mythology—prompting an ironical remark by one writer about the "vague science of anthropology and the exact art of myth"—has been confirmed by archaeology. The very close resemblance of its architecture to the cities of Mayapán, principally Chichén Itzá in Yucatán, confirms the trek of the Toltecs to that region in the twelfth century. Is this Tula, the legendary "Tollan" as described by the padre-chronicler Sahagún, the beautiful city "of rich palaces of green jade and white and red shell, where the ears of corn and pumpkins reached the size of a man, where cotton grew in the plant in all colours and the air was always filled with rare birds of precious feathers . . ."? If Tula is Tollan, eight centuries have changed the land. It is now dry, parched, dust-filled, and no "precious bird" in its right avian mind would go there.

And yet the description of the city is not as mythical as first believed. Archaeologists found elaborately carved and painted walls, a stepped pyramid with the remains of a temple at its summit, with the symbol of Quetzalcoatl—two stone-painted serpents fifteen feet high acting as caryatids for the elaborate façades of the temple; carved pillars for the temple of the warriors; immense stone-carved figures; and that sculptural idea which traveled farthest, the reclining figure of Chac-Mool looking blankly into space and holding a stone tray on which palpitating human hearts were placed as food for the gods. This same frightening figure, without any change, was to be carved and set up in the capital of the Aztecs, and was to find its way eight hundred miles south into Yucatán.

Xochicalco (A.D. 700–1200), of Toltec origin or influence, with its famous temple to the Plumed Serpent, was built more or less at the same time as Tula (A.D. 900). Lying lonely in the sun on top of bare hills, not more than twenty direct miles south of Cuernavaca, it was one of the first "ruins" to enter literature, having been explored by Antonio Alzate in 1777 and illustrations of it published in 1810 by Alexander von Humboldt.

Xochicalco, "Place of Flowers," was a ceremonial, perhaps administrative, center for the tribes which lived in this region. It is situated on the highest hills, looks down upon two freshwater lakes two miles distant, fish-filled, with much game and a fertile country and in a strongly fortified position. The hills were artificially flattened and terraced with strong points for defense. Four roads coming from the four cardinal directions led into the principal plaza, where the temple to Quetzalcoatl stands. The Aztecs knew of it and were influenced by it.

11. *Tula is Toltec. The fabulous city, north of Mexico, is presumed to have been built between* A.D. *900–1156 and ruled by Quetzalcoatl. Many Toltec architectural forms are found at Chichén Itzá in Yucatán.*

All the cultures listed here—and there are many more—were established on Mexican soil as long as twenty-five hundred years before the Aztecs made their appearance as an organized tribe. By the time they put in their appearance close on to A.D. 1200, the tides of these earlier cultures had swept back and forth across the face of the land, devastating one another, at the same time developing all the varied aspects of much of that which we call civilization.

And to all this the Aztecs were the heirs.

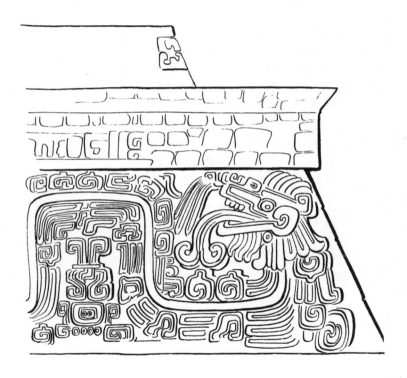

The People

The Origins of the Aztecs

6

T HE "AZTECS" came into Anáhuac, the valley of Mexico, in A.D. 1168. This, recorded in their written ideographic histories, has been synchronized with our calendar; no one has cast doubt on it.

The Tenocha-Aztecs were wanderers, a landless, "wanting" tribe who came out of the north of Mexico (some hold from what is now southwestern United States but there is no evidence of it); they were of Nahuatl speech, that language which was also the speech of the Toltecs. The Aztecs were of the "have-nots," moved about, settling here briefly, wandering there, nibbling at the nether edge of others' lands until a battle ensued; then peregrination began all over again. The date 1168, to be sure, does not tell us with certainty that the Aztec settlement in Mexico began then, but only, as Dr. Vaillant believed, that at that time the Aztecs, who were then cultural nonentities, had begun to use a calendar which had been in general use for a thousand years. Who were the Aztecs and from whence is answered in their mythohistories.* Like all other such origin myths, these differ in detail, not in basic content. The Incas came out of caves; Greeks were given divine guidance by an *autologos* in a darkened sanctuary; Christian myths overflow with heavenly inspired grottoes. And so the Aztecs. They found in a cave the Hummingbird Wizard, the famous Huitzilopochtli (a name the conquistadors

---

* The word "Aztec" as applied to the Tenochas is not of certain origin. They said that they came from some fabled land, *Aztlan;* because of this the Spaniards referred to them as "Az-tec"; of a certainty they neither called themselves that nor were they called that before the Conquest.

never mastered, calling it *Huichilobos,* "Witchy-wolves"). The idol
gave them advice. It sounded well: wander, look for lands, avoid
any large-scale fighting, send pioneers ahead, have them plant maize,
when the harvest is ready, move up to it; keep me, Huitzilopochtli,
always with you, carrying me like a banner, feed me on human hearts
torn from the recently sacrificed. . . . All of which the Aztecs did.

The number, even approximate, of the Tenocha tribe at that time
we do not know. It was minuscule—perhaps a thousand, perhaps
five thousand, not much more. At least in so thickly settled an area
as the valley of Anáhuac they were so insignificant that their arrival
at the lakes passed completely unnoticed, and there is no record of
their arrival in the stately forest of Chapultepec in the generation
about A.D. 1250. All this is understandable. No one regarded as "historical" the internal events of other tribes. History was perpendicular, not horizontal; it had no cross references. During these "wandering years," the Aztecs were absorbing the culture of their
neighbors. They grew. They made enemies. They expanded. Their
clans being too small for wife-yield, they took to wife-stealing, and
now for the first time their neighbors around the valley took cogni-
zance. They were set upon. One part of the tribe was swept into
servitude, another escaped to one of the swampy islets out in Lake
Texcoco. Those left behind were involved in the wars of their captors, wherein they displayed such valor that when asked to name a
boon, they asked for the daughter of the chieftain, so that through
her they could form a respectable lineage. It was granted, but they
sacrificed the beautiful girl, flayed her, and draped the skin over their
head priest so that he might impersonate the Nature Goddess. When
the chieftain of their captors, the father of the girl, arrived in gor-
geous array, he expected, naturally, to attend a wedding ceremony.
Instead he found—this. One can somehow understand his wrath.
Those Tenochas who escaped the butchery by his warriors fled and
joined their tribesmen on the second islet on the lake.

Tenochtitlán, the island city-state, began historically in 1325.
The lakes wherein the incipient Aztec capital lay, as shapeless as
free-swimming protoplasm, were five,* situated in the valley of
Anáhuac, a level plain over 7,000 feet in altitude. From the high
snow-covered mountains that surrounded it there poured the brawl-

---

* Contiguous but with five names: Chalco and Xochimilco were fresh-water; Texcoco,
brackish; the most northern, Xaltocán and Zumpango, very salty.

12. *Aztec temples and houses, with a chieftain in march toward them.*
Footprints indicate migration or movement. Redrawn from an Aztec codex.

ing streams that made these lakes, which were fifty miles long, five
hundred square miles in surface, and ringed with tall, slender marsh
grass. The lakes were deep in some places but shallow in others,
especially about the islets that formed the city of the Tenochas. The
exigencies of the moment called first for housing. Wattle and daub
houses thatched with the marsh grass came first. Later in the same
year, 4-Coatl (1325), the Tenochas dedicated their first temple. In
the beginning, and by agreement with the tribes that ringed the
shore, they had permission to use border lands for planting. This
land they augmented with *chinampa* agriculture, a method in which
outsized wickerwork oval-shaped baskets were made and then
towed to their islets, anchored to the shallow bottom and filled
with earth. In these they grew their crops. Mexico-Tenochtitlán thus
was hand-fashioned.

During the years 1403–55 (Aztec III period) the growing city-
state, through alliance and war, depressions and recovery, outgrew
the primitive stage and filled in the background with new and enlarged cultural horizons. Thereafter the Aztecs took the center of
the Mexican stage and became the principal directors of life within

and without the valley of Anáhuac. So they expanded as all peoples expand, as life itself lives, at the expense of other lives and of other peoples; this is reasonable, understandable, and natural.

Techniques moved slowly. Metalworking came up from South America by slow stages through indirect trade, arrived in Mexico about the eleventh century. Although advanced in many ways, these Americans were yet without the wheel, the rotary quern, and draft animals. Mexico in 1519, as C. A. Burland said, "was where Sumer and Egypt stood in 3500 B.C."; the picture, however, is not that clear.

At the same historical moment—A.D. 1100—that the Incas in Peru were emerging from a similarly obscure position to become a real empire,[32] the Aztecs were, by the same imperialistic means, evolving as the overlords of Mexico.

So, within these extreme dates of 1168–1521, the Tenochas, called "Aztecs," came into their own.

7 *Appearance — What Manner of Men*

T HE BASE of Aztec society was the plebe—the *macehualli* —the common Indian.

While his place was less that of an automaton than mere man under the Inca empire, where he was only a "head count," still he was, in labor terms, both rank and file. *Macehua* derived from "to suffer" or "to earn merits"—in reality he did both. He was a member of a clan and part of an earth cell, of a sort of mutual-aid society; he was, in summary, an able-bodied, taxpaying Indian. First and foremost he was a farmer, in European terms a peasant, and, in the still highly valid expressions of Oswald Spengler "the eternal man, independent of every culture ... one who preceded it, ... outlived it, a dumb creature propagating himself from generation to generation, limited to soil-bound callings and aptitudes, with a mystical, dry, shrewd understanding that sticks to practical matters."

Yet this common Aztec was something more. He was also a warrior, part of an agrarian militia. As the common Roman was a worker-soldier, so the common *macehualli* (plural: *macehualtin*) must be understood as a farmer-warrior.

Like most of the indigenes in Mexico, he was short—between 5 feet 1 and 5 feet 5—broad-headed and thickset. Tireless, he was used to walking since childhood and could carry a load of seventy-five pounds, fifteen hours a day. His arms were long and feet broad in proportion to his height; his gait straight and inclined to be

13. *The Aztec warrior-farmer, called* macehualli. *As plebe he was the base of Aztec society. These figures, redrawn from the* Codex Mendoza, *show two aspects of his life—as farmer and as warrior.*

pigeon-toed; the arches, as one can see in Aztec drawings of foot-steps, were very high.

The head was characterized by the jet-black eyes, lidded with the epicanthic fold, which gives the eye an almond shape. The hair was dark, coarse, abundant, except on his body and face. He was relatively beardless, and face hair was deemed objectionable, so that mothers used tweezers to pluck it out and applied hot cloths to stifle the hair follicles. They were "beardless," even though Cortés said that the Tlascalans had "barbers to shave you." The Aztec face was further made prominent by a hooked Roman nose (although any citizen of that *imperium* would have been shocked at so odious a comparison) which grew more so in old age. Their color varied from dark to light brown; the face could assume a fierce mien and often great dignity, an expression they carried into battle or palaver.

Aztec women were naturally smaller (4 feet 8), and delicate. Yet it was a false frailty. They bore children quickly, often in the milpa fields; they followed their men on long marches (the women attached to the Mexican army in recent times were part of the quartermaster corps), and carried their share of the load, including the inevitable baby. Many of them were of striking appearance; the Spaniards thought so, married them and found them attractive. Doña Marina, "The Tongue," an Indian girl who helped talk the Spaniards into victory over Moctezuma, was declared to be an "excellent woman . . . full of grace."

Dress was, for the common man, simple and expedient; the same raiment was worn night and day. All wore the loincloth (*maxtli*), a cincture that was passed between the legs and brought about the waist, its two ends hanging in front and back and usually embellished. In this he worked on marches where he carried cargo. The mantle (*tilmantli*)—in today's usage, the manta—was a rectangular piece of woven cloth tied over one shoulder, made at first from the coarse fibers of the maguey (*metl*) and later, when contact with the hotlands was general, from cotton. They used neither buttons nor pins. When the *tilmantli* was sufficiently flowing, it covered the whole body when seated. Many of these often were beautifully woven; of this however we have little or no evidence except their own pictures and the descriptions by their conquerors. The common Indian mostly walked with naked feet until he grew in social importance; then he traveled in sandals (*cactli*) made from animal skin or maguey fibers. For the chieftain or demigod, they were of gold.

Hair styles had some variation: in everyday use the hair hung in bangs and was cut in back by barbers with an obsidian knife—*Pagankopf* the Germans would call it—or it was allowed to grow long and braided into a thick pigtail. When at war it was decorated with two turkey or eagle feathers.

Woman's dress in this plebe class, while of only one cut, varied

14. *Aspects of Aztec cookery. In the upper left,* camoti *(sweet potatoes); to the right is the stone* metatl *on which corn is ground. The woman cooks red peppers on a* cumal, *and in the lower right-hand corner newly baked corncakes are covered to retain freshness.*

greatly in design, color, and pattern, for women were the principal weavers. The woman wore an underskirt (*cueitl*) of ankle length and often magnificently embroidered; when abroad she would put over this a poncholike dress (*huipil*), a rectangular piece of cloth with a slit through which the head passed, the sides sewn except for arm-holes—a prosaic description of some of the finest weaving in pattern and color found in the continent, which Bernal Díaz, then an impressionable young man of twenty-three, found "rich and beautifully ornamented." Her sandals, lighter than those used by men, she wore only on journeys or if her social position demanded it. Her hair, long and lustrous and black, grew to full length; it was braided with ribbons for festival days, allowed to hang when about the house; it was gathered and wrapped about the crown of the head when she worked in the fields. Cosmetics were used, mostly by those of the "directing classes" or courtesans (*auianime*) and even sometimes by women of the common sort when their souls were touched by things at the markets. Unguents, perfumes, and creams were available.

 ## *The Traffic of Speech* 8

NAHUATL (pronounced "*nah*-wah-t'l") was the language of the Aztecs.

It was neither their invention, nor perfected by them, since it was spoken by the Toltecs, Chichimecs, and numerous other tribes. It became, however, the lingua franca of Mexico and Central America (just as Quechua was that of the Incas in Peru) because of the conquest by the Aztecs, the penetration of their merchants and trade. And when later reduced to Spanish orthography, a further extension of it was made by the Church, which used it and translated the Christian catechism and other religious manuals into it, thus enlarging its speaking arena.

Nahuatl is one of the eight families of Uto-Aztecan stock. More detailed studies have been made of it, especially of Aztec, than of "any other American linguistic family." [121] This has been mostly because of the late B. L. Whorf, who was, *en passant*, a nonprofessional. Nahuatl speech is related to some of the language phyla of the Southwest Indians (Pima, Shoshoni, Sonora), hence the belief among some that the Aztecs were a fighting breed out of this region. There are seven hundred languages in Mexico; Nahuatl, which was somewhat confined to the central plateau but expanded following the Aztec conquest, belongs to one of the five large phyla of Macro-Penutian speech. Studies of it are highly specialized and its students use technical terms among themselves and in their publications which are never used in normal communications. If a layman were to read the one on "The origin of the Aztec *-tl*"—a suffix which the reader will find often in these pages—he would be as bewildered as Alice in her Wonderland when she came upon the "smile without the cat."

Nahuatl is a living language. Thousands still speak it, there are books and musical records in it, some of Mexico's foremost scholars converse in it; it is very graphic and plastic, as will be seen when the Aztec natural plant classification is discussed (see Medicinal Plants, page 110). The language was as compounded as the Aztec ideographic writing and capable of expressing great feeling and poetry, and although the early Spaniards found the suffix *-tl* very bewildering, sixteenth-century savants who mastered the tongue found it clear and harmonious, with an extended vocabulary.

Although there is no space here for a discussion of Aztec grammar, it had all the traffic of language—what one writer has called "the table manners of speech." Our modern grammar did not begin much before the Reformation; before that there was a cheerful indifference to syntax and spelling. Therefore it is amazing to find any people so removed as were the American Indians from the web of Old World communications who developed so involved a speech and grammar. There were derivative words and fusion "arising from context and pronunciation without regard to meaning"; agglutination was the natural result. What additions the Aztec made to his inherited speech, Nahuatl, is not known, yet it must have been substantial because, as a result of their conquests, new things were pouring into their world and they had to have some fixed grammar to receive them, with flections of person and tense. One of the first books printed in Mexico (1555) was Motolinía's *Vocabulario*. Grammars, catechisms, translations of texts from ideographic Nahuatl into Spanish orthography, have followed century after century until now there is quite enough for a serious study on "Aztec Literature." [42]

The speech of the Aztec *macehualli* had the same earthiness as the soil man's everywhere; practical and with careless speech habits, he fashioned his speech out of that usage stemming from need which is the living morphology of any language. Ordinary men were careless about the meaning of an affix, of the flections of person, number, case, gender; but in the *calmecac* schools of Mexico-Tenochitlán, where good Nahuatl speech was taught, corrected, extended so that high-placed persons could speak properly to the gods or impress visiting chieftains, this traffic of speech was carefully studied. It must have been. Those informants who worked with the first Spaniards in setting it down *knew* the grammar of their speech. This example will suffice; when Sahagún in 1529 began to take down the remembered sagas of the Aztecs, this is how he gave it in Nahuatl, using his own orthography, about the sun, the principal god-year:

> *Tonatiuh [sun] quautlevanitl*
> *xippilli, nteutl [god]*
> *tone, tlaextia motonameyotia,*
> *tontoqui, tetlati, tetkaati, teytoni, teixlileuh,*
> *teixtlilo, teixcaputzo, teixtlecaleuh.*

> *The sun, eagle, dart of fire,*
> *Prince of the year, God*
> *illuminates, makes things glow, lights them with*
>   *its rays,*
> *is warm, burns people, makes them perspire,*
>   *turns dark the*
> *countenance of people, blackens them, makes*
>   *them black as smoke.*[104]

One said much in Nahuatl with little. And while the language was by no means as far-flung geographically as Quechua in Peru, which spread for the same reasons—i.e., conquest from Chile to Colombia—the Aztec speech penetrated far enough—from Mexico down to Nicaragua.

ALL—OR ALMOST ALL—of early native American societies were democratic.

There was rank without class. The community, not the individual, owned the land, and most decisions were made by popular ballot, as, for example, by the American Plains Indians. Or done in the manner which Tacitus described in writing of how the Germans came to decisions in the depths of their forests: "When the mass is to decide they take their seats fully armed . . . silence is then demanded . . . such hearing is given to king or chief as age, rank, military distinction or eloquence can secure . . . if a proposal displeases them, the people roar out their dissent; if they approve, they clash their spears."

When once the Indian began to sustain himself wholly from agriculture, he became a member of a commune. This could be a clan or sib (kin, related by blood) as among the Plains Indians, replete with totem or badge (like a coat of arms that identified the group), or an *ayllu* among the Incas, or it could be a *calpulli* (from *calli*, "house") as it was among the Aztecs. Most of the idigenous American communes were based on this type of organization, a clan as an economic unit united by supernatural (i.e., blood) bonds.

An Indian was born into a clan or *calpulli*. A *calpulli* was a group of houses of extended families. This clan owned certain lands which it held communally. A married man was lent his piece of land directly from the clan. No one had title to the land he worked, he was allowed only the produce of it; if he died without issue or

15. Chinampas, *the "floating gardens" agriculture of the Mexican lakes. Into immense reed baskets, the Aztec put earth, then planted trees, anchoring the "floating garden" with staves. Out of these Mexico City grew.*

16. *The leaders of the Aztecs, heads of four clans (with their symbols above their heads), make their way toward the valley of Mexico in* A.D. 1168.

the land was neglected or he was "drummed out" of his clan, the piece reverted back to the holding corporation. So exact were some of these, that records were kept on *amatl* paper of the various land tracts along with a rebus drawing of the holder's name. According to their records there were seven original *calpulli;* once they settled on their island state, Tenochtitlán, these were enlarged into twenty.

Each of the clans owned, or held by treaty, land on the mainland. At first agricultural land was very limited; when a *calpulli* had none, its members industriously made *chinampas,* the so-called "floating gardens." These were the reed-woven baskets, eight feet in diameter, filled with earth and anchored in the shallow waters. Roots penetrating the basket bottom eventually firmly fixed them to the lake bottom. By this laborious method, a *calpulli* could enlarge its production and extend its clan holdings. Yet as their war conquests proceeded and more alien tribes were forced to yield terrain on the mainland, land grew plentiful and was divided proportionately among all the clans that formed the Aztec tribe. This system of land tenure was, as V. Gordon Childe calls it, "the fatal limitation of . . . Neolithic economy . . . the sole outlet for an expanding population was to annex more land for cultivation and suitable land was not unlimited." [33]

The Aztec clan system was not as rigid as the Peruvian system of the *ayllu,* which was overorganized. Yet it was so arranged that

69

the whole group-family, the *calpulli*, moved as a social unit. "Mexican society," observed Dr. Vaillant, "existed for the benefit of the tribe and each member was supposed to do his part in preserving the community."

An Indian born into a clan could not lose his clan rights nor his right to a piece of clan-held land of a size sufficient to feed the numbers in his family; no one except the duly elected clan chieftains could force an Indian to forfeit these rights by expulsion for crime or other antisocial acts.

10 *Marriage—the Tying of the* Tilmantli

TIED TOGETHER—"spliced," in the Menckenian American colloquial—was not merely a figure of speech in Aztec society. Marriage was symbolized by the actual tying together of the edges of the *tilmantli* cloaks of bride and groom, and once so joined, they were supposed to be "hitched" for life.

A man married at twenty, a girl at about sixteen. In this society there was not a prohibition against bachelors as there was among the Incas. But economic factors and especially the preparation of food made it impossible for a man to live without a woman—corncakes, the irreplaceable staff of life, made twice daily, took two hours for each preparation and this was a woman's task.

Marriage was permitted only between members of different clans, for since all clan members were considered to be of the same blood, to marry within it would be incestuous. Since marriage was exogamous, it had a formality more complex than ours. A young man who contemplated marriage had to consult with the clan council. While sexual attraction and affection played a part, they knew then as now that one does not only marry the woman, one also marries the family. In this case it was more than a family contract, it was a social contract, for by it one's child inherited the birthright of entrance into a clan.

Old women were the marriage brokers. There exists a curious ideographic picture history, a sort of comic-book history, of the whole proceedings in the *Codex Mendoza*. While love was doubtless a determinant in courtship, it was not strongly emphasized. There were too many taboos. Remy de Gourmont felt that one must associate the idea of pleasure with the idea of love if one wants to understand anything of the movement of life. Yet it is also true that there is not in the Aztec pantheon a goddess of love, nor are there drawings or pottery showing acts of generation such as exist in Peru.

On the night of marriage the bride was carried to the groom's house on the back of the old woman matchmaker. All the principal members of the family involved as well as the headmen of the clan sat on mats facing one another and listened or dozed over the long-winded homilies—"here we are present . . ."—and between the periods of discourse a servant would pour out generous portions of intoxicating *octli*. This was more than marriage: clan was involving itself with clan; new blood was being brought into the family holding corporation.

Once the torrents of speech ended, then, in an effort to thwart the supernatural forces that surround this new life adventure, the man and girl seated on their grass mat had the knot tied, and they were united.

There was no fixed rule as to whether the man went to live with the woman's clan or she moved to his. Of a certainty the man did not partake of his bride during the first nights; these rites of the first nights, always referred to in anthropology as *jus primae noctis*, were enjoyed by the uncles, brothers, and even father of the bride. This was not regarded as incest but was done to save them both from what Lévy-Bruhl called the "mysterious miasma of marriage"—the males, the "group-friends" of the bride and groom,

17. *Marriage—the tying of the* tilmantli. *An illustration from the* Codex Mendoza *depicts Aztec marriage customs. A man and woman, tied together, listen to homilies delivered by the old women who were the marriage brokers.*

taking on this "responsibility" in order to spare the newly married any contact with the forces of the supernatural. If one's Italian can encompass the libretto of Mozart's *Marriage of Figaro,* this is the underlying theme of the opera: the Count wishes to impose his ancient prerogative of being the first to sleep with the bride.

The Aztec woman had rights, although they were not as far-reaching as the male's. Thus she could own property in her name, go to the council for justice, and if she was cruelly treated she could obtain a divorce. If divorced, she could marry again; if widowed, she could only marry within the clan of the deceased husband. Sterility was the great onus, the one thing a woman feared, for if she bore no children her man could peremptorily divorce her. To a people so involved in wars and death, children were important and necessary.

Then as now woman's power was based on sex; she controlled mostly by her organism; she was given the privileges which men concede when they are intoxicated by the fumes of desire. Then as now, woman was supposed to be chaste; she could be executed for adultery. Woman was not supposed to have extramarital affairs; a man could, however, provided it was with a married woman. If a married woman was involved in multiple coition and became with child she was not so much a problem as an unmarried one.

Woman naturally did not have all the opportunities afforded to man. Nor did she have, as among the Incas, the opportunity, if she was comely, of being brought out of the remotest regions to Cuzco, there to be precipitated into fame as a *Ñusta,* a "Chosen Woman." The Aztec woman had to rise on her own merit, or body, and even when influential her moves had to be made obliquely like the bishop's on a chessboard. By mere chance, she might be at some strategic spot at an opportune moment and so become the "tongue" in history, as in the case of Doña Marina, who was first sold into another tribe by her mother, who had remarried and did not want her presence about her new young husband. But in general she had her place. A woman might escape it as an individual, but she was drawn back to it as a species. And for good reason. The sole aim of the couple in this or in any other society was to free the female from all that was not purely sexual so that she could produce children. "Like generation," wrote Remy de Gourmont, "mother love is a commandment, a second condition for the perpetuity of life. . . ."

Concubinage existed in Aztec life. This is a paradoxical condition in a semiwelfare state. The Soviets insist that in theirs prostitution could not exist—it does. Theoretically, in so organized a society as the Aztec, prostitution was not supposed to be. Yet the great warriors of the Aztecs had their concubines; Moctezuma had "many women as mistresses," writes Bernal Díaz, who saw them. As always, the permanence of war brought much change in the traditional mores of the tribe. Armed conflict, as it does everywhere, loosened the ties of home and parental authority. Moral codes, essentially unstable, are at best only a handbook on the ideals of human happiness. "Morality," Remy de Gourmont has said, "will modify itself according to the mobility of the ideal." We have no precise idea how widespread this concubinage really was, but the Aztecs had a word for it: *auianime.*

 Calli: *The House*   *11*

ONCE MARRIED, the couple built their own house. Like all else it was a communal affair. This was as true within Mexico-Tenochtitlán as it was without. The type of house the *macehualli* built depended on where he was and what he was. Finished, it reflected the "eternal man," the peasant-tribesman. Even the greatest Aztec temples and palaces had their origin in the simple native house. The Mayas knew this and immortalized such a peasant house as an element in the decoration of the south wing of the Nunnery Quadrangle at Uxmal. Dr. Vaillant confirms that "the great cities of the Aztec had their origin in the simple villages of sedentary tribesmen. . . . These were huts with thatched roofs resting on walls of wattles smeared with mud . . ." On the mainland, in the temperate zone of Anáhuac Valley, such houses persist to this day.

Within the "city" in a clan division, this house might be of adobe, sealed with adobe "cement" and painted. We know little about it—all has been destroyed. There is nothing left here as there was at Machu Picchu or Ollantaytambo in Peru, where one can follow the evolution of the *cancha* type of native house into the complexity of the Inca palace. In Mexico and in the Maya country there remain only the temples, pyramids, ceremonial ball courts; the link of evolution between peasant house and florid temple has dissolved.

The interior was partitioned between kitchen and sleeping-living portions. This can be clearly seen in the fragment of Aztec codex that gives the genealogy of the *tlatoani,* hereditary chiefs of Azcapotzalco, with its illustration of a typical Aztec house com-

18. *An Aztec kitchen. At the left, the woman grinds the corn. At the right, the woman shapes the corncake,* tlaxcalli. *In the center is the* cumal, *on which the corncake is baked.*

pound. At one end the fire and kitchen—not a fireplace as we understand it, but rocks of uniform height sunk into the beaten mud floor which merely contained the wood. There was no chimney, no window, no fireplace; the smoke found its own egress through the interstices of the grass thatch. The fire was banked at night and blown into life in the morning by the huff and puff of the women.

Because the city grew out of "floating gardens" it had as many canals as Venice, and usually a house of the common man in the city fronted on a canal. The greater number of houses, wrote Cortés, "were one story only." The materials, according to the importance of the buildings, "were *tezontli* [a volcanic stone easily worked, dull red in color] and adobes that formed the walls plastered with lime, and in the suburbs and shores of the island [the houses were constructed] of reeds and straw, appropriate . . . for the lower classes." Many had gardens in which flowers or medicinal herbs grew. By the house wall each had its own steam bath or *temascal.*

The corncakes were baked in the kitchen on a flat ceramic dish (*cumal*); about were three-legged pots for boiling and a variety of wooden spoons and other simple instruments for cooking. In the other section of the house there was a raised platform of earth on which a grass mat (*petlatl*) was spread. The highest chieftain in the land had nothing better. This surprised even Bernal Díaz, who

19. *The* temascal *(steam bath). Most of the Aztec houses had them. Steam was produced by throwing water over heated stones or a wood fire.*

wrote that they had "beds of matting with canopies above, and no better bed is given, however great the chief may be . . ." The floor was stamped earth; on it a *petlatl* or deerskin; windowless, the grass-thatched roofs were gabled or hipped. There were no doors; only a cloth hanging in front of the opening kept out the night cold. Clothes hung on pegs driven into walls. Paddles for canoes, weapons, shields with the totemic device of the clan were usually kept at the temple of the clan, and such personal treasures as the family possessed—jade, feathers, turquoise, festive clothes—were kept in a grass-mat chest, called *petlacalli* (literally "house chest," a word which for the Aztec was synonymous with "treasure"). There were no tables, few used chairs; there were braziers (see Pottery and Pottery Makers, page 91) to keep off the night chill, and for illumination long slivers of pine wood, heavy with pitch, which gave flickering light. Such, with variations depending on rank, were the houses of the common Indian.

12   *The Rhythm of Day and Night*

"I MUST ACT because I live" were the first words of the homunculus as he issued full-blown from the alembic of Faust.

Man must live. Before day's break the Aztecs throbbed to life with the beat of the wooden-tongued drums from the great temples, as each of the smaller *teocalli* throughout the city took its cue from the largest. As Venus, the morning star, appeared to them at about 4 A.M., day was born and the shell trumpets blown by the priests added to the din as all other temples responded in counterpoint. Fires that had been banked were blown to life and all over the city of Mexico-Tenochtitlán the pale smoke arose to a windless sky.

The Indian, as farmers do everywhere, rose at this hour before the sun; city or land, the instinct was general. He went to the steam bath, tossed water on the heated rocks, passed through the vapor, dipped into the canal—rich man, poor man, little man, chief, all responded in like manner to the rhythm of Aztec life. Even Moctezuma rose at the same time and went off to the courts to attend the dawn session.

All had morning ablutions. Aztec people were relatively clean since water was available. The Spaniards were unable to hide their surprise over this, coming from a Europe where it was rare to bathe monthly. Andres de Tapia, a companion of Cortés, affirmed: "Moctezuma bathed twice the day . . . and all [of the Indians] bathed frequently." Since there were no pigs and no fat, the Aztecs had no soap as we know it, but they had a natural detergent, the roots of the *copal-xocotl,* which the practical-minded Spaniard called the "soap tree" (*Saponaria*); it made a lather and performed the work of soap.

People newly married or too poor to have a slave (*tlacotli*), or too lately wed to have children help them, had to prepare the corn

mass for the tortillas (*tlaxcalli*) twice daily themselves. There were
no short cuts. Dry corn was steeped in lime, then boiled and the
corn skin pried loose; then it was brayed on the stone *metatl* with
a grooved stone roller. This technique of corn preparation is so
old that these artifacts appear among the first (as well as the last)
archaeological objects to be found in the yielding earth. The
unleavened cornbread, pancake-shaped, was baked on a flat *cumal*.
This was the unvarying base food of their lives. In addition there
were beans, chili pepper, fish, sometimes meat; maize could be
made into tamales or *atolli,* a gruel made of maize flavored with
honey and chili pepper. The culinary day began and ended with
the same food. There were no cattle, goats, pigs, horses until white
men brought them, thus no milk or cheese. There was nothing in
all Mexico such as the maté used in Paraguay. Chocolate (cacao
bean) was imported from the hotlands and only the well-provided
had it. There was no grease for frying—everything was baked or
boiled. Food was washed down with the mild intoxicant *octli*.

Corn was the base of life. All the tribes from Nicaragua to Arizona
predicated their lives on it; all the temple-cities reared their economy on it. One's day began and ended with corn, and no matter
how exotic were the foods of the Aztec leaders—which so surprised
their conquerors—the base remained the simple corncake. No
other plant has played so large a role in the development of cultures.

After this repast in semidarkness, man and woman put food
and drink into a basket slung from the neck and went into the
fields. If they worked in *chinampas,* these were cultivated; if they
had fields assigned to them by the clan on the mainland, they poled
their dugout to the fields, which they worked alone or collectively
with other clan members. However, the high frequency of Aztec
conquest and the need to put down rebellions among those newly
or anciently conquered made any able-bodied man subject to instant war call. Such was the life of the farmer-warrior.

At night before dusk they were home again and once more
there was the business of making corncakes. There were available
in the market turkey, duck, deer, beans, squash, *camoti,* and such
like; the evening meal, the largest, took place between four and
five o'clock. The man or men squatted on the reed mats, helping
themselves with their fingers from the pots of food brought to
them. Women ate apart.

At night the room was lighted by pine splinters. By this light the women spun or worked their loom or prepared the pulque intoxicant; the men made paddles for canoes, grass mats, split their knives, arrowheads, and fish needles from obsidian, or chipped out stone querns; these they would trade in the market. When children began to make their yearly appearance, they were first placed in a cradle, and then as soon as they could move they became a part of this fabric of life.

Above all—children.

In this state, where war was perpetual and death constant, a rising birthrate, even though it meant the overpopulation of the city, was one of the important duties of all. As soon as the woman was pregnant, she was put under the protection of the god Tezcatlipoca. There is a whole pictured history in the *Codex Mendoza* of the birth, naming, rearing, discipline of a child, of the details of swaddling and the type of cradle. When the child was born, a magician (*tonalpoulqui*) was brought in by the parents from their own local clan temple. He consulted a horoscope (*tonalamatl*), a sort of book of fate, which was unrolled to its twenty-foot length. This was to determine if the child had been born under good or bad auguries. The naming was important, and if they found that the day was unlucky, the naming was put off till a better moment—the avoidance of misfortune itself is the enjoyment of positive good. "What's in a name?" To the Indians, everything. It is a badge, a "handle" (in the colloquial of midwestern United States). Many primitives have two names, social and personal. The personal was known and used only by the immediate family in the belief that if used too often, it might lose its power. In times of illness, the witch doctor used the real name to call the dying back to life. Boys were called after their fathers or grandfathers, usually dynamic names, as "Smoking Crest" (*Chimalpopoca*), "Obsidian Serpent" (*Itzcoatl*), "Speaking Eagle" (*Quauhtlatoa*); girls, who seem always to evoke a sense of poetry, were named after flowers, stars, birds, as "Ibis" (*Atototl*), "Green Flower" (*Matlal-xochitl*), or "Rain Flower" (*Quiauh-xochitl*).[182]

Since there was rank without class, it was not necessary to remain in a lowly state, even if one were born into it. In Peru the state existed for the Inca as a whole; among the Aztecs the state developed for the good of the individual. A man, as Dr. Vaillant

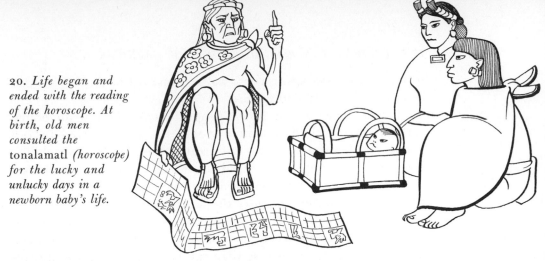

20. *Life began and ended with the reading of the horoscope. At birth, old men consulted the* tonalamatl *(horoscope) for the lucky and unlucky days in a newborn baby's life.*

pointed out, "could attain *rank* through his own efforts," but this rank his children did not automatically inherit "unless they earned it through equivalent tribal service." This could be accomplished in various ways—as a good farmer, hunter, artisan or soldier, or even merchant; excelling in any of these brought leadership.

Schooling of a sort was given at the clan's house for boys (*telpochcalli*). Each clan maintained a number of these under the administration of a master (*telpochtlatoque*). In charge was either a well-known warrior or an elder; here boys learned their own mytho-histories, rituals, and, above all, the use of war weapons. No doubt the master was soon able to ferret out those who showed dexterity with weapons—there was a small cadre of professional soldiers—and the young Aztec might be made to incline in that direction. Artisans and painters were revered too, or the boy might become a merchant, except that there was a tendency for this calling to go direct from father to son; or if he showed mystical leanings, he might be sent to the *calmecac* (which the Spaniards likened to a monastery), there to learn the intricacies of priesthood. In the expanding world of the Aztecs much was possible.

On the whole, training of the child remained in the parents' hands. Learning was by mimicry. One can follow the manner of this training in the recorded picture history. At three years of age, the child is allowed one-half tortilla per day—the tortilla being a foot in diameter; at thirteen he is eating two such outsized tortillas per day. The boy mimics the father; at first he carries a small bag suspended from his neck, for he must be his own draft animal; this is increased monthly until, like his father, he can carry sixty pounds. He fishes, plants, makes dugout canoes; he gathers rushes, weaves *petlatli,* makes sandals, carries, walks, runs. All of this is recorded in detail with word and picture.

Punishment was not always proportionate to the wrongdoing; certainly Aztec child discipline would not be approved by our overly timid society, which has created the "progressive child." For some infractions the father held the child's head over smoke; for others he was hand-pricked with a maguey thorn until the blood flowed. Since in these pictures the father is seen talking the while, admonishing while he is punishing (one sees by the speech scroll in front of his face that he is talking), the boy is being trained. This certainly was no worse than the fate Benvenuto Cellini suffered at the age of five when he thought he saw a lizard sitting on the coals of a fire: "My father . . . becoming instantly aware of what the thing was . . . gave me a great box in the ears which caused me to weep and howl with all my might." Cellini was pacified by his father's saying: "My dear little boy, I am not striking you for any wrong . . . but only that you remember that . . . you saw a salamander."

Daughters were like their mothers; dress was identical. At six the young girl is learning to spin; at eight she is sweeping the floors and eating one and a half tortillas per day; at thirteen she is making the tortillas, as she will do twice daily all the rest of her life.

This sense of dedication was the origin of Aztec social behavior. It was based on ancient mores dictated by custom, continued by custom and the authority of the parent. What was done is done; what was not, is not. Above all, their virtue was as the ancient Roman knew the word. The orientation of the Roman mind was as farmer-soldier, and although removed by time and distance, what has been said of Roman virtue in the farmer-soldier could be repeated for the Aztecs: "Unremitting work is the lot of the farmer, for the seasons wait for no man . . . accidents of weather and pest may frustrate him; he must accept compromise and be patient . . . routine is the order of his life . . . the life of the fields is his life . . . to him the knowledge born of experience is worth more than speculative theory. His virtues are honesty and thrift, forethought and patience, work and endurance and courage, self-reliance, simplicity and humility in the face of what is greater than himself." [9]

AZTEC LIFE revolved around the *milpa*—the cornfield.
And for good reason. No other civilization that has
left its footsteps on the road of time has been predicated on the use
of a single plant such as Indian corn (*centli*). Earlier than 3000 B.C.,
the cultures of the Middle East—Assyrian, Sumerian, Egyptian—
were cultivating such leguminous plants as pulses, peas, lentils,
vetches, whose high protein content made storage easy in semidesert
lands. As for cereals such as wheat, "that most important extra-
tropical grain," * it had been cultivated in India since Mesolithic
times.[224] "Wheat . . . barley, rye, millet, panic-grass" were all part
of the diet and economy of all who flourished in the Fertile Crescent. Yet none of these aforementioned civilizations depended solely
on one plant as did those of Mexico and Yucatán.

The Egyptians, to give one pertinent example, according to the
Papyrus Harris (Dynasty XX, *c.* 1200 B.C.) knew over thirty types
of bread—the Aztecs had one. The Egyptians' diet was varied: peas,
lentils, watermelons, artichokes, lettuce, endive, radishes, onions,
garlic, leeks. They had fats, both vegetable and animal—the Aztecs
had none. They had beef, honey, dates, as well as milk and cheese
and even butter, which was unknown to the Aztecs until A.D. 1525.
The stomach led in this refusal of man to accept his environment
as fixed—it is from the kitchen that so many technical operations
have sprung, e.g., furnaces, ovens, preservation, fermentation, grinding techniques. Independent inventions in the kitchen can be easily
discerned by comparing the Egyptian women making unleavened
bread, as shown in the drawings on the wall at Thebes circa 1900
B.C., with the Aztec method of making corncakes in A.D. 1520.

Corn made settled life possible in Mexico. Since these
people had but one such grain, it is understandable why it
played so great a part in ritual and in practice. The origin of this
grain is enveloped in botanical controversy. Although some geneti-
cists believe that the greatest diversity of varieties comes out of
Mexico, this is disputed. Paraguay is suggested as the point of dissemination by some, challenged by others. For the moment, "present
evidence points to a dissemination in all directions of the early forms

* Emmer, an early wheat, has been found in Troy II (2300 B.C.).

81

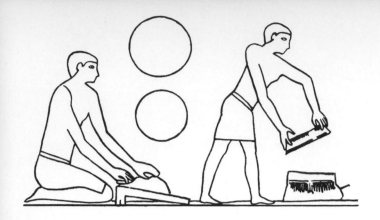

21. *Egyptians making bread; from a mural at Thebes dated 1900 B.C. The meal is ground on a stone mortar, and the unleavened bread is baked on a flat oven. The baked bread is illustrated by the two circles.*

from an unknown center." [169] In the beginning of the twentieth century, it was easy to state that maize—(the Awarak-Carib name for corn)—developed out of *teosinte,* which was considered by most to be the ancestor of corn much as wild grass was the ancestor of wheat. Today the botanical applecart has been upset by findings that point to a hybrid between a species of tripsacum and maize as the original corn, (both *teosinte* and tripsacum will cross with maize); and one of our great geographers who is not easily stampeded into accepting the idea of Asiatic contacts has stated—to make it still more complex—that the origin of maize "cannot even now be attributed with certainty to the New World as long as certain matters concerning Southeastern Asia remain unsolved." [169] Whatever the distribution centers, well-developed corncobs two inches in length have been found in graves on the desert coast of Peru, radiocarbon-dated 2500 B.C. Since one must begin at the beginning as Alice did in her Wonderland, we can begin at that date and allow those who wish to follow the maze of maize to pursue it. The starting point is in the bibliography.

Milpa culture has remained unchanged for three thousand years. What is true of Aztec farming technique is true of all others in this milieu. Milpas were located two to fifteen miles from the dwellings. If the land was forested, trees were ringed a year before and felled with ax-shaped stone celts. The bush and trees being burned, the ash was turned into the soil; larger trees were allowed to rot with time and provide humus. The earth was turned over and prepared by means of a digging stick (*coa*). March was the planting time. Corn kernels were placed in holes four to five inches deep; in temperate zones beans and squash were put in at the same time; corn, growing faster, acted as host plant for the vines. April brought rain, and

22. *An Aztec girl being instructed by her mother in the art of making corncakes. She grinds on a stone mortar. The circle in front represents the baking device, the* cumal. *On the wall are the baked cakes. From the* Codex Mendoza.

if the desired rain was withheld by the gods, sacrifice was made to Tlaloc, the rain god. Of the eighteen months of the Aztec year, almost every one had its ceremonies and dances connected with the growing and harvesting of corn. The corn ripened in July and there was a feast for the Goddess of Young Corn (see The Festival Days, page 97). In August the rain which had been petitioned in April had to be held back; the Aztec somehow had to cajole the gods not to send rain which would spoil the harvest. So, another sacrifice, this time to a mature woman representing the Goddess of Ripe Corn.

What did all this yield the Indian in food? The studies made among the Mayas can apply approximately to the Aztecs, even though Maya agriculture in the hotlands had slightly more yield.[130] An acre gave twenty bushels of husked corn, a bushel being fifty-six pounds, which, fortuitously, coincides with a "cargo," of what a man could carry on his back. The average size of a milpa in Yucatán was ten acres; it would have been slightly less in the land-hungry Aztec territory. This gave an Aztec family a yield of two hundred bushels of corn yearly, or 11,200 pounds. To fell, plant, weed, and harvest this land with the aid of his wife and, say, four half-grown children, the Aztec farmer would have to expend about two hundred days. In the same field he would also plant beans, squash, pumpkins, adding to the yield of the field and also to be included in the produce of these two hundred days. Now since the average consumption of corn for tortillas is one and a half pounds a person a day, the family consumed only one third of what it produced, or 3,380 pounds' consumption a year as against 11,200 of yield, allowing a surplus for barter, trade, work taxes, and religious taxes. With a surplus of 165 unused days unless he was called to battle, the Aztec could use these in his particular craft, making grass mats, fiber

83

sandals, canoes, weapons, etc. These he bartered for needed things at the markets.

Corn was the "basic." What else? Beans (*etl*) were grown in the same milpa, using the cornstalks for support, and squash and pumpkins, all of the genus *Cucurbita,* as well as the crooked-necked variety (*ayote*) were planted in between.

The Aztecs never had the other "basic," the potato, which nourished half of prehistoric South America; as a cultivated plant it was unknown throughout Mexico *until it was brought to them by the Spanish.* It first was carried to Spain, then it appeared in Europe as an article of diet for the poorer man, being introduced into England by Sir John Hawkins in 1565; then it returned to America. In Mexico it appeared "as an item of European diet," and in present-day Mexico, the potato is grown only for sale to those of a higher social position. Moreover, the potato was nowhere cultivated in Mexico or North America until after the Conquest. This is curious because wild tuber-bearing *solanums* are found as far north as Colorado. When the potato arrived, the Aztecs did not even have a name for it; they called it *pelon-camoti,* "the Peruvian sweet potato." As will be seen *there was never any direct communication between Peru and Mexico* until the white man appeared.[20]

The Aztecs had the sweet potato (*camoti*); it grew in the warmer valleys below 6,000 feet. An *ipomea,* a tuber-bearing morning glory, it is one of a great family of over one hundred species found throughout the world. The Chinese had the yam, which is Old World in origin; they called it *shu.* This yam, which is a *Dioscorea,* is found throughout Polynesia extending down to New Zealand, where it was assiduously cultivated by the Maoris. But one cannot botanically equate the *camoti* with the yam; they are different plants, though they are constantly confused with one another in the United States. Few Europeans are acquainted with one or the other so that when Thor Heyerdahl, the Wrong-Way Corrigan of anthropology, wrote didactically that "Tiki brought . . . in the fifth century the Peruvian sweet potato to New Zealand," it is the apogee of botanical ignorance.

The Aztecs developed, if not all the plants, then the names of much which is common on our table today: tomatoes (*tomatl*) grew below the frost line, planted in dormant milpas; the biting hot peppers (*chilli*), all varieties of capsicum, grew beside the *tomatl,* the gelatinous weeds valued as food for infants and the sick; various amaranth pigweeds, which they called *huautli,* were cultivated and made into flat cakes. Pineapples, which originated in the warmer areas from Panama to Brazil, reached Mexico probably from the West Indies and were grown as far north as Jalisco, appearing as high as 6,000 feet altitude. When they could, the Aztecs cultivated them. The very observant Jesuit traveler José de Acosta tasted them in Mexico in 1565 and found them "very coole, full of liquor and of easie digestion and in time of heate, fit to refresh." Cortés sent one to Spain "to our Emperor *Charles* which must have cost much paine and care to bring it so far . . . yet he did not trie the taste." [1]

Avocados—the Mexican word *ahuacatl* evolved into *ahuacate,* avocado—were grown in the warmer valleys of Aztec territory. The chewing-gum tree *chicle-zapotl* has come directly down to us in name and product. Chocolate (*chocolatl*), the beverage and the word, came to us from the Mexican farmer who cultivated the tree when his lands reached the lower, warmer areas; it thrived on the Pacific side as far north as Tepic. Everywhere chocolate appeared as an important element in native culture. It was an Aztec passion, sweetened with wild honey, perfumed with vanilla, tinctured with *achiotl.* Moctezuma quaffed it from pure gold cups: "a certaine drink made from cacao . . . served . . . with great reverence." [48]

The preparation and working of the milpa cornfield was collective. Members of the clan assisted one another, and when a farmer-warrior was away to the wars, his fields were cultivated by others of his clan. While the number of plants under cultivation seems impressive, agriculture was not as advanced as among the Incas. They

23. *Aztec cornbins in which the harvested grain was kept. At the right, one woman stores corn grains in a large ceramic urn, another woman holds the* tamale, *still a popular food after three thousand years.*

did not prepare elaborate terracing as was done in the Andes; they were not soil-makers, except in the expedient of the *chinampas*. They had no fertilizer other than their own feces, where the Incas had bird guano and llama offal. Irrigation was casually developed because of the nature of the land; the run-off of the rain could not be harnessed as was done in Peru. Irrigation techniques, which are inseparable from a developed agriculture, were of a poor order. The Aztecs' dependence on rain is the "reason why" for the ceaseless preoccupation with the appeasement of the gods and with conquests, the wars for more tribute and for more sacrificial victims in order to cajole the rain god into proffering the withheld gifts of rain. As the good will of the rain god could only be sustained by a diet of human hearts, and as these could only be provided by taking prisoners in battle, a long peace was a disaster. Only in perpetual war was there safety.

It was a nightmare.

14   *Tax Contributions to the State*

EVEN IN SUCH a moneyless society as the Aztec, everything, unfortunately, had to be paid for; taxes and death to the common Aztec *macehualli* were as inevitable as conception. Babylon invented money, this symbol that simplified life all over the world. But because of geographic isolation, no civilization in prehistoric America knew money, if one excepts the use of cacao money. "The Cacao is a fruit little lesse than almonds," José de Acosta tells us. "They use it in steede of money for with five cacaos they buy one thing, with thirtie another and with a hundred another, without any contradiction . . . from it theye make a drincke which they call Chocolate."

Taxes, whatever the reality of cacao money, were paid in service and seem to have been assessed through the clan. "The tribal council divided the land among the clans and the leaders of each in turn apportioned its share among the heads of families justly and equitably." [198] Sections were also reserved for the maintenance of the chief of the temple staff, for war supplies, and for the payment of tribute.

Other portions of this land controlled directly by the clan were worked communally and the yield—whether corn, beans, or agave fibers—was paid as tribute-tax to the central tribal council for the maintenance of religion, war, the "king" and his various non-taxpaying staff, (priests, army, craftsmen, concubines, keepers of the royal aviary), and for the engineering works in and beyond Mexico-Tenochtitlán and all the other paraphernalia of state with which we today are so fully familiar.

In addition to the foodstuffs which were sent to the central granaries and noted down in the account books by the Tribute Recorder of the Chief Speaker, the clan group was also called upon for levies of manpower to build public buildings. Under direction from architect-builders, who were tax-exempt, dikes, aqueducts, roads were built. The "king" of the Aztecs also had lands which were cultivated by clans in rotation, and the yield of this also went into the official deposits.

"Tell me what you eat, and I will tell you what you are," wrote Anthelme Brillat-Savarin in his *Physiologie du Goût*, written in Connecticut while he waited for the French Revolution to burn itself out. This aphorism could apply to all Neolithic theocracies, especially the Aztec. Frequent comparisons have been made between the temple-cities in America and those in Sumer. In primitive societies all were farmers, for "in a hypothetical pure Neolithic economy there would be no full-time specialist." [33] When farming improved, a surplus was produced and granaries were attached to the temples, in Sumer as in America. As man became completely dependent on agriculture and since sun and rain were derived from the gods, who "owned" the soil they tilled, the first fruit "tithes," in Christian parlance, were given to the temple to support the galaxy of priests who acted as the intermediaries for the gods. These surpluses were used to aggrandize the temple, secure the interest of the priestly class, and provide exchange for the import of raw materials they lacked. The administration of all this produced the temple-city, and so there came into being the specialists: craftsmen, administrators, clerks (*tlacuilo* writers in Mexico), who put down receipts and expenditures. These early temple accounts are among the oldest cuneiform writing in Sumer (3500 B.C.), and their Aztec counterparts constituted, until they were destroyed, some of the oldest Aztec records.

It is obvious that the directing class themselves did not personally consume all that poured into Mexico-Tenochtitlán. The surplus was used to compensate the specialists. It was also stored for general use during crop failures. Since accounts had to be kept, some archaeologists believe this was one of the factors which brought about the invention of writing.*

That the Incas, who also had a tribute state, should have developed only the *quipu* and not writing, remains one of the earth's mysteries.

15   *The Loom — A Woman's Art*

WEAVING was one of the functions that belonged wholly to woman.

She gathered the fiber, prepared it, spun, dyed, and then loomed it; no male interfered. It is a fact sometimes overlooked that, in this strange world where everyone was a craftsman in one form or another, the anonymous and communal weaving artisans were all women. Theirs was also an ephemeral art. None of the millions of pieces loomed has survived and all we know of Aztec design is that which has come down to us in the Book of Tributes or else what was painted on pottery and on murals.

The Aztec backstrap loom was simple. The type is known, with little variation, throughout all the Americas. Two wooden rods are fastened, one to each end of the warp, to stretch the cloth to desired length; the lower one is attached to the back of the weaver (hence the name "backstrap"), while the upper is tied to a post or tree. Three feet wide, the warp was loomed by means of a shuttle woven between the strands of the stretched yarn: that simple. And yet from these looms came, if one can trust the enthusiasm of the conquistadors, some of the finest weavings they had ever seen. "Eight damsels, they were," wrote Bernal Díaz, "all eight of them clothed in the rich garments of the country, beautifully ornamented. . . ."

* V. Gordon Childe writes that the "standardization of conventional graphic system" stimulated the invention of writing. "The art of reading and writing [he is writing about the lands of Mesopotamia] became an accomplishment with considerable prestige. The initiates were exempted from all manual tasks." Further, they were trusted with the task of thinking for the society. This was duplicated in Aztec society.

24. *Weaving was the woman's art. At the left, she uses the typical backstrap loom; to the right, carded cotton is put into thread on a spindle whorl which rests in a ceramic bowl.*

The Aztecs when they were wanderers used the fiber of the maguey (*metl*), a spined succulent which, after corn, was one of Mexico's most beneficent plants. It provided them with intoxicating drink (*octli*), rope fiber, which, under the name "henequen," is a well-known commercial product, and numerous other products too many and too varied to be noted here. This agave was a primary source of fiber. The pad (technically it is not a leaf) of this succulent is veined with strong fibers, which, when dried, combed, and spun, can be made sufficiently delicate to spin; from this fiber of the maguey, a very coarse linenlike thread, the Aztec women made their first weavings. Later, when they rose in social scale and could barter, they obtained cotton from the warmer valleys. Cotton soon passed from a luxury to a necessity, and one of the principal errands of their traders, who went to the south hotlands for goods or tribute, was to obtain the indispensable cotton. Women bartered for cotton in the market, or, when it arrived as tribute, it was distributed equally to the clans and each woman weaver obtained her share.

Cotton fibers were spun on the traditional spindle, a slender wooden stick ten to twelve inches in length, balanced at the lower end by a pottery whorl. This is "traditional" in that wherever there has been spinning and weaving the ancient technique of fiber preparation has been the same. It would be a well-versed archaeologist who could differentiate between the spindle rings of Palestine (3000 B.C.); Troy (2500 B.C.); Peru (2000 B.C.); Maya (200 B.C.), or Aztec (A.D. 1300). Curiously enough, all that is left of the greatest art of Mexico and Yucatán is the ceramic spindle whorl. All else—weavings, loom, even the sticks—has succumbed to time. The method of spinning the fiber, with the "business end" left in a small ceramic bowl, has been pictured by the Aztecs themselves.

The fibers after spinning were dyed, with urine as mordant to fix the color. Dyes were mostly vegetable: *achiotl* (the *Bixa* genus) yielded red—this, under the name of *anatto,* was later used in our own economy to dye oleomargarine; anil, a shrub, gave a dark blue; cochineal, a scale insect parasite, was gathered, as its Latin name, *coccus cacti,* implies, on the cactus by Indians, who obtained from it a carmine color; and there were others. The dark seed of the genipa, found on a tree in the hotlands, yielded a black color; a lavender color came, like the "royal purple of Tyre," from a mollusk found along the Pacific coast.

Color was more than color. It was symbolism, and, to the Aztec, very real. If red was used as blood, it became the actual equivalent of blood; it *was* blood. Black represented war because black obsidian glass was the cutting edge of battle swords (*maquahuitl*); it was also the symbol of religion: the priests dressed exclusively in it. Yellow was food because it was the color of corn; blue meant sacrifice; and green was royal, because it was the color of the quetzal plumes used only by chieftains. The French symbolists led by Mallarmé at the end of the nineteenth century used color in the same way in their poetry. And when they assailed all Paris with the allegories and esotericism of these ancient theurgies, what they believed to be so new was in reality as old as the world itself.

Design had no horizons—everything was allowed, everything permitted. Protected by the goddess Xochiquetzal, the weaver expressed anything that she felt. Of nature and realism, there were the things of the earth—sun, fish, snails, cactus, bird feathers, tiger skins, even falling snow were used as motifs; there were geometric designs, highly stylized animals, transformation of representational art into allover patterns. All this is suggested in the designs taken from the Book of Tributes and redrawn from the actual weavings delivered to Mexico-Tenochtitlán.

For themselves women wove the skirts ankle length, elaborately bordered, and for the top part of the costume the well-known *huipilli.* Their art sense ran riot. The striking effect of the women's dress was not exaggerated by the conquistador. Consider this description by a padre during the festivals of the month when the women, especially the beautifully dressed concubines, danced with the soldiers: ". . . and all were well clothed, beautifully adorned, all had wonderfully wrought skirts and pretty *huipilli*. The skirts were decorated with designs representing hearts, others a fish motif, others with spirals or leaves, some were of a simple weave; they all had frames, hems, and fringes. . . . As to the blouses, some had loose dark adornments, others motifs representing smoke or black stripes and some with houses or fishes. . . ." [163]

For the men, women wove two principal garments: the breech-clout (*maxtli*), a single piece with highly decorated ends which went about the waist, and a long cloak (*tilmantli*), which knotted at the shoulder, since they had neither brooches, pins, nor buttons. A portrait of Nezahualpilli, "king" of Texcoco, an ally of Tenochtitlán, shows such a costume elaborated for so exalted a person.

War kept the women further occupied. They wove a coarse cloth of cotton for the war dress (*xicolli*), and also, as a protection against arrows, a quilted cotton jacket not unlike that which the Chinese use against the cold. These jackets the Spaniards thought superior to their own steel armor.

The priests wore ankle-length black ponchos and got them from the looms of young virgins assigned to the temples. As befitting the necromancy of their beliefs, they were bordered with skulls and crossbones.

 Pottery and Pottery Makers   **16**

POTTERY, like weaving and housebuilding, was part of the Aztec cultural equipment. All made pottery in one form or another even if all did not make *fine* pottery. This self-sufficiency is what prompted Aldous Huxley in his Mexican travels to cite "the primitive's human wholeness." [86] Pottery making confirms the point that "a primitive is forced to be whole—a complete man, trained in all the skills of the community . . . if he is not whole, he perishes." All of the tribes were pottery makers, those of Cholula being especially famed for their red and black ware. It was mostly a craft

industry done at home with the leisure time allowed from agriculture. A number of pottery makers who rose in public esteem as artisans left agriculture entirely and organized the guild of pottery makers. Utilitarian pottery, coarse-grained and designed for heavy duty, was used for cooking. Three-legged pots, the large *cumal* which was a flat disk-shaped griddle for baking tortillas, bowls with roughened surface to act as graters for braying chili peppers—these, with pottery goblets for pulque, were part of every household. The finer pieces of delicate pottery almost as thin as good china, the beautifully decorated kind the archaeologists find in graves, were for the dead.

There was more to pottery than mere pots and drinking bowls. Spindle whorls, which weighted the spinning distaff like a flywheel, and spinning sticks too, were made of clay. Ceramic dolls were made with jointed arms. Toys were made with wheels, although the idea of putting the wheel to any other use never occurred to them. The little clay gods, gods of fertility and corn, were mass-produced in clay forms; the cult figurine was dropped by the farmer into his cornfield to conjure the good will of the local genii for a better corn crop. Each household had its charcoal brazier to snuff out the chill, and temples had large ceramic braziers the height of a man, coalescing beauty and utility, a ritualistic usefulness with architectural ornament; there were clay stamps and seals used for stamping cloth and *amatl* paper, a step in the evolution of printing. After ideographic writing, the next inevitable step (as the Chinese saw it) was to reduce the ideograph to a symbol and "print"—impress the seal on paper. Thus with these pottery stamps and *amatl* paper they were very close to true printing.

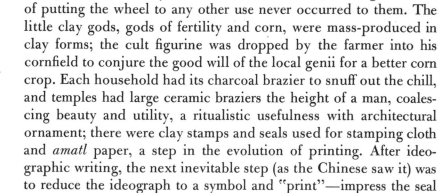

Pottery, apart from its beauty of form, provides an important record to the archaeologist. Potsherds may be dismal to read about and equally dismal to work over but they represent a type of history. A preliterate people give more precise information in their pottery than in their legends and architecture. Much can be determined from the stylistic changes effected in pottery. A new god cult arrives, a new epoch is ushered in, a new age—it is first reflected in pottery. A conqueror comes, and the temples remain standing, but the common people echo the change—we have seen the same thing in our late wars—reflecting the conqueror in style of clothes, manners, habits; pottery provides the sequence of advance and decline. By

using potsherds to establish spatial relationships, the archaeologist uses some of the techniques of geology: a stratigraphical cut at the kitchen midden of an archaeological site reveals the debris of the process of living. Pottery products are mixed with all the other artifacts and are imperishable. In painting, design, materials, techniques, they reveal age and establish a relative chronology.

Pottery was functional in this society of craftsmen. It brought psychological fulfillment—handicrafts are one of the therapeutic techniques of the psychiatrist. It had social utility—an economy based upon handicraft culture is not so liable to fluctuations as one based on mass-produced products. The Aztecs, who knew nothing of such reasoning, thought only of using the surplus pottery production as an exchange medium at the weekly market.

25. *Aztec ceramics.* FACING PAGE: *These are the types that were made for use and export at the height of Aztec power. The long-handled ceramic was used by priests in the burning of copal to remove the disease of newness. The other vessels were for eating and drinking.* THIS PAGE: *Various other pottery forms used in Aztec households. These were all utilitarian and were not placed in graves or tombs.*

THE MARKET was like Napoleon's measure of Switzerland; if such a thing did not exist it would have to be invented —an uninvolved ground in which warring nations trade. The idea that trade is sacrosanct is as old as society itself; the market did not have to be invented; it came into being wherever man lived and traded, sold and bartered. Yet even so the Mexican market was astonishing.

"When we arrived at the great market place," remembered the chronicler,[48] "... we were astounded at the number of people and the quantity of merchandise ... and at the good order and control that was maintained. ..." "Yes," agreed Hernán Cortés after visiting the same market, "there are daily more than sixty thousand people bartering and selling ... the square is twice as big as Salamanca ... every kind of merchandise ... is for sale. ... There is a street of game [partridges, turkeys, quail, pigeons, parrots, owls, kestrels]. ... There is a street of herb sellers ... roots and ... medicinal herbs ... and houses of the apothecaries in which they sell the medicines from these herbs. ... There are barber shops where you may have your hair washed and cut." And, as if they vied with each other, Bernal Díaz recalled "other wares," i.e., "Indian slaves [*tlacotli*] both men and women [brought in] as the Portuguese bring negroes from Guinea ... tied to long poles. ..." Next there were "traders who

26. *Activity at the* tiaquiz *(market) covered all the phases of Aztec life, interest, and consumption. Women are seen bargaining for food, men for luxuries.*

sold great pieces of . . . cotton, and articles of twisted thread. . . ."
Much in evidence was the coarse cloth spun from the fibers of the
maguey and used by those who carried cargo on their backs, and
the sandals made of the same fiber. Cortés wrote of the various animal skins for sale and the pottery "of very good quality"; and his
companion asked that they not forget the "paper" offered for sale,
". . . which in this country is called *amatl,* and reeds scented with
liquidambar . . . and tobacco . . . much cochineal . . . I am forgetting
those who sell salt and those who make the stone knives. . . ."
There were "dealers in gold, silver [this would have been impossible in Peru where the Lord-Inca 'owned' all metals], and precious
stones, feathers, mantles. . . ." And along with all this commercial
activity, there was order. "A very fine building," Cortés assured his
liege, Charles V, "stands in the great square and serves as a kind
of audience where ten or twelve persons are always seated, as
judges, who deliberate on all cases arising in the market and pass
instant sentences on wrongdoers."

Such was the market (*tiaquiz*), of which there were five on the
island. Every city on the mainland had its own *tiaquiz,* and the festive days were so arranged that the people could attend the various
ones within the circuit of the valley of Anáhuac.

While the Mexican market was large, perhaps the greatest, it was
not unique: the market at Cholula was a mecca because of its great
temple to Quetzalcoatl, which drew people from all over Mexico.
Even those who were traditional enemies held their enmities in

abeyance while they carried on trade. Trade was sacred. The Spaniards who on their march to Mexico entered Tlascala, a tribal state in perpetual war with the Aztecs, found a city which Cortés thought "larger than Granada . . . with a market in which more than thirty thousand people daily are occupied in buying and selling . . . nothing is lacking. There are gold, silver and precious stones and jewellers' 'shops' . . . there is earthen-ware . . . as fine as any in Spain . . . there are booths for washing your hair and barbers to shave you . . . there are also public baths . . . and good order for . . . they behave like a people of sense and reason . . . the foremost city of Africa cannot rival them."

If marching meant markets, men marched. It is incredible, until one sifts the evidence, the distances men walked from the earliest times to market surplus and buy up their lack. Long before 2500 B.C., man in many parts of the world was going to the markets. "The extreme parts of the inhabitable world," wrote the Greek historian Herodotus, who visited many of them himself, "possess the most excellent products." All of the early routes were luxury routes and the markets were luxury markets. Persia's roads were crowded "with men on the king's business"; people were drawn to trade in the remote Indus valley so early that when Alexander the Great ventured into it expecting something else "he found well-made roads built of clay-brick" and all manner of "trees bearing yellow fruits lining the way." Whether it was early China trade or the Danube traffic or the Fertile Crescent which drew man, all were bent on ridding themselves of surplus and gaining luxuries. Trade was the loadstone that drew man to its world markets.

The Aztec market, which included tribute in its wares, differed little in the beginning from the usual "American" system of war tribute. But the Aztecs systematized it, and every six months 371 vassal cities yielded tribute of products so varied and vast that elaborate account books were needed to keep track of it. The market was further fed by the activities of its wandering merchants. Bernal Díaz himself said: "But why do I waste so many words in recounting what they sell in that great market?—for I shall never finish if I tell it all in detail."

THE FESTIVAL was almost continuous in ancient Mexico. It is not easy to separate festive and ceremonial, sacred and secular, since everything was bound up together. It is not difficult, however, to find a parallel in times not far distant when hangings and garrotings were always an occasion for holidays, and to realize how, in affairs of this kind, festival and sacred ritual were interlocked.

Like all other advanced tribes, the Aztecs had a calendar, divided into eighteen 20-day months; every one of these eighteen months had ceremonies and festivals. Months had descriptive names. The first month was Atlcoulaco ("want of water") and there were ceremonies, parades, and sacrifice. The second month was Tlacaxipeualiztli ("boning of the men"), when for sixteen days there were ceremonies and parades with priests dancing in the flayed skins of sacrificial victims. This skin, naturally, had magic powers—it gave to the priest who danced in it the power of the undead (i.e., the sacrificial victim whose skin it was); nor was this skin merely a symbol, something that prefigures, as a symbol is to us—it was consubstantiality. We can grasp some of the meaning of this, perhaps, in the story told by Anatole France of an eighteenth-century burgher of Séez who was robbed of some doubloons by his servant. Knowing his rights, he exacted the skin of the thief after she had been tried and executed, and made pantaloons from it, and whenever the thought of his loss overcame him, he would smack his thigh and cry, "The hussy. The hussy."

The third month, Tozoztontli, began with "fasting," and if this did not touch the heart of the rain god, Tlaloc, another festival, the flayed-skin dance to Xipé, was performed by the priests. The fourth month brought the people into the city from the fields to celebrate the worship of the new corn; altars in their houses were festooned with cornstalks. This was a bloodless time and young girls gave virginal blessings to the seed corn. By the fifth month (May 3–22) rain was full upon them; there were god-impersonation ceremonies, and they sacrificed children to the rain god to thank him (they had sacrificed children in the third month to bring on the rain). It is of course pure calumny to say that anthropophagy was involved in this,

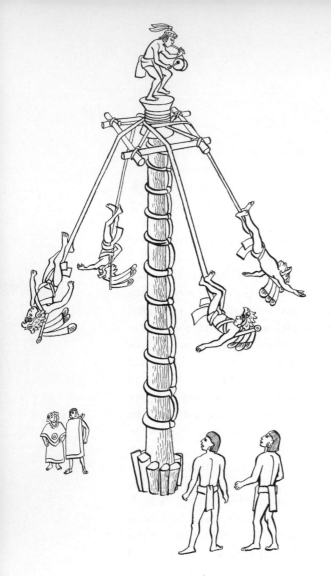

27. *The flywheel, a game-ceremony in which men, dressed as birds, hung from ropes and rotated, giving the effect of flight. This is still performed in some parts of Mexico.*

although Bernal Díaz wrote: "I have heard it said that they were wont to cook for Moctezuma the flesh of young boys." If that occurred at all, it was a ceremonial cannibalism.

The seventh month (June 12–July 1) was marked with the mimic dances of the salt workers, who leeched salt from the lakes of Anáhuac. The eighth month (July 2–21) was a joyous one—the adoration of the eating of the corn, an eight-day feast which could not get under way until the priests had dispatched a slave girl, beautifully attired to impersonate the Goddess of Young Corn. The ninth month, Tlaxochimaco ("birth of flowers"), brought feasts which lasted some days and was unusual in that the two sexes danced to-

28. *The dance of Xocotlhuetzi.*
This took place in the month
of that name, which celebrated
the "fall of fruits." Men
danced about a tree ornamented
with paper flags. From the
Codex Mendoza.

gether, "even touching the women," as an old Aztec explained. It was the rising class of merchant prince (*pochteca*) that gave these feasts, appropriately, for at the end it was to their god, Yacatecuhtli, protector of merchants.

The tenth month (August 11–30) was ostensibly to celebrate the "fall of the fruits." The people poured in in a festive mood, much as they once did in Europe to see someone drawn and quartered or, even better, beheaded. One has only to see Jacques Callot's mischievous drawings of the people of Paris rollicking during an execution to see the intermingling of holiday and bloodletting. In the Aztec world the rites to the fire god, Huehueteotl, were also certain to attract holiday crowds. Prisoners of war danced together with their captors and then, according to Dr. Vaillant, ascended to the top of a platform where *yauhtli* powder, an analgesic, was blown on their faces to anesthetize them somewhat during the next minutes. The half-awake prisoners were whirled about a dazzling fire and then dumped into the coals, fished out while still alive to have their still palpitating hearts cut out to be offered to the gods. There followed, after food and libations of intoxicating *octli,* a competitive climbing of a pole about fifty feet high to retrieve various paper insignia on top of it.

29. *Jugglers and musicians enlivened the festive days. Jesters and "merry-andrews" were part of the equipment of a high-placed Aztec.*

The eleventh month, from the end of August until September 19, was Ochpaniztli ("month of brooms"), with, of course, the usual sacrifices. It was also a military month with a review of all the clans parading with new arms, their own insignia on their shields; there was a procession of the knights of the Eagle and the knights of the Jaguar (who wore the animal skins as battle dress), a phalanx of warriors with special privileges; the festival ended in a gladiatorial contest.

The twelfth month, Teotleco, marked the return of the gods to earth (*teo,* "god," *tleco,* "return") and good fun for young and old, for ceremonial drunkenness was the rule of the day.

The thirteenth (October 10–29) had to do with Tlaloc, the demanding rain god. The fourteenth involved a general penance for four days; men were expected to abstain, with ceremony or without it, from their wives. Panquetzaliztli ("feast of the flags"), which was celebrated as the fifteenth month, honored the war god first with mock battles; then, says Sahagún, "the women sang and danced . . . intermingling with the men. . . ." They poured jugs of water over their heads—much as was done in the carnivals in Lima—took off their wet clothes, dyed their arms and legs blue, and dressed in *amatl* paper. The people marked for sacrifice also dressed in paper. It was raining again by the sixteenth month (December 9–28), and the month's name, Atemoztli, meant "fall of waters." The people prepared themselves by fasting five days previous to this feast. They spent the entire night cutting *amatl* paper "in diverse shapes, stuck them on poles, put them up in their homes and invited the symbol of the image they had cut to come together." They made vows, says Sahagún, "and at the same time took to their drums, their jingles and their tortoise-shell to play on." The seventeenth month brought the cold—it was the end of December. Now they tried to touch the rain god's heart, to persuade him to give them the withheld gift of rain. First the women wept, then the men; the men pelted their women with straw-filled bags to hurry on the tears. The eighteenth, the last month of the year, was to Izcalli. It was a time of mass sacrifice. The women who were to be immolated were dressed in *amatl* paper clothing, and after that they repaired to Cuauhtitlán, where prisoners of war were lashed to scaffolds, after the manner of the Pawnees of the western plains, and killed with arrows.

In all, the eighteen 20-day Aztec months accounted for 360 days. The imagination could not encompass more. It was satiated. There followed the *nemontemi,* the "five empty days" (February 7–11). One did nothing . . . no fire, no music, no love . . . one sat huddled waiting, waiting. . . .

To picture the life of the Aztec as one long joyous idyl cadenced by the beat of the drum to the frenzied dance of priests would, as one sees in this chapter, be wide of the mark. The Aztecs were terrorized as much by life as by the elements. The phenomenon of a snowstorm—understandably at 7,400 feet altitude—caused them to search their souls for portents; an involuntary loss of blood was disastrous; any contact with woman's catamenial flux would set off a concatenation of disasters.

Tenochtitlán may have been a paradise, but it was a troubled one.

AZTEC MUSIC—indeed all of American music—was tied up with dancing; any "pure" music has disappeared. What remains suggests that Aztec music was strong in rhythm but lacking in tone. This, at least, is what one infers from the instruments: the large upright drum, skin stretched over wood frame (*huehuetl*), was beaten with the bare hands and some control was exercised on the beat and quality of the tone; a smaller counterpart was hung around the neck and beaten with both hands, but contact with the body spoiled the resonance; the two-note wooden drum (*teponzatli*) was beaten with rubber-tipped beaters, sonorous but monotonous. The conch shell—all peoples who have had contact with the sea have had the conch, including the Inca and its use seems to have been world-wide—gave out an impressively deep blast: a chorus of them were used early in the morning with the rising of Venus to arouse the people out of sleep. Since they had no string instruments nor such instruments as the marimba—these were cultural borrowings from Negro slaves—their forte was the percussion instrument in various forms. They also had flutes shaped like Pan-pipes, in clay or of reed, and whistles, and in addition to the rattles, seed-filled gourds, and the seed or shell attachments on the ankles that kept the beat. These are still used by the present-day Yaqui people. There were also notched bones, usually human femurs, which, rasped with a stick, suggest modern *musica Cubana*. The thing to note was that the music was rhythmic, not melodic; its outward effect was cadence to the dancer, its inward effect, hypnotic.

30. *Music and musical instruments. Trumpet, drum, and gourd rattles produced the principal effects. The Aztec at the left blows a conch horn. The next man beats a* huehuetl, *an upright drum of stretched skin. Another beats a two-noted wooden* teponzatli *(the beaters were of rubber). The dancing figure shakes the gourd rattles.*

II. *Temple of the Sun, Teotihuacán. Artificially raised, this pyramid became the standard method of displaying the dignity of the gods.* (Victor W. von Hagen)

III. *Calixtlahuaca, near Toluca. The highest temple in Mexico at 9,517 feet, it is also one of the oldest. Its beginning is shrouded in mystery and is variously placed about* A.D. 500. (Victor W. von Hagen)

IV. *The frieze of marching jaguars and eagles at Tula, a temple-city of Toltec origin.* (Victor W. von Hagen)

V. *A detail of the frieze of marching jaguars and eagles at the temple of Tula.* (Victor W. von Hagen)

VI. *A detail of the wall (shown in Plate VII) of a serpent disgorging the skeleton of a man it has swallowed.* (Victor W. von Hagen)

VII. *The outside wall of the temple at Tula. About it runs the* xical-coliuhqui, *the symbol of the Quetzalcoatl derived from the stylized head of the sky serpent.* (Victor W. von Hagen)

VIII. *The figure of Chac-Mool, which first appeared at Tula, and then reappeared in Yucatán three centuries later. The hearts torn from sacrificial victims were said to have been thrown, as food for the gods, into the dish that the prone god holds on his stomach.* (Andor Braun)

IX. *The Temple of Quetzalcoatl, Teotihuacán, with its dominant feathered serpent heads.* (Victor W. von Hagen)

X. *A detail of a wall at Mitla, one of the best-known and best-preserved archaeological sites in Mexico. Its geometrical patterns seem inspired by and based on textile designs—"petrified weaving."* (Andor Braun)

XI. *Part of the North Plaza of Monte Albán, the present-day city of Oaxaca. It is surrounded by tall glyphed monoliths which, while not fully deciphered, suggest that they were set up during the occupation of the Mixtecs, the traditional border enemies of the Zapotecs, the first builders of the temple-city.* (Victor W. von Hagen)

XII. *Gold breastplate from Monte Albán.* (José Limón)

XIII. *Xochicalco.*
A figure of a priest with plumed headdress sitting cross-legged. It highly suggests the Mayas in handling and could be mistaken for Maya.
(Victor W. von Hagen)

XIV. *Xochicalco.*
A view of the temple (north side), showing relative size of carving and temple.
(Victor W. von Hagen)

XV. *Aztec art. A vase with a crouching figure, fashioned from the hard, brittle, volcanic obsidian.* (José Limón)

XVI. *A rabbit, carved from a piece of translucent quartz.* (José Limón)

XVII. *The Totonacs, on the coast of Vera Cruz (where Cortés first landed), produced a wide and varied art: here is a clay Faustian bearded figure, with lined face, immense headgear.* (José Limón)

XVIII. *An example of the curious original motifs in low relief on jade, from the Olmecs of Tabasco. The Olmecs are presumed to have been the cultural intermediaries between the Mayas and Central Mexico.* (José Limón)

XIX. *The celebrated laughing heads, shaped, perhaps cast, from clay molds. These are typical of the Totonac area, but quite unique in all Mexico.* (Victor W. von Hagen)

Dance was as inseparable from music as was singing or rhythmic stress. There were mass dances of various forms and there were certainly group dances. But, warriors or priests, merchants or chiefs—under whatever guise—the dance had but one function: to obtain aid from the unseen powers upon which Aztec prosperity depended. Drunkenness itself was ritual and sacred. The dance with music was to seduce the gods; the fundamental, the *raison d'être*, of the dance, to the dancers as well as the watchers, was "mystic communion," the fusion which made them one with the god they hoped would hear their call. Drumming was of supreme importance: it soothed the soul and made the gods amenable. Drumming also exerted a real mystical influence; it acted upon the disposition of the unseen as it acted upon the spectator, so that from the "mystic point of view the drum was an indispensable part of the magico-propitiatory apparatus." [106]

Drum and song were acclaimed together. With the beat of the bass drum and the two-noted wooden drums giving the added dignity of background, the singer (*cuicani*) gave out this to the national Aztec god:

> *I am Hummingbird Wizard, the warrior, no one*
> *is equal to myself.*

> *Not in vain have I donned my robe of yellow feathers;*
> *for me the sun has arisen.*

Song, music, rhythm, in addition to breaking the dull monotony of their lives, were used, as they always have been, for memory. There was little doubt of the effect sought after by the Aztec impresario. The various episodes of the dance, the same movements repeated without number, the volumes of sound, the ornaments and masks, all had one aim, one religious aim—emotional paroxysms in which all present were robbed of their self-possession and thus believed that their wish to secure the favor of the gods had been attained.

G AMES have always been immense fun. But to the Aztecs the "game" was not enough in itself. As with the present-day Russians, it was for them serious business, magical and ritualistic; it had no point of rest. They were more earnest in what was supposed to be unserious than in serious matters. This finds a counterpart in the pages of Anatole France's *La Rôtisserie de la reine Pédauque,* where, in a highly amusing card-playing scene, the author reflects that "men are more punctilious at play than in serious matters and they bring more honesty to bear on tric-trac where it is passable hindrance and leave it out in battles or in treaties of peace where it would be troublesome."

The passions which man displays in games were best seen in a game played from Honduras to Arizona and known as *tlachtli.* It began as a sport; it ended up as ritual. No one can say precisely where or when it began, except that the Olmecs who lived in the hotlands of the Gulf Coast, where rubber * grew, had the game as early as 500 B.C.—a ball court was found in their temple complex at La Venta— and their name was derived from the word for rubber, *olli* (*Ol-mec:* "rubber people").

Tlachtli was then already formalized. Yet the expressive pre- Aztec clay figures of tribesmen playing a variant of the game show it was as popular and ritualistic as baseball—if one must have an anal- ogy. It was played in a court shaped like an *I;* walls of tiered seats were on either side. In the middle of this was the "basket," a stone or wooden ring set, not horizontally as in basketball, but vertically; the object was to put the rubber ball through the ring. The ball was hard, not inflated. The players were allowed to strike it only with legs or hips or elbows; they were padded like a goalie in ice hockey. Although many played it, *tlachtli* was essentially a religious game performed before the rulers of tribes. In Mexico-Tenochtitlán, the ball court stood in the sacred enclosure in front of the racks of skulls of those who had been sacrificed at the main temple and was bounded on one side by the temple dedicated to the knights of the Eagle.

* Charles Marie de La Condamine (1701–74) was the first to experiment with rubber. He found it in use as a sort of syringe by Indians in the Amazon. Rubber from Vera Cruz was first mentioned by Oviedo, the Spanish historiographer, in 1500.

The Friar Bernardino de Sahagún wrote of the game: "the balls were about the size of bowling balls [i.e., six inches in diameter] and were solid, made of a gum called *ulli* . . . which is very light and bounces like an inflated ball." In playing, both players and spectators placed enormous bets, "gold, turquoise, slaves, rich mantles, even cornfields and houses [which reminds one that Cardinal Mazarin lost an entire chateau in a single play of bezique] . . . at other times the lord played ball for his pastime . . . he also brought with him good ball players who played before him, and other principal men played on the opposite team, and they won gold and *chalchiguites* and beads of gold, and turquoise and slaves and rich mantles and maxtles and cornfields and houses, etc. [feathers, cacao, cloaks of feather] . . . the ball court . . . consisted of two walls, twenty or thirty feet apart, that were up to forty or fifty feet in length; the walls . . . were whitewashed and about eight and a half feet high, and in the middle of the court was a line which was used in the game . . . in the middle of the walls, in the center of the court, were two stones, like millstones hollowed out, opposite each other, and each one had a hole wide enough to contain

31. Tlachtli *was the first basketball game. Popular as well as ritualistic, it was played in a rectangular court with stone "baskets" placed vertically. The ball was of hard rubber. The game was known and played from Honduras to Arizona.*

the ball. . . . And the one who put the ball in it won the game. They did not play with their hands, but instead struck the ball with their buttocks; for playing they wore gloves on their hands and a belt of leather on their buttocks, with which to strike the ball."

In other games also the Aztecs were certainly as "punctilious in play as in serious matters." *Patolli*, something like backgammon or parchesi, was a less sanguine sport and was played on a marked board or paper, with beans for counters. The object was to travel about the board and return "home" to win. It is doubtless the same game that Cortés used to play with Moctezuma when he was the Spaniards' captive in his own palace. Bernal Díaz called it *totoloque*. It was a gambling game, as he said, played "with some very smooth pellets made of gold. . . . They toss these pellets some distance as well as some little slabs which were also made of gold. . . . In five strokes or tries they gained or lost certain pieces of gold or rich jewels that they staked."*

There were other games, mostly played by children, that have their counterparts in our own life. But all this was the playtime of the little man before ritual and the gloomy pessimism of Aztec life turned his naturally gay exuberance into something lugubrious.

* There were only two players but each had his own official scorekeeper. Cortés had Pedro de Alvarado (called "the Sun" by the Aztec because of his white-blond hair), and Moctezuma observed that Alvarado always marked more points than Cortés gained and "courteously and laughingly he said he was being done ill because Cortés was making so much *yxoxol* in the game," i.e., he was cheating.

32. Patolli, *a game utilizing a board shaped like a cross, was played something like parchesi. Although a game of chance and used for gambling, patolli was semisacred and was watched over by Macuil-xochitl, the Five-flower Goddess.*

"CODES OF LAW," said Rabelais when he stopped panta-
gruelizing long enough to be very serious, "are
founded upon necessity and not upon justice." And the Aztecs
would have agreed. They were not versed in the dialects of "as if";
their justice was exacting, swift, and final. What was crime? Stealing,
adultery, blasphemy, killing, and drunkenness (unless it was ritual).

33. *Aztec justice as
shown in the* Codex
Florentino *and drawn
by an Aztec artist.
Three chieftains con-
demn a criminal for
an outrageous crime
and witness his execu-
tion by garroting.*

All these were capital crimes. It is difficult to understand that a
nation given to such overwhelming sacrificial slaughter would be
so aghast at death. But there was a fundamental difference: war and
ceremonial sacrifice, murder and rape during battle did not involve
the clan or tribe. This does not differ in practice from our own
moral phenomena—"There is no such thing as moral phenomena,
only a moral interpretation of phenomena"; we reward the killer
during war and consider murder beyond the pale during peace.

Aztec society, as do all societies, existed (in theory and mostly
in practice) for the benefit of its component parts. The Aztec ideas
of justice were ancient. Stealing to them was an aberration, for

which restitution in kind was the usual penance. For things that could not be restored, there was death or else expulsion from the clan (the same thing) or into slavery. Adultery brought death, although this varied much with the circumstances of the people involved. Punishment to tribesmen who misused the "king's way," the Aztec road, was severe; robbery of merchants carrying on "sacred business" was death by stoning—commerce and the royal way were sacrosanct. The penalty for murder naturally was death.

The most heinous were religious crimes. The robbing of temples, an offense that might provoke the disfavor of the gods, or doubting the efficacy of prayers, in short to blaspheme (to blame) anything that might bring disaster on the whole tribe—this brought immediate death. It was no different in the Christian world; an auto-da-fé reported from Seville in the *Fugger News-Letters* in 1579: "sentence the *third;* Juan de Color, slave, 35, reviled the name of Our Dear Lady and other saints—disputed her miracles . . . burning at the stake."

Witchcraft was the deadliest of crimes. Obsession with it is interwoven in the deepest fibers of the primitive mind, especially if it was directed toward someone of one's own clan. It was the worst crime that one could commit, and to cause death by witchcraft was considered worse than murder—it was anthropophagy, i.e., the eating of kin's flesh. The sentence of death was carried out only after protracted torture. To remain impartial, however, we must recall the prevalence of witches in our own world. There was the notorious witch Walpurga Hausmann, who, as reported in one of the *Fugger News-Letters,* confessed in 1587 to killing forty-three children over a period of thirty years. The bishop of Augsburg gave the verdict: "despatch from life by burning. . . ." And the verdict on another tried for misdeeds of witchcraft was changed to "as the result of her fervent petitioning her sentence has been lightened . . . first she will be strangled and only then burned."

The administration of justice was designed so that people would live in harmony among themselves. (It was not designed for their neighbors, for all other men were enemies.)

They lived by a code far more strict than the one we impose on ourselves. In the eternal theater of carnage and death that was Aztec, one had to conform.

Medicinal plants in the Aztec world were of a wide and interesting order. Few protohistoric peoples have left so extensive a description of plants, economic, aesthetic, and curative. The Aztecs, like all other "Mexicans" before them, were metaphysicians far more spontaneous than we ourselves. They wore amulets to protect against disease—an arm stricture, a nose ornament, a lucky shell or stone, a talisman to avert a baleful influence. Diseases, numbered among the disasters, were caused by unseen powers; defense was made by appealing to the same medium. Although not completely unaware of the pathological, their medicine was bound up with magic and religion. Yet since life is a lying dream and physics often saves one from metaphysics, the Aztecs, who were good herbalists, applied what they knew to ease the disease.

The cure doctor (*ticitl*) appeared in cases of serious illness; he brought with him all the appurtenances of the shaman (in the theatrical world, "props")—shells, eagle wings, a hank of hair, tobacco to purify by smoke. He began as a masseur by rubbing on the body to find and extract the "fairy dart"—a stone, a rock, a small arrow—which had entered the body and "caused" the illness. One of the names of the cure doctor comes from this: *tetla-acuicilique,* "he-who-recovers-the-stone." Illness was not natural; it had a mystical cause. It was carried down from the mountain on winds (we believed the tertiary fevers came from the bad air; hence "mal-

34. *The cure doctor* (ticitl) *at work. An old woman, as shown in the* Codex Florentino, *applies leaves to the back of a young mother.*

aria"); or Tlaloc, the rain god, for a lack of proper obeisance, sent leprosy, ulcers, even foot trouble (a disaster to people who were their own draft animals); or if man and woman in love breached the tabu of incest, they could die of *tlazol-miquiztli,* "love death." The best cure for such cravings was to invoke the name of the genie of desire, one Tlazol-teteo, and take a hot steam bath (not much different from the method described in the limerick "by thinking of Jesus/and venereal diseases/and the risk of begetting a child").

If the cause of the disease, after the magical object had been removed, was not easily diagnosed, the witch doctor gave the patient an infusion of the bark of *oloiuhqui.* Since this is of the *Datura* family and possesses narcotic properties, the patient dreamed and talked and supposedly revealed the cause of his illness. (The same principle underlies narcosynthesis treatment in modern medicine.) Once the hocus-pocus was over, the cure doctor used remedies, some sensible, others ineffectual, and still others (as in our own world) ridiculous and even harmful. Whatever it was, the Indian patient accepted it without protest, afraid to modify it by complaining and so spoiling its miraculous powers.

What were the diseases they had to cure? About the same as afflicted most of the indigenous Americans before white man's arrival: colds, grippe, and all the other respiratory diseases; malaria; swarms of intestinal infections and infestations; leprosy; skin diseases; and—most probably—syphilis.

The Aztec herbalists worked out a classification of plants, particularly of those having therapeutic value. Much of this information, fortunately, was gathered before time and the effect of conquest brought the society to an end. There are a few such herbals extant, *The de la Cruz-Badiano Aztec Herbal,* for instance, written in 1552.

The herbalist had a full command of curatives, as was known to José de Acosta, the learned Jesuit who traveled in Mexico in 1565: "I say onely that in the time of . . . the Mexican Kings, there were many great personages expert in curing of diseases with simples . . . having the knowledge of the many vertues and properties of hearbes, roots, woodes and plants. . . . There are a thousand of these simples fit to purge, as the rootes of *Guanucchoacan,* the *Pignons of Punua,* the conserve of *Guanucquo,* the oyle of Fig-trees. . . ."

They were, like all such Homeric simples, formed of equal portions of cure, hope, and magic. For boils take the leaves of the *tlatl-anquaye* root, apply morning and noon, wash after the application with urine. Loss of hair could be prevented by a lotion of dog's or deer's urine with the plant called *xiuh-amolli*. If the head was broken in battle, "the break should be smeared with plants growing in summer dew, with green-stone pearls, crystal and the *tlaca-huatzin,* and with wormy earth, ground up in the blood from a bruised vein and the white of an egg; if blood cannot be had burned frogs will take the place." [68] The cures suggest the diseases that afflicted the Aztec: he ate too much corn, too little

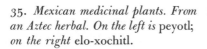

35. *Mexican medicinal plants. From an Aztec herbal. On the left is* peyotl; *on the right* elo-xochitl.

meat, not enough greenstuffs; the tropics brought their toll of intestinal diseases; birth was not always as easy as it is made out to be. Overheated eyes were cured by mixing the root of *matlal-xochitl* with mother's milk (note of warning: one suffering from this affliction would abstain from sex and wear on his neck a red crystal and on his right arm the eye of a fox). Bloodshot eyes, cataract, tumors in the eyes were all treated with plants that have been identified as having positive medicinal value. Catarrh and colds, common or otherwise, were helped by inhaling the odors of the plant *a-toch-ietl,* which is the pennyroyal of commercial medicine and is still used in some parts as a culicifuge.

Teeth, generally good, were often affected by swelling gums and toothache; the tooth was first punctured and a poultice made from the cactus *tenochtli* and farina then applied.

Tumors were cut out with obsidian knives, and after surgery the crushed leaves of a plant were applied. "Lameness of the hands" was to be cured by steeping the hands in warm water where the leaves of a bitter astringent had been crushed, after which the patient was to put his hand on an ant nest and "let him patiently allow the lame hands to be bitten by the ants' pincers." Heart pains, burning of the heart, pains in the side, all of which came from overdrinking of the fermented *octli,* were treated with other herbs.

36. *The maguey plant* (metl) *and the method of gathering the sweet sap of the plant and storing it until it became fermented* octli.

Stomach ailments were frequent among a people whose intestines swarmed with parasites; medicines to kill stomach worms, cures for tumors and dysentery appear often in the herbal. The bladderwort, which the Aztecs called *coanenepilli,* was used "when the flow of urine is shut off"; this was mixed with other bitter plants and "administered as an emetic." "If this medicine avails nothing," says the herbal, "it will be then necessary to take the pith of an extremely slender palm, covered with cotton, smeared with honey, and crushed with the herb *huihuitz-mallotic* and this cautiously inserted into the virile member."

Gout, rectal infections, rheumatism ("pain in the knees"), were frequent. More so were "cracks in the soles of the feet" for those who walked and had to carry burdens. There were remedies for "black blood" fevers (of which there is a good diagnosis in the herbals: "spit blood, body jerks and turns hither and thither, he sees little"). Hemorrhoids were present, and not, as often supposed, the result of modern occupational stresses; but if one had to go through the Aztec cure, perhaps it would be best to be left with the hemorrhoids ("before the cure, let him kill a weasel and eat it quite alone with dragon's blood"). Ringworm was endemic; the itch, dyspepsia, and warts were all part of the trouble of living. For all, specific cures were offered. Those who were "fear-burdened" had only to take a drink of the potion made of the herb called *tonatiuh-yxiuh* mixed with other plants and make a poultice of it with the blood of a wolf, the blood and excrement of an *acuecue-yxoyalotl,* ground together with sea foam.

Lice on the head, lousy distemper, and goatlike smell of the armpits could apparently be easily cured. There was much occupation with birth and many remedies were offered for recent parturition, to increase the flow of milk and for breast tubercles. The herbalist relieved pain in childbirth, but his methods would have appealed more to Jean Jacques Rousseau, who popularized the "noble savage," than to the gynecologist: "the womb of a woman entering childbirth is to be washed out with the juice of the plants. Into the womb you also inject the triturated herb *ayo nelhuatl* and eagle excrement. . . ."

There has been, to date, no comprehensive study of Aztec diseases. There is no evidence of surgery or of skull trepanning, as in Peru. However, this negative evidence is not decisive since we have few skeletal remains of these people. There is little doubt, however, that Aztec herbal medicine was far advanced. Certainly a people who could offer a remedy to relieve "the fatigue of those administering government and discharging public offices"* must have had a vast pharmacopeia or else a good sense of humor.

---

* The bark of the tree *quetzal-ylin,* the flowers of *elo-xochitl* and *izqui-xochitl,* the almond with its fruit, which is the *tlapal-cacahuatl,* the flowers *cacalo-xochitl, huacal-xochitl, meca-xochitl, huey-nacaztli,* and all fine-smelling summer flowers, leaves of the trees *a-ylin, oyametl, ocotl, a-xocotl, eca-patli, tlaco-izqui-xochitl, quauh-yyauhtli, tomazquitl, ahuatl, tepe-ylin, ayauh-quahuitl,* and *te-papaquilti quahuitl,* flower-bearing plants with their shrubbery, which you gather before the wind rises—these are expressed one by one in clear spring water, into new vessels or vases. This then stays for a day and a night, when the *huitz-quahuitl* wood, with a red juice, is added as coloring.

Also the blood of wild animals, namely the red ocelot, *cuetlachtli, miztli, ocotochtli,* white ocelot, *tlaco-ocelotl,* is sought for. With this and the above liquors the body is well anointed.

These medicaments give gladiatorial strength to the body, drive fatigue far off, and also cast out timidity and strengthen the human heart.

Yet there came a time, as it does to all, when medicines were of no help. From the time of a child's conception everyone in clan and tribe did his best to aid him through life; his mother was deflowered by others than the father so that evil, which was everywhere, would not harm him; at birth a priest had been called in to consult the auguries to be certain that the child was named on a lucky day; from cradle to fatal illness the fear of the "things" that moved through the supersensuous world never left him. What one did or did not do was only an attempt to steer successfully between Scylla and Charybdis on this uncertain sea of life. When the end approached, the dying must have felt that not enough had been done to propitiate the unseen powers, that perhaps somewhere along the way something had been forgotten, somewhere there had been a failure to conform.

Now that all had failed, the dying knew that the understanding alone was not enough to comprehend the world; somewhere the arguments of the heart must stand. The Aztec herbal gave final advice; the *ticitl*, "the cure doctor—will draw his auguries as to whether the patient is to die or get well from the eyes and nose. . . . A mark of death is a sootiness found in the middle of the eyes . . . eyes growing dark and unseeing . . . nose getting thin. . . . Also ever grinding of the teeth . . . and finally the babbling of words without meaning . . . in the way of parrots. . . . You may anoint the chest with pine wood crushed in water . . . or puncture the skin with a wolf's bone or that of an eagle or that of a puma . . . or you can hang close to the nostrils the heart of a kestrel wrapped in a deerskin. . . . If none of these avail, that fatal necessity is at hand . . . and death is complete."

23 *The Undead*

"IT IS A FACT," someone says in Thomas Mann's *The Magic Mountain*, "that a man's dying is more the survivors' affair than his own"; it certainly was a fact to the Aztec. Death complicated everything. The survivors had to do penance in many ways for the unsocial act of their kinsman's dying. Does death put an end to us utterly and entirely? The Aztec did not know how to answer this. He did not have the subtlety of the French poet who answered the question of death by saying: *"Je suis, elle n'est pas; elle est, je ne suis plus."* "To the Aztec," writes Jacques Soustelle, "death and life were but aspects of the same reality." He could not (any more than you and I) imagine himself as not being.

Then came the "confession"—it is as ancient as man's society; the dying had to confess. It is a very important part of Christian ritual and communistic political behavior patterns; it goes back to a far-reaching primitivity. Confessions had a virtue of their own; they were essential to neutralize the evil influences brought on by dying. For example, the Aztec believed that the act of dying caused uncleanliness, for dying was a form of social defilement. There actually existed a mystic bond between the dying man and death, some sort of participation like that which unites a living man and his belongings. Man is responsible; he is the silent accomplice of the evil which is being propagated. He must confess.

The sorcerer was called in to attend to it. He arrived, consulted the sacred roll, and tobacco smoke was blown across the dying man; invocations were made to the gods so that he would die like an Aztec of good sense. Then they prepared the body for burial. First in his mouth a greenstone to take the place of his heart. It was not like the obolus which the Greeks put into the mouth of the dead to pay the passage across the river Styx; rather it was a heart symbol—the "Heart of Jade"—for his journey to the unworld. Food was prepared, drink put in bowls, and the mummy bundle made complete. The next step was inhumation. Two courses were open to the Aztecs for the disposal of the dead, but the choice really depended on social position. If he was a common Indian, the body was swathed in cloth, tied with a cord, and festooned with paper flags; funeral chants (*miccacuicatl*) were put into the mouths of the dead by the living:

> *Where shall I go?*
> *Where shall I go?*
> *The road of the god of duality.*
> *Is your house perchance in the place of the fleshless?*
> *Perchance inside heaven?*
> *or here on earth only*
> *is the place of the fleshless?*

Death stirs both primitive and civilized, for to die, at least to the Aztec, was to accomplish an act of incalculably far-reaching potentialities. The dead were in reality living: they had merely passed from one phase to another; they were invisible, impalpable, invulnerable. The dead, or, better, in their feeling, the *undead,* had become the unseen members of the clan. The body of the common man, swathed in cloth, tied into a death bundle, had things of his life and other things for his death-life journey. He was then cremated and the ashes were put into a pot on which the piece of jade was placed, the pot being kept in the house.

Cremation was general except where those of elevated rank were concerned; the leaders were entombed. The "Anonymous Conqueror" found one of them after the rape of Mexico-Tenochtitlán. He found a mummy sitting with his personal device, sword, and jewels amounting to "three thousand castellanos."

The departed went to those tutelary genii who had protected them in life; the knights of the Eagle, warriors, and valiant women (considered the same as warriors) went to the land of Tlaloc, the rain god; he also cordially received those souls who died by drowning, since he was the god of water. How one acted or did not act in life had no relation to one's degree of immortality; conduct in life did not determine the soul's place in the shades. "The vertical world," says Dr. Vaillant, "was divided into heavens and hells [there were thirteen heavens and nine hells] which had no moral significance." It was one's occupation in life and manner of dying that determined it: warriors went to the eastern paradise, flower-filled; women who died in childbirth went into a western paradise and came to earth to haunt children and women in unspent spleen. Those of the undead who were unclassified made the passage to Mictlán; this was a veritable *via dolorosa:* rivers to cross, mountains to climb, deserts to cross, enduring of freezing winds and rains; the dead had full need of all the charms that the survivors put into the funeral pyre as talismans for the journey. When the soul arrived at the realm of the Lord of the Dead, he was assigned to one of the nine hells; the piece of greenstone tied to the mouth when the cadaver was swathed was left as a pledge in the seventh hell.

Poor human beings, we must needs furnish ourselves with illusions even in death. Since man, primitive or civilized, cannot endure the idea of a mechanistic interpretation of the universe, he cannot grasp the fact that when one is not, one ceases to be. Ignorance is not alone a necessary condition of happiness, it is a condition of life itself; the sentiments that make life bearable to all spring out of falsehood and are fed on illusions.

"We do not believe," said the Aztecs, "we fear."

Meanwhile, the living must go into mourning for eighty days. There were a variety of impositions and taboos on food, dress, and indulgence in sex; sustenance had to be regularly placed at the death urn, prayers given, blood offered from cuts made in the ears and tongue. All must be done to obtain the good will of the recent dead; their displeasure could have dire consequences and could expose the living to twofold retribution: from the justly offended recently dead and from fellow clan members, who collectively would have to suffer the consequences of the dead's anger. After eighty days the taboo was lifted. It was repeated on and off for four years: "For . . . it is a fact that a man's dying is more the survivors' affair than his own."

Such, from womb to tomb, was the daily life of the Aztec common man, base of the pyramid of Aztec society. Higher up in rank by election there were the clan heads; these in turn had representation on the tribal council (*tecuhtli*), and at the top of this curious *mélange* of elected officials were the "council of four" (*tlatoani*). Finally, at the apex was the semidivine Chief Speaker, the Uei Tlatoani, head of the army, high priest, the court of last appeal in the city-state of Tenochtitlán.

The well-remembered "king" Moctezuma was the Uei Tlatoani in that fateful year of 1519.

37. Aztec burial.

38. *Moctezuma Xocoyotzin—Moctezuma II, the Younger (reigned 1503–20). As Chief Speaker he ruled Mexico when it reached its apogee. Although the materials of his clothes were finer, basically they were the same style as his subjects: cloak, breechclout, and sandals. The headgear is his "crown."*

The Aztec 'Kings'

and the Directing Classes

 Moctezuma   *24*

THE RULER of the Aztecs had as title "One Who Speaks" (derived from the verb *tlatoa,* "to speak"); he was elected. So William Prescott was not entirely incorrect in calling their form of government an "elective monarchy." The leader was not absolute, as in the Peruvian theocracy—he did not claim ownership of the land, the earth, the people, as did the Inca—the Aztecs were in theory democratic.[198] Each family was a member of a soil community; a cluster of these families formed a clan, of which twenty made up the tribe of the Tenochas. Each clan had its own council and an elected leader; of these the oldest or wisest or more experienced were selected to make up an interclan council, the link between the clans and the tribe's governing body. This council was narrowed down to four principals, who were advisers to the leader of state and, as well, electors of the "king" (functioning, to pursue a convenient analogy, as did the electors of the Holy Roman Empire), since "kings" were not such by primogeniture but could be selected by the *tlatoani* from the brothers of the previous ruler, or, if he had none, from his nephews. These *tlatoani* were the key figures in Aztec government; they chose that "noble" descendant who in their mind was most distinguished in valor, war, knowledge. Such a one was Moctezuma, who was "crowned" in 1503. There is a description of him which is the most penetrating we have of any such ruler of any of the Sun Kingdoms of ancient America.

It was November 8, 1519, when Hernán Cortés arrived with his small army at Tenochtitlán. Where two causeways coalesced, "Here nearly one thousand of the chief citizens came out to greet me, all dressed alike and richly; on coming to speak with me each performed a ceremony very common to them, to wit, placing his hand on the ground and then kissing it, so that for nearly an hour I stood while they performed this ceremony.

"Moctezuma himself came out to meet us with some two hundred nobles. . . . They came forward in two long lines keeping close to the walls of the street. . . . Moctezuma was borne along in the middle of the street with two lords, one on his right and left. . . . Moctezuma wore sandles, whereas the others were barefoot."

Bernal Díaz, who did not have to content himself with lofty political remarks, kept to description where Cortés left off. "The Great Moctezuma was about forty years old, of good height and well proportioned, slender and spare of flesh, not very swarthy, but of the natural colour and shade of an Indian. He did not wear his hair long . . . his scanty beard was well shaped and thin. His face was somewhat long, but cheerful . . . He was very neat and clean and bathed once every day in the afternoon. He had many women as mistresses, daughters of Chieftains, and he had two great Cacicas as his legitimate wives. He was free from unnatural offences [i.e., sodomy]. The clothes that he wore one day, he did not put on again until four days later [the Lord-Inca never wore the same garment twice]. He had two hundred Chieftains in his guard . . . and when they went to speak to him they were obliged to take off their rich mantles and put on others of little worth . . . to enter barefoot with their eyes lowered to the ground, and not to look up in his face. . . . And they made him three obeisances . . ." (The Lord-Inca imposed a similar ritual.)

Moctezuma ate like a grand vizier. "For each meal over thirty different dishes were prepared . . . and they placed small pottery braziers beneath the dishes so that they should not get cold . . . he had such a variety of dishes . . . turkeys, pheasants, native partridges, quail, tame and wild ducks, venison, wild boar, reed birds, pigeons, hares . . . so numerous that I cannot finish naming them . . ." Moctezuma sat "on a low stool, soft and richly worked . . . Four very beautiful cleanly women brought water for his hands in a sort of deep basin which they call *xicales* . . . And two other women brought him tortilla bread, and as soon as he began to eat they placed before him a sort of wooden screen painted over with gold, so that no one should watch him eating. . . . four great chieftains [these were the *tlatoani*] who were old men came and stood beside [the women] and with these Moctezuma now and then conversed . . . They say that these elders were his near relations, and were his counsellors . . . They brought him fruit of all the different kinds . . . From time to time in cup-shaped vessels of pure gold, a certain drink made from cacao [was served]. . . . Sometimes at meal-times there were present some very ugly humpbacks . . . who are their jesters, and other Indians, who must have been buffoons . . .

"There were also placed on the table three tubes much painted and gilded, which held *liquidambar* mixed with certain herbs which they call *tabaco*, and when he had finished eating . . . he inhaled the smoke from one of those tubes . . . with that he fell asleep."

Moctezuma became a demigod. Although elected, with leadership he took on semidivinity. He was high priest, supreme commander of the army, and head of state, a plenary ruler, advised by council, with his power only held in check by ancient mores. Moctezuma was the ninth in succession, the nephew of the last ruler, Ahuitzotl, and grandson of Moctezuma I (surnamed "the Wrathy"). As an Aztec ruler-aspirant he was trained like all such in the "religious" schools, the *calmecac* ("house of the large corridors"). There, with the image of Quetzalcoatl painted on the wall, he learned by means of glyphic charts the history of the Tenochas. He was taught to read glyph writing, to remember the list of dates of rulers and history, which succinctly was:

Aztec history begins	A.D. 1168
Tenochtitlán settled	A.D. 1325

List of Aztec realm leaders after A.D. 1375:

Acamapichtli	ruled	1375–1395	Moctezuma I	ruled	1440–1469
Huitzilhuitl	"	1395–1414	Axayacatl	"	1469–1481
Chimalpopoca	"	1414–1428	Tizoc	"	1481–1486
Itzcoatl	"	1428–1440	Ahuitzotl	"	1486–1503

Moctezuma II   ruled   1503–1520

He studied the use of Aztec arms, swords, slings, and arrows, for it was expected he would be a military leader; once he knew and understood ideographic writing he learned about the stars, astrology, the calendar, and through constant reading of the *tonalamatl* (used as an aid in memory) he learned the rituals and interpretation of phenomena. As a youth Moctezuma had taken a very active part in the wars; later he devoted much attention to religion, "scrupulous in his attentions to all the burdensome ceremonial of the Aztec worship." José de Acosta also said that he was "grave and staid and spake little, so when hee gave his opinion . . . then he was feared and respected. . . . Hee marched with such gravitie . . . they all sayd the name of Moctezuma ['Courageous Lord'] agreed very well with his nature."

When elected, Moctezuma was found sweeping down the 133 steps of the great Temple of Huitzilopochtli ("to show that he desired not the Emprey," adds Acosta in an aside). "The electors . . . giving him notice that hee was chosen king . . . he was ledde before the harth of their gods . . . where he offered sacrifice in drawing blood from his eares & the calves of his legges."

First, war, where he went in person to an enterprise "necessary for his coronation,"[1] i.e., prisoners for sacrifice. He moved down to the Gulf, extended Aztec domination in both directions, and returned in triumph to Mexico and had his nose septum pierced for insertion of the royal emerald for his coronation. The number of sacrificial victims did not quite reach that of his uncle's piety; Ahuitzotl had immolated twelve thousand.

Moctezuma was "crowned" with a sort of miter; the color symbol of his power was blue-green. Immediately after coming to power he turned out the rankless people about him, commanding that "only the most noble and most famous men of his realme shoulde live within his pallace," thus severing the democratic base of Chief Speaker; it had been "custome" to have people of all shades and hues about the royal rooms ever since the time of "king" Itzcoatl, who had been born of a slave concubine in his father's house. Moctezuma seems to have taken on some of the prerogatives of a god; whether this was done before him by other Chief Speakers is not made clear.

Dress for Moctezuma was as the lower man's except that it was more elaborate. He wore the breechclout, elaborate sandals, the manta (*tilmantli*), and all the other accouterments so highly praised by the conquerors. These descriptions by the Spaniards, which were later dismissed by eighteenth-century historians as inspired by the heady fumes of war, have been confirmed by archaeology. Few— outside of the Maya kingdom—lived as sumptuously; the apparent overdrawing is no exaggeration of the real splendor of it all.

Marriage for the "first gentleman of the realm" was basically no different from the tying of the *tilmantli* among the lower orders, but, like royal marriages everywhere, it was often an alliance. There was one legitimate wife (although Bernal Díaz says two); the Spanish historian Oviedo elicited from Doña Isabel, one of the legitimate daughters of Moctezuma, that he had 150 children by his various concubines, but confirmed that he had only one legitimate wife. She was the executive; all others took orders from her. Indeed, our terms "legitimate" and "illegitimate" had no meaning.

The numerous progeny were trained for office. This is true of all polygamous marriages; the Inca used his enormous offspring as sources for leadership in the realm and the Aztec practiced a similar nepotism. Nezahualpilli, "king" of Texcoco, allied to Mexico, "had more than two thousand concubines." [198] In a society where war took men's lives faster than they could be created by simple monogamous birth, polygyny seemed most functional. Besides nothing so favors a marriage and consequently social stability as the indulgence of temporary polygamy.

Moctezuma ruled well. He spread the realm farther than all others before him; tribute was collected from 371 towns; justice in particular was well organized by him. "If there were any excesse of defect he did then punish it rigorously. . . . And also to discern how his ministers did execute their officers he often disguised himselfe . . . if they offended, they were punished. Besides that he was a great justicier and very noble, he was very valiant and happy . . . and he obtained great victories and came to his greatness." [1] But the times were out of joint: the heavens and the hells rose to plague him. What we would call natural phenomena, to them was evil omen: it snowed in Mexico; the volcano Popocatépetl, which had lain quiescent for a long time, became active. A child was born with two heads; the "king" of Texcoco (he of the two thousand women), who was a "greate Magitian," came over one day "at an extraordinary hour" to tell him that the gods had revealed he would lose his whole realm.

To give it all a sense of history, Quetzalcoatl, who had declared against human sacrifice and was the cultural hero of these lands, had sailed away in exile into the Atlantic saying that he would again return in the same year of his birth to "re-establish my rule." His birth had been in the Aztec year of 1-Reed (Ce-Acatl); in the Aztec calendar this fell in the years 1363, 1467—and 1519. For years Moctezuma had all but given up the military direction of his government and was surrounded by a corps of astrologers, augurs, necromancers, and mediums from whom he sought, by the interpretation of signs, symbols, and observation of the portents, to learn what to do to win back the favor of the gods.

What had happened was simple enough: white men had reached America's shores. In 1502, one year before Moctezuma's coronation, Cristóbal Colón, on his fourth and last voyage, had made contact with the Mayas; it did not take long for this event to boil over from the Maya councils and be carried over the trails from people to market and from tribe to tribe. Later, Yañez Pinzón and Juan Díaz de Solís skirted the shores of Yucatán, and once again rumor sniffed the breeze, as it were, traveled over the jungles, and somewhere was set down by a glyph writer to be sent to Moctezuma: strange bearded men in large boats have come from out of the ocean-sea.

No "king" in Aztec history had so terrible a problem to cope with as Moctezuma.

25  *The Function of Tenochtitlán*

THE RULE and organization of Tenochtitlán was activated through the system already outlined: the "king," Uei Tlatoani, gave his desires to the "council of four"; they in turn conveyed it to the larger body of clan heads (*tecuhtli*), then down to the clan body, where another official, who enforced peace and was the clan leader during a war, gave to members of the clan the programs promulgated from the higher reaches.

This clan, the basic unit of the system, enforced clan peace, organized for war, rounded out clan taxation; orders through these methods reached down to the very last rung of the social ladder. It seems that the Aztecs did not administer the affairs of conquered peoples. Perhaps they were not interested in doing so. The Incas in Peru had a system of sending *mitimaes*, a "safe" population of Quechua-speaking peoples, into newly conquered lands and removing the unsafe of the newly conquered. By this system the Incas conquered and amalgamated that which they conquered. The Aztecs had no such system. They imposed a tribute, not excessive, except for sacrificial victims, a contribution which fitted into the conquerors' economy. This was brought every six months to Tenochtitlán. Still the Aztecs won no friends and forged no empire. They went through all the social evolution of Neolithic states everywhere: they moved from the land, where at first all worked at agriculture, to the city which became a temple-city, where a social surplus produced nonfarmers—specialists in architecture, and sculpture, lapidaries, and priest-craftsmen, people who themselves no longer grew food. Then their society passed into the city-state with satellite towns, and Tenochtitlán developed an extended priestly class who exacted "first fruits" for the temples. Then lastly it became the conquering and finally the tribute city.

There were enough reasons for this. The Aztecs were fighting people. They had no luxuries on their land: cotton, brilliant bird feathers, chocolate, gold, rubber were not of their earth's bounty. If they wanted these things, they got them by conquest. Moreover, as they became specialized they manufactured and traded. It was difficult enough: each region was hostile to every other; there were few natural avenues; imbroglios had to be called off so trading could be carried on. There was a great lack of unity even among towns nominally Aztec. As Tenochtitlán, the conquering city, widened its horizons, new products, new ideas came into it, and gradually luxuries were converted into necessities.

Trade became vital to Mexico. And war was continuous; tribute, the result of conquest, poured in from many far-flung places and was distributed among the clans. As this gave people more leisure from the fields, leisure was devoted to manufacture, which in turn produced articles they traded for luxuries at the market. A new class of merchant (*pochteca*) came into being—a phenomenon in ancient America—traders who had their own guilds, their own gods, and were above the laws that applied to most. They set out from Mexico periodically with long trains of human carriers (*tamenes*), sixty

pounds on their backs, preceded by the lordly *pochteca*. Protected
in disputed terrain by soldiers, the human caravans penetrated into
southern Mexico, into and beyond Guatemala, down as far as Nicaragua. They traded Aztec manufactured goods for the raw products
of the hotlands: emeralds, which slowly found their way from Muzo
in Colombia (the only place they were found in pre-Hispanic
America), gold from Panama, feathers from Guatemala, jaguar skins,
eagle feathers, cotton, chocolate, chicle, rubber, live birds for the
royal aviary in Mexico (the source of plumage for the feather weavers). Roads of a sort were opened; Aztec garrisons were placed at
strategic places or among the newly conquered. The *pochteca* moved
freely.

There is a natural limit to conquest. The Aztecs had no definite
plan of assimilation. Conquest often followed trade as the Aztecs
got information on riches and defenses brought back by the merchants; sometimes the process went the other way: villages, city-
states, subjected to sharp wars of conquest, were made to yield
tribute. The number of these expanded until at the time of Moctezuma there were 371.

So during the growth of Aztec power all the riches of all these
cultures were pouring into their capital.

Mexico-Tenochtitlán was an island and a watery city.

It was something like Venice. There were the same type of *calli*
and *campi,* with hundreds of meandering streets, filled with canals,
bridges, and dikes. This Tenochtitlán began, as Venice, not out of
"feelings of men" who founded cities, but out of safety. Just as the
primitive Venetians took possession of the tide-washed sandbanks in
the Adriatic and turned this undefined swampy tract into a city with
its canals and waterways, so did the Aztecs, fleeing the mainland,
seek safety on the two marsh-bound islets three miles from shore
on Lake Texcoco.

Tenochtitlán was named after a cactus, *tenochtli,* which grew on
the islet; the people became the Tenocha, the city Tenochtitlán. The
name broken into radicals shows its origin: *tetl,* "rock," *nochtli,*
"cactus," *tlán,* "place of." An eagle is supposed to have perched
on the cactus during the founding; however, one of the Ten who,
according to legend, founded the city was called "Tenoch"; it could
be that this gave the city its name.

Tepeaca

Tlaltelolco

Lagunilla

Tacuba

Teocalli

Tiaquiz

Ixtapalapa

39. *Mexico-Tenochtitlán as it would have appeared to an Aztec artist. There were the same type of* calli *and* campi *as in Venice, with canals, bridges, and dikes. The plan is schematic, but seen in the center is the great temple, the* teocalli; *about it was the main plaza. To the north was Tlaltelolco, a rival city, until it was subjugated by swift conquest and made a part of greater Mexico.*

The oval-shaped valley of Anáhuac at 7,244 feet altitude, 30 by 50 miles, held the waters of the lakes, which were identified by five separate names although they formed a continuous body of water that varied from fresh to saline. The largest of the lakes was Texcoco. Directly out from Chapultepec forest, three miles more or less ("seven leagues" said Hernán Cortés), there were two islets, rock outcrops surrounded by mudbanks and reed-fringed. This was the base of Tenochtitlán.

The first buildings were structures of wattle and daub, the "immortal" house even today of the upland peasant. Then followed the temple, which, rebuilt from century to century, grew into the awesome Temple of Huitzilopochtli (the present site of Mexico's Cathedral). While developing the two islets * the Aztecs apparently maintained by treaty some foothold for cultivation on the mainland, augmenting this by the ingenious *chinampa,* the "floating garden," and the space between these formed the canals. Centuries of these operations enlarged the original mud flats until "Greater Mexico-Tenochtitlán," that is, Tenochtitlán and Tlaltelolco, formed a city 1¾ miles square and containing upwards of 2,500 acres. This was a sizable area: Rome's walls at the time of Marcus Aurelius enclosed a city of only 3,500 acres; London town in the time of Samuel Pepys was scarcely any larger.

Mexico-Tenochtitlán as a city grew as Venice grew: the Aztec raided the land about the lakes—a conquest here, a land treaty there—until by A.D. 1400 most of the city-states and their lands were under Aztec domination. Their safety assured, they began to build the great causeways that connected the island kingdom to the mainland. There were four; the best and most authentic description of them is by Hernán Cortés, the man who destroyed the city.

"The great city of Tenochtitlán . . . is two leagues [five miles] . . . to any point on the mainland. Four causeways lead to it . . . some twelve feet wide." The one which he took to enter the city in 1519 began at Ixtapalapa (". . . we saw so many cities and villages built in the water and other great towns on dry land and that

---

* There were two islets; one, Tlaltelolco, had been occupied by Aztec warriors coming over from adjacent Atzacoalco on the mainland; Tenochtitlán was settled by those coming from Chapultepec. The two grew up rivals like Buda and Pest or Minneapolis and St. Paul. A bridge connected them. Rivalry led to war in 1473; Tlaltelolco was conquered and incorporated into Greater Mexico.

straight and level Causeway going towards Mexico . . ." says Bernal Díaz). This causeway ("as broad as two lances and broad enough for eight horsemen to ride abreast") went for about a mile and there made junction with another causeway coming from the city of Coyoacán. Here there was a fort with battlements and a drawbridge; then the causeway went on some two miles directly north to the city. It was much used, "but broad as it is, it was so crowded with people that there was hardly room for them all . . ." [48] The second was an auxiliary causeway with aqueduct, which arched in a curve connected with some part of the mainland and entered this main causeway close to the entrance of the city. The third went westward toward Chapultepec (branching off to Tlacopán), i.e., Tacuba. This carried the aqueduct to the heart of the city. "Along . . . [this] causeway two pipes are constructed of masonry, each two paces broad [6 feet] and about as high as a man; one of which conveys a stream of water very clear and fresh." The other one lay empty to be used when the first was being cleaned. As the causeway had at intervals removable bridges in case of attack, the fresh water conduit, as explained by Hernán Cortés, "flows into a kind of [ceramic] trough as thick as an ox [twenty-five-inch conduit], which occupies the whole of the bridge." * The fourth and last causeway, the shortest, not much over a half-mile in length, connected the city with the mainland at Tepeaca.

This system of causeways, the greatest engineering feat of the Aztecs, had a twofold purpose: to facilitate communication and to serve as a dike or levee. The lakes were subject to rise and fall; rain could raise the level rapidly (there was no outlet); wind could raise huge waves that lapped up to and over the city, which was subject to frequent inundations (as it is still today). Since Tenochtitlán had almost been destroyed by flood in 1440, the then reigning Moctezuma I applied to his friend and ally, the ruler of the advanced city-state of Texcoco. The system of causeway dikes was constructed in such a fashion as to contain the waters of Lake Xochimilco. Moreover, by breaking up the lakes with other causeway dikes, the freshness of Xochimilco's water was preserved and Mexico-Tenochtitlán was protected from the rise of the water level. As much of the

---

* There were two aqueducts: one built by Ahuitzol (reigned 1486–1503), which went from Coyoacán over the arched causeway; it also emptied into a fountain in the main square.

lake was shallow (six feet), the causeways were doubtless first pon-
tooned and later replaced with *chinampas* firmly anchored to the
shallows. With all their records the Aztecs left us nothing illustrat-
ing their one great engineering feat.

The city, like Cuzco, capital of the Incas in Peru, was divided
into four sections, corresponding to the causeways, which entered
the city from three of the four cardinal directions. Each formal entrance to the city proper had a roadblock, where taxes were collected.

After the street ceased to be a causeway, the view along it was
clear and unobstructed ("one can see from one end to the other,
though it is some two miles in length"), and both sides of the streets
were lined with houses ("very beautiful, very large, both private
dwellings and temples"). House styles varied with the rank of the
owner. Those of the lower class were constructed with walls of wattle
and smeared with mud, grass-thatched; those of rank were raised
on a stone platform (in case of flood), made of sun-dried brick, plastered over, and brilliantly colored.

The ordinary house, invariably one-storied and with a pitched
straw roof, had its postern to the street, a patio garden within, and
by a narrow canal, which was its street, was the entrance. There was
also a jetty for the dugout canoe. The principal houses were two-
storied, made of *tezontli* stone, with flat roofs. The city "had many
wide and handsome streets," said the "Anonymous Conqueror";
they were in all probability of adobe, since to him they were
"formed half of hard earth like a brick pavement." Many if not most
of these "streets" were waterways, canals such as in Venice; "there
are principal streets, entirely of water which can only be traversed
by canoes." [7] Each dwelling had a small plot of earth, a garden;
this is evident in the fragment of an Aztec map (made circa 1480)
drawn on *amatl* paper and showing very clearly the individual
houses, ground plots, streets, and the great waterways.

Tenochtitlán was divided into twenty sections (*calpulli*). These
the Spaniards called *barrios* (wards); we refer to them as clans. Each
clan had its own *teocalli* (temple) and its school, each *calpulli* its
name and emblem (coat of arms). In the largest of the squares was
the great pyramid to Huitzilopochtli and Tlaloc. The 200-foot-high
structure was double-stepped and double-templed. The temple on
the left, painted white and blue, was to the national god, the Hummingbird Wizard; the other, white with blood-red background, was
that of the rain god and it very much impressed the Spanish. "It is

one," wrote Hernán Cortés, "whose size and magnitude no human tongue can describe" although Padre Acosta tried to do so: "Upon the toppe of the Temple were two . . . Chappells and in them were two Idolls." The structures rested on a forty-foot square, for the pyramids, like all in Mexico, were truncated. Bernal Díaz ascended the great pyramid and counted the steps—114 within the temples, where Cortés and Moctezuma had their famous discourse on the value of gods. The roof beams and the stone were beautifully worked. It was so sacrosanct that few could enter, and when Cortés wanted to dislodge them and plant a cross in their stead, Moctezuma cut short the visit, saying "he had to pray and offer certain sacrifices on account of the great *tatacul,* that is to say, sin, which he had committed in allowing us to ascend his great Cue . . ."[48] Near to the steps was the large sacrificial stone; Bernal Díaz shuddered to think of it: "[Here] they put the poor Indians for sacrifice, there was a bulky image like a dragon . . . and much blood . . ." *

The stone-paved great plaza measured, as do the boundaries of the *zócalo* of present-day Mexico, 520 by 600 feet, and within that square there was the great *teocalli,* with four lesser pyramids on its several sides: the Temple of Quetzalcoatl, a rounded structure entwined with green, open-fanged serpents; a raised dais on which gladiators fought; the sacred ball court, with, on one side, the residence of the officiating priests and, on the other, the house of the military order of the Eagle, an elite warrior class. The *tzompantli,* or skull rack, on which hung the craniums of the sacrificial victims, was close to the ball court. Three causeways terminated in the main square (just as in Cuzco, the capital of the Incas, the roads of "four quarters" that ran the length and breadth of their land terminated or began in the main plaza); of these, Ixtapalapa was the southern road and the causeway by which the Spanish made their entry. The water entered the city at the great square and was from there either piped off to other sections or was collected in water jugs, as one still sees women today collect it. The city, gleaming white in the sun, with barbarically colored houses and temples, surrounded by the blue lake, must have appeared to be a floating city, something

---

* Bernal Díaz described the view from the top of that "huge and cursed temple": ". . . we saw three causeways . . . that is the causeway of Iztapalapa by which we had entered Mexico . . . Tacuba, and that of Tepeaquilla, and we saw the fresh water that comes from Chapultepec [over the Tlacopán-Tacuba causeway] . . . we saw the bridges . . . we saw . . . the Cues [temples] and oratories like towers and fortresses and all gleaming white, and it was a wonderful thing to behold; then the houses with flat roofs . . ."

out of *The Thousand and One Nights,* with its gardens and aviaries
and multitudes of people, giving it a life as orderly as a termitarium;
and so it seemed to Bernal Díaz: "We were amazed and said it was
like the enchantments they tell of in the legend of Amadis." The
impression that the city made was so lasting that even when this
same Bernal Díaz was eighty-four years old, half blind, half deaf,
aching from the old wounds and having nothing for all his time and
effort, he could still write: "It was indeed wonderful, and, now that
I am writing about it, it all comes before my eyes as though it had
happened but yesterday."

The other half of the great square, empty of buildings, was the
market (*tiaquiz*). Here the people were addressed by the directing
classes. At one end was the sacred stone of war where the captains
met before going off to do battle; at the other end was the calendar
stone. In front of this was the new palace of Moctezuma. It was an
immense structure, as large in area as the plaza, a virtual city in itself
(the nineteenth-century modern Ayuntamiento occupies the same
area today); it repeated the features of the great square in miniature.
Two stories in height, Moctezuma's living quarters were on the
second floor. The rest of the magnificent structure was honeycombed
with rooms. There were sumptuous quarters for the "kings" of the
city-states of Texcoco and Tlacopán, to which the Aztecs were allied.
There were other rooms for at least three hundred accompanying
guests, always coming and going. Below there were the tribunal
rooms, especially for those held until given trial, rooms for the
"judges" (*achcauhcalli*), the public repository (*petalcalco*) where all
the tribute from the 371 tribute towns was delivered and stored for
distribution. It is to one of these rooms that Bernal Díaz was conducted to see the tribute: ". . . his steward was a great Cacique . . .
and he kept the accounts of all the revenue that was brought to Montezuma . . . Montezuma had two houses full of every sort of arms
. . . and in other quarters, cotton, foodstuffs, chocolate, feathers,
gold, jewels, all that was part of the tribute-economy." In other sections were the rooms of the administrators who kept record of the
economy of the theodemocracy.

On the second floor were the rooms of Moctezuma's wife, his
150 concubines and their offspring, his hundreds of guards and attendants. "Every morning at dawn," said Cortés, "there were over
six hundred nobles and chief men present in his palace, some of
whom were seated, others walking around the rooms. . . . The serv-

ants of these nobles filled two or three courtyards and overflowed into the street."

The rooms were decorated amazingly with carved cedar beams which "could not be bettered anywhere," said stout Cortés, "for they were cut with ornamental borders of flowers, birds and fish." The walls were presumably adorned with hangings. Bernal Díaz and his "merrie boyes" were lodged in the Palace of Axayacatl, near to Moctezuma's palace on the square, "where there were great halls and chambers canopied with the cloth of the country . . . [the walls] coated with shining cement and swept and garlanded." Moctezuma's was decorated with murals and bas-reliefs, with door hangings and so many rooms and doors that the "halls of Montezuma" seemed like a labyrinth, at least to Díaz, who confessed: "I entered it more than four times, and there was always more and more to see and always I grew weary from walking and for this I was never able to see everything."

Attached to the palace, or within it (for it was full of patios), was the royal aviary. This astounded the conquistadors, for there were no zoos in Europe—they were unheard of. "There were ten pools of water in which they kept every kind of waterfowl known in these parts . . . and I can vouch for it to Your Majesty," wrote Cortés to Charles V, fearful that if he described such a thing as an aviary the king would think him mad, "I can vouch that these birds, who only eat fish, receive some 250 pounds daily."

How large was the city, how large the fief of the city-state of Tenochtitlán? No one knew. Cortés admitted that he was "unable to find out the exact extent of . . . the kingdom." He thought it "as large as Spain." Certainly, even taking natural exaggeration into account, it was one of the world's largest cities; few of the temple-cities in the Old World seem to have been as large.

Of course it was not unique; ". . . a very unusual conjunction of circumstances," said V. Gordon Childe, "which occurred at most five times—in the Tigris-Euphrates delta, in the Nile Valley, in the Indus Basin, in Mexico, Central America, and . . . Peru." Neolithic peoples depended wholly on agriculture, went through what he has called "the Urban Revolution," changed their social structure radically, both psychologically and economically, by intensifying the exploitation of the land, creating social surplus, freeing many from agricultural work, and creating the full-time specialist. The city with all its complexities was the result. People crowding into cities was a radical departure from the "American pattern," where, either because of a basically unsocial nature or because of the extravagant methods of Neolithic cultivation (vast tracts of land were needed), clans or families were separated by considerable distances and only came together when the need was general.

How populous was ancient Tenochtitlán? The conquistadors said there were from seventy to a hundred thousand inhabited houses on the island kingdom; if each house had between four and ten inhabitants, averaging six to the house, the population would have been about one half million. Cortés's small army of one thousand men, even with his Indian auxiliaries, could not have beaten down *that* number. "Read eight thousand instead of eighty thousand houses," said Juan de Rivera, who—though he cheated at cards, tried to rob Cortés, and, to top it all, was cross-eyed—was nevertheless a keen observer and doubted the figures; so did Bernal Díaz. One historian gives thirty thousand for Mexico-Tenochtitlán,[219] but a modern French authority often quoted in this book falls back on the old figures; he says that the city had "a population certainly more than five hundred thousand and probably inferior to one million."[182]

The population of a historyless people is like the metaphysics of finance: it depends on how one reads the statistics.

Hernán Cortés should have known; he was a battle commander, and, while he padded his figures (as all commanders do), he had to have "an estimate of the situation"; of the population of Mexico he says flatly that Texcoco, one of the largest and most cultivated of the city-states on the mainland facing the city, "must contain some thirty thousand inhabitants"; double that sum, be utterly reckless and triple it, Mexico-Tenochtitlán had no more than ninety thousand inhabitants. Even "reduced" it was still one of the largest cities in the world: at that time London had no more than forty thousand, Paris could boast sixty-five thousand.

Although the Aztecs were not an empire (as the Incas were an empire), although they did not have what most regard as the essential elements of civilization—metal, the wheel, draft animals, the rotary quern—they had a form of organization, an intensification of older native techniques, which made possible the achievements that follow and stamped indelibly all things they touched with the word "Mexican."

○ ○ ○ ○

The Achievements

 What Mexico Wrought

AZTEC ARCHITECTURE perished with the Conquest.
We can mingle our tears with those of Hernán Cortés on that day of Saint Hippolytus, August 13, 1521, when Mexico-Tenochtitlán, ". . . one of the most beautiful sights in the world," was utterly destroyed in the process of being taken. With its collapse there was a complete loss of the scale and purpose of its architecture. What was left after the holocaust of conquest were the remains of temples and pyramids adorned with names which jingle like ponderous, brassy tassels, and not much more. Nothing has been left of the common houses, not even a ground plan to give an idea of how they were served by their architecture. However, from the existing codices, archaeological excavations, and descriptions by the destroyers, and by means of theoretical reconstruction, we know this: "Public buildings, of a secular character, like the clan or the chief's quarters, were large-scale projections of the domestic architecture." Dr. Vaillant develops this theme: "The addition of many apartments for attendants and concubines, a swimming pool and a menagerie, such as composed the palace of Montezuma, did not alter structurally or in basic plan the scheme of rectangular rooms set about a patio"—which was the home of the common Indian.

Most of Aztec architecture lay about the immediate vicinity of the lakes, dotted like satellites around Tenochtitlán. It is all gone. Yet enough has been found in the descriptive literature developed out of archaeology to attempt its reconstruction.

Tenochtitlán appears to have had one of the best planned urban centers of all ancient American cultures. It had not, to be sure, the mechanistic perfection of Cuzco, capital of the Incas, but its attention to human comfort for all the population, its zeal in transporting water through aqueducts, its hedonistic approach to life—often absent in the austere Inca city—doubtless surpassed all others. The only city-state to which it can be compared, where much of this luxuriousness obtained, was that of Chan-Chan, capital of the Chimor Empire in the desert coast of Peru and contemporaneous with the Aztec capital.

Beyond all else the thought of God is an incitement. Religion was the dominating factor in Aztec life and Tenochtitlán was "divine." The whole of it was, in its essence, religious; everything important within it was dedicated, in one form or another, to religion.

The symbol of it was the pyramid. The great *teocalli* stood in the plaza encircled by a high wall fashioned as writhing snakes, and hence its name, *coatepantli*. It measured at its base 150 by 150 feet and rose to about 160 feet high at its truncated apex, which was 70 feet square; on it rested two temples dedicated to the principal gods. While vastly inferior in size to the Temple of the Sun at Teotihuacán or the Temple of Quetzalcoatl at Cholula, it nonetheless was one of the largest and had a great architectural and dramatic effect. It commanded the city, the main road led to it, and it could be seen in the clear atmosphere miles away. The word "pyramid" has unfortunately persisted; these were not pyramids in the Egyptian sense, gargantuan tombs for dead kings catacombed within; they were lofty truncated structures on top of which were the temples, which had a real majesty. "The temple capped the substructure and was the culmination of a harmonious series of ascending planes, calculated to increase the illusion of height by emphasizing the effects of mechanical perspective." [119] The religious, administrative, and social aspects of life in the city were grouped, as previously explained, about the temple; this architectural pattern was repeated over and over again, throughout the city. The houses tended to be like squares on a chessboard and formed the basic plan of rectangular rooms set about a patio.

Water was kept potable by flowing through ceramic pipes and was distributed through the city to fountains. The small channels

40. *The building of the principal Aztec pyramid temple, the* teocalli, *in Mexico-Tenochtitlán. Reconstructed from early Spanish reports, illustrations.*

were kept open, the larger constantly cleaned; the engineering works and dikes to prevent the overflow of lake waters and the long causeways to provide access from the mainland to the island temple-city, the removable bridges and sluice gates, all were only part of city planning.

Sanitation was far in advance of anything in Europe until the end of the eighteenth century. So as not to pollute the lake, excreta was collected and brought to the mainland fields in canoes, to be used as fertilizer; urine was preserved as a mordant for dyeing cloth. Public latrines were seen by the conquistadors all along the causeways.

All this comes from history; there is little or no physical evidence of it. On the mainland, at Tenayuca, six miles north of Mexico, there are remains of an Aztec temple. It was mentioned during the Conquest; battles in 1520 swirled about it. The usually informative Bernal Díaz gives no more than its name, calling it the "town of the serpents." Tenayuca was not originally Aztec, having been built between A.D. 1064 and 1116. On excavating, Mexican archaeologists have found that is was enlarged six times in its history; the last phase, naturally, was Aztec and bears that stamp. Still their architects did nothing to disturb the chain of serpents which flow open-fanged around three of its sides.[119] What there was of its civic center has completely disappeared.

Tepotzitlán, a village fourteen miles northeast of Cuernavaca,

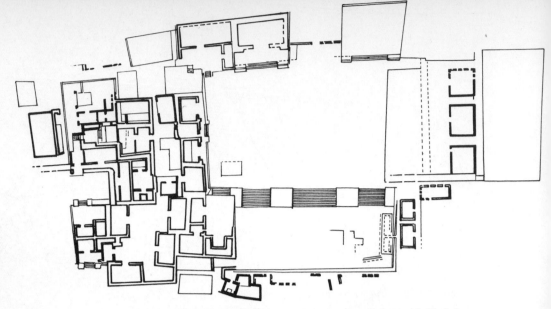

41. *The ground plans of an architectural complex at Calixtlahuaca, close to the circular temple, known as the house of* calmecac. *The uneven rectangle measures between 125 feet in length by 86 feet in width. Redrawn by Pablo Carrera from a drawing by J. A. Gomez, published by Ignacio Marquina in* Arquitectura Prehispánica.

has a small temple which crowns the hill overlooking it. A compact edifice once decorated with sculptured façade, it was not in a city, and no other structures remain except this form of triumphant temple erected by Ahuitzotl in 1487, which he dedicated when it came formally within the domains of the Aztecs. The temple of Teopanzolco, which also lies on the margin of Cuernavaca, is something like Tenayuca, with its exterior and interior stairway. But there is nothing beyond this. No houses stand here. All that is here is a mute symbol of the power of a militant religion. The essential quality of man, the civic city, the living structure of the house, is missing.

Calixtlahuaca, located near Toluca in the state of Mexico, and within the traditional boundaries of Aztec dominion, is an Aztec structure only by courtesy; it was captured by them in 1476 under the reign of Axayacatl and then destroyed by them in 1502. It is so ancient that it has seemingly no precise beginnings; its pottery reveals that the principal temple was begun about A.D. 500.[119] The highest placed site in Mexico, 9,517 feet in altitude, and located near a large lagoon in a valley now entirely devoid of trees, it is famous for its Temple of Quetzalcoatl, which was circular, like the convolutions of a seashell, with doors leading into sealed labyrinths

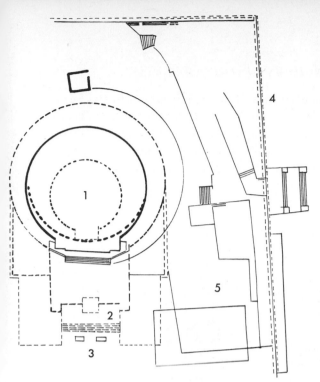

42. *Plan of the circular temple of Calixtlahuaca.*

Located within the traditional Aztec territory (near Toluca, state of Mexico), it is 9,517 feet above sea level, close upon the hill named Tenismo. The temple is circular 1), *and is approached by pyramid steps* 2), *in front of which are altars* 3). *It was surrounded by a wall* 4), *and other structures* 5) *served for the ceremonies held there. Excavation shows that it was enlarged many times. Calixtlahuaca has not been definitely placed in spatial culture sequence, but since archaic* (B.C.), *Teotihuacán* (A.D. 500), *Toltec* (A.D. 1000), *and Aztec pottery have been found there, it is presumed that its cultural history covers two thousand years. Redrawn by Pablo Carrera from the original plans of Dr. J. García Payón, published by Ignacio Marquina in* Arquitectura Prehispánica.

within; outside the traditional stairway mounted. The temple was built and rebuilt as tribes invaded the land and with each new conquest left their impress. In all probability it was one of the first such round structures raised in Mexico. Of particular interest are the remains of the *calmecac* portion of the site; these are the dwellings in which it is presumed the priests of the religious school attached to it lived. These remains give a basic plan of house structure and emphasize what Dr. Vaillant suggested: the most complex Aztec structure is only an elaboration, a large-scale projection, of domestic architecture.

Malinalco, also in the present state of Mexico, is the only site indubitably Aztec that lies outside of the immediate vicinity of Mexico-Tenochtitlán. The monuments and architecture, which date from 1476, during the reign of Axayacatl, were built sixty miles from the city, close to the village of Tenancingo. It is the only temple-city that is partly hewn out of the living rock. It is not, to be sure, a Petra, "the rose-red city half as old as time" carved out by the Sîk in Transjordania, nor is it as gigantic as the Egyptian rock tombs of Abu Simbel, but for America it is unusual enough to border on the unique. Malinalco (from *malinalli,* "grass") is self-contained, an architecturally composite site of six larger struc-

139

tures and a number of smaller ones. The principal building is hewn round out of the rock ledge, guarded by squatting pumas. At its entrance is a flight of fourteen steps cut out of the living rock. These lead to a temple, whose door once was the open mouth of a fanged snake head. This gives access to a circular chamber where eagles with

43. Malinalco. A drawing from a wooden drum (tlapan huehuetl), *showing the spirited dance of the Jaguar and the Eagle. This suggests its dedication to the warrior knights of the Eagle and the Jaguar. Redrawn by Pablo Carrera from a drawing by J. L. Quiroz, published by Ignacio Marquina in* Arquitectura Prehispánica.

furled wings and puma heads are carved in the natural rock wall. In another temple there are the remains of an impressive fresco of marching warriors, typically Aztec, with shields and spears "at ready." It is believed by Dr. García Payón, who carried on most of the excavations,[65] that Malinalco was reserved for the rituals of the military orders of the Eagle and the Jaguar, the two elite corps of warriors. A beautifully carved wooden drum found at this same Malinalco confirms this theory; around it circles a lively dance of jaguars and marching eagles, the symbols of the war cult.

That ends the melancholy parade of what is known of Aztec ruins, places which even in Bernal Díaz's time were razed into nothingness, for he wrote: "Of all these wonders that I then beheld, today all is overthrown and lost, nothing is left standing."

It shows also how utterly incorrect is the term "Aztec Empire." Theirs was not, like the Incas' or as the Mayas', a homogeneous empire, tribe and state; they had domination—not dominion—over the conquered lands. Held only by troops; there was no political or architectural unity. For instance, the number of Inca structures along the two-thousand-mile stretch of their empire is incalculable, there are so many. And the number of temple-cities in the old and new Maya empire reach beyond a hundred; each year sees more and more sites revealed out of the jungle. Unlike these, the Aztecs had no political method of absorbing the conquered populations into their system and imposing upon them an architectural formula. Theirs was essentially a tribute state. For this reason, to grasp something of Aztec architecture, which had its center in Anáhuac and which was destroyed by the Spanish Conquest, we must turn to those from whom the Aztecs borrowed and adapted.

Teotihuacán, the temple-city of the Toltecs, dwarfs in magnitude all else in Mexico and Middle America. It was in ruins and nameless when the Aztecs knew it. Its Temple to the Sun, 216 feet high and covering ten acres of ground, has no peer; all subsequent pyramids, including the great *teocalli* in Mexico-Tenochtitlán, were stylistically based on it. The remains of this great ceremonial city and center, which alone covers an area of eight square miles (and Mexican archaeologists are the first to admit that they have only found a fraction of the whole), date back to as far as 200 B.C. It continued up to 900 A.D. In this vast extent of time the immense Temple of the Sun, and its heavenly companion, the Temple of the Moon, rose to dominate the long avenues of religious structures which are part of Teotihuacán.

The Toltecs, famed as architects, craftsmen, knew how to handle mass; their buildings are impressive. The decoration, especially in the well-known Temple of Quetzalcoatl, with its great feathered heads as the dominant motif, has a massive awesomeness. Murals uncovered in the temple of agriculture show all the cultivated plants being grown—meaning that every domesticated plant had been developed one thousand years before the Aztecs appeared; the 260-day calendar, great monthly markets, writing, even the familiar Aztec speech scroll—the human tongue wagging in front of the speaker—had already been perfected long before A.D. 500. All were well-worn cultural elements, taken in the whole or inherited by the Aztecs.[198]

Temple-cities are not, to be sure, a purely American phenomenon, as V. Gordon Childe explains in his analysis of similar political

systems in the Near East; temple-cities functioned in the same way
on the Tigris-Euphrates delta, in the Nile Valley, and in the Indus
basin around 3000 B.C. They were the logical outcome of an advance in techniques of agriculture and, with the harvesting of surplus and improved methods of food conservation, the transformation
of luxuries into necessities. Since this type of civilization depended
on currying the favor of the gods, the result was the temple-city.

As early as 3000 B.C. in Sumer, the temple-city became the
repository of social surplus, and that surplus produced a new class
of people that never existed when society was in the hunting and
fishing stage or at the beginning of agriculture—in short, the nonfarmers, the specialists—artisans, writers, priests.[33]

Tula, which was such a temple-city sixty miles north of Mexico-
Tenochtitlán, is also of Toltec origin and very impressive even in
its ruins. It is a mutation of Teotihuacán. Until it was excavated by
Mexican archaeologists, its exact place in history could not be
gauged; now it is fully obvious that it was the model for the Maya
site of Chichén Itzá, eight hundred miles distant in Yucatán. Tula
originated new design concepts and new god concepts. The central
temple is of greatest interest since the two open-jawed, fifteen-foot-
high serpents which served as caryatids for the temple are the
model for a similar structure in Yucatán; the frieze of marching
jaguars and high-stepping eagles is repeated in Chichén Itzá (the
same motif was used by the Aztecs in Malinalco); the carved square
pillars of warriors are repeated in the Temple of the Warriors in
Yucatán; and the vacant stare of the expressionless and terrible
figure of Chac-Mool, a prone stone figure which holds a depository
for freshly torn human hearts, is also repeated by the Aztecs and
the Mayas. All these features had their origin in Tula.

Quetzalcoatl, the culture hero of this whole land, is closely associated with Tula. He was born on what was to be the most
momentous date in Mexico, Ce-Acatl, the year of 1-Reed. There
was a religious war during his reign, something like the Thirty
Years' War in Europe. The city was destroyed, and Quetzalcoatl
migrated to Cholula on his way to the coast to his "old home in
Tlapálan." The glory that was Tula ended with his departure. Civil
war worsened with a succession of "kings" and it was finally
destroyed about A.D. 1156, and so it disappeared except in tantaliz-

44. *The temple atop the pyramid of legendary Tula or Tollan* (A.D. 900–1156), *sixty miles north of Mexico City in the modern state of Hidalgo. Tula, belonging to the second phase of the Toltec empire, was a temple-city, and this, a reconstruction of what the main building may have looked like, was set on top of the truncated pyramid. Redrawn by Pablo Carrera from the water color of Ignacio Marquina in* Arquitectura Prehispánica.

ing myth until the Mexican archaeologist Dr. Jiménez Moreno in 1941 began to clean off the detritus of centuries.[119]

Cholula, the city-state of the Mixtec and now the city of Puebla, was the next culture to feel the presence of Quetzalcoatl. Forced to leave Tula, he made his way with a good-sized Toltec force into Cholula; there he stayed and became renowned as a builder of ball courts and the great pyramid which bore his name, so large that the people called it *Tlachi-hual-tepetl,* "Man-made Mountain." This pyramid, torn down by the Spanish to provide building material for Puebla's many churches, was measured by Alexander von Humboldt himself in 1804. He found it to be 187 feet high, its base covering the better part of forty-four acres, and it was judged to have been a larger mass than the Egyptian pyramid of Cheops. Its truncated apex, which he sketched, was almost an acre in size; a temple on top of it was dedicated to the god of the Air, which

was none other than Quetzalcoatl. The Mixtecs, very advanced in
architectural planning and in the making of pottery and in glyph
writing, existed as a tribal entity from A.D. 668 until they were
overrun by the Aztecs in 1467; their territory spread across the
width of Mexico down to the Pacific. When the Spanish arrrived
there in 1519 they were already under the domination of the
Aztecs: "Moctezuma," said Bernal Díaz, "kept many garrisons of
warriors stationed in all the provinces"; he had Aztec warriors
within and without their capital, Cholula. "The city of Cholula,"
says Cortés, "is situated on a plain with about twenty thousand
houses within its walls and as many in the suburbs outside. . . .
The city is very fertile (there is not a palm's breadth of land which
is not tilled). . . . There is an abundance of land. . . . As for its
city . . . its exterior is as fine as any in Spain . . . I . . . counted
more than four hundred pyramids." Bernal Díaz reports in the same
vein: ". . . it is a land fruitful in maize . . . full of Magueys from
which they make their wine. They make very good pottery . . . and
with it supply Mexico and all the neighbouring provinces . . .
there were many high towers in the city where the Idols stood,
especially the Great Cue [Temple of Quetzalcoatl] which was
higher than that of Mexico. . . ."

Although the Aztecs were doubtless influenced by Mixtec-
Cholula architectural planning, we have been left no details; like
the rest they disappeared totally with the Conquest. While at
Cholula, the Toltecs, who were by now reduced to a sort of
condottieri, made contact with some of the chieftains of Mayapán
at the famous trading center of Xicalango, at the edge of Maya
territory. There was a civil war in progress in the northern part of
Yucatán near Chichén Itzá. The Toltecs entered "in A.D. 1194,"
says the great Maya authority Dr. Morley, and loaded the scales for
victory and gained ascendancy over the Mayas. At the temple-city
of Chichén Itzá, at least, they imposed architectural forms that they
brought out of Tula. Whether it was Quetzalcoatl as man that led
this Maya invasion, or one bearing this name as a patronymic, his
name was imposed again on yet another temple-city. Myth or fact,
Quetzacoatl was to have a fatal effect on the Aztecs.[198]

The Aztecs, as they conquered, sought new ideas in living and
new forms of luxury. They found both in the hotlands of the Gulf
Coast. Ahuitzotl during the years 1486–1503 pushed his conquests

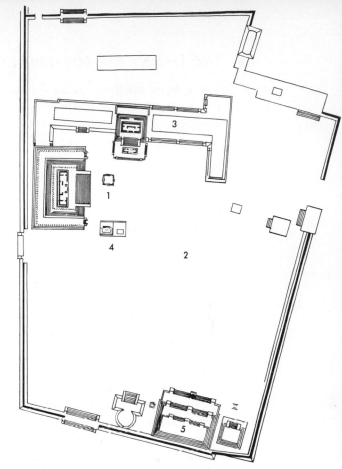

45. *Plan of the walled ceremonial center of Cempoala, in Vera Cruz, built by the Totonacs and occupied by them when the Spaniards began their conquest in 1519.*

This is the ceremonial center, but the temple-city had a known population of thirty thousand living in its environs. The great plaza had an area of 251,160 square yards. The principal temple 1) was seen and commented on by Bernal Díaz del Castillo. The great plaza 2) was walled, which was an unusual architectural feature. The Temple of the Chimneys 3), a rectangular building attached to the main temple, was occupied by the priests and chieftains; 4) a small edifice called the "Altar" and 5) the great pyramid, explored in the years 1946–47.

to northern Vera Cruz, where he encountered the Huastecs, who were of Maya speech. There he engulfed one of the oldest cultures, which began about 500 B.C.; he found them very well advanced in town planning.

The temple-city of Tamuin, close to the river of the same name in the modern state of Tamaulipas, is especially notable, since its main plaza covered some twenty acres and its temple walls were found to be covered with brilliant frescoes in a style reminiscent of the Toltecs. The Totonacs were the neighbors of the Huastecs. They occupied central Vera Cruz and held dominion over coastal territory close to the Mayas. They were, like the others, occupied by the Aztecs and tributary to them; they also influenced them in architecture. Moreover, many of their temple-cities are still extant, despite the encroaching jungle.

One of these, *Cempoala*, is utterly unique. We have a good description of how it appeared to the Spanish in 1519 to compare with the structure as it has grown out of its present-day restoration.

In 1519 the Spanish were following the ancient coastal road on the way to Cempoala; they passed, says Cortés, "a few large towns very passably laid out. . . . The houses in those parts which can obtain stone are of rough masonry and mortar, the rooms being low and small, very much after the Moorish fashion. . . . Where no stone can be got they build their houses of baked bricks, covering them over with plaster and a rough kind of thatch. . . . Certain houses belonging to chiefs are quite airy and have a considerable number of rooms . . . we have seen as many as five inner corridors or patios in a single house and its rooms very well laid out around them. Each one of the chief men has in front of the entrance to his house a large patio and some as many as two, three, four, sometimes raised a considerable way off the ground with steps leading up to them and very well built. In addition they have their mosques, temples . . . all of fair size."

Cempoala was twenty miles north of the modern port of Veracruz. As they approached it and saw the whitewashed buildings rise out of the green jungle, barbarically colored and vibrant, "we were struck with admiration," said Bernal Díaz. "It looked like a garden with luxuriant vegetation, and the streets were so full of men and women who had come to see us. . . . Our scouts . . . reached a great plaza with courts . . . and it seemed to be whitewashed and burnished . . . one of the scouts thought that this white surface which shone so brightly must be silver . . ."

The whole Totonac land, Cortés estimated, "included as many as fifty thousand warriors, fifty villages and strongholds." The Indians were "of middle height, disfigure their faces in various ways, some piercing the ears, introducing large and extremely ugly ornaments . . . others the lower part of nose and upper lip. . . . They wear as clothes a highly coloured poncho, the men wear breech clouts . . . and body cloaks finely worked and painted. . . . The common women wear highly coloured robes reaching from the waist to the feet . . . but the women of high rank wear bodices of fine cotton, very loose fitting, cut and embroidered after the fashion of our bishops and abbots."

Archaeology has confirmed all that Cortés and his minions said of Cempoala.[119] The temple-city alone with its surrounding houses had a population estimated at about thirty thousand; the walled plaza—which has been measured and in some parts restored by

Mexican archaeologists—had an over-all measurement of 210,000 square meters, or nearly 689,000 square feet. The general aspect revealed by research was that it was stone laid with soaring temples. There were fifteen, large and small, within the plaza, the ceremonial center surrounded by one-storied houses, gaily painted and grass-thatched. Dr. J. García Payón, who directed the excavations, found eight large groups of such buildings.

An Aztec garrison was close by. The *pochteca* merchants made frequent visits and the tribute collectors paid semiannual calls for tribute. Five of them were there at the time of Cortés's arrival, and they were "full of assurance and arrogance," writes Bernal Díaz. "Their cloaks and loin-cloths were richly embroidered, and their shining hair was gathered up as though tied on their heads . . ." The Aztecs thus had access to all this type of town planning and doubtlessly used it. It has been determined that Cempoala was built at the same time as the Aztec sites of Malinalco and Tepotzitlán.

North of this city there are remains of other Totonac city centers. *Tajín,* to name but one, 125 miles in a direct line from Vera Cruz and lying seventeen miles inland, is a temple-city known since 1785. It has been famous since then for its pyramid of the niches. There are 364 niches representing each day of the long year, which is an unusual architectural feature that somehow has withstood the insults of man and time. Mexican archaeologists have found an immense temple-city surrounding this pyramid, with at least fifteen large structures and numerous smaller ones. Here are all the elements of the city: pyramid, ball court, raised terraces, palaces. The ball courts are decorated with bas-reliefs, the style of the figures suggesting Mixtec. The subject matter includes all the familiar motifs used later by the Aztecs; the date 13-Rabbit has been found on one of the stone uprights of the Temple of the Columns. One of the favorite sculptural designs used on the buildings is the *xical-coliuhqui* "decoration-for-gourds," the most characteristic of Mexican art motifs, derived from the stylized head of the sky serpent, a symbol of Quetzalcoatl.

In the southern highlands of Mexico there are other cultural centers which influenced Aztec architecture. The one that has been the longest known and yet is still the least known is *Xochicalco,* "Place of Flowers" which lies twenty miles south of Cuernavaca.

46. *Plan of the ruins of Tzintzuntzán. Redrawn by Pablo Carrera from J. A. Gomez, published by Ignacio Marquina in* Arquitectura Prehispánica.

It squats lonely on the highest hills, overlooking two fresh-water lakes two miles distant, in a strongly fortified position. The hills were artificially flattened and terraced, with strong points for defense. Four roads radiate in the four cardinal directions and march up through the impressive buildings into the principal plaza, where the famous Temple of Quetzalcoatl stands. Another temple is reached by a paved ceremonial road sixty feet broad.

Xochicalco—its true name is unknown—was a ceremonial and, in addition, perhaps an administrative center; all the familiar edifices are here: palaces, temples, the ball court, and, when finally excavated, there will be found a house complex within the temple-city—the famous temple to the Plumed Serpent, which has one of the finest façades in all Mexico, has been uncovered. The handling of the figures would suggest Maya were it not for the fire snakes, which are a symbol of the Mixtecs; the glyphs and dates seem Mixtec and other features suggest Toltec.

Tzintzuntzán, located in the present state of Michoacán, represents a relative rarity. Known in detail only since 1941, Mexican archaeologists found these ruins near the modern village of San Pablo. The ruins, much destroyed by both time and man, have been reconstructed on what is now known. The platform, called *yacata* and approached by the familiar step pyramid, had on its top a concourse of other pyramidal towers. No spatial cycles have yet been put upon it, but Tzintzuntzán is early. Its pottery—an index of time—points to a time between A.D. 500–800.

Monte Albán lies southeast of this city in Oaxaca, isolated from the Mexican plateau by a range of mountains sufficiently difficult to prevent an Aztec invasion until 1469. A composite of cultures, Olmec, Maya, Zapotec, Mixtec, and Aztec, it was perhaps one of the longest continuously inhabited temple-cities known to us (500 B.C.–A.D. 1469). Located on top of the bald hills, 1,500 feet above the level of the valley, although 5,000 feet above the sea, the site has been modified numerous times. When the great Mexican archaeologist Dr. Alfonso Caso first began to excavate it in 1930 and finally concluded the basic part of his work, he found it to be a temple-city set on a large rectangular plaza 2,300 by 820 feet and containing ten large structures: an observatory, a ball court, palaces, and, in the center, a temple complex with four sets of stairways.

There were five marked periods of occupation: Olmec art adorns the early buildings and this links it to the coastal cultures. There followed a period of Maya influence until the Zapotecs exerted their control; this lasted the longest, from A.D. 534 until A.D. 1125. The fourth period found it under the sway of the Mixtecs, who brought new art, new gods, a variation in the calendar, tombs, murals, urns; it was they who made the superbly beautiful goldwork discovered by Dr. Caso in one of the unopened tombs.[28]

Aldous Huxley, when he visited it, found the site "incomparably magnificent. . . . An astonishing situation. . . . Zapotec architects were not embarrassed by the artistic responsibilities it imposed on them. They levelled the hill-top; laid out two huge rectangular courts . . . Few architects have had such a sense of austerely dramatic grandeur . . . few have been given so free a hand, religious considerations were never allowed to interfere with the realization of a grand architectural scheme; at Monte Albán they allowed nothing to get in the way of the architects."

The fifth phase of Monte Albán was its last; Moctezuma I, surnamed "the Wrathy," set out to conquer Oaxaca in 1469. The Aztecs needed it in order to give their merchants passage down to the Isthmus of Tehuantepec, from there to reach the untouched markets on the western Pacific side of Guatemala and into Central

America. They won the temple-city, lost it, and finally, under the next to last leader of the Aztecs, captured it and held it until the arrival of the Spanish. It was well known to the Aztecs and there is definite evidence that they were influenced by its urban planning.

Mitla, called in the Zapotec language *Yoo-paa,* "Place of the Dead," is part of the same culture; it lies twenty-five miles directly south of Monte Albán and is not only one of the best-known sites in Mexico but also the best preserved. There are five groups of buildings, extending to both sides of the mostly dry Mitla River. All of them constructed with the same basic plan which, Dr. Vaillant has emphasized, characterizes all Mexican structures: rooms formed around a rectangular patio. A cross section of one of the buildings at Mitla suggests how similar Aztec structures were roofed with giant wooden beams. The architectural façade is unique here, although used by the Mayas in Yucatán; the handling of its lines and proportions is unusual. The structures do not stand on pyramids; they are low horizontal masses and have a fortuitous beauty of proportion. There is an austere grandeur in their massive outlines. Aldous Huxley found them "strangely unlike any of the other pre-Colombian ruins . . . the walls of the temples . . . are decorated with geometric patterns . . . all are manifestly inspired by and based upon textile designs. . . . petrified weaving . . ."

All of these temple-cities, and there are many more, were the source of Aztec architectural ideas and Aztec urban planning. It is cause for regret that so much is gone. Yet, if the history of Aztec architecture is so fragmentary it is because there was so little. There was not, architecturally, any such thing as an "Aztec Empire."

27   Sculpture

SCULPTURE was the greatest Aztec contribution to art.
A work of art must be measured by its impact, and if one looks at the powerful and awesome goddess Coatlicue, her head of twin serpents, her necklace of human hands and hearts, her arms claw-handed, and her skirt a mass of writhing serpents, it has

the same terrible impact that the Assyrian basreliefs had on one explorer: "My hair alternately stood up and flattened down upon seeing them. . . ."

Much of Aztec sculpture is fearsomely awesome; death was much about them and somehow all this feeling that characterized their sculpture has been hammered into the raw stone. It was this that made Élie Faure, the French art historian, blanch and turn aside when he saw it: ". . . beautiful, almost always monstrous, contorted, blown up, crushed in, warped . . . one distinguishes nothing but heaps of crushed and palpitating flesh, quivering masses of entrails, a confused pile of viscera."

Realism was the high quality of Aztec sculpture. There were such pieces as that which revolted our Frenchman, but there are others of much delicacy—a rabbit made of white quartz, limpid and pure and very beautiful, a mask formed out of black obsidian, a woman grinding corn, bending over; sculpture had a wide range made to be seen from all sides. It was not like the Maya work, which Aldous Huxley described as "profoundly, incommensurably alien." Aztec sculpture had an uncanny vitality and unself-consciousness that makes it appeal to the modern eye. As the very observant Pál Kelemen wrote: "The nature of sculpture and the inherent possibilities in the material . . . make it perhaps the most immediately comprehensible of all the arts." [93]

Aztec idols were fearful things to the Spanish; they felt their impact. Thus José de Acosta: "They call this idoll *Tezcallipuca,* he was made of a blacke shining stone [obsidian] like to *iayel.* . . . It had earerings of gold and silver and through the nether lippe a small cannon of crystal. . . ." Yet an Aztec sculptor could handle material ranging from an emerald the size of a pea to immense masses as large as the great calendar stone, weighing twenty-four tons. His tools were the simplest: stone celts, awls, and drills.

Sculpture was closely linked with architecture. Almost in every structure extant one sees how closely allied were these two functional things—there were sculptured friezes, enormous stone-carved caryatids, columns; sculpture was not a superficial element as in our concept, but a fundamental part of architecture. All of their art was purposeful, functional, and it belonged to religion. *L'art pour l'art* had no meaning in Aztec life. Art was purposeful and hieratic; religion was life and life was religion, and sculpture along with all their crafts was tied to it. This is equally true of almost all the art forms of the other tribute states, Babylonia, Assyria, and Egypt.

Aztec sculpture subordinated detail to them—they had none of that fear of empty space which caused the Mayas to overcrowd design with detail; their aim was impact. The stone piece of Xipé has the flayed god appearing so simply quaint it seems as if the sculptor's small child was the model, until, looking at the back, one becomes aware that Xipé is attired in a freshly flayed skin of a sacrificial victim.

Different from all these and buried in a mass of ritualistic detail is the Aztec calendar stone. Two years in the carving (1479–81), it stood twelve feet high and weighed twenty-four tons. It embodies "a finite statement of the infinity of the Aztec universe," with the face of the sun god Tonatiuh in the center and twenty names of days circling it; it is filled with symbols of previous world epochs, symbols of heaven and color—a grandiose conception of the universe.

Aztec sculpture has quality. One does not have to be versed in all the intricacies of religious symbolism to enjoy it. Pál Kelemen wrote that it could be enjoyed as pure sculpture detached from any precise culture.

28  The Lapidaries, Goldsmiths, and Jewel Carvers

METALWORK came late to Mexico. It came up by slow degrees from South America.

None of the early cultures worked metal; it does not appear at Teotihuacán, which was already a memory when the technique of gold and copper working reached Mexico. It was unknown to the early Mayas, and the Olmec craftsman contented himself with making diadems of jade. It was not practiced in Mexico much before the eleventh century.

Gold makes life sumptuous; the Aztecs knew it and traded for it. As Bernal Díaz saw it, it was free to be traded in the market places: "placed in thin quills of geese, so that the gold could be seen through it."

Mining was rudimentary. Gold was panned or collected in nuggets; silver, which seldom occurs pure in nature, was more of a problem and was less used. Gold is a metal of great ductility, for a single grain can be drawn into a wire five hundred feet long. It was worked by the Aztecs with the simplest of techniques. It was melted in a furnace heated by charcoal, draft being supplied by a man blowing through a tube into the charcoal embers. There are few implements extant but we have been left illustrations of goldsmithery. They worked the gold by means of hammering, embossing, plating, gilding, sheathing. Out of this simple, almost crude technique came gold pieces which excited more than the cupidity of the conquistador. There were "three blow guns," said Bernal Díaz, "with their pellet molds and their coverings of jewels and pearls, and pictures of little birds covered with pearl shell."

Most of the gold extracted from Moctezuma, some 600,000 pesos weight of it, was melted down into ingots; some of it they thought too beautiful to destroy, like the pieces they received at Vera Cruz at the beginning of the adventure: "a wheel like a sun, as big as a cartwheel, with many sorts of pictures on it, the whole of fine gold; and a wonderful thing to behold . . . Then another wheel was presented of greater size made of silver of great brilliancy in imitation of the moon . . . Then were brought twenty golden ducks, beautifully worked and very natural looking, and some [ornaments] like dogs, and many articles of gold worked in the shape of tigers and lions and monkeys . . . Twelve arrows and a bow with its string . . . all in beautiful hollow work of fine gold." [48] All this was sent intact to Charles V. He being then in Flanders, Cortés's ship was sent after him. He was at last found in Brussels, and, on July 12, 1520, Cortés's ambassadors presented the Aztec goldwork to him. His comment, whatever it was, has not been recorded. That gold, like all the rest that came from the Americas, went into his crucibles to be made into ingots to pay the soldiery to maintain him on the nebulous throne of the Holy Roman Empire. Fortunately the great Albrecht Dürer was there at the same time and he left his impressions of it in his diary. Himself a descendant of a line of Hungarian goldsmiths settled in Nuremberg, knowing what he was seeing, Dürer wrote:

I saw the things which were brought to the King [Charles V] from the New Golden Land [Mexico]; a sun entirely of gold, a whole fathom broad; likewise a moon entirely of silver, just as big; likewise sundry curiosities from their weapons, arms and missiles . . . all of which is fairer to see than marvels. . . .

These things were all so precious that they were valued at 100,000 gulden. But I have never seen in all my days what so rejoiced my heart as these things. For I saw among them amazing artistic objects and I marvelled over the subtle ingenuity of the men in these distant lands. Indeed I cannot say enough about the things which were there before me.

That was the only commentary on these things by anyone whose opinion meant anything. Charles V ordered that henceforth all gold and silver coming from the Indies be melted down on arrival. Little survived—except the wonderful descriptions of the conquistadors, which, since there was no gold later to be found or seen, historians of the eighteenth century took as the natural braggadocio of such men. It was only in 1931 when Dr. Alfonso Caso found the undisturbed tomb of a Mexican chieftain at Monte Albán, containing superbly beautiful necklaces, earplugs, and rings, that historians realized that the simple, honest Bernal Díaz was making a magnificent understatement.

Goldsmiths had a guild. Those attached to Moctezuma's many-roomed household were nontaxpayers; they were supplied with placer gold and busied themselves making pieces for Moctezuma and other officials. Bernal Díaz speaks of the "workers in gold and silver . . . and of these there were a great number in a town named Atzcapotzalco, a league from Mexico." Since the gold was sold in the market, presumably any craftsman who had enough to barter for the goose quills of gold dust could work it up into jewelry for himself or else for trade.

Lapidaries, workers in precious stones, were many, and like the others: "skilled workmen Moctezuma employed." [48] Foremost of the stones was jade. This was found in southern Mexico and Guatemala and valued more than gold itself, which Bernal Díaz found to his satisfaction, for he took four jades during the first Spanish retreat from Tenochtitlán and they "served me well in healing my wounds and gathering me food."

Jade was an article of tribute and the glyph for it is found in the Book of Tributes. Now there is a difference, mineralogically, between the jade of America and that of the Orient, which should put to rest the idea that the American Indian got his jade from China; it is "American." It is utterly amazing how the Aztec craftsman achieved the delicate handling of so hard a stone; it required great patience. Everything of jade was saved, even the smallest pieces of the "precious green," to be put in the mouths of the dead to take the place of the stilled heart.

Masks were often made of jade, or, when it was not available, of less valued greenstone. Masks, with their expressionless slit eyes and swollen lips, were a feature among all of these cultures. Some are exquisite, others are repetitious and "vulgar," as the astute Pál Kelemen noted. These powerful artistic impulses "were stereotyped through constant repetition." The truth is that most art has always been either bad or indifferent, as Aldous Huxley said when looking at the same thing: "Vulgarity is always the result of some excess; and the means to vulgarity are therefore means to the realization in practice of an inward tendency toward the excessive." This holds for any who dominated: "Vulgarity has always been the privilege of the prosperous . . ."

The skill among the lapidaries was broad; the large objects doubtlessly were done by the "professionals," yet much was done by the ordinary craftsman. Crystal, a very hard stone, is not easily worked, yet the Aztecs shaped art forms out of it from the smallest of pieces to the life-size crystal skull. This latter symbiosis of beauty and death sits, divorced from its conception, before black velvet curtains in the British Museum.

Turquoise came by trade from the north. It was much in demand and traveled almost as far to Mexico and Yucatán as did amber (that "special act of God") in the Old World. The Aztec exacted turquoise as a form of tribute and it so appears from eleven towns on the tribute rolls; it was used with other materials for the making of mosaics on masks, knives, and even walls.

Obsidian glass was an Aztec specialty; it was exported as raw material and as finished product. Found close by, a product of volcanic action, obsidian was used for knives, razors, lip plugs, mirrors of high polish, and other objects of immense beauty.

Emeralds (quetzal-itzli) were the prize gem for the Aztec as for the Spanish. "The Kings of Mexico didde much esteeme theme;

some did use to pierce their nostrils and hang them therein," says José de Acosta, "on the vissages of their idolles." As soon as Moctezuma was elected as Chief Speaker, the first thing he did was "to pierce the gristle of his nostrils, hanging thereat a rich emerald."

The conquistador saw them as a symbol of riches. Hernán Cortés commandeered the whole of them for himself; he knew that Cleopatra wore emeralds and that a Christian pilgrim lately from India saw them in a temple of Buddha, "flashing their fire two hundred leagues on a cloudless night." As for the source, Moctezuma expressed ignorance; they were from "the south." In fact, they were from only one region, the mountain areas in Colombia, about Muzo, which was the only source of emeralds at that time. They were plenteous in Colombia, where they were used for barter to obtain cotton and gold dust. They were well known in Panamá and used to great effect in combination with gold. They were obtained for Moctezuma by the activities of his *pochteca* merchants who penetrated beyond Nicaragua. Emeralds are soft and chip easily, yet the Aztecs cut them in intricate patterns—flowers, fish, fanciful forms of exquisite workmanship. Hernán Cortés got his emeralds directly from Moctezuma, one in a pyramidal shape, "broad as the base of the hand," others so fabulous that Charles V is said to have coveted the fantastic baubles. Cortés refused 400,000 ducats in Genoa for them, saving them for Doña Juana de Zúñiga, his betrothed, a daughter of a ducal family. He gave her five Aztec-worked emeralds, "one in the form of a rose, one like a bell with a pearl for a tongue, one like a fish, one like a trumpet, one like a cup." [114]

29 *Feather Weaving*

THE FEATHER weaving was another of the Aztec accomplishments. Examples of it have disappeared completely because of conquest and climate. The only examples of real magnificence of this art are preserved by mere accident of history. The rest has perished. Similar feather weavings found in the desert coast of Peru, well preserved despite the passage of time, have given us an idea of the technique; we also have illustrations of artisans weaving feathers in the work of Bernardino de Sahagún.

Feather weavers (*amanteca*) were highly appreciated; they formed a guild and were of the professional class. In feather weaving, quills were inserted into the web, each quill was hooked over a thread and secured by a knot in the second row, leaving only the color part of the feather visible on the other side. The color pattern had to be carefully arranged as a mosaic before the feathers were applied. Shields, headgear, cloaks, banners, totem emblems were all done in feather weaving. Warriors so accoutered die beautifully.

Since colorful birds were limited in the altitudes of Mexico-Tenochtitlán, there was much activity on the part of the merchants to obtain bird feathers when the local supply did not meet the demand.

Birds of all climes were brought alive to Mexico and their habitats simulated; the waterfowl alone had separate pools, as attested by Hernán Cortés: "ten pools of water in which were kept every kind of waterfowl known." There was no such thing in Europe until Padua in 1545 erected a zoological garden. The type of food and water depended on the bird. There were three hundred men employed to look after them and "each pool was overhung by balconies cunningly arranged from which Moctezuma would delight to watch the birds." In another part were cages for the land birds, wooden trellises cleverly made, 9 feet high and 18 feet around; there were another three hundred men to look after these. Bernal Díaz could not even name all of the various species that he saw in that aviary: "birds of great size, down to tiny birds of many-coloured plumage . . ." The birds bred in the cages, too. As they molted, the feathers were gathered, selected, graded, and brought to the feather weavers.

Let no one doubt the magnificence of this art. One piece has been preserved, the headdress sent by Moctezuma to Hernán Cortés when he first landed at Vera Cruz and was believed to be Quetzalcoatl returning to reclaim his empire. This was sent in turn to Charles V, who passed it on to his fellow Habsburg, Archduke Ferdinand of Tyrol; it was long preserved in the castle at Ambras. When discovered and its history made known, it was sent to Vienna, and there today it rests in a burst of golden-green iridescence in the Museum für Völkerkunde—a double assurance, if that be needed, of the Aztecs' sense of beauty.

Everyone in Aztec society was some sort of craftsman. "Art" as a name for this is in all probability not the right word, yet is there another? The Aztec was a maker of things; everything was functional, real, purposeful. As Aldous Huxley pointed out when he examined all this for the first time: "Craftsmanship brings psychological fulfillment, a society of craftsmen is a society of satisfied individuals." More, it had a human wholeness. "A primitive is forced to be whole—a complete man, trained in all the skills of the community, able to fend for himself in all circumstances; if he is not whole, he perishes." But was the Aztec impressed by his craftsmanship, his "art"? Dr. Vaillant thought not: "They did not speculate about aesthetics." Yet a Mexican sociologist, going through Nahuatl texts,[104] believes they did and that they were animated by a real sense of beauty. He has translated the "song of the painter":

> *The good painter,*
> *understanding god in his heart,*
> *defines things with his heart,*
> *dialogues with his own heart.*

The Nahuatl texts now made available to us[67] show many expressions that suggest this attitude was not an isolated instance. In the presence of his "art" the craftsman felt the divinity of things. For listen to the song, well remembered and sung over and over again to later generations, of a birdkeeper who saw death fall upon Mexico-Tenochtitlán and the aviaries which he cared for all perish in the flames:

> *the plumes of the quetzal*
> *the works of iridescent jade*
> *all broken and gone*
> *the memory of a beautiful world,*
> *god-filled, truth-filled . . .*

If then, this real feeling is true, how explain the other world of the Aztecs, the "apparent incongruity," as Prescott wrote, "of a comparatively refined people of often gentle influences whose religion was of a spirit of unmitigated ferocity." Why did the Aztecs inhale the perfume of corpses as if it were some aphrodisiac perfume?

WAR AND RELIGION, at least to the Aztecs, were inseparable. They belonged to each other. "It is no exaggeration to say," observes a recent writer on the subject,[41] "that the
government of [Aztec] Mexico was organized from top to bottom
so as to be able to sustain, and thereby mollify, the unseen powers
with as many human hearts as it was possible to give them."

Blood was the drink of the gods. To obtain appropriate prisoner
victims as sacrifice for the gods, there were ceaseless little wars, for
one could hardly expect the Aztecs to offer themselves in endless
lines for immolation. At the outset it would serve little to explain
this attitude in moral terms. All militant religions have been involved
in bloodletting in one form or another.

The object of Aztec religion was to attract favorable forces to it
and repulse or at least mollify those which were not. They knew
that nature moved in a series of rhythmic patterns. They put all their
observatory powers to work to discover what these rhythms were
and to harness them, not alone for their own good but for all mankind's survival. "From this point of view," wrote Dr. Alfonso Caso,
"magic and science are alike: both are techniques which aim at the
control of the world and both consider that magic or nature are a
necessary link between phenomena."[29]

Since man always turns things into an image of himself, it would
have been impossible for the Aztecs to have a mental image that was
not anthropomorphic; natural forces among them were personified.
As the society grew complex, the gods grew in complexity and they
took on specialized functions.

In the forefront of the Aztec pantheon was a sun god who
brought life by his daily appearance; sun worship was an essential
part of Aztec religion. There were the gods of the four cardinal directions, each symbolized by his own color, "since," as Dr. Vaillant
wrote, "the Aztec universe was conceived on a religious rather than
a geographic sense." Gods were appointed, with their colors, in
keeping with the preconceived prejudices of their own life history:
east was red; south was blue, and evil; west was white (it had good
auguries); north was black, a pallor of gloom and presided over by
Mictla-tecuhtli, Lord of the Dead.

There were personal gods, each plant had its god, each function its god or goddess, even suicides had one. Yacatecuhtli was the deity of the merchants. In this polytheistic world all gods had clearly defined traits and functions. So the pantheon grew more complex as the people took to worshiping the different manifestations of the gods, and this duality made the pantheon so bewildering that only the priests, whose function it was, could keep track of them all.

The Aztec gods warred in Aeschylean grandeur. The gods of evil—for the Aztecs believed in immanent evil—fought with the beneficent gods. Light and darkness struggled for man's soul.

Yet all this was beyond the pale of mere man. He kept to the little gods. The image of the corn goddess he purchased at the market—a stamped clay figure which he buried in his *milpa* field with prayers and tears. There were household gods set up in some remote corner. There was the goddess of the maguey, Mayahuel, whose spirit was evoked when he drew the sweet syrup and converted it into an intoxicant.

All these earth gods were their life. The complicated religious pattern they left to the priests, who told them when to weep, when to get drunk, when to rejoice, when to die. The people seemed content to resign themselves to those who spoke of the unknowable with so great a certainty.

Huitzilopochtli, the Hummingbird Wizard, was the Aztecs' own. They were his children, the "chosen people." He it was who led them out of the dry misery of the north into the promised land of Mexico-Tenochtitlán; he took his place among all the other gods, from the ancient past and from other cultures. He was the sun, the ever-youthful warrior who fought battles with the other gods for man's survival. Each day he rose, fought the night, the stars, the moon, and, armed with sunbolts, brought on the new day. Since he fought these battles for them, the Aztecs could only repay him by nourishing him for his eternal wars. The proffered food could be neither the watered-down intoxicant pulque, nor corncakes such as mortal man ate—the god must be nourished on the stuff of life: blood. It was the sacred duty of every Aztec—for all were part of an agrarian militia—to take prisoners for sacrifice in order to obtain for Huitzilopochtli the nectar of the gods—human hearts and blood.

War, eternal war, then, was bound up with religion. How else could human hearts be obtained? A long peace was dangerous, and war thus became the natural condition of the Aztecs, for if the beneficent gods were not nourished they would cease to protect man from the other gods, and this might lead to the total destruction of the world. When the great temple pyramid to Huitzilopochtli was dedicated in Mexico in 1486, "king" Ahuitzotl, after a two years' war campaign in Oaxaca, amassed more than twenty thousand prisoner victims. These were lined up in rows waiting to be spread-eagled over the sacrificial stone. Their hearts were cut out and held briefly to the sun, then, still pulsating, deposited in the heart urn of the recumbent Chac-Mool figure.

The ritual for all this became as complex as that which now surrounds the religion Norman Douglas described as the "quaint Alexandrian tutti-frutti known as Christianity."

The priests directed the intellectual and religious life of Mexico. At the top of the pinnacle was the Chief Speaker—the "king," to the Spanish. He was more than an ex-officio high priest; his was the final tribunal.

Two high priests (*quequetzalcoa*) lived in Mexico. Under them was another who administered the business end of tribute tithes and who supervised the schooling of new priests (*tlamacazqui*) and the establishment of the faith in the newly conquered villages. There were, it is said, five thousand priests attached to the temples in Mexico-Tenochtitlán alone. They dressed in black, their *tilmantli* were ornamented with a border of skulls and entrails. Bernal Díaz said that the priests had "long robes of black cloth and long hoods like those of the Dominicans . . . The hair of these priests was very long and so matted that it could not be separated or disentangled . . . and [it] was clotted with blood."

They elaborated cult rituals, taught in the religious schools, helped train those who traced out the rituals, worked with the *tlacuilo* artists, taught and extended the knowledge of hieroglyphic writing and the symbols of the complicated mathematical and astronomical computations. They helped the architects to delineate the temples and buildings, and when the buildings were completed arranged the ritual of sacrificial dedication. They helped to create music and dances, arrayed them, prescribed the things to be heard, proscribed those not to be heard. They intervened with the unseen powers, remembered and chanted the historical events until they became fixed in human memory. This theocracy pervaded everything in Aztec life.

"The gods ruled," wrote Dr. Vaillant, "the priests interpreted and interposed and the people obeyed."

31 *The Calendar*

THE CALENDAR was at the base of every action of the Aztecs.

There were two calendars, the ritualistic one (*tonalpohualli*),* a parade of 260 days; and a second which was a form of solar calendar. The latter consisted of eighteen 20-day months, a lunar reckoning of 360 days plus five uncounted days, the empty *nemontemi*.

The first calendar was magical and sacred; it bore little relation to astronomical observation, and the origin of the cycle has never been satisfactorily explained. It was very ancient; the Aztecs gave it nothing, for it had been known to the Mayas under the name of *tzolkin* for fifteen hundred years. The divinatory cycle consisted of twenty periods of thirteen days. There were twenty day names—*calli* (house), *coatl* (snake), *malinalli* (grass), *tochtli* (rabbit), etc.—which, combined in sequence with the numbers one through thirteen, designated the days, such as 1-Grass, 2-Reed, 3-Ocelot, etc., to 13-Lizard, when the next period began. In this example, the name "Grass," coming up in its regular position, would coincide with the number 8 in this next period, followed by 9-Reed, 10-Ocelot, etc., to 13-Motion. This pattern recurred again and again in a continuous fifty-two-year solar cycle, or 18,980-day period, in such a way that no day could be confused with any other, since the name of the day and its associated number precluded repetition within the fifty-two years. Each year was named after the day on which it began; thus a year known as 1-Reed would recur every fifty-two years.

The solar "year-bundle" (*xiuhmolpilli*), as the Aztecs called it, consisted of 365 days, divided into eighteen months of twenty days

---

* This is often mistakenly called the *tonalamatl*, which is really the physical book in which the *tonalpohualli* was recorded.

Miguiztli · Mazatl · Tochtli · Atl

Itzcuintli · Ozomatli · Malinalli · Acatl

Ocelotl · Cuauhtli · Cozcaquauhtli · Ollin

Tecpatl · Quiauitl · Xochitl · Cipactli

Ehecatl · Calli · Cuetzpallin · Coatl

47. Aztec day signs. A solar calendar was divided into eighteen 20-day months (with five empty days); the sacred calendar was divided into twenty 13-day months. The day signs were used in both calendars.

each. The remaining five, "the empty days" (*nemontemi*), were the unlucky days and neither named nor counted, just as in New York City many buildings do not have a thirteenth floor.

The least common multiple of 260 (20 by 13) and 365 (whose primes are 5 and 73), as Franz Boas graphically explained,[18] is 18,980 days. This was the fifty-two-year cycle; after this period the same divinatory combination repeated itself. In another form the

Aztec astronomer-mathematicians, or those from whom they obtained this most complicated, ingenious calendar, determined that seventy-three years of the divine calendar (20 by 13 by 73) resulted in the same 18,980 days, making again the magical fifty-two-year cycle.

Why this fifty-two-year cycle? Why was fleeting time so great an obsession with the Aztecs? Why did it become a national fetish so that they really believed that at the end of a fifty-two-year cycle the very future of the world was in balance and might be destroyed? Did the very cleverness of the mathematicians seduce them? Did the fact that these two calendars just happened to coalesce in the various calculations to make the fifty-two-year cycle seem so magical that they conceived their inventions to be really a basic fact of nature? No one really knows.

The Aztecs' relation with time was fundamentally emotional. Their priest-astronomers had put great intellectual effort into the elaboration of the calendar. As a calendar, it was more advanced than in either Egypt or Greece. Egypt and Mesopotamia had lunar calendars, i.e., the beginning of every new month was determined by the waxing or waning of the moon. They made up for the discrepancy between lunar and solar by having "hollow" and "full" months, and this crude form of calendar existed down to Roman times. All peoples strongly agricultural in character gave great importance to the solar year, but the cities in the Fertile Crescent had different calculations, which produced chaos in comparative time reckoning. The Egyptians (as did the Mayas and Aztecs) had two systems: a religious lunar calendar and a civil 365-day calendar; and a twenty-five-year cycle.

The Greeks in the time of Hipparchus (150 B.C.), taking over the whole of Babylonian science, began to use "the methods of computing sexagesimally and the place-value notation, including a symbol for zero," [136] but the use of the zero symbol never came into general practice until the Hindus perfected it in the eighth century A.D. Yet the "American" cultures were far, far in advance of all this; the Mayas invented zero and could calculate their day count as far into the past as 23,040,000,000 days.[136]

Why all this? Why this extraordinary preoccupation with time? Did they find the endless continuity of time so appalling even though they marked it into spatialized periods with rituals and festivals? No one knows. The dominant note was the fifty-two-year cycle; the whole of the tribe's intellectual forces was put to work long before its advent to allay the wrath of the gods.

The priests had to calculate ritual by most involved methods; they had to know the precise interconnection between each particular god and "time" as given on the calendar. Sacrifice had to be correctly calculated so that it would benefit the particular god to whom they were appealing. All the developed intellect of the Aztec was turned toward this one thing: how to propitiate the right god at the right time. So sacrifice was not mere butchery, it was a parade of elaborately conceived ritual with only one object in view: to preserve human existence.

For the Aztec was threatened not only at the end of each fifty-two-year cycle; when the priests announced the end of each year there came the dreaded *nemontemi,* the "five empty days." Fires were extinguished, fasting was general, sexual intercourse ceased; artists left off their work, business lay idle. The same thing occurs in the Austrian Tyrol when the *Föhn*—the warm south wind— blows: important business grinds to a halt. No transaction on these days have legality. On the dawn of the fifth day, when the priest-astronomers, consulting their calendar books, observed the Pleiades rising in the heavens and knew the world would not end, they reached out and found a sacrificial victim, slashed open his chest, pulled out his heart, and in the freshly weeping wound kindled a new fire; from it all the fires in the temples were rekindled; and from it people all over Mexico-Tenochtitlán gathered the new fire for the new year.

All was right once more with the Aztec world.

 ## *War and Weapons* 32

WAR was the director of this religion.

It was, as is seen, related directly to religion (captives for sacrifice). It was related to economy (supplying tribute for the tribute state). War was an Aztec preoccupation; it was sacred; it had a mystic religious quality which made it all the more ferocious. Every able-bodied man was a warrior, part of an agrarian militia; the only professional army in the Aztec confederation was

the small coterie of well-born warriors who formed the bodyguard of the Chief Speaker. The Aztecs had universal service hundreds of years before Napoleon returned to nature by using a mass army without regard to losses (instead of the artificial maneuvers with small bodies of troops favored in Baroque times). The Aztec warrior was hard and spartan; he was trained to be so from childhood. His land was not lush, life was not easy, he was given only one choice: victory or death by sacrifice. Life, if it would be great, the Aztec attitude emphasized, is hard, and to victory belongs the sacrifice of victory.

War is the primary of politics. It was to the Aztecs then; it is the same to us, the living. Politics is the way in which a fluid being maintains itself, and the character of war and politics is quite the same:[87] tactics, stratagems, material forces applied at the moment of truth are the same in both, ". . . the growth of one's own way of life at the expense of the other." [183]

War as a branch of politics began with the powwow. Ambassadors, called *quauhaquauh nochtzin,* were sent to the village or tribe under pressure to join the Aztec "commonwealth"; trade and road protection were offered. With the compact came the demand that the Aztec national god Huitzilopochtli be placed alongside their local deity. They were to be allowed to keep their own dress, manners, and chieftains; they would yield tribute every six months. Negotiations were long and involved;[198] they were given the length of a lunar calendar month to capitulate.

When war was decided in council, the leaders gathered in front of the stone of Tizoc in the great plaza. Set up during the reign of Tizoc (1481–86), the large cylindrical block of trachyte, eight feet in diameter and carved with figures in low relief, shows Aztec warriors capturing others in battle, symbolized by the warrior grasping a lock of the enemy's hair.[171] It was set up facing the great *teocalli;* there or near to it the final act of war was set in motion.

The war lord held office only for the duration of a particular campaign. He was generally related by blood ties to the Chief Speaker. His war dress was elaborate; there are murals still extant that show him accoutered in quetzal feathers, ofttimes with a fantastic headgear. It was impossible not to discern him in battle and one of the prime objects was his capture. The elite of battle, the military order of the Eagle, wore a mimicry of an open eagle's beak and feather weavings of eagle feathers; the military order of the Jaguar dressed in jaguar skins; the soldiers, other common warriors from the clans, wore distinct tunics. Their shields also bore a totemic device of their clan. Before they set off, priests had to consult the *tonalamatl* to divine if the moment was propitious for victory. And why not? The Incas consulted the lungs of sacrificed llamas to see if the auguries were right, the Romans consulted chicken livers; the Aztecs, consulting the stars in their orbit, were at least a bit more governed by reason. If observations suggested dubious victory, they did not enter into war until later.

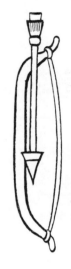

The Aztecs, in comparison with the European standards of 1519, were lightly armed. Headgear when worn was more decorative than protective. They did, however, wear quilted cotton tunics, soaked in brine; as Bernal Diaz observed, they "wore armour made of cotton reaching to the knees." For the hot country it was supe-

48. *Aztec warriors, showing their weapons, elaborate headgear (to aid in overawing the enemy), shields, and face painting, all part of war equipment. The round object was a shield* (chimalli) *which bore the crest of the clan. The most-feared weapon was the* maquahuitl, *the sword toothed with obsidian blades; there was also a sort of tomahawk. The bow* (tlauitolli) *was a Toltec weapon, used by the Aztecs and introduced into Maya country in the tenth century. The javelin* (mitl) *was thrown with the aid of a spear thrower and had great force.*

rior to Spanish armor. All carried shields (*chimalli*) to deflect arrow or sword. Made of wood covered with animal hide, many were extremely decorative, with the totemic device of the clan. The closing-in weapon was the *maquahuitl;* it was of hardwood edged with blades of obsidian sharp enough for a warrior to sever a horse's head. The bow (*tlauitolli*), with obsidian-tipped arrows, they used with deadly effectiveness "and with great skill," confesses Bernal Díaz, who received many in his own hide in his time; "the first flight of arrows wounded fifteen soldiers." In addition to these they had the sling, which hurled an egg-sized stone, and, most effective, the obsidian-tipped javelin (*mitl*), which was thrown with great force by means of the *atl-atl* spear thrower. Bernal Díaz remembered that in one of their battles on the coast, the Indians "let fly such a cloud of javelins . . . that they wounded seventy of us."

The nature of the land conditioned Aztec strategy. Wars had to be of short duration. They had no beasts of burden; everything had to be carried on the backs of human carriers. There was no system of supply such as the Incas in Peru set up along finely developed roads. Siege wars under these conditions were almost impossible since no Aztec army could be kept on the field for more than a few days. Besides, the Aztec plan was not to slaughter unnecessarily or destroy; death and destruction would imperil tribute, which was the primary aim of the battle, along with the need for sacrificial victims.

In general there were no walled cities, although the Mayas had several in Yucatán and the hereditary enemies of the Aztecs, the Tlascalans, built a wall fifteen feet high surrounding their large towns.*

The watery defense of Mexico-Tenochtitlán was a deterrent to any save the Spanish but in general there were no fortifications. Fighting was in the open. There were no "secret weapons," all had the same type of arms; what counted most in battle was surprise, ambush, morale. Battle began with a war of nerves: there were military promenades to overawe the enemy; warriors came with drums, conch-shell horns (the type seen in the Maya murals at Bonampak). The Spaniards in their first encounter got the same

---

* A part of this defense wall can still be seen at Huexotla (state of Mexico).

treatment; the Indians were "drawn up in battle array whistling and sounding their trumpets and drums." [43]

Before the campaign got under way, ambassadors had to be sent to towns and villages, subject or not, to arrange for supplies. It was almost impossible to hide intent in a major undertaking. In some instances the Aztecs deliberately refrained from use of surprise, not only giving their enemy time to arm, but sometimes even sending them arms, to develop the premise that the outcome on the battlefield was, in truth, the will of the gods.

When at a distance of an arrow flight from each other, the opposing warriors released their shafts over the heads of their forward forces; then they hurled rocks, accurately enough, from plaited cotton slings. Spears followed, which really wrought havoc, then in a welter of noise and fearful shouting they fell on each other with the *maquahuitl,* the closing-in weapon. The object was to capture the leader. Often this alone was enough to decide the issue—a single battle could suffice; again enmities could be protracted over the years. Slaughter was only to cause a rout; when that happened prisoners were taken. The retreat was followed up by the Aztecs into the principal tribal city; usually the priests with some warriors put up a determined resistance on the steps of their sacred *teocalli.* In token of victory the Aztecs burned the temple, for that was the symbol of conquest in their glyph writing. Peace was arranged as quickly as possible and normality restored. Then the tribute tribunal fixed the amount and kind to be yielded every six months. The warrior-prisoners were sent to Tenochtitlán to be held for sacrifice; if the tribe was unreliable, an Aztec garrison was placed close by and their chieftains were sent as hostages to the Aztec capital. No attempt was made at absorption of the newly conquered into Tenochtitlán. "The idea of absorbing conquered towns into the victorious state . . . never occurred to the Mexican," says Dr. George Vaillant, "and even defeated towns retained their local autonomy." There were revolts, naturally, and the Aztec militia had to be kept constantly on the go; this one defect in their political system was their Achilles' heel.

There never was an "Aztec Empire." They were never able somehow to transform domination into dominion.

THE AZTEC state was a tribute state.

Although trade was vast, extending down to Nicaragua and perhaps beyond, although things Mexican traveled as far north as Arizona for an interchange of products (Moctezuma was said to have had a bison in his zoological gardens), although the Aztec people were good craftsmen and produced for "export"—still the state in its later development depended on tribute exacted from conquest. The Aztecs knew, without the benefit of an Oswald Spengler, that "war is the creator and hunger the destroyer of all great things" and that whole peoples have lost force through the gnawing wretchedness of living. When an Aztec warrior died, he died *for* something, not *of* something. Total war was not part of their policy, nor did they want to liquidate or force the erstwhile enemy into abject poverty; they wanted tribute.

This imperial appetite began after A.D. 1400. It continued under the various "kings" until by 1519 the Aztecs dominated—with tribute yield—those parts of Mexico beginning in the north about Tampico across to Lake Chapala, thence southward including almost all of the southern part of Mexico up to the domain of the Mayas. It was large enough to include 371 tribute towns and sufficiently complex that they had to keep tribute rolls so extended that Hernán Cortés had to admit to his King-Emperor: "I was unable to find out exactly the extent of Moctezuma's kingdom. . . . The king has fortresses in all those provinces armed with his own men and also overseers and tax-collectors." And: "the tribute is inscribed in written characters and pictures." These were the tribute rolls (or, since they were folded screenwise—books), the same that Bernal Díaz saw at Tenochtitlán: "a great Cacique . . . kept the accounts of all the revenue that was brought to Moctezuma, in his books which were made of paper which they call *amatl,* and he had a great house full of these books."

A copy of one of these is still extant, with names, products, and amounts from tribute towns. Antonio de Mendoza, the first viceroy to Mexico (1535–49), had one of these tribute charts copied. It was drawn by a native artist, the glyphs translated and written in parallel Spanish orthography. It was intended as a gift to Charles V;

49. *The collecting of tribute was done every six months. Various objects of tribute collected from conquered tribes or those living under Aztec hegemony are seen here. There is a shield, blankets,* huipilli; *in another section Indians bring in corn and squash. One of the tribute collectors studies the tribute charts.*

instead French pirates seized the Spain-bound vessel at Vera Cruz, and by a chain of events too complicted to follow, it came to rest in the hands of André Thévet, the famous cosmographer to the King of France. He sold it for twenty crowns in 1584 to the English traveler and publisher of discoveries, Richard Hakluyt; it was translated with the idea that Sir Walter Raleigh would publish it at his expense, but he left his head at Whitehall before this could be accomplished. It then came into the hands of Samuel Purchas, the clerical publisher of travel literature, and so it first appeared in *Purchas his Pilgrimes* in 1625. After being "lost" for two centuries in the Bodleian Library at Oxford, the *Codex Mendoza* (named after the one who had had it made), was included, in 1831, in Lord Kingsborough's *Antiquities of Mexico.*

Tribute covered every phase of Aztec wants and Aztec luxuries. Foremost were various elaborate war costumes: helmets, shields, jaguar skins for warriors of that order, eagle skins of the other; other clothing included all that man wore in Mexico.

Precious stones formed an important part of the tribute list: gold, turquoise, and jades are listed; gourds, copal for incense, copper, shells, skins and bird feathers, dyestuffs, cotton, rubber— all were part of the economy. Chocolate, which every well-placed

171

chieftain quaffed, flavored with honey, vanilla, and, of all things, red pepper, must have come to Tenochtitlán in great quantities: "it seems to me," wrote Bernal Díaz, "that they brought out . . . over two thousand jugs of cacao all frothed up . . ." Foodstuffs were a dominant item in the tribute rolls; one can see very clearly the quantities of corn, beans, pepper, honey, vanilla that made their way into the Aztec capital.

The *calpixque*, tribute collectors, were naturally hated and feared. Their arrival every six months to supervise collections meant that towns had to disgorge much of their surplus. A good description of the *calpixque* is in the literature; they appeared in 1519 at the selfsame Totonac villages in Vera Cruz then occupied by Hernán Cortés and his small army: "five Mexicans, who were Moctezuma's tax-gatherers, had just arrived. . . . [They approached] with the utmost assurance and arrogance . . . Their cloaks and loin-cloths were richly embroidered, and their shining hair was gathered up as though tied on their heads; and each one was smelling the roses that he carried, and each had a crooked staff in his hand. Their Indian servants carried fly-whisks . . ." [48]

The Vera Cruz area was garrisoned by Aztec warriors; some were at Ceycoccnacán, said Hernán Cortés, "a fortified town which belongs to Moctezuma," so that any discourtesy to the tribute collectors or any delay could bring swift retribution.

To give historical balance, not all tribes nor all towns under Aztec dominance were in opposition; the Aztec overlords freed them from the petty tribal struggles, commerce widened, prosperity was heightened by protection, roads were freed from attack, and Tenochtitlán was a good consumer. Many accepted the Aztec peace willingly.

Who had title to the tribute and how did it enter their economy? Presumably the state, i.e., the Chief Speaker, who officially received the tribute at his capital. There, as we know, it was entered into his "account books." Some of it, such as excess foodstuffs, must have been distributed to the various clans on arrival; some of it was stored in the official storage chambers to be used against periodic famine or to pay, in lieu of money, the wages of those specialists attached to the royal household. Bernal Díaz said that "Moctezuma has two houses full of every sort of arms . . . There were shields great and small, and a sort of broad swords . . .

lances . . . which cut like razors . . . quilted cotton armour . . . casques or helmets made of wood and bone"—all the things that appeared on the tribute-lists.

Distribution of all this was made on a per capita basis. Aztec society existed for the good of the whole people, and while the tribute won by Aztec armies was in practice held by the Chief Speaker, all of it, in one way or another, found its way back to the people. Arms were distributed to each clan and held in part of the local temple; foodstuffs were distributed. Doubtless, based on the designs of the shields, each clan had the right to ask a tributary village to make shields carrying their own coat of arms on it. Some of the tribute was used to pay the tax-free artisans, the specialists— priests, masons, goldsmiths, featherworkers, sculptors, etc.—who produced the vast array of beauty which the public enjoyed.

Such a tribute state is not new in history; as has been pointed out, it has its parallel in Sumer, which, around 3000 B.C., maintained itself similarly. Before 2500 B.C. all the temple-cities of Mesopotamia within the same general region had been independent states until Sargon of Agade extended his conquests "to the silver mountain and the cedar forest," making, like the Aztec, a conquest of all the petty states and forcing tribute from them in the form of raw materials, and this imperialism "became a new instrument in the concentration of a still vaster social surplus." [33]

It was not enough that the Aztec state was a tribute state, for while the common man did not own land, he owned—after work tax—the usufruct of the worked lands. Surplus was traded at the various markets; leisure time used up the raw materials which filtered down from top to bottom and were made into manufactured goods for "export" trade. So, to extend this economy, a new class came into being—something unknown among nations of other indigenous "American" organizations—a merchant class.

THE GUILDS of "commercial travelers," the *pochteca*, were a law unto themselves. They had distinct prerogatives. They lived in their own wards or *calpulli* (Pochtlán was one); guild rights passed from father to son; they paid no taxes; they had their own gods, and before setting off on a long journey they evoked the protection of Zacazontli, the protector of roads and travelers; and they were not subject to the ordinary law tribunals.

The *pochteca* were a rather late development in Aztec society. Their own chronicles said, "commerce began in Mexico-Tenochtitlán in the year 1504"; assuredly it was earlier. It rose out of the great social surplus piled up in the city as a result first of tribute and then of the manufacturing activities of a people somewhat relieved from constant attention to agriculture. In and about the city they manufactured cotton cloth, rabbit-fur robes, obsidian and copper mirrors, cosmetics (a tincture of cochineal with grease) for face painting, medicinal herbs, flower pastes as a base for perfumes. Salt, which they leached out of the lakes, and other stuff that was light enough for long journeys, were also in the list. In return for these things the directing classes and the common man alike wanted from the hotlands cotton, feathers, precious stones, chocolate, rubber. The *pochteca* were purveyors of luxuries.

All of the early Old World routes were luxury routes: the amber road (still known as the *Birnsteinstrasse* where it passes through Bamberg, Germany) was the longest haul in ancient times —from the Baltic to Egypt. From 10,000 B.C. people journeyed these thousands of miles to obtain amber.

Salt, a luxury for many, made one of the great life lines in history. The *Via Salaria* was one of the first Roman roads. Grain eaters needed salt; for them it was an essential. Those in highland Mexico who had no coastal connections were dependent on the Aztecs who controlled the salt-leaching works about the saline lakes. One of the plaints of the chieftains of the Tlascalans, hereditary enemies of the Aztecs, was that "they had no salt; since there was none on their lands and they did not venture out." [43]

Still the greatest traffic has always been in luxuries. It was frankincense and myrrh, or silk loaded on camel caravans, or delicacies for "frolicking and chewing and sucking" for Greek or Roman banquets. In the New World the Aztecs craved chocolate and feathers, jade, emeralds, and gold dust. The *pochteca* in this world were the alchemists who turned the base metal of necessities into the gold of luxuries.

Trade was a monopoly of the *pochteca*. Days, weeks, months were spent by them acquiring the articles for trade at the various markets; they then assembled carriers who were capable of carrying sixty pounds on their backs, and the human caravan set off. In regions where conditions were not fully secure they were accompanied by Aztec warriors. Trade has always been sacrosanct. The way to bring down swift reprisal was to plunder them. If one of their numbers died in a far-off land he was given the same rites as a warrior slain in battle.

Aztec trading colonies under the *pochteca* penetrated to Guatemala, going down the Pacific Coast (which was not controlled by the Mayas) as far south as Nicaragua. Their caravans were often gone for a full two years. They also left colonists behind, small "islands" of Nahuatl-speaking peoples called *pipil,* who, even now, show their Nahuatl origin in their designs on pottery and weaving and their use of the symbol of Tlaloc, the Aztec rain god.[112]

The *pochteca* were often accused of being "warriors in disguise,"[198] ferreting out information as to the weakness and strength of tribes outside the pale of Aztec dominance. There seems to be no direct evidence of this, but as conquest often followed their trading incursions, the "other peoples" received them suspiciously when they bore gifts.

50. *The* pochteca *were commercial travelers of the imperial Aztecs. With the aid of their human carriers, they extended Aztec commerce as far south as Nicaragua.*

LITTLE is known of Aztec roads or communications. That there *were* roads and good communications must be assumed. Yet there have been no connected studies of Aztec roads such as have been made of the network of the Maya *sacbeob,* nor has there been such an extensive survey as the von Hagen expedition study of the Inca highways on the west coast of Peru.[209]

The best-known Aztec road, since it was the one that Cortés and his small army followed from the hotlands to the uplands of Mexico, was that which ran from Vera Cruz to Mexico-Tenochtitlán; the precise route has been identified. The first prerequisite of empire is communications. Rome had it, the Incas had it, but since the Aztecs were not an empire, their roads were undeveloped. The nature of Mexican geography worked, it is true, against direct communications, and the engineering science of the Aztecs was not oriented in the manner of Peru. Yet the Incas would have found Mexico's obstacles minor; they had roads that crossed the bare Andes as high as 15,000 feet.

Roads in Mexico followed the path of least resistance. The ancient trade route was on the warm Gulf Coast, the main road which ran from Xicalango (Sahagún called it "the land of Anáhuac Xicalango") as far north as the Tropic of Cancer. Xicalango was located in the Laguna de Términos, into which four rivers debouch. Here Maya trading missions had contact with central Mexican tribes. It is from here that Toltec troops were introduced into Yucatán in the twelfth century; it was from Xicalango that the Aztecs had first news of the arrival of white man.* It was one of the great trading centers of central Mexico; trade from Yucatán and Central America was brought to it by giant canoes arriving along the coast.

The road ran northwest from here along the jungle coast through the Olmec country into the lands of the Totonacs where a road (followed by Hernán Cortés and his small army) led to their villages, and to the large city of Cempoala. Cortés does not describe it. There were no bridges—rivers which rose with callous

---

* Sahagún said: "They had news of the arrival of the Christians from some merchants [*pochteca*] who had gone to the markets of these coasts . . . at Xilanco [Xicalango]. . . ."

ease would not permit them, and natives crossed by canoes or by swimming. In fact, in all Mexican literature there are no descriptions of bridges other than the small removable ones used by the Aztecs in their causeways. Presumably this coastal road continued up as far as Tampico (22° N. lat.).

Mexico-Tenochtitlán was connected with a road from Vera Cruz and the conquistadors followed it. Only from them do we have a description: "The way was rugged"—understandably, since it rose from sea level to 8,000 feet; in a few miles it was narrow. When they entered Xicochimilco (now Xico) in the heights, it was defended by "a town of great strength" and the road "was a narrow defile cut in steps." Beyond this the road passed through the frigid unpopulated heights of Cofre de Perote (13,000 feet), where the traveler was assailed by "whirlwinds of hailstones and rain."

Once the land mass lowered into a warmer plateau, Cortés speaks of a "royal road"—it is not further described. They found rest houses at intervals and occasionally small temples "with idols" which Cortés likened to roadside chapels built along Spanish roads. Near to Cholula they found two roads: "The best road was by way of Cholula," now the city of Puebla. This "royal road" passed between the volcanoes of Popocatépetl and Ixtaccihuatl ("my men proceeded along it until they came to two mountains between which it runs"), and went straight to Mexico-Tenochtitlán by way of the town of Amecameca; another branched off to Chalco near to the lake's edge and it was "well swept and clear."

Along this route, which is often subject to sleet and snow in the winter, there were way stations like the Inca *tampus:* "groups of houses which they build like inns or hostels where the Indian traders lodge." At the edge of the lake they entered the wide causeways which lead to the capital of the Aztecs.

Some of the Aztec roads were doubtlessly paved with *tezontli,* a pink pumice traprock, abundant and easily worked, composed of silica and volcanic ash. This is suggested by the fact that the name of the god of the road whom all travelers invoked was Zacazontli. But there is little physical evidence of pre-Hispanic paved roads throughout Mexico. There are remains of ceremonial ways at Teotihuacán; there is a sixty-foot-broad paved road at Xochicalco that leads to a hilltop temple, but it is only half a mile in length. There is nothing like the Maya *sacbeob* ("artificial roads") built of limestone with a width of 15 feet, rising above the plain and extending for 62.3 miles from Cobá to Yaxuna in Yucatán.[200]

Two roads went southwest out of Mexico-Tenochtitlán. One was that already described which ran through the snow-topped volcanoes to Cholula and on southward to Oaxaca toward the Pacific; the other leaving Mexico went due west of Cuernavaca and paralleled the first to Oaxaca, making junction at Huajolotitlán; it then proceeded to the Pacific Ocean, terminating at Huatulco. There seems not to have been any direct Aztec communication to the Pacific Coast; indeed, there was no need for it. The Aztecs did not use the sea; they had no maritime connection with any other land, and there is no evidence of any direct communication, to use an example, between Mexico and Peru. All the evidence has been sifted; there were no communications between the Inca Empire (or those that preceded it) and the cultures of Mexico. The Spaniard had to develop Mexico-Peru communications *ab ovo*.

The southern communications of the Aztecs—a mere development from existing older routes—we know only because after his Mexican conquest Hernán Cortés used the road, enlarged it, and created a port at the Indian fishing village of Huatulco on the Pacific (the best natural port southward from Acapulco). The manner in which Cortés enlarged the ancient trails to provide space for cart traffic suggests how it was done under the Aztecs. The work of building and maintaining the roads, writes Dr. Woodrow Borah, who was the first to thread his way through the maze to plot the road, was carried out by *corvée* levied on Indian towns near by.

51. *Water transport was limited to lakes. The canoes were as large as the trees which could be brought down. Although the Aztecs had some coastal trade, this was usually carried on by allied tribes.*

Each village took care of the twenty-mile section nearest it. They also maintained the inns or *mesones* on the route. The southbound Aztec-Zapotec road joined up with another transcontinental route at Tehuantepec, which crossed the flat isthmus at sea level. Where precisely the southbound road went from there is conjectural.

Although the Aztec reached considerable heights in luxury, he never escaped carrying his own burdens. The llama and its relatives were unknown in Mexico until the estate of Hernán Cortés (Marquisate del Valle) brought a herd of sixty llamas, "*ovejas del Perú.*"[1] They were taken to the highlands of Penol del Xico for domestication in Mexico; they died out and that was all. Although most Indians carried their own produce, there were some of the baser sort who formed the human caravans. These *tamenes* were well-known; Bernal Díaz called them *hombres de carga:* "There arrived thirty cargo-Indians called *tamenes.* . . ." The regular accepted weight was a little less than sixty pounds, the rate of travel fifteen miles a day.

The wheel, except as used in children's toys, was totally absent in Mexico. The whole principle of the wheel as arch was unknown, as was the potter's wheel and the rotary quern. Even if the wheel had been known, it is doubtful that it could have served much without draft animals. Instead the Aztecs used the litter. This conveyance for the exalted was universal in the Old World as well as the New; few advanced cultures were without it. The Aztecs seem to have considered it only a ceremonial device and not, as among the Incas and the Chimús in South America, a mode of transport. To the Spanish, Moctezuma first appeared being carried in a litter along the great causeways out of the city. There is no mention, however, of the litter being used beyond this; when Cortés took along the unfortunate last Aztec "king," Cuauhtemoc, on his expedition to Honduras, he walked as did the rest of the Indians.

Water transport was limited to the lakes. The Aztecs constructed dugout canoes—almost everyone seems to have had one in this Venice-like city. Much of the lacustrine commerce was carried on by water. Canoes brought in produce. They removed the excreta from the public toilets so as not to pollute the city and used it for fertilizer. There were special canoes used to transport fresh water: "The water is sold from canoes," wrote Hernán Cortés. "The canoes place themselves under the bridges where the aqueducts are

52. *Courier runners employed to carry messages over Aztec roads.*

to be found . . . filled by men who are specially paid for this work." The Aztecs used no other type of boat larger than the dugout; when Cortés built two moderate-sized sloops on the lakes of Mexico, he took the captive Moctezuma for a sail to a distant isle, skimming over the wind-swept waters, so that "Moctezuma was charmed and said it was a great thing, this combining sails and oars together." [48] The Aztecs had nothing larger than these for the Pacific; in the Gulf the Mayas had enormous dugouts, and Caribs sailed the turbulent seas with no difficulty, but the Aztecs like the Incas were landlubbers.

Couriers were employed on the roads to carry messages. Beyond the fact that they existed there is little more reference to them, whereas those Spaniards who went from Mexico to Peru were astounded at the Inca system of *chasquis,* who, running in relays, could cover a distance of 1,250 miles in five days. The Aztec courier was trained to run; there were competitions for the fleet of foot and this tradition is still kept up by the present-day Tarahumara Indians living in Chihuahua.

Pictographic communications were put into a forked stick. It is not known for certain but it is probable that an artist accompanied the runners on important missions. At Vera Cruz Cortés was amazed upon receiving an embassy from Moctezuma who "brought with them some clever painters . . . and ordered them to make pictures true to nature of the face and body of Cortés and all his captains, and of the soldiers, ships, sails and horses . . . even of the two greyhounds; and the cannon and cannon balls . . ." [48] Later he found when in Mexico that Moctezuma had known by such means every action of theirs since they touched the shores of Mexico.

Thus the Aztecs had roads, wayside rest houses, roadside gods, couriers, and, through their pictographic writing, a good form of communications. The Europe of 1519 had not as much. "To journey in Europe," wrote Awaliyal Effendi in 1611, ". . . is like a fragment of hell." Roads in the sixteenth century were paved like hell in the proverb, and many the complaint that travel was a purgatory "in little." To move over Europe's roads one had to have "a falcon's eye, an ass's ears, a monkey's face, a merchant's words, a camel's back, a hog's mouth, a deer's feet."

It is small wonder that the conquistadors praised the Aztec roads.

 Paper, Writing, Literature   *36*

ALL ADVANCED civilizations (with the amazing exception of South American cultures such as the Inca, Chimú, Mochica, and Tiahuanaco) had some form of paper, some form of writing, and some form of literature. In all these phases of culture the Aztecs excelled.

Paper (*amatl*) was an article of tribute.

On the tribute lists of Moctezuma one reads: "twenty-four thousand reams of paper are to be brought as a tribute yearly to Tenochtitlán." Twenty-four thousand of these reams would be 480,000 sheets of paper and judged by any standard this is an enormous consumption of paper.* [39]

While it is not necessarily true, as someone once wrote, that the quantity of paper consumed stands in direct ratio to the intellectual development of a people, still the prevalence of paper and writing had much to do with the particular intellectual direction of the Aztecs.

* "Ream" is adapted from the Spanish *resma*, which in turn is derived from the Arabic *rizmah*, "a bundle, especially of paper." It is only an expression which fortuitously coincided with the Aztec numeral *pilli* and has no connection with our ream.

"True paper" (the product of a technique by which beaten fibrous material is felted on a mold while suspended in water) was not the paper of the Aztecs. The inventors of true paper were the Chinese in A.D. 105. They used the fibers of the mulberry. The technique was transmitted by Chinese papermakers captured by the Arabs in 751 after the battle of Samarkand. Papermaking was perfected by the Arabs, brought by them to Spain in 1150 when they

53. *Two forms of Aztec papermaking. On the left, an Indian pulls off the bark of the wild Ficus tree (related to the mulberry which is also used in paper-making). The bark was then beaten into large rolls of paper which were folded double to make books. On the right, a woman makes smaller pieces of paper from branch fibers of the same tree.*

settled in Xativa, from whence paper went around the Western world.[85] The Egyptians did not have true paper either; papyrus was made by laminating strips of the stems of a water plant; they were able to produce rolls of papyrus "paper" twelve inches wide, forty feet long. The most widely used method of obtaining a paper substitute, the one used by peoples in such widely separated regions as Polynesia, Melanesia, Southern Asia, Africa, South America, and the method that was the source of Maya and Aztec paper was that of peeling off the bark of the *Ficus,* which is related to the mulberry, and felting it into sheets as thin as paper by beating it with a ribbed mallet. This is called "bark cloth," but it is not cloth since it is not woven; it is bark paper.

A functional form of paper made in this manner appeared very early in Yucatán and Mexico. There is no manner of dating its appearance, but probably it was used as paper among the Mayas as early as 1000 B.C.[203] The Mayas folded their *huun* paper and made polychromic books of it. The paper prepared from the inner bast fibers of the wild fig trees was, in use and appearance, like true paper. There are only three such Maya "books" or codices left of those that escaped the "burning of the books" in Yucatán by Bishop Diego de Landa.

All of the advanced cultures in Mexico had paper and writing. The Toltecs had glyph writing and the same graphic techniques; they are credited with having an encyclopedic *teoamextli,* a divine book compiled in A.D. 660; neither it nor others like it have survived. The Mixtecs at Cholula had paper and writing; several of their codices are extant. So did the Zapotecs in Oaxaca and the Totonacs in Vera Cruz. Bernal Díaz saw piles of books near the Totonac city-state of Cempoala: "Then we came on some towns . . . [and] found idol houses . . . and many paper books doubled together in folds like Spanish cloth . . ."

Paper and writing, then, were not an Aztec invention; the Aztecs, however, perfected them.

The fact that the Indians had books and writing greatly astonished the conquistador: "There is so much to think over," said Bernal Díaz, "that I do not know how to describe it, seeing things as we did that had never been heard or seen before or even dreamed about." So much so that they sent back to Spain, along with the first gold collected, two of such books. Fortunately these fell into the hands of the Italian humanist Pietro Martire d'Anghiera, who was then in Seville; he, corresponding with the learned, wrote about "books such as the Indians use." Later Dr. Francisco Hernández, who was neither priest nor clerk, came to Mexico in 1570 in the capacity of *protomédico* on the first botanical expedition to the new world. In the course of his five-year plant explorations he saw the paper craft at Tepotzitlán: "Many Indians are employed at this craft. . . . The sheets of paper are then polished (by means of a *xicaltetl*) and fashioned into sheets." These *xicaltetl* were stone flatiron-shaped celts which, when heated and pressed upon the paper, closed the pores and gave it surface, more or less the same technique that European papermakers used during the Renaissance to burnish paper by means of an agate stone. "It is something like our own paper," he wrote, "except that theirs is whiter and thicker." The paper was called *amatl*, the tree the *amaquahuitl* (literally "paper tree"), of the genus *Ficus*.

The Aztec glyph for *amatl* was a roll. Yet there were other types. A yellow paper always sold in sheets came from the town of Amacoztitlán on the Rio Amacuzac in the state of Morelos; it derived from the fibers of the yellow wild fig, the *Ficus petiolaris*. This whole area, in a tropical setting of under 5,000 feet, was *the*

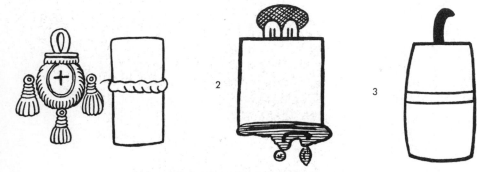

54. *Three types of Aztec* amatl *paper:*

1) *A paper roll attached to the symbol for 8,000.* 2) *A yellow paper, made in sheets, which came from the town of Amacoztitlán. Above the paper are teeth symbols for* tlan *(place); below, the symbol for water.* 3) *A long roll-type paper (which came from the town of Itzamatitlán) made from the* Ficus *tree, whose leaf was shaped like a dagger (*itzli*).*

paper manufacturing center of ancient Mexico. Itzamatitlán, a village in Morelos on the Rio Yuatepec, was the source of yet another type of paper.

The Aztecs were like the Chinese in their reverence for paper, for "all classes of Chinese," writes Dard Hunter, "from the aristocratic scholar . . . down to the most illiterate coolie [showed] a pronounced reverence for every scrap of paper." This, more or less, was the attitude of the Aztecs.

Paper on arrival went first to the priests, writers, artists; then it passed into the market where is was purchased or traded. Bernal Díaz saw it there: "[There was] paper, which in this country is called *amatl* . . ." Sahagún, the observant Franciscan monk, in his great work on the Aztecs (in the chapter entitled "The Gods Which the Ancient Mexicans Adored") tells us that "for the merchant's god Yacatecuhtli . . . they made offerings of paper . . . for the image of Napatecli—the patron god of the rush-mat makers—

they gave him a crown of paper . . . and in his hands flowers made of paper." Each of the Aztec months dedicated to a god was "honoured by strips of paper covered with copal and rubber . . . for the goddess who lived in the house of the sun . . . they adorned with paper." So it went on, every phase of life or worship used *amatl* paper. Even today the descendants of the Otomis remain papermakers. They make their paper from the same plants as did the Aztecs.

The greater bulk of the paper, however, was used to keep the genealogies, trial records, land records, for each ward or *calpulli* had its land registers and tribute rolls. There were hundreds, perhaps thousands, of such "books." Bernal Díaz thumbed through them when he wandered into the endless rooms of Moctezuma's palace; he followed an "accountant" and he saw "all the revenue that was brought . . . [and recorded] in his books which were made of paper which they call *amatl,* and he had a great house full of these books."

Those not destroyed by the Spanish siege of Mexico perished in other ways. After the Conquest Fray Juan de Zumarraga collected all the "books" that could be found, especially in the "royal library" at Texcoco, east of Mexico, and "the most cultivated capital of Anáhuac," wrote Prescott, "and the great repository of the national archives." The "burning of the books" by the monks was so thoroughly done that only a pitiful fourteen of these now remain.

Like all early writing, Aztec writing was nonphonetic. It was not capable of any general statement nor could abstract ideas be expressed. Only in its later evolution was a change sensed and the Aztecs seemed to be arriving at the beginning of syllabic phonetics. This would have occurred when signs no longer stood for pictures, or even ideas, but for sounds. Instead, Aztec writing, in 1519, was still pictographic: a wrapped mummy figure was a symbol of death; migrations or movements along the road were expressed by footprints; seeing was expressed by an eye projected beyond the viewer; speaking was a wagging tongue; a mountain was symbolized so obviously that even one untrained in reading Aztec glyphs would know it. These symbols could be compounded so that if a "rememberer" wished to chant about a notable historical fact such as *"In the year 2-Reed (1507) Moctezuma conquered the village of Itztepec,"* the *tlacuilo* artist would have first drawn the year 2-Reed, then the offi-

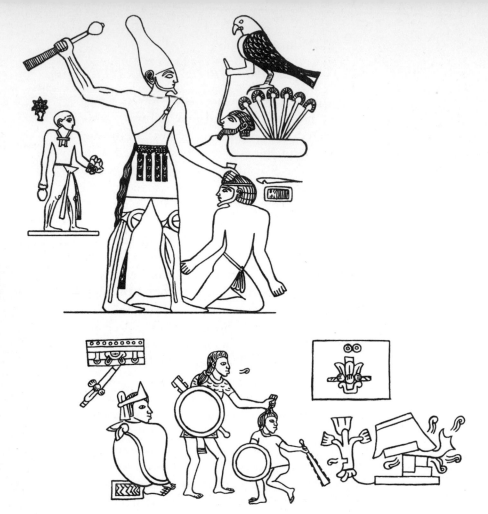

55. *An illustration showing the comparative glyph writing of the Egyptians and the Aztecs.* ABOVE: *A detail from King Narmer's palette, Hierakonpolis, Egypt, 3100 B.C. The first sign of the man symbolizes a fish, the n'r fish and its phonetic value* nar. *The second sign represents a chisel,* mer; *hence the name of the king, Narmer. Narmer holds a warrior by the hair—the symbol of captivity. Above this a falcon sits on six lotus buds. Each lotus (kha) has the sound value of a thousand. So it is read: "King Narmer brings six thousand foreigners captured within their land."* BELOW: *An arrangement of Aztec history, as given in the* Codex Mendoza, *to show similar thought and glyphic pattern. This depicts one of the military achievements of Moctezuma I (1440–69). A rebus drawing of his name is above. An Aztec grabs the hair of another—the symbol of battle. To the right is a symbol of a temple on fire, meaning conquest; attached to the temple is the rebus drawing of the village, a tree which has a speaking tongue—Quanahuaca (modern Cuernavaca). Above it is the date, 1469.*

cial accepted symbol of Moctezuma; a thin line would have run to a burning temple and above it the rebus drawing of the town of Itztepec (an obsidian dagger on top of a mountain).

There was naturally no alphabet to this system, yet the Aztecs did combine a series of pictorial elements, often abstract, to give complicated meanings; by these methods as well as by puns, color, position, they produced a staggering amount of records.

The thought of God and the exigencies of economy were the origins of writing; at least this was true in the Near East. Early Sumerian writing (about 5000 B.C.) developed as did the Aztec. The clay tablets were impressed, says Dr. H. S. Hooke in *A History of Technology,* with a cow's head, an ear of grain, a fish, a mound; later they were compounded and show the "first attempts to express verbal notions." By 4000 B.C. the Sumerians had a syllabary or sign-list of five hundred to six hundred signs. Egyptian writing developed similarly. The motive that furthered writing was the need to record tribute. In the temple-cities of the Near East, God was regarded as the owner of the land and the people as occupiers of the land, and they had to pay rent to the temple-city, to the priests who were the gods' vicars.

In the beginning early Egyptian pictorial writing did not differ a great deal from that of the Aztecs. Later, in the Middle Kingdom, it was reduced to 732 conventional signs, moved into syllabary, developed homonyms, and, as it progressed, divorced sound from meaning. Still later it evolved into a cursive form of glyphic script and by 800 B.C. into demotic, which is one of the forms found on the Rosetta stone. In the beginning the pictographic glyph to express a historical event was not much different. Take for example a historical event of King Narmer's dated 3100 B.C.[81] This is a mixture of pictorial and phonetic elements: *"King Narmer brings six thousand foreigners captured within their land."* When the two forms of writing are compared in descriptions of similar events, they tend to show similar evolution.

This speaks very well for the perception of the Aztec, for although his cultural attainments appeared forty-five hundred years later in time than those of the Egyptian, it must be remembered that man migrated to the Americas during the early Neolithic stage of his history. At the time of the early American's arrival into the Americas the other Neolithic cultures, in the Middle East, Europe,

Greece, had no greater wit nor ornament than he. But the "American" became isolated from the main currents of cultural evolution. The art of writing, the wheel, the alphabet, metalworking, etc., came out of the Fertile Crescent and thence made their way throughout the Old World. Even then diffusion worked slowly. It took two thousand years for the principle of the wheel to reach Britain and other inventions were even longer in arriving.

"The fabric of the Old World history," writes Pál Kelemen, "is like a vast web stretching from the Roman ramparts of England to the delicately drawn woodcuts of Japan, from the Byzantine icons of the Russian steppes to the wondrous world of the royal tombs of Egypt. . . . It is an enormous territory . . . yet remote as certain points lie from one another, as different the styles, it is clear that details and even whole ideas were incorporated, adapted, and developed inter-regionally."

The Aztecs had literature. The term perhaps is incorrect, just as saying that their functional crafts were "art" is not wholly right; while both expressions are true, they are, in fact, misleading. As is obvious, the Aztecs had no literature as we understand it, even though the word can be defined as "the total of preserved writings belonging to a given language or people." Yet, since one must always put a truth or a conclusion at the end of a chain of reasoning, like the knot at the end of a thread—since otherwise the thread would not hold—so therefore Aztec literature.

Aztec literature was mostly history. Annals of ancient times, year counts, books of the day and the hours—even diaries. There were observations of planetary events, eclipses, movements of stars, observations of celestial phenomena which had affected or might affect their present. There was much out of the past; for their mythopoetic faculty was well developed. They were poets and most delighted when writing and singing of the past—for only the past is really poetic. One of their chief concerns was this; their "histories," recorded on paper, showed the migrations, the stopping-off places, the wars, conflicts, founding of cities. Their sacred almanacs were scarcely literature nor were their tribal records, land registers, lines of descent, and tribute charts.

Their tribal history approached more closely to what we know as literature. Even then, what was put down was only enough to aid the memory; there were no cross references to other tribes. The

Aztecs would have seemed to any who read their glyphic charts as if they lived alone in Mexico. No reference is made to other tribes. Aztec interests extended "vertically from tribe to pantheon." [198]

Aztec literature really consisted of that which was unwritten, that which was transmitted orally, and glyph writing served to provoke the memory of the "rememberers," helped them to recall the passing of events. These twice-told sagas, hymns, elegies, chants only became "literature" when they were set down by a bilingual scribe (Spanish Nahuatl) after the Conquest. [67]

Many of the great sagas which form our world literature were orally transmitted before they were set down. For how long were the wanderings of Ulysses chanted before some nimble-fingered scrivener put it down? All the stories of the Cicones, the Lotophagi, the Cyclops, and the Laestrygones were repeated in chant before being made "immortal" by letters.

And so with Aztec literature. Present-day Mexican scholars, who speak Nahuatl as easliy as they do mellifluous Spanish, have translated the original texts set down by scribes who transcribed them from the original sixteenth-century Nahuatl speech. Dr. Angel María Garibay has filled two volumes of things Aztec (which are here translated into English for the first time), and it is amazing how wide the field of the Aztec concern was. Reading them we are brought in closer connection with these people whose spectacular history has here been set down. They were always curious about their relation to the universe as a whole; they questioned themselves about life and afterlife.

> *Is it true that one lives only on earth?*
> *Not forever on earth: only a short while here.*
> *Even jade will crack,*
> *Even gold will break,*
> *Even quetzal feathers will rend,*
> *Not forever on earth: only a short while here.*

Those who may go into the place of the underworld chant about the day:

> *[If] in one day we leave,*
> *In one night descend to the mysterious regions,*
> *Here we only came to meet,*
> *We are only passers-by on earth.*

Let us pass life in peace and pleasure; come, let us rejoice.
But not those who live in wrath: the earth is very wide!
That one could live forever, that one need not die.

The poetic side of their lives, their imagery and the love of nature and flowers, which even Hernán Cortés first recognized, is expressed in an agony of soul:

My heart wishes with longing for flowers,
I suffer with the song, and only rehearse songs on earth,
I, Cuacuauhtzin:
I want flowers that will endure in my hands . . . !
Where shall I gather beautiful flowers, beautiful songs?
Never does spring produce them here:
I alone torment myself, I, Cuacuauhtzin.
Can you rejoice perchance, may our friends have pleasure?
Where shall I gather beautiful flowers, beautiful songs?

The *Codex Florentino*, written in Spanish, translated directly from ideographic Nahuatl speech, sermoned how the boys studying in the *calmecac* religious schools "must learn artfully all the songs, the songs of the gods . . . which are written in the books," such as these:

Where shall I go?
Where shall I go?
The road of the gods of duality,
Could your house perchance be the place of the fleshless?
Perchance inside heaven?
Or is only earth here,
The place of the fleshless?

And others, which reaffirmed God's possession of this celestial globe:

In heaven you live;
The mountains you uphold,
Anáhuac is in your hand,
Everywhere, always you are awaited,
You are invoked, you are entreated,
Your glory, your fame are sought.
In heaven you live:
Anáhuac is in your hand.

One American scholar, John Cornyn, opines that in the whole range of indigenous "American" literature no other tribe has left such a variety of expressions and feelings. For it is through chants that literature left the realm of the priestly intellectual and entered the people. Here they stress ideas, both hieratic and secular, a fact unusual in itself. A poet, perhaps a worker in fine stones, sings of the beauty of gems:

> *Jades I perforate, gold I cast in the crucible:*
> *This is my song!*
> *I set emeralds . . .*
> *This is my song.*

And that he *felt* as a literate artist feels is expressed by the phrase "understanding God in his heart":

> *The good painter;*
> *Toltec artist of the black and red ink,*
> *Creator of things with the black water. . . .*
>
> *The good painter; understanding*
> *God in his heart,*
> *Defies things with his heart,*
> *Dialogues with his own heart.*
>
> *He knows colors, applies and shadows them.*
> *Draws the feet, the faces,*
> *Sketches the shadows, obtains a finish,*
> *As if he were a Toltec artist*
> *He paints the total colors of flowers.*

Does one suspect these sentiments? Does it appear that the original Nahuatl-Mexican text has been improved in the translation, gilded by Spanish poets who love to tint the past with new colors? This is how a fragment of the original text appears in parallel translation in the manuscript *Leyenda de los Soles* (*Legend of the Suns*)[104] which was set down originally in 1558:

My flowers shall not perish	*Ah tlamiz noxochiuh ah tlamiz*
Nor shall my chants cease,	*nocuic*
They spread, they scatter.	*In noconehua*
	Xexelihui ya moyahua

Mexico, like Peru, was a sun state. Above all was the sun god and no matter how many the manifestations of the gods, how widespread their influence, the sum of all things came from the sun. Mexico was virtually a Sun Kingdom.

Now our father the Sun
Sinks attired in rich plumes,
Within an urn of precious stones,
As if girdled with turquoise necklaces goes,
Among ceaselessly falling flowers. . . .

Such is an idea, an idea, nothing more, of Aztec literature. It has recently been carefully scrutinized by Dr. Miguel León Portilla in a book, *La Filosofía Nahuatl* (not available in English), which casts a new light on the human qualities of the Aztec. There is more Aztec literature extant than one would at first surmise, even though much has been lost. But what *is* here tallies very well with what the first conquistadors said they saw of Aztec life and what has been confirmed by archaeology.

As the world spun into 1519, the Aztec could look back on a history which for sheer will to power has few peers. They came out of nothing and made themselves in a relatively short time heirs of thousands of years of culture even greater than their own, a culture which was adopted and assimilated by them. They gave the Mexican land its first direction toward some form of economic synthesis. They gave it a new concept of commerce by extending trade beyond traditional borders. Their knowledge of geography and of plants was vast. They developed paper into a veritable industry. They had writing which tended more and more to evolve into the phonetic. They had literature. They were using wooden and clay stamps to impress designs and symbols on their *amatl* paper. Thus the Aztec had all the ingredients—paper, writing, literature, and stamping—which ancient China had and which brought about the first steps toward that reproduction of ideas by printing which extended civilization.

It is, however, useless to speculate what might have been. In that year of 1519 a small fleet of vessels anchored at Vera Cruz: Hernán Cortés had arrived.

Hail and Farewell

THEY FELL.
It is a drama which, no matter how often told, never seems to lose the patina of its romance. The Spanish who took active part in it felt the historicity of the moment: Hernán Cortés penned his famous *Five Letters* even while wading through the sea of Aztec blood. Three other Spaniards who participated left their impressions as well, including that wonderful Bernal Díaz del Castillo, one who even at the age of eighty-four could not forget its impact: ". . . it all comes before my eyes as though it had happened but yesterday." The Conquest will be a source for literature for a long time and none perhaps will replace William Prescott's historical narrative. All the others that have followed—be it General Lew Wallace, D. H. Lawrence, or Samuel Shellabarger, or even Madariaga's *Heart of Jade* and Maurice Collis's *Cortés and Moctezuma*—are only pallid copies of the original piece forged by William Prescott.

They fell. Why they fell can be found in the literature it was inevitable. Once white man began to probe into the new world, contact with the Aztecs and conquest of the Aztecs were a certainty; if it had not been Hernán Cortés, it would have been someone else.

Hernán Cortés arrived at a psychological moment in Mexico (just as in Peru Francisco Pizarro came when the Incas had just gone through a civil war). A god, Quetzalcoatl, was expected from the east. Columbus made contact with the Mayas in his fourth and last voyage in 1502. This amazing bit of intelligence, enlarged every time it was told and retold, came to the ears of Aztec merchants who were trading near Yucatán at the ancient market of Xicalango at that time. Moctezuma came into power in 1503. During his reign white men continued to appear and disappear along the Gulf shores. Quetzalcoatl, the culture hero of these Americas, who was expelled from his land, vowed as he sailed away into that selfsame Gulf sea that "on the date of my birth which is Ce-Acatl, the year of 1-Reed—*I will return.*" According to the Aztec calendar this year 1-Reed could only fall, in the Christian calendar reckoning, in the years 1363, 1467, or 1519. In 1519 Hernán Cor-

tés appeared on the shores of Vera Cruz, and one of the first gifts
sent to him by Moctezuma was a magnificent headdress of quetzal
plumes, the same headdress which today is in the Museum für
Völkerkunde at Vienna. Long before this the whole Aztec people
had gone through years of tribulations; they felt their insecurity as
their priests searched the heavens and the earth for portents of disaster. Long columns of sacrificial victims were taken from tribute
villages and immolated on the sacrificial block so that the gods
might bring them answers to their questionings about the strange
creatures that were appearing and disappearing on their shores.
It was natural that these demands upon other tribes for sacrificial
victims would alienate them; even those tribes who had been
friendly for two hundred years were desperately angry over the
drain on their own kin; bonds between conqueror and conquered
were loosened. But the Aztecs in fear and uncertainty increased
the pressure.

Then Hernán Cortés appeared. He came with new weapons,
horses, steel armor, and new gods. Two different worlds, two different human natures, met. The Aztec had no concept of himself
as a separate absolute entity; he thought in terms of clan. The
Spaniard believed in his own person; the most real reality of his
world was his own individual soul.[58]

They fell. They fell, suggests William Prescott, under the
weight of a different, "if not in some respects higher, civilization;
none of its achievements could save it and its own internal weak-
nesses helped to destroy it." Moral history is not good history;
historical action, judged under the Spinozan "aspect of eternity,"
lies beyond good and evil. By its very nature history is amoral, and
yet . . .

And yet what Prescott wrote bears some relation to the reality
of the facts of this book: "The Aztec monarchy fell by the hand of
its own subjects. . . . Its fate may serve as a striking proof that a
government which does not rest on the sympathies of its subjects
cannot long abide; that human institutions, when not connected
with human prosperity and progress, must fall . . . by the hand of
violence from within or from without."

Thus on Saint Hippolytus' Day, August 13, 1521, in the stench
of a thousand fires, the Spanish Conquest was complete and the
Aztec civilization passed into cultural limbo.

MAYA

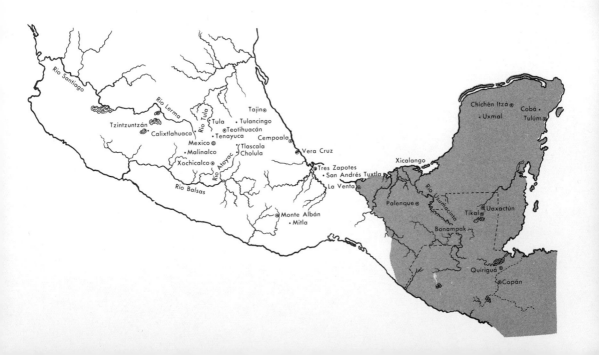

XX. *Pottery figurine in the classic Jaina style of the Mayas. This was also used as a whistle; the mouthpiece is under the left knee.* (Nikolas Murray)

The Historical and
Geographical Background of
The Mayas

 Of Man, History, and Fable   *1*

"MAYA" WAS, naturally, not their name. No one knows what they called themselves or what the name of their language was. Nor do we know, with any degree of certitude, the names of their stone cities, which are now entwined with tree and vine much as Laocoön was enveloped by the tentacles of serpents. The Mayas are as little known as the other side of the moon once was, despite the fact that their civilization has been subjected to an unusually intense study.

All this is very disturbing. For the Mayas were the only people of America's high cultures who developed glyph-script language capable of recording events, yet so far as is known they have left us little or nothing of themselves beyond certain calendric dates. No other culture in the Americas, perhaps in the world, in so confined a space has had so much attention paid to it from every possible angle of approach. Few lost civilizations have had so distinguished a list of investigators. From the time of Christopher Columbus,[129] the first white man to see them (1502), down to the present turbulent times, when the Russian Dr. Yuri Knorosow[98] claims to have a key to Maya glyphs, there has been a veritable parade of people drawn by the air of mystery that hangs over the Maya civilization. Conquistadors, priests, historians, explorers, adventurers, geographers, astronomers, engineers, botanists, epigraphers, not to mention a generous sprinkling of picaros, have walked the Maya earth and left their impressions.

A preliterate people can only be seen through their art, for they are otherwise inarticulate. From the vague Maya beginnings, somewhere around 2000 B.C. down to A.D. 987 there are no tangible records and no traditions, nothing but the evidence—and this in an overwhelming degree— of their existence contained in the remains of buildings, sculpture, murals, and pottery. All that which the Mayas really were is known only through inference.

It is not that there is any lack of literature on the subject. On the contrary, there is an abundance, and of wide variety. Literature on the Mayas is often written with so much profundity that discussions tend to go far into the empyrean. The simple Indian, creator of it all, sometimes wholly disappears.

The Mayas have been characterized as the "intellectuals of the New World" because of their highly developed calendar, their glyph writing, and the ornamental complexity of their architecture. For a long time theirs was considered to be the peak of American civilizations. They were unique in their culture. Pacific, they fought few wars; they viewed life from their jungle fastness with Olympian detachment, working out complicated calendric inscriptions that could trace their history back 23,040,000,000 days.

This archaeological daydream has been shattered by the new discoveries. The Maya culture was a feudal theocracy. Apart from being "intellectuals," the Mayas were just as cruel and ruthless— i.e., human—as any of the other tribes around them. The murals of Bonampak, discovered in 1946,[77] have provided data for an analysis of Maya character, for depicted here is the full interplay of Maya life forces that most of their sculptured monuments have only hinted at. They were human, all too human.

Moreover, the Mayas were not the landbound people once pictured, living in the splendid isolation of their stone-built ceremonial centers. They were seafarers; setting out in large canoes that held as many as forty people, they cruised for thousands of miles along the Gulf coasts and in the Caribbean, one of the most dangerous of seas. They, and they alone of the great theocracies— Inca, Aztec, Chimú, Mochica—regularly used the sea for maritime traffic.

The Mayas will be treated here neither as "intellectuals of the New World" nor as fossilized archaeological specimens. Instead they will be shown as they depicted themselves or else told of themselves to others: feeling, sensing human beings, as contradictory in thought and action as we ourselves are.

Maya history begins with Columbus. On his fourth and last voyage, Christopher Columbus landed in 1502 at Guanaja, one of the Bay Islands off the coast of Honduras. There the Admiral of the Ocean Sea met an Indian trading party in an immense dugout canoe. When asked from where they came, the Indians replied: "from a certaine province called Mayam."

Some years later another Spanish navigator skirted the coast and saw the well-constructed buildings. When he landed and inquired in Spanish about the builders and asked the Indians who they themselves were, the reply came back: *"Ci-u-than."* It actually meant, "We don't understand you," but the Spaniards took it for an answer to their questions, and with time's alchemy the land became "Yucatán." However, a conquistador who wished to preserve the "true history of things" wrote that the Mayas "now say their country is called 'Yucatán' and so it keeps that name, but in their own language they do not call it by that name."

In 1511 Captain Hernández de Córdova Valdivia, sailing his ship from Panama to Santo Domingo with twenty thousand golden ducats aboard, ran onto the reefs of the Jamaica shallows. Escaping in an open boat without sails, oars, or food, he and his twenty men drifted thirteen days until they came upon Cozumel Island. This was within sight of Yucatán. The natives, who were Mayas, promptly put to death all the survivors except two and these were traded as slaves to the Lord of Zamanzana on the Yucatán mainland.

Gerónimo de Aguilar [120] of Écija, Spain, was one of these two first white men to live in Yucatán, and the first to learn Maya. He kept a breviary which he continued to read in order to keep track of Christian feast days. When rescued in 1519 by Hernán Cortés he became, with the Indian woman Malinche ("The Tongue"), one of those who helped to defeat the Aztecs.

After the fall of the Aztecs it was the turn of the Mayas. The Spanish conquest of the Mayas[126, 32] had neither the terrible fierceness nor the dramatic impact of the conquest of the Aztecs. It went on for nineteen years in Yucatán, from 1527 to 1546, and was not totally completed until 1697 when the Itzás, who carried on the Maya way of life in the area of Lake Petén, were finally engulfed by time and man.

Unlike the Aztec campaigns, these wars of extermination did not inspire the writing of first impressions by the Spanish captains

56. *La Malinche (Doña Marina), "the Tongue" of Cortés's conquest of the Aztec and the Maya, spoke both Nahuatl and Maya. She was given to Cortés at Xicalango, the great trading center in Tabasco, in 1519.*

who took part in them, but Hernán Cortés [44] gives in his fifth letter a general narrative of his almost unbelievable march through Mayadom; and the invaluable Bernal Díaz, who accompanied him in 1524, penned in considerable detail some wonderful factual accounts of Maya life that picture this as a still-living and functioning community. [48]

Once Yucatán settled down under the yoke of peace the Christian priests took over. It was under the priests, who were at once destined to be the destroyers and conservers of Maya culture, that history was written. All or almost all we know of Mayas living then—and so, by inference, of those who lived a thousand years before—comes from the writings of these God-inspired *frailes.* Much of their written material was in the form of *relaçiones,* a sort of informal history intended to instruct and guide the Spanish court. Like so many of the accounts of Spain in the New World, these were not published until three hundred years had passed, and then under the title *Relaçiones de Yucatán.** There was an occasional padre, such as Antonio de Ciudad-Real, who could rise above the prejudices of his cloth and deal objectively with what he saw. The brief *relaçion* in which he describes his discovery of "the very renowned edifices of Uxmal" is a classic.[35]

But of all these creator-destroyers the most notable was Fray Diego de Landa. His small book *Relaçión de las Cosas de Yucatán* ("Account of the Things of Yucatán"), written in 1566, is the principal source of late Maya history. The details Landa gives of Maya lives,[100] the description of food, history, and tribal mores, the delineation of the *katuns,* or twenty-year periods, of Maya history (which made possible the modern reduction of Maya dates), and his insistence that the Mayas in his time were the very same people who built the stone cities found in the jungles (which even then were ascribed to Roman, Greeks, and Jews)—these have given him a unique place in the literature on the Mayas.

Landa was born at Cifuentes, Spain, of noble parents. In 1524, at the age of sixteen, he joined the Franciscans. He set off for Yucatán in 1549. In time he became adept at the Maya language. Landa had prime informants, and his interests were broad. Considering what he had to do, he was amazingly objective. He is our one source of the habits and foibles of the Mayas, and the immense historical value of his work is attested by the number of editions of his little book.

From the late sixteenth century to the beginning of the nineteenth the Mayas were the specific charges of the padres. The earth during this time went about its appointed rounds and the great stone cities of the Maya were gradually grown over with jungle verdure; in time they were blotted out of human memory. There was, to be sure, an occasional chance discovery of a Maya city. In 1576 Diego García de Palacio** on his way to Guatemala discovered the city-state of Copán. He sent a report to Philip II:

* Published by Spanish scholars in 1898–1900, these are the reports and demi-histories written in the sixteenth and seventeenth centuries.

** García de Palacio was a lawyer and judge of the Royal Audience of Guatemala. In his report to Philip II, dated March 8, 1576, he describes the Indians of Guatemala.

"I have tried to find out . . . what people lived here . . ." The report made no impression. The Spaniards were making their own history.

If the final conquest of the Itzá tribe in 1697 had been delayed until a half century later, the extent of the known history of the Mayas might have been somewhat different. The interest in the antique which occurred in Europe around the middle of the eighteenth century began the fashion. When Palenque was discovered in 1773 and a report was sent to Charles III of Spain, he ordered a royal commission sent to the ruins with artists and engineers, specifying that artifacts be gathered there so as to illustrate an *Ancient History of America.*

Maya archaeological history began at Palenque. These ruins, buried in the jungles of the state of Chiapas, would seem the least likely place for it to begin. No roads led to it. Once one of the great centers of the Maya, this city had been deserted since the ninth century and promptly reclaimed by the jungle. Palenque was discovered by Indians who carried their information to a priest. Upon visiting the ruins himself, he promptly prepared a *memoria.* This excited interest and resulted in numerous expeditions. The account of one of these, that of Captain Antonio del Rio, was translated into English in 1822 and its drawings were inaccurately redrawn by one "J. F. W.," none other than Jean Frédéric de Waldeck, who later went to the ruins himself. The bibliography of Palenque is immense.[170]

The drawings of Waldeck set the Mayas on the road to Rome, for he stated that Palenque was either Roman or Phoenician, and he even altered his drawings of the monuments to give proof of the theory. At the same time he gave aid to Edward King, Viscount Kingsborough, the gently mad Irish aristocrat who was then compiling what was to be the monumental *Antiquities of Mexico.*[95]

One shudders to think what might have been the fate of the Mayas had not John Lloyd Stephens, the well-traveled New York lawyer who had seen Roman and Egyptian ruins, rediscovered the Maya ruins in 1840. Stephens, as we have seen, had an excellent historical sense and, moreover, a facile pen. Frederick Catherwood, his English-born companion, had limned many of the known ruins in the Near East and had made detailed architectural drawings of the Mosque of Omar, gaining entry by submitting himself to circumcision. Although his illustrations have overtones of Piranesi, they are so accurate that scholars can read his renderings of the Maya glyphs.[186] Histories of Yucatán began to appear, by both Mexican and Spanish scholars. In the following years these works filled something of the void. In the first decades of the twentieth century the Mexican archaeologists worked mainly in the immediate Mexican milieu, but now much work is being done by Mexican archaeological explorers who are well equipped with the intellectual tools to solve the Maya problem.*

The French have sustained an interest in the Mayas for centuries. Their contributions have been mainly in scholarship, deduction, and literature rather than in systematic archaeological excavations. From the time of Jacques de Testera, who came to Yucatán in 1539 and invented the "Testerian Hieroglyphics," ** to Waldeck, to Brasseur, who discovered Landa's *Relación* collecting dust in Spanish archives and first published it, down to the present-day controversial Jacques Soustelle, an ethnographer known for the lucidity of his texts, the French have maintained a creative interest in things Maya.[71]

The English have been investigating these grounds ever since the early seventeenth century when Thomas Gage,[59] the "English American" who traveled in Guatemala between 1625 and 1637, first gave them insight and interest in the Mayas. He was followed by Juan Galindo[60] and then by Captain Herbert Caddy,[26] who anticipated the famous trek of Catherwood to Palenque. Alfred Maudslay combined excavation with exploration and published well and effectively. He wrote numerous papers and edited the journal of Bernal Díaz. He is the first Maya archaeologist. English interest has continued unabated; the British museums contain some of the choicest documentation on the history of the Mayas.[63] J. Eric S. Thompson,[193] English-born and educated but attached mostly to American institutions, is the outstanding figure in Maya archaeology.

* To mention only a few of these scholars: the work of Miguel Angel Fernandez on Jaina and José García Payen on El Tajín, in Vera Cruz; the fascinating work done by Alberto Ruz Lhuillier at Palenque, resulting in the discovery of the tomb under the Temple of the Foliated Cross; that of the artist-anthropologist Miguel Covarrubias; and the work on the correlation of the Maya calendar by Juan Hernandez Martinez have given much to the literature on the history of the Mayas.

** Testera, a brother of the chamberlain to Francis I, on the king's order came to America in 1529; he and four others were the first to arrive. In Mexico he devised a method of putting the Catholic catechism into a picture writing similar to that used by the Mexicans.

Interest in the Maya civilization has not remained the exclusive concern of any one nationality. The truly great figure among the German contingent was Alexander von Humboldt.[83] Arriving in Mexico in 1803 after four years in South America, he spent a year there preparing what is now a classic and encyclopedic work on Mexico. He also gave much attention to American archaeology. His critical judgment stands as a landmark in this field, and although he himself did not enter Maya territory, he did reproduce and comment for the first time on several pages of the now celebrated *Dresden Codex*. While French interest in the Mayas was literary and speculative, the German was geographical and exploratory.

Captain Teobert Maler,[115] who escaped the debacle of the Emperor Maximilian in Mexico in 1867, was the first German to make explorations of Maya ruins. He went down to Guatemala and became enmeshed in the mystery of the Mayas. Alone except for native carriers, Maler plunged into new archaeological grounds, photographed, described, and published accounts of them for Harvard University. Then, unsettled by his privations and convinced that others were making money from his reports, he filled his letters with insults and execrations and bitterly withdrew into himself. His contemporary Eduard Seler,[172] as thorough as Maler, made outstanding contributions, as did Karl Sapper,[166] the geographer, Walter Lehmann,[103] the linguist, and Förstemann, a librarian who evolved a way to decipher the Maya "dates." Förstemann wrote numerous important papers on Maya writing, and there were many Germans who followed him, such as Hermann Beyer.[14]

The dominant names in Maya archaeology have been North American. Ever since Stephens initiated the Maya interest in 1840, the largest amount of field work, the restoration of Maya ruins, and especially excellent and solid publications have resulted from the American contribution. A list of the important work done and published is long and impressive.* Most of it has been linked to the Carnegie Institution of Washington. Ever since that institution en-

* E. W. Andrews has done much work on Yucátan's north coast; he is now excavating the ruins of Dzibilchaltún, which may change our concept of the Mayas (see "Dzibilchaltun: Lost City of the Maya," *National Geographic Magazine*, January, 1959). Other important American studies, listed alphabetically by author in the Bibliography, include: Blom and La Farge, Brainerd, Brinton, Gates, Goodman, Homes, Kidder, Lothrop, Morley, Morris, Redfield, Ricketson, Roys, Ruppert, Satterthwaite, Smith, Spinden, Teeple, Wauchope, and von Hagen.

tered the Maya field in 1915, scarcely a year has gone by when they did not have a dozen men representing various fields of research somewhere in Mayadom. However, with the expanding atom and the expanding universe, its interest has been stifled.

Out of these two centuries of frenzied activity has come a bewildering mass of literature; it would be difficult to encompass it all unless one gave it a lifetime. Much of it is highly technical—specialist talking to specialist—so that the general reader, unless he is as tough-fibered as General Grant ("I propose to fight it out on this line, if it takes all summer"), may, out of sheer bewilderment, leave the Maya theater all too early and never really come to see the drama of a people's sheer will-to-culture finally conquering nature by raising tall stone towers which loom over the tallest jungle.

Eric Thompson, one of our finest scholars on the Mayas and a graceful writer, said that his impression is that "travelers as well as most readers of books on Maya civilization return from their journeys, physical or mental, curiously unsatisfied. . . ."[194]

The monuments remain, the people have disappeared. So the whole human business is so inextricably bound up with prehistory, conquest, epigraphy (the study of ancient inscriptions), and astronomy that the Maya story by its very nature is disconnected. Thompson feels that he and his fellow archaeologists are partly to blame for the frequent failure of the nonprofessional to get a coherent impression of past civilizations: ". . . the very nature of the material that an archaeologist handles, exacting excavations, the shapes of cooking pots, the reduction of Maya dates, the abstract speculations of time and space," the minutiae out of which archaeological history is fashioned, does not make for inspiring reading.

In this Maya section of *The Sun Kingdoms* I depend heavily, as will be seen, on this mass of technical literature; I would be the last to denigrate it or to underplay the privations and difficulties that were its birth pains.

My attempt here is to tell of the Mayas as human beings. Speculations have been held to an absolute minimum; I have used my own experience as ethnographic explorer to test if what I culled from the literature had the weather tints of reality.

And so if out of this the Mayas emerge from their fossilized archaeological limbo as sentient and living people, perhaps then the reader will not go away "curiously unsatisfied."

2 *The Country*

"PROJECTING northward into the Gulf of Mexico like a giant thumb between North and South America, lies the Peninsula of Yucatán. . . ." The words are those of the late, great Dr. Sylvanus Morley. We might expand the simile to note that the Yucatán thumb broadens out at its base to include most of Mayadom.*

Towering ranges of volcanic origin (Mount Tajumulco, at 13,816 feet, is the highest) lie along the Pacific slopes, and the climate here is variegated. The soil is cultivated from sea level to 10,000 feet. The whole area is characterized by deep valleys and pine-fringed mountains; there is an excessive dryness on the western slopes and excessive wetness on the eastern. In this high zone the Mayas found volcanic stone to make the *metatl* for braying corn, and here is found obsidian, volcanic glass, which made mirrors, knives, and razors; from the streams came jade, as important to the Mayas as life itself; in the high cloud forests were the red-green parrot and the far-famed quetzal bird that yielded the jade-green tail feathers used to deck the headgear and cloaks of the chieftains.

In the lowland areas where the great temple cities were located—Tikal, Uaxactún, Yaxchilán, Calakmul—is El Petén. Here rain forests alternate with depressed areas, which are seasonal swamps called *akalches,* and high bush with alternating savannas of tall grass.

---

* "Meso-America" is the hybrid word now used by many to designate that portion of the world wherein the Maya kingdom lay. It lacks as much meaning as that other hybrid "Amerindian." "Middle America" is used to designate that land which lies roughly between the Rocky Mountain system of Mexico and the Andean Mountain system of South America. This term is better but still inadequate, since Panama, reaching to the border of Costa Rica, is historically, linguistically, and biologically South American. But if the specialists wish to speak of "Meso-America," this terminology must then be extended. North America would be "Proto-America" and South America, "Meta-America." This *reductio ad absurdum* is enough to show how undescriptive the term "Meso-America" really is.

It is the least likely place one would choose for developing a culture, yet it is precisely here that the earliest-known Maya cities are found. The lowland jungles are set upon plateaus of limestone and are amazingly fertile, yielding valuable trees and plants which were of great use to the Maya economy. Giant cedars were fashioned into outsized canoes eighty feet long for navigation on the Caribbean. Copal, an odoriferous resin, as essential to the Mayas as amber was to the Greeks, was a commodity of "very great business for them"; it was burned on all priestly occasions. There was the brazilwood, used for dyeing Maya cloth; and the sapodilla, or "chewing-gum tree," which yielded a fine-tasting fruit as well as the chicle sap. Lignum vitae, as hard as iron, was "a specific against syphilis and buboes."

These jungles were rich in birds and animals: quails, woodpeckers, pheasants, and the ocellated turkey with feathers "as beautiful as the peacocks in Spain"; pumas, jaguars, and "wonderful many deer"; brockets (red deer) and tapirs, which were common and killed whenever possible.

The tropical jungles thin out and disappear in the "thumb" proper, which is the present state of Yucatán. This limestone zone, low and flat as a tortilla, characterizes the whole northern part of the peninsula. "It was a country," remembers Diego de Landa, "with the least amount of earth I have ever seen. . . . it all seems to be one living rock . . . this because there is only a small cap of earth over the limestone and in many places it is less than six inches in depth." Despite its apparent flatness, the land is broken up into limestone outcrops and depressions with a profusion of loose stones —*dzekel*, the Mayas called these hillocks of limestone rubble. It was doubtless a good source of rock for the inner core of their buildings, yet most difficult for traffic. It is because of this that the Mayas built their famed *sacbeob*, or causeways, in order to make trade and travel easier.

As slight as is the earth cap covering the porous limestone base, the land is amazingly fertile. Now only a high bush grows in most of Yucatán, yet there is evidence, botanical and traditional, that trees, and even jungles, once flourished there. There is a Maya folk tale —which might well be pure history—that about 1467, after the fall of Mayapán the capital of coastal Maya, "during a winter's night about six o'clock there arose a wind, a hurricane. There followed a

great devastation—villages, temples, game, trees, were all destroyed
. . . and it lasted until noon next day . . . there were thousands
killed." Another Spanish chronicler remembers that "Yucatán is
heavily wooded but of so uniform a height it seems that the trees
were all cut with scissors. . . ."

"So much was lost [on that night] and so much changed," said
Diego de Landa, "that even the name of the land disappeared, that
land which was once called *The Land of the Turkey and the Deer.*"

There were turkey and deer and much other game besides; here
were rabbits "large and good to eat," the agouti, "a little animal,
sad by nature," and opposums and coati-mundis (these last the
women suckled at their breasts and deloused as they did their own
children). Along the coast there was an abundance of birds: frigate
birds, cormorants, herons, and egrets. The Muscovy ducks, a source
of plumes, were raised in the houses from eggs and did not run away.
On the beaches sting rays were killed for their tails, which, armed
with a razor-sharp bone, were used as saw knives to cut and bleed
the body in blood sacrifice; it was "the duty of priests to keep and
have many of them."

Iguanas were found everywhere along the shore; they yielded flesh
that tasted like chicken. Turtles and turtle eggs were plentiful. As
for *ain,* crocodile tails, they were considered a rare delicacy. In the
lagoons, of which there are many along the coast, the Mayas hunted
for the manatee. The manatee was killed with harpoons and gave
them more meat "than a yearling calf."

Fish were plentiful and an important native industry. Chieftains
of the sea towns in the Maya province, called *chikin-cheel,* were the
"lords of the sea," and they controlled fishing rights. They used their
slaves as fishermen. Fishing in these lagoons, with net, harpoon, bow
and arrow, was a vast operation. "Their fisheries," says Landa, "are
on a very large scale."

And there was salt in great quantity, very important to grain
eaters such as the Mayas. It had preservative qualities and was used
as a tonic. The salt taken from long coastal lagoons around Ekab
was "very white and highly concentrated . . . the operation was
simple and salt was a great trade commodity."

In the interior the cultivated maize fields gave other subsistence
crops in addition to corn. Stingless bees were bred in tree hollows;
"the land abounds in honey used for sweetening and, more impor-

tant, for a meadlike intoxicant called *balche*." There was much cotton, which was spun and woven into mantas. Cacao, the seed which when dried, toasted, and ground is chocolate, was the Maya elixir. It was raised in the lush tropical extreme of Mayadom.

In the northwest of the base of the Yucatán peninsula was Campeche, a rolling country of forests and rivers, and west of it the

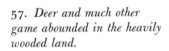

57. *Deer and much other game abounded in the heavily wooded land.*

lushly tropical Tabasco, covered with swamps and quagmires, a network of bayous, creeks, rivers. The land was made for cacao plantations and the Indians planted little else, depending on the exchange of cacao for cloth, salt, and corn. South, at the other extreme of the Maya domain, was Hibueras—Honduras—also possessed of rivers. On the banks of these rivers there were "wide roads bordered with cacao trees."

Such was the geography and such the environment of natural riches of the Mayas. The entire area was equivalent in size to the state of New Mexico.*

Water, however, was the one element the Yucatán Mayas could not command. Although water was everywhere, there was often not a drop to drink. Great quantities of rain fell, varying from 39 inches a year in the driest parts of Yucatán to over 150 inches in the wetter zones. During January and February there were light rains. June

* The lands occupied by Mayadom totaled about 125,000 square miles and included present-day Guatemala, Yucatán, Campeche, Tabasco, the eastern half of Chiapas, Quintana Roo, British Honduras, and the western section of the Republic of Honduras.

through August were heavy rain months, and even September brought light rainfall. The temperature varied with the seasons, as low as 45 degrees in December, as high as 105 degrees in April. Still, there was no way to hold the rain. There are no rivers on the Yucatán peninsula.

To meet the water problem the Mayas constructed reservoirs and cisterns. At their greatest city, Tikal, they hollowed out an immense reservoir between two temples, cementing the porous limestone so it would hold water. In northern Yucatán, where all the rain water percolates underground, Maya cities developed around natural wells. (These wells were formed by the collapsing of the friable limestone shelf, which exposed the subterranean water table. Some of these natural *cenotes* are two hundred feet in diameter, with the water one hundred feet below the surface.) At Chichén Itzá there were two of these, one for drinking, the other for watery sacrifices. Where the natural *cenote* (Maya, *dzonot*) did not occur and they wished to build a city, the Mayas in Roman fashion made underground cisterns. These were called *chultunes*.

Water, or the lack of it, was the curse of the Maya paradise (it was equally so to the Aztecs), and drought and its disastrous consequences play an important role in native Maya literature.

Aside from their periodic plagues with drought, the Mayas lived in a land which might be characterized by the Biblical phrase "flowing with milk and honey." No other tribe in the Americas had so balanced a wealth of natural resources. Although the Maya society was Neolithic (the Mayas had neither metals nor the wheel nor draft animals, and needed none), they had a soil and climate that gave them maize in such awesome quantities that it allowed them leisure. A rich and varied flora and fauna yielded all they needed for food, clothing, and medicine. Limestone rock for temples and dwellings was easily quarried, even without metal tools. The same stone was burned and easily reduced to lime. The material for a durable stone-mortar masonry was everywhere available.

Sometime, circa 2000 B.C., these who were to be the "Mayas" filtered slowly into this land. Once in possession, they were to hold it for thirty-seven hundred years, in continuous cultural sequence, before the last city was subdued.

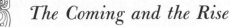

THE MAYAS, as a culture, developed within the Americas; nothing came from without.

As man, the Mayas developed out of the various peoples whose common ancestors were those Mesolithic wanderers that century upon century poured across the Bering "land bridge" once connecting Outer Asia to Alaska. It is one supposition that finds support in geography and paleontology, and considerable inferential proof in anthropology. It has a closer relation to fact than those will-o'-the-wisp theories of the "diffusionists," who explain the origins of such civilizations as the Maya, Aztec, and Inca would have whole peoples, their cultures already full-born, being wafted across the sea on rafts or canoes.

The controversy over the origin of American man that has raged since the discovery of the Western Hemisphere has already been discussed (see page 41). It is sufficiently diverting, but one must be on guard against seeing the obvious and missing what is significant. And the significant thing is that Maya culture was an attenuated, and in some ways a rarified, variation of a culture that was basically Middle American–Mexican. Its characteristic elements are to be found in every culture which bordered it. This one must insist upon, for since the beginning the Mayas have been described as everything—Roman, Jewish, Egyptian, Phoenician—but what they really are: *Maya,* a tribal group as American as the Sioux or the Pawnee, as American as the Inca or the Fuegian. Maya society was an American society. It was organized on a cognate kinship basis. Like the other tribes that developed from the primitive hunting-fishing stage and turned farmers, the Mayas eventually became temple builders and mythmakers.

In the beginning there were "other people" who lived in the lands that later became Maya. Around 2000 B.C. a longheaded people, in thinly scattered tribes, lived on most of the land which became the Maya area. We know little more. They were rudimentary farmers and were perhaps the proto-Maya. Tribes using Maya speech were widely scattered along the hotlands of the Mexican Gulf Coast, from Yucatán to Tampico, and doubtless inland into the low, flat Tehuantepec isthmus, and certainly in the high hinterland, since they followed the Rio Usumacinta along the fringe of the tropical highlands of Chiapas.

At this theoretical date, 2000 B.C., the intellectual equipment of the Mayas was certainly no better than that of any of the other tribes about them. Their agricultural traits were the same. Society was primitive and agricultural techniques were on the same level. Their safety depended on the beneficent gods. They counted the stars in their balance, watched the seasonal rising of planets, noting the portents in the sky for rain or sun, and in this way gradually roughed out their primitive calendric system.

There is no tradition that can be taken as uncritical history; even the Maya chronicles are reasonably obscure as to the place of Maya origin. It is only after the tenth century that history becomes alive, as in the *Popol Vuh,* the sacred book of the ancient Quiché Maya, which chronicles the arrival of the highland Mexicans, the Toltecs, into the land of the Maya. The latter day theory, inspired by missionary zeal, that the Mayas came from the eastern sea and expected for centuries greater gods and men to follow is a part of the Maya mythos. The general reliability of tradition can be trusted if corroborated by archaeology. Corroboration is missing here.

There *is* linguistic evidence, however, that sometime early in Maya history—the date 2000 B.C. may, for convenience, be assumed to be it—a non-Maya-speaking group drove a wedge between the tribes, thus isolating the Huastecs (who speak a language definitely Maya) from the bulk of the others. It is presumed that by this time the Mayas were scattered throughout the lands which became Mayadom in small tribes, various kinship groups formed into self-contained social units. They were corn-growing, pottery-making peoples. In appearance, although there is little skeletal evidence, they were perhaps not much different than they appeared a thousand years later.

What these people did, said, and wore can only be inferred. At the moment all we have of early Maya man is a collection of potsherds. These are fragments of a utilitarian pottery which is called *Mamom* ("Grandmother"); the term was suggested by the *Popol Vuh,* the sacred book of the ancient Quiché Maya. (See Pottery and Pottery Makers, page 266.) Their houses, circular and thatched with palm leaf, were of wood. A crude flat stone was used for braising the maize for the unleavened corncakes. Open woven bags held beans and squash. Their crude beds, over which rush mats were thrown, rested on stilts. Until cottom was developed and the loom perfected, clothes were beaten from the bast of wild fig fibers. The fire-hardened planting stick (never improved upon by the Mayas in 3,700 years) they already possessed, and their weapons were spears and arrows tipped with flint or obsidian. For hunting they had the barkless dog.

To infer more about these "before people" would involve fiction. It would be pleasing to be able to embroider around these minor facts a wealth of the incident that gives history its sparkle. But the cultural sequence is missing, as is the archaeological evidence that shows the slow evolution of the primitive into the sophisticated. Strange, and yet not surprising. Even with exhaustive records, there are wide gaps in such histories. Suddenly, it seems, archaeology reveals mounds and small pyramids; there is a developed pottery and much other evidence of the formed Maya type of social organization.

These Mayas are revealed as people with wit, passion, and interest. Superbly painted polychromatic pottery depicts the already formed upper classes, a stratified society where inequality is stressed. Man has set bounds to his fields, and he wars, hopes, fears. All this was Maya, but also it was essentially as old as man in the Americas. Similar communities were spread from the Pacific to the Caribbean. Trade was already advanced. Tribes were in touch not only with each other but also with foreign ones in Mexico, principally through the great trading center of Xicalango. Glyph writing was known and used by all tribes, and each one of them also had its calendric system based on the twenty-day lunar calendar.

Archaeology reveals that population centers, small, compact, and self-contained, were springing up over all these areas during the long formative period, i.e., between 1000–300 B.C. Trade, language, and common culture rather than political ties held them together as "Maya."

El Petén is the name given to a region which is composed of vast swamps, jungles, and savannas, with a medial chain of lakes, and grassland surrounded by tall tropical forests. It is here that the people begin to show the characteristics of their culture which

58. *Archaeological map of the Maya area. From S. G. Morley,* The Ancient Maya, *Stanford University Press, 1946, Plate 19.*

define "Maya." The potters depict representational human forms on their bowls; painting and coloring is rich, imaginative, and polychromatic. Much of the pottery is dated with glyphs. Thus far no one has traced the evolution from utilitarian pottery into aesthetic ware. It appears suddenly, full-born.

Maya epigraphy no longer suggests that the Tikal-Uaxactún triangle was the birthplace of this civilization. Dzibichaltún in northern Yucatán is perhaps a thousand years older. Yet before A.D. 200

Uaxactún is already on its cultural way; the oldest stela there is dated A.D. 328. Eleven miles west is Tikal, another temple-city. After this there is a quickening of building throughout the entire length and breadth of the land. The cities can be listed by their dated stelae in the order of their appearance in Maya history.

But this was not a unique performance. There was a florescence of cultures throughout Mexico and Middle America. The perfection of the calendar, the progress of glyph writing, the perfection and use of paper, the ritualistic calendar, and dated monuments were common to all advanced peoples. Cultural exchange of ideas and techniques through trade had gone on since the beginning. So far as is known now—although this concept is subject to re-evaluation at any time owing to new and continuing discoveries in the Maya area—the early Maya city-states had a common trade, a common language, and similar cultural traits. There was a cultural union but not a political one. There is no known center or Maya capital. These cities endured between the extreme dates of 500 B.C. and A.D. 1000.

It is believed through inference that they ceased to function after the year 1000. The archaeological evidence gained through the superb deductions of the epigraphers would indicate that after this date the Maya tribes within the area of what is called the "Old Empire" no longer raised dated monuments, and so far as is known now, the cities ceased to function. This does not imply that the temple-cities disintegrated at once; it was perhaps a long, slow process. The explanations for the decline and fall have been many; all explanations have been examined and none can withstand the catapult of criticism.

To us it seems illogical that a people numbering no less than three million would abandon stone cities which took them centuries to build. Yet the archaeological evidence shows that city-states as widely separated as Copán and Tikal "ceased to erect monuments at the end of successive periods—one of the fundamentals of Maya life," and gradually melted away.

These Maya temple-cities (numbering in the hundreds) were not in most cases abandoned because of conquest. The temples, the priestly houses, the pyramids, and the dated stone monoliths stand as they were left. There is no evidence of any cataclysmal climatic change nor of diseases that had not appeared elsewhere in the Americas, nor is there evidence of large-scale wars. The cities, some of the most impressive monuments built by man anywhere, were just left to be enfolded by the tentacles of the jungle flora.

The Mayas themselves have compounded their own mystery. Their involved glyph writing, even though capable of expressing the abstract quality of numbers, tells nothing about themselves beyond such facts as that a certain building or stela was completed on such and such a date. Of themselves—nothing. They have not left a name, even of a chieftain or a city. Until formulas are found to decipher the remainder of the glyphs which are not concerned with the calendric system, we shall be a little longer in the dark. Even the Incas, who had no writing, left an oral history which, confirmed by archaeology, has at least given us the great names of their kings and the epochs in their history.

Whatever the causes, the cities within a wide range of the humid forest were abandoned. What happened to the people? Where did three million people go? Or did they go at all? We know only that after A.D. 1000 the bulk of the population was concentrated in the Guatemalan highlands and in the northeastern part of Yucatán.

Once upon a time, the centering of the Mayas in the Yucatán area was known, in the language of archaeology, as the "New Empire." It was neither new nor an empire. Some of the stone-built cities here are as old as those in the interior. Tulum, high on the cliffs facing the Caribbean Sea, has a date of A.D. 564. Cobá, inland from the sea, was connected by road with Xelha, a walled coastal city a few miles north of Tulum. This causeway runs inland for sixty-seven miles, connecting Cobá with Yaxuná. A stone stela there gives the date of A.D. 361. These and many other temple-cities were existing in full panoply during the last four and a half centuries of the interior "Old Empire."

After A.D. 900 there was a concentration of the Maya tribes, for reasons unknown, into the northern part of Yucatán. In the tenth century this brought the Maya in direct contact with the highland Mexicans. These Toltecs, who even to their enemies were the classic people, originally had their capital at Teotihuacán, northeast of Mexico City. They practiced crafts such as weaving, had a calendar, used rebus writing, and made paper. From A.D. 300 onward, the Toltecs carried on trade with the highland Mayas. After the decline of Teotihuacán, the Toltecs built a new capital city called Tula (900–1156) which lies sixty miles northwest of present-day Mexico City. Here they were concentrated, and it is here, at Tula, that the man-god Quetzalcoatl takes up his strange and haunting history.

Quetzalcoatl, in various guises, was the cultural hero of the land. His motif, a plumed snake's head—an exact translation of his

59. *Kukulcán, the Plumed Serpent god of the Maya, who is identified with the Mexican Quetzalcoatl. Various symbols are included in the snake's body and in the god's head.*

name—existed long before Quetzalcoatl, as person, took on flesh as political leader of Tula. It is believed that this chieftain, named Ce Acatl Topiltzin (he was born in the year of Ce Acatl, One Reed), took the patronymic of the cultural-god Quetzalcoatl, and under this aegis ruled the Tula Lands. He was still leader of the Tula as late as 968 A.D. since a monument dedicated to him on that date has been found near this city. In 987, according to the latest deductions of Mexican archaeologists, Quetzalcoatl was forced out of leadership and was exiled with many of his followers. Although the precise dates are confusing in the various native chronicles, this same Quetzalcoatl, or another of the same name, arrived with an army of exiles at Tabasco, "the place-where-the-language-changes," (i.e. where Nahuatl speech becomes Maya speech) and from there went to Xicalango, which for centuries had been a sort of free port, a place of exchange of goods between the Mayas on the one hand and the Mexican tribes on the other. The time was the end of the tenth century.

At about the same time, a tribe called the Itzás, who were originally Chontal-speaking Mayas (who had their origin about the lands of Tabasco) were, after many years, becoming revitalized. They had apparently once lived at Chichén Itzá and had been either thrown out or left there; they had settled in the sea-girt town of Chakanputún (now Champotón). For forty years as a tribe, so say the Maya chronicles of Chumayel, they had wandered "under the trees, under the boughs, under the vines to their sorrow." Sometime in the latter part of the tenth century,* these people joined up with the tribesmen of Quetzalcoatl who had settled 100 miles to the southwest close to Xicalango. Together the Itzás and the Toltecs reoccupied Chichén Itzá. Sometime during the period A.D. 968–987 this became their capital. The verbal histories, the chronicles, and even archaeology are for once in agreement. ". . . the Itzá," wrote Landa, "who occupied Chichén Itzá 'arrived' with a great lord . . . named Kukulcán. They say he arrived from the west (i.e., Mexico) but they differ among themselves as to whether he arrived before or after the Itzás . . . or with them."[26]

Following the reoccupation of Chichén Itzá, a splinter group of the same people, those ruled by the dynasty known as the Tutul Xiu, began to build Uxmal, and at the same time Kukulcán began to rebuild a city which they called Mayapán. It headed the league of that name and became the first known capital of the Maya.

It is at this point that the actual documentary sources of Maya history begin. *The Books of Chilam Balam* lay down the divisions, or *katuns*, of Maya history. The sources of it are many and widespread. Several chronicles, taken from Maya picture histories and written in Spanish characters, such as the Tizimín manuscripts, give historically verified accounts.

The highland Mayas were also subject to the Toltec invasion

---

* Historically a Nahuatl-speaking people, Toltecs had been in Tabasco long before this date. The original inhabitants were of Maya stock and spoke Chontal, a Maya variant. The Mexican intruding peoples spoke Zoque and Nahuatl, and were called, at least by the Mayas, "Itzás."

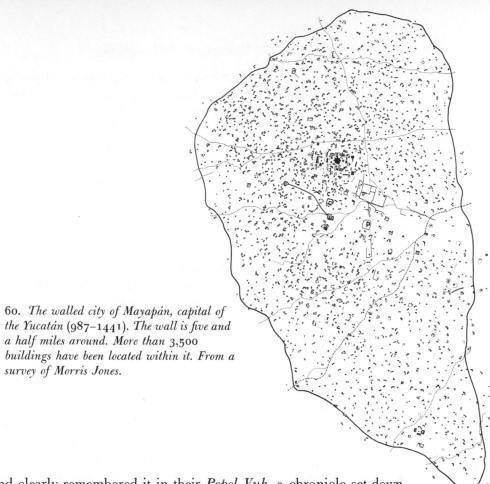

60. *The walled city of Mayapán, capital of
the Yucatán (987–1441). The wall is five and
a half miles around. More than 3,500
buildings have been located within it. From a
survey of Morris Jones.*

and clearly remembered it in their *Popol Vuh,* a chronicle set down
in Spanish script in 1550. The Toltecs followed the course of the
Usumacinta River inland and upward into what was the heartland
of the Old Empire, and then on into the Guatemalan highlands
where the Quiché tribes were established. The "priests," says the
Popol Vuh, "as they journeyed toward [Yucatán] took all their
paintings [books] in which they recorded all the things of ancient
times [i.e., of crafts and calendar and magic] and [Quetzalcoatl]
gave to the Quiché Lords among other things *u tzibal Tulán* . . .
the paintings of Tula, the paintings as those were called, in which
they put their chronicles."

This was the time of the Maya renaissance; art and architecture flourished anew. There was an introduction of Toltec motifs
throughout the region of the Puuc and around Chichén Itzá, the
plumed-serpent caryatids, the prancing jaguar, the eagle with un-
furled wings—talisman of the warrior-knights' cult of Toltec origin.

A new architecture introduced wooden beams, instead of the self-limiting corbeled arch, and buildings took on new graces. During this time Uxmal, the most beautiful city of the entire region, was built. New or extended rituals came into religion, with human sacrifice and its bloody bath. New weapons made war more fearful, and the Spartan principle for warriors stiffened the flaccid spines of the old Mayas. The old causeways were rebuilt and extended. Cities were walled along the coast. Seafaring Mayas moved as far as Panama and up into the Nicaraguan lakes. Trading posts were spread along the coasts, and contact was said to have been made with the Arawaks from the isles of Cuba and Jamaica. Maya learning was revived and extended, painted books were multiplied, and the *Dresden Codex,* a beautiful example of Maya draftsmanship, was made into a "new edition" in about the twelfth century.

The League of Mayapán endured, according to Maya chronicles, from A.D. 987 to 1194. In the latter year occurred a civil war, the origins of which are obscure, between Mayapán, the capital, and Chichén Itzá, the larger and most-famed city of Yucatán. Mayapán emerged as the leading city-state.

In 1441 war broke out again between the Cocoms, who claimed they were "natural lords of the Maya," and the Itzá. The Cocoms, with the aid of Toltecs, had invaded Yucatán and reoccupied Chichén Itzá in A.D. 987. The Cocoms, who thought of themselves as "classic Mayas," had at first joined with the Itzás and formed the League of Mayapán. In 1194 the Cocoms rebelled and expelled the Itzás from Chichén Itzá, occupying the city. This marked the ascendency of Mayapán. A century later, this hurt still lying in the Itzá memory, they planned a mass attack on Mayapán when all of the Cocom leaders were present. They were slaughtered to a man except for one who then was on a trading expedition to Honduras. Mayapán was sacked and destroyed; ". . . that city," wrote Landa, "after having been established for more than five hundred years [941–1441 A.D.] they abandoned it and left it desolate."

These are the bare *katuns* of Maya history. They mark the rise of a people from, technically, the Neolithic age to one of the highest cultures of the ancient Americas. Thus, from 2000 B.C. to the fall of Mayapán in A.D. 1441, the world of the Maya was forged.

The People

The "Lower Men"—
Appearance and Reality

4

Lᴵᴷᴱ ᴀʟʟ theocratic societies, in which god-men rule the roost, Maya society was a pyramid with the common man at the bottom. The precise generic name for him is not known, but early Maya-Spanish dictionaries interpreted *yalba uinicob* to mean the "lower men."

The common men were maize farmers. When war was upon them they were soldiers, acting as an agrarian militia. Their labor erected the soaring temples. They built the immense ball courts and terraces. They felled the trees, dressed and then transported the limestone blocks, carved the glyphs, and sculptured the Maya art. They built the raised causeways, the *sacbeob*, that bound city to city.

Like all Americans, the Mayas belonged to a soil community. It is presumed, although we have no precise knowledge of it, that the Maya society was a clan society. The prevalence of an exogamous surname marriage taboo (Landa says: ". . . they always called their sons and daughters by the name of the father and mother. . .") suggests that there was a clan system and that each bore a totem name.

Each member of such a clan was part of an earth cell. The lower and higher man were both wedded to the soil. One's taxes were paid out of it; either a portion of the crops went to the *batab* (tax collector) or else the cultivation of the fields was in the form of work tax. Agricultural surplus provided leisure that was used in the building of temples, palaces, and roads.

There were more than three million Mayas around A.D. 800. Since no one really knows, the estimates of Maya population vary; the lowest given is 1,250,000, the highest 13,000,000. Eric Thompson's figure of 3,000,000 seems the most reliable.

Although Landa called him "tall," the Maya's average height was 5 feet 1 inch. Still, he was robust and strong. The Mayas were brachycephalic, one of the most broad-headed peoples in the world. Even today their features closely resemble the faces on the ancient monuments. As soon as a baby was born his head was artificially flattened by being placed within two tied boards. This custom, as it was explained to Landa, "was given to our Maya ancestors by the gods. It gives us a noble air . . . and besides our heads are then better adapted to carry loads."

Ear lobes were pierced for pendants and so was the septum of the nose. The left side of the nose was also pierced—as is the practice of certain peoples of India—and, the gods willing, a topaz was set into it. The hair was long, black, and lustrous, wrapped around the head, and "braided like a wreath, leaving the queue to hang down behind like tassels." Tied to the hair was an obsidian mirror disc. "All of the men wore mirrors," but the women wore none, and for one man to call another a cuckold, "he need only say that his wife put mirrors in her hair."

The hair on top of the head was cropped short, singed in fact, so that it looked like a monk's tonsure. Facial hair was disliked. Mothers stunted the hair follicles of the young, and therefore beards were scant. Such hair that appeared was pulled out with copper tweezers. Despite this, old men had straggly beards, which are often represented in Maya sculpture.

"They tattooed their bodies . . ." a fact confirmed by archaeology, since quite a few sculptured stone heads show tattooing "the design being pricked in the skin with a sharp bone into which pigment was rubbed, and accompanied with great suffering." For this reason, the more tattooing one had the more one was thought brave and valiant.

Maya eyes, dark and lustrous, appear to be more Mongolian than those of most American peoples; the position of the eyes in the face emphasizes the epicanthic fold that gives them their "slant." Many were cross-eyed; in fact, to be so was considered both a mark of beauty and distinction. Itzamná, god of the heavens, is always featured as cross-eyed, and so are some of the other gods and personages that appear on the carved monuments. Bishop Landa wrote: "Maya mothers hung a pitch-ball in front of their children's eyes so close that both eyes focused on it and in this way began to cross." The practice must have been widespread, for Bernal Díaz, in the early days of the conquest, "took prisoners . . . many of them cross-eyed."

Maya skin color varied from *café au lait* to dark copper; the men for some unaccountable reason seem lighter than the women. At least such was the opinion of Landa, who had much occasion to see both bathing in the nude. Painting of face and body was

61. *The basic dress for all Maya men was the breechclout, elaborately decorated. These are redrawn from sculptured monuments.*

general among the men. Black was used by young unmarried men and those enduring a fast. Red was used by warriors, and blue by priests and those about to be sacrificed. Warriors painted themselves red and black "for the sake of elegance"; and when captured, the greatest degradation was for a warrior to be "despoiled of his insignia and smut." One could gauge the social condition of a Maya by the color of his paint.

Men dressed for the climate. The basic dress was the *ex* (pronounced "eesh"), a woven-cotton breechclout which the "women made with great care." This was wound around the waist several times and passed between the legs. The ends hung down in front and back. This is the most common article of Maya dress and is pictured from the earliest times. Men wearing the *ex* are found on painted pottery, and certain sculptures dated A.D. 600 show the ends of it elaborately embellished and decorated.

Around their shoulders the Mayas wore a covering like a poncho (*pati*); it was elaborated according to one's life station. The same piece was used as a covering for the night's sleep. If this sounds rustically simple, it must be remembered that the classic Greek wore no more; he also used the sheet in which he had slept as clothing, shaping it elegantly around himself in the morning when he set out to face the world. Sandals were the final item in the attire of the lower man. Almost all wore them, especially in Yucatán, because of the roughness of the terrain. These *keuel* were made of either tapir or deer hide and tied to the feet by two thongs.

The women were comely. Diego de Landa, that observant bishop, thought them better looking "generally . . . than Spanish women, larger and better made." Maya women were small, in fact dainty. Their average 4 feet, 8 inches in height is not much taller than a fair-sized nymphet. They pierced their ears, as did the men, and tattooed their bodies "but not their breasts." They had their teeth filed to points by old women using pumice stone as an abrasive. They thought this dental style very elegant. The hair was worn long and intricately braided. The outsized necklaces and richly woven dress that one sees modeled on the clay statuettes from Jaina indicate the high position of women in Maya society.

They bathed often, using the same *cenote* wells as the men. The bishop also noted, and it has been since his time confirmed, that the women had an irregularly shaped blue-purplish mark near the base of the spine, just above the buttocks—the "Mongolian spot." This is prevalent throughout Asia and the Americas, but is especially marked in Yucatán.

The women painted their faces. Red, obtained from the seed of the *achiote,* was a blood symbol. It was mixed with the highly perfumed *ix tahte,* the liquid amber resin that was "odoriferous and very sticky." It was supposed to be a prophylactic against sun and insects. In reality, it was a blood surrogate. Women were fond of perfumes and they "anointed their breasts, arms, and shoulders" with it. In addition they walked abroad with nosegays of flowers, "arranged with great care," which they smelled from time to time.

Dress was the *kub,* a single piece of decorated woven cloth with holes for the arms and a square-cut opening for the head (the original chemise). The style, which one sees on the famous murals

62. *Around their shoulders the Maya wore a covering like a poncho* (pati); *it was elaborated according to their life station. Women wore the* kub, *and their hair was elaborately dressed. Late figurines from the island of Jaina, Campeche.*

of Bonampak, has survived for two thousand years; it is still worn throughout Yucatán. Underneath, the women wore a lighter white petticoat, decorated and fringed. About their shoulders they draped a stole (*booch*). They walked barefoot.

Women married young. They spawned from seven to nine children, of which unfortunately only half survived. "They had children early and many," Landa comments, "but they were excellent nurses because the continued grinding of tortillas constantly agitated their breasts, and they do not bind their breasts as we do in Spain and so they have large ones that have a good deal of milk."

Bishop Landa found the women "marvelously chaste" and correctly estimated them as the "soul" of the household. Good housekeepers, they labored to pay the tribute tax. Good managers, they worked at night at their weaving and raised ducks to obtain plumes for feather weaving. They reared deer, monkeys, and coatis which they suckled at their ample breasts. They worked in the fields and when needed were the transport animals; they educated their children and in leisure time spun and wove cotton in the company of other women. They had a robust sense of humor. They danced only among themselves, and they got properly drunk with other guests, but not so much as to be unable to lug home their drunken husbands. They were "prudent, polite and sociable . . . and not given to any erotic practices and they had no gods of love."

The women's goddess *Ix Chel,* which some scholars had hopefully thought was the goddess of desire, was in reality only the patroness of pregnancy.

5   Maya Speech

". . . in this country there is but one language." Landa, who first studied it, stated this as bald fact, and time has borne him out. The Mayas did not always fully understand one another, but a lowland Maya generally could understand a highlander, just as a peasant from Naples can understand a peasant from Milan. Since there was common trade between the diverse areas—coast, highland, jungle—and common communications, and the same glyph-written language was used in cities that might be five hundred miles apart, it is presumed that there must have been a basic common tongue. Although more than fifteen dialects were spoken (such as Chontal, which extended across the humid center of Mayadom, and the dialects in Guatemala, Tzeltal, Ixil, Quiché, etc.), the languages must have been, as Eric Thompson suggested, closely related to one another as are the Romance languages. The modern conclusion is that one can properly speak of only two Maya languages at best, highland and lowland Maya, the dialects being only variants of these.

Although Maya speech is not closely related to any other language of Central America or Mexico, this does not imply that it is derived from "something" outside of America. Walter Lehmann, the German linguist, believed from his study of all the known Maya vocabularies that the language was related to Mixtec-Zoque-Huave speech, which in turn was derived from some common parent language.

There were linguistic links between Maya and Mexican on the north coast, especially at the great trading center of Xicalango, and archaeology in the Guatemalan highlands has shown the close contact that the Mayas there had with the cultures of Teotihuacán. When the Toltecs made large-scale penetrations into Mayadom in the ninth century, they were Maya-speaking.

Upsetting this neat linguistic package, however, are the Huastecs. All Maya-speaking peoples lived contiguous to one another, with the exception of the Huastecs. This tribe dwelt three hundred miles northeast of the nearest Mayas and was separated from them by several distinct tribes—Nahautl, Popoloco, Totonac, etc.—and they spoke, and still speak, a language which is definitely Maya. Yet their cultural sequence (archaeologists have found a ceramic sequence of more than two thousand years) has no Maya characteristics at all (in dress, hieroglyphics, architecture, and so on). This suggests that before the formative period of Maya culture a cultural wedge of people of another linguistic stock split the primitive Mayas who once, by this implication, occupied a large area along the Gulf Coast. It is the only way to explain the linguistic schism.

The precise name of the Maya speech is unknown. Mayathan was that language used by the Mayas of the League of Mayapán in the area controlled by them in Yucatán. There was doubtless a certain unity of speech among the lowland Mayas as there was among the highland Mayas; that the name glyphs were uniform throughout Mayadom did not mean that the language itself was without variants. In the eighteenth century one who spoke Low German could read Schiller, but in verbal contact with a Hoch Deutscher he could have hardly understood him. We know that in the seventeenth century a priest in Yucatán, when talking to Cholti-speaking Itzá-Maya peoples gathered about Lake Petén, needed Indian interpreters who understood both dialects. This shows the great divergent linguistic evolution which had taken place within Yucatán in two hundred years. Despite his statement that "in this country the language is but one," Diego de Landa admitted that there were some differences in usage between the speech of the coastal inhabitants and that of the inlanders, and that "along the coast they are most polished in their language and behaviour."

It is not possible here to give more than an idea of Maya speech. Maya is spoken today by most Indians and many white people throughout Yucatán and Guatemala (just as Quechua is spoken by both whites and Indians in the Peruvian Andes). The bibliography on Maya speech is voluminous. Most authorities have found it "musical and pleasant." Several letters and sounds used in our speech are absent, i.e., *d, f,* and *r.* The speech, which is low-pitched, has many glottal stops and fricatives, and its pronunciation is not easy to learn unless one has been reared in Yucatán. The Mayas wrote simple sentences. It is doubtful that even after scholars have translated the 60 per cent of the corpus of the still-untranslated Maya glyphs, we will find the Mayas had glyph affixes to express verb tenses and pronouns. The Mayas were weak in verbs, and made much use of the verbal noun. Thompson has given us an example of it.[194] A literal translation of the glyphs would read like this: "His influencing the maize, the death god heaped up death."

Transposed into our literary forms this fractured Maya would read: "Much death will be the result, for the death god now rules the growing maize."

6  *Social Organization*

Maya society was composed of man higher and lower. There was a noble class, *ah mehenob*, from which all officeholders—and there were many—were selected. At the base of the social pyramid were the *yalba uinicob*, the lower men, as well as multitudes of slaves. This much is certain, but it is readily admitted that "we have no direct evidence as to the type of government and social organization prevalent among the Maya." The evidence gathered from art, sculpture, murals, and painted vases shows the nobleman in full command. Maya lords are shown being carried in litters. Armies are led by superbly accoutered leaders in panoplies of jade and quetzal feathers. Chieftains are seen laying down laws, the captured warriors being judged and put into slavery. Yet these vignettes refer only to limited aspects of the social organization. The Aztecs had a well-known clan organization wherein the land was communally owned and communally worked. The Incas developed the *ayllu,* which was collectivistic in principle, as their basic social unit. The Mayas are thought to have had some similar form of organization, yet its name and precise form is unknown.

The Mayas were not an empire, as the Incas were, with one

ruler controlling vast lands maintained by tribute tax. Nor did they have a complex tribute-gathering organization as did the Aztecs, who had domination but without dominion over vast lands. There was, so far as we know, no center of Maya organization, no capital, no Cuzco, no Tenochtitlán, no central ruler.

Explanations are needed, since what we now know about this stirs the curiosity without satisfying the reason. There was a common Maya culture, language, and religion. There was a system of roads, some the finest constructed in the protohistorical Americas, binding coast and highland together. Trade was general and far-flung. Why, then, did not someone of imperial ambitions force the whole into a single imperial state? Perhaps because of the hazards of geography? Yet, this did not prevent the Incas, whose empire was geographically far more complex than that of the Mayas, from uniting Andean South America under one realm.

Maya society has been likened to that of the city-states of Greece. The comparison is most apt. Although Sparta, Athens, and Corinth had, like the Mayas, a common language, culture, and religion, they were fiercely independent and often warred with one another, sometimes even supporting foreign invasions against other Greek cities.

The Greek word *polis* is translated "city-state." It is, thinks H. D. F. Kitto, a bad translation because the polis was more state than city. The largest polis in Plato's time was Syracuse, with a population of only twenty thousand, approaching in numbers the smaller city-states of the Mayas. Like that of the Greeks, Maya society had a household economy and was self-contained. Writing of the Greeks, Kitto says, ". . . the nature of their society was that the group is socially more important than the individual. The individual is a member first of the family, then of his polis. A wrong done to him is a wrong done to his family or his polis." This was also the case among the Maya. And it is the nature of clan society everywhere.

The temple-city organization is well known. The archaeological evidence of the Near East shows that farming peoples living in a Neolithic economy bring agricultural offerings to a center. It might be formed about a rock outcrop or a lake, or a *cenote* as in Yucatán. This is a waste from an economic point of view, but if the location of such a temple-city is chosen for religious reasons it becomes, as in Peru, a *huaca*, and a temple is built on the site and the priests make contact with the gods. The first fruits of the harvest are brought to the temple. The people know, of course, that the produce does not go directly to the gods. They are aware that it is eaten by the priests. All of the early peoples, who were farmers, believed that they were dependent on the favor of the gods and that they needed the hierarchical priesthood to secure it for them. The priests maintain the temples and are themselves maintained by the products and the service of the farmers. As the local shrine grows into a temple and the temple into a city or a ceremonial center, houses are grouped about it.

Because a high culture must originate with an aristocratic class, for only such a class has the time and energy to create it, a corporation of priests is developed who act as god contacts and see to it that all rituals are followed. In this way the lower man, whose tribute and service help to build the temple-city and maintain it, finds the temple ceremonial center to be useful. His maize grows better. He is told the time to plant and harvest (the priest is also the astrologist-astronomer), and the nature of mysteries are explained to him. Generations repeat this performance and, since useful habits when repeated finally become invincible, this type of life becomes in time veritably instinctive.

Out of this develops the clan organization. The lower man is convinced that the gods are the owners of the land and that the priests in parceling it out are acting on behalf of the gods. The various clans are allotted areas of land by the temple-city councilors (among the Aztecs actual maps drawn on *amatl* paper gave the rebus names of the owners), and the councilors presumably officiate at the division of the land. Among the Mayas, each family was assigned a piece of land of four hundred square feet, a *hun uinic*, measured with a twenty-foot measuring tape. We are ignorant of further details. Whether the land was held in trust by the ruler, as among the Incas, and was returned to the clan on the decease of the user to be reallotted, or whether it belonged to the *calpulli*, as among the Aztecs, we just do not know—at least no more than Diego de Landa, who says, ". . . each married man with his wife . . . sow a space four hundred square feet . . . which they call a *hun uinic*, measured with a rod of twenty feet."

The land was worked communally: ". . . the Indians have the

habit of helping each other in all their labors . . . they join to-gether in groups of twenty and do not leave the communal property until everyone's own is done." This would indicate the existence of a clan organization. Clans are the closest bond, the most intel-ligible relationship. The Mayas were held together by supernatural bonds, i.e., blood bonds, "for to be of the same blood is to possess the same vital principle and in this sense all who are of like blood make one single living being. It is in this that the clan relationship really consists." [106]

That the Mayas were organized into clans can be also inferred from Landa's remarks on the prevalence of an exogamous surname marriage taboo: ". . . they always call their sons and their daughters by the same name of the father and the mother . . . and this is the reason why the Indians say that those bearing the same name are all of one family . . . and on this account when an Indian comes to a place in which he is not known and he is in need . . . he at once makes use of his name and they receive him with kindness."

 Marriage   7

"THERE ARE no monogamous animals save those who love once in their lifetime," said Remy de Gourmont. The Mayas were well aware of this and tried, as do all other civiliza-tions, to make rules so that permanent marriage could be main-tained. Yet mating, the most natural of functions, has never been treated by human beings, civilized or primitive, as either natural or normal. Marriageable ages were considered to be eighteen for the Maya men, fourteen for the girls. One of the stringent taboos was that a man could not marry a woman having the same surname as himself. But he could marry any woman stemming from his mother's line, even a first cousin.

The Mayas had a professional matchmaker; she was called *ah atanzahob*. To the Mayas it would have been mean-spirited for men to seek wives for themselves. Sometimes fathers arranged marriages between sons and daughters in infancy and treated each other even before formal marriage as in-laws.

63. *The Maya married early—women at fourteen, men at twenty. The marriage broker stands at the left, while the priest "purifies" the couple with copal vapor.*

For this reason, among others, Diego de Landa thought that the Mayas married without love. But, despite the bishop, the Mayas were fully aware of the force of romantic love, though perhaps like the Greeks they believed passion to be a destructive thing. Besides, primitives are always superstitious about marriage; go-betweens acted, they believed, as the first barrier to defilement. Still, it is true that the ancient Mayas were not lascivious.

Aldous Huxley, after viewing Maya sculpture *in situ*, concluded with a certain amount of irritability: "There is no sex in the art of the Maya . . ." He reasoned that perhaps it was because the native's nervous excitability was less than ours and their sexual imagination very sluggish.[86] He also noted the infrequency with which the female form appears in Maya art.

Had Huxley traveled in that region of Yucatán called the Puuc, where lies the superb stone city of Uxmal, among others, he could have seen enough evidence of ithyphallic traditions. On the façade of the building called, ironically, "the Nunnery" there are sculptured naked male figures with full emphasis on the ithyphallic. In front of the Governor's Palace, at the same site, are the remains of a gigantic phallus. Throughout the Puuc and extending to the ruins of Chichén Itzá, the phallic symbols stand around like toadstools to shock or amuse the visitor. There is enough evidence that the Mayas had, in some yesterday of their tribal life, a full share of libidinousness.

There was sexual liberty, whatever that means, among the Mayas. Young men, who lived apart from the old, had in each village "a large house, whitened with lime, open on all sides," where they met for amusements, dice, ball and bean games. Their bodies were painted black as was the custom for a man before marriage. They slept together, but, says Bishop Landa in a quick aside, they did not practice the "abominable sin," that is, sodomy. Bernal Díaz said that he saw on the island of Cozumel in 1516 murals in which Indians were shown in the act of sodomy. He is contradicted, however, by Landa's contemporary, Padre Ciudad-Real, who wrote that there were three things for which the Mayas should be commended: "The writing of books, absence of cannibalism, and their lack of interest in the abominable vice of sodomy." We do not know whether they, like the Greeks, regarded homosexual love as a normal thing and treated it as frankly as heterosexual love, but we do know the young men brought public women (*guatepol*) into their quarters. "Although the women received pay for it [a handful of cacao beans] they were besieged by such a great number of men—one after the other—that they were harassed almost to death."

Monogamy was the rule among the lower men. "The Yucatecans never took more than one wife." When a young man thought of marriage and his father put the thought into action, he took good care, writes the bishop, to seek a wife in good time and of good quality. An *ah atanzah* matchmaker was engaged, a dowry (*muhul*) and marriage settlements were worked out. To ward off the evil spirit that hung over marriage, they consulted a priest, an *ah kin nec chilan*, who read the astrologic book of days to determine whether their birthdays, their names, and the date of the contemplated union fell on unlucky days. The mothers-in-law then wove new garments for bride and groom, and the bride's father prepared the house for ceremony and feast.

Marriage customs here are not as detailed as among the Aztecs, nor is there data on the practice *jus primae noctis,* in which the father-in-law or other male relatives partake of the bride during the first nights of the marriage to prevent the bridegroom from being menaced by malign influences. Many tribes do not allow husband and wife to live together until several months have passed, so as to avoid the evil influence that marriage brings—since to all primitives new experiences, and marriage is certainly that, are regarded as dangerous. In primitive society virginity is not generally highly valued. A Maya girl could not be overzealous about a mere hymen, a thing which she shared in common with a rabbit. But the evil thing that might come from improper consummation of marriage was something else again, and she and the whole clan could be menaced by it.

Marriage for the Mayas was matrilocal: the son went to the father-in-law's house and worked for him, as part of his family, for about five years. It was called "marriage in service." As such, Maya marriage was fundamentally permanent and women played an important part in society. This much can be seen without the help of Bishop Landa, for the murals found at Bonampak show women taking part in important affairs, and the grace that the sculptors gave to women in the statuettes found at Jaina, Yucatán, shows the respect in which they were held.

Women were jealous. Fights often occurred among them over men, yet Landa found them "marvelously chaste" because they turned their backs on men whom they met on the road, or stepped aside to let them pass. They had a great desire for children, praying to their own goddess for many and asking Ix Chel, goddess of pregnancy, to ease their pains—and with reason. A man could repudiate marriage if there were no children. Just as among the Greeks, a "childless union could be dissolved at the instance of the wife's relatives." [97]

Women could not hold public office. That they had some property rights is evident, but they were not allowed within the precincts of a temple. But then Greek women, too, were not enfranchised, nor could they hold property; and from birth to death they were, so to speak, the ward of their nearest male relative.

The best reputation a Maya woman could have was not to be spoken of among men for either good or evil. If women were accused of adultery they had to be found *flagrante delicto;* then they were disgraced. They seem to have undergone no other punishment except that the husband could, if he wished, repudiate the erring wife. The aberrations of marriage are understandable; in all societies, primitive or civilized, the couple is natural, but the permanent couple is not. Man the world over and at all times has become monogamous with difficulty. In all human societies there is a radial polygamy that is concealed behind a façade of monogamy, and "nothing," says Remy de Gourmont, "so favours marriage and consequently social stability as the *de facto* indulgence of temporary polygamy; the Romans well understood this and legalized polygamy."

But the Mayas were not Romans. A Maya of the lower orders found engaged in temporary polygamy with another man's wife had his arms bound behind him and was brought before the husband, who had the right "to kill him by throwing a large stone upon his head from a great height."

Divorce was by repudiation. If the woman was barren, or if she did not properly prepare the husband's daily steam bath, she could be repudiated. She might also take similar action against the man; although that was not as easy. When a couple was divorced, the younger children stayed with the mother. If older, the sons went to the father, but the daughters always remained with the mother. Divorce was common in Diego de Landa's time (1550–1570), although the elders of the tribes did not countenance it and "those of better habits condemned it." Men left wives and wives left husbands, and there seemed to be no proscription against remarrying. However, when death put an end to marriage, it was something else again. The widowed husband could not remarry for a year after his wife's death. He was not supposed to have any women during this time, and the Maya community had little regard for him if he did. A widow was bound by taboo; remarriage for her was complex and problematical.

Death, like sex, complicated everything.

 NA: *The Maya House*   *8*

THE HOUSE of the lower man was like that of the eternal peasant everywhere, simple and practical.

After marriage a Maya built first a small house opposite the dwelling of his father or father-in-law. Later his larger house was built with the aid of the community. The house could be constructed round, square, rectangular, or as it is best known in Yucatán, apsidal, rounded at both ends. Its frame was made of withes and rested on a stone foundation. The withes were then covered with adobe. Later the house was colorfully painted. The high-pitched roof was made of trunks and saplings and wonderfully thatched, then as now, with palm (guano) "of very good quality and in great abundance," wrote Landa. In ancient times (A.D. 500) the Maya house was usually square and mounted on a low substructure. Maya houses, while not always the same, tended to resemble one another in specific areas.

The interior of the house was divided by a wall. One part became the kitchen, and the other contained their sleeping racks. "They had beds made of small saplings" says Landa, "laced together by withes which . . . gave way to the movement of the

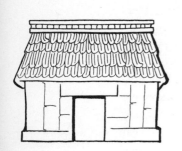 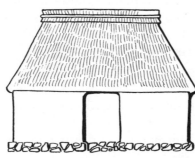

64. *The Maya house, past and present;* LEFT, *the* na *of the common Indian immortalized in a stone frieze at Uxmal, and* RIGHT, *the present-day Maya house.*

body like a mattress." This was covered with a woven grass mat. They used their cotton mantas as blankets. Whether the hammock later used by the Mayas was known to them before the arrival of the Spaniards, who brought examples of it from the island of Hispaniola, would seem doubtful.

There was one entrance and it had no door. Across the entranceway was placed a light string from which hung small copper bells. One brushed against these to give the owner notice of arrival. People seldom entered a house without permission, for "they considered it a grave crime to harm the houses of others."

This functional house has varied little in two thousand years. The terms for various parts of the structure are the same in various Maya dialects and may be thought of, writes an archaeologist, as "linguistic paleontology." The roof purlin is called "the road of the rat," the entrance "the mouth of the house," and the main roof post "the leg of the house."

The common man built the houses of the nobles, which were larger and more spacious than the others. Some were made of sculptured stone. "The slope of the roof comes down very low in front on account of their love of sun and rain" (as protection against the sun and the rain). The walls of their houses "were painted with great elegance," an observation which has been confirmed by archaeological excavation. The single entrance, also without a door, could be closed with a drapery, usually a woven hanging of much richness. Certain structures that are now found in the temple-cities may have been nobles' homes, although no buildings have been found which can be definitely associated with the ruling class.

A house endured for little more than a generation. The excavations of the house mounds reveal a "complete ceramic period." As the inhabitants of a house died, they were buried beneath the hard mud floor ("they bury their dead inside or in the rear of their houses,") After several burials the house was abandoned and was then treated as a sacred burial plot.

 ## The Round of the Maya Day   9

THE WOMAN rose first, between 3 and 4 A.M., rousing the flames from the smoldering ash in the *koben*, the three-stone hearth; if a household had a slave, he or she carried out this task.

"Their principal food is maize [*chim*], from which they make various foods, also drink . . . in the morning all they ate was maize water [*pozole*]." The evening before, the woman, with the aid of daughters or slaves, had prepared the dried maize. It was boiled with ash until softened and then husked, after which it was brayed on a stone grinder until reduced to a thick paste from which the women prepared tortillas.

When the Maya farmer departed in the early dawn for the fields, he took with him several apple-sized balls of ground maize wrapped in leaves. Steeped in water and flavored with burning hot chili peppers, these became his lunch, to which he added perhaps a piece of dried venison. His diet, mainly carbohydrate, was less than twenty-five hundred calories a day, yet many waxed fat on it, as Maya wall paintings and ceramics reveal. But then, gluttons are many on this terraqueous globe.

The farmer returned early in the afternoon. The women, by custom, had a hot bath ready for him. In the large centers such as Tikal and Chichén Itzá, there were communal steam baths. Where these were not available, the common man contented himself with a crudely made steam bath or hot water in an improvised tub, with a dip later in the local well.

The evening meal was the only elaborate one of the day. The menfolk sat in a circle, some on low wooden stools, the others on woven grass mats, and were served by the women. Stews were prepared of deermeat, wild or tame fowl, or fish, fresh or sun-dried; sometimes this was supplemented by the flesh of a tapir, *tzimin*. Deer were to be had, as were rabbits and agoutis. Armadillos (*zub*) were considered a great delicacy. There were also iguanas, turtles (*ac*), and on occasions flesh of the *baclam*, the manatee or sea cow. Fowl was varied and many. Foremost was the wild ocellated turkey, famed for its gamy flavor. Its feathers were used for making cloaks and head-dresses, "as beautifully feathered as the peacocks of Spain." The domesticated turkey shared the house and the land with young ducks (*axix*), "which when home-raised do not fly away." The Muscovy was raised more for its feathers than for food, "and as well a certain white mallard-duck." Doves were reared in cages. Almost as abundant as the turkey was the yellow-crested curassow.

All these found their way into the Maya *olla podrida*. Yet eating was disciplined; they ate well when there was food and could endure hunger when there was none. Washing preceded and followed meals. A natural detergent was used, the roots of the soapberry tree (*Sapindus saponaria*), "from which they washed their bodies and clothes like soap."

Maize, the "principal sustenance," was supplemented by several varieties of beans (*buul*), squash, and pumpkins. The chayote, a vine bearing a squashlike fruit, was found everywhere. The pale sweet

65. *The deer caught in a snare shows the hunting methods of the Maya. From the* Codex Tro-Cortesianus.

potato appeared on the warm coasts. Fruits were many. The avocado was cultivated, as were the papaya and sapote. Mulberries and melons were gathered, and the vanilla bean of the orchid was found in the jungle. Maya boys ate the fruit of the "chewing-gum tree" and chewed its gum (*cha*).

66. *The bee god as a bee coming in to swarm at the hive. Honey and wax played an important part in Maya lives.*

"The land," said Bishop Landa, "abounds in honey . . ." Then as now, it was gathered from the hollow of trees, and easily extracted because the bees were stingless. Fermented, the honey became mead, an intoxicant. Mead is one of the world's earliest beverages; it was nectar, the mythical drink of the gods. An illustration of an Upper Paleolithic honey collector has been found in the Cueva de la Arana, Valencia, Spain. Maya honey mead was fortified by the addition of an alkaloid-yielding bark called *balche*.

Like the Aztecs, the Mayas were enthusiastic drinkers of chocolate. "They made it of cacao and ground maize . . . a foaming drink which is very savory." Since it was grown in the humid lands on the periphery of the Maya country, it was expensive, so much so that the beans served as money.

Yet, turkey, chocolate, or fish notwithstanding, the mainstay of the Maya diet (as with all of the Central American and Mexican tribes) was—maize. Maize was eaten on every occasion. During the main evening meal each male would consume upward of twenty large-sized tortillas. Water was never drunk pure but always with the addition of maize meal. Does the type of food suggest the civilization? Does the bon mot of Brillat-Savarin—"Tell we what you eat, and I will tell you what you are"—correctly gauge a people?

The diet of the Greeks and the Romans was mainly farinaceous. Until 600 B.C. the Greeks ate *artos,* a coarse leaven bread baked in ashes. When baking became a profession, a form of porridge, groats made from emmer, was the basic food of the Greek common man. Flavored with honey, salt, and olive oil, it was not much different from the Maya maize *pozole.*

Greeks only rarely had meat and fish, and only the well-off could afford and obtain game. In general, meat was eaten freely only at sacrifices. The people of ancient Rome ate mostly unleavened bread dipped in milk, relieved by onions, peas, and turnips. Only those in close contact with the sea had fish, and only the farmer had meat, which consisted mostly of goat, pork, and lamb. While Oriental fruits—cherries, peaches, apricots, and the like—were introduced into the Roman diet in the first century B.C., active citriculture did not develop until the fourth century of the Christian era. It was only after the fall of the Roman republic that the rich lived in the Lucullan fashion; they constructed refrigerators, kept cold with snow and ice, to preserve foods. In the year 1000 man in Europe ate like a poor poll when compared with the Mayas of the same period. The diet of the masses was vegetarian and frugal, and they usually ate but two meals a day.* The impression given by medieval chroniclers of colossal meals washed down with quantities of wine, mead, and beer was true only of rare occasions in the lives of nobles.

The classical archaeologists, seduced by the honeyed words they have used to conjure up the classical past, still turn up their noses at the thought that the Mayas (in culture, art, or mathematics) could be dimly compared to the early Greek or Roman, and this is often because of these archaeologists' belief in the bucolic savagery of the Maya life and diet. As seen above, the Mayas had a list of available foodstuffs which most Europeans of their time would have thought "paradise enow."

At sundown a breeze springs up from the sea, churns up the Caribbean, and wafts across the Yucatán flatlands and up into the highlands. At this hour the Maya man retired to his home and had

---

* A medieval proverb had it that "angels need to feed but once a day, mankind twice, beasts thrice or more. . . ."

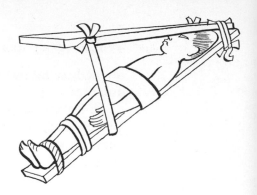

67. LEFT. *The "squint," a Maya beauty feature, was created by hanging a ball of wax in front of the eyes. The concept is ancient.* RIGHT. *The method of artificially flattening the head. The custom ". . . was given to us by the gods and gives us a noble air."*

his principal meal. Then, in Yucatán, he sat in semidarkness and worked wood, jade, or cotton into articles of trade, or made weapons. His wife spun cotton and wove mantas. In the highlands they made light with pine splinters, as bright as candles.

Time was found for love. Children were born, early and many. Women made pilgrimages to the island of Cozumel, a hazardous twenty-mile trip in an open dugout canoe across the wind-whipped channel separating it from the Yucatán mainland, so as to worship at the shrine of Ix Chel, the goddess of pregnancy. It was an act of devotion that outstripped that of those pregnant women of the eighteenth century in Europe who were wont to put the printed hymns of Saint Marguerite as a poultice on their extended bellies to ease the pain, "as it acted better than when recited."

Within five days after birth, which was attended by a midwife, the head of the child was placed between boards and bound so that it would become "flattened and molded as was the custom of all." The child was bound into a rigid cradle, over which balls of pitch were dangled to cause it to become cross-eyed. Later, when released from the cradle, the baby was carried *hetzmek*, i.e., astride its mother's hip. This caused its legs to be bowed. Children were weaned at four, and in their first years the young Mayas were "pretty and plump, good and frolicsome, running about naked as they played at hunting games." Later the boys put on a sort of G string, and the girls tied a shell over their mound of Venus.

Names and naming were of cosmic importance. Each Maya had four names: (1) the given name, *paal kaba;* (2) a patronymic; (3) a combination of his father's and his mother's family names, *naal kaba;* and (4) a nickname, *coco kaba.* Names were magical. A name could be worn out by excessive public use; only intimates knew the real one. If a doctor wished to use the name of his patient to call the soul back, he chose the private name which possessed strength, rather than the social one, which was hackneyed and worn from use.

Influence began, they believed, as soon as the woman was pregnant. The position of the planets, the advent of the unlucky days played a part in the fortunes of the child-to-be. All primitives believe that an enterprise must be begun on an auspicious day—days exert favorable or unfavorable or malignant influence. Much attention was given to the suprasensuous realities.

The Mayas were not far wrong. After long-term study of prenatal factors, modern researchers have reported that there is some connection between seasonal conception and birth and mental disorders, and that there is a greater possibility of mental deficiency in children born in winter as opposed to those born at other seasons. Children conceived in summer reduce the protein intake of a pregnant woman.

After the child was born, the priests consulted the horoscope for the best time to name the child, taking into consideration when it was conceived. Names were given only on lucky days; the ceremony could be put off until an auspicious time. Names once given were the Maya badge. Masculine given names (*paal kaba*) began with the masculine prefix "Ah," the feminine with "Ix." Some typical names for boys were Ah Kukum (Feather), Ah Cuy (Owl), Ah Tok (Flint Knife), Ah Balam (Jaguar); for girls: Ix Chan, Ix Can, Ix Kukul. The *naal kaba* name, which was taken after marriage, was made up of the prefix "Nah," the mother's matronymic, and the father's patronymic. Landa mentions as example a man named "Na Chan Chel"—Chan was his mother's maiden name, Chel his father's family name. Thus the names of the families of both father and mother were perpetuated.

As mentioned earlier, the Mayas believed that all people bearing the same surname were of the same family, which points to the clan origin of the system. Each Maya of the same name was treated as part of the clan family even though he could not work out the precise genealogy. Name exogamy still holds true in Yucatán, and there still remains a taboo for marriage between people of the same name.

Inheritance was patrilineal; the sons inherited and divided what the father had accumulated, the mother acting as guardian, and when not the mother, then the deceased father's brother. When the boys were of age they received their inheritance before the town officials,

68. *The coming-of-age ceremony (girls, twelve, boys, fourteen). The rope is held by four* chacs, *who restrain "evil" while the children are purified by a priest.*

which illustrates the primitive's system of "legality by publicity."

At the age of puberty (girls, twelve; boys, fourteen) there was a coming-of-age ceremony. This custom, *em ku,* was seen by Diego de Landa, who describes it minutely—except that in his unsullied innocence he thought it was baptism. Those parents who had pubescent children banded together to share the costs, just as today socially ambitious mothers introduce their daughters to society by means of a collective cotillion. On a lucky day, old "honorable men" (*chacs*) were chosen to help the priest (*chilan*) to officiate. Food and sexual abstinence before the ceremony were required of parents and officials. The courtyard in front of the local temple was swept clean and spread with leaves. At the four corners sat the *chacs* holding a cord. Within the square so formed were the children.

The *chilan* purified them with copal and tobacco smoke, and they were asked to "confess their sins." This is Diego de Landa's interpretation, and since there is no one else to gainsay him, it must stand as given. If any present confessed an "obscene act" he or she was dismissed from the circle. To the primitive, confession was imperative. If one was unclean and did not confess it could cause social misfortune. But confession made the evil nonoperative. So before the primitive undertook anything hazardous, he confessed and overcame social defilement.

Water is the great purifier, not only among the primitives but also in our own "civilized" religions. At the end of the long cere-mony, after the children had been admonished and the *chac* had recited age-old homilies of respect to parents, society, and so on, the priests put on their feathered robes and headdresses and anointed each child with "virgin water," "showing," says Landa, "exactly the same gravity as the Pope shows in crowning an Emperor."

Then the boys took off the white bead which had been stuck to the top of their tonsured heads since birth. The mothers then knelt down and removed "from each daughter's midsection . . . the little shell which all wore as a symbol of their purity." It was, Landa in-sisted, "a very dishonorable thing for any man to take this off before the ceremony." It was so for the Greeks: it was death to a man to remove the aegis, the goatskin chastity tunic worn by Libyan girls, at least without the owner's consent (hence the prophylactic Gor-gon's mask set above the chastity belt). After the shell had been removed the girls were allowed to "marry whensoever it pleased their fathers." Today's matron who presents her daughter to society is practicing an exquisite archaism; she is figuratively kneeling down like the Maya mother and removing the little shell. However, people everywhere make gestures that are explicable only on the hypothesis that they once had a different intention.

Young men had great respect for their elders; boys listened to their fathers, worked with them. Companionship was very real. Fathers helped them choose their brides and counseled the sons in marriage. At an early age the boy followed his father to the maize milpa. Education was by imitation, by rote; knowledge followed by observation. The boy hunted and learned of nature. He was told and believed that everything had soul. To the gods of the earth, who were very much alive, he addressed his prayers. When hunting he learned to whisper a prayer before killing: "I have need." And when he killed he made an amulet of the slain animal so that other animals in the future would allow themselves to be killed to fill his need. Rather than eat his kill, he gave it to others, who then returned part of it. All this so that the animal would not feel that he was lacking in respect. How widespread this code is can be seen from the Austrian Tyrol. There, too, the hunter does not eat his kill, but takes only the horns and head and, symbolically, the loin of the chamois. Some of the hair is made into a *Gamsbart* and put into the hunter's hat. The head and horns are mounted and kept as a trophy, which could be said to have the same significance as the amulet of the primitive.

Maya morality was a group morality and co-operation of the individual with everyone in the community was "virtue." Custom demanded that the Mayas be hospitable and provide guests with food and drink. A boy learned through custom that when he visited he must always bring a gift. He must be humble and repeat over and over again a person's title, especially if he addressed a lord. Another custom ordained that while listening to someone he must make a soft affirmative sound in his throat, as if to say, "indeed," "you don't say," "you do tell me."

Because everything in the Maya world was alive, sentient, and possessed of soul, an object made by a person took on something of the soul of its creator. Theft was an aberration (unless decreed by tribal war, in which, as in our own world, everything then is permitted). Maya scribes have asserted: "Before the coming of the Spaniards there was no robbery or violence. The Spanish invasion was the beginning of tribute, the beginning of church dues, the beginning of strife." Actually the Mayas had wrung tribute out of the defeated and had practiced slavery. Yet in the face of the new threat from without, this was forgotten—which reminds one of the validity of Nietzsche's apothegm: " 'I did that,' said my memory: 'I could not have done that,' says my consciousness, and remains inexorable. Eventually the memory yields."

The moral code was essentially as old as the Maya himself. Clan co-operation, respect for family, and personal discipline brought about what Eric Thompson believed to be a living form of the

Delphi motto "Nothing in excess." This idealized portrait of the Mayas does not agree with the violence and lack of restraint shown in the murals of Bonampak. They were no freer than other people from paroxysms of savagery. It is much to be doubted that the Maya was any more moderate than was the Greek who wrote the motto and invented the "mean." The motto did not, as a modern author stated, "imply the absence of tension and lack of passion, but the correct tension."

Daughters were the images of their mothers, disciplined from the beginning and made to repeat useful actions. They were lectured, too, pinched on the ears, and when really intractable had red pepper rubbed into their eyes. They learned to make corncakes, to spin and weave cotton, and they learned those prayers which were concerned with their part of the Maya world. Instinctively, when they were born they were already old, more rooted to earth than man. Man made history but woman is history, and Maya women knew that the great Maya calendar had first been based on her menstrual cycles. She was the producer, the foundation. As with the Aztecs, so with the Mayas: when woman died in childbirth she was honored among the heroes.

She was not allowed to go into the temples or to take part in the ritual of religion; still, she was the seeress. True of women everywhere, her principal conquest was man.

10   Maya Agriculture

CORN was the epicenter of the Maya world.

The cornfield, the *col*, was their preoccupation; "the greatest number of them were cultivators . . . who applied themselves to harvesting maize," said Diego de Landa. These observations are confirmed by another priest in a sixteenth-century document written in the Maya highlands: "If one looks closely he will find everything these Indians did and talked about had to do with maize. . . ." The grain is ancient; the latest dating through maize finds in the Bat Caves of New Mexico places it as cultivated plant before 2000 B.C. Dr. Paul Mangelsdorf, whose studies on the origin of corn in the Americas are classic (and never given to undue speculation) believes that "the present-day races of maize in Mexico . . . are the product of four thousand years or more of evolution under domestication." Its place of origin within the Americas is still undetermined.

The Mayas had corn as a developed plant. This corn (*ixim*) after life itself was their greatest preoccupation. Yum Kaax, believed to have been the corn god, is always represented as youthful and wearing an ear of corn in his headdress. Prayers were offered to him. The head of Yum Kaax, found at the ruins of Copán, is among the most sensitive in primitive American art.[152]

Methods of agriculture seem not to have changed much since the earliest times. The Mayas felled trees and brush with a stone ax (*bat*) and burned them during the dry season. The earth was turned with a fire-hardened digging stick (*xul*). Each Indian was allotted by his clan organization a portion of corn land, a *hun uinic,* of four hundred square feet. Land was communal property: ". . . the land was held in common and so between the towns there were no boundaries or landmarks to divide them except when one [city-state] made war on the other." [11] The technique of corn culture was the same everywhere in the Americas: the felling of trees, burning, fencing, planting, weeding, bending the stalks at harvest (so as to deter the birds), harvesting, and shelling. The Mayas preserved the corn in storage bins; "they kept it in fine underground granaries called *chultunes.*"

Water was, as mentioned earlier, always a Maya problem. Those in the hinterland built huge reservoirs. At Tikal an immense one was located in a deep ravine, the porous rock cemented and held by a masonry dam. The sites of Piedras Negras, Palenque, and Yaxchilán were located on rivers. Cobá, in Yucatán, was set felicitously between two lakes, but most of the cities in Yucatán had as their only permanent source of water the well, the *cenote.* A Maya farmer tried to locate his milpa as close as possible to the wells. As new fields were needed, there was a tendency for the Maya farmer to move farther and farther from a given center. This in time doubtless loosened his connection with the city-state. Agricultural decentralization could well have been one of the factors which loosened the social structure of the Old Empire and contributed to the disintegration of cities.

Between January and February, at the time of light rains, trees were felled. From March to May was the hot and dry season; the living trees blossomed and the cut trees were burned. The larger unburnt logs were dragged to the edge and built into a crude but effective fence against deer and other animals. Ash from the burned plants was turned over with the digging stick, and the land was cultivated. From June through August, the rains fell heavily.* These were the planting months.

Planting was ritually controlled. Maize, the gift of the gods, was sacred, and planting had to be done with the proper ritual. The rain god Chac was properly propitiated and those days when rain should fall were selected for planting, in order that the newly planted seeds would sprout. Astronomy was mostly astrology. But the almanacs for planting were based on empirical observation; in one of the Maya codices it is stated: "This is the record of the year-bears of the *uinal.* . . ." Actually, this was weather forecasting based on observation of previous years. In the ninth month, Chen (Moon), and the tenth, Yax (Venus), planting was to be done during certain lucky days. Typical interpretations of the Maya planting almanac were these: "Cimi, the 5th day of the 11th month Zac [February] . . . bad day for planting . . . with rain incantations there is a good downpour . . . The month and day of 9 Caban [February–March] . . . good day, lucky day, heavy rains, good for planting everything."

For every detail of planting, sowing, and harvesting there was ritual, yet much of it was based on the shrewd observations of the earthbound man, who related them to the priest-scribes. The priests in turn set it all down in glyph script so that it could be remembered. During his excavations at the ruins of Copán, in Honduras, Dr. Sylvanus Morley found that two stone time markers were placed four and a half miles apart in such a position that the sun set directly in line with them on April 12 and September 7. It is thought that April 12 was the date chosen for burning the brush in the fields around Copán.

Chac was the rain god. He is represented in the Maya glyphs in

---

* Rainfall is heavy in the jungle regions, eighty inches a year. In El Petén (near where the first great Maya cities, Tikal, Uaxactún, etc., were located) it rains sixty-five inches a year; in Yucatán, forty-six inches. There is a high incidence of rain but water is not held by the shallow soil; it percolates down through the porous limestone into the *cenotes* one hundred feet below the surface. Some water remains in pockets called *aguadas*.

books, on sculpture, and in painted murals as the long-nosed god. His eyes, T-shaped, suggest tears and, symbolically, rain. His importance in the Maya pantheon can be gauged from the fact that the Chac name glyph occurs 218 times in the three surviving Maya codices. Chac was a benevolent deity and considered to be man's friend. The Maya farmer always evoked his name when planting. He was *the* god. So in the months of Chen and Yax there were great festivals to honor him. (See Religion, page 352.)

Planting was simple and effective. All that was required was a bag to hold the maize kernels and a fire-hardened planting stick. A hole was made in the soil, four or five inches deep, and into it three to six kernels were dropped. After that, Chac willing, the Maya waited. He frequently weeded the fields and waited for the maize to grow. "And when it rains," exclaimed Diego de Landa, "it is marvelous to see how maize grows." September and October brought light rains; they were also the hurricane months. In November, when the weather was cool and dry, the corncob was bent downward to keep it from the birds. Dry, it was harvested.

What did it yield? From exhaustive studies made in Yucatán over a ten-year period an idea has been gained of how much maize was harvested. How many fields of four hundred square feet the Maya farmers planted, we have no precise idea. "They plant in many places, so that if one fails, the others will suffice." The yield of corn from a given field would vary. Production was higher in the humid areas than in Yucatán, where the statistical studies were made. The present-day farmer in Yucatán plants an average of twelve acres. A hundred and ninety days of the year are given to preparing the field, burning, planting, weeding, harvest. The average cornfield produces 168 bushels a year. An average family of five consumes 6.55 pounds of maize per day, 64 bushels a year, including that fed to the livestock. From the fruits of his 190 days of labor the Maya feeds his entire family and still has a corn surplus of 100 bushels, which he uses to buy the luxuries that he cannot produce. It is presumed that since the Mayas in ancient times cultivated less land than at present, and kept no draft animals, his farm labor consumed only forty-eight days of the year. In the surplus time of nine to ten months a year, he built the great city-states.

The Maya cultivated much besides maize. In the same cornfield, using the maize stalk for support, the farmers planted beans; on the

ground, squash and pumpkins grew. Chili peppers were grown at
the edge of the fields or in the houses as an ornamental shrub. In
separate fields in the warmer areas the Mayas grew the pale sweet
potato. The sweet cassava (*dzin*) was known, as was *chicham* (from
the Mexican *xicamatl*), a root shaped like a turnip. They had one
good green vegetable, the chayote, the fruit of a herbaceous vine
that when cooked tasted like summer squash. Around the gardens
which surrounded their houses the Mayas planted papayas (*haaz*)
"which they esteemed very highly." The avocado (*u cheel*), a "very
large and fresh tree with fruits of great delicacy," appeared in groves,
while the soapberry tree they put near their houses to obtain the
roots from which they made a kind of soap.

The fruit of the *achiote* tree, mentioned earlier as a source of
color, was also used in food, giving "color to their stews, like saffron." The gourd tree, which produced large, unedible melon-sized
fruits, provided very thin but durable drinking cups that, as Diego
de Landa observed, "they paint very handsomely." The *balche* tree
was planted; its bark yielded the strong alkaloid used in making
honey mead.

Hemp was raised for its fiber, "from which they made an infinite
number of things": sandals, ropes, twine, bowstrings, fishing line,
and so on. Cotton was of two kinds; both were grown and "gathered
in wonderful quantity." It was of great economic importance because
of the cloth manta woven from it. The ceiba (*piim*), a sacred tree
that was supposed to hold up the Maya heavens, yielded a fine cotton made into pillows for Maya heads. The sapodilla, or "chewing-
gum tree" (*ya*), the source of our modern chicle, is a large tropical
fruit tree growing to a height of sixty feet. The Mayas boiled its sap
to a sticky mass and used it in making blowguns and for adhesion
when a strong glue was needed. It was an article of trade; Maya boys
chewed it, calling the stuff *cha*. The search for chicle to fill modern
needs has done much for archaeology; many of the Maya ruins were
discovered by *chicleros,* who spend the rainy season searching for
sapodillas.

Copal, which yielded a resin burned in all religious ceremonies,
"was a commodity and is very great business," wrote Landa. Cedar
(*kuche,* which meant "tree of God") was used for the large dugout
canoes. There was brazilwood, the famous dyewood called *cachte;*
"when thrown into water it turns to red." It was used for dyeing

cotton cloth. Palms were many, and their leaves were used for thatching house roofs. Cacao was grown on the two extremes of the Maya domain, Tabasco to the northwest and Honduras to the southwest. It was a Maya passion and farmers in Tabasco grew it exclusively, even to the detriment of the traditional maize, and traded "that gold of the country" for their needs.

One fruit, the banana, was not native to Maya land: "There are many bananas . . . the Spaniards brought them; for before this there were none."

Droughts were frequent and of great intensity and their "disastrous consequences play an important role in Maya literature." As explained in an earlier section, rains were usually heavy, but the greater part of the lowland is only a thin soil cap laid over a limestone outcrop ("the country with the least earth that I have seen," says Diego de Landa). The rain trickled through the porous limestone and down into natural cisterns. The Mayas tried to combat this; at many of the city-states they built artificial cisterns. During the rainy season water was gathered from the roofs by means of cemented run-offs and was directed into wells, which were elaborately roofed to prevent evaporation in the hot weather. Tikal, although in one of the wettest zones, suffered repeatedly from drought. There the engineers cemented up an entire ravine of porous limestone around the principal plaza, to create giant-sized reservoirs. Over these passed causeways which served as both dams and roads. All this was to no avail for the maize fields. When rain did not fall at its stated interval, the soil quickly dried up, cracked, and became cement-hard.

When this happened (and it is obvious from the frequent appeals to the rain gods that it happened often), the Mayas abandoned their cities, went into the jungles, and were reduced to eating the bark of trees. The old, who were unable to come, were left to die. Human sacrifices to the gods were frequent on these occasions. Other Mexican tribes suffered in the same measure from drought, and the Aztecs sacrificed thousands to the rain gods.

One of the enigmas of the Mayas is that Neolithic mental block which prevented them from devising a way in which to obtain the water which lay immediately below the land surface. Landa noted that there "are few places where one digs down that water cannot be found, sometimes within one meter." Irrigation techniques are inseparable from a developed agriculture. The pre-Inca civilizations in Peru, whose rainless coasts were more of a challenge to the primitive mind than the situation which faced the Mayas, solved their problems by the construction of an elaborate system of irrigational aqueducts, water often being brought down for hundreds of miles.

Although they were able to perfect a calendar as good as the Greek or Egyptian and raise stone cities from the jungle, the Mayas used the wheel only in toys for children. It would not have been beyond Maya technique to install a treadmill that dipped into the giant *cenotes* and raised the water to the surface, conveying it then, by means of an aqueduct, to their fields. In arid Numidia and Mauretania (present-day Algeria and Morocco) the Romans used reservoirs, ponds, and underground cisterns, linking them with canals and aqueducts to convey water to field and home. The water tunnel widely used by the Achaemenian kings in Persia (circa 600 B.C.)—and later introduced into arid Egypt—was a product of the intelligent use of gradients and the natural flow of water into waterless areas. Could it not have been worked out by the Mayas? The giant wheel built by Romans in A.D. 113 in the town of Fayum, in Egypt, lifted water from the Nile by a human tread method and fed it into reservoirs, which in turn flowed to fountains, baths, a brewery, and even to two synagogues. Such a device was surely not beyond the means of the Mayas.

There was a mental block against the principle of the wheel in the Americas, where man was the draft animal. None of the practical uses of the wheel, in whatever form, were known: pulley, arch, roller wheel, rotary quern, potter's wheel, or water wheel. Had the Mayas had the latter in that terrible year of 1464, when there was drought followed by a locust swarm so thick that the weight of it broke the limbs off large trees and engulfed the land until "nothing green was left," they might have survived and weathered the great hurricane which followed and destroyed houses, trees, and fields. "After this the land of Yucatán remained so destitute of trees that . . . casting one's eyes over the country from some high point it looks as if the whole land had been cut by scissors. . . ."

ONLY THE GODS seem to have been able to create something out of nothing. That something cannot come out of nothing is the reason for taxation. The Romans used the word *taxare*, meaning "to touch sharply," and most people of all times have felt it to be a burden. To the Mayas, whose closest approach to money was the cacao bean, the tax burden was in the form of service.

Little is known of its details. With the Aztecs we have some idea of how each clan or *calpulli* was collectively taxed. Aztec charts give a precise idea how tribute (which was a form of tax) was levied from the conquered. That other great theocratic state, the Inca realm, had a form of work tax called the *mita,* in which every able-bodied man was obliged to give a stated amount of service to the state, which service was recorded in their knot-string quipu. Though it is possible that the Mayas had such records, they have left none behind.

The Near East civilizations, such as the Sumerian and Mesopotamian, kept precise tax accounts in cuneiform writing, and it is thought that this necessary business stimulated the invention and perfection of writing. This was also true in the case of the Aztecs. From the name glyphs in their tribute books, we know the precise towns that lay within the Aztec orbit. If such lists existed among the Mayas, the overzealous padres must have destroyed the evidence.

Maize was the first tax. Part of a farmer's surplus was turned over to the tax-collecting *batab,* who brought it to the "state" depositories. Then, as a form of work tax, the personal maize fields of priest and nobility were cultivated and harvested. Writes Landa: "[the common men] improved the lands of the lords . . . planting them with wine-trees [*balche*] and they sowed cotton, chili peppers and maize."

Construction was also a part of personal tax. The houses of the directing classes were built by the common people, at their own expense. The causeways were built as part of the work tax; it was carried out by *corvée* by the clans that lived near the road. The nobility were carried in a litter, as were the Aztec "kings," who allowed themselves to be carried short distances. The Inca nobles

used the litter as a conveyance and picked groups of hardy tribesmen who carried them for thousands of miles. It is not known
whether the litter convoy was used among the Mayas, but "if the
lords went out of their fief, they took with them a great many
people."

Public building was the principal labor tax. It is fully evident
that immense religious centers, temple-cities such as Tikal—a city
covering many square miles, complete with reservoirs, giant causeways, and ball courts, whose façades are intricately carved—pre-
supposed a complex social organization and effective use of labor.
The Indian could always be counted on to work willingly on the
construction of a temple-city, since in the long run it would benefit
him. All wished to gain favor with the gods. It would be wrong to
believe that this was slave labor. It greatly differed from the labor
to which the Maya was later put by his white conquerors. The
latter benefited the Spanish, not the Indian.

Many in Maya society were exempt from taxes. The nobles,
priests, and civil and military officials lived on the tax tribute of
the lower man. In addition a sizable number of artisans, who
decorated the temples, carved the stelae, and directed if not actually
carved the wooden lintels and the masks for the actors, were supported out of the accumulated surplus brought to the official storage
chambers by the taxpaying Maya.

The gods, no matter in what guise they came, have always cost
Mexico dear.

12   Weaving

IX CHEL YAC, daughter of the goddess of pregnancy, was the
patroness of weaving.* Because weaving was done exclusively by the woman and because she was almost continuously
pregnant, the association was perhaps made in Maya minds between the two otherwise unrelated activities.

* Eric Thompson believes that Ix Azal Uoh, the wife of the sun god, was the goddess of
weaving, that Ix Zacal Nok was the "lady clothweaver," and that the figure shown in the
Codex Tro-Cortesianus, (102, b, c, d) may represent the moon goddess spinning. Dr.
Thompson, who has spent more time than any other living man exploring and writing
about the Maya, may well be right.

Weaving was both for home consumption and for trade. The women wove *huipilli* for themselves and breechclouts for their men. Unfortunately we have no examples of these garments beyond the representations of them on murals, pottery, and sculpture. So far as we know, Maya weaving was secular. They did not, like the Incas, appoint "Chosen Women" to live and weave in the sacred precincts.

69. *Ix Chel Yac, the goddess of weaving. She was the daughter of Ix Chel, the goddess of pregnancy and the wife of Itzamná, the Maya god of learning. From the* Codex Tro-Cortesianus.

Spinning invariably has been *woman*. The very tools are symbolical: an unmarried woman is a *spin*ster; and the female is "the distaff side," since the yarn was always spun from a distaff held under the woman's arm.

The spindle whorl is universal. The Maya spindle was a stick ten to twelve inches in length, with a pottery balance ring three inches from its end. It was spun about in a small ceramic dish. These pottery whorls are all that survive of Maya weaving.

Cotton was "gathered together in wonderful quantity and grows in all parts of the land . . . there are two kinds of it." One type was an annual: ". . . they sow it every year." The other was a perennial, a sort of tree cotton (*Gossypium herbaceum*), as its classification suggests, "and this lasts five or six years and bears cotton every year." Tree cotton was known and used by the pre-Inca cultures; it grew in the coastal drylands about Piura.

Dyeing was done before weaving. Colors, vegetable and mineral, were symbolic. Black was the symbol of war, since obsidian tipped arrow and spear; black was obtained from carbon. Yellow, the color of ripe corn, was the symbol for food. It was extracted from hydrous iron oxide. Red was a blood symbol; it came from several sources: red iron oxide and, from the vegetable world, *achiote* and brazilwood. Cochineal (*mukay*) was highly prized, "the best in the Indies coming from the dry land." It was obtained from the insects that Maya boys "herded like cows" on cactus pads. (In the sixteenth century the insects found to yield cochineal of a good color were extensively cultivated in Italy and Greece, replacing all other sources of red dye.)

70. *The spindle whorl is universal. The spindle stick was rotated on a small pottery dish as shown here in an illustration from a Mexican codex.*

Blue was the color symbol of sacrifice. That particular "Maya blue" which one sees so vividly on the murals of Bonampak, came from a mineral which has been identified as a blue chromiferous clay. "Colors of many different kinds were made from dyes of certaine trees." The Mayas also made them from the wild tomato, the blackberry, and the green-black avocado. The most prized, because it was difficult to obtain, was the deep purple obtained from a mollusk (*Purpura patula*). It is almost identical with the famous Tyrian purple derived from several genera of mollusks, *Murex* and *Purpura*. Dyes were pounded in stone mortars, which are sometimes found in graves. The dry colors were doubtless kept in small bags, which one does not see among the Mayas, but their counterpart in Peru has been preserved.

Independent invention is an archaeological fact. Peoples living under similar geographical conditions will resemble one another in various practices. Like the Mayas, the Egyptians used carbon for black, and got their purple from the *Purpura* mollusk. Ancient weavers needed a mordant to fix their dyes. The Peruvians used copper. The Mayas first used urine, as did the Aztecs and the Egyptians. That it was so used in Egypt is attested in a papyrus dated 2000 B.C.: ". . . his hands stink [referring to a dyer working in the urine vat] and he abhorreth the sight of cloth." When the cloth trade was extended, the Mayas obtained alum from the Mexican highlands, using it as a mordant for dyes, an astringent, and a preservative for leathers. The whitish astringent alum came from Aztec-held territory and was brought to the trading center of Xicalango by the trading delegations. (The people of the classical lands always used aluminum sulfate, to cause the dyestuffs to adhere to textile fibers. It was called "alum of Yemen" and was important in trade from the earliest times. Alums were extensively used as mordants in Europe in the Middle Ages.)

The Maya loom was identical with that of all the other American tribes. The backstrap loom had a horizontal rod that was attached to a post or tree. The warp was then fastened to the lower wooden rod (*xunche*), which had a thick hemp cord (*yamal*) that went around the ample rump of the woman weaver. The essentials of weaving vary little, be it Aztec, Inca, Egyptian, Greek, Roman, or Maya. The weft is interlaced with the warp. But the arrangement of colors and pattern is the art, the genius of weaving. The designs of the cloth produced from these Maya looms must have been fantastic, judging by the scant evidence which is shown on their murals, sculptures, and vase paintings. There were fabrics made of the imported rabbit-wool yarn from Mexico, others with bird plumage tied in to form feather mosaics, and tough manta cloth padded with cotton and soaked in salt brine for body armor. Designs and colors ran riot, and yet all we know of them are from the scant, tantalizing illustrations. All of the art of those looms has perished with war and conquest, time, and the elements. Except for the fragments found at the bottom of the wells of Chichén Itzá, there is no other evidence. It is a great loss to the history of art, for we know from an analogous source—the weavings of Peru, where dry desert conditions have preserved many superb pieces—how wonderful it must have been. Since, as said an old report, "the traffic of this land is in mantas of cotton," and this cloth was produced over an immense period of time, 1000 B.C. until A.D. 1670, the amount produced could have certainly stretched around the world.

From the simple manta woven in strips eighteen yards long, used for trade, came the colorful *huipil* for women, the breechclout for men, the robes of the priests and chieftains, the cloth for dressing idols, the portieres for temple doors, and the body armor referred to above.

All this has perished.

THE ART of featherwork was highly developed. It was equally so in the other great American theocracies, Inca and Aztec. Only the featherwork of the Incas has been preserved, owing to the enveloping sands of the dry coast of Peru. Of the Aztec work only two feathers pieces have been preserved, and those by mere chance. From the Mayas, nothing.

Since the Mayas did not have a centralized capital, we have no knowledge of craft guilds within such a center. The Aztecs had feather weavers (*amanteca*) and a centralized aviary where birds were raised for their plumes. This was not necessary for the Mayas; in their lands the birds were abundant. In Yucatán there was the motmot (*toh*), with its iridescent tail, and the blue Yucatán jay (*paap*), which traveled in flocks and yielded a wide variety of blue plumes. There were the modest-plumed quail, woodpeckers, pheasants, and the yellow-crested curassow, whose blue-black feathers were made into a feather mosaic for high priests. The ocellated wild turkey gave feathers which were used in Maya rituals. Along the seashore were ducks, egrets, herons, and the sun bittern. In the tropical area of El Petén there were toucanets, parrots, and trogons, and farther up, in the high, cold forests of Guatemala, were the long-tailed green and red parrots and the fabled quetzal, a bird the size of a pouter pigeon, which yielded two long, golden green tail feathers. The quetzal lives in the highlands and breeds in the cloud forests, above 4,000 feet. "In the province of Verapaz [in Guatemala] they punish with death he who kills the quetzal bird, the one of the rich plumes . . . for these feathers were of great value. . . ."

Birds were caught in bird lime or else felled with clay pellets propelled from a blowpipe,* a method of capturing a bird without killing it. The author, in fact, used this means when he caught,

---

* This blowpipe, *dzonche*, was an effective instrument. Diego de Landa, who saw it in action, said that an Indian using a blowpipe (with a pellet the size of a marble) could knock down a bird however large. Moctezuma had dozens of blowpipes, made of gold, which he used for hunting. He gave one of them to Cortés. The same type of blowpipe is still used among the remote tribe of Jicaques in Honduras, who once bordered the Mayas. The ingenious method of manufacture, with a botanical identification of the plants involved, the making of the pellets, and the methods of hunting have already been described by the author in *Jungle in the Clouds* and *The Jicaque Indians of Honduras*.

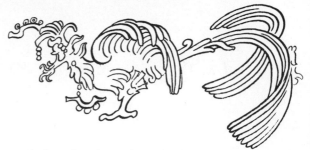

photographed, and studied the quetzal for the first time in its history.

The technique of preparing a feather mosaic began with the preparation of the loom as in cloth weaving. The feathers were then laid out in the desired pattern by the weaver. As she wove, the quill of the feather was tied into the warp and weft of the weaving.

The Mayas made much use of the feather mosaic. The ends of the man's breechclout which hung down, fore and aft, were decorated with elaborate featherwork. The priests and chieftains wore woven cotton-mat helmets ornamented with the magnificent golden green feathers of the quetzal. There were feather fans for actor-dancers, and for the nobles, long fans mounted on poles, which kept away the insistent insects. One sees these on the murals of Bonampak. For the festival of Xul five magnificent banners of woven feathers were presented to the temples by various artisans. Warriors dressed in featherwork, which made them look something like Papageno in *The Magic Flute*. There were feather shields similar to the one made for the Aztec "king" Ahuizotl (died 1503), which is still preserved at Vienna. In many dance ceremonies feather dress was used, as Diego de Landa saw and noted: ". . . one woman clothed in a feather dress danced for the people . . . and the lords of the land went clothed in certain *xicoles* of cotton and feathers woven into a kind of jacket . . . and the very lofty in fine feathers, especially the quetzal feathers, which are so valued . . . they are used as money."

71. ABOVE. *The sacred quetzal bird from a relief found at Palenque. Only the feathers are formalized.* LEFT. *A parrot, drawn realistically.*

14 *Mats and Matting*

POP WAS the word for the woven grass mat.

The mat was the symbol of authority to the Mayas as it was to the Aztecs. The *holpop*, "he who sits at the head of the mat," was the title given to an official of the directing classes who sat in the place so designated. In the sixteenth-century Motul Maya dictionary, the word *pop* means both "throne" and "mat." More, Pop was the first month of the eighteen-month Maya year.

The importance of the rush mat to the Mayas may be seen in the varied uses of it. In ordinary houses the mat was used as a floor covering. Food was served on the mat, and mats were used as mattresses for beds. On one of the temple walls, at Tikal, where some Indian circa A.D. 700 doodled the things of his life (one sees a man being ceremonially killed with an arrow, a jaguar with tail at the alert, a throne, a lord being carried on a litter), there are two sketches of the woven rush mat. The same type of decoration appears on the stone Stela J at Copán and again on Stela H at Quirigua, not far from Copán. At Chichén Itzá, on the small truncated platform in front of the great pyramid, the woven rush mat shares the decoration with the symbol for the planet Venus.

Mats were woven by men and women in their homes, during the round of the day. "They have in the fields and forests many different kinds of osiers," says Landa. The woven mat no doubt antedates weaving. Mat weaving and basketry are found in all of the Neolithic cultures dating as far back as 5000 B.C.

No examples of Maya matwork have survived.

15 *Basketry*

BASKETRY was highly developed. There seem to have been four types, but time has effaced them all. We know the Maya basket only from wall paintings, pottery, and sculpture. The Maya used reeds, rushes, sedges, grass, and vines for making baskets. "They have a certain plant [*Cyperus camus*] which they raise or grow in their *cenote*-wells and in other places from which they make their baskets . . . and they are accustomed to dye them in colors, thus making them very pretty."

The drawings show that some baskets were twilled, others made in a design of stepped frets and small squares. Inca baskets, as the hand of the maker left them, have been found in the preserving, desiccating sands of Peru and give a good idea of how well developed basketry was in the Americas. The techniques of basketmaking have changed little throughout the centuries; the earliest found in certain Neolithic sites in Iraq (5000 B.C.) are almost identical with those found in the Americas.

 Rope and Ropemaking   16

AS MASTER BUILDERS and seafarers, the Mayas had much use for rope. Rope was plaited out of the tough fibers of the henequen, or hemp. It is one of the agaves, a genus of the large and important amaryllis family, with spined fleshy leaves. All of the agaves were of considerable economic use to most of the American Indian tribes. The Aztecs had 317 uses for the agave, which included the fabrication of a beverage called pulque from its fermented juice. The Incas plaited the same agave into thick cables, "as broad as a calf's body," and used them for sustaining the suspension bridges which they hung over Andean gorges. The Mayas used it for a number of items, sandals, bowstrings, fish lines ("they tie their harpoons with buoys at the end"). They used it as cordage for sails on their long coastal sea voyages. One of the most frequent uses for rope was in temple building.

We may assume that the use of rope cables was analogous to that of the Egyptians (henequen was superior to their date palm fiber ropes). Rope and ropemaking was of the greatest importance to theocratic empires. It was a basic source of power, for men with ropes suspended from their shoulders pulled huge rock masses into place. A bas-relief at Nineveh (circa 700 B.C.), at the Palace of Sennacherib, shows legions of men, bearded in the Hittite fashion, pulling huge carved monuments on wooden sledges. At the Tomb at Thebes (circa 1450 B.C.) there are scenes of ropemaking. Men are seen plaiting palm fibers into wrist-thick cables.

Unhappily for us the Mayas were so preoccupied with the hierarchy of numbers and so intoxicated with time's flight, that they forgot to record all the daily events of their lives. They have left us no illustrations of the craft of ropemaking.

17   *Pottery and Pottery Makers*

Monsieur d'asterac, the gently mad alchemist of Anatole France's *La Rôtisserie de la Reine Pédauque*, said that "Jehovah's artifice in making man did not go beyond that of a very able potter capable of molding beings such as we are, in clay. . . . We are, in fact, nothing but animated pottery."

The ancient Mayas themselves are not much more now than animated pottery. Pottery is a chronological frame upon which to gauge historical perspective, so Maya potsherds have been studied to the point of delirium. The preoccupation with pottery design and techniques is ofttimes carried to extremes.[174]

In the study of prehistoric cultures art is given undue attention because it is far easier to photograph a temple than to detail a form of life. Moreover, the Mayas are inarticulate except through their art. So those Mayas, anonymous and communal, who raised the stone temple-cities and out of the chaos of the jungle built a concourse of roads, have now been reduced to being only a sequence of pottery.

The Mayas were pottery makers of the highest quality.[45, 177] The imagination, design, and form is as good as anything of the Greeks, far surpasses the Roman ceramic arts, and is superior to the pottery of almost any of the cultures of the ancient Near East. All of the wonderful Maya pottery forms—too varied to detail—were done without the potter's wheel. Pottery was done by coiling. The technique is almost as old as man. Clay molded into long coils, a sort of outsized spaghetti, is laid down in successive rings and worked and pressed into a single form with the hands. The clay form is then smoothed with a shard, the same sort of thing that Job used to scrape his boils. If the vase is large—and some were gigantic—the pottery maker walks around the vase, becoming himself the potter's wheel. This technique is not limited to the Mayas; all the tribes and cultures covering the wide area of the Americas employed it, and many used it in Africa and the peripheral Asiatic world.

These time-consuming methods have changed little since the earliest Neolithic times. The pottery wheel would have simplified the process, but we have seen that the wheel was almost unknown to the cultures of pre-Hispanic America. The potter's wheel presented mechanical problems not easily solved unless a people were fairly advanced in metallurgy; it must turn true and tight on a bearing. It is not, however, to be supposed that because the Mayas and other American potters used the primitive technique that their pottery was primitive. The wheel brought, as in the Greek vase, repetitive forms. Maya potters achieved greater individuality in their work because of a lack of mechanical devices.

Pottery was turned out in mass. They had molds for pressing designs on finished pots. Excavations have turned up such molds with decorations in vertical, horizontal, and pinched stripes for rouletting and comb markings, and molds of baked clay to impress patterns. There is no technique (other than the wheel) used by the best "mechanical" potters of the classic era that was not known and employed by the Maya.

After being decorated, the pottery was fired in an open kiln (wood-, charcoal-, or grass-burning) and baked at a heat of 450 degrees upward. All Maya pottery was made in this fashion: simple utilitarian bowls and cooking pots, decorated dishes, pitchers to hold chocolate, beakers to be filled with the heady mead. Braziers were made, to warm a chilly room or to burn copal. There were plates to hold sacrificial urns for the ashes of the dead ("the nobles had their ashes placed in great urns"). They made man-sized jars, as large as the knotted and corded jars found in Knossos, Crete; the Mayas used immense ones for underground water storage. Those found at Tabasco had an elaborate appliqué decoration. Life-sized idols were fashioned from clay, and each of the twenty thousand houses in Mayapán had one such. Even in Landa's time "they earned a great deal by making idols of clay."

Decorated with scenes of Maya life, the most beautiful of pottery was made for the dead. The Jaina clay figures already mentioned are

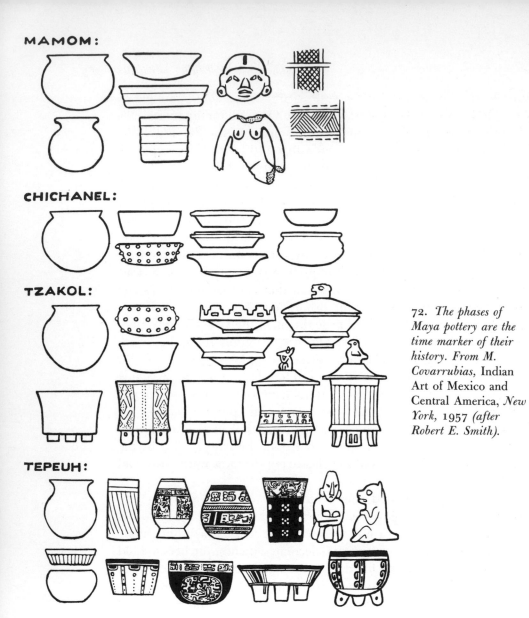

MAMOM:

CHICHANEL:

TZAKOL:

72. *The phases of Maya pottery are the time marker of their history. From M. Covarrubias,* Indian Art of Mexico and Central America, *New York,* 1957 *(after Robert E. Smith).*

TEPEUH:

freely molded yet exquisite in detail, showing Maya chieftains elegantly dressed and women richly clothed with necklaces and elaborate coiffures: "an extraordinary mastery of handling, realistic knowledge of form and movement; they are elegant and refined, majestic and monumental . . . excellent examples of the Maya aesthetic ideal." Their pottery has left us many details of Maya life, especially the life of the women, which is never indicated in the carvings on the monuments. Clay modeling was in a large sense a secular art; the clay figurines show Maya man as he saw himself. They were the expression of the lower man and the world about him, not an art form designed for the dominating elite, grandiose, elegant, and remote. The modeled figures give a picture of appearance and habits, the dress of men and soldiers, houses and games. Figurines which came from the coast of Vera Cruz greatly influenced the later Mayas. They show the Indian as gay; the laughing heads and the soft modeling of bodies emit a sort of contagious happiness and embody sophisticated elements. The God-obsessed Mayas, austere in their religiosity, were considerably influenced by the art of these figurines; they borrowed much from it for their Puuc-style architecture.

Pottery was woman. All we see of the remains of the Maya ceramic art was done by women. It is a fact that should be stressed. Almost everywhere that pottery making was on an archaic level, Africa or Melanesia, pottery was woman-made and its design woman-inspired. Throughout the area of the Amazon, pottery is a woman's task. Women were the potters, so far as we know, in ancient Peru. Early Greek and early Egyptian pottery was also woman-made until the introduction of the potter's wheel. Sir Lindsay Scott is "certain" that it was only after the introduction of the potter's wheel that pottery became—as the drawings on the walls of Thebes show—exclusively masculine. This suggests that all the superbly beautiful patterns found on pottery (as well as weaving) were conceived by woman.

Perhaps Art *is* a woman.*

Pottery is a time marker. For the archaeologists who reconstruct the history of a preliterate people, the most important evidence is the shape, decoration, and temper of pottery. Ceramics record stylistic and therefore social development.

Very primitive pottery is little known in Mayadom. When pottery appears it is already fairly well advanced. Archaeologists have

---

* A paraphrase from Nietzsche's *Jenseits von Gut und Böse,* which open with: "Suppose that Truth is a woman—what then?" Is there not ground to suppose that all archaeologists, insofar as they have been dogmatists, have failed to understand woman? That the terrible seriousness they have attached to pottery shards as a measurement of cultural time has been misguided, and their efforts to understand the meaning of symbols in art—of which woman, the determiner of history, is the maker—have been seriously inept? Later in his book Nietzsche confirms that "Truth is a woman—and one should not use force with her." If one replaces the word "Truth" with "Art," one need not change the context or the conclusion.

given Maya pottery, and therefore Maya history, five phases and to each (except the fifth) a name drawn from the *Popol Vuh*.

Mamom, "Grandmother," pottery (2000–500 B.C.) is strictly utilitarian; it has been discovered at the lowest levels in El Petén (where the earliest dated records begin). Most in evidence are the rounded cooking pots (*cum*) which remain relatively unchanged throughout the length of Maya history. They are simply decorated, grooved, and incised. Naked clay figurines also appear and flat eating dishes.

73. *"Thin-orange" pottery of late Maya history, from the region of Chichén Itzá.*

Chichanel, "Concealer," is the Maya formative period (500 B.C.–A.D. 300). There now appears some of the superbly painted polychromic Uaxactún pottery. The human form is treated literally, and it is often glyph-dated. Between this and the Mamom phase there has seemingly been no evolution of form; Chichanel suddenly appears full-born. The Chichanel styles vary widely throughout El Petén and Yucatán. The shapes are low, flaring; bowls have an orange color, decorated by what has been called the *abatik* process. It is also the beginning of the culture of Maya cities. The oldest dated stela thus far found (A.D. 328) is at Uaxactún.

Tzakol, "The Builders" (A.D. 317–650), is the period of the rise of the great ceremonial or temple cities throughout Mayadom. The pottery is sophisticated and polychromic. "Thin-orange," a very delicate pottery, appears. Widely distributed far outside the Maya area, it was developed from some unknown center. This period, archaeological stratification proves, lasted about three centuries.

Tepeuh, "Conqueror" (A.D. 650–1000), is dominantly Maya. All the traits that are Maya appear. The pottery is facile, sophisticated. One senses that the potter has now full control of clay and design, and it turns into decorative baroque. The arts, technically perfected, seem to lose their original creative vitality. The same flamboyance appears in Maya sculpture (which is less sensitive to periodic change than pottery). It is an ornate phase in Maya art. There is a change from static to dynamic composition; the richly dressed personages in the sculptures are presented in anecdotal scenes, and there is an unrestrained elaborateness, an exaggerated love of ornament. The greatest temple-cities, Tikal, Copán, Palenque, Piedras Negras, have all been built and there follows what most have called a period of decadence—the mass of building stops and grinds to a halt. There seems to be some relation between this baroque period and the abandonment of Maya cities. The ceramic arts, at the same time, show a shift in frame of reference; decoration becomes secular, religious motifs no longer hold, and the artist becomes increasingly concerned with the world about him. The overelaboration of sculpture, the tendency of the lower man to concern himself with secular subjects, the cessation of building, the ruinous destructive methods of Neolithic agriculture, the disintegration of central authority, all combine to show that "something" is happening in Mayadom. It is rash to base a theory of disintegration on flamboyance in the arts. Still, the condition of a people's art is often a symptom of its society. "Vulgarity is always the result of some excess," says Aldous Huxley. "Wherever artists find much technical difficulty in imposing form on brute matter, art tends to be simple . . . Luxuriance, unchastity and consequent vulgarity become possible only when men have acquired almost complete mastery over matter."

If all this is not explanation enough, in the Tepeuh period, the "Conqueror" phase, "something" caused millions of people to abandon their cities.

Maya-Toltec, unnamed in the *Popol Vuh,* is the final phase (A.D. 1000–1500). It begins with the introduction of new styles in architecture and pottery—the effect of the Toltec incursions—and ends with the occupation of Yucatán by the Spaniards.

Although the *cum* cooking pot retains its shape and function through all these periods (a confirmation of Spengler's "eternal peasant" theme), new ideas, new shapes of pottery, and especially new design and ornament appear in northern Yucatán, which was invaded by the Maya-speaking Toltecs. *Pumbate,* the only glazed pottery in the Americas, appears. Manufactured perhaps at Soconusco, in Chiapas close to the Oaxaca border, it is decorated with Aztec-like gods and animals. In the Puuc a new form of Maya architecture develops and along with it a hard, gray, slatelike carved pottery. Fragments of it from the ruins of Uxmal show this pottery to have been as limpidly beautiful as anything out of early Egypt. Toltec motifs, themes from the military orders of the Jaguar and the Eagle appear, as well as variations on themes of the cult of the plumed serpent. Tradition and known history are confirmed by pottery and it by archaeology. Thus, pottery is an "index fossil" of Maya history.

18   Trade

T HE OCCUPATION to which they [the Mayas] had the greatest inclination was *trade*."

This inclination toward trade early manifested itself among the Mayas; they were the only one of the three great American theocracies which maintained it by sea as well as by land. Ever since man has appeared on the earth, he has traded. Wars ceased so that man might trade. As man was willing to go vast distances for things he lacked, the early trade roads were luxury routes. He went vast miles, from the Mediterranean to the Baltic, to obtain amber, "that special act of God." Camel caravans traveled even greater distances through hostile lands to effect trade and bring in luxury items. Trading areas throughout the world had rights of asylum. Few were hindered in passing through hostile tribes when trade was the object. Strabo, the Greek geographer, stated that wayfarers whose object was business went under divine protection (Mercury was the god of travelers). In the Middle Ages, Edward the Confessor gave travelers protection on the four main Roman roads in England, declaring them "under the truce of God." And today, though it means imprisonment and perhaps death for anyone to pass into East Germany, daily trade missions cross over the border with complete freedom. It is not surprising then to find that the supreme occupation of the Mayas was trade.

The trade routes date from the origin of the Mayas. The Guatemalan highlands were linked with both coasts by trails and later by man-maintained roads. The *Popol Vuh* speaks of "where the four [trade] roads joined." Colors were direction symbols. "One of the four roads was red, another black, another white, and the black road said to him, I am the one you must take."

The one great river of the Mayas, the Usumacinta, which rises in the high mountains, was navigable to above the city of Piedras Negras; traders went up and down the entire distance of 240 miles. Trade traffic on land used a well-developed system of roads and causeways (*sacbe*; plural, *sacbeob*); many of these connected with the interior Maya cities. (See Land Communications, page 365.)

Early trade routes have been traced by articles found in Maya graves. In Maya Guatemala, at the site of Kiminaljuyu, there are artifacts which derived from Teotihuacán, in Mexico, showing that early Toltec trade lines moved along the Pacific side. Graves in the temple-city of Tikal, deep in the jungle, have yielded sting-ray barbs (used for blood sacrifice) that came from the Caribbean Sea. Social surplus stimulated trade. The highland Mayas traded in obsidian (all the active volcanoes yielding obsidian were on the Pacific side). Jade, a Maya symbol and passion, came from the highlands (although the geological source has not been found), as did the feathers of the quetzal. Copal, an incense, was an export item, along with flint, alum, and cochineal. These were exchanged with the lowland Mayas for cotton, salt, cotton yardage, honey, wax, *balche,* cacao, dried fish, and smoked deer. So trade flowed in both directions. It brought with it new influences. New ideas accompanied the march to market— patterns for weaving, deadlier weapons, new foods, all these followed commerce.

The routes are best detailed in Yucatán, for here the Mayas were concentrated in the last centuries of their cultural existence, and here they were conquered by the Spanish, who chronicled the details of their lives. Christopher Columbus was the first man to make a record of Maya trade. His caravels, on his fourth and last voyage to the Americas, met a Maya trading canoe on the isle of Guanaja in 1502. The canoes were forty feet long. They brought obsidian razors, copper hatchets, and cotton draperies of many different colors, and the Maya chieftain explained that they had come to this island, which lay twenty miles off the coast of Honduras, to trade for green parrot feathers and crystal.

When Cortés was in Xicalango in 1524, seeking the route to

GULF of MEXICO

XICALANGO

TERMINOS LAGOON

74. *Xicalango was an important Maya-Mexican trade center.*

Honduras, one of the Maya traders there gave him a well-made map, painted on finely woven cloth, showing the entire inland routes through Mayadom, from Xicalango in Campeche to Nito, on the Gulf of Honduras, a distance of four hundred land miles.

All sea or land communications led to the great emporium of Xicalango. To the Aztecs it was Anáhuac Xicalango and called "the place where the language changes," that is, the tribes to the southeast of Xicalango spoke Maya.

Xicalango lies a few miles inland from the Laguna de Términos. Into this outsized lagoon debouch four rivers, the largest of which is the Usumacinta. At the northeast end of the forty-mile-long lagoon there is a smaller one, the Laguna de Pom; on its shore was Xicalango. It was strategically placed. To reach it traders coming southward had to use canoes. It was surrounded on three sides by bog and swamp. On the northeast side there was a causeway leading to Vera Cruz and Aztec Mexico. Xicalango was a meeting place of Maya, Aztec, Toltec, Mixtec, and Totonac.

Merchants brought salt, dried fish, cotton yardage, copal, honey, wax, corn, beans, and feathers woven into cloaks, shields, and caps. Certain tribes of the Mayas had a virtual monopoly on salt. "There is a marsh in Yucatán worth recording," says Diego de Landa, "more than seventy leagues long and entirely of salt. . . . here God . . . has made the best salt." The lagoon began at Ekab (which was the first town seen by Grijalva in 1518; he called it "New Cairo"), a large commercial trading center with an extensive canoe trade dealing mostly in salt. Only certain Maya clans were allowed to gather the salt, and the lords of Ekab demanded a royalty on it.

Salt has been important in the history of most peoples. Rome's first formal stone road was the *Via Salaria*, built to obtain salt. In

270

Colombia the landlocked Chibchas grew rich because of it; they had mountains of salt at Zipaquira (8,500 feet in altitude). Salt cakes in ceramic dishes were one of the most familiar trade items in pre-Hispanic Colombia. Along with emeralds, it was a Chibcha monopoly. Salt routes are found all over the world. There are many around the Fertile Crescent; grain eaters had great need for salt.

Fish, turtles, turtle eggs, and large conch shells (used for trumpets and for making cement lime, the conch shell also became the symbol for zero in Maya arithmetic) were brought into Xicalango

75. *Sea animals drawn by a Maya artist: realistic turtle, sting ray (much used in Maya blood rituals), crab, barracuda, snail, and, in the lower right-hand corner, a spheroid mollusk that the Maya used for the symbol of zero. From the murals of Chichén Itzá.*

from the sea. Cotton mantas were widely exported. Maize was sent in sacks. The Mayas lacked metal, but flints were used for knives and were a large trade item. "God," said Landa, "provided them with many outcrops of flint . . . and so flint served for metal."

The Maya merchants, called *ppolms,* belonged to an honored profession. Like the Aztecs' *pochteca,* they were counted among the more important people. They had their own god, Ek Chuah, and their own rules of social conduct. They were nontaxpaying Maya, with special social privileges. The merchants operated canoe fleets, and maintained warehouses for exchange along the Gulf Coast, as well as deep into the interior of Mayadom. Hernán Cortés, in his famous trek across Mayadom in 1524 to punish a revolt, found evidence of stone-laid roads with "rest-houses along the entire way," and beyond Lake Petén he captured a high-placed Maya who told him he was a merchant trader and that he with his slaves had voyaged to these parts in his ships.

At Xicalango large, palm-thatched, stone-built warehouses awaited the cargoes. The merchants gave and extended credit, solicited terms and payment dates. Contracts were oral; there were no written documents. Deals were closed by public drinking, emphasizing "legality through publicity," a system of the Mayas. Yet failure to pay or dispute over oral terms often led to wars. Trade was on a truly vast scale. Post-Hispanic tribute lists record that twenty-six villages in the Maya province of Maní paid an annual tribute of 13,480 cotton mantas, each 16 yards long by 24 inches wide. This was 215,680 yards of cotton fabric from this small area alone!

There was a considerable trade in luxuries—cacao, stone beads, green stones called *tuns,* "emeralds" (*popzil tun*), topaz nose beads, cochineal for dyeing, alum, and, from the distant Maya-speaking Huastecs, bitumen, which those tribesmen gathered from oil seepages around Tabasco, now Mexico's primary oil fields.

On the upper reaches of the Usumacinta River were the large city-states of Piedras Negras, and Yaxchilán, and near to it, on a small tributary, was Palenque. Traders from these cities brought down copal, the odoriferous and magical resin. It was used as incense throughout Central America and much in demand in Mexico. Pelts of jaguar and puma, fruits, vanilla beans (to season the chocolate), wood, lime, and clay were items in the trade picture. In Cortés's fifth letter to Charles V, dated September 3, 1526, telling of his awesome trek of four hundred miles through Maya territory, he spoke of the province of Acalan:* "Of great size, containing many people and towns . . . many traders with slaves to carry their merchandise from here to every part [and Xicalango] . . . cloth, colors for dyeing, candlewood for lighting [long splinters of pine], so full of resin they burned like a candle." Most of this went overland to the Usumacinta, then by canoe down the river. There are firsthand reports on how trade was carried out.

After cacao, slaves. An excellent market for slaves was in Tabasco, near Xicalango. It was here in 1518 that Cortés on his way to the Conquest of Mexico was given the famous woman Malinche, "The Tongue," later honored by the Spaniards with the title of

* Scholars discovered in the Spanish Archives in Sevilla an important manuscript containing a narrative history of the Chontal and Acalan, fourteen generations before Cortés. See Roys, *The Indian Background of Colonial Yucatán,* p. 126.

Doña Marina for her part in the taking of Aztec Tenochtitlán. She was "from the town of Paynama, eight leagues from Cotzacoalcos in Tabasco," writes Bernal Díaz. Her father had been the chieftain of the town. When her mother remarried, her presence was found inconvenient and she was given into slavery.

Slaves (*ppentacob*) were big business. The Mayas trafficked widely in them. The basic cost of a slave was one hundred cacao beans. They were used for heavy manual labor, as fishermen, paddlers, and cargo carriers. Women slaves helped to draw water, grind maize, and dye cloth. Men slaves had their hair cut short and were given ragged mantles to wear. Slaves can be seen in ancient Maya sculpture.

Since there was always an acute labor shortage in theocracies, slavery was practiced throughout the whole of classical antiquity. All the extensive states in history—be they Egyptian, Hittite, Greek, Roman, English, Spanish, American, or in our time, German and Russian—had slaves. There is no basis for the oft-given assertion that slavery impeded the use, development, and evolution of the machine. In Rome, free and slave worked together, and the manumission of slaves had much influence on business and politics whether it concerned a Greek philosopher like Epictetus, an Aztec chieftain like "king" Itzcoatl, or a Booker T. Washington in America. Among the Mayas, the Spaniard, Gonzalo Guerrero, who was first a slave, rose to captain when freed. He led the Chetumal Mayas against the Spaniards.

Maya traders, who were given a high status in their society, purchased slaves by the hundreds in Xicalango. They were tied together, as Bernal Díaz saw them in Mexico, by their necks to long poles, "just as the Portuguese bring Negroes from Guinea." Slaves were often treated well and considered as part of the family. Yet when times were out of joint, that is, if it did not rain, they were sacrificed and pushed into the *cenotes*. At Chichén Itzá, their skulls have been dragged up "somewhat inordinately battered."

19 The Maya Market

THE NORTH STAR was the protector of the travelers. Under it, loaded down with luxury goods, they converged at stated times on the local Maya markets. Travelers (*ah ppolom yoc*) were expected to burn copal while moving over the roads. Merchants stopped at the resthouses used only for that purpose. They were expected to stay no longer than a single night or one trading day, and when there they paid for their own food and entertainment as part of "business expenses."

Concerning markets the only details that have come down to us are from northern Yucatán, where the Mayas were mostly centered at the time of the Spanish conquest. Along the coast the market towns were many and included Cachi, Chauche, and Ekab, the first Maya centers seen by the Spanish explorer Grijalva when he skirted the coast in 1518. Juan Díaz, chaplain of the fleet, remembered that Cachi, which he visited, "had a large market square and beside it was a building which houses the court where disputes were settled; it also had a place for execution for those who dealt badly in business." There they were summarily tried and summarily executed.

Of all the market places known to the Spaniards, Chichén Itzá was the greatest. This sacred city, with its sacred wells and imposing buildings of Toltec-Maya origin, was a place of pilgrimage with an extensive market. "Pilgrims came from foreign parts to trade as well as to worship." Within the court of the "thousand columns" of the Temple of the Warriors is a large area which Landa called the *mercado*. Open on four sides, it had a thatched roof supported by tall stone Doriclike columns, which still stand. There are also remains of a stone dais, on which the official sat to administrate sales and trading. In the open courtyard, squatting under white cotton awnings, men and women bartered the goods that they created in the surplus time allowed them by the cultivation of maize. In appearance it probably did not differ from the Aztec market so often described. Each product had its place. There was a section where fish, deermeat, and birds were sold. Cloth and cotton dealers had their precise area, as did those who traded in plumes, arms, and the other items of commerce.

The lords who had accumulated a surplus of maize, beans, shells, salt, and cotton, through tribute tax and "gifts," offered these things in trade to merchants who brought cacao, gold, obsidian, feathers, or jade, things the lords needed to uphold the dignity of office or to adorn their persons. Local merchants traded their surplus for the things of other lands, principally slaves and cacao. They did business in gross. The goods in turn were traded to the lower man, who then resold or traded them under the shadow of the cotton canopies.

It is strange that the Mayas did not use their highly developed glyph writing for writing contracts. It seems generally agreed so far as the Near East is concerned that trade, tribute, and taxes gave rise to the scribe, "that agent of its acquisition," and that writing was perfected out of the need for exact transactions. Some of the earliest writings left us are contracts in Hittite-written cuneiform, pressed into clay tablets and fired for permanence. If the Mayas used writing for trade, evidence of it had disappeared by 1500. But the Aztecs used their writing for this purpose. Books of tribute have come down to us. Bernal Díaz saw "great houses full of these books" on the coast of Vera Cruz and in Mexico itself.

"Cacao was the gold of this country . . . and it serves for money in the plaza . . . of Chichén Itzá," wrote Bishop Landa. The cacao tree grew on the periphery of Mayadom, for it had need of much rain and thick jungle loam. It is a thick-trunked, low-growing tree that produces oval pods the size of small papayas. The pods when matured are allowed to rot and the seeds ferment. Cacao seeds are almond-sized and almond-shaped; dried in the sun they become dark, chocolate-colored, with a parchmentlike skin. It is these beans that were used as money. A rabbit was worth ten cacao beans, a pumpkin four, a slave one hundred (the amount of cacao that would make about twenty-five cups of chocolate), and so on. Maya public women, always around the markets, "gave their bodies for a price. . . . he who wants them for his lustful use can have a run for eight or ten cacao beans. . . ."

Cacao bean money had its counterfeit. There were traders who cleverly took off the thick cacao skins, filled them with earth or sand, and mixed the spurious beans with untampered cacao. For this reason wily Indians always pressed each bean to make sure it was solid, just as elsewhere in the world people would bite a silver coin to see if it had been minted of lead. Cacao bean counterfeiting was one of the offenses most frequently judged by the Maya courts.

There is little data on the revolving Maya market (*yaab*). Among the Incas the *catu* markets were regularly held but the dates for them were staggered among cities so that the trader could have time to attend them all. In Mexico City the main Aztec *tiaquiz* market was every day while markets in other cities were held at different times so that the merchant was able to make the rounds. Of the Maya practice we know little.

20   *Festivals*

THE FESTIVALS were religious in nature. To the Mayas, religion was man and man religion; much, if not all, of what they did had a magical or religious purpose.

The month of Pop, which would fall in our calendar in July, was the Maya New Year. It was the time for renewal. People put on new clothes, destroyed their old pottery and fiber mats. There was a sense of re-dedication. It was a solemn occasion.

Uo, the second month, was a period of festivals for all the special patron gods, those who served the fishermen, hunters, travelers, and so on. The Maya gods seemed innumerable to the Spaniards, for most gods had different aspects. Uo was the month of vocational festivals; it ended in drink, dance, and fornication.

Part of month five, Tzec, was the bee god's turn. All those who kept bees—and there were many—joined the festival. The object was obvious; they wanted to cajole the bee god into increasing the flow of honey. Honey, with its by-product, wax, was a trade item, and as mentioned earlier, their principal drink, mead, was made of it. In these months all participants became uproariously, albeit ceremonially, drunk.

Xul, which fell in November, was the sixth month. This honored Kukulcán, the plumed-serpent god. In Chichén Itzá it was believed that he, or another of the same name, had rebuilt the sacred city and given it new laws. Rich gifts were exchanged. Featherwork, principally headdresses and shields and cloaks made of quetzal feathers, was displayed by the Maya lords in gala array. There were also processions of priests—and clowns. Although the ceremonies were most solemn, clowns carried on buffoonery; there was much burlesque.

So it went, month to month. Each had its special festivities. On Chen, the ninth month, new idols were finished, paid for, and presented. Yax was the renovation month. All over the land hunters made amends for shedding the blood of the animals they had killed. To the Mayas all animals possessed soul force, and when they were killed the hunter had to show them respect. If this was not done, other animals of the same species as the one insulted would not allow themselves to be killed. So the feelings of the animals had to be humored and nothing done to offend them; antlers, jawbones, and wings were hung in the houses.

All festive months had dances prescribed for them. The fifteenth month, Muan, was the time of rains, so the choreography of the dance had to do with rain and crops. In the sixteenth month, Pax (so different in meaning from the Latin word), war was celebrated. People poured in from all the smaller Maya settlements to the large ceremonial temple-cities and there witnessed their *nacom*, the elected war chieftain, make obeisance to the god of war. He was carried in a litter. There were five days of dancing and drinking. Landa was horrified when he saw it: "... in the month of Pax the rites of which were paid by the wealthy, the Indians made wine-skins of themselves ... and at the

POP   YAXKIN   MAC

UO   MOL   KANKIN

ZIP   CHEN   MUAN

ZOTZ   YAX   PAX

TZEC   ZAC   KAYAB

XUL   CEH   CUMHU

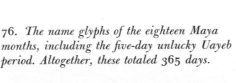

UAYEB

76. *The name glyphs of the eighteen Maya months, including the five-day unlucky Uayeb period. Altogether, these totaled 365 days.*

end of the five days the *nacom* were escorted back in their litter." Everyone (except the *nacom*, for whom it was taboo) got royally and ceremonially soused.

In the last three divisions of the Maya year, the months Kayab and Cumhu, and the five-day *uayeb*, there were also festivals, except that most pleasures were of a private nature. There was much drinking and—judging from the frequency with which it is discussed —considerable adultery. "They had no fiesta," says Landa in clerical disgust, "in which they did not get intoxicated, drinking a kind of mead into which a certain root was added by which the wine became strong and stinky."

The nobles gave many private parties. Those who accepted an invitation to one were expected to give one in return. On arrival each noble presented to the host a beautifully woven manta and a ceramic vase "as beautiful as possible." Food was offered in plenty—turkey, deer, duck, chocolate—and all were served by the most comely women. The guests separated in pairs or in groups of four, and dances were performed. Drink was brought by the cupbearers, who themselves were not supposed to get drunk. Women drank little, for they were expected to "get their drunken husbands home." There were scufflings and fights, and sometimes the "violation of conjugal rights followed," said the bishop, "the poor women thinking they were receiving their own husbands, whereas . . ."

21   Music, Dance, and Drama

MAYA MUSIC was group music, and as with the Aztecs, percussion instruments were important. There were no string instruments in pre-Hispanic America, and music and song were one.

Drums gave the group a hypnotic feeling of oneness. The *tunkul* (called *huehuetl* by the Aztecs) was an upright kettledrum, coming up to the beater's chest. It was made of a hollow log of light decorated wood, with a deer membrane stretched across it. It was beaten with the hands. Another rested on the ground and the drummer sat on it while it was beaten. A third was like the Aztec *teponzatli*, horizontal and hollowed of wood, with two wooden tongues; it was beaten with "beaters tipped with rubber." If beaten when the wind was right, the drums could be "heard two leagues off." When dancing the Mayas held a small drum, called *pax,* "which they played with the hand and there was another drum made of hollow wood with a heavy, sad sound." Still another type of drum was made from the shell of the small land tortoise, the carapace carved and lacquered. This same type of tortoise drum is used by many other Mexican peoples. "They strike it with the palm," wrote Landa, "and the sound is doleful and sad."

The Mayas also used an ingenious ceramic drum shaped like two connecting vases; across one end was stretched a membrane.

77. *Maya music was percussional. In the center, the upright* tunkul *drum, to the left, musicians scrape the hollowed-out carapace of a land tortoise, to the right, gourd rattles. From the murals of Bonampak.*

This type of drum still exists among the primitive Maya-speaking Lacandons, who called it a *kayum.* That it is very ancient is confirmed by its appearance in the *Dresden Codex,* where an illustration shows musicians playing about the head of the corn god; one of them plays the *kayum,* and musical speech-scrolls pour from the mouth of the drum.

Trumpets were of various kinds. The large conch shells found abundantly in the waters off Yucatán were made into trumpets that emitted one full awesome sound and were used to call down the gods. Similar horns were used by the Incas as well as the Aztecs.

78. *Trumpets were of wood, ceramic, or conch shell. Twin trumpets set in a different key always played together. Behind the trumpeters, the leader sets the beat with whistle and rattle. From the murals of Bonampak.*

Trumpets carried "melody." The largest of them were of wood and ceramic, five feet in length. One can see these instruments painted in the murals of Bonampak. They were always made as twin trumpets and blown in unison, although each part was set in a different key.

Flutes were of wide variety. The six-noted flute was made from a human leg bone, a deer's femur, reeds, or baked clay ("they had whistles made of the leg bones of deer—and flutes made of reeds"). The five-noted Panpipe, almost identical with the Old World type, was known to the Mayas; it also was extensively used in South America. The place of its origin is unknown.

Bells of copper and of gold or silver, tied on legs, waist, or wrist, gave sound to the dancer's prance. There were *raspadores*, various grating instruments similar to those used widely in present-day Cuban music. These were made of bones—deer, tapir, or human—which, notched and ribbed, were grated by means of a stick. They gave rhythm for the dance. Archaeologists have found many types. In Monte Albán, 150 miles inland, was found one *raspador* made from the rib of a whale.

In the vivid murals of Bonampak is depicted a twelve-piece orchestra. The music is being played by two matched ceramic trumpets, one kettledrum, three turtle-shell drums, and four musicians shaking gourd rattles. Music was ritual and sacred; all instruments were kept by the *holpop* official ("to his care the drums of *tunkul* are entrusted as well as the other musical instruments").

Punishment was meted out to those who did not keep time. The leader was the principal singer; he set the key and the rhythm. "This man they venerate."

There was no such thing as "pure" music. The song was a recital of "their fables and their lore," and the dance was in great part a ritual to cajole the gods into giving rain, sunshine, or whatever was needed at the moment. There were so many dances that an early Spaniard who witnessed some thought the Maya dance repertory could reach a thousand. There was a shield dance—presumably for warriors, who used their fighting shields as props—a monkey dance, a grandfather's dance-song, and one called the "Shadow of the Tree." There was an erotic dance (*nuaul*), called "bawdy" by a shocked friar. Dances are mentioned in the *Popol Vuh* of the highland Mayas. "They performed the dance of the *puhuy* [owl], of the *cux* [weasel], of the *iboy* [armadillo], the *xtzul* [centipede], and the one called *chitic*, performed on stilts (an illustration of this appears in the *Codex Tro-Cortesianus*). The Yucatán Mayas danced on stilts when the New Year fell on the day of Muluc.

Landa saw fifteen thousand Indians come from miles around to attend the dances. There were two dances which he thought "worthy of seeing": *colomche*, the "Dance of the Reeds," was performed in a large circle of 150 dancers, who moved to the rhythm of drum and flute. At a signal from the leader two performers

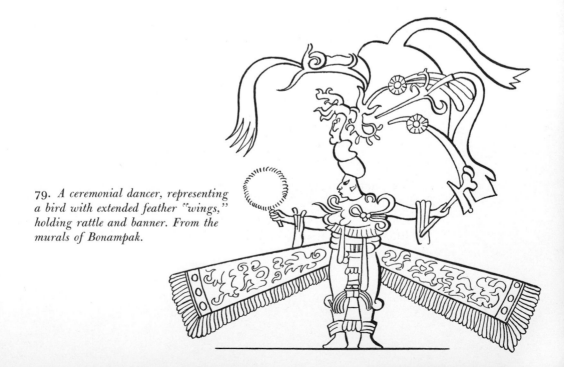

79. *A ceremonial dancer, representing a bird with extended feather "wings," holding rattle and banner. From the murals of Bonampak.*

leaped into the center of the living wheel; one was the hunter, the other the hunted. The hunter threw rubber-tipped reed lances at the other, who caught them "with great skill." All the while the circle moved and kept time to the music. The other dance, which Landa does not name, was performed by eight hundred dancers carrying cloth, paper, and feather streamers. The choreography was based on a deliberate, warlike step. They kept time (punishment was meted out if they did not), and danced the whole day without stopping, for food and drink was brought to them without their breaking formation.

For the most part men danced with men, women with women. The only dance which men and women performed together was the one that Landa thought "not very decent."

Dance was a mystical communion between participants and the onlookers. The object of the dance was by group participation to gain victory over the unseen powers. To the Mayas, drumming, singing, hand clapping, and ululation exercised a mystical influence, formed a social bond in which they all felt in contact with the supernatural.

Dramatic presentations in which actors took part, their actions set to musical stresses, were also performed by the Mayas. Landa tells us that "their players act with a great deal of wit," and he unhesitatingly says that there were "professionals."

Stages were both indoor and outdoor. At Chichén Itzá in 1560, Landa saw "two stages built of stone with four staircases . . . and paved on top; here they recite their farces . . . and comedies for the pleasure of the public." These two-stage platforms, now restored, can be seen at Chichén Itzá. One is the Platform of the Cone, a twenty-foot-high stage with four stone staircases on a direct line between the pyramid-temple and the *sacbe* roadway. It has a flat space on top for performances. The other referred to by Landa is the *Tzompantli* stage, decorated on all its sides with, as its name implies, stone-sculptured human skulls. It is in front of the Great Ball Court.

The actors were graceful, witty, and elegantly costumed; generally they were masked. This is confirmed by the murals of Bonampak, which show actors impersonating birds, animals, and sea life. One has his face encased in an alligator mask; another has the long tentacles of a crab. They seem relaxed, as if awaiting their cue to enter the stage. Another has water lilies dangling from his earplugs (the water lily is the symbol for abundant earth), and yet another is a god-impersonator, wearing a mask with a *T* for the eyes (the *Ik* sign, symbol of fertility and germination).

This is pictorial confirmation of all that has been said of their cleverness, for the costumes were well made and imaginative. We can well believe Landa when he says that the actors had so great a wit and so wonderful a sense of mimicry that the Spaniards often hired them "to make jokes and burlesque of other Spaniards." Maya terms found in the old dictionaries show that there were humorous parts in their repertoire—parts for the parasite, the pot vendor, the cacao grower—which parodied phases of their own life and made fun of their own foibles.

To the primitive, the moment that an actor is masked he actually takes the place of the thing he represents. If he plays a god, he *is* that god. It is magic and magic "is a counterpoise to a state of unrest . . . really a waking dream," as Lévy-Bruhl pointed out in reference to other primitive societies. "Life is a lying dream," says one of the characters in a Japanese *nō* play, "he only wakes who casts the world aside."

Drama was all part of the collective hypnotism.

 Games 22

B OYS PLAYED at "beans" on a board something like our parchesi, and they played the game of the young everywhere, hunter-and-hunted. Landa remembered that the children "never stopped going around with small bows and arrows and playing with one another." But the passion of the adult Mayas— which they shared with most Indians from Nicaragua to Arizona— was the game played with a hard rubber ball and known to the Aztecs as *tlachtli* (Taxco derives its name from it). The Mayas called it *pok-a-tok*.

No one knows where the game began. Rubber came from Tabasco among the Olmec Indians, who are believed to be pre-

80. *The religious game*
pok-a-tok, *played with a
rubber ball in the form of
a basketball, was the
principal sport. This is the
immensely large ball court
at Chichén Itzá, 545 feet
long by 225 feet wide. A
ball is aimed at the basket,
which is shaped like a
millstone.*

cursors of the Mayas, or at least contemporaneous with the cultural
rise of the Mayas. As we have seen, the word for rubber in Toltec
was *olli,* and the Olmecs were called the "rubber people." All of
the larger Maya temple-cities that have been found have their ball
court. Those who have visited the ruins in Mexico or those of
Copán or Chichén Itzá will remember the ball court's appearance:
long and rectangular in shape, like an *I,* with tiered seats on both
sides for the spectators. In the exact middle on either side of the
court, often as high as thirty feet from the floor, a stone ring is set,
not horizontally as in basketball but vertically.

Because *pok-a-tok* was no longer being played by the Mayas in
Landa's time, we must fall back on the description of the game as
played by the Aztecs (see p. 105), written by the Friar Bernardino
de Sahagún. No such detailed description of the game as played by

the Mayas has come down to us, but the *Popol Vuh* chronicle refers briefly to the sport:

"Let us play ball, said the lord of Xibalba.

"Then the lords seized the ball and butted directly at the ring of Hunahpu."

Chichén Itzá had seven ball courts. The largest one, the greatest seen in any temple-city in the Americas, is one of the exciting features of the site. It was built by the Toltec-Mayas and decorated with motifs derived from Tula, eight hundred miles away. It is 545 feet long, 225 feet wide, and the millstone "basket" is decorated with an open-fanged snake, thirty-five feet above the playing field. It is so high, in fact, that the rule of the game cited by the friar— that the player could not use his hands, but only butt the ball through the "basket" with elbows or hips—cannot possibly hold for this court. As in Aztec Mexico, the Maya lords wagered high on the game, and if the player put the ball through the hole—a feat that seems rare enough—he had the right to demand as forfeit all the clothing and jewels of the spectators present.

With the Mayas, as with present-day Americans, games were sometimes given more consideration than serious matters.

 Crime and Punishment   23

THE MAYAS "were governed by laws and good customs and they lived in peace and justice." That is the opinion of Torquemada. What is meant is that, while war was waged with other clans and tribes, there was still "peace and justice" among those living in the same tribe. There is no doubt that the Mayas had a highly developed sense of justice, but definitely the form of justice meted out by a preliterate people. After three thousand years or more of living within the same area, tribal mores had become dicta. What is done, is done; and what is not, is not. Any infractions of this brought retribution. It was executed rigorously. Crimes to the Mayas were basic—theft, homicide, adultery, lese majesty—and punishment often "fitted the crime," like being punished with like.

Theft of course was antisocial. Since all the clans within the tribe were of one blood, it was considered distinctly unethical to take something not one's own. Maya houses had no doors, no locks, only a drapery or a string of bells to inform the owner that someone had entered. For theft the punishment was slavery. The thief had to "work off" the theft; or should his immediate relations feel the social defilement brought on by his enslavement, they paid off the debt. Second offenses could bring death. Theft perpetrated by any member of the directing classes brought disgrace; his face was scarred by deep tattooing and carried notice of his crime

81. *Justice was dispensed by the* holpop, *he-who-sits-at-the-head-of-the-mat. The mat* (pop) *on which he sat was the symbol of justice.*

throughout life. There was no social atonement for theft. The thief did not pay society, the Mayas having no form of imprisonment except for sacrificial victims; the culprit paid the victim.

Even if accidental, homicide carried a death penalty—unless the relatives were willing to pay the victim's survivors. There was no such thing as accidental death; homicide was treated as willful murder. "The penalty of homicide," says Landa, "even when death was accidental, was to die in the snares set by the victim's survivors."

To their mystic mentality (this is true of primitives everywhere) there was no such thing as chance or accident; what we call accidental was to them purposeful. It revealed that evil influences were at work even before the "accident" and that the intended victim had been "selected"; it was a sign of malignant influences. We acknowledge accident; they thought about the supersensuous realities of the incident.

Any form of death was defilement. The greatest social uncleanliness came from the shedding of blood. The Mayas even had to atone for the killing of an animal. That is why the hunter hung up something of the animal and usually pierced his own tongue and/or penis and spread a few drops of his own blood over the recently killed animal. Killing an animal gratuitously was the same as homicide, and anyone who took life and shed blood brought about social defilement; he was subject to tribal discipline.

Loss of property by accident was treated the same as if it had been caused deliberately. If an Indian knocked over another's beehive, he had to pay the owner. If it was proven that an Indian committed suicide because of blameful commission or omission on the part of another, the latter had to pay.

Adultery brought death. The only legal loophole was that one had to be caught *flagrante delicto*. If so caught, the wife's paramour was brought bound to the judges, was heard, sentenced, and then handed over to the husband, the offense being not so much a violation of virtue as of property. The adulterer was summarily executed by the husband, who "dropped a large rock on his head . . . from a great height." Or should the case involve the woman of a noble, the adulterer might have his navel cut open and his intestines pulled through it until he died (an illustration in one of the Maya codices shows an Indian being slowly executed in this manner). Among those of high rank, adultery was much detested because "there was no need," that is, the noble was polygamous and had ample women to satisfy his longings.

Crimes of malice were always satisfied with bloodshed. If complex, the case was heard by the *batabob,* the town rulers. Nothing was written down; everything was verbal. In complicated cases, speakers who took the part of lawyers were chosen and they "argued" the case. Accused and accuser alike brought "gratuities" to the judge. The Mayas were talkative; a case could be prolonged by talky-talk for days. A suit, criminal or civil, might be so involved that it could run the gamut of sound, with complicated legal abracadabra such as Bridlegoose uses in the third book of Rabelais' *Gargantua and Pantagruel.*

24   *Cures and Curers*

AMONG THE MAYAS, illness arose from a mystical cause. The one who cured disease and one who was able to cause it, *ah men,* were identical to their minds; "the physicians and the sorcerers . . . are the same thing," observes Landa.

Magic and medicine have always been bound together. One has only to call to mind the magical panaceas of the Middle Ages or, for that matter, some of the curatives of modern times to be made aware of this. Disease is thought to be caused by a someone rather than a something. It may be brought on by the malevolent influence of someone in the community, by someone who has broken a taboo, or by someone who failed properly to observe the rituals of life. This idea was interwoven into the deepest fibers of the Maya mind. The Maya was aware of the connection between disease and cure. Sacrifice—the tearing open of human bodies, the flaying of skins, the removal of skulls from the dead—had given the Maya some idea of anatomy and function, yet he was not able to turn this knowledge to account, for the Maya mind was orientated in another direction.

Illness, like death, was brought on by supernatural causes.

When ill the patient called the *ah men,* who diagnosed the malady by divination. He evoked the goddess of medicine Ix Chel (who was also the goddess of pregnancy), placing her image before the patient. Copal incense was burned and tobacco smoke blown across the patient. The *ah men* brought along the appurtenances of his trade, "the bundles of medicine." This fetish bundle might contain roots, jawbones, or anything that was deemed magical. The divine stones were rolled out in front of the patient to find the prognosis of the disease. Priests have been found buried with these *am* stones. An illustration in a Maya codex shows an Indian tossing six stones, and in another there is a divination conference between two doctors. The patient had to combat the mystical forces which caused his disease with power of the same kind. Divination was, and still is, one of the accepted forms. After all, the Romans consulted chicken livers before battle to look for good augury and the Incas looked at the lining of llama stomachs for signs of good or ill fortune.*

Maya cures were effected by extensive questioning of the patient along mystical lines; and only after this, when the doctor believed he had found the cause, the physical cure began.

What were Maya diseases? There was asthma, rheumatism, stomach worms and other parasites ("It is difficult to make love on an empty stomach," wrote Aldous Huxley, "and still more difficult to make it on a duodenum that is full of *ankylostoma*").

Pneumonia was frequent among Indians, who were often soaked by the rains and later scoured by the winds. It was usually fatal. A Maya herbal, addressing the doctor, says: ". . . you will not be able to cure him of this because he will die vomiting." Malaria, termed "nightfever," was present; chills recurring every three days were the symptoms. Diarrhea and dysentery, which must have been endemic, are often mentioned. The Maya was subject to jaundice, cancer, tumors, and skin diseases of various kinds. Erysipelas was known graphically under the name of "hell eruption."

As the Maya diet was excessively starchy—beans and maize—they suffered from flatulence, vertigo, depression, nightmares, and epilepsy ("He is speechless and will fall," says the Maya herbal).

Yellow fever was doubtless present. Spider monkeys in the area about Tikal have been found to have it. It was called *cil*, "blood vomit." It appears historically about 1480, twenty years before the first Spanish contact with the Mayas, and is mentioned in a Maya chronicle: "On 4 Ahau [1482] the pestilence, the general death swept over the land."

Syphilis is not described nor is there any disease mentioned that would seem to be syphilis (it is graphically described on Mochica pottery in Peru). The Mayas do mention "a bubo of the groin" which arose when one "overcopulated."

* Anyone who thinks this so primitive should think back on how long the tomato was regarded as a poisonous "love apple" and not eaten. The potato at one time was not accepted as edible because it was "liable to cause disease." In 1764 a Prussian edict signed by Frederick the Great forced it upon the Germans and then not as an enjoyable food but only as a source of starch.

Despite the generally good condition of Maya teeth—which women brought to early ruin by their custom of filing them to points because it "looked well"—there was decay and toothache. Said the Maya herbal: ". . . now to cure this, take the bill of a woodpecker." Teeth inlaid with jade have been found in graves. The inlaying was done, not to fill cavities but because it was thought attractive.

When bones were broken the patient got a specialist called a "bone-binder" (*kax bac*). The Mayas seem to have been able to diagnose cancer. "There is a crab called *ah buk* . . . take its claws and powder them and apply this to the cancer . . . or else . . . [and here the archaeologist will wince] powder a potsherd, which is not so bad."

No matter how advanced the Mayas were in architecture, in working out their calendars, or in glyph writing, regarding illness they were not much different from the most primitive of tribes. They did have cures and remedies and, in glyph writing, "books" on astronomy, divination, prophecy, and incantations. It may be that among those hundreds that were destroyed there were herbals. It is true that there is none now extant comparable to *The de la Cruz-Badiano Aztec Herbal,* written in 1552 by an Aztec who knew Spanish and Nahuatl (it was illustrated with pictures of the precise plants used in the remedies). None of the known Maya herbals, with which Ralph Roys worked to produce his *Ethno-Botany of the Maya,* are dated much earlier than the eighteenth century. In his study of them Roys believed that the *ah men* doctors who survived the calculated massacre of Maya "intellectuals" had copied these from some glyph book and then dictated in spoken Maya.

Cures, as seen by the remedies proffered by the Maya herbals, were often worse than the disease. Many were sensible, some just ridiculous, and not a few, as will be seen, exceedingly harmful. Pleurisy, "extreme pain that attacks the ribs," could be relieved by drinking turkey broth, or *balche* mead* containing the ashes of

---

* *Balche* (*Lonchocarpus longistylus*) bark was steeped in fermented honey. Elsewhere —the Amazon and Central America—*balche* was used for a stupefacient; cattle when they drink water containing the juice of the *Lonchocarpus* will abort; *balche* in mead not only made the Mayas drunk, it also must have acted as a violent purgative. The Mayas regarded it as healthy; it "purged their bodies . . . they vomited up worms when they drank it." Landa, who called *balche* mead "the wine of the country," admitted it was wrong for the Spaniards to prohibit it. The drinking of *balche* mead is illustrated in the Maya codices.

dog excrement that had been burned. Dysentery (*kik-nak*) was called rightly a "blood flux." For its cure an extended pharmacopoeia was offered: the sap of the rubber tree, a fungus, a euphorbia (which was perhaps better than anything else prescribed). *Kik-nak* was also cured by "taking the tender tips of the guava-plant mixed with the excrement of a dog, adding a little tapir dung as you boil it, and after resting until dawn, adding a bit of honey." The herbal states that the *kik-nak* "will cease by these means." There is little doubt that the patient would cease also. *Ta-kik-zok*, blood in the feces, could be cured by putting a freshly killed bat into a *balche* brew. (As the blood-sucking vampire bat emits a bloody stool, one can see that here like was being treated with like.)

The description of yellow fever, "blood vomit" (*xe-kik*), is given thus: *U cacale yitz xpomolche, chactez, u macil u capil kaxil-koch, xtuzil, chac-kan-cab, chac-piliz-mo, chac-piliz, chac, cicib, macap-lum huchbil, macoc zum, kankan u top y kuxubcan y xanab-mucuy ukbil y cacal. U cacal xe tik tu tamil ca chabac cincan y xcantacii y chilimcan y u yalaelel, chacmuc y canchacche ak ca chacac hunppel akab ca ukue lai ppiz y zappal yalil hun ppul cabin chacace.*

The remedy includes the gum of a species of *Jatropha*, the pith of the Cecropia moth (*ix-tuzil*), a certain reddish earth, the feathers of the *chac-pilliz-mo* (a small red parrot) and of the Yucatán cardinal (*macap-luum*) ground up with the *mac-oc*, and the euphorbia. The remedy is to be drunk.

An epileptic was described as a "man who falls to the ground among the plants." The Maya herbal states that "this is the cure for one who falls on the ground, waves his arms and froths at the mouth . . . seek the horn of a deer, powder it, drink it, or else the testicles of a cockerel which has been shredded in cold water . . . if all this fails . . . have him remove one sandal, urinate in it and drink it." Nosebleed could be stopped by administration of a drink made from various roots and plants, "but if this fails, then the cure-doctor should bleed his foot." The nosebleed might cease, but there may be another complaint: ". . . the foot may continue to bleed."

There were ten types of scabies (*kuch*) and each was treated with a different plant. The plant one used depended on the type of scab. There was the contagious scab, the behind-the-ear scab, and there was one that "looks like the rectum of an old turkey hen." Smallpox was included by the Mayas among the types of scabies; it was called *cim-ex*.

Women had their problems which, then as now, were usually combined with the menstrual period or pregnancy. The Maya herbal stated that the type of womb "which rises and falls and cuts off menstruation" was easily cured: ". . . an old leather sandal should be burnt under her nose, or even better, the feather of a woodpecker." For delivery the Maya women employed a midwife, *ix alanzah*, but if there were complications she called in the *ah men*. "To deliver the foetus which was already dead in the womb" it was recommended that "the best [way] was to take dog's milk and mix it with *balche* mead and after she drinks it set a smoking dish of coals under the woman so that it would reach her inside womb to smoke her out."

There was frequent mention of infections of the kidney (blood and pus in the urine) and gallstones. All this suggests that the excessive drinking of *balche* took its toll of Maya health.

However, when the patient recovered from these diseases through the various specifics proffered by the doctor (which speaks more for the rugged Maya's constitution than for these un-Homeric simples stuffed down him) and his thoughts turned to love, the doctor could offer him one of several aphrodisiacs, such as the heart of a hummingbird or the testes of a crocodile (the head-hunting Jivaros in the Upper Amazon extract, dry, and scrape the penis of a crocodile and offer it to a woman candidate in a bowl of manioc beer). As the average Maya was as libidinous as a two-toed sloth, he had need of it. They lacked sexual imagination, which is the only true aphrodisiac; and Aldous Huxley, as we have seen, gave them up completely.

Finally, if a patient survived illness and cure and escaped the witchcrafts which caused the illness, the successful doctor could change his role and become a sorcerer (*ah pul yaah*) and bring disease to the one suspected of causing the malady. He could return the disease and so parlay malevolence into death.

WHEN DEATH approached, the Mayas feared it and bewailed its coming. And why not? One always feels to excess the bitterness of any departure. After all, what is life but a succession of little deaths? We lose a little bit of everything hourly. The dying Christian could say, "Now I am going to live." Not so the Mayas. Despite the fact that much of his waking life had to do with death and the appeasement of the dead, he did everything to stave it off. He was not *too* sure of a future life, and he believed only in the sensuous here and now. Thus he wailed.

"They have a great and excessive fear of death," said Bishop Landa, who after all was sure he would sit on the right hand of God; "all the services performed for their gods were for no other purpose than that they should give them health and life... when death occurred they wept the day in silence, and at night they wailed."

A dying man confessed to a priest in the same manner as the dying Aztec, for confession was necessary to neutralize the evil influences brought about by one's death. Dying was a form of social defilement; it was an antisocial act. It was individual, setting one apart from the clan wherein all acts of life were collective.

Dead, a man was wrapped in a shroud, usually his own manta. Into his mouth was placed ground maize (*koyem*) with a few jade beads, "which they also used for money so that they should not be without means to get something to eat in the other life." The lower man was buried in the hard mud floor of his house with the things of his life; if he was a fisherman, nets and harpoons, if a warrior, shield and lance. All had pottery filled with drink and food. Time has caused all of this to disappear except the pottery, and it is on this pottery that the Maya archaeologist depends in order to formulate a historical stylistic sequence of Maya history.

Houses were abandoned after a generation of burials, becoming in effect family shrines. The possessions of the dead man were usually taboo, and most of them were buried with him. "If he was a priest they buried with him some of his witchcraft stones." A *chilan* (soothsayer) was often buried with his "books" (Kidder found evidence of one so buried at Kaminal-juyu, in Guatemala), which may account partially for the disappearance of many of these writings.

Very few well-preserved graves have been found. Nobles, which included priests, were often buried in small stone-lined vaults; they were laid out full-length and surrounded with pottery vessels. In A.D. 500 a chieftain at Kaminal-juyu was buried in a sitting position along with two adolescents and a child "elected" to be killed and sent with him into the afterworld. Even the chieftain's dog accompanied him, so as to guide him to death's abode.

The noble dead were buried in the plazas of the temple-cities. In Chichén Itzá the high priest was found in a sumptuously appointed stone-lined grave. Around what had been his neck were baroque pearls brought back from Venezuela by the seafaring Maya tradesmen. A chieftain's tomb found recently under a temple at Palenque is as elaborately splendid as anything found in the Old World.

In Yucatán, nobles were cremated and their ashes placed in an urn (made of ceramic or wood) which portrayed their features. Portrait statues were made of deceased people of position. The back of the head was left hollow and the ashes of the dead placed in it. "They preserved these statues with a great deal of veneration." The Cocoms, the dynasty that ruled Mayapán toward the end of the "empire," devised a unique burial; they decapitated their dead "and after cooking [the heads] they cleaned off the flesh and then sawed off half the crown at the back, leaving entire the front part with jaws and teeth. Then they replaced the flesh . . . with a kind of bitumen [and plaster] which gave them a natural and lifelike appearance . . . these they kept in the oratories in their houses and on festive days offered food to them. . . . they believed that their souls reposed within and that these gifts were useful to them." Landa was confirmed when archaeologists dragged up from the sacrificial *cenote* of Chichén Itzá a skull with the crown cut away, just as he described it, with remains of the plaster and wood that had given the skull a lifelike appearance.

The Greeks made similar burials at their tombs in Myrina, where archaeologists have found mirrors, spatulas and strigils, ornaments, diadems, cups, plates, and statuettes of the lesser gods in baked clay. Both Maya and Greek suffered from the same pious illusion. The living wanted to surround the dead with the familiar objects among which their lives had been spent; for if the dead found it disagreeable to go alone to the afterworld, they might wish to carry along the living to comfort them. The dead had malice toward those who still had the light of day; thus the living had to propitiate them with living comforts.

The Mayas believed in immortality and a form of heaven and hell. Those who kept the rituals, that is, "the good," went to a place shaded by "the first tree of the world," and drank their fill of cacao under it. Where the others went is not clear. The Aztecs elaborated gods and places of the underworld in a complexity which could have drawn praises from a Greek himself. We do not know how closely the Mayas paralleled these concepts. The name glyphs of the nine Maya lords of the night and the underworld have been identified (the Aztecs had thirteen heavens and nine hells), but remain unnamed. This is evidence that the Mayas had, like the Aztecs, a vertical world, layers of heavens and hells to which the dead souls journeyed. These afterlife dwelling places had no moral significance. In the Maya mythology one was not rewarded, as in the Christian mythology, for pious or useful acts. Where you went after death depended more on what you were in life than on what you did. Warriors, fishermen, priests, mothers who died in childbirth, all went to that departmentalized heaven or hell where their tutelary genii lived. Suicides went to their own heaven; they were sacred. They even had their own goddess, Ix Tab. Depicted as hanging from a halter, she can be seen thus illustrated in the *Dresden Codex*.

As everywhere, the survivors had their taboos. They were socially defiled; by the clan custom they must keep the rituals or the dead would come back and claim something from the living. Privations of various kinds were imposed upon them. Her husband's death made a widow "unclean," and so long as the tie to the dead was unsevered, the uncleanliness persisted. As for the dead, they were occupied with getting out of life into death. Martin Luther remarked that he envied the dead because they rest. He was wrong. The dead have much to do—they prepare life.

Thus went the daily round of life (and death) of the Maya lower man. He was the taxpayer by whose tribute in service the temple-cities were built. Above him were the directing classes: the town councilor, the *batab* who collected the tribute, the governor who "sat at the head of the mat," the *chilan*, or soothsayer, the war chief, and highest of all, the hereditary leader—both high priest and great lord, functioning like a baroque archbishop—an embodiment of temporal and secular power, the "true man," the *halach uinic* who sat at the very pinnacle.

○ ○ ○

The Ruling Classes

 The Maya Lords 26

AT THE HEAD of the Maya city-state stood the *halach uinic.* He was *the* man, the "real man," the "true man," endowed with plenary powers and restrained only by a council who were presumably related to him by blood ties. He was absolute and, as in all theocracies, a demigod. When one of these lords met the Spanish conqueror Francisco de Montejo in 1542, even though his lands were laid waste he was still carried on a litter and surrounded by an imposing retinue.

A Maya *halach uinic* surrounded himself with suffocating ritual. He was, said the Spaniards, trying to define him, "the [state's] father, lord and *halach uinic* . . . which in our language is Great Lord. . . . they were absolute and what they ordered was carried out without fail."

Like other demigods the Maya lords were given obeisance by their inferiors. This was similar to the Aztec practice; when a chieftain entered Moctezuma's presence, "he had to take off his rich mantle and put on others of little worth . . . to enter barefoot and not look at his face." The Inca lord was of so exalted a position that all who came before him, even rulers of vast provinces, had to put a symbolical cargo on their backs, as if they were the lowest of Indians.

The Maya lord wore the breechclout, and it was superbly embroidered. The wealth of information on this has been minutely analyzed.[151, 196] His skull was flattened so that it reached a narrow peak at the top, and his face was tattooed, actually scarified. He remodeled his nose with putty, making it a hooked beak to "con-

form with the concept of beauty." The prominent nose is the dominant feature of many stone bas-reliefs (at Yaxchilán, Palenque, and
Tomb Stela 9 at Oxkintok, Yucatán). Hair was allowed to grow
long and into it were braided various ornaments. Ears were perforated and gradually enlarged, and enormous ornaments were passed
through the lobe. (This custom recalls that of the Inca nobles, the
"Big Ears," whom the Spaniards called *Orejones*.) The nose septum
was pierced and a jade ornament passed through the perforation.
The left side of the nostril was perforated and kept open by wooden
plugs, replaced on festive occasions with a topaz that the Spaniards
called "amber."

The Mayas' horror of empty space caused their art to be con-
fusingly luxuriant; every part had to be covered with ornament. Their
bodies were similarly treated; heads flattened, ear lobes widened until
they would admit a turkey egg, the nose perforated and artificially
deformed, the eyes purposely made crossed, facial hair pulled out,
teeth filed and inlaid with jade, face and body tattooed. Finally, even
the penis was transmogrified; this was often so cut that the glans
looked as beribboned as a tassel.

The Mayas sported jade rings on their fingers and toes; wrists
and ankles were cuffed with ornaments. Sandals were often as gaudy
as their loincloths. The Maya lord put over his breechclout a long
skirt, often ankle-length; sometimes the skin of a jaguar was attached
to it. Belts had rows of small human heads, symbolical of course,
but suspiciously like those *tsantsas* made by the head-hunting
Jivaros of the Upper Amazon.

The headgear of the Maya lord was monumental. Often it was
as large as himself. The headpiece was a mask, symbolizing the rain
god or the sun god, and carved of wood or made of wickerwork.
On this framework was elaborated a superb feather ensemble topped
with swirling masses of iridescent green quetzal feathers.

He dressed differently for each of his various offices, religious,
military, or civil; for each he carried a symbol of authority. As
statesman he carried a scepter, and often he is depicted carrying a
shield (a symbol of the sun god). In his religious role he held a
double-headed ceremonial bar of snake heads resting in hallowed
arms. As war leader he wore a sort of body armor and carried lance
and shield; sometimes he is shown standing on the body of a squatting Indian, symbolizing victory.

82. *The ruling chieftain of the Maya was the* halach uinic, *the "true man," as pictured on the Bonampak murals. He is dressed in full costume with the symbols of office. From the murals of Bonampak.*

The glorious headdress of the Maya lord, the focus of his attire, was in contrast to the simple cloth "crown" worn by Moctczuma and a far cry from the "crown" of the Inca, which was a mere *llautu*, a sling worn about the head to which was added "royal fringe." The headdress worn by the Maya "true man" and his cohorts was often so elaborate that it is difficult to think of their moving through the jungle while wearing it. A scene in which headdresses are being made ready appears in the murals of Bonampak. Detachable feather ornaments, mounted on winglike wooden elements shaped like inverted *U*s, are attached to the belt of the Maya lord. The headdress is again as tall as he is and certainly restricted normal movement.

Color was the outstanding feature of Maya costume. In fact, everything in their life, including themselves, was painted. Stucco ornaments were a riot of color. Even the great stone sculptures were colored (traces of the color still remain). They made no point of being drab. It was quite the same with the Greeks, who painted their sculptures in garish colors, a fact which came as a great shock to many modern scholars.

The *halach uinic* had one legitimate wife. Her title is not known. He also had his concubines, although there are no figures as to their number. (Moctezuma had "many women as mistresses," and the Inca rulers has a ménage of royal concubines, *pallas;* one of the last of the Lord-Incas had, in the male line alone, five hundred descendants!) Whatever her title, the wife of the Maya lord was herself "lordly." She was held in high respect, as can be seen from the superb modelings in clay of women of the upper classes. In the Bonampak murals the wife of the *halach uinic* can be seen with head flattened and ears pierced, wearing earrings and a necklace. Her hair is tied up and made into a swirling coiffure. A white *huipil* hangs off the shoulder, and a red stole is draped carelessly around her arms. Her hand holds a folding fan. So modern is her appearance—except for the flattened head—she could walk right out of the murals, which were painted in A.D. 800, and take her place in modern society. There is a queenly aura about her.

The office of the Maya *halach uinic* was neither elective like that of the Aztec ruler, nor selective like that of the Inca, but hereditary. The office descended from father to son. "If the lord died . . . it was the eldest son who succeeded him." However, if the sons were not fit to rule, a brother of the ruler became head of state; and if no one was available for succession, a capable person was chosen by the council, probably a relative of the late lord, with the same patronymic. Such methods of succession were also employed in the valley of Mexico.

Of the precise functions of this "man of the greatest importance" we know no more than a philologist can ferret out of the scant factual material that exists. For the period from 2000 B.C. to A.D. 928 we have nothing other than the interpretation that each scholar wishes to make of what he *feels* that he sees on the sculptured monuments. From A.D. 1000 until the first appearance of the Spaniards in 1502 we have records of a sort, that is, verbal recitative history with Maya glyphs used as mnemonics, and later an interpretation by the men of conquest and the men of God of what they

83. Batabob, *the functional officials in the hierarchy, concerned themselves with administration and the collection of tax tribute. From the Bonampak murals.*

believed to be the order of things. The personal equation is never missing. There is no such thing here as impartial history, for each orders and interprets events according to his own idiosyncracy.

What seems to be fairly clear, however, is this: the functions of the "true man" were as a leader, spiritual and temporal, of a given territory within a Maya city-state. There were many such in Mayadom before A.D. 1000. "They were ruled not by one head, but by man," wrote Diego de Landa. It was not until Mayapán functioned, after A.D. 1194, as "kingdom of the Maya" that one *halach uinic* controlled a great number of cities and geography. "The Kingdom of Yucatán which extends for a length of three hundred leagues [approximately nine hundred miles] was not only filled with people but was ruled by individual lords. . . . they were governed by laws and good customs . . . which is a proof of good government. This was aided a great deal by the fact that they were all of one tongue. And this is a cause of not a little wondering that such a large race and so widely extended, stretching for so many leagues, should be understood with one single language."

First this *halach uinic* was executive of his own city-state. The head chiefs of other towns allied to his were *ahaus,* or, since the word is more dominant, *batabob.* They were local governors of territorial divisions. The lord laid down his extratribal relationships or "foreign policy" through them. They were more than likely related to him by blood ties.

Batabob were "they of the axes." One might almost find the title equivalent to the modern slang term "hatchet men." They carried out the upper man's orders with force, if need be. A *batab* was responsible first for the well-being of his own resident city. He had a staff of bailiffs or deputies to aid him. However, there was a town council composed of chiefs from the various subdivisions of the

84. *Detail of Maya* batabob *conversing over a filled dish. Highland Maya from the Nebaj vase, Chixoy Valley, Alta Vera Paz, Guatemala.*

town, who, though nominally under him, had a veto power on his actions. These councilors were called *ah cuch cabob*. To explain the power and the functions of the council, a Spaniard wrote: "Next in order were the town councilors . . . of whom there was said to be two or three; each had his vote like an official voting in a municipal government in Spain and without his vote nothing could be done. . . ." The council then had direct contact through the clan heads with the lower man. The arbitrary powers of the governor were held in check by these means.

A *batab* had much discretionary power. He was held in awe much as a viceroy would have been. The office was hereditary and the functions were judicial and military. Manpower was raised on a selective proportional basis to build temples, roads, or residences for the nobles. He settled disputes in judicial matters, usually contract violations and land disputes, if the disputants belonged to his own administration (otherwise it went up to the "true man"). When the priests made known their oracles as to when the people should sow, reap, or make merry, the *batab* saw to it that the functions were carried out. In time of war, although he was *de facto* head of the province, actual command was in the hands of a war captain (*nacom*) elected for three years. But when there was an all-out war, such as that against the Spaniards, the *batab* was expected to—and did—appear at the head of his army. When he traveled he was carried on a litter and attended by a large retinue. The people were scattered to allow him passage, and cloaks were spread on the roads for him to pass over. Women served him. He was attended by fan bearers who waved beautiful feather fans and beat the air to drive away the blood-sucking flies and sweat-loving bees. In short, he was treated as a demigod. When Captain Montejo visited the *batab* of Loche in Yucatán during a lull in the battle, the Maya received him reclining à la Récamier, fanned and fawned upon by his flunkies. He spoke to the Spaniard through a cotton cloth curtain suspended between them.

There was enough bureaucracy to satisfy the most exacting—governors, bailiffs, war captains, and so down to the very lowest, the *tupil,* a kind of constable.

All were of the upper classes and nontaxable.

The state's, or rather the *halach uinic's,* income to maintain all this was derived from the food tax, produce tax, and service performed by the lower man. Each inhabitant of village, town, or city-state, collectively or singly, contributed maize, beans, chili, poultry, deer, honey, wood, wax, copal, cloth, salt, fish, jade, or whatever he produced. There are no records of Maya contributions such as are available for Aztec history. However, one known record of tribute is enough for an example. One small village, Tahdziu, of twenty households, paid an annual direct tax to their lord of twenty loads of maize (approximately twelve hundred pounds) and twenty turkeys. If one then considers a city-state of fifty thousand people, the amount of tribute tax would be considerable. The chieftain then traded this in the gross through merchants for cacao or slaves, which in turn were retraded in the local markets for feathers, jade, and, later in Maya history, gold and silver.

There are no details of the court that surrounded the *halach uinic.* The Spaniards have left word pictures of Moctezuma attended by a concourse of lords, wives, and concubines; of a table where he ate like some grand vizier; of retinues of servants who attended chieftains from other lands and how these chiefs and their wives and concubines "filled two or three courtyards and overflowed into the street"; of how the royal aviary had ten large pools of water and was attended by 150 people. And as to the Inca who lorded over Peru, we have exquisite details of his life, concubines, royal will; of the thousands who attended him; of his clothes, woven of the finest vicuña, which were never worn more than once. But if the Maya *halach uinic* led a similar existence and was similarly attended, we must be content to surmise it. The stone monuments and painted murals suggest it, but that is all. The Maya glyph writing, which was intricate enough to count the steps to the moon, is silent on the details of their lives.

27   *Government — City-State and Village*

How WELL did such a theocracy function? Diego de Landa thought it functioned very well: "Before the Spaniards had conquered that country, the natives lived together in towns in a very civilized fashion. They kept the land well cleared of weeds, and planted very good trees. The manner and order of their towns was as follows—in the middle of the town were their temples with beautiful plazas; all around the temples stood the houses of the lords and the priests, and then came the houses of the most important officials. Next were the homes of the rich men, and then those of the merchants who were held in the highest estimation, and at the outskirts of the town were the houses of the lower classes."

The theory of most archaeologists is that the Maya city "was not a city at all in our sense of the word because it was a ceremonial, not an urban center." There is indeed little archaeological evidence of Maya cities; most of the buildings found are temples, pyramids, and ceremonial structures. Dwellings were built on clay platforms and made of perishable materials, wattle and daub, and thatched with straw. These were obliterated by the centuries of cultivation about them. However, among those towns of the highland Maya recently studied [176]—which have been subject to less destruction than those in the humid areas—there are those that do show an urban Maya pattern. Of the hundreds of sites that were surveyed (dates range between A.D. 300 and 1200), these highland towns reveal the essentials of urban planning. Whether the town conformed to the terrain or to the caprice of the builder, it contained certain common features: the central ceremonial court, surrounded by a large plaza where markets were held, and in the following echelon were the houses of chiefs, priests, and the other functionaries— and after them the houses of the common people. A ball court, if not part of the sacred precincts, was close by. A. Ledyard Smith found these sites "with buildings arranged in orderly fashion and orientated with each other." Thus archaeology agrees in general with Diego de Landa's description of the form and function of a Maya city. The Mayas' theocratic spirit was similar to that of the absolute monarchs of the European baroque, who were aware of the emotional interplay between power and a monument of enormous dimensions and a parade street. Absolutism and enormous plazas belong together.

The immense city-states built by the Mayas presuppose a high degree of social organization. A city structure must be planned. Manpower has to be organized and close at hand if the buildings are elaborate, as most Maya temples were. Artisans had to be trained and available. The earliest and the greatest of Maya cities was Tikal. It was so immense that its full size has not yet been determined. At present it is calculated to cover over twenty-five acres of jungle. The great court, lying roughly in its center, is 400 by 250 feet in size. About it are its tallest pyramids, the largest of which towers 229 feet above the plaza. There are many other such and hundreds of structures, from small plazas to enormous reservoirs, broad causeways, ball courts, and a still undetermined number of lesser monuments. Each of these large pyramids contains something like 260,000 cubic yards of filling. It would require something like 100,000 man-hours merely to place the core. The number of skilled artisans needed to cut and lay the stone, to plaster, carve, and cast, can not be determined readily. Tikal consists of forty large structures and two hundred lesser ones. How much manpower was needed to raise these immense piles in a hostile jungle is incalculable, especially when it is remembered that the Mayas had neither metal instruments nor draft animals. Moreover, there was presumably no professional labor force, since every man was a craftsman of lesser or higher degree.

The Maya temple-city was a civil as well as religious center. It was *le fait urban,* a townscape with buildings. [141] The reason one

finds no evidence of city housing at such sites as Copán, Tikal, and
Palenque is that the dwellings were made of very perishable materials and have vanished, leaving nothing behind except the remains
of postholes. To find and to outline such a city is a laborious and
often unrewarding archaeological labor, but to argue that such a city
as Tikal could have been built by a people whose houses were
scattered at random throughout the jungle, miles from the center,
provides no idea of how the cities were erected or how such a
society functioned.

Mayapán was the only known organized Maya capital. The evidence of its existence is authentic—a written glyph history, a long
tradition, and the proof offered by archaeological excavation. Since
it is the only Maya site that has all these, it is the site that one must
examine to form some idea of the structure and function of the
Maya city. Mayapán was founded in 987 (or 941) after the Itzás, with
the aid of the Toltecs, had taken possession of Chichén Itzá and
the surrounding areas; it was, however, not really functional as a
capital until after 1200. The Itzás were Maya-speaking, using
Chontal, a Maya dialect. They came, it is believed, from Tabasco,
the lands that produced much of the cacao-chocolate which was a
Maya obsession. The precise time of their appearance in Yucatán is
still not fixed. Although the date for their reoccupation of Chichén
Itzá is generally given as 987, Eric Thompson reads certain dates
at this city to suggest that Mexican architecture had already made
an appearance there in 889. Precisely who the Itzás were, and what
the name of their leader was also confused Diego de Landa
when he was gathering his histories. ". . . . the indians differ
among themselves, as to whether Kukulkan arrived before or after
the Itzás or with them." But they did arrive. And those who came
with the Itzás were not Maya. The Toltecs brought with them so
precise a rendering of the temples which stood in faraway Tula in
Mexico, seven hundred fifty miles from Chichén Itzá, that many of
the architectural motifs and decorations are echoes of Tula, the last
capital of the Toltecs.

Mayapán gave its name, which means "standard of the Mayas,"
to the league of city-states in which it was, according to tradition,
associated with Chichén Itzá and Uxmal. The league probably
controlled much more than this. A Spanish report states that
Mayapán "conquered all these provinces," and time and explor-

XXI. *One of the four stairways of the Pyramid of Kukulcán at Chichén Itzá. While restoring the pyramid, archaeologists of the Carnegie Institution found that it was built over an older, inner one. The original pyramid contains a startling life-size jaguar with jade spots.* (Victor W. von Hagen)

XXII. *Temple of the Warriors at Chichén Itzá. It is so called because of the hundreds of columns with carved warriors. The temple is a copy, in all of its main features, of the Toltec temple at Tula, Mexico, 800 miles northwest of Yucatán.* (Silvia von Hagen)

XXIII. *The observatory at Chichén Itzá.* (Victor W. von Hagen)

XXIV. *The building called the Monjas in the Nunnery Triangle at Chichén Itzá. It is south of the main group, in what is regarded as the older part of the city. The structural features are typical of Puuc architecture. The same motifs appear in Uxmal, Kabah, and other Maya sites far removed from Chichén.* (Silvia von Hagen)

XXV. *The Pyramid of Kukulcán at Chichén Itzá in Yucatán. Chichén Itzá was founded by Itzá-Maya emigrants from central Mayadom in the fifth century and was occupied by the Toltecs between the tenth and thirteenth centuries, during which time this pyramid was built.* (Victor W. von Hagen)

XXVI. *View of Uxmal from the Governor's Palace. On the right is the Temple of Kukulcán.* (Andor Braun)

XXVII. *Detail of the Governor's Palace at Uxmal. It is 320 feet long, 40 feet wide, 26 feet high, and rests on an artificially raised triple terrace that is 50 feet high. It covers five acres of ground, and was probably the administrative center of the city-state of Uxmal, which included many other sites, some known, some lost.* (Andor Braun)

XXVIII. *Sayil (circa* A.D. *800) is five miles northeast of Kabah. It has one imposing building, Casa Cerrada, with Doric-like pillars. In the hills beyond Sayil are other structures, as yet unexplored.* (Victor W. von Hagen)

XXIX. *Chac, the long-nosed rain god (the nose is broken here), as seen on a façade of the ruins of Sayil.* (Victor W. von Hagen)

XXX. *The gateway and the building presumed to be the priestly residence at Labná. This impressive site lies ten miles beyond Sayil. The architecture is Puuc in character.* (Victor W. von Hagen)

XXXI. *A stone disk from Chiapas. The figure represents a ballplayer in full action; note how the arm and diaphragm are covered for protection (arch- aeological evidence that the ball was butted through the stone "basket").* (José Limón)

XXXII. *Copán is famed for the majesty of its stelae. This is Stela P, erected in* A.D. 623. (Victor W. von Hagen)

XXXIII. *A grotesque head of a serpent god, one of two similar figures guarding the approaches to the Hieroglyphic Stairway at Copán.* (Victor W. von Hagen)

XXXIV. *The beaches of Tulum, showing a portion of the central temple. On calm days the sands gleam whitely, but during a storm immense waves are hurled against the limestone cliffs.* (Victor W. von Hagen)

XXXV. *This stela is one of the twenty sculptured time markers at Tikal; the other sixtythree are plain.* (Victor W. von Hagen)

XXXVI. *Sculptured profile of the sun god in low relief, found in the debris about the court of the Hieroglyphic Stairway at Copán.* (Victor W. von Hagen)

XXXVII. *Dzibilchaltún ("where-there-is-writing-on-flat-stones"). The Temple of the Dolls, the first of the restored buildings of an immense Maya city, dating back to 1500 B.C., near Mérida, Yucatán. The stela on the platform is not carved; it is believed that the inscriptions were done either in stucco or painted.* (Victor W. von Hagen)

XXXVIII. *The windows in the Temple of the Dolls at Dzibilchaltún are an unusual feature in Maya architecture. Ungraceful, almost crude in concept, this is the beginning of Maya architecture.* (Victor W. von Hagen)

ation in this area will reveal through the roads that lead to Mayapán that it was specifically erected for the purpose of controlling most of the north of Yucatán. The towns, villages, and city-states controlled by the league were so many, said Diego de Landa, "that the whole land appeared to be one town." In 1194, as victor in a war with Chichén Itzá, Mayapán became the major power in northern Yucatán.

There had been a previous settlement at Mayapán, but its name is not known. Since the "natural Maya lords" had warred with one another for a thousand years over slave-raiding expeditions, it must have been difficult to determine where among the three cities the League of Mayapán should place its capital; presumably the old site was chosen to avoid squabbling. The availability of water must have been inviting; within the walled enclosure have been found at least nineteen usable *cenotes*. Around the city was built a wall of dry-laid stone over twelve feet in height, from nine to twelve feet in thickness, and five and a half miles long. It had nine formal entrances; the gates measured between three and six feet in width and so were easy to defend. The area within the city has been calculated to have been two and a half square miles. "In the center of Mayapán they built a pyramid, which is like that of Chichén Itzá" (except that it was smaller). Archaeology has confirmed Landa's statement. The four stairways of the pyramid were oriented in the four cardinal directions.

The houses of the principal nobles were located close to the central plaza. In fact, all of the "natural lords" of the country were obliged to build a house within Mayapán and dwell therein for certain seasons of the year. This was similar to a custom of the Incas; when they conquered new territory the chieftains were required to reside in Cuzco to insure their loyalty.

Mayapán was divided for administrative purposes into four quarters, corresponding to the cardinal directions. It had its markets, its officials, and even a system to care for the socially unfit. "It was the custom to seek in the towns for the maimed and blind and there they supplied their needs." An early Spanish report said that Mayapán, "walled in like those cities of Spain, had within sixty thousand dwellings." A modern survey by Morris Jones reveals more than thirty-five hundred houses, but to account somewhat for the discrepancy between the two estimates, there have been four hundred years of tree growth and destruction. Moreover, the modern calculation was made from an air survey. Take then the thirty-five hundred houses; this would presuppose a population of over twenty thousand inhabitants. As it was, there was overcrowding. The Maya informants of Diego de Landa told him—since the city had been destroyed and abandoned only in 1441, the information was still un-clouded—that the governing lords "ordered that houses should be constructed outside the walls."

In each house a Maya lord kept his *caluac,* a sort of major-domo, who made himself known by a wand of office which he sported when he went to the center of the city "for what was needed . . . birds, maize, honey, salt, fish, game, cloth, and other things because each of these houses outside of the walls was, as it were, the office of his lord." The merchants, a rising new class within the Maya realm, also had their houses in the city. As in all urban societies, the dollar patricians tended to move into the orbit of the upper classes.

Mayapán was administered jointly by two tribal dynasties, the Cocoms, who claimed the closest descent from the Toltecs, and the Tutul Xius, who, through the Itzás, believed themselves claimants to the rule left by Kukulcán. "These lords of Mayapán," explained Diego de Landa, "held the entire country in subjection and the natives of it were tributary to them. All the citizens and inhabitants who lived within the walled enclosure of Mayapán were exempt from tribute tax and in it dwelt all the nobles of the land. . . . the lands were held in common so that between the towns there were no boundaries or landmarks. . . . salt beds were also held in common [which bears out the author's contention that the League of Mayapán extended beyond the three cities] in those provinces on the northern sea coast which supplied all the inhabitants of the land."

During the two and a half centuries that Mayapán functioned as a capital, its administrators were appointed by the *halach uinic.* Selection of qualified men was based on some sort of examination. It was called the "interrogation of the chiefs" and occurred every *katun,* i.e., every twenty years. A candidate had to offer proof of his legitimacy, his nobility, and that he knew the traditions and the occult "language of Zuyua." In this way there was a weeding out of misfits. However, most offices were hereditary. "The lords appointed the governors and if they were acceptable they confirmed their sons

in office," so that the office of *batab* became in time like the
Italian podesta; it was *de facto* hereditary.

Mayapán, then, had all the elements, physiognomic and political,
of an urban organization. Moreover, it was not unique. Tulum is a
walled city which lies on the open sea; it was Mayapán on a
smaller scale and dates from the Old Empire. Another walled city,
Xelha, lies a few miles farther north on the same coast. It also
antedates Mayapán and was connected with the interior city of
Cobá by one of the longest and best-known causeways. Cobá itself
dates from the Old Empire. Although modified in some ways by
the Itzás, the idea of the city as shown by Mayapán is doubtless
Maya.

Mayapán did not have the ordered beauty of Chichén Itzá. It is
considered to be a "sad degeneration" of the latter; the stones are
roughly dressed and the masons covered up the casual construction
with stucco. The Castillo is almost a replica of the one at Chichén
Itzá, except that the former is smaller. The citizens of Mayapán
built four rounded structures therein, fashioned something like the
famed Caracol at Chichén Itzá (which is presumed to have been a
form of astronomical observatory), and there are remains of a long
colonnaded hall as at the Temple of the Warriors in the more
famous city. However, it is not worked stone but plaster. The word
"decadent" has been applied to it by some archaeologists. The fine
Puuc architecture—which includes Uxmal, Kabah, and Sayil—is
also sometimes referred to as "decadent." This architecture is different, not decadent. There is nothing in the records that allows
so moralistic an appraisal of Mayapán as has stirred the otherwise
judiciously calm Dr. Eric Thompson. Thompson believes that
Mayapán represented a shift from a fairly peaceful theocracy to a
warlike lay autocracy. Insistence on the "peaceful" attitude of the
Mayas, in view of the blood and rapine shown in their sculpture
and the murals at Bonampak, is an atavism of archaeology. Thompson refers to "militaristically organized groups . . . aggressive dic-
tatorships," and insists in the face of overwhelming evidence that
the earlier Mayas were peaceful stargazers and compilers of data
on astronomical phenomena. The contrary screams at him from
most of the sculpture and mural illustrations. There are, said
Nietzsche, no such things as moral phenomena; there is only a
moral interpretation of phenomena.

Though founded very late in Maya history, Mayapán is as "early" as the capitals of the other theocratic Sun Kingdoms of America. Cuzco, the celebrated capital of the Incas, was not the capital before 1100, and the island capital of the Aztecs, Tenochtitlán, was not even founded until 1325.

In 1194, this "dual monarchy" of Mayapán, after two hundred years of joint administration, exploded in violence. Chichén Itzá, one of the cities of the League of Mayapán, was held by the Tutul Xius, the hereditary rivals of the Cocoms. Since the strength of each of them was almost equal, the Cocoms went to Xicalango and hired a small army of Toltecs who had gathered there, for in 1156 Tula was burned and destroyed by the Chichimecs and this forced more of the Tula-Toltecs to migrate (as had Quetzalcoatl and others in the last part of the tenth century). Their bows and arrows and spears, with the deadly atl-atl, the throwing device, were for hire. Huanc Ceel, leader of the Cocoms, introduced the Mexicans into Yucatán. All sources, for once, agree on this; the very same names given for their chieftains is Mexican. Their capture of Chichén Itzá is pictured on the frescoes, the bas-reliefs, and even on the golden disks that were thrown into the *cenote* and dredged up in the nineteenth century. The contrast between Mexican and Maya, in dress, person, and weapons, is easily discernible. With the rivals of the Cocoms expelled from Chichén Itzá and its environs, this city was rebuilt.

Mayapán was now the dominant city, and the Cocoms the ruling element. The other contending dynasty, the Tutul Xius, were not fully quiescent; they nurtured their hate for two hundred fifty years. (This contention for the rule of Yucatán is reminiscent of the struggles of the Guelphs and the Ghibellines which were occurring about the same period in Italy.) In 1441 (or a date within ten years of that) a chieftain named Ah Xupán of the Tutul Xius, in conspiracy with others within the walled city of Mayapán, engineered a carefully arranged revolt. It was planned to occur when all the ruling members of the Cocoms were within the city walls. When the slaughter occurred, all of the chieftains were killed, save one who at the time was off on a trading expedition to Honduras.

There are native records of the fall of Mayapán, for it was a live and throbbing story when the Spaniards arrived seventy-five years

later. There survives in one of the Maya chronicles a murky echo
of it in deep and powerful poetry:

> *This is the pronouncement of 7 Ahau.*
> *This was when there occurred the death of Mayapán.*
> *Evil is the pronouncement of the Katun in its great power . . .*
> *Thus is reoccurred when the great priest Chilam Balam*
> *painted the aspect of the Katun 8 Ahau.**

Collective hatred is an easy thing to drum up. As Aldous
Huxley says, "Hate is like lust in its irresistible urgency; it is, however, more dangerous than lust, because it is passion less closely
dependent on the body. . . . Hate . . . has what lust entirely lacks
—persistence and continuity. . . ."

The attack on Mayapán had just that sort of "persistence and
continuity"; the walls of buildings were pulled down, and the
statuary, principally of the god Quetzalocoatl, which most of the
inhabitants seemed to have kept in individual shrines, was smashed,
showing the violence of the onslaught.**

It was the end of the only known capital of the Maya.[150]

* Ahau is the name of a *katun*, a period in the Maya calendar, 7,200 days (twenty years
of 360 days). 8-Ahau ran from 1441 to 1460; within that time it is certain that the
destruction of Mayapán occurred.

** John L. Stephens and Catherwood first observed Mayapán in 1841. No archaeologist
thought much of Mayapán until Morley in 1938 made the first investigation. This was
followed by Carnegie's "first team" under the direction of H. W. S. Pollock in 1952.
A. Ledyard Smith and Karl Ruppert were assigned to study the houses and burials; Edwin
Shook, superintending Tikal, worked on and investigated pottery styles; Gustav
Stromvik had charge of some restoration; Robert Smith worked on pottery sequences;
Tatiana Proskouriakoff worked on mapping and architectural restorations. The data still
await publication.

O O O O

The Achievements

28   *Architecture*

T<small>HE MAYAS</small> have left behind a mass of structures that forever will remain a monument to their aesthetic sensibil-
ities—and their muscular energy.[149] Cities and ceremonial centers
are found geographically everywhere throughout Mayadom, and in
every conceivable landscape—on the edge of the sea, in the flat,
dry interior along the sides of rivers, beside lakes, and in the
jungles. The cities varied in size and purpose. There were those,
such as Tulum and Mayapán, where the whole seemed to be a city
in miniature. There were others, such as Tikal, where pyramids
soared 229 feet high to dwarf the jungle. Others stretched along
the rivers. Most structures were built of stone, since limestone was
usually available. When it was not, they used baked brick with
stucco for ornamentation.

This architecture differed from that of the other Sun Kingdom
civilizations because of the use the Mayas made of lime mortar.
Their buildings, said one writer, "are essentially monoliths of rubble and lime with an exterior veneer of cut stone."

Just as the use of the arch and a superior, almost imperishable,
mortar were the distinguishing characteristics of Roman architecture, lime mortar and the corbeled arch distinguish that of the
Maya. Pulverized limestone makes a cement that forms so tight a
bond with the cut stone that the whole structure appears to
be monolithic. When the cement had hardened, the building was
polished and glazed. Bark was stripped off the *chocom* tree and
soaked in vats of water. The resulting solution was applied to the

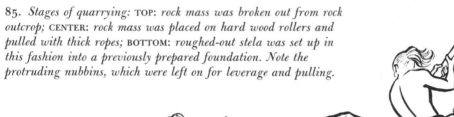

85. *Stages of quarrying:* TOP: *rock mass was broken out from rock outcrop;* CENTER: *rock mass was placed on hard wood rollers and pulled with thick ropes;* BOTTOM: *roughed-out stela was set up in this fashion into a previously prepared foundation. Note the protruding nubbins, which were left on for leverage and pulling.*

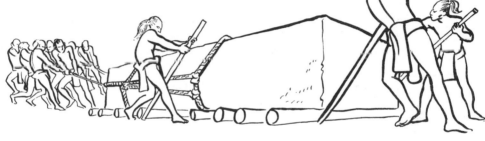

walls, which when dry took a superb polish, becoming impervious to rain and in time turning a bright brick-red.

Stone was quarried, shaped, and sculptured with stone, metals such as gold and soft copper coming very late to the Mayas. Danish Neolithic peoples used thin-butted, polished-stone blades, and a reconstruction of such axes shows them to be empirically effective; a large tree can be felled within one hour. The cutting edges of stone axes are almost as sharp as steel, and they can be sharpened by rechipping. Similar stone hammers and chisels were the tools of the Maya builder.

Plans for Maya buildings were made on either paper or wood, all perishable. There must have been a unit of measurement, although no one has succeeded in discovering it. They doubless had, like the Incas, professional builders or architects, that is, nontaxpaying specialists. Yet as great as is Tikal, not one architect's name has come down to us.

The *na*, the simple fascine house daubed with wood and thatched with palm leaf, was the humble origin of Maya architecture. The Mayas acknowledged this on one façade of the finest building in the Puuc, the Nunnery Quadrangle at Uxmal, where some sculptor depicted a series of these houses as decorative motifs.

Inca architecture also evolved from the simple native house, in their case the *wasi*, built of field stone and adobe cement. The Vitruvian theory, which holds that features of stone temple construction derive from wooden house prototypes, can apply to many cultures.

Out of this house of the "eternal peasant," the Mayas shaped the most distinctive feature of their architecture, the corbeled arch. In this, the stones are placed so that each projects beyond the one below it; eventually the walls meet and a vault is formed. To support this type of arch, a weight mass was necessary. This developed into the roof comb, an overhang to act as cantilever to the vaulting, that became for Maya sculpture a façade on which to lavish intricate and swirling design. The Mayas have been known to raise a massive pyramid with an estimated 260,000 cubic yards of fill, only to place at its pinnacle a building of less than 150 feet square. Aware of the self-limiting aspect of the corbeled arch, the Maya later used massive wooden beams and wooden lintels as well; these were made of sapodilla, a metal-hard wood. They counted on everything but the termites.

The sheer number of Maya remains is staggering. No one has yet tried to give them a precise figure. Those ruins which have been surveyed and photographed run into the hundreds while those which have been merely noted total even more. It can only be surmised that the scrub jungles and the rain forests yet hold hundreds more from man's sight.

Aside from cities and ceremonial centers, there is in the Maya architectural vocabulary a variety of other specialized constructions —ball courts, gateways, sweat baths, vaulted bridges, and raised platforms where plays were performed. Much of this the early Spaniards saw while it was still in its pristine form. When Grijalva sailed along the coast he saw "three towns separated from each other by about two miles. . . . There were many houses of stone, very tall towers . . . and then a city or town so large that Seville would not have seemed more considerable." Uxmal had been seen and described (looking "like a painting of Flanders") by Antonio Ciudad-Real, a priest of facile intelligence who wrote *Of the Very*

86. *The carving of Stela E at Quirigua, close to Copán. The intricate design and complicated calendric computations were first worked out on paper and painted boards. The base material here was a coarse red sandstone; the tool was the basalt stone celt.*

Renowned Edifices of Uxmal. He described the façades, "carved with wonderful delicacy," and remarked on the glyphs that appeared on the sides of the buildings, "carved with so great a dexterity as surely to excite admiration." Diego de Landa said that "there are in Yucatán many beautiful buildings, which is the most remarkable thing that has been found in the Indies." In Izamal there was, for example, "a building of such height and beauty that it astonishes one. . . . And Chichén Itzá, a very fine site where there are many magnificent buildings . . . and around the sacrificial *cenote* can be found . . . buildings of the country almost like the Pantheon at Rome."

So many of these stone cities were there that Landa said "the whole land appeared to be one town." And so many are the remains of these cities today that neither this nor any one book could hope to cover all in full detail. Besides, to say everything is to say nothing. Here then is a selection of Maya cities with brief accounts of their form and function.

Uaxactún (A.D. 328) is located where one might believe that men with a wide choice would never found a city, in the low, humid junglebound El Petén. It is (at this moment of writing) the oldest known Maya city. Here are found, too, the finest examples of polychromic pottery, and until Bonampak was discovered, it had the finest murals extant—spirited figures painted in red, orange, yellow, gray, and black on a whitened background.

There are eight principal groups of buildings. The low-lying hills were artificially leveled and then built up into a series of large and small plazas. These lie close together and are connected by wide causeways. The principal temple pyramid, although only twenty-seven feet high, is interesting since it shows the evolution of the pyramid form, which in near-by Tikal was to soar over two hundred feet in height. The wide stairway is ornamented by grotesque stucco masks eight feet high. An interesting study has been made of the evolution of the temple complex from the original palm-thatched native house. In a series of isometric drawings it can be seen that the first structure was a raised stone-adobe platform on which rested a wooden house (the postholes of this have been found). In the next stage of development, three identical temples were built with similar stairways and decorated roof crests facing each other. A high priest, having died, was buried in the plaza;

the floor level was raised to contain his tomb and a similar temple, presumably above the grave, was added. Slowly, with the accretion of years and techniques, the temple evolved into a complex of buildings.

Tikal (A.D. 416) was the largest of Maya cities. Although it is only thirty-five miles from Uaxactún (they were connected by a causeway), its format is different. Tikal rests on a gigantic limestone outcrop. The surrounding forest is as thickly treed as the Amazon.

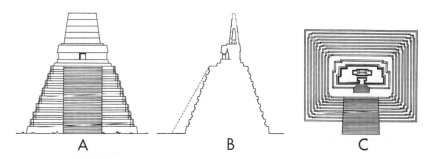

A   B   C

87. *Architectural form and structure of Temple V, Tikal. This temple, south of the great plaza, faced the south ravine, which was a water reservoir,* A) *The elevation, showing handling of mass.* B) *A profile that exhibits the manner of crowning the truncated pyramid.* C) *The structure; note the narrowness of the room caused by corbeled arching. Taken from the drawings of Maler, Tozzer, and J. A. Gomez.*

Cedars, mahogany, palms, and the strangler *Ficus* are dominant. Jaguars, tapirs, and snakes prowl the jungle floor, while monkeys and a variety of birds rule the treetops. It is here that these machineless men built their greatest city.

On an artificially leveled tongue of limerock, between two ravines, the center of Tikal, civil and ceremonial, was built. Since there was a lack of dependable water supply, even with a high incidence of rainfall, the two ravines were converted into reservoirs and spanned by a raised causeway that is also a dam. There are five separate groups of buildings all connected by wide causeways, covering a square mile. Beyond this in every direction Tikal stretches out for several miles. So immense is the site that no one has yet even attempted a definite calculation. Since 1956 the long-held dream of archaeologists has been in the process of realization: the

University of Pennsylvania is now at this moment of writing excavating and restoring the ruins.

Tikal is best known for the number of its monuments; thus far
eighty-three stelae and fifty-four altars have been found. The city
has the finest wood carvings known in the entire Maya area, twelve
doorways and lintels carved on sapodilla wood, of which the first
and the finest was carried off to a Swiss museum.

The pyramids of Tikal, which push their verdure-covered heads
above the jungle, arrogantly towering above all else, were, one may
well assume, its pride. Interior space was sacrificed to height and
grandeur. In the great court, in the center of Tikal, two of these
massive pyramid-temples face each other. In the plaza, which measures 400 by 250 feet, stands a structure not unlike a Mesopotamian
ziggurat; it rises to 229 feet. A stone staircase follows the setback
structure to its apex. There, with decorated roof crest, is the
temple—three dimly lit rooms with a gross space of less than 150
square feet. It is for this that Maya laborers worked incredibly long
years to carry on their backs enough limestone rubble to fill
260,000 cubic yards. It is estimated that twenty-five thousand man-
hours were required merely to build up the core of one of these
pyramids. To cut, set, and finish the stone of the surface and rear
the temple, with its florid and decorated roof crest, cannot be easily
calculated. This must have cost the skilled masons twice as many
man-hours as were required to build the inner core.

Next, lime mortar had to be made. It has been estimated that
one sixteenth of most Maya structures is lime mortar. To reduce
limestone to cement, which was done by burning, required four
times as much wood, by volume, as limestone. For every twenty-
one cubic yards of lime cement, a cord of wood was consumed.
The immense labor service needed merely to fell trees with stone
axes, then carry the wood to the lime kilns, can be grasped if not
precisely calculated.

At Tikal there are eight such immense temple pyramids. Lesser
structures—palaces or habitations—total ten times this number.
There were acres of stucco surface to cover, and many of these
structures are covered with glyphs. The mind reels at the thought
of the organization required merely to supply labor to a city such
as Tikal.

According to its own records, Tikal survived from A.D. 416

until 869, though it is possible that it was reoccupied briefly in the fourteenth century by the Itzás. Its existence was made known to the outside world in 1696, when a Franciscan monk, Andrés de Avendaño, on his way to "reduce" the remaining Mayas about Lake Petén, stumbled upon "a number of ancient buildings which although they were very high and my strength very little, I climbed."

San José (A.D. 435), minuscule when compared to the other Maya centers, is situated in British Honduras, less than fifty miles from Tikal, with which it was, in all probability, bound by causeway. No one knows what its Maya name was. San José lies in the ancient Maya area called Chetumal Province, where cacao was raised and canoes manufactured. Here Gonzalo Guerrero, Spanish castaway-slave turned Maya war chief, repelled the Spanish conquistadors.

San José is small, still it conveys an idea of what smaller ceremonial centers were like. There are four building groups set on artificially leveled hills. The larger is composed of temples and a habitation complex; another has a modest pyramid fifty feet high. There is also a water reservoir and the inevitable ball court. The decoration shows sophistication. The head of the maize god is a lively piece of imagery, and the polychromic pottery found there is similar to that of Uaxactún, where the best in Mayadom has been found. This pottery shows a continuous occupation from A.D. 435 up to the Toltec period (987) and perhaps beyond. A thousand or more families lived about the center or within reach of it. Although small, its tastes were cosmopolitan; trade pieces found within the graves show that it imported shells from the Pacific, obsidian from Zacapa, copper from Mexico, marble drinking vessels from Ulúa in Honduras, spindle whorls from faraway Huasteca (which, as the *zopolote* flies, is a good thousand miles north). San José is listed here not because of anything spectacular, but because Eric Thompson, its excavator, thought it to be a "small-scale ceremonial center of which there must be literally scores" still buried in the jungles.

Copán (A.D. 460) the most southern of the great Maya cities, lies at an altitude of 2,000 feet in what is now Honduras. It was bound to those cities already mentioned by sea road and land road. Copán was built at the edge of the Copán River, which flows into the Motagua River, which in turn debouches into the Gulf of Honduras near Omoa, in ancient times a large Yucatán trading post.

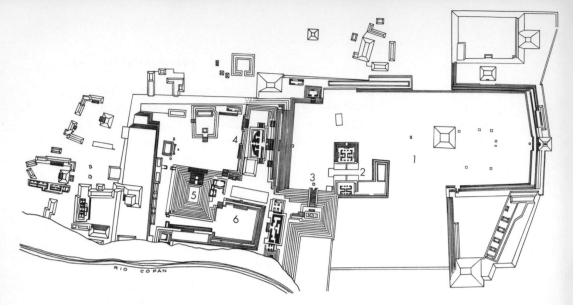

88. *Plan of the Maya acropolis at Copán, Honduras.*
1) *The main plaza; its extreme length is over eight hundred feet. Scattered about the plaza are the dated stelae for which Copán is famed.* 2) *The ceremonial ball court.* 3) *Temple 26, crowning the Hieroglyphic Stairway finished 756 A.D.* 4) *The eastern courtyard, dominated by the feline heads with snakes issuing from the mouths.* 5) *The pyramid with adjoining structures.* 6) *The western courtyard with the Jaguar Stairway. Taken from S. G. Morley,* The Ancient Maya, *Stanford University Press, 1946, Plate 34, with additions.*

The region was known for its cacao and obsidian, its fine Ulúa marble vases. In the high rain forests was the habitat of the red-green *guacamayo* and the quetzal. It was the only Maya city to be known, at least in the literature, outside of the Yucatán peninsula area. Diego García de Palacio, a judge of the Audiencia Real de Guatemala, was led to Copán in 1576. He wrote in a speculative letter to Philip II; "They say that in olden times a great lord of the Province of Yucatán came here, built these buildings . . . returned home and left them empty. . . . According to this book, which I have . . . it seems that in ancient times people from Yucatán did conquer these provinces." It was the same Copán that was purchased for fifty dollars by John Lloyd Stephens more than two and a half centuries later.

Copán covers seventy-five acres; beyond this rather vast acreage lived the people. It is the second largest of Maya cities and composed of five main plazas and sixteen subgroups. The enormous main plaza, surrounded by tiers of stone seats, has been likened to the Roman Circus Maximus. The compact acropolis, overlooking the Copán River, is an amazingly wonderful complex of temples. In the eastern courtyard are tiers of stone seats and, at one end, the Jaguar Stairway, flanked by the stone jaguars from which its name is derived. The animals are rampant, one forepaw outstretched, the other akimbo. Their coats were spotted with rounded pieces of inlaid obsidian. The architects of the temple that dominates the courtyard made use of a squatting stone Maya figure to support a panel that is obviously allegorical—a cacoplastic *mélange* of arms, gnomelike figures, dragonlike heads, a design that is mobile, moving out into space, formless yet form-consuming.

In the western court is the Reviewing Stand, which is dominated by a god entwined by a snake, in the fashion of Laocoön. From the same courtyard rises the famed Hieroglyphic Stairway, thirty feet in width and sixty-three treads in height. Each tread is decorated with a running commentary of glyphs. The dates, which alone have been deciphered, show that it was dedicated in A.D. 756. It is calculated that there must be twenty-five hundred glyphs in the stairway.[132] Stephens hoped that when read they would reveal the "entire history of the city," but since only ten treads were found in their original positions, the restoration, completed in 1942, is at best tentative and conjectural.

Beyond this is the great plaza, at one end of which is a small temple. Carved and dated stelae, the most beautiful in Mayadom, are scattered throughout this area.

Copán was no isolated city. Near by is Quirigua, which is believed to have been intimately connected with its history.[131] Northeast of it are several other known Maya sites.

Palenque (A.D. 642) is 280 miles northwest of Copán. No direct trade contact between the two cities has been established, but their art, sculpture, calendric system, and glyph writing are similar. The two cities are separated by rivers, high mountains, deep ravines, thick jungles, and almost three hundred miles. Geography did not prevent the interchange of intellectual ideas between independent Maya city-states. Despite political disunity, there was a cultural unity.

Palenque is the Spanish for "palisade." The Maya name for the city has not been revealed by its multitude of glyphs. Palenque is unique in that modern Maya history began there. What it has lately revealed and is expected to reveal has changed our concept of Maya history.

89. *Stucco figures in relief from the façade of House D at Palenque. The art of stucco sculpture reached its height at Palenque during the ninth century* A.D.

The city is barely visible in a sea of jungle. Set at a 1,000-foot altitude in the Chiapas forests, near a small river (the Otolum, a tributary of the Usumacinta), Palenque by river travel is less than eighty miles from Xicalango, the great trading center, with which it had trade connections. The city became known in 1773, when an Indian brought it to the attention of a priest who, amazed by all he saw, drew up a report. It was later visited by a Spanish captain of engineers, who wrought havoc there with his battery ram techniques. He was accompanied by an Italian architect, Antonio Bernaconi, in the Spanish service. When these reports were brought to the personal attention of Charles III of Spain, a ruler of the Enlightenment, he ordered that all antiquities found at Palenque be well preserved so that they could illustrate an *Historia antigua de América.*

The history of the exploration of Palenque covers two centuries. Many of the explorers of Palenque were later persons of distinction, such as Count Waldeck, a wonderfully baroque character.[36] He showed up at Palenque in 1832, at the age of sixty-four. The places of his birth are given variously as Paris, Prague, and Vienna. Waldeck was characterized by an observer as "a racy and on the whole, despite dubious foibles, attractive personality." Of himself he modestly said, "I am the first competent person who occupied himself with the ruins of Central America." However, his facile drawings were deliberately falsified so as to give the impression that Maya ruins had been built by Phoenicians or Romans. "He talks so big," said William Prescott, "moreover his drawings do not have the true weathertints of antiquity. . . . I have a *soupçon* that he is a bit of a charlatan."

Stephens arrived at Palenque in the spring of 1840 with his companion, Frederick Catherwood. Since their publications, the history of the city has been set on a firm archaeological basis.

That part of the site thus far uncovered consists of two groups of eight structures divided by a small ravine with river water that has been canalized to flow through a corbeled-arch sewer (an unusual Maya engineering feature). On the west bank is the Palace, an irregular rectangular structure 340 by 240 feet and sixty feet high. This is where Stephens lived. It is thick-walled and many-chambered, and has an interior court from which rises—unique in Maya architecture—a tower four stories in height with an interior stairway. At the entrance to the Palace are archaically carved stone figures, and the sides of the edifice are decorated with stucco figures in high relief, regarded by all as the finest anywhere. Within, there are carved stone panels with a remarkable series of well-preserved Maya texts. Four of the other structures, the temples of the Cross, the Sun, the Inscriptions, and the Foliated Cross, are outwardly similar—an artificially raised pyramid, with a single structure atop that is crested by an immense, decorated roof comb. The engineering purpose of the latter is to act as a cantilever to the corbeled arching beneath. All are decorated on the exterior with figures and ornaments in stucco, which were once brilliantly painted.

90. *A cross-section of the Temple of the Inscriptions at Palenque showing the long-lost stairway that led down to the grave of the high priest. It was found in 1951 by Alberto Ruz Lhuillier, a Mexican archaeologist.*

Each of the large rooms has an altar and a carved wall panel. In one, the Temple of the Foliated Cross, are two life-sized figures (Maya dimensions) holding a mannequin up to the gaze of a bird which despite embellishments is the sacred quetzal. There are many inscriptions on the tablet. On the altar of another, the Sun Temple, the two figures stand upon the bodies of prostrated men. In the center is the symbol of the sun, the face of which some have likened to a Gorgon's head. Once again mannequins are held up in reverence. The Temple of the Inscriptions, which lies near the Palace, has lost its roof comb. It retains its decorations. The date that has been deciphered is A.D. 692.

In 1951 the Mexican archaeologist Alberto Ruz Lhuillier was assigned to restore some of the structures at Palenque. When his investigations brought him to the Temple of the Inscriptions, he noticed in the inner room a large slab set neat into the floor, with finger holes in it so it could be raised. He raised it, and following a narrow corbeled stairway downward, first in one direction and then another, he reached another large slab poised horizontally, sixty feet below the surface. In front of the door were the skeletons of six Mayas who had "elected" to remain as guardians of the tomb. Beyond the stone door, a few steps down, was the tomb. When discovered it was a veritable fairy palace. Through the centuries the dripping water, lime-saturated, had formed many stalactites.[161]

Over the tomb was a beautifully carved slab in relief. A portrait with hieroglyphics, it weighed five tons. Within was the skeleton of the "true man," bejeweled with enormous jade earrings, a jade necklace, and a pear-shaped baroque pearl. It had been long held that the Maya pyramids were built solely to support temples and did not contain the tombs of important personages, as pyramids do in other lands. The findings at Palenque changed this attitude.

Piedras Negras (A.D. 534), one of the great cities of the Mayas, is sixty bird-flight miles from Palenque. On the south bank of the Usumacinta River, it is set in the jungle. The city begins at the river's edge, and the structures go from the simple to the complex, the latter occupying the undulating hills. The palaces, even though in advanced decay, give the effect of one huge monument. The sculpture of the stelae and lintels in low relief is of the finest, sharply delineated and sensual. War motifs dominate many of such sculptures; often Maya overlords appear looking down on massed prisoners. There are over seventy-five dated stelae (between the dates of A.D. 534 and 800), altars, lintels, thrones, and even sculptures chipped out of the *piedras negras,* the black stones that lie above the river. One of the features is the *zumpulche,* a building which housed the sweat bath. It had two large rooms, one hot and one cold, reminiscent of the Roman baths, if not as magnificent. In the steam room were two stone benches, and the steam was made by throwing water onto hot stones. This description might seem contrived were it not supported by a combination of good archaeology and good reconstruction.

Yaxchilán (A.D. 514) lies higher up on the Usumacinta, twenty miles from Piedras Negras. Yaxchilán (called thus from a rivulet that flows through it) lies on the north bank, where the river makes a large curve. The structures of this city are spread along the river

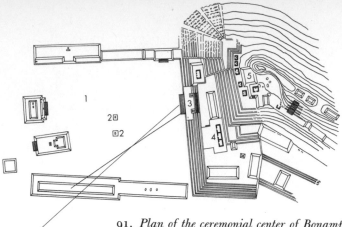

91. *Plan of the ceremonial center of Bonampak (eighteen miles southeast of the well-known ruins of Yaxchilán on the Usumacinto River), where the famous murals were discovered during May, 1946, by Mr. Giles G. Healy. Bonampak is small but carefully laid out.*

Its plaza 1) measures 270 by 370 feet. Two dated stelae 2) stand in the center of the plaza. Approached by a series of steps 3) is the principal structure 4) of Bonampak. This is the building that houses the famous murals. Other smaller buildings decorated with stucco 5) dominate the rise of ground called the Acropolis. From K. Ruppert, J. E. S. Thompson, and T. Proskouriakoff, Bonampak . . . , Washington, D. C., 1955. Surveyed by Ruppert and Stromsvik.

for almost a mile. Eight undulating hills overlook the esplanade, and on each is a temple structure. Its sculpture, chipped out of finely textured limestone, is dramatic. In one lintel a priest is seen passing a thorn-studded cord through the center of his tongue, dripping blood onto a piece of *huun* paper, while a servant fans him to ease away the pain. The surface of Yaxchilán has only been touched by archaeologists.

Bonampak (A.D. 540) was an architectural satellite of Yaxchilán, some eighteen miles from the other city. Because it was recessed in the jungles away from the river, no one ever heard of Bonampak before 1946. In Maya the word means "painted walls." When the city was discovered, the interest created by the paintings found there was second only to that caused by the earlier discoveries of John Lloyd Stephens. Bonampak lies in the area where the Maya-speaking "wild" Lacandones live, they who carry on many traditions of the old Mayas. It is also a region much penetrated by the chicle gatherers, who search for new stands of gum-yielding sapodillas.

Giles G. Healy, a photographer pursuing a Maya chase under the aegis of the United Fruit Company, pressed the search for Bonampak when he heard the Indians say "painted walls." He was

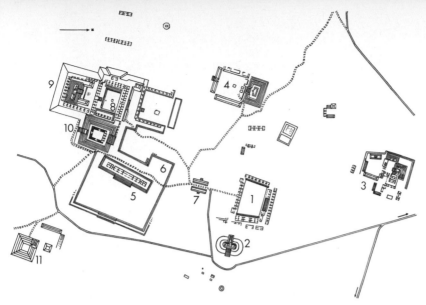

92. *Plan of the civic and religious center of Uxmal.*
1) *The Nunnery Quadrangle.* 2) *House of the Magician.* 3) *North group (unrestored).*
4) *Cemetery group (unrestored).* 5) *House of the Governor.* 6) *House of the Turtles.*
7) *Ball court.* 8) *House of the Pigeons (partly restored).* 9) *South group (unrestored).*
10) *Great pyramid (unrestored).* 11) *House of the Old Woman (in ruins).* From
S. G. Morley, The Ancient Maya, *Stanford University Press,* 1946, *Plate* 49.

led to the city on May 21, 1946. Hidden in the innermost recesses
of the Lacandon jungles, Bonampak proved to be one of a constellation of unrecorded sites. There Healy found a local ceremonial center, with eleven buildings and part of a carefully laid
compact plaza 270 by 370 feet. Here were several dated stelae and
decorated, carved, and dated altars. On a slight rise were several
structures; one had three doorways. Its façade revealed marvelously
molded figures in stucco. (All of the sculpture found here is
superb; it much resembles that of Yaxchilán.) Within this building
Healy found the murals. Painted in A.D. 800, these rank as art with
anything of similar antiquity, be it in Crete, India, China. As
history they are one of the best sources of information of Maya life
patterns, showing warfare, dress, musical instruments, religious
ceremonies, sacrifice, and above all, the attitudes and expressions
which make a new analysis of Maya social organization possible.[160]
(For a more detailed discussion of the Bonampak murals, see
Painting, page 343.)

    Uxmal (A.D. 987) lies in the Puuc of Yucatán, a range of low
hills, rolling limestone ridges, with alternate pockets of soil. It is
not only the most uniform of Maya cities; it is also the most beautiful. Moreover, it is quite probable that Uxmal is what it was

327

called by the Mayas themselves. It has history, written, recitative, and traditional. Uxmal was part of the League of Mayapán. It even has a date in the literature: "In Katun 2 Ahau [A.D. 987] the Maya Lord Ah Suytok Tutul Xiu was established in Uxmal."

There was a time when archaeologists cast Maya culture into two chronological categories: Old Empire (the cities of older date described were such) and New Empire, those which were concentrated in Yucatán. It is now known that those of the New have dates almost as old as the Old, so these terms are no longer very meaningful. It is not known with certainty whether the Maya cities in the humid interior were abandoned after A.D. 890 with a precipitous mass migration of people toward Yucatán. Still, Maya tradition and history speaks of descents of invaders great and small, to account for the fact of the abandonment of the interior for the dry, coastal Yucatán.

Uxmal was a city of the Maya renaissance. The Maya-speaking Toltecs had already invaded Yucatán and permeated the land with a renewed vitality in religion, trade, and welfare. Ritual was dominated by the mystical Quetzalcoatl cult. All this found a reflection in Maya architecture.

Uxmal is fifty miles from the sea and a hundred from Chichén Itzá. It is the main city of the Puuc. About it are scores of cities, small and large, all of a similar style. The site of Uxmal is unusual because it was built near a *cenote*. The region has rich soil and plenty of rainfall, but no wells. So, as the Romans did at Capri, the builders of Uxmal relied on underground cisterns that collected the run-off of rain from roofs. It has been calculated that the plaza of Uxmal if used efficiently as a cistern could have kept six thousand people in drinking water throughout the year. All the Puuc cities provided themselves with underground cisterns, an engineering feat which would have brought encomiums from the Romans themselves.

There are eight groups of buildings at Uxmal, covering an immense area. The House of the Governor and its related structures stand at what is considered to have been the secular administrative center of the city. Mounted on an artificially constructed mound, fifty feet high and reached on all sides by stone steps, the group covers five acres of ground. The palace itself is 320 feet long, 40 feet wide, 26 feet high, and it is the single most magnificient building ever erected in the Americas. The whole is covered with a veneer of ornamented stone, the joints fitting as perfectly as a mosaic. Each stone is an element in this immensely beautiful façade, which is a masterpiece of precision and craftsmanship. On an altar in front of it rests a double-headed jaguar, heads fore and aft. In front of the main flight of steps was an enormous stone phallus, which is broken in half and for "moral" reasons never restored. It stood ten feet high when in its pristine state.

Around the House of the Governor are pyramids, other palaces, and the House of the Pigeons, so termed by someone because the roof comb resembles a dovecote. Close upon the palace, on the same raised plaza, is the House of the Turtles (the decorative motif on the façade is a parade of realistically carved box tortoises). South of this, where the great *sacbe* causeway passed (it ran directly in front of the House of the Governor and led to Kabah), there are other buildings, now mostly amorphous except for the Temple of the Phalli, where there are enough reminders of the worship of the ithyphallic to make even Aldous Huxley change his assertion, "There is no sex in the art of the Maya. . . ."

Stephens lived in the Governor's Palace during November and December, 1841, Frederick Catherwood sketched that monument for two months, making so many detailed drawings that he had "materials for erecting a building exactly like it." It was here too that Count Waldeck lived in 1836 (his drawings of Uxmal are still extant).

The ball court is north of the palace, and beyond it is the second group of buildings: the Nunnery Quadrangle and the temple-pyramid of the Dwarf. The latter is an oval-shaped pyramid. On one side a broad flight of stairs mounts at an almost perpendicular angle 125 feet high to the temple, which had as its motif Chac, the open-mouthed god, patron of rain. Immediately below the pyramid, so close that in the late afternoon it shadows it, is the Nunnery. This is a somewhat irregularly shaped quadrangle, enclosed by a low range of buildings, each with different motif. Like the Governor's Palace, the whole is faced with a veneer of cut stone set into designs which "project"—the white stones are set so as to create a chiaroscuro of light and shade. One of these buildings is multistoried, a temple dramatically set back with intricate ornamentation. On another the corners have the long snout of the rain god as decoration. The third has as its motif the simple *na* house of the common Indian, immortalized in stone. The fourth shows another variation of the fret design, over which stone snakes coil, twist, and entwine. At intervals there are figures of men with abnormally large penes.

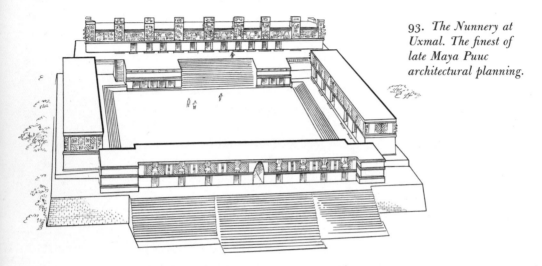

93. The Nunnery at Uxmal. The finest of late Maya Puuc architectural planning.

Although still little explored beyond its immediate confines, Uxmal has been partially restored. There is much contradiction here. Mentioned in the Maya chronicles as having been built by the Maya-speaking Toltecs, it possesses the least of Mexican architectural traits. Uxmal is supposed to have been one of the triumvirate of the League of Mayapán, but archaeologists suggest that it was abandoned before the league was in operation. It has been called decadent, whereas it has a style wholly its own. Sixteen dated stelae have been found in and about Uxmal. When read, the dates are within the tenth century. The style of the sculpture, ornate and flamboyant, is also decadent, says one writer, in comparison with that of Tikal.

Kabah (A.D. 879) lies nine miles southeast of Uxmal. The ancient Maya *sacbe,* which leads to it, leaves Uxmal in front of the Governor's Palace and goes past the Hacienda San Simón (which belonged to Simón Peón, host to Stephens and at that time owner of Uxmal). Near by is a stone arch similar to the one at Kabah. It stands in isolation and is not related to any other structure. Six miles farther, following the *sacbe,* one comes to Kabah. The main road continues southeast, but a branch of it makes a sharp left turn and comes up and passes under the Great Arch of Kabah. Stephens discovered it and Catherwood made a drawing of it, but later archaeologists, who could not find it, politely smirked at this "triumphal arch." Today it stands restored, and is the formal entrance to Kabah.

As Kabah now stands, there are three groups of buildings visible to the eye, and uncovered mounds and temples abound. Around Kabah, in the eleventh and twelfth centuries, was one of the densest populations in Yucatán. The Palace of the Masks— for once rightly named—is Maya baroque; the long-snouted masks of the god Chac are repeated over and over again along the whole range of the 151-foot-long building. The effect of this lavish use of the motif is simply overwhelming. In front of it there is an altar filled with a running commentary of glyphs. Before it and underground is a huge cistern, a *chultun,* which was the depository for water collected from the roofs. Kabah had two dated wooden doorjambs (A.D. 879) showing warriors with spear throwers—an indication of Toltec presence in the Puuc.

Labná (A.D. 869), one of the constellation of cities about Uxmal, is only six miles from Kabah. Its architecture is characteristic of the Puuc. Labná lacks architectural continuity. One feels that the project was larger than the labor supply and that buildings grew by accretion; many structures were left unfinished. There are only two known dates from Labná. One of these, A.D. 869, is carved on the elongated proboscis of the god Chac.

The Palace, imposingly set on an artificial hill, has two immense cisterns, one within the building itself and another that takes up its whole front (the very one into which John Lloyd Stephens lowered himself, despite all warnings, to make sure that it was a cistern). This palace, presumably an administration center, was joined to the other group of buildings by a causeway, a ceremonial road 450 yards in length, ten feet wide, and varying between two and eight feet in height. There is here, as at Uxmal and Kabah, a gateway; it is part of a building. As at Uxmal, the native house, the common dwelling of adobe and thatch, is immortalized in stone. Here it is used on either side of the gateway as a decorative motif.

Sayil (A.D. 800) is the oldest of the group. The dating is based more on its style than upon any dated stelae. Its center of interest (there are many other structures in ruins about it) is its palace of a hundred rooms arranged in three stories. The second and third are set back, leaving terraces as rest areas for the occupants. A great stone staircase beginning at the bottom leads to all three terraces. It is 210 feet long and seventy-five feet wide; it has magnitude, proportion, order, and sensibleness. The style is massive and simple and has the classic qualities of Greek Doric architecture. Around its façades is the ubiquitous mask motif. It has, wrote Tatiana Proskouriakoff, "a freedom from the oppressively monotonous intricacy of ornament that mars many *Puuc* structures." There are so many late Maya cities within the Puuc, each with something individual about it, that we can mention only the more important: Xcalumkin; Chacmultun, with its interesting murals; Holactun; Almuchil; Kickmool; Keuic, visited by Stephens, who spelled it "Kewick"; Huntichmool; Sabacche; Yache; Xcalumpococh.

Chichén Itzá, thrice founded (A.D. 432, 987, and 1194), was the greatest of the Maya cities near the Yucatán tip. On a plain so flat that its great pyramid can be seen for miles around, Chichén Itzá was joined by road to Izamal and to the seacoast at Polé, in direct line with Cozumel Island. Important in the history of the city are its two enormous natural wells, one of which was used for human sacrifice and the other as a source of water.

The first founding of the city (A.D. 432) was by immigrants from the Old Empire during the "Little Descent." They formed their city around the salubrious Xtoloc well, where they built two masonry stairways descending precipitously sixty feet to the water's edge. The architecture of old Chichén is reminiscent of the Puuc style. Many of the buildings have almost identical motifs, masks, colonnettes, and frets, especially the building named the *Abab dzib*. Traditions and dates give this further proof. The rounded "astronomical tower," certainly one of the most interesting in the area, is dated A.D. 900.

Chichén the "new" was founded at the north end about the sacrificial *cenote*. This well is 190 feet in diameter and now contains thirty-six feet of water, green with algae, and forty feet of detritus. Its water level stands sixty-five feet below the surface. The "new" part of Chichén Itzá was occupied by the Itzás between the years 987–1194. There were two distinct Mexican invasions into

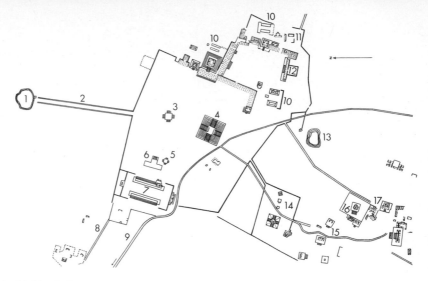

94. *Plan of Chichén Itzá.*

1) *The sacrificial* cenote. 2) *The* sacbe *causeway.* 3) *Temple of Venus.* 4) *Pyramid of Kukulcán.* 5) *Platform of the Eagles.* 6) *Tzompantli, or Place of the Skulls.* 7) *Ball court.* 8) *The modern road to Mérida.* 9) *Temple of the Warriors.* 10) *Ball courts.* 11) *Sweat baths.* 12) *The market.* 13) *Fresh-water cenote.* 14) *High priest's grave.* 15) *House of the Deer.* 16) *Caracol, the observatory.* 17) *Sweat baths.*

Yucatán and Chichén Itzá. The first was peaceful, of Maya-speaking Itzás who, although of apparent Mexican origin, had an understanding with the Toltec leader, Quetzalcoatl, who had been exiled from Tula with an army of his followers. They jointly descended upon Chichén Itzá, then unoccupied. It was the period in which many people, both in the Mexican highlands and throughout the Maya country, were in mass movement. Famine, drought, or disease may have been the concomitant causes. Tikal, Palenque, Piedras Negras, and doubtless hundreds of smaller inland Maya cities were putting up their last time-markers and passing into cultural silence. This was the time of great dispersals almost everywhere in this part of the Americas. Among the Mayas it was known as the "Great Descent." It is recorded in their traditions.

Chichén Itzá was apparently unoccupied when the Itzás with the Toltecs of Quetzalcoatl took it over. Some time after 900 (there is a confusion of time sequences between archaeological and native history) they built the first large truncated pyramid at Chichén. This was discovered when archaeologists of the Carnegie Institution, while restoring the pyramid-temple of Kukulcán, found a smaller one underneath it that served as core to the larger. It was Maya in style, but with Toltec motifs, e.g., marching jaguars such as are found at Tula in central Mexico. A secret stairway led to the Red Jaguar

95. *The Pyramid of Kukulcán at Chichén Itzá. Although a great part of the city is late Maya, Chichén Itzá was occupied as early as the fifth century* A.D.

throne room. Here a life-sized effigy of an open-mouthed jaguar, painted a mandarin red, stood guard. Its spots are seventy-three round disks of polished jade.

Chichén Itzá, by a strange concatenation of events, was now bound up with the culture of Tula which lay about eight hundred miles to the northwest. This ruined city, near Mexico City, had been the capital of the Toltecs, after the collapse of ancient Teotihuacán. Between the years 900 and 1156 it was again the center of Toltec culture. The temple of Tula had the plumed serpent motif, an immense snake rampant, formed into fifteen-foot-high caryatids. Inside the temple were immense warrior figures as colonnades. About the lower portions of the temple were motifs of marching jaguars and rampant eagles. Above all else there appeared the terrible figure of the Chac-Mool, a prone stone figure with a vacant expressionless face. Its hands held a stone dish, and into this freshly torn human hearts were flung during sacrifices.

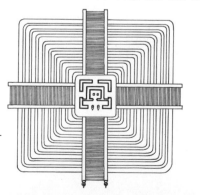

96. *The Temple of Kukulcán, Chichén Itzá. When the city was reoccupied, this temple was set over an older one that had Tula-Toltec characteristics. The new temple is notable for the use of wooden beams, making larger rooms possible. The figure of the Plumed Serpent is a direct architectural borrowing from the Toltec temple at Tula. The temple also served as a fortress during the brief occupation of the Spaniards under Francisco de Montejo.*

Quetzalcoatl was the leader (for spiritual and military were one) of Tula. He was actually named Ce Acatl Topiltzin, and had taken the patronymic of the god Quetzalcoatl who in many guises had been the cultural hero of the Americas for centuries. He ruled Tula for twenty years (there is a monument to him near Tula which bears a date corresponding to 968); he fought and lost a civil war and was forced into exile with a sizeable number of warriors. Various dates (and all are conflicting) have been given for this historical occurrence. However, he is known to have moved south to Cholula, capital of the Mixtecs, where he acquired fame as a bringer of laws and as a builder (there, at Cholula, the largest pyramid ever built in Mexico bears his name).

This much is certain; some time in the tenth century, Chichén Itzá was occupied for the second time and those who came with the Itzás were of Toltec origin. Archaeology, history, and tradition, except for precise dates, are for once in full agreement; "it is believed," wrote Landa, ". . . that with the Itzás who [re-] occupied Chichén Itzá, there reigned a great lord named *Kuk* [quetzal] *ul* feather [*can*] [serpent], and that the principal building, which is called Kukulcán, shows this to be true." This temple, called the *Castillo* by the Spanish (because a conquistador once mounted his cannons at its pinnacle), the temple one now sees, was erected over the first; its ninety-one steps rise on all four sides and terminate at its truncated summit with an elaborate temple. The Toltec builders under Huanc Ceel, the conqueror of Chichén Itzá in 1194, introduced carved wooden beams to provide larger space, since Maya rooms were severely restricted by the use of the corbeled arch. The walls had murals which still survive to show many aspects of Toltec-Maya life. An open-mouthed plumed serpent is on the balustrade on each of the four stairways ascending the pyramid. On top, at the temple, the serpents appear again, this time as sculptured columns—precisely like those at Tula. To make doubly certain that people knew it was the Temple of Kukulcán, the top of the building is decorated with the symbol of the sky god, Quetzalcoatl.

The square where the temple rests is a huge, roughly trapezoidal walled square, 1,600 by 1,400 feet. Within this is a gigantic ball court (its tribunes carry architectural motifs derived from Tula). There are low platforms, "theatres," reached by stone stairways (Landa refers to "two small stages of hewn stone where they gave farces . . . and comedies for the pleasure of the public"). Near by is a thirty-foot-wide ceremonial causeway, leading nine hundred feet to the sacrificial *cenote*.

The Temple of the Warriors faces the great square. Its corridor of the "thousand columns" is below, within another walled enclosure. This, smaller than the great plaza, has at one end another group of buildings, one of which is called the "Market." There is no doubt about this feature; from indisputable archaeological data Tatiana Proskouriakoff has made a restoration of it, and early Spanish reports speak of the great market at Chichén Itzá "where pilgrims came from foreign parts to trade as well as to worship."

The Temple of the Warriors in many of its features resembles the Toltec temple at Tula: the plumed-serpent columns, fanged-mouths open and tails rampant; the motifs of marching jaguars and eagles, symbolizing the military orders of highland Mexico; the dwarfed figures at the temple's edge that held feather banners; and that Tula fixture, the reclining figure of Chac-Mool. Finally, the "thousand columns," which once supported carved wooden roof beams, bear the same martial motifs as those at Tula: armed spearmen with helmet and body armor of Mexican origin.

Tula, near Mexico City, lies about eight hundred miles in a direct line to Chichén Itzá, but as man then had to move through mountain passes, swamps, jungles, high mountains, not to mention hostile tribes, all of which necessitated wide detours, the distance was actually more than a thousand miles. "The extraordinary fact," states Eric Thompson "is that nowhere between central Mexico and Yucatán have buildings or sculptures [such as the Temple of the Warriors and the temple at Tula] in this distinctive style been found." Another archaeologist says flatly that "the draftsmen and architects must have been Toltec . . . the craftsmen, Maya." There is no other instance in pre-American history where two tribes, so distant from one another, erected identical temples in places so widely separated. How did the Toltecs remember the details, for Tula was built between A.D. 900 and 1156, the Temple of the Warriors in Chichén Itzá about 1200. The *Popol Vuh* of the highland Quiché Maya, which, though written in European characters, is a literal translation from a Maya painted book, confirms that "Quetzalcoatl . . . after his departure from Tula . . . left . . . with those Toltecs who escaped . . . went to the region of Xicalanco [Xicalango]

. . . later at Chichén Itzá . . . and the priests as they journeyed . . . toward Yucatán took all their paintings in which they had all things of ancient times and of their arts and crafts . . . and other things that were what they called *u tzibal tulan* . . . the paintings in which they put their chronicles."

This, then, supported by tradition, written record, and archaeology, is the history of Chichén Itzá; and with it, the architectural history of the Toltec-Mayas.

Tulum (A.D. 564) is a walled city lying on the open Caribbean sea coast opposite (and twenty-five miles from) the extreme southern tip of Cozumel Island.[113] The present-day Mayas have in their folklore a tale that in ancient times Tulum was connected to Cobá, Chichén Itzá, and Uxmal by *cuxan san,* a road suspended in the sky. This *cuxan* (living) *san* (rope) is based on considerable archaeological fact; stone-laid causeways at one time did connect these cities.

The beginnings of Tulum, anciently called Zama, stretch back into the earliest time. It was being added to during the late Toltec period in Yucatán, and it was populated when the Spaniards in four ships under command of Juan de Grijalva sailed along the coast in May, 1518. The chaplain, Juan Díaz, reported seeing "three large towns separated from each other by two miles. There were many houses of stone . . . we perceived a city or town so large that Seville would not have seemed more considerable. . . . there was a very large tower; on the shore was a great throng of Indians, who bore two standards which they raised and lowered to signal us to approach." There were really four towns—Xelha, Soliman, Tulum, and Tancah— situated so close to one another as to give the impression of one continuous city. At that time the chieftain of Tulum was the captor and master of the Spaniards Aguilar and Guerrero.

Tulum is the largest and most impressive Maya city on the east coast of Yucatán. Although, as we have seen, the city had been sighted in the sixteenth century, John Lloyd Stephens and Frederick Catherwood, who journeyed to Tulum during the ides of March, 1842, may be considered its discoverers.

Tulum is mounted on the summit of a limestone cliff forty feet high, lashed by waves of the open sea.

The cliff is covered with a cheval-de-frise of cactus and thorned plants, a veritable barbed wire. On its other three sides the city is protected by a great wall, thirty-six hundred feet in length and averaging fifteen to twenty feet in height. It is pierced by five narrow gateways, each of which will admit only one person at a time. Guardhouses are placed at the western end. Beyond is a solid mass of vegetation growing out of swamps that stretch for many miles inland. The northeast gate was the sally port to the causeway that led to Xelha, six miles distant, and somewhere near it was the turnoff for Cobá and thence to Chichén Itzá. A three-roomed structure was built inside this gateway; it stood over the only water supply, a *cenote* into whose deep hollow there is an underground drainage from the land thereabout.

The Castillo, the largest structure at Tulum, stands close to the cliff that faces the open sea. It is twenty-five feet high. On the top is a squat temple that had a wooden-beam roof and was ornamented on the exterior with stucco figures. The frescoes inside still reflect something of their original beauty.

Within the walled enclosure dominated by the Castillo are ten other structures, exhibiting various periods of construction. The largest, at the southwest end, is the Temple of the Diving God. Twenty-seven feet wide by twenty in depth, and nine feet in height, it is not only the most picturesque building at Tulum, but one of the few that have been preserved. The interior, the outside walls, and both sides of the doorway are painted with frescoes. Over the door, in a niche, is a winged deity plunging earthward. This particular god also appears on the multistoried palace at Sayil; it has been identified as Ah Muzen Cab, the bee god.

97. The diving god. A stucco decoration from the Temple of the Diving God at Tulum.

On the coastal causeway, north and south of Tulum, were a number of Maya centers, large and small. In the sixteenth century, Maya villages and cities were almost continuous along the east coast—from the large city of Ekab at Cape Cotoche, the most northern point of Yucatán, 150 miles southward to the Bay of Zamabac (now called Bahía de la Ascención). Some of these were settlements that dated back to early Maya times; others were erected during the suzerainty of the League of Mayapán—Tulum in particular was expanded then—but most found final flower when the Maya earth took on new vigor, during the Mexican Toltec political absorption, from the tenth century far into the fifteenth.

 Sculpture   *29*

THE FUNCTION of sculpture was twofold. It was first architectural; in most Maya buildings sculpture was an integral part of the building. Secondly, it stood on its own as an art form; this sculpture had various voices and various mediums—stone, stucco, wood, and clay.[93]

Most conspicuous, since they are massive and impressive, are the carved stone monoliths called stelae. These large, shaftlike obelisks appear scattered throughout the Maya cities that existed between the dates A.D. 328 and 889. They represent portraits of priests or rulers, and are carved in relief or in the round, with rows of glyphs that record their dates. Since they served a hierarchic purpose, the figures are formal, austere, overpowering. Only the backgrounds have freedom, and some are vehemently alive, the sculptor having been allowed to carve animals, birds, and men that flow about the religious format. One such stela is thirty-five feet high and weighs fifty tons.

Maya sculpture is of wide variety, gods in various forms, doorways, busts, masks, tablets, panels. The material for study is enormous. There are over four hundred examples of monumental sculpture that fall within the extreme dates given above, enough for Tatiana Proskouriakoff to have made a minute analysis of styles, traits, and mannerisms. Six broad phases can be distinguished in the evolution of Maya sculptural art.[151]

The sculptor's tool was the stone celt (either made from basalt or diorite). His usual medium was limestone, which often had the texture of marble. Inexhaustible patience had taught him to transcend the limitations of Neolithic techniques. Despite what we would regard as inadequate tools, he was able to simulate in stone the delicate shimmering swirl of quetzal plumes and the texture of a drapery, to represent elaborate bead necklaces and even tattooing, so cleanly carved that the sculpture provides important data on the customs of the ancient Mayas. Hieroglyphics are so delicately carved that they have survived the awesome centuries of tropical destruction and can still be read. So complete was the mastery of the Maya sculptor over his material that he seems to have handled large rock masses as dexterously as a Chinese craftsman handles ivory.

Stylistic changes in Maya sculpture make it possible to follow the shift from static to dynamic, from the simple to the ornate. Overemphasis in design, a baroque trait, seems to appear just when Maya society itself becomes ornate. There is a shift from religious to secular themes, from communal emotions to particular ones, that coincides, as Maya history is now read, with a breakup of the older cities, a shift from the purely theocratic to the secular.

Aldous Huxley thought most Maya sculpture to be "incommensurably alien." The Mayas, like other peoples of the Americas, developed an ideal of beauty untouched by historical influences of the kind that figured in the development of European art. Their art is florid and austere, and yet at its best ranks without question with the best of the art of other world civilizations. At least Roger Fry believed so: "In the finest works of Maya culture . . . we find . . . a plastic sensibility of the rarest kind. I do not know whether even in the greatest sculpture of Europe one could find anything exactly like this in its equilibrium between system and sensibility, in its power to suggest all the complexity of nature."

Stucco allowed the Maya artist greater freedom than stone, and one feels this in the swirling movement of designs modeled in stucco. This form of sculpture is found at widely separated areas, from Tulum on the coast to newly excavated Dzibilchaltún, and up to Palenque in the humid jungles. Stucco is a natural outgrowth of hand-modeled clay. As sculpture, it also was closely allied with architecture, since it appeared usually on the façades of buildings. It is at Palenque, however, that "stucco came into its supreme expression. . . . whether frugal or abstract it speaks one idiom. . . . it is highly articulate and technically pre-eminent." There are in Palenque whole galleries of stucco figures that are almost Oriental in feeling.

Stucco as an art form is very old. The immense eight-foot-high masks that decorate the temple in Uaxactún, the oldest in Mayadom, were of stucco, as was the heroic-sized head found at Izamal that a French explorer sketched in the late nineteenth century. Wherever the Mayas went, stucco was sure to go.

Clay sculpture preceded stone sculpture and modeling in stucco. The small clay heads made to propitiate the gods are among the earliest artifacts to be found. While Maya modeling does not have the force of the Aztec, it has great merit. The life-sized funeral urns seen by Diego de Landa and dug up in fragments show how large a clay mass the Maya artists could handle with elaborate appliqué decorations.

Figures in sculptured clay have been discovered throughout the Maya area, but the finest are those found in a cemetery on the island of Jaina, off the Campeche shore; these are the jewels of any Maya collection. The Jaina figures are portrait statuettes. Although small, ranging from six to twelve inches in height, they are majestic in concept. Little else in the whole range of Maya art is more sensitively wrought. Of the Jaina pottery the late Miguel Covarrubias, one of the few creative artists who weighed these as art, said: "it shows an extraordinary mastery in handling, a realistic knowledge of form and movement." The statuettes reflect the Maya ideal; there are figures of warriors and actors with arms outstretched in dramatic movement, chieftains sitting cross-legged and festooned with elaborate headgear; in a sort of "Susanna and the Elders" theme, an elderly man caresses a young woman. This is the kind of detail for which a historian searches when trying to construct what the Mayas looked like behind the luxuriant façades of surface decoration. In these the faces are so exquisitely modeled that every nuance of expression can be seen. Calm, defiance, lust, all can be discerned. More than half of the Jaina statuettes found are of women. These meet Huxley's complaint ("the most conspicuous absence from Maya sculpture is that of the female form—*et tout ce qui s'ensuit*"), for here women as subject matter are treated with concern and feeling.

Wood carving was for the Maya only another form of sculpture, except that wood is a more obedient medium than stone. A considerable number of wood carvings have been found in Yucatán, but the finest are those discovered at Tikal.

Before the Maya carved their calendars on stone, they carved on wooden stelae. When they used wooden beams for ceilings in-

stead of stone corbeled arching, the beams were carved. Landa
referred to some he had seen as "great beams standing erect and
ornamented with carvings." At Tikal several of the temple-pyramids
yielded, even after a thousand years, wooden panels carved of sapodilla wood. One, with a spread-winged quetzal and a fantastically
conceived god, is seven by seven feet; a carbon-14 dating confirms
the date given on its own glyphs, A.D. 741. Several such have been
found at Tikal; they are now all in European museums. Wood
carving was practiced extensively by the Mayas. They made idols,
helmets, ceremonial masks (which were adorned with feathers),
masks for actors, intricately adorned wands of office, and carved
boards that served as bindings to their "folded books." Landa admitted even in his time that the Mayas earned "a great deal making
idols and carvings . . . of wood."

Yucatán produced neither gold nor copper. It was just as well.
The lack of it delayed its conquest while the Spaniard followed the
golden scent to the Aztec realms. Metallurgy developed in South
America—all of the very ancient cultures there had it—with its
greatest florescence in Colombia. On this point there are no dissent-
ing voices. The art of goldsmithery was centuries old in Panama and
Costa Rica when Columbus set up a colony at Veragua in 1502 and
found the natives gold-spangled. He called the place "Golden
Castile," and the king of Spain conferred on him the Duchy of
Veragua. Today his descendant still carries it as one of his titles.
Veragua (its precise location has not been determined) was a center
for casting gold ornaments, and through trade many of these
traveled north to the Mayas.

By the early eighth century gold began to filter into Mayadom.
After 900, when the Mayas were concentrated in the Yucatán peninsula and trade was extended, gold and copper began to appear with
some frequency. It was further quickened by the coming of the Itzás.
Copper brought from Oaxaca to trade at Xicalango was made into
bells; gold plate and leaf brought from Panama was fashioned into
ornamental disks and crowns. All that is now known of Maya gold
concerns the objects dredged from the *cenote* at Chichén Itzá by
Edward H. Thompson. Reposing in the Peabody Museum at Harvard for many years, they have recently been the subject of a splendid brochure.[111] Many of those objects found are in the style of
Veragua, suggesting that they were cast there. The gold plates a foot

in diameter are interesting for the history of the Mayas, for despite the Maya glyphs that rim the disks, they are decorated in Toltec themes—the ritual of tearing the heart from a sacrificial victim, the scenes of naval battle between Itzás and Mayas—evidence of how late goldwork came to the Mayas.

The Spaniards never found much concentration of gold among the Mayas. At Potonchon in 1524 Cortés found various gold objects: crowns, headbands, necklaces, earplugs, little cast figures of gods, lizards, and ducks. The forms show that these were imported from Panama. The only gold cache which was enough to whet a conquistador's appetite for metal was seized in Chetumal Province in the early days of the conquest. Chetumal, the center of seagoing-canoe construction, was also a large trade area. There the Spaniards seized gold bullion and objects to the value of two thousand pesos in weight.

 Painting   *30*

M AYA PAINTING, as revealed in the frescoes, shows a realistic perception and a more advanced realistic style than that of any of those other civilizations numbered among the Sun Kingdoms of the Americas. Art was not for the masses. Despite this, the Maya approach to form is realistic. It was not meant to be educational and rarely designed to commemorate historical events; it was religious, symbolic. It never so completely lost its symbolism as to become purely decorative. Like all symbolic art—including the present-day avalanche of nonrepresentationalism —it was antisocial. Colors, arrangements, signs, symbols meant nothing to the viewer unless he was of the *cognoscenti.*

Because art was religious it concerned itself little with the secular. Despite this the Maya artist limned real people in naturalistic poses, there is an emphasis on movement and an attempt at perspective, people are differentiated by headdress, costume, action. The earliest-known mural—that found at the ruins of Uaxactún—depicts what is easily seen to be a conversation between Maya lords (precisely what they are talking over the glyphs do not reveal). It has gesture, color, movement. Those found at Chacmultun, in the Puuc region of Yucatán, removed by a distance of 210 miles and six hundred years from the one at Uaxactún, reveal a continuity of the same spirit.

Murals have been found elsewhere in Mayadom, unfortunately in fragments. The narrative quality of the murals at Chichén Itzá, created during the Toltec period, is almost wholly secular. Those within the Temple of the Warriors, which covered a wall space 9 feet high by 12½ feet wide, belie the name of the temple, for they show scenes of everyday life in a coastal village in Yucatán, a type of picture seldom found among the Mayas. Here are realistic and genre drawings of Maya dugout canoes, trees, houses, and even the tall feather-and-wood markers that were used to signal the landfall for sea traffic. The artist here does not depict temples and priests, but as a sort of Maya Pieter Breughel he shows the simple native house, women at work and at rest, men "who were the oxen of the land," carrying their trade goods to market. On the walls of other structures at Chichén Itzá—the ball court, the Temple of the Jaguars—there are animating scenes of battle. Instructive as to Maya armor and weapons and military technique, they are also revealing tableaux of dress and postures.

Bonampak as place and architecture has already been discussed, but the murals of Bonampak, discovered in 1946, have so revolutionized our earlier concept of Maya society that the literature has yet to come fully to terms with the change.

There are three rooms of murals at Bonampak. Taken together they form a continuous narrative: a raid on enemy territory, a consultation among the chiefs, a judgment of prisoners, and a festival to commemorate the victory. The figures are almost life-size and give a sense of arrested movement, as if they had been caught by a daguerreotype plate. It is a dynamic composition with a superb handling of masses of color.

The technique was done in classic fresco. Cement was applied to the walls, and while it was still wet the artist drew his cartoon on it. Then his assistants—and there must have been many—applied the colors. As analyzed by the Mexican muralist Villagra, who aided in the copying of the Bonampak pictures, the whole of the three rooms must have been painted in forty-eight hours. Plasterer and artist have to work together in this medium, and since Villagra could not detect where the plaster was laid, the making of a fresco

98. *Mural painting is related to book illustration. It is quite possible that both were directed by the priests. Here artists paint the murals of Bonampak. The room is precisely drawn. Adapted by Alberto Beltrán.*

must have been a continuous process. The palette of the Bonampak artists was rich. The famous Maya blue dominates, and there are yellows and browns and a lustrous black. The colors were mostly mineral; the reds and yellows were oxides; Maya blue came from a blue chromiferous clay; and black was carbon. One authority believes that the ground colors were mixed with the resin of the *pom* tree, from which varnish is now produced commercially. The murals of Bonampak show us the Maya artists' mastery of line and color, and a passionate movement of figure, a limitless freedom of posture, that has never before appeared in primitive American art.

Although the Bonampak murals have disintegrated, they were superbly copied, and the small temple ruin duplicated; the latter can be seen in the Archaeological Museum at Mexico City.

The decoration of polychromic pottery can also be considered painting, and there are many superb examples of it. The Maya "book" itself was only a continuation of the mural. And in turn, many murals, especially those found at the ruins of Tulum and Santa Rita (in British Honduras), would appear to be copies of pictures in the "books."

31   *War and Weapons*

MAN HAS a double nature. There is scarcely any situation where man will not display, "simultaneously or alternatively," thinks Aldous Huxley, "repulsive characteristics combined with heroism"; this dichotomy is nowhere more clearly shown than in the character of the Mayas. They were master builders and architects, carvers of wood and jade, potters of some of the finest and most sensitive ceramics in America, if not in the world. They were artists working in fresco and water colors; they were sculptors fashioning little clay portraits of extraordinary mastery in realistic handling of form and movement. They were aesthetes. They were astronomers of no mean sort who charted the course of the planets and formed a calendar which in precision was better than that of either the Greeks or Egyptians. They were builders of roads, the finest form of communications the Americas knew (outside of Peru) until 1800. And they were seafarers of unusual courage, trader merchants with far-flung interests.

They were also warriors: "for any little cause they fought." "They never knew peace," said a chronicler, "especially when the corn harvest was over." The old myth of a peace-loving people passionately dedicated only to erecting dated monuments, tracing the planets in their flight, and preoccupied with writing complex glyphs, has been fully exploded. At every turn the scholar is confronted with sculptures showing Maya lords sitting on the necks of slaves, of battle captives being seized by the hair. The murals of Bonampak bristle with the sound and fury of battle. Yet one reads again and again about the peace-loving Mayas. All this has the odor of exquisite archaism.

War was continuous. It could not be otherwise. There were contending city-states with no set boundaries; farmers by the very nature of their agriculture moved back and forth in trespass. Commerce was carried on, then as now, at friend or enemy's expense. Slaves were important, and the only way to get them was in battle. Victims were needed for sacrifice, since an individual was not expected to immolate himself for the gods if someone else was available.

The war chief, *nacom*, was a professional. There were two. The

99. *The farmer was both agriculturist and warrior. There were no professional soldiers as war was of short duration. War dress was magnificent. From the Bonampak murals.*

office of one was hereditary and dealt with sacrifices. The other was a military leader elected or chosen for three years, and held in high honor. During this time he could neither drink nor have traffic with women. The *nacom* had to conduct the war festival during the month of Pax (beginning May 12). At this time "they bore the *nacom* about on a litter in great pomp, perfuming him with copal smoke as if he were an idol." Armies were gathered in the villages and towns. Every able man who knew how to use bow and arrow and lance was liable for service. The *ah holpop,* a town official, raised the troops. There was also a trained group, called *holkans,* who acted as mercenaries; they were led into battle by their own captains and "guided by a

100. *The* nacom (RIGHT) *holding judgment over prisoners of war. There were two such war chiefs—one was permanent, the other was elected for a three-year period. From the Bonampak murals.*

tall banner they went out in great silence . . . and when upon those marked for attack . . . with loud cries and great cruelties fell upon the unprepared enemy."

In present-day military terms, the Mayas, especially the Old Empire Mayas, were lightly armed. Their primary weapons were the spear, the obsidian-edged war club (called *maquahuitl* by the Aztecs), and the spear-throwing *atl-atl,* the last a very effective weapon as Bernal Díaz confirms ("our captain was wounded in no less than twelve places by these arrows"). For close-quarter fighting they used a broad-bladed flint knife and a three-pronged claw knife, made out of a large shell, that could work havoc. Slings (*yuntun*) were used; there is extant a sculpture showing a warrior carrying into battle a basket of stones the size of hen eggs.

The *nacom* died gloriously. No knight went into battle more panoplied than he. His wooden headgear had a magnificent stream of quetzal and parrot feathers cascading over his shoulders, his face was gaudily painted, and his jade bracelets and necklaces flashed like emeralds under the Maya sun. A marked man in battle, he was its primary object. When he was captured, his warriors usually fled—and he was sacrificed.

War, although continuous, was waged in relatively short battles. They often occurred in October when the farmer-soldier did not have to work his cornfield. Surprise was the desired tactic. Where it could not be effected, as in the wide grass savannas of Campeche, there were elaborate ritualistic promenades to overawe the enemy. If the land was high bush or jungle, tactical surprise was used. An attacking force sent out scouts—"road weasels," the Mayas called them—to feel out a town's defenses. These might be barricades, wooden palisades, and pits dug on trails with spikes to impale the unwary. Barriers were erected in a semicircular fashion and camouflaged. Larger cities were sometimes surrounded by a deep ditch as at Champotón or walled as were Mayapán, Tulum, Xelha, and others. The argument that the old Mayas were not warlike because their cities were not walled lacks historical perspective. Very few Inca towns were walled; the Inca people retired to a fortress (*pucara*) in case of attack. The Aztec cities were rarely fortified or walled. Many of the Maya towns were, however. Hernándo Cortés in his wonderful march across Yucatán and El Petén found a Cehache village encircled by a wooden rampart raised back of a dry moat in early American frontier fashion. At another village Cortés found the Indians waiting for him behind a veritable cheval-de-frise of cactus.

When defenses were plumbed, the Maya warriors attacked en masse. If the defenders were too firmly entrenched, the Mayas hurled entire hornets' nests into the enemy and set thatch roofs afire. Then in a chaos of sound, drums beating, conch shells and whistles blowing, they fell to. Slaughter was not the primary aim of warfare. Like the Aztecs, the Mayas wanted prisoners—the distinguished ones for sacrifice, the less worthy as slaves. After a victory the dead were decapitated and their jaws cleaned of flesh "and worn on the arm." Captains were sacrificed immediately; they did not wish "to leave anyone alive who might injure them afterwards."

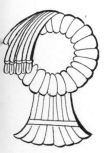

The Mexican intrusion in the ninth century gave these wars even more ferocity. The motives for war remained the same—commercial aggrandizement, slaves, tribal insults—but the Toltecs reintroduced the bow (*chulul*) and arrow (*halal*), which "they shot with great skill and force." The spear was better made, and the lance (*nabte*) was fitted with sharpened flint. The *atl-atl* spear thrower made this weapon deadlier. All this is well illustrated on the walls of the ball court at Chichén Itzá.

Defense also improved; shields (*chima*) were heavier and warriors now wore a quilted cotton jacket (*euyub*) that was soaked in salt brine to toughen it. This was, in fact, the Aztec *ichcau-ipilli.* The Spaniards later adopted it as better for tropical warfare than their own steel armor. It covered the chest and the entire left arm, which held the bow. The spearmen were armored with the *euyub* from neck to ankle.

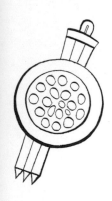

When the Spaniards met the Mayas in 1517 for their first formal battle, they encountered a well-organized foe. Even though the whole of Yucatán had been torn by internecine wars for a hundred years, the Mayas united against the foreign invaders, and neither the shock of hearing and being torn apart by firearms nor the surprise of seeing horses deterred them in the defense of their land. Bernal Díaz, who was twenty-three at the time, recalls that day in 1517. The battle had begun at dawn, with "troops moving towards us with flying colours." Maya battle techniques were similar to the Spaniards': divide, surround, outflank. They "divided themselves into different groups; arrows were released by the bowmen, some three hundred feet in the rear, and acted as a barrage for the advancing spearmen and rock-throwers; when close they used the two-handled obsidian-bladed swords." Díaz concedes the effectiveness of the Maya assault: "eighty of our men were wounded at the first onset." Even when fighting white men, the battle objective of the Indians remained the same—to capture their captain alive. Over the din of battle could be heard *"halach uinic,"* and the warriors pointed to Captain Valdivia. In their practice, battle was usually broken off when the *nacom* was killed, and warriors slung their shields on their backs, dropping their lances. This was called *cuch chimal,* a term used for anyone cowardly. This battle technique, which the Mayas never altered, worked to their disadvantage.

In the field the Mayas were supplied with food, drink, and fresh

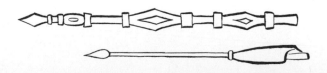

101. *Techniques of war: Mexican-Toltec invaders swing the spear-throwing* atl *and shields. They are raiding a Maya village. From the murals at Chichén Itzá.*

The weapons include (FROM TOP TO BOTTOM) *shield made of mat, other types of shields, wooden club set with flint or obsidian, throwing spears, obsidian-tipped arrows.*

supplies of stones, lances, and arrows. They showed, said the Spaniards, good military discipline and sound tactics.

The defects of Maya warfare were in its ceremonial and ritual characteristics. When the chieftain died, war ended; they did not fight at night, for the farming instinct was stronger than the warring. The Inca revolt against the Spaniards in Cuzco in 1536 might have been won had not the soldiers melted away as the planting season came upon them. The Mayas had the same obsession; as late as 1848, during the "war of the castes" the badly used Indians had Mérida, the capital, surrounded—until there came the time to plant maize.

Was war bad? One might put it paradoxically thus: Is evil necessarily evil? Could not that which began as bad end in becoming good? The Mayas thought so. If evil did not exist, neither could

good. War was evil insofar as things that Maya man made were destroyed, but it was good insofar as it brought new ideas in art, weapons, commerce, government; it helped in its way to develop the great Maya achievements.

32   Religion

RELIGION pervaded everything. The whole of Maya life was religiously oriented—birth, death, agriculture, time count, astronomy, and architecture; life itself was bound up with religion and its rituals.

The Maya cosmos was much like that of the highland Mexicans. It had thirteen heavens and nine hells. The heavens were a number of horizontal layers, one above the other, where the gods dwelled, and they were sustained by four gods who stood at the four cardinal directions and held up the heavens and the world. Each of these four gods had a symbolical color; this was important to the Maya mind (and also now to the archaeologist who is trying to understand this complex cosmology, since elements in the Maya calendar are connected with gods, direction, color).

The Chinese believed the world rested on a tortoise; the Mayas thought it rested on the back of a crocodile. The Greeks pictured the Pleiades as birds, while the Mayas thought them rattles of a snake and called the constellation *tzab*.

The world of the Mayas, according to them, had suffered cataclysmic destructions four times. When the veil lifts on Maya history they are living in its fifth re-creation. They even had traditions of a flood, and on one of the fascinating pages (page 74) of the *Dresden Codex* is a symbolical destruction of the world by a universal deluge, *haiyococab*, "water over the earth." The earth-upholding gods "escaped," the Indians told Diego de Landa, "when the world was destroyed by the deluge."

Gods pervaded the underworld, walked the earth, and animated the sky. Itzamná—the word meant "Lizard" and is symbolized as an old cross-eyed man with a lizard's body—headed the Maya pantheon. He had various attributes, as food-giver, patron of medicine, inventor of writing. There followed all forms and fashions of gods in all walks of life, all crafts, all professions; each had its patron. The beekeeper, the corngrower, the fisherman, the warrior, the traveler, the merchant, even the comedians and the dancers had their own deities. Ix Tab, the "Lady of the Rope," was the goddess of suicides; and Ix Chel, whom we met earlier, was patroness of weaving and childbirth. Her shrine on Cozumel Island was visited

102. *Itzamná* (LEFT) *was always drawn as old and therefore wise. He was the sky god and also the god of learning. Yum Kaax* (RIGHT), *god of corn, is always pictured as being youthful.*

by women who were in labor or expected to be. All women were expected to visit this mecca once in their lifetime. Bemoans one of the friars, "Those two wicked sanctuaries of Cozumel where they sent an infinite number of poor wretches to sacrifice."

Because each had so many different aspects, the Maya gods were considered multitudinous by the Spanish prelates who were trying to suppress them. "They have such a great quantity of idols, that as if their own personal gods were not enough there was not an animal or an insect of which they did not make a statue." A Spanish mayor, ordered in 1565 to put down idolatry in his city, was aghast at what his harvest of gods yielded: "In my presence, upwards of a million were brought."

The idea of god is an excitant. It also has mystery, and all mankind suffers from the same great uneasiness in the presence of the unknown. The Mayas thought of the gods as do all primitives. Life is subject to external powers; man cannot control the weather, even though he can count the steps to the moon. The best thing, the Mayas thought, is to keep on good terms with the gods and cajole them. Images of the rain god, Chac—an old man with an elongated nose and T-shaped eyes that symbolize tears and, therefore, water— are found as a decorative motif on almost every building in the Puuc. He was a quadruple god, with four directions or beings just as the Christian deity has three. Chac was indiscriminate. The rain he caused fell equally on the just and the unjust. Still, he had to be propitiated. In Mexico the same rain god was fed human hearts; in Yucatán, where drought was not as severe, human sacrifice occurred less frequently. In Peru, where agriculture was highly developed— with terracing, aqueducts, and so on—the rain gods were given short shrift.

Yum Kaax, thought to be the corn god, was youthful and depicted as holding a flowering plant. His portrait found at Copán is as moving as anything in Old World sculpture. Death was called Ah Puch and represented as a skeleton; he was the patron deity of the Maya day Cimi. The war god was painted red and black just as warriors were painted when going into battle. Wind, war, death, all had their individual traits and symbolical glyphs. All these were the unseen partners allied with man in the problem of survival. All gods had to be treated with scrupulous respect. Sacrifice had to be offered to them in a prescribed form and at the right time. Since the gods were so numerous and complex, the priests had to observe the rituals with almost legalistic exactitude based on long-observed formulas.

Religion is a system of ceremonies. The most primitive myths, ours included, attest the fatal chain of causation. The Maya lower man, who was told when to sow, reap, weep, and rejoice, must have found that ignorance had immeasurable consolations. Still he feared. And he gave eager ear to the god-man who provided the oracles, the *chilan*, "he who had the duty of giving the answers of the gods."

Ah kin (*kinyah*, "to divine") was the title of the Maya high priest. At the time of Mayapán there were twelve. In the Bonampak murals, which provide such an interesting picture of Maya social organization, the high priest is flanked by eight others no less resplendent than himself. This suggests that priestly power was not concentrated in the hands of one individual. Yet in plural or singular form the priests had a social power almost as great as the Maya lord. Their functions were to train the *chilanes,* examine them in the sciences, ceremonies, and duties of teaching, and send them, when trained, to villages and towns in the necessary numbers. "They taught the sons of other priests and the second sons of the Lord Maya." The Aztecs, it will be remembered, had a similar school, a *calmecac* for teaching the occult. Moctezuma was so trained; when chosen as Chief Speaker, i.e., "king," he was found sweeping down the steps of the great temple of Tenochtitlán.

"In the high priest," states Diego de Landa, "was the key of their learning and it was to these matters that they dedicated themselves." What they taught was "the computation of the years, months, days, the festivals and ceremonies, the administration of the sacraments, the fateful days and seasons, their methods of divination and their prophecies, their events and the cures for disease [disease was magical], and their antiquities and how to read and write with the letters and characters . . . along with the drawings which illustrate the meaning of the writings."

103. *The Maya high priest* (ah kin) *taught the ruling classes and others "the letters and reckoning of months and years."*

Beyond what we can infer, we have no idea of education among the Mayas. It is presumed that they had institutions analogous to those of the Aztecs, wherein sons of the lower man attended a clan school and sons of the directing classes went to a *calmecac* school. What is certain is that the lower men could not read the glyphs; they did not know how to calculate time nor interpret the almanacs. This was reserved for the nobles and priests who taught the sons of other priests "and provided them with books."

In contrast to the Aztec, who had rank without class, the Maya found it was not easy to escape the confines of caste. But, while we do not know enough to analyze the Maya social system, it can be said that a slave might obtain rank through his own efforts. One of the two Spaniards captured by the Mayas and held in slavery was Gonzalo Guerrero. He lived as a slave for eight years and, when Cortés arrived, refused to return to the Spaniards.* Instead he went to Chetumal near the Honduras border and when the Spaniards began their conquest, he was elected war lord by the Indians and led attacks on the conquistadors until he was killed in Honduras on August 14, 1536. He had married a woman of rank and reached one of the highest positions in the land. His case supports the idea that rank and class were not fixed and that a man could obtain rank through tribal service.

Generally, however, all culture was in the hands of the directing classes, since they alone had the time and energy to create it. "All cultures," as Oswald Spengler developed the theme, "are town cultures." This was especially true among the Mayas. The lower man's roots were in the soil that he cultivates, "earth becomes the earth-mother . . . the town is *not* his habitat and so all great cultures developed in towns."

History, as Spengler envisioned it—and this is confirmed by what we know of the Mayas—is the history of civic man, and all effectual history begins with the primary classes, the nobility and priesthood. The lower man is history-less; he is the eternal man and independent of every culture, which he precedes and outlives. Writing and written history belong to the nobleman. Priests of the

* Bernal Díaz gives this version of Gonzalo Guerrero's apostasy; to his companion Aquilar, who went to Cortés, Guerrero said: "Brother Aguilar, I am married and have three children and the Indians look upon me as a Cacique and a captain in wartime— You go, and God be with you, but me, with my face tattooed and ears pierced, what would the Spaniards say if they saw me in this guise? . . ."

Mayas were, as Diego de Landa said, the key to their learning, and it was to this matter that they dedicated themselves. In all high cultures the script was in the keeping of the priesthood, and knowledge, technical knowledge, in the hands of the few. It is not otherwise in our modern world. "A selective massacre of three or four thousand technicians . . . would bring the whole economic and social life of England to a standstill."[86]

Under the *ah kin* were various priestly officeholders; *chilan, chac,* and *nacom* (to be distinguished from the war chief of the same name), and the cure doctors. The classification was almost the same as that found in Mexico. The *chilan,* an interpreter of the gods, was carried on a litter. When about to make a prognostication, he retired to a darkened room and fell into a trance; later he delivered it in "measured words." He read the *tzolkin,* book of days. The *chacs* were four old, honored men whose function was "to aid the priest." The *nacom* was the one who cut open the chests of the sacrificial victims and jerked out the beating hearts.

The *ah kin's* office was hereditary; his sons or nearest relative succeeded him. The *ah kin* paid no taxes and lived mostly on contributions. His dress was of monastic simplicity. In a sense it was symbolical, being a long, white, sleeveless robe of bark cloth, beaten from the fiber of the wild *Ficus* tree. Its edges were sometimes ornamented with shells. His miter was a bark cloth "crown." The hair, left long, was unkempt and unwashed, "stinky" from the blood of sacrifice.

Sacrifice had the magic virtue of a charm. It has been common to all cultures, our own included, even though it is often represented as something else. It was practiced by the Mayas, one supposes, from their very beginnings. The fact of human sacrifice has been sicklied over with a pale cast of thought by those archaeological historians who, having made of the Mayas the "intellectuals of the New World," believe that sacrifice is not compatible with their calendric system and glyph writing. But then the Greeks, too, were bloodthirsty and had human sacrifices, and this has not marred our interest in them. Besides, most civilizations have their private horrors and it has been said "to understand is not necessarily to pardon, but there is no harm in trying to understand."

Like any other living beings, the gods had to be nourished, and since the gods proceeded necessarily from the Maya brain, they were imperfect and had human faults. If rain was withheld or disease appeared, it was because the gods were not properly propitiated. Blood and, most of all, throbbing human hearts were cherished by the gods. War yielded prisoners for sacrifice; in addition women and children were immolated, "and were made much of before sacrifice and feasted up to the day; they were well guarded so that they would not run away or pollute themselves by any act of carnal sin."

A victim marked for sacrifice was painted blue, that famous Maya blue which is found on murals and stone carvings. If he was to be sacrificed by the arrow ceremony (we do not know the Maya word), he was tied in crucifix fashion to a wooden frame high off the ground, and they "danced a solemn dance about him." The priest wounded the victim in the "place of shame" (i.e., the penis), and the blood that dripped from the wound was smeared on an idol near by. Then at a given signal the dancers one by one, as they came in front of him, released their arrows: "in this way they made his whole chest look like a hedgehog of arrows." There are those who would like to believe that this sacrifice is un-Maya (the Plains Indians, such as the Pawnees, did it the same way), yet an illustration of the ceremony is found scratched on the walls of a temple at Tikal.

The most spectacular sacrifice was, literally, heart-rending. The blue-painted sacrificial figure was spread-eagled over a sacrificial stone so shaped that it arched the chest. The arms and legs were held by four priestly *chacs,* and the *nacom* ripped a flint knife across the victim's chest, exposing the heart. Then, says Landa, "the Arm of God plunged into it and seized the heart like a raging tiger and snatched it out alive." This was a common ceremony among the Mayas and shown in murals and sculpture—though, to be sure, they were not so demonically devoted to it as the Aztecs, who in the year 1486 sacrificed twenty thousand persons.

Another form of sacrifice was to throw the "selected one" into wells. The great *cenote* at Chichén Itzá was the best known depository, and Landa described it. Four hundred years later Edward H. Thompson proved him correct when he dredged that sacred well and found the skeletal remains of men, women, and children, as well as the artifacts that had been thrown with them into this clouded water.

Blood has for primitives a mystical significance. The folklore

104. *Sacrifice was made at the* cenote *at Chichén Itzá. This occurred only on unusual occasions of drought, epidemic, or invasion. The remains of bodies and ornaments have been found at the bottom of the well.*

connected with it lies so deep in the human consciousness that it has slipped over into most religions; "washed by the blood of Jesus" is only a passing reference. Smearing the body with blood, or with a blood surrogate, increased the vital principle. The Mayas, however, "offered sacrifices of their own blood." They pierced their cheeks, their lower lips, "and their tongues in a slanting direction."* Blood so obtained was smeared on an image of the god that was being propitiated, or onto their own hair and bodies. Like other primitives, they did not consider blood as we do. Blood to them expressed vital principles even when outside the body. Its magic arrested witchcraft; it made the gods beholden. So obsessed with blood and its magical qualities were the Mayas that "they even," wrote Diego de Landa, "split the superfluous part of the virile member, cutting it and fraying it as they did their ears to obtain blood on account of which some were deceived into saying that they practiced circumcision." Blood from the penis was considered

* There is a sculpture, done in low relief, at Yaxchilán in the province of Chiapas (dated A.D. 750) that shows a kneeling Maya passing a spine-decked cord through his tongue while a fan bearer waves away with a feather fan the agony of his hurt.

especially efficacious. Another friar witnessed the ritual: "I saw the sacrifice. They took a chisel and a wooden mallet, placed the one who had to sacrifice himself on a smooth stone slab, took out the penis and made three cuts into it an inch long in the center; all the time they murmured incantations." Landa says: ". . . it is a horrible thing to see how inclined they were to this ceremony. A group of Indians who initiated this form of sacrifice had holes drilled completely through their virile member . . . obliquely from side to side and through this hole . . . they passed a thin cord." Thus fastened together, "they danced and the flowing blood was caught and then the idol annointed with it. . . ."

All this was done so that the gods would be properly propitiated and so that they would not withhold the gifts of life. A nineteenth-century philosopher summed up man's religious history with an ironical apothegm: "Blood and cruelty are the foundation of all *good* things."

33   The Calendar

THE THOUGHTS of Hans Castorp as he contemplates the flight of time on top of the Magic Mountain, in Thomas Mann's novel, would have found a sympathetic response among the Mayas, for no other people in history made of time so great a fetish.

The whole of Mayadom with its hundreds of stone cities and thousands of sculptured stones may be said to be one vast monument to their extraordinary preoccupation with time and its consequences. On ball courts and temples, on lintels, sculptured panels, shells, jade, polychromic dishes, on wood, on stone and modeled stucco, the Mayas over a period of a thousand years carved the date when each particular piece was finished or begun, or a date that marked some important event of the past or present. At Copán the famed Hieroglyphic Stairway—composed of sixty-two flights, thirty-three feet wide—has more than two thousand individual glyphs carved on its risers. The dates of completion can be read from these, but little else.

People of other civilizations were beset by time. What is a calendar when all is said and done but a method of classifying time into periods—days, weeks, months, years, centuries—for the convenience of civil life and, in the realm of religion, for fixing the precise moment for rituals. The Greeks bewailed, with a rare eloquence, the transience of youth and the flight of time. Other peoples have felt the pressure of endless continuity so depressing that in order to make it reasonably bearable they organized it into cycles—hence our calendar. Almost everyone, at one time or the other, is made aware of time's flux, and one often feels to excess the bitterness of departure; but the Mayas are a special case. One scholar found a Maya inscription that probed ninety million years into the past. Time, the Mayas concluded rightly, had no beginning and eternity was an everlasting moment. Still, why this obsessive preoccupation with time?

There have been attempts ever since the dawn of man to work out a satisfactory calendar. Man began to observe and record the positions of planets, the phases of the moon, and the eclipses of the sun to organize these celestial phenomena into calends, months.[91]

Greek chronology before the appearance of the philosopher Eratosthenes was absurdly inadequate. A Greek lunar calendar was calculated on the appearance of the first crescent moon, yet the city-states differed among themselves on when to insert the intercalary month, so that there was great confusion as to the correct date. Aristophanes made great sport of this confusion in his *Clouds,* where he makes the moon complain that days were not being correctly kept according to her reckoning.

The Egyptians after 3000 B.C. used a lunar calendar and divided their seasons into three: flood, seed, and harvest time. Like the Mayas, they had both a religious and civil calendar. The Jewish calendar was also lunar; it featured the seven-day week and the Sabbath. The Roman lunar calendar was hopelessly confused until Julius Caesar called in Sosigenes, who suggested that the Romans use the uneven month and the leap year.

The Mayas believed that time was cyclical, that the same influence and thus the same consequences would be repeated in history.

The Mayas had not one calendar but three. The *haab* year was made up of eighteen periods, or months, of twenty days each, plus a terminal period of five days called *uayeb* (the empty or unlucky days). The second was the *tzolkin,* a sacred calendar of 260 days. The Aztecs and Toltecs also had the *tzolkin.* No one knows why they settled on this precise number of days, unless it comes out of some "crystallized pantheon," for it has no astronomical significance. The third calendar was the "long count," which reckoned the number of days since the mythical beginning of the Maya era, which was dated 4-Ahau 8-Cumhu for reasons unknown (equivalent to 31111 B.C.). What occurred at this date? We do not know. There is no clue, for archaeology reveals that at this time the Mayas as such did not even exist. Still, all of the known calendars of the world hark back to a date which represents the beginning of time.*

Twenty *kins,* or days, made up the Maya month (*uinal*). Eighteen *uinals* made the 360-day year (*tun*); this plus the five-day *uayeb* brought the total of the Maya year to 365 days (*haab*). Next came the *katun,* a period of 7,200 days, or twenty *tun* years. Then there was the period of fifty-two years now called the "calendar round." Each day of the *haab* year had a name and number, as did each day of the sacred *tzolkin.* The coincidence of any given *haab* day with any given *tzolkin* day occurred every 18,980 (*haab*) days, or every fifty-two years. The Aztecs had a similar obsession with the fifty-two-year cycle.

Maya calendric system was not mere intellectual gymnastics. The farmer had to know when to plant and when to sow. He depended on the priest-astronomer to tell him when rain could be expected. The seafarer had to know when to expect a full moon, an eclipse, or a hurricane. The Mayas were dominated by fear and superstition, and used astronomy as a handmaiden of astrology, but they were sometimes remarkably accurate observers of the heavens. Maya astronomers calculated that the synodical revolution of Venus took an average of 584 days. The count made by modern astronomers, using precise instruments, is 583.92. The famed *Dresden Codex* is apparently a table of eclipse syzygies showing the revolutions of the planet Venus over a period of more than three centuries.

* The starting points of other world calendars are as follows:
1. Jewish—the supposed date of the creation of the world, 3761 B.C.
2. Greek—776 B.C., when the first Olympiad began.
3. Roman—the date of the foundation of Rome, 753 B.C.
4. Islamic—A.D. 622, the year in which Mohammed left Mecca.
5. Christian—the birth of Christ.

KIN

UINAL

TUN

KATUN

BAKTUN

PICTUN

CALABTUN

KINCHILTUN

106. *The mechanics of the Maya calendar, as worked out by J. Eric Thompson.
A schematic plan to work out the calendar as a mechanism. In the center is the
god of number 13; he prepares to set down the load of 13 Ahau at the end of his
day's march. In the center, the sacred 20-month calendar, at the right, the sacred
260-day calendar, which bears no relation to the solar year. The larger is the
365-day calendar (eighteen 20-day months plus the five unlucky Uayeb days).
It represents the calendar round or 18,980 different combinations of days,
numbers, names, and months. From J. E. S. Thompson,* The Rise and Fall of
Maya Civilization, *University of Oklahoma Press, Norman,* 1954, *Fig.* 12.

They had names for Venus (*chac noh ek*), the North Star
(*xamann ek*), Ursa Minor (the Maya name meant "guards of the
north,") the Pleiades (*tzab*, "rattles of the rattlesnake"), the Gemini
(*ak ek*, "turtle stars"), and Scorpio (*zinaan ek*, which curiously
enough meant the same as the Latin, "scorpion stars"). They believed that eclipses—they could predict the lunar eclipse every
173.31 days—were caused by ants eating at the planets.

Every moment of their lives was involved in the position of the
planets. They feared that if the gods were not propitiated they
would put an end to the world, and that is perhaps the reason for
their obsession with having an almost exact calendar, so that each
god at the right moment might have his prayers or the sacrifices
meant for him.

105. *The nine known Maya time periods with the corresponding
glyphs. Kin was a day; uinal, twenty days or a month; tun, 360
days; katun, twenty tuns (7,200 days). Time proceeded in this
manner until alautun, which was 23,040,000,000 days in length.*

ALAUTUN

Many scholars seem in agreement that the Mayas, no matter how widely dispersed, exchanged astronomical data to perfect their calendar and that there was a "congress" at Copán in A.D. 765 to adjust the calendar and the accumulated errors of the fifty-two years before that time. The month of Pop began their year, and they gathered at Copán to put Pop in order. The presence of the same date on Maya monuments as distant from one another as three hundred miles suggests intimate contacts for exchange of this data.

Diego de Landa was the first to call attention to their calendar. "They have their year as perfect as ours, consisting of 365 days and six hours. They divided it into two kinds of months, the one kind of thirty days . . . and the other kind of twenty days. . . . The whole year had eighteen of these months plus five days and six hours . . . for these . . . they have twenty days or characters by which they name them." Landa fortunately had the good sense to copy down the glyphs of the day signs, with their Maya names in Spanish script, and upon these sketches all subsequent study by epigraphers has been grounded.

Of the *katuns*, Landa said: "by them they kept an account of their ages marvelously well . . . and thus it was easy for an old man to whom I spoke . . . to remember traditions going back three hundred years. . . . whoever put in order this computation of *katuns*, if it was the devil, he did it, as he usually does, ordaining it for his own glory." The *katuns* set down in books were the mnemonic devices by which past events were remembered. Here were records of eclipses of the moon, and of unlucky days (floods, hurricanes, pestilence). If a pestilence had occurred on the date 13-Ahau, the Mayas were certain that pestilence would occur again on the same day. Typical is this prophecy in the Maya books: "13 Ahau. There is no luck for us on this day." Another entry: "5 Ahau . . . harsh is the face of this day-god and harsh are the things he brings."

Thus Maya religion made use of every possible device to exert control over the people, for as in all theocracies, astronomy, religion, ritual, and science were interlinked.

Aᴘᴀʀᴛ from the famous Inca road system which they somewhat resemble, the Maya communications were the best in the hemisphere until the Lancaster Turnpike was opened in North America in 1792. Those Maya *sacbeob* which are best known are ceremonial, for roads everywhere played a part in religion. Those who took part in sacred voyages were sacrosanct, and the curious custom of right of asylum extended to roads; wayfarers were under the protection of the gods. Anyone who dared attack Aztec merchants moving on roadways underwent swift retribution, and travelers walked the Inca royal road in perfect safety even though it went through hostile territory.

Early Spanish settlers in Yucatán noted the remains of Maya roads. "There are signs even today," says Diego de Landa, writing in the sixteenth century, "that there was once a handsome causeway from T'ho [now Mérida] to the other city, Izamal." This Izamal, another Spaniard noted, was a center of great pilgrimages: "for which reason there had been made *four roads* running out to the four cardinal points which reached to all ends of the land, Tabasco, Guatemala, Chiapas, so that today [1633] in many parts may be seen vestiges of those roads." In 1883 there were still, as reported by a traveler, remains of it; "a road from this Izamal ran to Polé, facing the sea and island of Cozumel." Polé was in a direct line with Cozumel Island and the road from Izamal was "used by pilgrims going to Cozumel to visit the shrine."

107. *Inland communications. Raised causeways connected many of the Maya centers.*

And there were other *sacbeob* connecting various ancient cities. "There are remains of paved highways which traverse all this kingdom and they say they ended in the east on the seashore. . . . these highways were like the Spanish *caminos reales,* which guided them with no fear of going astray." Roads were also seen in the jungles. A Spaniard reported that on his journey in 1560 from Chiapas to Champotón one league from Mazalan (near Lake Tacab in El Petén) they came upon a fine road, broad and level, which led to the city. Other *sacbeob* led through the jungle from Campeche to Lake Bacalar, one of the centers of Maya canoe building. A padre states in 1695 that he "followed roads through the swamps which had been built in ancient times and still were well preserved." Aerial photographs recently taken by oil geologists confirm the existence of these roads.

Hernán Cortés, in his celebrated march through the heartlands of the Maya in 1524, proved the reality of these roads. He was given by some Xicalango merchants a detailed map, painted on cotton cloth, which showed the route. At various places he followed causeways which went through mangrove swamps. He took the river route, up the Usumacinta; it was the interior route followed by Maya merchants going from Tabasco to Honduras. They made the first portion of the journey by canoes, but Cortés was impeded by his cavalry and was forced to build bridges. Above Iztapan "a fine large town on the back of the magnificent river [Usumacinta] he ordered a bridge to be built. . . . it was done in four days . . . and horses and men passed over it. . . . it contained more than a thousand logs the smallest of which was the thickness of a man's body. . . . I do not know what plan these Indians used to build this bridge; all that one can say is that it is the most extraordinary thing one has ever seen."

Once into the interior of Acalan Province, Cortés found his map listed seventy-two towns all connected by road; again he followed the route used by the Tabasco merchants. Itzamkanac was the Acalan capital. It had temples and nine hundred houses; and beyond it Cortés had found resthouses. Since Cortés's route lay near the ancient cities of Tikal and Uaxactún, he was crossing remains of roads that once connected these to all of the other Maya cities. At Tayasal, the Itzá-Maya capital of El Petén, Cortés found many merchants, their produce carried by slaves, on their way to the fairs of Nito and Naco; he shaped his way there. South of the river Polochic, which feeds into Lake Izabal, in turn flowing into the Gulf of Honduras, Cortés entered the city of Chacujal (it remains unexplored). There he found a city with several roads leading into and out of it. The Spaniards followed one to Nito (now named Lívingston), which is on the left, or north, bank of Lake Izabal; this was an important trading center frequented by Maya- and Nahuatl-speaking traders. From Nito travelers were transported by canoe to the other bank, where the road began.

The road wound for fifty miles through the rugged mountains of the Sierra de Espíritu Santo, down into the lower Motagua River valley and across the Sierro Mico. It was the same route taken by Stephens and Catherwood in their memorable journey. Stephens remembered those five hours, "dragged through mud-holes, squeezed in gulleys, knocked against trees and tumbled over roots; every step required care and physical exertion." When Catherwood was thrown clear off his mule and struck his head on an outsize tree, Stephens felt that their inglorious epitaph might be: "tossed over the head of a mule, brained by the trunk of a mahogany tree and buried in the mud of Mico Mountains." Yet three hundred years before there had been a fine road, and Bernal Díaz, that honest conquistador, mentions the wide, "direct" road he followed from Nito to Naco; others with him commented on the wide roads "bordered with fruit trees."

Maya roads constructed during the classical period (A.D. 300–900) seem to have connected most of the inland cities with those of the coast. A recent aerial oil survey in El Petén has revealed the scars of roads comparable to the known Maya road axis at Cobá. Tikal was bound by a causeway to Uaxactún and thence onward toward rivers which by canoe connected them with the sea in the province of Chetumal. Although there has been one very limited study of a Maya causeway, it may be presumed that many of the Maya centers in classical times were bound together by roads; trade routes have everywhere been reported by the early padre-explorers. Typical was that of Las Casas, who was poled up rivers and followed roads from the Rio Tacotalpa to Chiapas by way of Teapa and Solosuchiapa, thence took the old trade route over which came the yellow topaz beads that the Spaniards called "amber."

Maya cities in the Puuc, of which Uxmal was the center, were connected by roads, as Stephens first noted in November, 1841. The writer of this book has explored those roads during his various

periods in Yucatán. A causeway fifteen feet wide, varying in height
from two to four feet, runs from Uxmal to Kabah (where it still can
be seen). One part there makes a 180-degree turn to enter the gateway of Kabah; another leads on to Sayil, Labná, and other cities of
the Puuc. Northwest Uxmal was connected with Mayapán and from
there to Chichén Itzá. The latter has eight *sacbeob* within the city,
and at least two of the roads lead out of its environs toward other
Maya centers. Best known at Chichén Itzá is the ceremonial causeway that leads from the Temple of Kukulcán. Nine hundred feet in
length and thirty-three feet in width, it goes to the edge of the sacrificial *cenote*. Not so well known are the *sacbeob* that led out from
Chichén Itzá. These have been traced by the writer from an air survey. Photographs reveal that a road went from Chichén Itzá toward
Chabalam, where it doubtless connected with the well-known
(and only really surveyed) road that leads from Yaxuná sixty-two
miles toward Cobá.

Ceremonial roads within some of the greater Maya city centers
are, of course, well known. As was mentioned earlier, those of
Tikal, built between A.D. 400 and 900, were economic as well as
ceremonial. A causeway in the south ravine of the city acts as a dike;
the ravine itself, its porous limestone cemented, served as a reservoir.
The wide surface of the dike was a ceremonial road which passed
from one center to another. All of Tikal is bound by wide stone
causeways. Many other Maya sites have causeways. The one at
Labná, six hundred feet long and twenty-five feet wide, is well
known; it went from the principal temple to a smaller one famed
for its gateway. The newly uncovered ceremonial road at Dzibilchaltún, twice the width of the one at Labná and possibly
a thousand years older, reveals the form and function of a Maya
ceremonial road.

And at the shrine on Cozumel Island the first Spanish expedition there in 1517 reported that "this town was well paved . . . the
roads raised on the sides . . . and paved with large stones."

The only *sacbe* which has been formally explored is the so-called
Cobá-Yaxuná axis. The study took twenty days, and is described in
a small brochure.[200] The known length of the road is 62.3 miles. It
begins at the site of Yaxuná, thirteen miles southwest of Chichén
Itzá. Like most *sacbeob,* it is a causeway, raised above the surface of
the land, and despite the depressions it keeps an even level. It varies

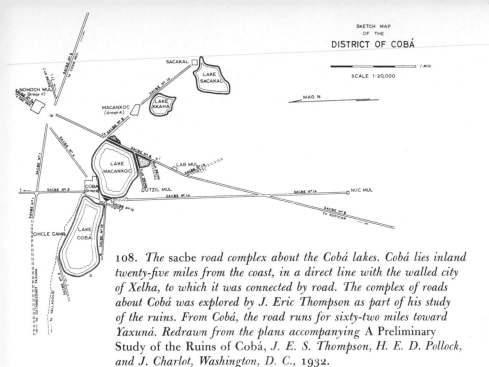

108. *The* sacbe *road complex about the Cobá lakes. Cobá lies inland twenty-five miles from the coast, in a direct line with the walled city of Xelha, to which it was connected by road. The complex of roads about Cobá was explored by J. Eric Thompson as part of his study of the ruins. From Cobá, the road runs for sixty-two miles toward Yaxuná. Redrawn from the plans accompanying* A Preliminary Study of the Ruins of Cobá, *J. E. S. Thompson, H. E. D. Pollock, and J. Charlot, Washington, D. C.,* 1932.

in height from two to eight feet, and is thirty-two feet wide. Maya *sacbeob* have various widths, so that we do not yet have a standard. The Inca coastal road, 2,520 miles long, had as its standard a width of twenty-four feet. The Incas, of course, used llamas for transport, but with the Mayas "the people were the oxen themselves." Although Maya architecture has been minutely studied, no one as yet has suggested what the Maya standard of measurement was.

The *sacbe* was dry-laid. The Maya engineer first laid down a roughly dressed limestone bed; the stones in this varied in weight from twenty-five to three hundred pounds. On top of this went a limestone gravel which when wetted and tramped down made a hard, smooth surface. The result was the *sacbe,* the white road which the early Spaniards found "fine, broad and level."

In its 62.3 miles the Cobá-Yaxuná road makes six changes in direction. There is no topographical reason for this, but the remains of a Maya city lying in the direction of every shift suggest that the road was built to reach towns already in existence.

At stated intervals ramparts cross the *sacbe* transversely; it may well be that these held "stations of the road," as was first suggested by Teobert Maler. The Incas maintained rest stations (*tampus*) along the entire length of their royal road, every twelve to eighteen miles. We know from the literature that the Mayas had a similar system,

SCHEMATIC MAP OF MAYA

(SACBEOB) ROADS

0   25   50   75   100 Miles

GULF OF MEXICO

GULF OF HONDURAS

N

109. *A schematic plan of the Maya* sacbe *road, based on the scattered observations of 400 years, some excavations and explorations, and one specific, although limited, study of a road. The map is based on that of S. G. Morley,* The Ancient Maya, *Stanford University Press, 1946, Plate 19, with additions.*

but we have neither its name nor precise function. We know much of the Inca *tampu* system, but nothing of the Maya other than a post-conquest reference to an *alcalde meson* who in each village was designated to keep up the traveler's house and see that wood, maize, and other provisions were always at hand. Markers have been found along the road every five miles. Señor Alfonso Villa, who explored the road, believes them to have been boundary markers rather than distance markers. It would be strange, however, if the Mayas did not mark distance, since most peoples did this on their roads. The Incas marked theirs by a *topo;* the Persians set up "pillars to indicate distances"; the Greeks, as bad as their roads were, marked them at intervals with piles of rocks onto which travelers were expected to toss an "absolution stone." Roman roads were marked; when Ptolemy built the African desert road, distance markers were placed every four miles. There must have been some sort of markers on the Maya *sacbeob,* for Landa stated it as a fact that travelers on the roads were expected to burn copal to honor the Ek Chuah, the god of traders and merchants.

Cobá was a large city.[164] Built between two lakes, it contained clusters of interrelated buildings. The city was the hub of a series of roads. More than sixteen have been found within the environs. One of them even crosses the arm of one of the lakes. On some roads there were near-by gateways with rectangular pillars and buildings, which suggest that tolls were collected or at least passage was controlled. The main road (*Sacbe* 1) continues in a southeastern direction from the junction point, goes through Nohogh-mul, and is then lost. No known exploration has been undertaken from this point eastward. The author, first by ground then from a low-flying plane, saw the unmistakable welts of a road running toward Xelha, which lies directly adjacent to the Caribbean Sea facing the southern end of Cozumel Island. Xelha lay on a road, fragments of which remain, that followed the coast twelve miles southward toward Tulum; north of Xelha the *sacbe* led to Polé and Mochi.

This road complex unmistakably exhibits that the *sacbeob* were not only ceremonial; they were trade arteries as well.

Having no draft animals, the Mayas carried all produce on their backs. The chieftains were carried in litters. Though no litters survive, there is an illustration of a very elaborate one scratched on the walls of a temple at Tikal; a chieftain being carried in a wicker-

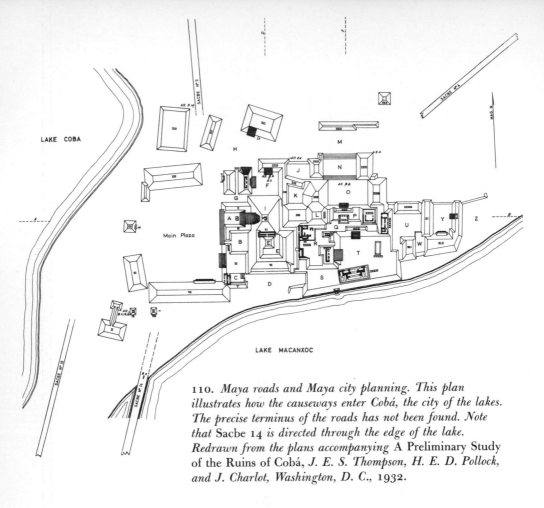

LAKE COBA

Main Plaza

LAKE MACANXOC

110. *Maya roads and Maya city planning. This plan
illustrates how the causeways enter Cobá, the city of the lakes.
The precise terminus of the roads has not been found. Note
that* Sacbe 14 *is directed through the edge of the lake.
Redrawn from the plans accompanying* A Preliminary Study
of the Ruins of Cobá, *J. E. S. Thompson, H. E. D. Pollock,
and J. Charlot, Washington, D. C., 1932.*

work palanquin is pictured on a vase from Guatemala; and there
are several eyewitness accounts of Maya chieftains being carried "in
large litters decorated with plumes."

All people who possessed roads had a developed messenger
service. The Incas had the *chasqui* courier system, which continued
down to the nineteenth century in Peru as an integral part of the
Spanish post-office system. The Aztecs had runners who carried
ideograph messages in a forked stick. Of the Maya system nothing
is known except that when Cortés sent a letter to the two Spaniards
living as slaves among the Mayas, an Indian carried it "wrapped up
in his hair."

On the methods of Maya road building again there is nothing.
Presumably, it was carried out by a corvée levied on the Maya villages through which the road passed and each particular village or
city was required to keep up its share. Maintenance makes the

road. The Mayas had to fight constantly with the plant life; a tree
seed here needs only a handful of earth to fructify. The Cobá road
has now been destroyed by trees growing on top of it, spreading
their roots through the interstices of lime rock. On top of the
Cobá-Yaxuná road, near Ekal, a large cylindrical stone thirteen feet
long was discovered; it weighed five tons. It was first thought to
have been a roller to flatten down the road, but now most achae-
ologists question this interpretation for technical reasons. Since the
whole of Yucatán is a mass of lime rubble and building lies close
at hand, it was not a herculean task to build these roads. It did
require considerable engineering knowledge to pass through
swamps and to lay down a straight undeviating roadbed. Since an
Indian can move fifteen hundred pounds of lime-rock rubble on his
back per day, a road could be fairly rapidly built. There is one
record; when the Spaniards in 1564 wanted to open a road from
Mérida to Maní, a distance of fifty miles, it took three hundred
Indians only three months to open the forest and build the *sacbe*.

 Sea Communications   35

THE MAYAS also used the sea road, which required no upkeep. They and they alone of all the great civilizations of
the ancient Americas were a maritime people, going out in large ocean-
going dugouts, traveling over thousands of miles of coastal sea.

The first thing that Columbus met when he landed at Guanaja
in 1502 were Maya boats. At one of the islands he saw and
examined one "as long as a galley, eight feet in breadth, rowed by
twenty-five Indian paddlers," and laden with commodities—cacao,
copper, bells, flint-edged swords, cotton cloth—brought from the
mainland, twenty miles distant.

As Spanish voyages began to multiply, others reported seeing
immense dugout canoes that held as "many as forty Indians." In
1542 at the siege of Omoa, a trading colony in Honduras, fifty war
canoes were sent at one time all the way from Chetumal, a distance
of over two hundred sea miles, to aid in resisting the conquistadors.
Many of the early Spanish accounts mention the tremendous num-

ber of canoes and the amount of canoe traffic along the entire coast from Tabasco to Panama.

The Maya canoe (*chem*) was usually made from cedar, and carved out of a single tree trunk often as long as eighty feet. It was built with a high bow and stern more or less as the Mayas have themselves pictured it in the murals of Chichén Itzá. There were several well-known canoe-building areas. The fallen cedars were dragged from the woods over log rollers by means of rope cable and manpower. At the town of Buct-zotz, a little west of Cape Cotoche, there was a special enterprise for cutting cedar and making it into canoes; these were largely used for the salt trade at Ekab.

In the province of Uyamil, near the inland lake of Bacalar, there is an immense area of cedar. The Mayas at Mazanho made a specialty of dugout building destined for the coastal sea traffic. Small rivers flowed out of the lake (the ruins of Ichpaatun, which date from the sixth century are close by) into the large Chetumal Bay. Between A.D. 400 and 800 Tikal and other interior cities had contact with the sea, using the river roads that emptied into Chetumal Bay. Farther north at Bahía de la Ascención—anciently, Zamabac—was a place for the embarking of "maritime traffic destined for Honduras and other regions south." [158] By the time of the Spanish arrival, circa 1511, trade had shifted farther north to Tulum. This city was connected by road to Xelha, thence to Cobá and the interior cities such as Chichén Itzá. So complete was their dominance of the coastal sea that the Mayas of Chikin Chel were known as "lords of the sea," while those seafarers about Chetumal were called "guardians of the sands," presumably because they protected the coast from the incursions of the Mosquito Indians from Nicaragua (who were still attacking up to the eighteenth century) and perhaps from stray Carib raiders who followed the spoor of trading canoes.

The whole coast about the Laguna de Términos—where Xicalango was located—was a network of rivers, bayous, and creeks. A Spanish map of the seventeenth century shows inland waterways and describes in detail routes by narrow channels, such as appear on the Florida coast where boats of small draft can move without actually going out into the open sea. This coast was difficult for European ships, which had to stand out to sea, but not for the Maya dugouts.

111. *Immense seagoing canoes "with as many as forty passengers" sailed the Gulf Coast, said Bernal Díaz (1517). A Maya drawing of canoes with houses along the coast, from the Temple of the Warriors, Chichén Itzá.*

Inland waterways led to the Usumacinta River, up which (by portage and prayer) the Indians managed to navigate two hundred miles. The rivers of Honduras were navigable for canoe traffic many miles inland, and salt, for example, was carried in sacks direct from the Yucatán salt ponds to the interior of Honduras. There the sacks were filled with cacao and obsidian for the return voyage. The whole coast was a Maya economic bloc with some concessions to the Nahuatl-speaking traders from Xicalango. Seafaring was coastal. Signs were erected, feather banners, to help sailors navigate the flat shore. The murals of Chichén Itzá, which illustrate Maya canoes, also show signs that could be so interpreted. One writer with lively imagination says they had a "lighthouse service"—perhaps there was an occasional fire, but scarcely a "service." The Romans, who hated the sea and called it "the pasture of fools," hugged the coast with their ships. So did the Mayas. Only in dire emergency, one gathers, did they navigate at night, at which time they used the North Star to guide them. The large canoes used a lateen sail—Bernal Díaz saw it—but mostly the trading canoes were "paddled by slaves just like the galley slaves of Venice."

There were limits to Maya seafaring. There is no evidence that the Mayas had contact with Cuba, even though it is only 125 miles away, perhaps because a bewildering and dangerous current runs between Cuba and Yucatán. Yet there was an occasional accidental, if not purposeful, contact with the Antilles. Bernal Díaz met at Cozumel Island "a good-looking Indian woman" who—spoke "the language of the Island of Jamaica . . . As I . . . knew the language

. . . we were very much astonished, and asked the woman how she happened there. . . . two years earlier she had started from Jamaica with ten Indians in a large canoe intending to go and fish . . . the currents had carried them over to this land where they had been driven ashore . . . her husband and all the Jamaica Indians had been killed and sacrificed to the Idols."

One wonders how far Maya sea traffic extended. There is evidence, archaeological and historical, that these voyages carried them from Tampico down to Panama. Following the coast line, this is over twenty-four hundred sea miles, and it would reach an impressive three thousand miles if they went as far south as Margarita Island, which lies fifteen miles off Venezuela opposite Araya Peninsula and was one pre-Columbian source of pearls. A baroque pear-shaped pearl was found in the tomb at Palenque under the Temple of Inscriptions (dated A.D. 700), and another was found in the tomb of the high priest at Chichén Itzá.

The Mayas maintained trading stations along the Caribbean coast in Yucatán and Quintana Roo; at Nito, where Lake Izabal debouches into the sea; inland at Naco; and along the Honduran coast at Omoa and Trujillo. Trujillo was seen by Cortés in 1524: "there was a mighty and haughty lord who commanded ten thousand people or more. . . . the Maya traded for birds, feathers, salt, and achiote."

From here the Mayas skirted the treacherous Mosquito coast, full of shoals and cays—where Columbus floundered on his last voyage in 1502—down to the San Juan River in Nicaragua (the same river for which William Walker and Commodore Vanderbilt contended in 1856, seeking for control of the Nicaragua Interoceanic Canal). There a trading station was maintained. Their canoes, we know from historical evidence, were poled up the San Juan River well over a hundred miles to Lake Nicaragua. "Other nations," stated a Spanish historian. "traded in the province of Nicaragua . . . especially those [Mayas] of Yucatán who came by the sea in canoes." The Spaniards immediately went there, guided by Maya traders, "because gold was carried from there."

After A.D. 900 the Mayas seemed to have extended their commerce to Panama, for from that time on gold frequently appears. Emeralds, if the Mayas had them—and the writer has seen none which are really emeralds—would have come from the same

Panamanian source. The goldworking Indians about Coclé, in Panama, traded with the Chibchas of highland Colombia, who exploited the emerald-producing lands about Muzo and Chimor, then the only source of emeralds in the New World.

There is no evidence of any direct Maya penetration into South America. No pottery has been found in South America which is unquestionably Maya. Finally, there is no hint in the traditions of any southern cultures that they were even dimly aware of the existence of the Mayas.

The Mayas navigated to islands only if those islands could be seen from land. Cozumel—its real name was *Ah-Cuzumil peten* (Swallow Island)—lies close to the mainland. Yet since an arm of the Gulf Stream runs between it and the mainland, sailing is treacherous. When Captain Montejo tried on one occasion to force the Indians to make the run when the sea was high, they refused. The water was *homoc-nac kaknab*—it boiled yellow. It is just this *homoc-nac kaknab* that kept Carib and Maya from any certain contact. Nothing Antillean has yet been found in Maya graves. However, as evidenced by the instance of the Jamaica woman and the famous castaway Aguilar, there must have been enough casual contacts to make the Mayas aware of "something out there." It is even possible that Carib canoes occasionally came purposely into Maya territorial waters; many of the coastal cities were walled for some reason.

Archaeological evidence shows that trading voyages went as far north as Tampico, to land of the Huastecs, who spoke a Maya dialect. Bitumen, which was widely used for boat caulking, at that time could be obtained only from oil seepages, and the latter were in Mexico. The Mayas also used bitumen in the preparation of effigy masks. Spindle whorls for making cotton thread, Huastec-made, are found in Maya graves. Even Tikal, which seems so hemmed in by jungle, yields sting-ray barbs, seaweed, and shells from the Pacific; Palenque, pearls from Margarita; the wells of Chichén Itzá, gold from Panama; and other sites, pottery from Vera Cruz.

Evidence of their use of the sea roads considerably changes the tribal portrait of the Mayas, who were so often pictured as cloistered in their green mansions and occupied only with the metaphysics of time.

"THE MAYA," said a sixteenth-century writer, "are commended . . . among all other Indians in that they have characters and letters with which they write their histories and ceremonies." And Diego de Landa agreed: "These people made use of certain characters . . . which they wrote on their books." Maya glyph writing was, in all of its aspects, the most advanced in the Americas, even though it was not of course unique. Many tribes of Mexico had lesser forms of it. It is fully possible that the Olmecs, who were northern neighbors of the Mayas, were the originators of glyph writing.

What Maya writing really *is* is disputable. For a long time it remained an utter enigma until Bishop Landa's manuscript *Account of the Things of Yucatán* was uncovered in 1864. He thought that this was an alphabet in Maya writing. What the Maya informants gave the bishop was no alphabet at all. When he asked for a letter, his informant drew "a glyphic element resembling the sound." For example *e* (pronounced "ay" in Spanish) was in Maya *be,* which means "road"; so the artist-informant drew the ideograph for "road," a pair of parallel lines representing the *sacbe.* When the outline of a human footprint was drawn between the parallels, it was the glyph for "travel." The discoverer of the Landa manuscript was the diligent though erratic scholar Charles Etienne Brasseur (the title "de Bourbourg" he had discarded with the fall of Napoleon III), who had held an administrative post under the ill-fated Maximilian of Mexico. He rushed into print with Landa's book and tried with fervid imagination to use it in reading the Maya *Codex Troano,* which lay in Paris. The result was catastrophic: "the master is he of the upheaved earth, the master of the calabash, the earth upheaved of the tawny beast; it is he, the master of the upheaved earth of the swollen earth, beyond measure, the master of the basin of water. . . ." All attempts to read Maya glyphs with this "alphabet" have been dismal failures; still, Eric Thompson believes that what Landa recorded is still as close to a Maya Rosetta stone as will ever be found.

Maya writing was ideographic, so thought William Gates, a very lucid writer-scholar. It had system; there are main elements, names

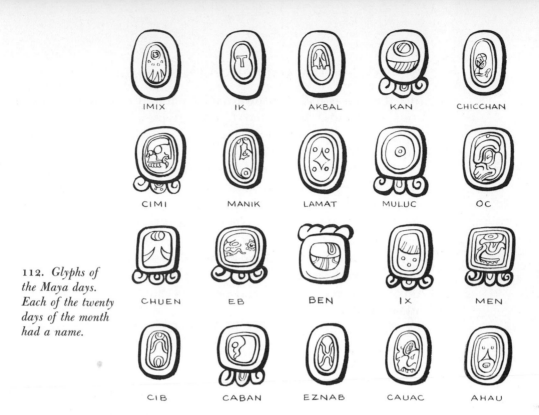

IMIX   IK   AKBAL   KAN   CHICCHAN

CIMI   MANIK   LAMAT   MULUC   OC

CHUEN   EB   BEN   IX   MEN

CIB   CABAN   EZNAB   CAUAC   AHAU

112. *Glyphs of the Maya days. Each of the twenty days of the month had a name.*

of things, words of action (which imply verbs). There are a number of adjectival glyphs, such as those representing colors, and a set of minor glyphic elements wholly undefined, which could be "very necessary parts of a written language." Gates set out to make a tabulation of Maya glyph forms, a sort of Maya dictionary (which is not too highly approved by scholars now because casting the glyphs into type, it is felt, reduces their value for students). The work was left unfinished at his death in 1940, and his materials were dispersed.[69]

Maya writing is ideographic, since the characters stand for abstract ideas. It also has rebus writing elements. It is pictorial and symbolic but not syllabic, yet there is a considerable amount of phonetics in the writing. Aztec writing is simpler in form, and is capable of a form of iconomatic punning: a grasshopper (*chapul*) is drawn on top of a mountain (*tepec*) resulting in the word "Chapultepec," which can be easily read. The system was exact enough so that the names of every Aztec city, village, province, and chieftain are known, whereas among the Mayas not a single glyph has been identified that is associated with any person or place. It is known

379

that the Mayas had their own names painted or tattooed on their arms or hands. If, in the future, glyphs that "identify" are recognized, then one may have the material to read a Maya sentence.[192]

The Maya glyph was self-contained. It filled its appointed place. There are glyph compounds. The main element has various affixes which modify it and extend it. A prefix could be placed to the left or below a postfix, to its right or below; where it was placed depended on the space that was being allowed for it. William Gates, when redrawing all the known glyphs that occur in the three surviving codices, found that there were many different types of affixes, subfixes, prefixes, and postfixes. Some were pictographic, others symbolical.

Of this extensive corpus of Maya texts, 60 per cent remains undeciphered. Those glyphs which deal with dates and calculations can be read; those that deal with ritual and history cannot.

Since much of the preoccupation of the Mayas was with the calendric system, calculation was well developed. Our counting system is decimal. Theirs was vigesimal; twenty, the total number of toes and fingers, became the base. As numerical symbols the bar (—) had a value of five and the dot (•) a value of one. They counted in groups of twenty. Twenty was represented by a shell (the symbol of zero) with a dot over it. Independent discovery of the abstract zero gave the Mayas a system of place notation, and with it they were able to calculate immense sums. As a system it was far better than the Greek, Egyptian, or the cumbersome Roman method. The early Spaniards were most impressed with the facility the Indians had for counting cacao beans, which were not sold in dry measure or weight but counted bean by bean and sold in lots of from four hundred to eight thousand beans, which could be calculated very quickly.

Maya scholars, having worked out a method of determining the dates from the glyphs, have had many of their deductions confirmed by the carbon-14 system of dating. Of the greater mass of glyphs, beyond those of calendric significance, little else has been deciphered; and the best minds admit that they have reached a stalemate. We are all in the dark together. The only difference is that while the scholar keeps loudly knocking at the door, the ignoramus sits quietly in the center of the room.

Yuri Knorosow, a member of the Russian Academy of Sciences, has announced that he possesses a "key" to the Maya glyphs. While those who have long worked on the subject state that "it is hazardous to estimate the number of glyphs because most of them are compound, and mostly undecipherable since there is no alphabet," Knorosow has no such qualms. He seems to have carefully studied all the literature, and the most famed of Maya codices, the *Dresden*,

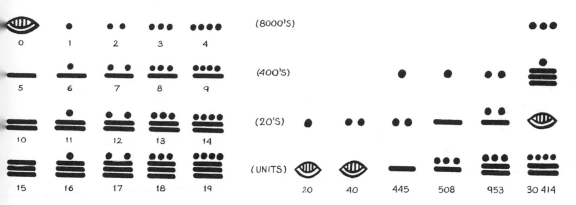

113. *Maya numeration. The mollusk shell is the symbol for zero; the dot is one, the bar is five. By combining forms, large totals could be calculated. From J. E. S. Thompson,* The Rise and Fall of Maya Civilization, *University of Oklahoma Press, Norman, 1954.*

is in Russian hands. He states that the number of Maya glyphs amount to 270, of which 170 are generally used. He places them in three categories: the ideographic, which are mostly self-explanatory; the phonetic, which appear most often; and the determinative, which are rare and not meant to be read. Knorosow asserts that he is now ready to "read" all of the existing codices. Those who have given much of their lives to the study remain rightly skeptical about the Russian Maya experts. But the Russians have been the first to see the other face of the moon. Can it be that they will show us the other face of the Mayas?

It is a historical fact that almost all of the pioneering in the deciphering of the texts of "lost" civilizations has been done by nonprofessionals, i.e., those who were not primarily trained in archaeology and did not gain their livelihood by it.

Jean Francois Champollion was only nineteen and certainly not an archaeologist when he used the Rosetta stone to decipher Egyptian texts. Georg Grotefend, a simple German schoolteacher, unraveled cuneiform writing that looked "like bird tracks on wet sand." Diego de Landa, who gave us the clue to the Maya glyphs, was of course a friar; Juan Pío Perez, who worked out the Maya numerical system, was a local administrative official in Peto, Yucatán. "I have discovered the secret of the ahua and Katun count . . . I determined the character of the great cycles"—in this manner J. T. Goodman announced his discovery of the reduction of Maya dates. A newspaperman, he was the editor of the *Territorial Enterprise* who gave Mark Twain his start as a journalist. Goodman had never seen a Maya. Nor had Dr. Ernst Förstemann, the librarian at Dresden where the famed codex lay. Developing an interest in Maya hieroglyphs late in life, he worked for fourteen years until he "had wrest the secret of the Maya calendar from codex and stela." Benjamin Whorf, professionally an insurance actuary in Connecticut, was an authority on American linguistics. And to shift the archaeological scene but not the theme, it was only recently that Michael Vestris, a young English architect, succeeded where all other scholars had failed in unraveling the Cretan linear script, which he long insisted was really primitive Greek. The talented nonprofessional is an important figure in archaeology because, of all the art-sciences, it is the one that he can enter without an academic gown.

37   *Literature*

THE MAYAS had books. Mentioned earlier was the chronicler Cuidad-Real, who thought that they were to be commended for three things: absence of cannibalism, lack of interest in sodomy, and the writing of books. These were naturally not our kind of book; they were in effect illustrated glyph texts. But the fact that they had books astonished the Spaniards most. When young Bernal Díaz thumbed through them in a Totonac temple at Cempoala, he saw "many paper books doubled together in folds. . . . it gave me much to think over. . . . I do not know precisely how to describe it." And, as we have seen, among the things sent back to Charles V along with gold and feather ornaments were "two books such as the Indians use." Many of the scholars in Spain were "wrapped in astonishment" at this proof of high culture. For not only the Mayas but the Totonacs, Aztecs, Mixtecs, and almost all other Indians of high culture had books. The Mayas, however, had them over the longest period of time—perhaps as long as eight hundred years.

At the time of the Spanish conquest, almost every large center in Yucatán had its depository of books. As late as 1697 a Spaniard reported seeing records still being kept in hieroglyphic writing at Tayasal in El Petén.

There cannot be any doubt of the extent to which books were used; the comments left by Spaniards are unusually complete on the subject. "The natives had [written] characters and understood one another by means of them." Said a report to the King of Spain: "These *Ah Kines* had books of figures . . . and they knew what happened many years before." Diego de Landa confirms all this. The Mayas "knew how to read and write with letters and characters with which they wrote and drawings which illustrated the meaning of the writings. . . . their books were written on large sheets of paper doubled in folds, which were enclosed entirely between boards which they decorated, and they wrote on both sides in columns following the order of the folds. And they made this paper from the roots of a tree."

Maya paper was made of bark pounded from the inner bast fibers of *Ficus* trees. The bark was pulled from the tree two palms wide and as long as twenty feet. It was soaked first in water to soften it and to extract the heavy white sap, then beaten with a ribbed beater. This action stretched the fibers so that a piece of bark twelve inches wide was extended to paper forty inches in width. It was beaten until it was, as a Spaniard said, a "leaf the thickness of a Mexican real of eight," i.e., two millimeters (.079 inches) in thickness. This form of papermaking is widespread; the methods, instruments for beating, and the species of plant involved are almost identical in widely separated areas—the Amazon, Africa, Polynesia, and Easter Island. The author, in his book on Maya papermaking,[203] thought then that the Mayas were the earliest American papermakers. He is now not so certain. The craft, like so much else, was practiced by most of the tribes of Middle America.

The Mayas used bark paper as clothing before they learned to weave cotton cloth. Their priests continued to wear bark paper clothes even after they had weaving. The transition from clothing into paper has an old cultural history.*

This Maya paper (*huun*) had wide usage: plans for building were made on it; it was used in puzzling out the intricacies of glyphs; designs on stelae were worked out on it before carving. We know the Mayas had maps. Their contemporaries, the Aztecs, used *amatl* paper for land charts, tribute charges, histories, and genealogies; paper itself was an item of tribute.

A Spaniard who saw the Itzás' books in 1697 gave a fully accurate account of their size and appearance: "Books of a quarter of a yard high [i.e., nine inches] and about five fingers in width, made of the bark of trees, they are folded from side to side to another like screens. These are painted on both sides." [100] The physical appearance of the three surviving Maya books, in particular the *Dresden Codex*, fits this description. It is made from a single piece of bark paper beaten from the fibers of the *copo* (*Ficus padiofolia*). It is eight inches high, 126 inches in length, and folded like a screen. It was sized by means of warmed stone irons (such as the Mexican *xicaltetl*), which would have given it surface (the Renaissance papermakers polished their handmade paper with an agate stone), or it may have been given a sizing with a mixture of lime and the starch yielded by a plant similar to manioc. Diego de Landa remarks that Maya paper was given "a white gloss upon which it was easy to write." The paper was folded into a book by doubling the paper screenwise; each leaf or page measured about three inches wide by eight in length. The ends were glued to wooden boards presumably carved with glyph titles. A Mexican codex that survives is similarly bound and is ornamented with inlaid jade on the order of the jeweled bindings of Europe's Renaissance. The *Dresden Codex* has thirty-nine leaves painted on both sides, or seventy-eight pages. These pages are the "folds of the katun," of which the codices speak. The Maya priest-scribes

---

* In Europe, fiber sources were not available for paper until men began to wear linen underwear. The cast-off garments were eagerly sought by thirteenth-century papermakers. The Abbot of Cluny, on a visit to Italian paper mills, was shocked: "God reads the book in Heaven . . . but what kind of a book? It is the kind we have in daily use, a parchment made from the skins of goats, or is it the rags of all cast-off undergarments . . . and some other vile material?"

worked with brushes made from bristles of the wild pig. The colors used were dark red, light red, black, blue, yellow, brown, green, and a lustrous black.

There is no precise date on the beginnings of the Maya book. The Maya after A.D. 889, for reasons unknown, abandoned the practice of erecting dated carved-stone stelae. After this, it is deduced, they kept similar records on a more obedient medium such as paper. Sometime around 889, then, it is conjectured that the first Maya book came into being.

The *Dresden Codex* is the finest of the three surviving Maya books, and gets its name from the Royal Library at Dresden, where it was brought from Vienna in 1739. The precise provenance of the book is unknown, but since its latest date corresponds to A.D. 1178, Dr. Eric Thompson believes it was a new edition made about the twelfth century from an original executed in the classical period (A.D. 323–889). The contents (admittedly only half of the glyphs can be deciphered) are in the form of a divinatory almanac, dealing with women, childbirth, and weaving. There are multiplication tables for the synodical revolutions of the planet Venus and prognostications. The book ends with the sky god, Itzamná, as a celestial monster, pouring water out of his mouth and destroying the Maya world by flood. Of the three codices, the *Dresden* is astronomical, the *Tro-Cortesianus* astrological, the *Peresianus* ritualistic. They present almost nothing that can be regarded as history.*

The Spaniards said the Maya books treated "of the lives of their lords and the common people" and spoke of "the history they contained." Seventy years after the conquest and the burning of the books, a Spaniard still spoke of seeing "books" painted in color, "giving the count of their years, the wars, epidemics, hurricanes, inundations, famines and other events." And as late as 1697 an isolated Itzá chieftain knew all about the history of Yucatán because "he had read it in his books." It has been stated that "their

---

* Of the other two surviving Maya codices, the *Codex Peresianus* and the *Codex Tro-Cortesianus*, are respectively in Paris and Madrid. The *Peresianus* is so called because the name "Perez" appeared on its wrapping when it was found in a chimney corner of the Bibliothèque Nationale, with a basketful of other old papers, in 1860. The *Tro-Cortesianus*, discovered in the 1860s, was found in two pieces (the *Troano* and the *Cortesianus*), each in a different place in Spain. It is composed of fifty-six leaves of 112 pages, and when extended is 23½ feet long. A late Maya product (circa 1400), it is crudely done and concerned with divinatory ceremonies. The codex has many illustrations of Maya crafts—weaving, pottery, deer snaring—all very instructive to the ethnographer.

hieroglyphic literature seems to have covered nearly every branch of Maya science," but there are no examples of it. That they regarded their books as most sacred is shown by Landa's remark, "the most important possession that the nobles who abandoned Mayapán [on its destruction] took to their own province was the books of their sciences."

Learning was aristocratic and belonged only to the ruling classes, for "priests were the key of their learning. . . . they employed themselves in the duties of the temples and in teaching their sciences as well as in writing books about them." Although their interest in their own genealogy was intense, no personal names or names of cities have been identified in the old Maya glyphs. Yet we know that there were painted charts and maps, and it is stated as a historical fact in the *Popol Vuh* that when the Toltecs journeyed toward Yucatán they "took of their paintings, in which were recorded all the things of ancient times," and that the highland Mayas received *u tzibal tulan,* the paintings of ancient Tula (last capital of the Toltecs) "in which they wrote their histories." In fact, the similarity between some of the buildings at Chichén Itzá and Tula, seven hundred and fifty miles apart, is so exact that the architectural data could have been transmitted no other way than by drawings painted on paper. They had, in addition, books on medicine, eighteenth-century copies in European script, no doubt first translated from the glyphs into written Maya. José de Acosta, who traveled widely in Peru and Mexico (1565), wrote: "there used to exist some books in which the learned Indians kept . . . a knowledge of plants, animals and other things." However, they did not use their glyph writing for contracts—"in sales and contracts there were no written agreements"—and this was a source of confusion and friction, which often led to war.

The Aztecs, whose writing was less developed than that of the Mayas, kept precise accounts of tribute and income, maps of property, and a detailed map of Tenochtitlán. We know the correct succession of their leaders and the names of all the ancient Aztec towns and provinces. (The Aztecs also left behind an impressive literature, which was set down by Aztec-Spanish scribes in the sixteenth century.[67]) Among the Mayas, we do not even know the names of their "kings" at least not until very late. Even the Incas, who had no other writing, had (after A.D. 1250) a *quipu* string recorder; this acted as a mnemonic device which gave them, and now us, a chronology of their history. It is possible that Maya glyph writing is not really a written language at all, but rather a mnemonic system by which, with dates, glyph pictures of gods, and symbols, the reader had his memory jogged. The fact that they had songs in meter raises this question. The early Greeks, guided by Mnemosyne, sang in meter the history of things past; the *Iliad* was chanted long before Homer set it down. The Druids employed bards to record in mnemonic rhyme their chronologies and treatises on geography, the sea, and the techniques of husbandry. Henry III employed a *versificator regis* to chant rhymed chronicles, epitaphs, and the like.

But if the Maya books covered fields other than those of the extant codices, we will never know, because the Spanish friars destroyed them. Says Diego de Landa flatly, ". . . we burned them all . . ."

It was decreed that idolatry must be stamped out. Diego de Landa himself signed the decree in 1562. As part of the Spanish religious program, all Maya books were seized and brought to the town of Maní.* "We found a large number of books," wrote Landa, ". . . and they contained nothing in which there was not to be seen supersition and lies of the devil, so we burned them all, which they regretted to an amazing degree and which caused them much affliction." This is confirmed by a historian writing in 1633. In Maní, Landa "collected the books and he commanded them burned. They burned many historical books of ancient Yucatán which told of its beginnings and history, which were of so much value." José de Acosta, that learned Jesuit who traveled in Peru and Mexico in the springtime of that world, was angry at this iconoclasm: "this follows from some stupid zeal, when without knowing or wishing to know the things of the Indies, they say as in a sealed package that everything is sorcery. . . . the ones who have wished earnestly to be informed of these found many things worthy of consideration."

Diego de Landa carried out this work thoroughly enough; of the hundreds of books, only three somehow escaped this holocaust.

* "And . . . this witness being in the said pueblo of Maní and Homun, saw the said friars suspend many Indians by their arms, and some of them by the feet and hang stones from their feet and whip them and spatter them with tapers of burning wax, and mistreat them grievously in such a way that afterwards, at the said time, when as he has said they were given penance and brought forth in the said public auto [da-fé], there was not a sound place on their bodies where they could be whipped. . . ."

The general content of the Maya texts is known. It is doubted, even by the best-informed scholars, that historical events were recorded on the monuments. Here is a typical example of a Maya text found on a superbly carved stela at Tikal: "6 Ahau 13 Muan, completion of the count of 14, the completion of the *tun*." Its concern is calendric. There is no mention of the name of the city, the ruler, or any historical events that occurred during "6 Ahau 13 Muan." Such is the nature of inscribed texts elsewhere among the Mayas.

How very different are the records of the Middle East. They are tautological, chatty, and informative, as for example, *The Sixty-Two Curses of Esarhaddon*.* In Maya terms this Assyrian talking tablet is miniscule (18 by 12 inches). In style it differs not much from the tablets at Palenque: king-gods thundering down at kneeling vassals. In May, 672 B.C., Esarhaddon, King of Assyria, swore his vassals to a covenant and called down on them an awesome array of curses if they violated it. He demanded that his son Ashurbanipal be his successor. The tablet is alive with furor; the very names clang like the crash of cymbals: ". . . may Sarantium, who gives light and seed, destroy your name and land . . . may Ishtar, goddess of battles and war, smash your bow . . ." and so it goes on until sixty-two curses are uttered. Out of it come dates, history, people, character.

What can one find out about the Mayas from their glyph texts such as this?

> Katun 11 Ahau is set upon the mat: is set upon the throne. When the ruler is set up: Yxcal Chac sits face to their ruler.

> The fan of heaven shall descend; the wreath of heaven, the bouquet of heaven, shall descend.

> The drum of the Lord 11 Ahau shall resound; his rattle shall resound.

> When knives of flint are set in his mantle; on that day there shall be the green turkey; on that day there shall be Sulim Chan; on that day there shall be Chakanputun.

> They shall find their harvest among the trees: they shall find their harvest among the rocks, those who have lost their harvest in the *katun* of Lord 11 Ahau.[171]

* Transcribed by Donald J. Wiseman, Assistant Keeper in the Department of Western Asiatic Antiquities in the British Museum.

Such is the nature of the inscribed texts found throughout Mayadom.

Only on the very rarest occasions is there anything other than this almost pathological concern with time's passage. Years were burdens carried by the gods, who were good or malign, none indifferent. The bad could be influenced by appropriate ceremonies, and it was "possible to ease the woes of Ix and apply balm to the ills of Cauac." Like ourselves, the Mayas judged human actions by the pain and pleasure caused by them. That which was carved on Maya monuments was to influence the gods, but it had scarcely anything of what we think of as literature.

In addition to the three surviving Maya codices and the vast corpus of Maya glyph texts on the monuments, there are *The Books of Chilam Balam (The Books of the Jaguar Priest).** There are many of these. The text is Maya, written in European script. The dates of their composition vary between the first half of the sixteenth century, when the Maya conquest was a fact, and the late eighteenth century. The themes are of a similar tenor to that which has been deciphered in the Maya books. Maya priests dictated from the books that had escaped the burning to a bilingual scribe who set it down in Maya in European script. They are not chronicles in our sense. As to whether they are literature, let the books speak for themselves. The opening lines of one of them read:

> This is the order of the Katunes since [the Itzás] left their land, their home of Nonoual.

> Four Katunes stayed the Tutul Xiu, Ahau-10 Ahau, [A.D. 849-928] at the decline of the Zuyua.

In these books there is much on the "language of Zuyua," a cabalistic form of speech used by priests to determine if those of their kind were worthy and knew the details of rituals. One will notice how antiphonal is the text. It suggests that much of Maya literature was oral, like that of the other earlier cultures.

There are few surviving chants, history chanted to meter and drumbeat:

> *A tender boy was I*
>
> *at Chichén*

---

* There are many different texts of *The Books of Chilam Balam*. For an excellent summary of them all, see *El libro de los Libros de Chilam Balam*, by Alfredo Barrerra Vasquez and Silvia Rendón, Mexico, 1954.

> *When the evil man*
> > *the army master*
> *Came to seize the land*
> *O at Chichén Itzá*
> > *godlessness was born*
> *Yulu uayano*
> *One mix was the day*
> > *when he*
> *When he was taken at*
> > *Chikin Ch'en*
> *Behold how I remember the*
> > *the song*
> *Godliness was favored*
> *Yulu uayano*

We know that the Mayas had dramatic presentations. Dances were many, reaching into hundreds of distinct choreographies. Rhythm was considered so important by the Mayas that a drummer could lose his liberty or perhaps his life for a wrong beat.

This is the song of one of the dances, which Diego de Landa once witnessed and thought "worthy of seeing":

> *Take three light turns*
> *around the painted stone column*
> *where virile is tied that*
> *boy, impollute, virgin, man.*
> *Take the first; on the second*
> *take your bow, place the dart,*
> *aim to his heart; you need not*
> *employ all your strength to*
> *pierce him; not to*
> *wound deep into his flesh*
> *and so he may suffer*
> *slowly, as wished*
> *the beautiful Lord God.*

Eric Thompson, the most literary of Maya scholars, has praised the mythopoetic qualities of Maya verse, calling attention to its free use of iambs and the repetitive antiphonal rhythms of the Old Testament. The Mayas told their history in cadence. Verse is one of the most ancient of forms among all people and was originally a clumsy artifice to aid the memory of people who could not read. If one finds it hard to believe that a mnemotechnical expedient has been transformed in the course of time into beautiful poetry, it is enough to reflect that in Greek architecture a beam laid upon wooden pillars became the architrave of the temple and the ends of the beams became the marble triglyph, or that the simple Maya house evolved into a temple such as that of Tikal, which soars to 229 feet in height. But to liken the cadence of Maya verse to the powerful rhythms of the Old Testament goes too far. The fault belongs not to the Mayas but rather to ourselves, who have labeled them the "intellectuals of the New World."

The Mayas have been the subject of much romantic misconception. Ever since Chateaubriand sat on a riverbank in 1791 with some Indian girls of the Natchez tribes and, beguiled by his longings and vexations, conceived his two Floridians, Atala and Celuta, Rousseau's Noble Savage theme has kept the stage. This imaginary exoticism has entered the blood stream of American protohistory, where it ferments into an intoxicant that every new generation drinks.

Maya literature was symbolical and abstract. It was antisocial; only the initiated could understand the value and meaning of its symbols. Yet what has one when the glyphs are translated? The Maya says nothing of himself or his history. A mere date is fleshless; it lacks blood and passion unless it is connected with meaningful human events. Time knows its business. What is abstract and symbolical in literature disappears and vanishes into the air. What is purely sonorous vaporizes into wind.

 XUL — *The End*   38

THE MAYAS, first of the Sun Kingdoms to feel the presence of the white man, were curiously enough the last to fall under that presence. For there was no escaping the wave of the future once Columbus noted the presence of a very superior people, the "*Maian,*" in 1502. The Spanish persisted. The relationship was violent from the beginning. The Mayas were fierce warriors; they gave no quarter and asked none. When the report reached the Spanish governor at Cuba—"we have discovered thickly peopled countries with masonry houses, and people who cover their persons in cotton garments"—more conquistadors poured over to break a lance; hundreds left their bodies on Yucatán shores.

When Cortés arrived he gave a practiced military eye to the inhospitable shore and, somehow sensing that there was little gold, remained only long enough to pick up the castaway Aguilar. In 1523, Mexico having been conquered and organized, Cortés sent Pedro de Alvarado to undertake the conquest of Guatemala and dispatched Cristóbal de Olid in 1524 to Central America to sniff out the tribute channels of the Aztecs. Instead, the latter set up an independent government in Hibueras (Honduras). So Cortés set off after him, making the famed trek through quagmires and rivers and jungles. He cut a wide swath through Maya territory, meeting little resistance. It was known that the Aztecs had been toppled and that he, Cortés, was the toppler. The Mayas were in awe of that energetic man who, undismayed by the terrible geography of the land, came down upon them replete with mistress, falcons, buffoons, and jugglers.

In 1527 came the turn of the Maya tide. Francisco de Montejo, who had played his part in the Conquest of Mexico (it was he who had carried its treasure to Spain), used this to advantage; he emerged from an audience with the king with a contract to conquer, settle, and convert all Mayadom. He arrived in Yucatán in 1527 with 380 men, 57 horses, and high hopes. Montejo was, says one who knew him, "middle-sized and with a merry face. He was fond of rejoicings but was a businessman; and a good horseman. When he came over to Mexico he may have been about thirty-five. He was liberal and he spent more than his income warranted." The lives he would spend were even more unwarranted. The party settled at Xelha, where skirmish and sickness whittled away his forces. He then moved up the north coast, encountering one large Maya city after another. At every turn the Indians attacked, chewing up his small troop.

Even so, Montejo was attacking a people completely disunited, for they were as much at war with themselves as with the Spaniards. Even the example of Mexico had brought the Mayas no unity.

Mayapán, which ruled most of Yucatán, had collapsed and the land
was split up into warring factions. In 1464 came the horrendous
hurricane that caused a fearful loss of lives and devastation. In 1517,
in the wake of the first Spanish contact, came smallpox (*maya-
cimil*, the "easy death") killing thousands upon thousands. Family
rivalries caused constant intertribal wars. Despite all this the Mayas
routed the Spaniards. After trying to gain lodgment without success
in Yucatán, the expedition sailed down to Chetumal, at the great Bay
of Zamabac. Here was a large city of two thousand houses. Cacao,
honey, and canoe building were its interests. At this city, which
traded with Panama, the Spaniards found gold and, within days, war.
They hoped to be helped by the other Spanish castaway, Gonzalo
Guerrero, but he would have none of them. As a Maya *nacom*, Guerrero prepared the thrusts and counterthrusts against the Spaniards.
He soon tossed the would-be conquistadors out of their foothold
in Chetumal. They then embarked and continued southward to put
in at Ulúa, a Maya trading post in Honduras. When knowledge of
this was transmitted to Guerrero, he lead a flotilla of war canoes to
relieve that outpost. He was killed by a shot from an arquebus, but
his death did not change Spanish fortunes. By 1535 there was not
a white man left alive in the whole Yucatán peninsula. Those who
had not died or wearied of unsuccessful war had heard the clarion
call from Peru, where Francisco Pizarro was engaged in the conquest
of the Incas.

Montejo, full of years and scars, resigned from his title and
authority in favor of his son. Furiously renewing the conquest in
1542, the conquistadors occupied half of the peninsula and founded
their capital, Mérida, within the buildings of ancient Tiho. In 1546
they put down with terrible and indiscriminate slaughter those Maya
tribes who refused the yoke of peace, and the conquest was over.

The Mayas were engulfed by the waves of conquest. They had
known slavery, which was part of their social system, but their new
masters improved upon it. Five hundred thousand free men were
sold into peonage, ancient Maya centers were destroyed, and the
chieftains who did not submit were killed. The priests were disposed
of and their books burned. Their learning died with them.

Still the conquest was not complete. After the fall of Chichén
Itzá in 1194 to the forces of Huanc Ceel with his Mexican mercenaries, one part of the Itzá tribe moved, en masse, out of Yuca-

tán into the humid area of El Petén. On an island in the center of what is now Lake Flores, they built their capital of Tayasal. Around the edge of the lake and into the Petén's interior were the houses and cornfields of the people. This was classical Maya territory; the ruins of Tikal lie only fifty miles from the lake. There the Mayas lived unmolested from 1200 until 1618 (except for the brief, friendly visit of Cortés in 1524). The Spaniards became aware of them soon enough. It was a neo-Maya state and its mere existence encouraged rebellion among other Mayas living under the Spanish yoke. It was similar to the neo-Inca state in Peru which, under various Lord-Incas, existed for thirty-six years after the Spanish conquest.

In 1622 Fray Diego Delgado, in search of martyrdom, offered to Christianize the Itzás. He was accompanied by soldiers, who, not as delicate in these matters as himself, cut a swath of destruction on the way to El Petén. Leaving the soldiers behind, Delgado and a large group of Indians he had converted to Christianity proceeded to the Itzá capital of Tayasal, on friendly invitation of its lord, Canek. But when they reached the town, Delgado and his entire party were put to death as a sacrifice to the Itzá gods. Throughout the century there were repeated attempts to enter Itzá territory: they were repulsed. Construction was begun on a Guatamala-Yucatán highway designed to bring two economic units together. The Itzás were in the way, and that decided their fate. "I, Fray Andrés de Avendaño y Loyola . . . who had no other wish than to sow in their hardened hearts the pure grain of evangelical seed," set off to the Itzás in 1696. After years of hardship, on his second attempt he entered Tayasal alive. It had twenty temples, not unlike those in Yucatán, and numerous houses; other islands were similarly inhabited, as were the immediate shores of the lake. Avendaño, with a subtle play of dialectics —he had earlier mastered the language and glyph writing—finally broke down the Itzás' mental resistance to Spanish contact; they agreed to come peacefully into the Spanish fold.

January, 1697, found Martin de Ursua, governor of Yucatán, with his soldiers at the farthest point of the new road. On March 13, a force of Spanish soldiers crossed the lake in a large galley to accept the peaceful surrender of the island capital of Tayasal—or to make an assault on it.[126] As it made its way, a canoe flotilla of two thousand armed Indians encircled the galley. The soldiers were

under orders to withhold their fire, which they did even though pro-
voked by accurate arrow thrusts from the Itzás. But near the shore
of Tayasal a soldier, wounded to fury by an arrow, fired his arquebus at close range. At this, the other soldiers fired, and the lake soon
was strewn with Itzá dead. As the troops landed, the remaining
Indians fled. On March 14, 1697, the Spaniards formally took
possession, in the name of the king, of the last living city of
the Mayas.

The Mayas had endured as a cultural entity for thirty-seven
hundred years. This is a long time in human cultural history.

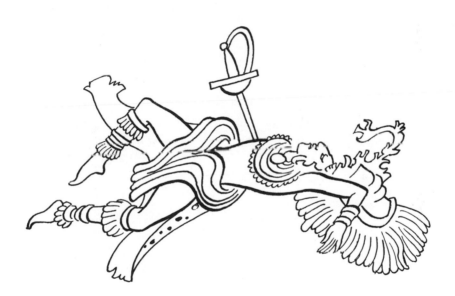

INCA

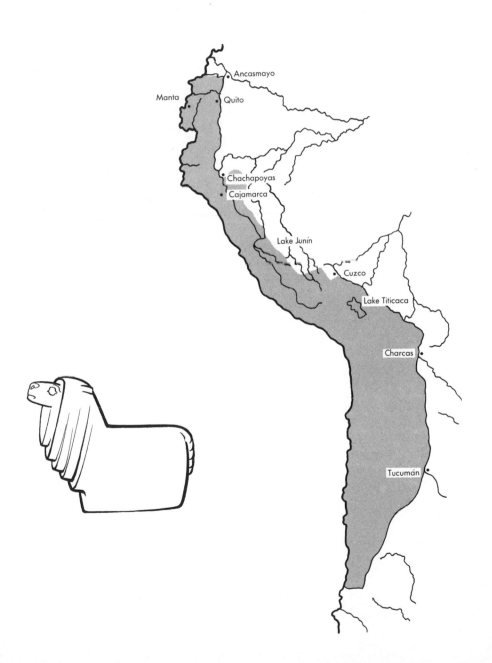

Ancasmayo

Manta

Quito

Chachapoyas

Cajamarca

Lake Junín

Cuzco

Lake Titicaca

Charcas

Tucumán

XXXIX. *Massive tumbaga (copper-gold alloy) pendant representing an anthropomorphic alligator god. The upper part of the face apparently is a mask with a diamond-shaped plaque over the nose and two bird torsos over the eyes.* (Nikolas Murray)

О

The Historical and
Geographical Background of
The Incas

 How We Know What We Know
About the Incas

THE INCAS arrived late.
This is a fact—it might have been otherwise—yet it
has long been known and accepted that man in South America
had fashioned many amazing civilizations before the advent of
the Incas.

There are thousands of books and pamphlets about the Incas.
Merely to collect them all you would have to have much of the
golden loot that was to ransom Atahúalpa, for many of the best
books about the Incas are scarce and expensive; further, only to
thumb through all the published material that deals with them in one
form or another, involving oneself in the disputes over trivia, is alone
a life study.

The whole history, from the beginning, will be both paradox
and puzzle. Since the question will spring up within the very first
pages it might as well now be asked and answered. All of the prehistory of the South Americans is shadowy: not one of their cultures
had writing; we do not even know with absolute certainty the name of
any of these people, and not even the name of the people of the Incas

(for that term was applied only to its rulers). The knot-string records —the famous *quipus*—have no key without the aid of the professional "rememberers" who could read them; now to us they are only lifeless strings. There are here no "talking stones" such as appeared among the Mayas, no folded books with rebus writing as the Aztecs had; there was no kind of writing of any form, no matter how much some scholars may strain their imaginations. There is not even a single absolute time element one can seize upon. The only certain date is 1527, for in that year Francisco Pizarro touched for the first time the shores of the realm of the Incas.

How then, if all this is true, does the archaeological historian speak so knowingly about the Incas? From what sources all the detail that follows? How can an archaeologist, like a theologian who talks of eternity, speak so knowingly of the unknowable?

Somewhat this way.

The records started immediately with the Spanish conquest in 1532. An "Anonymous Conqueror" [6] first wrote down in vivid homespun prose the matter-of-fact details of this fantastic conquest of a fantastic kingdom; of how millions of Indians were brought to heel within an hour by 130 foot soldiers, and this, published in 1534 only a few months after the event (even containing a crude woodcut of the Lord-Inca himself being borne aloft by his litter-bearers), began the literature.

Next came the reports made by the soldier-secretaries of *the* conquistador; these are earthy and informative, couched more in the style meant for the daily business of human lives than with the lyricism one expects to herald the death throes of a barbaric kingdom. It is true, these reports lack details, their concepts of geography are vague, yet they convey a good picture of the Inca peoples, their land, roads, buildings, and there are wonderfully descriptive pictures of the golden ransom sent by the empire to free their Lord-Inca held captive by the small band of Spaniards. One of these, Pedro Pizarro (who actually participated in the conquest), wrote down his memories—larded, however, with highly sententious fantasy.[143]

Then there are other reports which in effect begin the literary avalanche on the "Inca," for following the unadorned soldierly reports came those scribes who spent the night scribbling their reports. They were attached to the officials whose job it was to root out the riches of the Incas. They are full of contumely. But in 1547 a simple soldier named Pedro de Cieza de León ("simple" here synonymous with "intelligent") turned up in Peru.[34] He came riding down the full length of the Inca highway from Colombia. At last one is on solid ground. A man of infinitely good sense, he has provided much that is in this book. His first book, published in 1553, went through six editions in as many years. Soldiers, scribes, and lawyers cribbed from him. Then come the narratives from the new race—the Cholos, half-Inca, half-Spanish. There are a goodly number of them. The best-known writer is, of course, Garcilaso de la Vega, son of a knight and a royal Indian lady, who wrote his *The Royal Commentaries of the Incas* in Spain.[66] Another, not so well known, is Felipe Guamán Poma de Ayala, who wrote and illustrated *The First New Chronicle and Good Government*[144]—it is difficult to read but valuable since it is profusely illustrated with pen drawings; it is a primary source for the dress and customs of the Incas. Yet no one in Peru or Spain ever heard of the author,

114. Self-portrait of the Inca-Spanish chronicler Felipe Guamán Poma de Ayala in Spanish attire of the sixteenth century, seen talking to Indians, from whom he gathered the basic material and drawings for his book The First New Chronicle and Good Government *written between the years 1560–99. It was lost until found in the Royal Library at Copenhagen in 1908.*

the book was never printed until 1927, and when it was found in the beginning of the twentieth century it turned up, of all places, in the Royal Library at Copenhagen.

The seventeenth and eighteenth centuries ushered in the epoch of the priest-chronicler; and even though the material on the Incas is manipulated to fit into an existing Christian pattern, much of the details on dress, customs, religion, food, government are excellent. Of these histories, that by Bernabé Cobo is "the best and most complete description of Inca culture in existence."[155]

The eighteenth century brought in the period of enlightenment and with it began the scientific explorations to Peru, and from out of these came many detailed observations, culminating with the works of the great Alexander von Humboldt,[83] who gave us the first truly accurate descriptions of Inca roads and buildings. It is with these that the modern era of archaeology begins.

After William Prescott had written the *History of the Conquest of Peru,*[148] long-lost or forgotten manuscripts came to light and were published; three more of Pedro de Cieza de León's wonderful Inca histories were found, and hundreds of other reports were brought to light under the impulse of renewed interest in the *Conquest.*[118] And they still are. Sir Clements Markham followed Prescott and himself appeared in Peru (Prescott never did), and although Markham himself penned no epics, he did fan the fire of Inca enthusiasm by translating numerous old Spanish chronicles which have been the fount and source of scholars for a century.

The Peruvians themselves began now to take an interest in their own past, so much so that when E. George Squier appeared in Peru in 1863 as Abraham Lincoln's representative, Peru was already conscious of its past greatness. One of the first "dirt" archaeologists, Squier began the physical examination of the "evidence"; his book, *Peru: Incidents of Travel and Exploration in the Land of the Incas*[185] (1877) marks the beginning of this modern approach, and still can be read with pleasure and profit. The next writer of real consequence to appear is a German. For forty years Peru and other countries occupied by the Incas were examined by Max Uhle. He collected widely and well from funds sent to him by Mrs. Phoebe Hearst of California, the result being that those selfsame archaeological pieces have nurtured in California three generations of archaeologists. Many of the most prominent ones cut their archaeological teeth on Max Uhle's collections.

If one examines the literature one can see how the wand of the archaeological relay is handed from one to another. In 1911 Hiram Bingham, a young American historian, appeared in Peru. He was actually looking for Vilcapampa, the last capital of the Incas, when he accidentally discovered the fabulous stone city of Machu Picchu. That discovery gave the new generations as much impulse toward Peruvian archaeology as Prescott's writings had given the past. With Bingham was another young historian, Philip Ainsworth Means. He remained behind and over a period of years wrote a series of books that nicely mingled scholarship and archaeology. His *Ancient Civilizations of the Andes* (1931) and the *Fall of the Inca Empire and the Spanish Rule in Peru, 1530–1780* (1932) will remain source books for all time.

The last twenty-five years have been the years of systematic excavation and stratigraphical archaeology. Peruvians, notably the late Dr. Julio C. Tello, following the scent of oral history, dug up cultures such as Paracas and Chavín and many others, which had never been in the archaeological lexicon. Regrettably, Tello wrote little, but he was in his way (even though much criticized by his fellow archaeologists as having been a sort of Giovanni Belzoni, who broke into the pyramids with a battering ram, trampling on golden-plated mummies as "thick as leaves in Vallambrosa") an archaeological pathfinder and has opened myriads of new avenues into the roads of the past. Peruvians, a few French, Germans, and many Americans have published widely and thoroughly on far-ranging aspects of Inca and pre-Inca cultures. In 1931, the Shippee-Johnson Aerial Expedition to Peru discovered many unknown sites from the air. Since that time aerial exploration has given a new dimension to Peruvian archaeology and the aerial mosaic is now standard equipment for the investigator. With new techniques, principally the carbon-14 tests—a method of dating through the measurement of the rate of disintegration of radioactive carbon in active matter—and with controlled stratigraphical surveys of ancient sites, the archaeologists have in some instances "fixed" the dates of some of these ancient civilizations.

All that was known up to 1945 of the material culture of the Incas, along with other South American cultures, was published in the encyclopedic-sized *Handbook of South American Indians,*[187] written by the world's leading authorities on the subject. For the nonspecialized reader it will perhaps tell him more about South

American Indians than he wants to know, yet it is all there—and in full measure.

So the hero of this, if there is one, is the archaeologist, he who has sat in the dust of history and patiently pushed back the layers of detritus, in a way like turning the leaves of a book, out of which he has read the past.

2　　*The Geographical Background of a Culture*

IT WAS Bartolomé Ruiz, the first Spanish navigator to sail the windlashed Peruvian seas, who provided those others who followed him with sailing instructions. When asked how in all this incomprehensible desert land they could know when they had made the correct landfall to the "Kingdom of Gold," he replied: "When you no longer see any trees, you are in Peru." It was not wholly true, of course; still it was good enough to serve a navigator for laying down a course to Tumbes, the first port of call of the Spanish conquest.

Tumbes, or Tumpiz as it was then pronounced, was in fact the last northern coastal city of the realm of the Incas. North of this frontier city there is a sharp topographical line, and the humid tropics, a luxuriant jungle begins and continues northward to Panama. South of Tumbes, or rather at Tumbes, the brazen desert begins and extends, except when broken by occasional valleys, for two thousand miles southward.

The forces of nature in this extremely confined coastal desert (it varies between one to twenty-five miles in depth between the sea and the Andes) have always been of supreme importance; here, as in few other places in the world, climate was (and still is) the vital factor that shaped human lives.

First, the strange sea, the cause of it all. It rushes onto the coast in huge unhurrying rollers roaring in from the turbulent coastal current without. The phenomenon of a cold current in a tropic sea has had marked effect on the land, for here normally rain never falls and the entire length of this coast is reduced to an extreme waterless desolation. The mountains loom up out of the desert like dry bones; the whole aspect of it in its entire length is hollow and fainting: "A place where," said one of the first Spaniards, "there is no water, no trees, no grass nor any created thing except birds which by the gift of wings wander wherever they will." [34]

For more than half of the year the heat of the sun is of such force as to broil one's brains, but between May and November the skies, due to a further cooling of the cold current, cause heavy mists to pour over the littoral, and the days are overcast and grim. A haze overhangs the land during the day, and at night it dulls the glamor of the stars.

Plankton is carried on the bourn of this ubiquitous current, the passively floating animal-plant life, so minute as hardly to be seen by the naked eye but in so incalculable a multitude that it pigments the ocean stream. This life is avidly fed on by the sea fauna, rich and varied, which in turn attracts the sea birds (in such astronomical numbers as to darken the skies). These birds, to complete this interlocked life cycle, nest on off-shore islets where they deposit their guano dung, the most concentrated nitrogen-rich fertilizer known in the world.

Although along this 2000-mile-long desert coast there are more than forty valleys, between each lies the lifeless void of desert. Rivers, large and perennial, others small and occasional, which have created these valley oases cut through the towering Andes and rapidly descend into V-shaped valleys bringing every year a renewal of fertile silt.

Early South American men filtered into these valleys and formed into tribes; in time they extended these valleys by careful irrigation, increasing artificially and unnaturally the areas of fertility. And so, as each tribe was isolated by desert from the other, they developed over great reaches of time highly individual traits and cultures.

Since trees were rare here in ancient times, the idols of these coastal dwellers were of wood; since mud and sand were the base of their material culture, they built of sun-dried brick, and their most fabulous cities were in reality only plastic mud. Since here the sun was always menacing and was *not* to be appeased, they selected as their principal deity the moon, which controlled the sea.

So Man here became the catalyst of the desert.

Yet one of the most remarkable civilizations did not originate in this environment. The *Incas* instead were one day to emerge as a tribe and empire in the Andes. They appeared in a high, treeless tableland, a region of long grass, a land which is seared by the noonday heat and made frigid by night. This was the land of the *Keshwas* (or Quechuas), the "warm-valley people"; their name in time was to be given to the language of the Incas.

There is not one Peru but three, and all these three Perus lie parallel to each other: coastal deserts, high mountains, and low-lying jungles. It is these three discordant geographies which the Incas were to coalesce into empire.

The temperate zone in the Andes lies in the grass areas at a land height above 9,000 feet; it is a region that is capable of sustaining an intensive agriculture. Here in this purlieu, trees were also rare but there was rock, so stone became the source of these Andean peoples' culture. As the sun's appearance was limited and the making of sun-dried adobe hampered building with it, stone became the primary building material, and the fabulous cities of these mountain tribes were put together with intricate stonemasonry. Since the life-giving sun was life-warming, it became their principal deity.

Man here became the catalyst of the Andes and bent this rock-hard world to his will.

The imposing Cordilleras in Peru's center march southward in a double array of mountains as in two chains; they spread apart into a vast oval at 14°3″ south latitude, and this becomes the basin of Lake Titicaca. Still farther southwest and down into Argentina and Chile the Andean chains break into a tangled mass of mountains and salt marshes, and eventually emerge into immense rolling pampas which are also treeless. On these plains primitive man, intensely wild and untamed, hunted the ostrich and wild guanaco.

The deep valleys of the Cordilleras (as the first Spaniards called the mountains) take the run-off of the water and form it into numerous rivers, which emerge into the gigantic rivers Huallaga and Ucayali, both tributaries of the Amazon. This is the jungle, the third of the three Perus.

Actually the forest begins as montaña at 6,000 feet altitude, for it is ceaselessly wetted from the rain-bearing trade winds which collide with the Andean spurs that slant sharply east. The Montaña

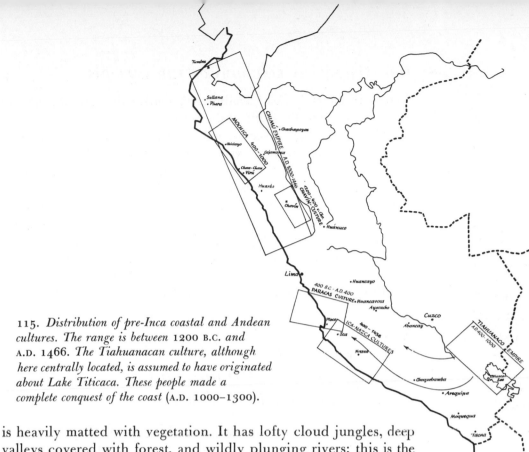

115. *Distribution of pre-Inca coastal and Andean cultures. The range is between 1200 B.C. and A.D. 1466. The Tiahuanacan culture, although here centrally located, is assumed to have originated about Lake Titicaca. These people made a complete conquest of the coast (A.D. 1000–1300).*

is heavily matted with vegetation. It has lofty cloud jungles, deep valleys covered with forest, and wildly plunging rivers; this is the *yungas*, a Quechua word applied both to the hotlands and to the people living there.

The eastern slopes of the mountains are inexorably flattened until they become finally a vast carpeted forest broken only by rivers which flow through the green mansions of trees, propelled by the eastern slant of the land into the Amazon. Here to plant one tree you must first cut down twenty. In this terrifying luxuriance a totally different people lived—fierce, independent, cityless warriors who were armed with poison-tipped darts which curdled the blood when stuck in flesh. They too were farmers, jungle farmers, but they resisted any form of organization and so only the margins of the jungle yielded to the soldiers of the Inca.

These, then, are the three Perus, and out of these three contrasting geographies—desert, mountain, and jungle—the Incas hammered out, *á la repoussé* their fabulous realm. No matter what form of society that lived in this ancient Peru—whether it was the effete Chimú, who surrounded himself on the desert coast with gold and ease, or the head-hunters in the jungle, who made out of their slain enemy's head a mimicry (tsantsa) the size of a fist, all were brought into the orbit of the Incas.

All phenomena, it seems, felt the Inca influence: the people, the plants, the animals, the very names over the land.

The whole Andean area, as Philip Ainsworth Means once wrote ". . . is colored indelibly with the Inca dye. And to this day, in every part of the territory once ruled by the Incas [from Colombia through to Argentina, from the desert coast to the jungles] one is hourly conscious of the ghost of the Incas' supremacy manifesting itself in scores of ways: through speech, customs and material culture."

All this, even though the Incas arrived very late.

 The Pre-Inca Cultures: Chavín — Mochica — Paracas — Nazca — Tiahuanaco — Chimú

3

EVERYTHING, or almost everything, in Peru, as is evident, had antecedence over the Incas. Archaeologists have peeled back the layers of Peruvian prehistory until their spades have come to rest on sterile cultural earth, and they know that the story that archaeology tells us in Peru is this: a succession of cultures endured for millennia, and in many instances died out, before the Incas arrived to engulf the whole land and to organize its conquest-acquired inheritance into an empire.

That we have almost no history of many of these pre-Inca cultures other than that which archaeology reveals, we owe principally to the Incas themselves, for in their conquests they snuffed out the others by their own "selective manipulation of remembered history." [140]

For not only were the earth and the peoples organized by the triumphant Incas but memory as well, and the theme of the Inca as *the* "civilizer" became their dominant theme. Their thesis was that before their arrival all of South America was a cultural void. This official history was forced upon all those conquered. Memory of past peoples and cultures was systematically purged and subjected to a "sort of editing and selective distortion not entirely

116. *Chavín. The dominant design of this culture (1200–400 B.C.) is the Cat God.*

unlike the tendentious distortion to which the Spanish themselves subjected it [the Inca history] in their turn." [140] An "official" Inca history was created, local oral traditions of the tribes whom they had conquered supplanted and allowed to lapse. The official "rememberers," who were the Incas' historians, no longer bridged the gap between legendary man and those innumerable pre-Inca cultures, so that this "selective manipulation of history" which was to represent the Incas as being alone the culture bearers, emerged as *the* history of preliterate Peru. All the rest of the pre-Inca histories were allowed to be lost in oblivion.

What then, and who, were all these civilizations, now without name and barely with legend, that preceded the Inca? Who were these people who pioneered in that triumph over life that forced nature, that exigent mistress, to yield plants where there had been none before, who were these who sent water into a waterless land and created domestic animals out of a wild fauna, animals needed for the new burgeoning societies of American man? Space does not permit us, nor is it the object of this book, to detail all of those cultures which preceded the Inca; that alone would be a book. To say everything is to say nothing; to show everything is to make one see nothing.

The thing is to light up what is pertinent, and an archaeological excursus, admittedly limited, will I believe show readily enough that which has already been put forward: that for two thousand years prior to the Incas there was in Peru a long steady cultural growth.

As regards precise time, no one can be absolutely sure in Peru of anything in this regard. There was no written literature or history except the litany of "remembered" historical events that was orally passed down through the ages. There were no dated coins, as there were among the Romans, where a Caesar had image and date stamped thereon; the Incas had no money. There is only the one date (1527) which we know with absolute certainty.

And yet with painstaking persistence archaeologists have made progress in unraveling, in the broad, the space-time divisions of these pre-Inca cultures. Archaeological stratigraphy has rolled back the layers of history. The designs on ceramics, which are among the best aids for time analysis (see Pottery and Pottery Makers, page 466), have been carefully studied, and archaeologists have set up for themselves a table of such "horizon styles"; excavation and reconstruction of material cultures, a re-examination of Inca oral traditions, in this new light, have yielded a broad cultural time sequence. The deductions from these are obviously only the bare outlines of history which wait to be detailed with further facts; yet from all this, the late Dr. Wendell Bennett (accepted by his colleagues as the best in this field) conceived the *six periods of South American archaeological history*, admittedly tentative.[12]

The curtain rises (at approximately 1200 B.C.), with Period I. Man has already been on the north desert coast of Peru for a long time. He has had pottery and weaving since 1500 B.C. He builds structures. He is already growing maize (no doubt with bird guano as fertilizer), and he raises the tuber called manioc. But he is not the first here; there were others long before him, for the remains of their weaving and agriculture, as proven by the carbon-14 tests, show them here as early as 3000 B.C.

The first culture of prominence in Period I is *Chavín;* its leitmotif is a ferocious-looking Cat God found on pottery and stonework and in weavings. This motif was to haunt the cosmology of the ancient Peruvians for the next thousand years.[57] Chavín's center (presumably it was a mecca even during late Inca times) is the site of Chavín de Huantar, which lies in a narrow valley in the Andes beyond the Cordillera Blanca. Here are the remains of impressive buildings characterized by well-laid stone walls and ornamented with stone-carved human and animal heads set in the wall.

Period II, which, it is deduced, fell between the centuries 400 B.C. and A.D. 400, is called, with some exercise of the imagination, the "Experimenter" period because of the supposed experimenting in weaving and pottery by many widely scattered cultures.

Paracas, which lay below Central Peru to the south of Lima near Pisco, is a pre-Inca culture of Period II. It is famed for its textiles, believed to be the finest ever loomed. This culture is wrapped in mystery; we do not know its tribal name nor anything more positive about it than the evidence in their caverns found in the brazen desert and close upon the sea on the Paracas Peninsula. In deep subterranean rooms four hundred or more mummy bundles were found: the flexed bodies were adorned with superbly woven shawls, turbans, and robes, all in the most exquisite polychrome embroidery. Little is known about them beyond these remains. They, and the culture which preceded them by five hundred to a thousand years (and which used the same area for their burials), made use of the natural desert sands for mummification. The Paracas appear in no remembered annals and are unmentioned by the Incas.

By the time of Period III, between A.D. 400 and 1000, man has completely dominated his environments of the desert coast and the Andes. He has acquired wit and cities. It is the period of high craftsmanship in architecture, ceramics, and weaving. On the coast the *Mochicas*

117. *Nazca pottery. Finely made, it is characterized by the use of abstract decoration. Its motif: the Cat God holding severed heads.*

(we have no idea what they called themselves) are a caste-minded empire; they lord it over the northern Peruvian desert and one can still see the remains of their temples, one of which, called Huaca del Sol, in the Moche Valley is constructed of approximately 130,000,000 sun-dried adobe bricks. This suggests, natu-

118. *Paracas culture (400 B.C.–A.D. 400) is easily defined by its superb weavings. This is the complete costume of a man from the acropolis of Paracas Peninsula.*

119. *Mochica pottery, coastal culture (A.D. 400–800). 1) Historical evidence of the successful amputation of legs as shown in the realistic representations of warriors who underwent operations. Drawn from the coastal pottery of the Mochicas A.D. 400–800. 2) The pottery of this period is so realistic it might be considered as portraiture. 3) Man riding a llama. Drawn from Mochica pottery circa A.D. 800. A coastal llama with a rope through its ear is guided by a man with an amputated foot.*

rally, a complex social organization to accomplish so effective a construction; the advancement of their society is given further emphasis by their skill in gold casting and wood carving. Their weaving is thought to have been done on a shop basis, for on one Mochica vase a man, obviously a chieftain, sits under a frilled sunshade and directs rows of women busily engaged in weaving on their back-strap looms. The Mochicas had warriors, messengers, weavers, and "doctors"; they built roads and organized a courier system, and perfected many a social pattern that appeared later in the political organization of the Inca.

In a verdant valley, Nazca, south of Paracas, which breaks the naked misery of the desert, is another lost culture, lost to history

1

2

3

because its own history was purposely "disremembered" by the Incas—the *Ica-Nazca*. This cultural area is now somewhat less of a mystery and is being unraveled by the archaeologists. Fine weaving and excellent ceramics were emphasized, and not too distant in design from those of Paracas. Architecture, however, is not a dominant feature, and little remains to tell us how they lived. Like the others, they are anonymous. The greatest mystery of the Ica-Nazca cultures is the vast network of "lines," a fantastic assembly of rectangles and squares that have been etched into the sand and waste gravel. Outsized birds, spiders, whales, and surrealistic figures are also present. These lines, some running for miles in length, have remained in a good state of preservation, showing this land to have

413

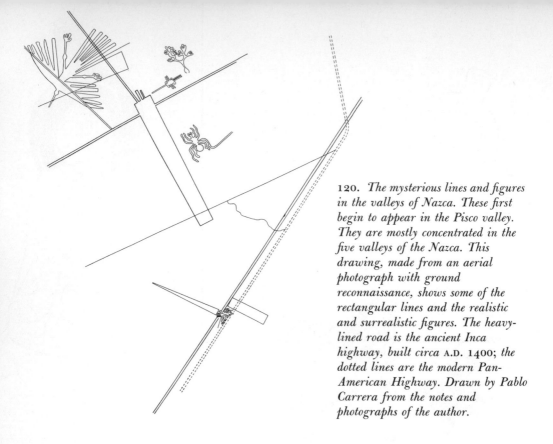

120. *The mysterious lines and figures in the valleys of Nazca. These first begin to appear in the Pisco valley. They are mostly concentrated in the five valleys of the Nazca. This drawing, made from an aerial photograph with ground reconnaissance, shows some of the rectangular lines and the realistic and surrealistic figures. The heavy-lined road is the ancient Inca highway, built circa A.D. 1400; the dotted lines are the modern Pan-American Highway. Drawn by Pablo Carrera from the notes and photographs of the author.*

been, then as now, a desert of everlasting drought. These lines are approximately fifteen hundred years old. They could be calendary observations or they could be genealogical symbol "trees." What is now positive, at least, is one date: an American archaeologist found a wooden "sighting" stump at the end of one of the lines and carbon-14 tests have placed it close to the date of A.D. 500.

It is known that sometime close to A.D. 900 a mountain people called the *Tiahuanaco Empire* came to the coast in a religio-military invasion, sweeping down from their stronghold centered about Lake Titicaca. They had then an interest in astrology, a solar calendar, and, as well, a sort of shadow clock. It is highly possible that the Tiahuanaco culture brought the technique of the "lines" to Nazca before their cult of the Weeping God.

Whatever the origins of all this, the Incas allowed nothing about them to come down to us. For the "lines" of Nazca, they had full contempt; those practical Inca engineers ran their 24-foot-wide coastal road directly through them.

The empire of Tiahuanaco is the dominant civilization of Period

IV (A.D. 1000–1300) in Peru and Bolivia. Like all the other pre-
Inca cultures, it has left us only unexplained mysteries. The remains
of what must have been the greatest ceremonial center in all the
Andes are still to be seen on the Altiplano in Bolivia, near Lake
Titicaca at an altitude of 12,500 feet. Dr. Wendell Bennett thought
"Tiahuanaco the most elaborate and the purest manifestation of the
culture yet to be found up to this time."

The stonework of Tiahuanaco developed centuries before the
Inca work, and until their advent, it was the best in the Andes.
Stones are fitted together with insets and tenons; larger stones are
bound with copper clamps. All this architectural megalithic stonework presupposes a social organization, a strong central government which could divert the use of manpower into non-food-pro-
ducing channels of so large a scale. All this must have been done
by a large supply of workers with a long technical tradition.

And yet nothing is precisely known of these people or their
empire. They too, like the others, are nameless.

That this great culture, Tiahuanaco, should have no oral history
points more than any other evidence to the success of the Incas
(who were, in some stage of their development, doubtless contemporaneous with them) in deliberately obliterating all memory of
them. For when Pedro de Cieza de León made inquiries in 1549
about the people who built the ruins at Tiahuanaco, the oldest of
the Indians then living could not even recall a single fact, and to

121. *Man receiving a blow on the
head. Drawn from a Mochica vase,
dated circa A.D. 800. Blows such as
this resulted in head fractures, which
were often cured by skull trepanning.*

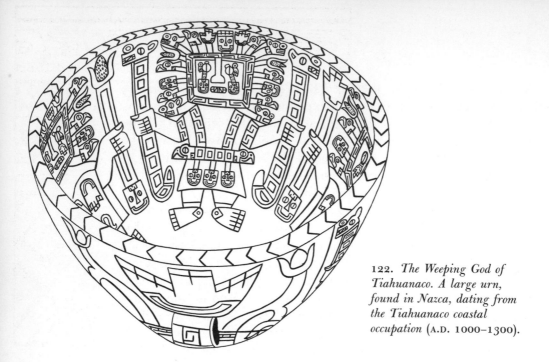

122. *The Weeping God of Tiahuanaco. A large urn, found in Nazca, dating from the Tiahuanaco coastal occupation* (A.D. 1000–1300).

these inquiries they replied that it had been built long before the Incas ruled but that they were unable to say who had built it.

Yet the Tiahuanaca cultural conquest penetrated many of the remote corners of Peru. Many of the contemporary cultures, even the early Inca, adopted the symbol of the Sun God. This Weeping God wept all manners of tears—zoömorphic tears—condor-head tears and snake-head tears. These and other design motifs, such as the puma, trident, and step designs, are widespread along most of the thousand-mile coast. But that conquest, motivated by religious fervor, was not systematically organized, for the Tiahuanaco left behind them little social impress—only those unmistakable designs on pottery and cloth, and the cult of the Weeping God.

The *Chimú Empire* (A.D. 1000–1466), called the Kingdom of Chimor, also belongs to this period even though it extends beyond it into that of the Incas.

The Chimús were coastal people, workers in plastic mud and worshipers of the moon. Their capital, Chan-Chan (which is close where the Spanish-Peruvian city of Trujillo now stands), was eight miles square, replete with enormous step pyramids, rows of houses, great walled compounds, irrigated gardens, and gigantic stone-lined reservoirs.

123. *The Chimú culture, centered about the Virú and Chicama valleys, existed between* A.D. 1000 *and* 1466. *The Chimús were workers in plastic mud, and the walls of their capital, Chan-Chan, were covered with designs such as these. Drawn from photographs of the author.*

From Chan-Chan, the Chimús ruled over six hundred miles of coast from Rimac (now Lima), up to the humid tropics of Ecuador. Indirectly, they ruled over much more territory. Everything here was on a large scale: weaving was on a mass basis; pottery, mostly black ware, was produced in molds; whistling jars and cooking pots were mass-produced. Their weavers made superb feather tunics and goldworking was also on a large scale, for the amount of gold yielded to their conquerors, the Incas, was staggering and even that which the Spaniards found much later (which was a mere nothing) reached into the millions. The Chimús developed the roads, taken over from their predecessors, the Mochicas; they developed further the courier communication system, and they extended their political alliances beyond the coastal desert far up into the Andes in order to protect their water supply.

The Chimú Empire was the last of the larger cultures to offer opposition to the Incas. That we know a good deal about the Chimú culture is due only to the fact that before the Inca methods of historical selectivity could be brought into full effect to eliminate the Chimús from human memory, the Spaniards arrived.

The listing of these pre-Inca cultures will seem, as it indeed is, foreshortened; there were many others, but only those of the

417

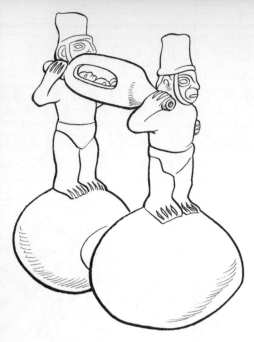

124. *Coastal Indians carrying a child in a litter. Drawn from a Mochica vase circa* A.D. 800.

greatest cultural influence in Peru have been named in order to show how steady was the cultural evolution that had been going on for three thousand years in Peru before the advent of the Inca.

Many of these civilizations were of the highest level, and from them the Incas drew heavily in order to form the material culture of their own empire. In a sense, and the analogy has often been made, the Incas were like the Romans—inheritors of a vast skein of cultures which became, in the weaving, a complicated tapestry of human progress.

Thus archaeology stands in direct opposition to the form of history which the Incas told of themselves, which is that all of the Andean (and coastal) peoples were savages until the Incas came upon the scene. This special twisting of events by the Inca history-makers is something that bears an ironic resemblance to the living history of the Russians as described in George Orwell's book *1984*.

The story that archaeology does reveal—if one will have the patience first to locate and then go through the infinite number of articles, monographs, and books on this fascinating subject—is this: there was a long succession of cultures before the Inca, and the Incas arrived late and were the organizers rather than creators of Peruvian civilization.

However, as this book will reveal, they were incomparable organizers.

"Inca History Has Its Origin in Myth and Continues in Legend"[140]

4

W<small>E KNOW</small>, curiously enough, no more about the origins of the Incas than that which they tell us of themselves in their "remembered" history and mythology. This "official" history embodies a vague legendary memory, but what part is myth, what part history, what mere dialectic, we do not know. And, moreover, there is as yet no precise answer from archaeology. The "remembered" history has it that they came out of, or about, Lake Titicaca, wandered north between the double array of the Andes, came to the valley of Cuzco and there laid the beginnings of empire. That the Incas and their empire *did* evolve within the valley of Cuzco has been at least confirmed by archaeology.

What do the myths say? The Sun God created the first Inca, Manco Capac, and his sister, on the Isle of the Sun in Lake Titicaca.

The Sun God instructed them to set out and teach the arts of civilization to all the other Indians then living in barbarism. Thus begins the apostolic succession of the Incas from the creator-god. Manco Capac carries a golden staff; he has been instructed by the Sun God that when he reaches a place so fertile that the staff will sink out of sight when thrown into the ground, there he is to build his city. The brother and sister set out northward, encountering, as mythical characters do, the usual difficulties, until they arrive at the Cuzco Valley. Manco is moved by what he sees, he throws the golden staff, it sinks out of sight—and Cuzco is born. There are variations on this theme: there are four brothers surnamed "Ayar" (wild quinoa grain), and there are four sisters called "mama," and they live in caves some twenty miles southeast of Cuzco. They set out, find the fertile Cuzco Valley, and then three of the brothers metamorphose themselves into stones or shrines, allowing Manco, with his sisters as his harem, to found Cuzco and begin with them the tribe and the empire. This is the sort of folklore that most peoples invent about themselves. If the mythos of Christianity were reduced to a five-line synopsis, it would have much of this naïveté.

Doubtless the Inca legends are the personification of a small tribe (one of the many which were then living about the fertile regions of Lake Titicaca) who in search of new lands fought their way northward until they came to the valley of Cuzco; there they defeated the original possessors of this Andean glebe. The precise time of Inca emergence is not known. At this time the entire Andean region was broken up into "an almost unbelievable number of small political units," [155] all of different speech, all with different myth patterns. At this time these divers tribes were on about the same cultural level; i.e., they had the same plants under cultivation, they tilled land with the same techniques, and all had the domesticated llama. So the story that the Incas tell of themselves, that they were especially chosen by the Sun God to raise the other Indians from their subhuman ways, to bring arts and culture to those other Indian tribes, *has found no support in archaeology.*

The people called the Incas began—and this is precisely what makes their history fascinating—with the same cultural weapons as all other Indians then living in the Andean regions.

"In the year 1000 A.D.," wrote Pedro de Cieza de León (whom we will meet often in these pages), ". . . in the name of *Tici Viracocha* and of the Sun and the rest of his gods, Manco Capac founded the new City.

"The origins and beginnings of Cuzco was a small house of stone roofed with straw which Manco Capac and his wives built and which they named 'Curi-cancha,' meaning 'Golden Enclosure.'"

This, Pedro de Cieza de León had from the "rememberers" of history in Cuzco in the year 1549; it is as good and simple a historical premise as any.

The Incas stress that they developed within the Cuzco Valley, and the excavations of Dr. John Rowe have confirmed this. "Enough has been done . . . to show that the Inca civilization *was* the product of a long development in the valley of Cuzco itself and that consequently it is unnecessary to look farther afield for that civilization's cultural origins." [155]

It is important that this tangible evidence of archaeology be stressed, to balance, as it were, the present-day insistence that the Incas originated elsewhere; for since the sixteenth century the Incas have been variously described as descendants of the tribes of Israel, the sons of Kublai Khan, Armenians, Egyptians, Chinese and—even Englishmen. Sir Walter Raleigh had it from someone that Manco Capac, the first Inca, was actually a corruption of Ingasman (i.e., Englishman) Copac, "the Bloody Englishman."

The latest spectacular attempt to prove that Polynesia was peopled by Tici Viracocha, the creator-god, this by an expedition on the floating balsa raft *Kon-Tiki,* also has no support from archaeology, nor, still more important, from botany. The Peruvian civilization was built up of *intensified* pre-existing American Indian cultures and not by anything additional or foreign. The Incas developed within the valley of Cuzco and the whole cycle of their mythology contains not even the slightest suggestion of any tribal migrations outside of the Andean region.

They occupied the valley, liquidated the earlier possessors (although just *whom* they replaced is not clear in the archaeological sequences), and they began their polygamous society. They had, it is only repeated for emphasis, the same cultural tools as all other Andean folks: the polished stone celt, forms of agriculture following the same irrigational techniques, the domesticated llama (it had been domesticated for two thousand years *before* the coming of the Incas). And finally they had as the base of their society the earth-cell commune, the *ayllu,* or communally held land.

All this was Andean in pattern. And yet they had something more. They had an innate sense of organization. War was no longer an elaborate façade to overawe an enemy; war was to be won and conquest was to be organized. The particular genius which was Inca came out of Cuzco, that small hollow of land and valley, that very Cuzco which is the longest continuously inhabited city in the Americas.

The Incas expanded; they expanded as all empires do—by conquest.

Centuries passed like the moving arm of a weaver's shuttles. The people of the Incas, call them Quechuas, for Quechua was their

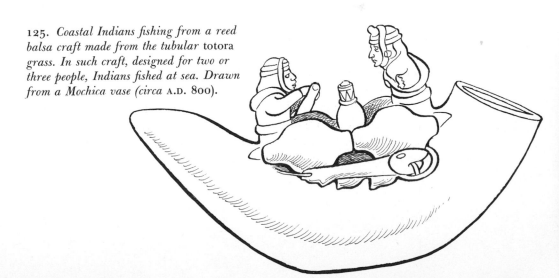

125. *Coastal Indians fishing from a reed balsa craft made from the tubular* totora *grass. In such craft, designed for two or three people, Indians fished at sea. Drawn from a Mochica vase (circa* A.D. *800).*

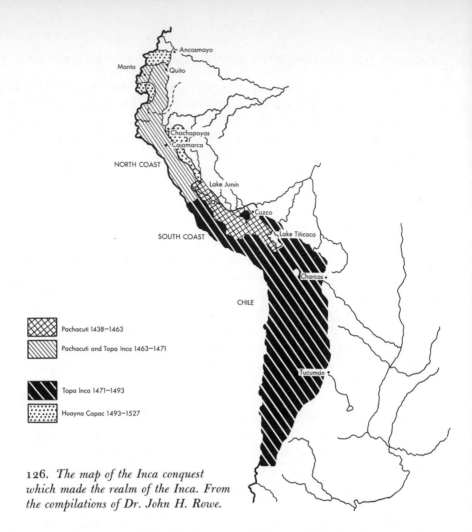

Legend on map:

- Pachacuti 1438–1463
- Pachacuti and Topa Inca 1463–1471
- Topa Inca 1471–1493
- Huayna Capac 1493–1527

Map labels: Ancasmayo, Manta, Quito, Chachapoyas, Cajamarca, NORTH COAST, Lake Junin, Cuzco, SOUTH COAST, Lake Titicaca, Charcas, CHILE, Tucumán

126. *The map of the Inca conquest which made the realm of the Inca. From the compilations of Dr. John H. Rowe.*

language, became a disciplined people living within the framework of the Andes, and out of this discipline came the solid base of people, who, born to this type of society and thriving on it, went about the daily business of ordered human lives; and, in so doing, became an empire.

It took time to mold people in this manner, and its passage we must accept; and so we come to that period of Andean history (between the dates of A.D. 1200 and 1438) when their rulers, the "Incas," have pushed the expanding realm beyond the narrow confines of their "origin" valley and have established lordship over much of the surrounding mountains.

Within this Andean crucible the character of the people of the Incas was forged.

The People

 Appearance 5

THE QUECHUAS, the people of the Incas, were (it need hardly be stressed at this juncture) American Indians, and native to the Andes. Although there are, as anyone who has personally seen them, marked variations between the multifarious tribes strung out along the thousands of miles which are the Americas, there is an underlying appearance and trait in them all which is American. The Quechua was (or better *is,* since there remain some five million of them) of medium height and inclined to be thickset, with large hands, small wrists, a disproportionately large chest (developed for breathing in high altitudes), well-developed legs, and widespreading feet. They are broad-headed, with high cheekbones, prominent aquiline noses, and small, almond-shaped eyes.

The eyes appear to have a Mongolian tilt, actually produced by an epicanthic fold over the eye. This marks the American Indian and suggests as his remote ancestry a Stone Age migrant from somewhere out of Asia.

The women, as is natural, are smaller and more delicately constructed, yet they wear a false frailty for they are capable of arduous physical exertion; they give birth and return to the fields within twenty-four hours. Many of the Quechua women have delicate features; some could be called beautiful. At least the early Spaniards found them so and married them. The early Spanish portraits of them exhibit very delicate features, and a Spanish soldier, commenting on the women of Chachapoyas, wrote: "We found them the most fair and good-looking of any . . . seen in the Indies . . . exceedingly beautiful fair and well formed." [34]

Actually the Quechua's skin color runs from light chocolate to the color of beaten bronze, but to their conquerors, at first, they were all "brown and noisy." [143]

The factor which places the Peruvian really apart from many others is his physical stamina; he is capable of great physical endurance even in high altitudes—between 10,000 and 16,000 feet above sea level. This would make normal life impossible for most others.

He also has, remarks Harold Osborne, an exceedingly observant writer: "A high degree of physical insensibility which is [now] artificially enhanced by masticating the natural anaesthetic *coca* [see Medicine, Magic, and Curing, page 482] which renders him impervious to the effects of hunger, cold, exhaustion, and pain to an extent which is perhaps unequalled in another race."

Centuries of acclimatization in the Andes have developed his body so that he can, even in these antipodes, carry on normal functions. His chest, as well as his lungs, are abnormally developed so that the high altitude does not render him anoxic, his large lung capacity frees him from anoxemia (shortness of breath); he carries in his organism the hereditary and ancestral *soma* which allows life at these high altitudes. [128] However, it must be pointed out (so that one is not carried away by this uniqueness of the Andean man) that *physiologically* a 12,000-foot altitude in the Andes—for some reason not altogether clear—is equivalent to 6,000 feet in the Alps. And so, while at first the unacclimatized will suffer at these heights, time rapidly brings about an adjustment.

So it was this man, copper-colored, hard-working, tireless, robust, and by nature attuned to his surroundings, who became the broad base of the social pyramid which was the Inca Empire.

He was classified as a *hatun-runa* or *puric*, [195] an able-bodied worker; he belonged to an earth-cell commune, and as such was given a head count in the decimal pyramidal pattern of the Inca Empire.

 *Dress* **6**

THE DRESS of a *puric*, a man of the people, was simple and unpretentious. He wore a sort of poncho, much like a shortened version of a Victorian nightgown, made by folding a piece of cloth down the middle, cutting a slit for the head, and sewing up the edges, leaving a gap in the folds for the arms. This was called an *onka*, woven usually from the wool of the alpaca. He had another woolen cape garment (*yacolla*) which he threw over his shoulders at night or when the day was cold. This costume is well known, having been drawn by a native artist at the time of the conquest.

The last item of his dress was the breechclout; this was passed between his legs and the two ends held in place by a colorful woolen *chumpi* belt. He assumed this when he was fourteen years of age. Among those of mean birth, coming of age simply meant doing a man's business when he assumed the breechclout. Among the higher men, the *wara cicoy*, putting on the breechclout was a symbol of manhood and was attended with gaudy ceremonies.

So then, this breechclout, tunic, and rustic cape were all the Indian had to wrap his body in this frigid Andean clime. When working in the fields, he merely braided his long hair with colored woolen strings, but when traveling to a market or to a festival, he wore a distinctive headgear which distinguished him from other clansmen traveling on the royal road. On festive occasions he had a longer tunic, reaching to his ankles, on which he or his wife expended their finest talent; he usually went shod in *usuta* sandals.

Woman's dress was equally simple. It was a long rectangular piece of woven alpaca cloth (*anacu*) passed over the head and made wide enough to overlap and be held in place with a sash. It fell to the ankles, almost to her sandals. Over this she had another woolen cape garment woven from the wool of the alpaca, a *yacolla*. This she threw over her shoulders at night or when the day was cold. This costume is well known, having also been drawn by a native artist at the time of the conquest. Over her shoulders a shawl was held together by a copper, silver, or, if fortunate, a golden metal pin; this *topo* was universal with the women and still is. The hair was braided, bound, and tied with woolen ribbons, the ears pierced so as to hold copper, golden, or shell earplugs.

425

127. *A puric or* hatun-
runa, *an able-bodied worker
of the Quechua tribe,
dressed in festive clothes.
Redrawn from Felipe
Guamán Poma de Ayala
(circa* 1565).

The men cut their hair in bangs with copper or obsidian knives;
the women's hair was similarly treated, but hair styles differed from
place to place and tribe to tribe, and were the most distinctive
feature of the Indian. These variants in coiffure continued on direct
order from their Inca; each *ayllu,* or clan, was to keep its distinctive hair style. They had small combs made of rows of thorns or
polished jungle *chonta* wood.

The higher men and the "Incas by privilege," which included
the governing *curacas,* dressed in a style similar to the common
Indian, but the quality of the material was sumptuous. They were
easily distinguished if not by their tunics then by the massive earplugs, usually in jeweled gold. The Inca himself dressed much as
did his people except that his tunics were spun by his women

attendants from the finest vicuña wool. While the man of the people seldom took off his tunic, the Inca never wore the same one twice. It was destroyed on the changing. "And I asked them why," wrote one of the soldiers. "They replied . . . because everything touched by the Inca-kings, who were children of the Sun, had to be burned and made to ashes and scattered to the winds so no one else could touch it." [143]

 The Language 7

"QUECHUA" was applied to the language of the people as well as to the Incas themselves. The word "Quechua" (it can also be written "Keshwa") means "warm-valley people"; in this sense it was the name of a tribe which lived in the *keshwa* grasslands. It is at once a geographical term, a region, a tribe, and a language. It is as a language, however—and written "Quechua" —that the word now has meaning.

The Quechua tribe originally lived in the region of Curahuasi, in a mild Andean climate close to the great canyon and river of the Apurimac. They were a large and dominant tribe when the Incas were still struggling in the Cuzco Valley. [155] After the Quechuas had been attacked by the powerful Chancas and deprived of their dominant position, the Incas moved in, took over the traditional Quechua territory, absorbed the people into their empire—and, presumably, took over the language.

It is not known what language the Incas spoke before this.

After 1438 the Inca Pachacuti made Quechua his language. It then became the language of administration; every official had to know it. Teachers of Quechua went along with the conquests, so that gradually it superseded all the other bewildering number of native dialects. It is now spoken by whites and Indians alike in highland Peru; there is a variant of it in Ecuador, Colombia, Chile, and Argentina. It is a living language; there are many dictionaries of Quechua. It is a language of commerce as well as a literary one, and there are also musical records in Quechua. As a language it has marked characteristics and the closest related tongue morphologically is Aymara, but it doubtless is part of a large language phylum.

The Incas had, as aforesaid, no writing. Their "literature" was transmitted orally and thus subject to the modification of the transmitter (see page 561), but it does not follow that because there was no writing Quechua had no grammatical rules. All the South American languages, even though they differ from one another, have rules of speech, but even to approximate the voice stops is a problem: the sibilant sounds and the fricative variants which give Quechua so expressive a sound have made it a problem to linguists, who have set down its voice sounds in varied orthography. There is considerable confusion in the writing of Quechua place names, towns, and gods.

Soon after the conquest, the Spaniards set about the task of preparing a vocabulary manual and a grammar, yet it was not until 1595 that the first Quechua grammar and vocabulary was published. Since that time many have been published; surprisingly enough, the most thorough and complete were done at varying dates in the nineteenth century by two physicians, one Swiss, J. J. von Tschudi, and the other German, E. W. Middendorf.

One of our foremost authorities on Inca culture has tried to explain the workings of the language in this way (an explanation seemingly far more complicated than the language itself): "A noun can be made from a verb merely by adding nominal suffixes instead of verbal suffixes to the stem, and the finest gradations of meaning can be expressed in inserting affixes between the stem and its grammatical ending." [118] In point of fact, Quechua has a very rigid phonetic pattern, yet it is at the same time plastic in its ability to make new word formations.

There is a surging emotion in the language, which doubtless comes from the fact that almost all Quechua words are accented on the penultimate syllable. It does not have the letters *b, d, f* and *j,* for example, but *p, t, v* and *h* take their place. There are guttural sounds, written *cc,* which are coughed up from the bottom of the throat, as the word *ccapac* (rich). There is a double *t* at the beginning of some words which is almost impossible for one to use unless he has long spoken Quechua; thus between *tanta* (a crowd) and *ttanta* (bread) there is a vast distance in thought and pronunciation.

Although it has no articles, Quechua has all the traffic of language: to form a plural the particle *cuna* was added.* The language has adjectives, genders, pronouns and verbs (*Cani,* "I am"; *Canqui,* "you are"; *Can,* "he is"), particles and adverbs. It is so complex that one wonders how a people could verbally, without writing, transmit so expressive a tongue.

To give something of its flavor an Inca chant would appear in this manner:

Caylla llapi	In this place
Pununqui.	Thou shalt sleep.
Chaupi tuta	Midnight
Hamusac.	I will come.

Whatever the grammar of the language (and it cannot be dwelt upon), Quechua was one of the instruments for carrying the Inca way of life throughout the length and breadth of the Andes, for by the Inca system of population transference (see The Organization and Assimilation of Conquered Lands, page 576), Quechua-speaking people were moved into newly conquered regions. This unification by language is one of the reasons why today more than 46.8 per cent of Peru's inhabitants speak Quechua, and why, in various dialects, it is heard throughout the Andes.

Quechua, then, whether it was traditional in his tribe or whether it was imposed upon him by conquest, was the communicative language of the *puric*.

 ## *The* Ayllu

8

THE *ayllu* was the basic social unit, an early collectivist principle, which seems to have been indigenous throughout the Andean region. It was upon this *ayllu* principle that the Inca Empire was built.

The *ayllu* has been defined as a clan of extended families living together in a restricted area with a common sharing of land, ani-

---

* In this book, however, *s* has been used in most cases, since this complicates an already complicated matter.

mals, and crops so that everyone belonged to an *ayllu*. An Indian was born into it. This commune could be large or small, extending itself into a village or a large center (*marca*) or even into a complex city; for even Cuzco, the capital, was itself only an aggrandized *ayllu*. This social organization must be emphasized for the entire structure of the Inca society is based on it.

Individually no one owned land, it belonged to the community. The *ayllu* had a definite territory and those living within it were "loaned" as much land as was necessary for their well-being. Again, the Incas did not invent or create the *ayllu*—it was already there, part of the long development of primitive Andean society—but the Inca systematized and extended it. Everyone belonged to an *ayllu*. Each was ruled by an elected leader (*mallcu*) and guided by a council of old men (*amautas*) who, when asked, or even when not asked, gave their collective advice on matters affecting it. A number of these scattered communes came under the dominance of a district leader; these in turn formed a territory, and finally they coalesced into "one of the quarters of the world" which was ruled by a prefect (*apo*), who answered only to the Lord-Inca himself.

"The political pattern, and in turn the economic, can be described as a basically decimal pyramidal pattern. At the base of the pyramid was the *puric*, an able-bodied male worker. Ten workers were controlled by a straw boss [*cancha-camayoc*]; ten straw bosses had a foreman [*pachaca-curaca*]; ten foremen in turn had a supervisor, ideally the head of the village. The hierarchy continued in this fashion to the chief [*hono-curaca*] of the tribe, reportedly composed of ten thousand workers, to the governor of a province, to the ruler of one of the four quarters of the Inca empire, and finally to the emperor, the Sapa Inca, at the apex of the pyramid." [12]

For every 10,000 people there were 1,331 officials.

Normally an Indian, unless he died in battle in some faraway land or was transferred by orders, was born, matured, and buried in his *ayllu;* it was his primary and principal loyalty.

AT THE AGE of twenty a man was expected to marry; if he did not, a woman was chosen for him. There seem not to have been, nor was there allowed to be, voluntary bachelors in the realm. While there is considerable detail on how the upper classes married, there is little or nothing on the common man. Marriage was motivated by economics rather than by abstract love. They did not have our own concept of prolonged wooing. If a man wanted a woman, he appeared with frequency at her father's house and joined in the work, and there were premarital sexual relations since absolute virginity was not overly important.

If a man did not find a woman, or the other way round, and had reached marriageable age, marriages were "arranged" during the visitation of the *tucui-ru-cuc*, the chieftain, "he-who-sees-all." Man and woman were arbitrarily selected as mates.

The marriage rites of the common Indians were simple: there was a joining of hands, later followed by a charming arcadian ceremony of an exchange of sandals. It must be understood that, though the life was hard, woman's lot here was no unequal concubinage, nor a weary servitude.

Marriage for the lower man was strictly monogamous, and since the woman prepared food and drink, the death of an Indian's mate was calamitous. Polygamy existed only for the nobility, the Inca himself having as many as seven hundred concubines. All of the ruling classes had plural wives. The first, however, always remained head wife; all the others were secondary. The death of a wife among those blissfully polygamous was not so difficult for the male, except that his secondary wives wept "noisily and lengthily" hoping by the attraction of sentiment to be upgraded to the position of head wife. Among the upper classes, sons of officials grew up with nurses their own ages who became their concubines until they were ripe for marriage, and orphan boys of the same class were often given to childless widows who instructed them in sex techniques and brought them up in exchange for this "servicing" of the old by the young. But none of this was within the reach of the common men; their lives were monogamous with little opportunity for variations on the theme of love. Their excessive sexual appetites, if any

431

existed, were lost in the gross fatigue of ritually controlled labor.

Once a year, every autumn, the communal lands of the *ayllu* were divided among the members of the commune. Each couple united by marriage was given by the headman of the village, who presided over it, a *topo* of land, roughly 300 by 150 feet. The distribution of land was based on the amount of mouths to feed; those with larger families were given an increased acreage for each child. After the division, each family was responsible for its own particular piece of land.

The communal land of the *ayllu* was divided thus: first for the people, then for the Inca (that is the state), and thirdly for the Sun religion (call it tithes). Those two parts of the land for state and religion were tilled communally and harvested communally as part of the labor tax.

10   *Domestic Architecture*

THE INDIAN, with the mutual aid of his kin (*ayni*) within the commune, built his house. His house was, as it is now, a rectangular, windowless room built of field stone plastered with adobe mud or made up entirely of sun-dried adobe bricks. It had one entrance; the "door" was a woolen drapery. The supports which held up a roof, either gabled or hipped, were made from gnarled poles cut from mountain shrub. The roof was very thickly and beautifully thatched with *ichu* grass. The house had neither chimney nor fireplace; the smoke rising from the cooking was left to find its way out between interstices of the thatch. One can see the houses of rustic stonework at the fascinating ruins of Machu Picchu and observe very clearly this type of house. The floor was of beaten earth; perhaps skins of llamas or alpacas might have been laid upon it. There was no furniture; only the head of the tribe was allowed a stool. The Indian sat on the mud floor or on an old weaving, or squatted on his haunches. He slept on the ground either upon llama hides or on a blanket. Niches in the wall served as shrines for a local god. Pegs were used to hang extra tunics, robes, shawls, festive cloaks, slings, or if one belonged to a militia, a warrior's fighting tunic, helmet, shield, and distinguishing headgear with the totem mark of the village *ayllu*. Stones were arranged to hold up the clay cooking pots; the kitchen utensils, clay dishes for eating, copper or bronze knives, bone skewers, and a large stone mortar where the Indian women brayed their corn stuffs were in this section. All was simple and expedient.

The peasant's house (and one may here use the words "Indian" and "peasant" interchangeably) was rustically simple, yet the Inca architecture, which has excited so much attention, grew out of this type of house. Adobe, when ill-kept, has neither dignity nor grandeur, but when painted and thatched it can be, and undoubtedly was then, attractive. All architectural styles have had their roots in the homes of the peasants. The early rustic Greek or Roman peasant house was no better than this of the people of the Incas; those of the Iron Age in Britain were even ruder. Great architecture came out of all of these.

The houses might proliferate at random until the *ayllu* grew to be a *marca*. Then the village was built on a rectangular plan and laid out, presumably by professional architects sent out by the state. Three or four rectangular walls formed a sort of common wall, a *cancha*, a form of co-operative backyard; out of this grew the organized village. This type of architecture is still to be seen in the ruins of the village of Ollantaytambo under the fortress of the same name, which lies on the upper Urubamba River some twenty-four miles from Cuzco.

 A Round of Daily Life   *11*

THE ROUND of daily life began at daybreak. The Indian *puric* slaked thirst and hunger by quaffing fermented *aka* (spoken of now as *chicha*), a mildly intoxicating, thick, malt-smelling beverage. A family had no breakfast as such; aside from *aka* the Indian ate what was left of yesterday's evening meal. Then he went to his fields.

The people were primarily farmers. With few exceptions all preliterate men in the Americas were tied to the earth; everything in the Inca culture must be understood in these terms. They were all members of an earth cell, and each thereby a symbiont of a soil community. After taking his *chicha,* he went to the fields, came back to eat at nine, then returned again to the fields. There he was joined by his wife and entire family; he labored all day in his fields.

The Indian, like agricultural people the world over, did not resent this incessant toil. His work as well as his relaxation was ritualistic and he would never have understood our separation of work and worship; for him, as Harold Osborne said: "Work that was not ceremonial lacked sense and meaning." "Unlike modern society," wrote Osborne, "in which work is regarded as a necessary evil undertaken to secure a leisure which society is untrained to utilize, in Inca society work was regarded as an end in itself."

In late midday the family gathered for their second meal. Cooking was mostly done by boiling; grease and frying were unknown. Corn was cooked with chili peppers and herbs until the corn split; this was *mote.* Sun-dried llama meat (*charqui*) was made into a soup into which *chuñu* (dehydrated potatoes, reduced to a thick whitish powder) was put to make a stew called *locro.* Popcorn was known and considered a delicacy. Ground corn was made into a paste and baked in the ashes like bread. Bright-eyed *cui* (guinea pigs), which ran about the darkened corners of the house, were raised for food. These types of food, certainly not inspiring to a gourmet, were, with variations, the food of the common Indian.

The evening and final meal was taken between four and five o'clock. Men squatted about the pots laid upon a cloth on the ground, helped themselves from the pot with fingers or quaffed the soup from ceramic bowls; the women sat outside of the circle, their backs to the men. When their *ayllu* was visited by the governor, the people of the commune joined together in long lines facing each other (all having brought their own food), and the *curaca* at the head of the "table" sat on his golden stool.

In the tropic latitudes night falls quickly. The door tapestry was lowered and all the members of the family sat upon the animal skins or cloths either about the coals of the pallid fire (for at these altitudes the fire is short-breathed), or about an open-mouthed ceramic brazier which gave out an exceedingly limited warmth. Fuel then, as now, was limited in the naked misery of the soil at 10,000 feet. There are few trees, only gnarled, low-lying scrub for their wood needs. They mostly used the dried *taquia* dung of the llama. The Indian had no artificial light beyond this. Night was spent listening to the oft-told tales of battle, of death, and of the little gods, and the father in these moments passed down to son the remembered things. Men repaired their tools, sharpened their bone knives, worked on weavings, or on the other things of their lives. Women labored quietly on the preparation of *aka,* the beverage that all drank. She first boiled the corn; then she put it into her mouth, chewed it, and in that process her saliva converted the starch, an enzyme distate, into sugar. The chewed mass was placed in a large pot and the enzymes further converted the malt sugar into dextrose, then into alcohol. The chewed corn mass was then mixed with water, boiled somewhat to add to the fermentation, and set aside for a day. The taste for this—to us a noisome beverage—must be acquired; certainly its gray color and heavily maltish odor of stale beer are not, as it was described by William Prescott, "sparkling *chicha*"—but it *was* their life. Women, when they did nothing else, were eternally preoccupied with it.

Cooking, as in almost all societies, was strictly woman's work. She, besides making the *chicha,* prepared all the food. It was her feet that crushed the liquid out of the potato, alternately frozen by the night and dried by the sun, forming *chuñu.* It was her hands which brayed the corn on the stone mortars, a type of millstone slab with ears for handgrips and made with a stone rocker quern for the grinding of corn, spices, and condiments. When woman was not preparing food, she was spinning; then and now it was the most common sight of the Andes—the Indian woman with wool distaff under her arm, walking that particular half-trot, half-walk, spinning the wool onto a straight spindle stick topped with a pottery whorl.

When the woman was not working in the fields or cooking or spinning, she was begetting; sterility was considered an abomination, and a man could leave his woman for it. The essential wealth of the empire, the Inca knew, was the people, and there were tribal rules about childbirth.

There are no precise details on children and childbearing, but need there be? Pleasures and pains are universal; amidst the eternal illusion that envelops us one thing is certain—suffering. It is the cornerstone of life. Before the birth of the child, the Indian woman went to the local *huaca* shrine and there prayed for a good birth. Both man and woman fasted.

After the birth the child was washed at the nearest stream, and on the fourth day placed in a cradle, called a *quirau*. It was carried on the mother's back and put always within easy reach. The child was suckled until two to three years of age, and then after that he began to imitate the parent's life. The child was not named for the first two years, being called nothing else than *wawa* (baby); then there was a family festival and the elaborate ceremony of *rutu-chicoy* (hair cutting) took place. The child was given only a temporary name, and the permanent name was given when he reached puberty.

An Indian's education was the mimicry of his parents in every act of their lives. Parents had no life apart from their children; all acts of their daily lives—eating, sleeping, and working—the children took part in. Sexual acts, too, were witnessed by the children, so that when a boy reached maturity he was in fact a miniature man.

At fourteen, a boy, having reached puberty, put on his breechclout. Among the peasant men it was a simple growing-up theme with all the broad ribald peasant humor reserved for such moments: the boy-turned-man then took his permanent name, either that of an uncle or of his father, or that of an animal.

It was far different with the sons of the upper classes: their putting on the breechclout meant a pilgrimage to the birthplace of the Inca state at Huanacauri up the Cuzco Valley, the sacrifice of llamas with priests officiating, and the smearing of blood on his face (our initiations into secret fraternities are not much different). Later he took on the aspect of a warrior, replete with shield, earplugs, and slingshot, and made public avowals to the Inca. Then the boy of the upper classes was given the type of traditional education which fitted him for a later administrative post within the realm.

Young girls became of age about the same time in a charming hair-combing ceremony, and they, too, took their permanent names; as befitting them their names were, in our sense, and I believe in theirs, somewhat poetic. One could take the name of a star and be called *Coyllur*, or that of the plant called coca, or a blue egg, and perhaps even *Ima Sumac* ("How Beautiful").

Strangely enough, a woman, much different from lowly man, had a chance to leave the *ayllu* and better the existence into which she had been born. She could, if she had special talent in weaving,

128. *Men and women, working together in teams, harvest potatoes. Redrawn from Felipe Guamán Poma de Ayala.*

or grace, or was very beautiful, be selected as a "Chosen Woman" (*Ñusta*). Under these conditions she was brought to Cuzco, or some other provincial capital of one of the quarters of the world, there to learn specific things such as weaving, cooking, and rituals of the Sun, the state religion. She might, as she usually did, become the wife of a high-placed official, or if fortune favored her, a concubine of the Lord-Inca himself.

But normally men and women of the realm of the Incas were born, reared, and buried within their *ayllu*. There was no escape from it. In this society a man was, in the words of Epictetus, "a factor necessary to complete the sum"; he was anonymous and communal. In this womb-to-tomb society everything was prescribed; work, love, festival, death. The price of this security was his absorption into the state.

Religion naturally played a great part in the Indian's daily round of life. The fundamental, enduring principle, the all-prevailing religious idea for this simple Indian was the *huaca.*

There are almost everywhere two aspects to religion. In its first aspect, it is the simple expression of natural man who faces the unexplainable and stands in awe of the supernatural and makes his obeisance to it. It has much to do with death, and among the Incas such fear was animated by the priests of the religion of the Sun; the simple Indian was frightened into a lugubrious phantasmagoria of illusions. And so he made his prayers and paid his homage. In its second aspect, the organized religion took his simple faith, here

129. *Woman opening the irrigation locks to water the fields. The artist shows an advanced form of irrigation reservoir. Redrawn from Felipe Guamán Poma de Ayala.*

as in all other religions, and embroidered these fears with elaborate borders of hocus-pocus.

For the Indian the *huaca* was first the religion of the family, then of his *ayllu*—and then only lastly, that of the Sun, the state religion. He practiced the movingly simple rites of natural man. A prayer was offered up to the local *huaca* for the safe delivery of a child, or there was an invocation to the gods for a good harvest. There is a woman's prayer to the earth god to give the withheld gift of rain:

> *The most distressed of your children,*
> *The most distressed of your servants,*
> *With tears implores you*
> *Grant the miracle*
> *Of water,*
> *Grant the gift of rain*
> *To this unfortunate person,*
> *To this creature*
> *Pachacamac has created.*

The prayers to the gods which accompanied the offerings of first fruits were words well known to the head of the family. In primitive religions, power or spirit resided in everything, and the spirits had to be propitiated. *Huaca* was animism and was what the Romans called *numen*. How could man mitigate the awe of this power and win for himself, his family, and his *ayllu* the peace of the gods? In this way the simple arcadian rites were practiced; only on great feast days did the common man see his prayers festooned with gaudy rituals by the priesthood.

Such, more or less, was the daily round of an Indian's life, a life which, if it were reduced to a moral platitude, could be summed up in one short sentence: *Ama sua, ama llulla, ama cheklla*—"Do not steal, do not lie, do not be lazy."

THE STATE of mind of the Andean Indian, like that of the Roman peasant, was the mind of the farmer-soldier, not farmer, not soldier alone, but farmer-soldier. Although part of an agrarian militia, his life was based on agricultural routine. The caprice of weather might frustrate him and undo his work, but planting, growth, and harvest followed in appointed series.

He was a head count in the decimal system of classification, and a call for so many heads for war could take him from his fields and put him into battle, but no matter how grave the crisis, war was not his life rhythm. So deeply ingrained was this agricultural cadence that when the Inca, with his people, rebelled against their Spanish overlords in 1536 and subjected Cuzco to a terrible siege of sixteen months, it failed principally because of this. For even with his very way of life threatened if he did not succeed, still the farmer instincts dominated the soldier instincts and the uprising failed; the army melted away, demobilized so that the farmer-warriors could go back and cultivate their fields.

In the sense of the farmer-soldier, the Andean Indian must be understood.

Under the guidance of the Inca's "professionals," the whole of the realm—which included Andes, desert, and Upper Amazon— became a great center of plant domestication. *More than half of the foods that the world eats today were developed by these Andean farmers;* it has been estimated that more kinds of food and medicinal plants were systematically cultivated here than in any other sizable area of the world! One has only to mention the obvious: corn—that is, maize—(twenty varieties); potatoes (forty varieties); sweet potatoes, squash, beans of infinite variety; manioc (from which come our farina and tapioca); peanuts, cashews, pineapples, chocolate, avocados, tomatoes, peppers, papaya, strawberries, mulberries; so many and so varied the plants, and so long domesticated in the Old World, one forgets that all of these originated in the Americas.

The potato is dominant in the high Andes. Nowhere else are there so many localized varieties or colors of potatoes as in Peru: white-yellow, pink-gray, brown, purple, black, spotted, and streaked; they are planted from the hot coast seemingly to the sky; the *tatu* variety is planted up to 15,000 feet above the level of the sea and is fully able to withstand the heavy frosts.

A member of the nightshade family, the potato was avoided by the European for three centuries because he believed it caused leprosy. In the seventeenth century the lowly "spud" was considered to be an aphrodisiac. The origin of potato (*papa* to the Incas) is so remote that its beginnings are lost in antiquity. Moreover, few plants have had the social influence of the potato.[164] Since it grew in the utmost livable heights of the Andes, it was the vegetable base of the Inca realm, but since the potato, unlike the other cultivated plants raised by the Andean farmers, was perishable, someone invented the *chuñu* process of potato preservation, and the Inca rulers systematized this by-product into an industry; in a large sense it prevented famine. *Chuñu* (pronounced "ch'un-yu") was the first really dehydrated food, and it was prepared in this manner: the potatoes were left outside to freeze, and on the following morning the people squeezed out the water with their feet. The process was repeated on five consecutive days. *Chuñu* may be preserved whole or made into a very white, light potato flour, and in this powdered dry state it can last for years. *Chuñu* was one of the principal foods stored in the public granaries throughout the Andes.

The grass we call "corn"—maize to the Mexicans, *sara* to the Incas—shared the social base with the potato, and it was, as now, the great food staple of the American Indian. The origin of corn is a fascinating botanical puzzle, and to the problem Dr. Paul Mangelsdorf and his associates in plant genetics have given much patient time.[117] Its place of origin is still unknown; "present evidence points to a dissemination in all directions of the early forms from an unknown center." Not able to withstand as harsh climate as the potato could, corn reaches its highest limits of cultivation in sheltered slopes about Lake Titicaca, at an altitude of 12,700 feet. *Sara* also has great antiquity; it is found in pre-Inca graves dating back to 3000 B.C.; it was even then fully matured as the Indian maize we know. The varieties are many. To the Incas, sweet corn is *choclo;* parching corn was *kollo-sara;* corn for the making of *chicha, saraaka;* corn for making a sort of hominy (*mote*) had kernels the size of hazelnuts.

These two staples were supplemented by quinoa (a pigweed, member of the goosefoot family), a tall reddish stalk, whose seed is much used as oatmeal is in the Scottish highlands, and *oca*, a tuberous plant which, like the potato, grows in the altiplano uplands. These four were the basic subsistence plants, although there were many more. In the warmer valleys, below 8,500 feet, a whole cornucopia of fruits and vegetables appeared: chili peppers, the principal condiment along with salt, tomatoes in considerable variety, beans (all world varieties except the European broad bean and the soybean), squash, pumpkins, wild gherkins, and fruits known and unknown to the world—papaya, chirimoya, avocado, guavas, and the granadilla, the fruit of the passionflower.

In the wet zones of the Montaña, the *yungas*, that part of the Upper Amazon under control of the Incas, peanuts, chocolate, two varieties of manioc, pineapples and soursop were cultivated—all of which originated in the Americas. And from the hot desert coast, fully under Inca control after A.D. 1450, came sweet potatoes, corn, squash and gourds, and a large variety of other plants long developed by the pre-Inca coastal peoples and immortalized in the realistic ceramics of the Mochicas, who existed between 400 B.C. and A.D. 800.

The archaeological world is today besieged by the "diffusionists" who once again (as has been done often in the past centuries) wish the Incas to come from some place else, much in the same manner as those who argue that Shakespeare could not have been Shakespeare. It is impossible for them to accept that indigenous man evolved culturally in this American world. Some claim that the Incas, unsatisfied with their vast Andean realms, went off into the Pacific on a fleet of balsa rafts and so colonized Polynesia; a contrary school suggests that the Incas owe their culture instead to the Polynesians, and to test it a raft was also launched in the opposite direction, that is, west to east. The Mayas must come from Angkor Vat, the Incas from China; the Hy-Brazilians, replete with alphabet, must be immigrants from the sunken continent—Atlantis.

Diffusion has long been known to be an essential dynamic factor in human culture. And it is agreed that many common cultural elements are due more to diffusion than to originality. In our own historical times we have seen how countries have benefited by

130. *Men and women working together, sowing the land. Note the difference in the* puric's *dress (see Figure 131). The first plowing then was festival; now work is at hand, and he wears common work dress. Redrawn from Felipe Guamán Poma de Ayala.*

borrowing—mostly through agricultural borrowing of domesticated plants.

But the Western Hemisphere, once it had its successive waves of migrants from somewhere out of Asia, was apparently sealed off by a geological transformation (as is equally evident in the diffusion of the primitive camel and llama from a common protocameloid ancestry from out of North America—see The Llamoids, page 456), and American man developed from man-as-animal into man-as-culture-bearer without any appreciable "outside" influence.

To show this, here is a comparative list of what man was using in the Old World and in the New in, say, 500 B.C.

EURASIA

1. *Green vegetables:* cabbage, lettuce, spinach, onion, cucumber, egg plant, okra, asparagus, cress, garlic, artichoke
2. *Roots:* beet, parsnip, carrot, radish
3. *Fruit:* apple, pear, plum, cherry, grape, lemon, fig
4. *Nuts and oilseeds:* walnut, linseed, poppyseed, olive
5. *Legumes:* peas, lentils, soybean, broad bean
6. *Cereals:* wheat, barley, rye, oats, millet, rice
7. *Condiments:* mustard, cane sugar

INDUSTRIAL PLANTS:

1. *Vessel gourds*
2. *Fiber plants:* flax, hemp, cotton
3. *Dyestuffs:* madder, saffron, indigo

AMERICA

1. *Green vegetables:* cabbage palm, chayote
2. *Roots or tubers:* potatoes (many varieties), manioc, *camote, oca, olluco, añu*
3. *Fruit:* chirimoya, papaya, avocado, tomato, cacao (chocolate), pineapple, soursop, gerkin, strawberry, raspberry
4. *Nuts:* cashew, brazil, peanut, hickory
5. *Legumes: canigwa, tarwi, molle,* beans (all world varieties except European broad bean and soybean)
6. *Cereals:* maize
7. *Condiments:* peppers (chili—*aji*)
8. *Pseudo cereal:* quinoa
9. *Beverages:* mate, guayusa

INDUSTRIAL PLANTS:

1. *Rubber*
2. *Vessel gourds:* many varieties
3. *Fiber plants:* cabuya, cotton, etc.
4. *Dyestuffs:* cochineal, *achiote, genipa*

It will be immediately noticed that the two lists are almost completely different; only one item—cotton—is common to both continents, and that is wrapped in great mystery.

From the Fertile Crescent came wheat, rye, barley, and the pulses (leguminous plants with high protein content); wheat appears as early as 2500 B.C., and of course never appeared in the Americas until it was brought there by the Spaniard. Eurasia knew no beans other than the soy and the little-known broad bean, *Vicia faba,* descendant of a wild African variety; all other beans, no matter where they appear in the world, are American. White man, after the discovery of the Americas, was the intercontinental plant distributor; it was white man who brought tobacco, maize, tomatoes, chocolate, vanilla, strawberries, squash, potatoes, cranberries, pumpkin, red peppers (hence paprika), pineapples, papaya, and cashew nuts, to be cultivated in Europe and elsewhere. It was white man who brought the banana from Africa to the Americas in 1535, coffee from Mocha in Turkey in the late eighteenth century, sugar cane from out of the Fertile Crescent to the tropics of America in the first days of its discovery; and rice. White man brought the pineapple to Hawaii, and in turn brought back, in one of the early voyages from the Philippines, the coconut—completely absent from the Americas. It is curious that in all the hypothetical diffusion contacts which play so great a part in the anthropological literature, the people of different continents did not make any plant exchange; they also forgot to bring to the Americas the vehicular wheel, the architectural arch, or the potter's wheel or the spinning wheel. In the matter of diseases, after the first contact, they did better; white man brought smallpox, the Indian gave him syphilis.

Cotton is the great puzzle, and it is riddled with mysteries. It was first cultivated in the Nile Valley after the fifth century B.C. The first exact date is 370 B.C., but Junius Bird, of the American Museum of Natural History in New York, found cotton in Peruvian graves which date back to 2000 B.C. At that early date, early Peruvian man cultivated cotton, spun and wove garments from it, and this *before it was cultivated by the Egyptians.* It was known to the Assyrians as "tree wool," yet the Greek etymology of the word points to the fact that it came originally from India.

Cotton as a botanical puzzle causes botanists genetic nightmares, for American varieties show that the chromosomes of cotton point to a trans-Pacific passage west to east by an Asiatic parent, an incompleted return movement of the tetraploid ancestry, which means that the "distributor" must have been birds if not man, who in the early history of the Americas "brought" cotton from the Old World, then several millenia later picked up the American cotton, which had developed new chromosome patterns, and brought it back again to Eurasia.[169] But what a thing to assign to birds, especially as birds do not eat the *Gossypium* seeds? And winds cannot distribute them for three thousand miles. Then, how to account for the same cotton, containing the same genes, in both continents?

Still, until someone presents us with something more positive than the accidental resemblance of sculpture between the Old World and New, it is safe to assume that man in America created his own culture without contact with the other continents, and if the American Indian shares, as he does, forty-nine cultural traits with the Polynesian, then it merely shows how severely limited the human animal is. In twelve thousand years he has been unable to think up another deadly sin. There are traits shared by the Tibetan living at 13,000 feet and the Inca living at the same altitudes—and why not? Geography itself is a determinant.

Agriculture was the soul of the Inca Empire; it determined everything. The Andean farmers' year was divided into two seasons: wet and dry. The wet season began in October and extended to May; the dry season, starting in May, although subject to considerable caprice (hence the Inca's preoccupation with obeisance to the unseen powers), continued into November.

In the autumn the lands of the commune were divided fairly between the members of the *ayllu,* the earth cell which controlled the communal land tenure. First the lands (*chacras*) assigned to the Inca, that is state lands, were cultivated communally (part of the Indians' *mita* tax of service), then the lands of the Sun, the state religion. The fruits thereof were harvested and stored for the use of these agencies. These state granaries were stocked, so the early Spaniard remembered, with maize, quinoa, *chuñu, charqui* (dried llama meat), fish, cords, hemp, wool, cotton, sandals, and military arms, stored in hampers, each item in its appropriate warehouse. They were seen by Francisco de Xerez, the first soldier-chronicler of the conquest in 1533, who remembered these storehouses as

131. *Men and women plowing the fields together. The men use the foot plow, called* taclla; *the women break up the clods of earth. Another woman brings corn* chicha *to drink. Redrawn from Felipe Guamán Poma de Ayala.*

being "piled to the roof, as the Merchants of Flanders and Medina make them." [223]

The work of tilling these fields done, the *puric* then turned to his own.

August was plowing time, and work in each other's field was—like all else—communal. It began with a festival. The nobility took it all most seriously and always participated. "If," wrote the Jesuit historian Padre Cobo, "the Inca himself or his governor or some high official happened to be present, he started the work with a golden digging stick which they brought to the Inca, and following his example all the other officials and nobles who accompanied him did the same." (No different in idea today than some state official turning the soil with a gold-plated shovel or else laying a corner-stone with a golden trowel.)

They had no plow as such, and no draft animals. Men used, as they still do, the *taclla,* or foot plow, which was a thick pole six feet in length with a fire-hardened point; sometimes it was bronze-tipped. There was a footrest near the tip and it was driven deep into the soil by a thrust of the foot and shoulder pressure. The clod of earth was then prized up. The digging stick, like all else in the realm, was a group tool and was seldom used by only one man. His kinsmen of the *ayllu* formed a long line across the field to be plowed, and with a rhythmic chant *"Jailli"* (pronounced "whay-lyi," which means "triumph"), ". . . they triumphed over the soil," writes Garcilaso "the Inca," "plowing it and disemboweling it." The chant went something like this:

○	Free translation
QHARICUNA:	THE MEN:
Ayau jailli, ayau jailli	Ho! Victory, ho! Victory,
Kayqa thajilla, kayqa suka!	Here digging stick, here the furrow!
Kayqa maki; Kayqa jumpi!	Here the sweat, here the toil!
WARMICUNA:	THE WOMEN (answering):
Ajailli, qhari, ajailli	Huzzah, men, huzzah!

The men worked backward, the women followed facing them and breaking up the clods with a sort of hoe called *lampa. Sara* (corn) was planted in September, potatoes when the rains began to fall, i.e., between October and November. After plowing the fields of the Inca, the Sun, and their own, they next turned to those fields of kinsmen who were serving in the army, and then finally to those of the sick and the halt. Their principal tribute (it was part of their tax), said Garcilaso, was "the working and cultivating and harvest-ing of the lands of the Sun and the Inca."

Agriculture was bound up very closely with terracing and irriga-tion, since the amount of flat land was severely limited and the Andean valleys are deep and narrow. The sides of the valleys were wonderfully terraced (see Plate XLV), and these terraces are very exciting when seen for the first time. The rainy season run-off carries away soil; terracing prevented it. Terracing further extended the soil community where the earth surfaces were scant; so the Indians, too, were soil-makers.

Under Inca rule, terracing of the Andean valleys was a systematic part of their methods of soil preservation and soil creation. In the greater projects, those, for example, of Pisac—where the terraces stand poised over the heights of the Urubamba River—or at Ollantaytambo (where the workers cut into the living rock), professional architects were sent out from Cuzco to plan them. It was an enormous expenditure of labor. That these terraces still stand after five centuries is sufficient testimony to the foresight of those Inca rulers.

Irrigation was tied closely with terracing and so naturally with agriculture. It was the lifeblood of empire. In the wet season rain does not always fall nor does all this borax-filled earth hold the water, so irrigation was the answer, and the Inca engineers harnessed the brawling streams pouring out of glaciers and brought them down in the most careful manner to water fields, even though separated by immense distances from the watercourse. These techniques helped to control the density of population and gave the social body a meticulous balance between population and productivity. Much Inca-directed skill was devoted to irrigation. There were immense water reservoirs in the fortress of Sacsahuamán above Cuzco; water was laid underground in superbly made stone-laid sewers in many widely spaced areas. Rivers were straightened, canalized as one sees the Urubamba River, a few miles east of Cuzco and below the great fortress of Pisac. This type of advanced engineering once extended throughout the empire, but is now only dimly seen since so much has been lost to the insults of time.

Irrigation techniques are inseparable from a developed agriculture, and their elaboration marked man as a settler, brought about a corporate life with settled habits; irrigation also created the city-state.

Irrigation, it need hardly be said, was not an Inca invention, but it *was* an Inca perfection. On the desert coast the Mochicas, to mention one great pre-Inca dynasty, had vast irrigation works, and their heirs, the Chimús, built their cities on the ruins of those of the Mochicas and extended the irrigation system so that their cities were supplied by gigantic stone-laid reservoirs.

In the Ica-Nazca coastal regions, west of Cuzco on the Pacific Ocean, these cultures, between the years A.D. 500–800, also elaborated immense irrigation works; the underground reservoirs are still known as *puquios*. Of all this, the Incas were the inheritors.

Yet under the Incas terracing was perfected and extended. Water was so engineered as to be introduced at the top of the terraces, thence it ran down from one gigantic terraced step to another, the whole area being watered by a single stream. Water conduction demands careful design and must be determined by a knowledge of hydrologic conditions, the nature of the soil, and the general conformation of the land. To secure the flow it must run down a slight incline: too fast, it will erode the banks; too slow, it will allow weeds to grow and silt will choke up the channels. It is scarcely curious that wherever in this variegated globe water conduction has been practiced, the techniques of it are almost identical. In ancient Mesopotamia, after its conquest by Hammurabi in 1760 B.C., land exploitation was centralized, which led naturally to the erection of canals, reservoirs, and irrigation dikes.[175] King Hammurabi's "Water Code" is written in a form that sounds like an Inca text: "Each man must keep his part of the dyke in repair." Royal letters were dispatched to governors giving them over-all responsibility to keep the waterways open and the dikes in repair: "Summon the people who hold the fields on the side of the Damanu Canal that they may scour it."

This is only one instance of parallelism in human inventions, for after all it is the stomach that is the all-compelling motive of invention, and man through his ages tested, tasted, and tried the fruits and grains that fell within his ken; he learned to evaluate them, select and plant them—for this reason one need not become unduly overexcited about the parallelism of means and methods in terracing used by peoples out of contact, for where geographical conditions are similar, agricultural methods and water induction will also spring up naturally. One need not fall back on diffusion as an explanation. The peasant is landbound. He may be a Peruvian *puric* or an Egyptian *fellah,* but he remains the "eternal man." He is, in the Spenglerian dictum: "the eternal man, independent of every culture that ensconces itself in the cities. He precedes it, outlives it: a dumb creature propagating himself from generation to generation, soil bound, a mystical soul, a dry, shrewd understanding that sticks to practical aptitudes."

132. *The drum was a part of the festival in which tribesmen imitated the things of their lives. The men are dressed as birds. Redrawn from Felipe Guamán Poma de Ayala.*

In Peru, after the September planting, especially in those lands unreached by irrigation, October was always the "critical" month; if rain did not fall, there would be a crop failure. In instances of prolonged drought the Indian fell back on the "mysteries" and the high priests took over.

Throughout the planted land llamas were sacrificed to the rain gods. If that did not seed the rain clouds, then a man, a woman, perhaps even a child, was sacrificed. The procedure was repeated in Cuzco on a greater scale. The people paraded dressed in mourning; black llamas were tied without food or drink in the belief that the gods could not withstand the plaintive wail of the llama and would send rain to assuage it.

When the corn was ripe, the Indians faced another crisis: birds and animals in the Andes converged on the grain to get at it before it was harvested. Boys, disguised with wolves' skins over their heads, waited to plague birds with slingshots; at night women stayed up to beat on a small drum. Everything, it seemed, conspired against the Indian.

When the crops survived all of this, then there occurred the corn harvest festival; all joined together in the field, and that part of the grain that would not be immediately consumed was stored in the public granaries.

It was after this that the Incas offered the first fruits to their local shrine—the *huaca.*

The idea of the *huaca* is intimately bound up with religion; it combines that which is magical and charm-bearing. *Huacas* were varied and numerous. A *huaca* could be a natural feature of land, a mountain crag; rivers were *huacas,* such as the Apurimac, "the Great Speaker," over which the Incas hung their greatest suspension bridge; and *huacas* were lakes, springs, or other natural objects. All were worshiped in one form or another. But since religion was practical and life was religion, agriculture as such was holy too, and any ritual connected with it was *huaca.*

The best-known and incontestable *huacas* were those built in the fields; they are still to be seen throughout the Peruvian coast. Some near Lima contain upward of twelve million individual bricks. They began, certainly, as a stone deposit; as an Indian worked the fields he tossed stones onto a common pile. This became a shrine and was formed into a stepped pyramid, as most *huacas* are built. Then on top was added a gaudy canopy, where a wooden or stone effigy was placed. That was the *huaca:* "a primordial synthesis in which the conceptual differences of content have never been made analytically distinct." [140]

These *huacas* erected in the people's fields were the primary source of religious expression of the people. Here the first fruits of the harvest were laid. The *huaca* is certainly not wholly Inca nor is it exclusively American; the farmers cultivating their soil, as in Mesopotamia, built their shrines, called *Tells,* more or less in the same manner, and they were placed in the wheat fields. The

133. When the corn is ripe, everything conspires against its harvest. A boy protected by a wolf's skin kills animals and birds with his sling. Redrawn from Felipe Guamán Poma de Ayala.

Sumerian civilizations in the fertile Tigris-Euphrates delta believed also that they, as farmers, were dependent on the favor of the deities, and to secure, to maintain these favors, such as rain and sun, they paid tributes from their first produce in quite the same manner. Human beings everywhere act like human beings. They knew that the gods were dead, but they persuaded themselves that they were living and fell, just as we ourselves do, into inextricable contradictions.

DEATH AND TAXES are not a modern preoccupation; they were just as inevitable if one lived under the rule of the Incas. Since they did not have money, that "great human convenience," [89] the Indians' taxes were in service, called *mita*.

Money began in Babylonia, where it was at first a thin golden ribbon that could be told out from a wheel attached to a wall, but the "eternal man," the farmer who lived away from city cultures, kept firmly to the barter system. The primitive Romans—the pastoral folk—reckoned their values in cattle; the very word money, writes R. H. Barrows, was *pecunia* (whence "pecuniary," from *pecuniarius* which means "head of cattle").

The Incas, even if they did not have money had value; value here was work performance.

The first *mita* of the *puric*, the common taxpayer, was, as already noted, paid in the form of agricultural service, which consisted of a communal cultivation of fields assigned to the Inca and the Sun, the harvesting of the crops, and their storage and attendance. The other form of *mita* was work on government-controlled projects (a similar system was set up under the German National Socialist government as *Arbeitsdienst*).

Each taxpayer was obligated to give a stated amount of work annually to the government. It might be as a laborer in the mines (an odious service which all resented, and the Inca recognized it by rotating the miners rapidly), on roads, or in bridgebuilding or the building of temples or fortresses under professionals (i.e., non-taxpaying individuals, architects)—or any other of the multiple services that a fully organized state needed. There was a constant need of specially trained runners for the *chasqui* courier service.

All labor levies were based on the decimal classification. If one thousand Indians were needed to repair, say, a suspension bridge which would mean cutting cabuya fibers, spinning thick cables, and suspending them across an abyss, then each leader of a given *ayllu* would be asked to furnish one hundred Indians. Within the space of time it took for the courier to arrive with his instructions, the men would be gathered and marched off to the task. Accurate records of service for each community were kept on the knot-string record (see The Knot-String Record, page 561).

Some communities had a permanent service. The village of Curahuasi, which is still extant, lay closest to the great suspension bridge, the Huaca *chaca* (so wonderfully described by Thornton Wilder in his *Bridge of San Luis Rey*), which hung across the Apurimac gorge. Its *mita* was the upkeep of that bridge, the restringing of the cables every two years. So ingrained was this system that even during three hundred years of Spanish occupation, even into the republican period of Peru, the village of Curahuasi performed that task; they strung the suspension ropes, three hundred feet long, for the last time in 1879.

Mita could be paid in transport of military equipment or by service as litter bearers (see Chapter 30, Transport). To appreciate how organized was the *mita* service system, when the great fortress of Sacsahuamán was begun circa A.D. 1438 to defend Cuzco from attack, upward of thirty thousand Indians were set to work quarrying, dressing, and putting into place the gigantic megaliths. It took labor shifts of thirty thousand Indians eighty years to build this structure—a work which ranks in scale with the pyramids.

The small professional class (other than the Inca and his enormous family, who were in effect the administrators of the realm, the *curacas,* or governors, the "Incas by privilege") was made up of the bodyguards of the Inca (who were in effect a cadre of warriors), accountants (*quipu-camayoc*), silversmiths, tapestry weavers (all had titles of their craft), the architect-engineers, and, of course, the priests, as always and as everywhere; none of these paid *mita*. But all others of the millions who formed the realm did. The *mita* tax seems to have been administered fairly and seems not to have been resented by the Indian. Pedro de Cieza de León, writing in 1550, explains how when the Inca wanted to determine what tribute was due from all the provinces between Cuzco and Chile, he dispatched his governors along with the account keepers. They went from village to village examining the condition of the people and their capacity for payment. An inventory, kept on the colored strings of the *quipu*, recorded the various products: the number of heads of llamas, the number of taxpayers, and the quantity of metals, for the Inca automatically owned all the gold and silver of the realm. This done, they returned to Cuzco with the reigning chieftains, and so with *quipu* in hand and his governors to interpret them, the Inca "addressed them lovingly saying that as they received him as their sole lord . . . they should take it in good part and without feeling it burdensome, to give the tribute that was due to his royal person. . . . Having been answered in conformity with his wishes, the lords of provinces returned to their lands, accompanied by the Inca's people who fixed the tribute." [34]

Since the Indian paid his taxes in time rather than in money, it is fully obvious why laziness was a capital offense. For, wrote William Prescott (1847) in his immortal and still largely valid *Conquest of Peru:* "The whole duty of defraying the expense of government belonged to the people . . . Even his time he could not properly call his own. Without money, with little property of any kind, he paid his taxes in labor. No wonder that the government should punish sloth with death. It was a crime against the state and to be wasteful of time was, in a manner, to rob the exchequer."

Yet the *mita* system did not seem burdensome to the Indians themselves; they were happily content in work so long as it was ritualistically controlled, and since there was no ambition to accumulate wealth by surplus production, all the work they did for the state came back to them later when famine made them fall back on the stores in the public granaries—the direct result of their *mita* tax.

Such were the advantages of a womb-to-tomb society; its disadvantages will appear later.

14 *The Llamoids: Llama, Alpaca, Vicuña, Guanaco*

THE AMERICAN Indian did not have, it scarcely has to be repeated, draft animals of any form. Outside of woman, who was the first carrier, the closest that indigenous man got to a domesticated animal was the llama. Before the coming of the white man, America had neither horse, nor steer, nor bovines of any form, nor domesticated pigs or goats. The only animal, and it was not a draft animal since the vehicular wheel did not exist in prehistoric America, was the llama and its wool-bearing relatives.

The llama is the most stylized animal in nature's book; it has a camel's head, large eyes, a split nose, a harelip, no upper teeth, and two-toed feet, which look cloven but are not. Its usual gait is as leisurely as that of a *grande dame* entering a salon, but it can leap like a deer, and when it stampedes it runs as fast as a train (an Andean train).

Along with its remote ancestor the camel, it has (at least for the subject of this book), an amazing history. As far as is known now, the animals known to us as camels and llamoids (which include the llamas, guanacos, alpacas, and vicuñas), originated out of the proto-cameloids who were the dominant types in the Eocene period of geologic time. The particular group which, it is believed, gave rise to the present-day llamas and camels has been found only in North America. Due to the increasing aridity and a floral change which affected the food supply, there was during Tertiary times a continual faunal readjustment through migration. Associated with the proto-camels are rhinos, and particularly tapirs, which are found today only in Malaya and Central and South America.

These, like the *Protylopus* which had camel-like features, in that geological epoch preceding the appearance of man, must have followed a land bridge that most likely connected the roof of America—Bering Strait—with Outer Mongolia. Whatever the "missing links," that animal which was to evolve into both camel and llama appeared in North America in the Lower Eocene times, was forced by the "general floristic change affecting the food supply of herbivorous groups" [70] into migration out of its origin zone: one offshoot moved south into South America and became the llamoids, others moved into Mongolia and became in time the well-known dromedary camel (of one hump) and the Asian (or Bactrian) with two.

The llamas are cameloids: they differ in lack of hump, sternal knee, and hock callouses; the camels grow to a weight of twenty-two hundred pounds, the llama to, at best, four hundred. Their relationship to man, his cultures, and the highways he constructed on differing continents is amazingly similar.

Nobody knows when the first camel appeared in the recorded history of man. There are no records of any in a wild state, yet they have a longer heredity of variation and adaptation than any of the cattle. They do not appear on the early monuments of Egypt, and Julian Huxley has recently confirmed [87] that they did not appear in Egypt until 300 B.C. Camels were apparently still relatively new to the Fertile Crescent since when Xerxes in 480 B.C. started on his invasion of Greece, Herodotus says, that vast army had only one camel corps: "The Arabians equipped . . . on riding camels which in speed are not inferior to horses," but they "brought up the rear to avoid spreading panic amongst the horses who cannot endure the presence of camels."

Camels apparently did not appear in North Africa until late Roman times: at least Sallust says the first time Romans saw camels was in Asia Minor when they were fighting Mithridates (which would be 88–84 B.C.), and Julian Huxley affirms that they were not abundant there until the fourth century A.D. Yet camels formed the main transport along the ancient Silk roads, just as llamas formed the transport on the highways of the Inca.

The camel was the first boxcar. And more; it is a veritable walking commissariat; alive and dead it contains almost everything useful to man. Its wool is made into the "black tents"; [49] its meat is tender. The camel only walks and gallops; fully loaded, up to fifteen hundred pounds, it can travel twenty-five to twenty-eight miles a day. When urged to gallop it can move at the speed of an express train, and it outstrips a horse traveling one hundred miles a day. Its paunch holds enough water for days (it can be drunk by man in dire emergency); it has trapdoor nostrils to keep out the sand drift, and its great liquid eyes are so heavily lashed that not a grain of sand can enter in during the wildest windstorms. There is something *right* about a camel; it can withstand the temperature of the Gobi Desert at 140 degrees and also be impervious to Arctic cold. The camel, says the author of *Travels in Arabia Deserta,* can be "clothed on the high days with glorious pall of green velvet" with a seat of a four-poster litter and march through the empty way of the desert, or it can lie for weeks in the spring pastures "laying up flesh and grease in their humps for the languor of the desert summer." [49]

Whatever one says about the camel one can say about the llama: it furnishes food, wool, transport, and fuel; it is a social beast, i.e., although it has no love of mankind such as horses and dogs display, none the less it is part of man and his society.

After twelve months of gestation the camel cow gives birth to a calf "as big as a grown man," observed Charles Doughty; "the herdsman stretches out the newly-born's legs, draws it out of the womb, claps it on the chest, revives it, and within three hours it stands, suckles, and gives first voice, sheeplike in complaint." After that the camel cow will yield three pints of milk daily (the llama was never milked). Like the llamas, the camels have no upper teeth after they mature; grass, thorny boughs of sweet mimosa leaves are ripped off by a stiff upper lip. Since there is little fuel in the desert lands of the camel, its dung, called *jella,* is used as fuel. When overburdened camels will protest the vast bulk with a groan but march to the end in silent fortitude.

They give everything—even their urine, which is used by the nomads to wash their babies in the belief that the odor will keep

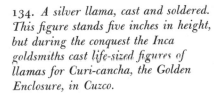

134. *A silver llama, cast and soldered. This figure stands five inches in height, but during the conquest the Inca goldsmiths cast life-sized figures of llamas for Curi-cancha, the Golden Enclosure, in Cuzco.*

away insects. Resigned, unreproachful, uncomplaining, the camel goes plowing across the vacant land, with the nomad women walking barefooted, spinning, beside their slow-pacing camels. A camel is like some graceful, hideous woman, someone wrote, who has magic in her way of walking—like Baudelaire's courtesan: "worn-out, heroic . . . the indestructible elegance in her."

Whoever says "camel" says "llama," for in all or almost all of their habits tied to man they are comparable even though distant by a hundred thousand years of variant evolution; both are man's transports along some of the most extraordinary roads built by him. The llama mimics the camel except for bulk, but their mechanism of water storage, even without the hump, is quite the same (metabolism of subcutaneous fat and body carbohydrates). They are seldom ridden, although there are Mochica ceramics showing Indians mounting llamas; they are not milked and never used for wheeled drayage. Yet they have, like the camel, that amazing plastic ability for adaptation; they can live in the range of perpetual glaciers, 17,000 feet altitude, or acclimatize themselves to the desert. The Mochicas (A.D. 400–800), in their pottery show them carrying heavy loads through the desert, with a woolen fringe over their eyes to keep down the glare of the sun. Normally a llama loaded with half its weight will walk between six and twelve miles a day; if pressed it will travel longer. As the camel was to the Asian, so the llama was to the Inca; its wool was used mostly for heavy blankets, strong cords, sacks for cargo (the wool is very greasy); its meat was made into sun-dried *charqui* (hence our western word "jerky"); its dung, *taquia,* like that of the camel, was a fuel, and was gathered in their communal voiding places.

To have been a llama herdsman in Inca times was a complex and honored profession, since the llama not only yielded all material things, but its lungs were consulted in times of dire stress for the omens they would reveal, just as the Romans consulted chickens' entrails.

The Incas, it need hardly be said, did not "invent" the llama; it was present in Peruvian culture twenty-five hundred years before the Incas even appeared; it is so old that it appears mummified in Paracas graves, where it has five toes instead of two! But the Incas did systematize llama husbandry.

There now seems little doubt that the untamed guanaco is the wild progenitor of the llama; the llama itself is a hybrid, but these two are most closely related. Of the other two of the llamoids, the alpaca, which now, as it did during Inca times, furnishes wool for weaving, seems to be a hybrid of the llama and the vicuña. The alpaca does not "carry"; it is not much larger than a large sheep and is confined mostly to the altiplano, about 15,000 feet altitude. The vicuña (pronounced "ve-kuhn-ya"), the most delicate of the llamoids, is completely wild. "A delicate animal with plenty of fine wool," said Cieza de León, ". . . it stands higher than a goat and the color of its whole is clear chestnut. They are so fleet that no dog can overtake them and they frequent the loftiest fastnesses near the line of snow." Possessing the finest wool in the world (worthy of Jason's Golden Fleece), the vicuña was taboo to ordinary man: only the Inca and his circle might wear garments from its wool. They were obtained in hunts, as Cieza de León explains: "When the Yncas desired a royal hunt, they ordered three, four, ten thousand, twenty thousand Indians to surround a wide track of country and gradually converge until they could join hands . . . They made very precious cloth from the wool of the vicuñas for the use of the Ynca." Very often, "there were as many as forty thousand head of guanacos and vicuñas alone in this great circle; most of the female vicuñas and some of the males were released, but they were shorn of their wool before they were allowed to go free . . . that of the vicuñas, as fine as silk, was reserved for the Ynca's service."

For transport during war, for carriers of trade goods during peace, the Incas depended mainly on the llama. It was the principal pack animal (outside of the Indian himself), and in conquests thousands were used along the ways of the Incas.

The llama herds were an integral part of Inca economy. Each *ayllu,* or earth cell, had its own contingent of llama herds, which were counted by the *quipu-camayoc*—the knot-string-record accountants—so the Inca could know the precise number of llamas within his realm; they reached, if we are to believe the chroniclers, into the hundreds of thousands.

As llamas are a hybrid, the Indians had to give them constant attention during the reproductive act; the males were aided during copulation and Indians were on hand to aid the birth of the single llama calf given at issue. Because of this intimacy a considerable folklore has grown up about the llama: one, that as the Indian found the female llama attractive, a male herder must always have his wife present during his chore. Then, since *all* anthropologists (if not all physicians) agree that syphilis was American in origin, and that it had never appeared in the Old World until Columbus returned to Spain after his first voyage, it was presumed by some that this disease came from the llamas and that Indians must have practiced zoophily (literally: love with an animal). The supposed result was syphilis. And this was transmitted to white men. It is good folklore but not good science: no llama was ever found to harbor *Treponema pallidum,* the spirochete of syphilis. Which fact does not ruin the theory of this social disease as originating in the Americas, but only disposes of the llama as the original carrier. What is it that Herbert Spencer said when he excused himself for bringing up an ugly fact to ruin a beautiful theory?

THE WEAVING skills occupied both men and women. The wool stuffs collected by their *ayllu* were divided among them according to their needs, i.e., depending on the number and demands of each member of the commune. The residue was stored in the official storage bins, the precise amounts accounted for by those officials who recorded this on their *quipu* string counters, so that the governor of a given province could know precisely down to the last fiber how much wool was available in this district.

Wool, until Inca conquests opened up the channels for trade to obtain cotton fiber, was *the* Andean material. The wool of the alpaca, generally white, but mixed with grays and natural browns, was used for wearing apparel because of its superior fineness and long fiber; llama wool, coarse and greasy, was spun, in a distinctive brown-white color, as fiber for heavy blankets, durable sacks for llama transport, and ropes and llama halters. Vicuña, soft, silky, the finest in the world, was reserved only for the highest, luxury weaving. The wool was dyed before carding and spinning, although where the particular weaving called for the natural colors of the wool they were fully utilized.

"Virtually nothing is known of the dyeing procedures," writes Junius Bird,[13] the most experienced of America's "dirt archaeologists." This is surprising since the pre-Inca graves of Paracas have yielded so fantastic a collection of weaving techniques and colorings that one textile expert distinguished 190 hues! Mordants, metallic substances such as copper and tin, were definitely used to give permanence to vegetable dyes; *achiote* is a tree whose pod yields a red dye, the genipa, a jungle pod which yields a jet black, and the seed of the avocado long has been known to have yielded a permanent bluish dye; one recent experimenter extended to 250 the number of plants from which good dyes could be obtained in Peru. In Mexico, they used the cochineal, a scale-insect parasite (*Coccus cacti*), but this seems to have been absent in Peru. The wool dyers certainly made use of a shellfish dye, just as the people of the Mediterranean obtained the famous *purpura* and *murex*—the Tyrian purple—from the molluscs of the inland sea.

After dyeing, the wool was tied to a distaff and spun. The

spindle was a straight stick with a piece of ceramic whorl (usually nicely decorated) which one spun between the fingers as one would a top, while the other fingers, well moistened with spittle, fed the fibers from the wool ball on the distaff. This system of spinning is world-wide. The spindle whorls found in Palestine or in Egypt as early as 3000 B.C., or in Troy of the same period, are so similar in design and purpose that, placed beside those found in Peru dating from the same time-epoch, they can hardly be told apart.

Cotton was spun in the same manner. As is well understood, the Inca people were out of the range of cotton; but by trade and barter they secured it from the Upper Amazon, famous for a long-stapled naturally brown cotton, and from the coast where it was extensively planted.

Tree cotton was known in India as early as 3000 B.C., and is mentioned in the writings of Herodotus. Presumably the cotton stalk plants as grown today were not those cultivated by the ancient Peruvians; rather they were "cotton trees." When cotton, through extensive trade, came to the Incas, they used it for certain weavings with considerable eagerness; it has, since its early cultivation on both continents, Old and New, been an important fiber because it is so easily processed. The things that these people could do with hand-spun cotton are utterly amazing: it could be gauzy tissue, or a gossamer of muslins of extraordinary whiteness and thinness (mummies on the coast were wrapped in it); guilds of cotton weavers were attached to the Peruvian coastal temples just as factories of cotton weavers were connected with temples in Egypt.

The looms to spin wool and cotton were of three kinds: the backstrap or belt loom, wherein the upper part is tied to a tree or upright and the belt for tension is passed around the back of the weaver (hence the name); the horizontal loom, put upon the ground, the warp being supported by a forked-stick support a foot above the ground; and the vertical loom, built against the wall, upon the cloth of which the weavers—usually men—worked standing. "As yet," says an authority, "no one has made a comprehensive study of the loom types still in use and of their distribution in Peru." [13]

What is certain is that the art of the loom was widespread throughout Peru, and that the Incas were inheritors of the techniques that had been thousands of years in the perfecting. Almost all authorities seem to agree that most of the fabrics found in graves came from the backstrap loom; these looms have often been found in graves—usually in that of a woman so that in the netherworld she could occupy herself as she had in this one—and on these backstrap looms cloth is found half completed. By comparing these with the present-day looms of tradition-bound Peruvian communities, one can see that the techniques have changed little in two thousand years.

Weaving has had a long history in Peru; the most advanced was that produced by that unknown people called Paracas, on the desert coast of southern Peru. From this culture (which endured with some interruption between 400 B.C. and A.D. 400) have come pieces of embroidery and weaving which are admitted to be without peer in the world. The prodigious expenditure of time to weave so complex and startling an array of ponchos, turbans, shawls, skirts—all for the dead—is quite incalculable; the designs, the craftsmanship, are amazingly consistent.

On the north coast, five hundred miles from the Paracas, the Mochicas, whose culture extended from A.D. 400 to 800, pushed weaving to such perfection that it seems to have been done on a factory principle. At least a celebrated Mochica ceramic exhibits a row of women (all with backstrap looms) weaving industriously, while a male supervisor sits under a sunshade and directs them. So the Incas inherited complete techniques; their notable contribution was to perfect a method of obtaining the wool of the vicuña which was made, as said elsewhere, into weavings of such fineness that they were mistaken by the first Spaniards to be of heavy silk.

As in spinning, so with looms (*ahuanas*). Those used by the ancient Peruvians are identical with those of other civilizations with which they had absolutely no contact. A form of backstrap loom was used in Egypt, a horizontal loom appears in predynastic Egypt, and the one pictured on the tomb of Khnem-hotep (at Beni Hasan), circa 1900 B.C., is identical with those of the Andean and coastal Peruvians. The same may be said of the vertical looms which appear in the tomb of Thotnefer at Thebes: in form and function they are quite similar. Man is like the earth, repetitious in form. As Charles Doughty had it, "The carcass of the planet is alike everywhere; it is but the outward clothing that is diverse."

135. *Woman weaving at a backstrap loom. This was the common type of loom throughout the Americas. It is still used. Redrawn from Felipe Guamán de Ayala.*

The weaving methods of the Incas, like all else about them, were functional. Three grades of wool cloth, all distinguished by names, were woven. The common was *awaka* woven material. The finest and most finished (on both sides) was *kumpi*. Many Inca materials were done in tapestry weave, but much of this has perished due to the climate. The thick and heavy weave, *chusi*, was a baizelike material used for bed or floor coverings. The looms on which the finest *kumpi* materials were woven were ". . . made on frames of considerable size, the function of the lateral beams being to give rigidity and a proper tautness to the warp. There were no needles in these frames, all the work being done by the weaver's fingers and by the spindles or bobbins carrying the colored weft-threads which were beaten up after insertion by the use of the weave dagger." [124]

Men were weavers (*kumpi-camayoc*) as well as women; the latter, however, were entrusted with the finest wools of the alpaca and the vicuña. One of the functions of the Chosen Women was to produce the fabulous vicuña tunics for the Inca—the kind which he never wore more than once before it was destroyed. They also fashioned the feather tunics, a mosaic of jungle-bird feathers put quill-first into the warp of the weaving. "The luster, splendour and sheen of the fabrics of feather-work," said the Jesuit Bernabé Cobo, "were of such beauty that it is impossible to make them understood, unless by showing them," and what he said then applies equally now. They are indescribable except to call them feather mosaics. In addition to the feather weaving, other cloth was richly adorned with bangles of gold or tiny bells and golden particles called *chaquira;* there were tunics completely covered with gold, silver, or burnished copper pieces. I can go no further except to urge those near a museum to seek them out.

Now if the Indian was an automaton in all else, he seems to have been allowed full freedom in design for his weavings. The selection of bright and vigorous colors is bold and startling; here the weavers have achieved an effect of heightened colorfulness by discords of adjacent hues, the kind of color effect which was developed by Gauguin and a few other postimpressionist painters. Each weaver, presumably, selected his or her colors and designs so fanciful that they seemed to come as a protest to the confined circle of his life. Having been allowed full individuality, the weaver made the most of it. One finds similar pottery, since it was mold-produced; one rarely finds weaving designs repeated. A collector of modern art would not consider it out of line to place the most abstract of modern designs beside those of the Peruvians; their ability to dissolve images into symmetrical and geometric patterns, the stylization of subject matter, their innate sense of transforming representational art in an over-all decorative pattern, has been eulogized ever since this art has been recognized as art.

16  *Pottery and Pottery Makers*

Pottery is one of the oldest of skills in the Americas. The Indians did not have the potter's wheel (the whole idea of the wheel being completely absent in all forms). The ancient Peruvians, as all others in the Americas, used the coil method, and yet despite the primitive techniques this pottery is among the world's best, and its graceful forms rival the Greek vases of the best periods. Taken as a whole, the "arts" in these higher Peruvian civilizations are "fine arts in the best sense of this term." [2]

Inca pottery is well made, fine-grained, with a hardness almost metallic. Pottery shaping was made by first rolling clay into sausage form, then building spirally into the projected pot, one hand feeding the sausage-shaped core, the other pressing it into shape. This was then smoothed and molded by a small flat wooden disk; then it was dried, painted, and fired.

136. *A pottery brazier* (LEFT); *when placed in a room and filled with charcoal, this was capable of giving localized heat. A three-legged urn* (RIGHT) *was placed over a fire for cooking.*

Inca pottery has a wide range of shapes. There are the utilitarian, three-legged pots used by the warriors on campaign, the household pottery, strong and crude red, the enormous, beautifully shaped aryballus (although not like the Greek, from which its name derives)—a bottle-shaped pot with a pointed bottom, which fell to its side when emptied, but was so exquisitely balanced that a jar, capable of holding six to eight gallons of fermented *chicha*, could, when filled, balance on that single point. The Inca aryballus had a long, graceful neck and two band-shaped handles, used for holding a rope passed through them for carrying; it was the most characteristic of Inca pottery. There were shallow dishes for food, a type of service all seemed to have, and sometimes wonderfully decorated. There were beaker-shaped vessels for drinking, and three-legged braziers, wide and open-mouthed for heating the otherwise unheated rooms.

All, or almost all, of Inca pottery is a reflection of function; they made no contrast between art for its own sake and art for a practical purpose. It is even misleading to speak here of "art" in the aesthetic sense of today; the Incas, as all other ancient peoples, were unaware of such distinctions. Most of the world's ancient art was religious, except that of the Mochicas, who had a secular "art." There is an intimate relation in most of these societies between art and religion, particularly in agrarian societies such as the Incas', where art was bound up with religion for the purpose of humoring the gods, cajoling them, or even compelling them by these objects to grant rain. All objects were made for use. There was naturally,

who could deny it, a real sense of beauty in the craftsman. His absorption in geometrical ornamentation must have come from his enjoyment of attractive lines and forms, but everyone was a craftsman and leisure from the fields, when it existed, was used for "thing" producing.

The designs of Inca pottery are very distinctive: usually elaborate geometric patterns, so unalterably Inca they were as identifiable as a Roman coin; for Inca pottery, as indeed is equally true of other Peruvian pottery, is a diagnostic for spatial relationships.

A history of preliterate people is mainly written in, and determined by, the stylistic changes which can be seen in their artifacts, and the artifact most sensitive to stylistic change is pottery. An archaeologist seeking to understand the time factor involved in a particular site makes a stratigraphical cut through a ruin; the potsherds that are found associated with other items of an Indian's life (worn clothing, spindles, cordage, slings, bags, warheads, etc.) help to establish a typology of all other artifacts about them, included in that time-space area. Through potsherds (design, shape, firing), the archaeologist can establish certain time subdivisions. The knowledge derived from archaeology is more explicit than literature or oft-told tales. Literary statements can be challenged, but potsherds and artifacts are tangible and visible and reveal much. In the specific case of Inca pottery, it is so distinct that wherever it is found —with other collaborating material—it marks the fact that the Incas were there. "Virtually all of these [archaeological] techniques,"

137. *Inca pottery types.* (FACING PAGE) *a tall, fragile ceremonial vase, unusual for the utilitarian-minded Incas; polychrome eating plates (diameter about six inches);* (THIS PAGE) *varying forms of eating pots; a type, also found in wood, for drinking corn* chicha.

wrote the late Dr. Wendell Bennett, "depend heavily on ceramics, since these are not only well preserved but also reflect styles." Such a thing must have occurred to the first Persian ambassador sent to China, for when fingering a beautiful bowl he said: "The date and the maker of the pot can be told by the touch."

Pottery, too, can become language, as one sees among the Mochicas. Their pottery is so realistically modeled that every cultivated plant can be identified. The designs of their garments, the dyes they used, the various social castes in their society—rich man, poor man, beggarman, merchant chief—are found in their ceramics. Animals and birds are there in profusion and so realistically done that it is almost better than glyphic writing; for the maximum number of mouth gestures is 144, but by rotating wrist, hand, and fingers, a man can produce 100,000 distinct elementary signs. "The human hand is about twenty thousand times more versatile than the mouth." [89] This is reflected in the realistic Mochica pottery, which, with its wide range of subjects (even the sexual approach and attitudes are so many and varied that they promise a corpus of unplumbed sexual positions), constitutes a veritable plastic alphabet. [101]

While most were by necessity housebuilders or pottery makers or even weavers, there was, as in all complex societies, a class of specialists: some worked in gold, silver, wood; there were weavers of special fineness and specialized pottery makers—those living in regions of better clay. And as in all craft cultures, there was an excess; this was the lifeblood of trade. So while the Indian did not own his land nor the wool of the llamas which he herded, he was allowed his leisure time, and with this he created things in excess of his own consumption. He had no money, but he had value and he knew barter; out of this grew the market (as ancient as the Andes), which the Incas systematized into the *catu.*

17   CATU: *The Market*

M AN first knew peace through trade.
Throughout the prehistoric world, be it in the Americas or Africa or within that Fertile Crescent, hostilities were often suspended so that trade could be made. Trade, exchange, diffusion—through these activities man became more human. All the early routes of and for trade were luxury routes: "The extreme parts of the inhabited world," wrote Herodotus, "possess the most excellent products," and to these "extreme parts" men of all hues and colors passed in search of luxury products; the *Via Salaria*— the route to salt—was one of Rome's oldest roads. And in the Americas, one of the conquistadors, by following the route of the salt trays (a ceramic dish about the size of a bread pan) coming down from the interior of Colombia, traced that salt road and discovered the Chibchas, and with it the golden treasures of El Dorado. [215]

Man sought out amber from the earliest times, and the oldest road through Europe is the amber road over which man traveled from the Mediterranean to the Baltic to secure that wonderful fossilized soft rich pitch—that "special act of God." Other luxury items came over early pathways: *murex,* which yielded that Tyrian purple, silks, frankincense, and myrrh. So trade, when man became a city-dweller, was part of his urban revolution, perhaps not so much a revolution at all but the outgrowth of his gradual control of nature and the production of an excess of local products. It was just these concentrated surpluses that made possible the luxury tastes.

In addition to the amber routes, there were lapis lazuli routes, and silk roads; caravan cities such as Petra, Palmyra, Damascus, and many other famous caravansaries sprang up to meet the demand for luxury goods. So in the world search for luxury goods and transit, men often held roads under general amnesty; when men met for trade, hostilities were called off so that an exchange of products could take place. Markets, too, were the principal vehicles of diffusion—the essential dynamic factor in human progress. The market as a means of interchange of ideas and information gave the needed stimuli to human progress.

In preliterate America it was also luxury goods that stirred the Indian, although he was handicapped by geographical barriers and the lack of the "idea" of the wheel or draft animals. He was severely limited in his desire for luxuries (that "damned wantlessness" which Lenin complained of in the Russian peasant). But agricultural discoveries were exchanged rapidly through the medium of the trade market, so that within the entire Western Hemisphere almost every type of cultivated product was known throughout the three Americas. Obsidian for knives traveled thousands of miles from the place of origin; emeralds, which were found only in the narrow corner of a mountain called Muzo in Colombia, found their way to Mexico and south into Peru as luxury items. The Mexican markets brimmed with luxury items: chocolate, vanilla, gold and silver objects, feather weavings, ornamented sandals. And thus, the Peruvian.

Markets under the Inca Empire were frequent and general, but trade was purely local and commerce a government monopoly. The need for markets within the empire was an important element in the economic structure of the realm. "In order," wrote Garcilaso de la Vega, "that labor might not be so continuous as to become oppressive, the Inca ordained that there should be three holidays every month in which the people should divert themselves with various games. He also commanded that there should be three fairs every month, when the laborers in the field should come to the market and hear anything that the Inca or his council might have ordained." They called these markets *catus*.

This system of using the market as an official decree-dispensing method is remembered in one of the smaller market centers of Cuzco itself; it is known as Rimacpampa, the "Speaking Place," where the people gathered to hear the Inca equivalent of "Hear ye, hear ye. . . ."

The orbit of the people was limited; fairs were mostly local, and an Indian used the royal roads only with the consent of the local chieftain. In many of the larger Inca cities (and still to be seen on the fragments of the Inca road that winds its way through the Andes) are the posts, the halting places, where guards made certain of who used the road and for what purpose. Tolls were set up at all the large bridges for travelers to markets, as was recorded by the first European observation. On January 14, 1533, when Hernando Pizarro made the journey to the coast to hurry up the flow of gold which was to ransom the captured Inca, they came to the Andean village of Piga along the royal road which there crossed the Santa River which was "spanned by two bridges close together made of network . . . By one of these bridges the common people cross over and a porter is stationed there to receive transit dues. . . ." [54]

The economic interdependence of the various provinces did not require complex trade, and so the markets were not warranted alone by economic necessity; the stuff and products wanted were luxury goods, mostly interchange between the mountain and coastal people on one side and the mountain people and the jungle people on the other.

What was luxury to the Indian? From the coast came cotton— soft and different, easy to weave, and although not as warm as alpaca wool, yet luxury; all classes of society sought it and the Spanish on their arrival found the public storehouses full of it. There was a different set of dyeing colors—always important to the weaver—and many types of rock mordants from the coast that gave cotton subtle hues; there was *achiote*, which rendered a carmine color, and purple from seashells. Among the foods there were seaweed (still beloved by the Indian and still to be seen in their markets), seashell food (the great shell conchas were used as trumpets), dried fish of every description, reeds for basketmaking, and many forms of hotland food products. The jungle people brought feathers for the feather mosaic weavings, *chonta-palm* (an iron-hard wood) much used by the Incas; there were birds, jungle game, and batwings' fur (from which a silklike cloth was made for the Inca), dyestuffs, and many Homeric simples such as quinine, ipecac, sassafras, *guayusa* (used for a febrifuge), rubber, and gum latex from the sapodilla tree, strong tobacco leaf, and narcotics.

The Andean people brought to this type of market their excess manufactures: weavings, bowls, carvings, potatoes, *chuñu,* corn—that which they did not themselves consume; and since the empire levied no property taxes, only *mita* labor service, they were free to exchange any accumulated movable property.

There was, as aforementioned, no money, "that great human convenience" says Madge Jenison in her stimulating book on *Roads,* "by which a symbol of life is simplified." Without coinage the monetary principle was barter. Nor did the regime intervene in the spirited exchange at the markets. "No value," says Garcilaso de la Vega, "nor standard was fixed in these exchanges by any public authority, for this was left wholly to the satisfaction of the bargaining parties." Although the Incas, as the rest of the native Americans, were out of the stream of Old World culture that brought in its current the wheel, the horse, coinage, and writing, they were forming, none the less, a society similar to the early Egyptian and Sumerian civilizations. They were already part of the urban revolution that changed man from a food-gatherer to a food-grower, part of the settled community that produced the city-state and class society.

In ancient Sumer the land was also communally held: "owned by a god who stood for the community which formed his people . . . but it was parcelled out among god's people—the citizens—to be worked as individual allotments . . . The surplus accumulated," writes V. Gordon Childe, "was deposited in the Sumerian temples and made it worth-while to organize caravans."[33] The Inca system was somewhat similar except that there was no such thing as a merchant class in this empire, in fact no merchant at all. Yet, as everywhere, the stomach was the guiding impulse, and markets and trade, no matter how different the society nor how far removed, followed the pattern that was man's.

Pedro de Cieza de León, that most accurate of observers, tells something about them in 1549, long after the departure of Inca glory. The barbaric pageantry that went with these markets can only be dimly surmised: "In all parts of this kingdom of Peru we who have travelled over it know that there are great fairs or markets, where the natives make their bargains. Among those the greatest and richest was formerly in the city of Cuzco, for even in the time of the Spaniards its greatness was caused by the gold which was bought and sold there and by the other things of all kinds that were sent into the city. But this market or fair at Cuzco did not equal the superb one at Potosí, where the traffic was so great that among the Indians alone, without including Christians, twenty-five or thirty thousand golden pesos exchanged hands daily. This is wonderful, and I believe that no fair in the world can be compared to it. . . ."

18 *Holidays and Games—Dance and Music*

THE HOLIDAYS, which were public ceremonials, were many and elaborate, bound to the markets and to the ceremonial year which was tied up with the agricultural year.

The Inca year was divided into twelve months, each month named after its ceremony. The year began in December with *Capac Raymi*, the "magnificent festival" month. There were many sports and games attached to the festivals, and the coming-of-age rites were held, with the boys of the upper class receiving the breech-clout. There was the month of the "small ripening" and the "great ripening"; there were others which were called the month of the "dance of the young maize," and later the "festival of the water"; a complete list as given by Dr. Luis Valcárcel[199] appears opposite:

GREGORIAN MONTHS	PERUVIAN MONTHS*	TRANSLATION
December	*Capac Raimi*	Magnificent festival
January	*Huchuy Pocoy*	Small ripening
February	*Hatun Pocoy*	Great ripening
March	*Paucar Warai*	Garment of flowers
April	*Airiway*	Dance of young maize
May	*Aimuari*	Song of the harvest
June	*Inti Raimi*	Festival of the sun
July	*Anta Situwa*	Earthly purification
August	*Capac Situwa*	General purification—sacrifice
September	*Coya Raimi*	Festival of the queen
October	*Uma Raimi*	Festival of the water
November	*Ayamarca*	Procession of the dead

Although these were observed throughout the empire and re-enacted wherever there were great Sun temples, Cuzco, as Rome, was the focus of most of the important events; here they were the most elaborate. The stirring pomp and meticulous ritual connected with all of the festivals has not been exaggerated by the first Spaniards; they are fully documented in the remains of the gaudy garments that were worn by the participants which have been recovered from the tombs.

The ritual attending was naturally part of the whole trance of being; the mimetic dances and songs, movements and voices, were all part of the elaboration given to the earth mysteries by the priests of the Sun. It was precisely the color format needed by the Indian, who was, by the nature of his environment, hemmed in and dulled by the narrow corner of his world. Inca festivals gave ordinary man a sense of belonging; this collective hypnotism, these ecstatic states of ecstasy robbed him of his self-possession, and to paraphrase a French anthropologist,[106] "transported him to a life beyond life," and gave him the feeling that the particular plea to the gods, at the moment, had been attained. And it provided him later, in the long, dark hours in his mountain house, with the subject for talk to fill in the interstices of extended night.

* Spellings have been modified to conform with the usage of Quechua words in this book.

Holidays might last for a day or for a week. There might be public dancing, such as when hundreds of radiantly clothed Chosen Women danced with Huáscar's Chain. There could be games and sports. There was always drinking, for the Indian was expected to get drunk, which he did, quaffing immense quantities of fermented *chicha;* ritual drunkenness was as essential to a good festival as agricultural discipline was to a good harvest.

Conch-shell horn
(potóto)

Games at the festivals differed from those played by the Indian boy (which consisted mainly of spinning a top by whipping, a sort of "pile-on" game with potatoes, flipping small counters against the wall—called "lagging" in the United States—and a game called "Puma" which was something like Run, Sheep, Run). Sports at fair days were Olympic: there were foot races, such as described by Padre Acosta, during the "magnificent" month, when "young sons of the nobility used to race one another up Huanacauri hill"; there were mock battles in which village would be pitted against village, or group against group in a large square arranged for the purpose; there was the sport of throwing the bola (similar to roping steers), where the young man watched the practiced hand quickly enmesh a running llama by a skillful toss of the lariat ingeniously balanced by three stone or metal balls, which entwined the animal in a moment as the snakes ententacled Laocoön.

There were other variants in the games. In the month of December, on the day fixed for the feast, men and girls came to a predetermined place among the fruit gardens, whose ripening they were to celebrate. Men and women were completely naked. At a given signal they started off in a race, upon which bets were placed, toward some hill at a distance. Each man who overtook any woman in the race "enjoyed her on the spot."

Bone flute (piroro)

The musical instruments of the Incas were as limited as the variation of their dance. By their nature they were self-limiting; they were mostly percussion and wind instruments, and strictly bucolic. Drums were made of a hollow log and covered either with llama or tapir hide (they varied from small drums used by women to war drums used by warriors). Whatever the variety, they were beaten by a rubber-knobbed stick, and their drumming had nothing of the quality of the sensuous music of the Mediterranean world. A tambourine (*tinya*) was used in dances. There were copper and silver *chanrara* bells, attached to clothes and hung on bracelets and dangling from wooden maces. On the dancers' legs were attached

Tambourine (tin-ya)

anklets of silver bells or shells, and snail-shell (*churu*) rattles.

The most stirring of the trumpets was the *potóto*, made from an enormous seashell; it is monotonic, but the effects of a massed chorus of these in war ritual must have been stirring. The Incas seem not to have had, or at least did not use, the large trumpets known to the coastal people, which have been found both in metal and ceramic forms.

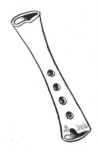

Reed flute (quena)

Flutes were many and varied; the flute, *quena*, made like a recorder, ranged from two to six notes. There were flutes made from the femurs of jaguars and human beings (*piroros*), but the most typical was the syrinx or Panpipes of cane or pottery made in a minor scale. This *antara* is still found throughout the Andes.

There have been few studies of Andean music. The music was strange to the ears of the conquistadors. It was anathema to the padres, who feared its pagan overtones so that they scarcely mention it; and the d'Harcourts, who made a collection of "Inca" music, the type of which is still heard throughout the Peruvian Andes and now obtainable in records, used uncontrolled sources so that it may be said with considerable conviction that we know little about Inca music, and that "detailed studies of native music are urgently needed. Time is fast running out for this sort of survival, and will soon eclipse all memory of it." [75]

Music was bound up with the dance and the dance with religion; all forms of religious expression involved dancing.[90] The dance (*taki*) itself included singing; it was part of the collective hypnotism. The songs were repeated endlessly, monotonously; the evolutions of the dancer, the ornaments, and the furiously rapid movements robbed all of the onlookers of their self-possession and gave them a feeling that their needs—for which the dance was designed—had been supplied. Masks and costumes were important in these dances, and they have survived to a surprising degree among the Andean Indians of the present day. There were dresses in mimicry of animals (and the dancers were always accoutered in the pelt of the animal depicted); there were victory dances (*cachuas*) limited to warriors who, holding hands and in full military panoply, formed a great circle, moving and writhing as a snake. The drumbeat for this was usually performed on what had been the body of an enemy: the skin of the whole body of a dead man had been flayed and the belly stretched to form a drum; the whole body acted as a sound box, throbbings coming out of the open

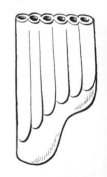

Reed-made Panpipes (antara)

138. *Types of Inca musical instruments.*

mouth—grotesque but effective. Such dances, widespread through-out Peru, can be seen illustrated on the pottery of the famed pre-Inca culture of the Mochicas.

There was a farm dance (*hayl-yi*) of the common people; here the Indian farmers carried the instruments of their work, and they moved through the dance in mimicry of tilling the fields; such a dance is still seen in the Andes today. Those who watched the dance and those who acted in it had in common the mystical com-munion, the fusion of the participants with the particular god which they were attempting to pacify.

The most elaborate was the *way-yaya*, the formal dance of the Inca family, not much different in idea and substance from the dance of that other Sun King, Louis XIV, which opened the minuet. It was performed very solemnly and in a stately manner, self-limit-ing and self-sufficing, two steps forward, one step backward, as the line of dancers moved slowly toward the golden stool on which sat the Lord-Inca.

African dances are sensual, Arabian, erotic, but the dances of the Andean Indians possess a monotony that, if watched long enough, can make one howl. It is so now—and might well have been then—yet it must have been a very wonderful thing to see, and how one wishes at this moment to turn back time's clock to see all this Tawantinsuyu, "Land of the Four Directions," dancing beneath the Andean sun.

Still the picture of the life of these people as one long joyous idyll cadenced by dance and the hypnotic beat of the tom-tom has been terribly overdrawn. Distance, of course, has lent this barbaric empire enchantment; it was hardly that. From birth to death—and even beyond—their lives were saturated with the supernatural: their entire preoccupation was with the "unseen powers"; they were magicbound every moment of their lives. Although in this Inca welfare state, man moved as close to Utopia as he ever would in the Andean world, judged by any other standard it was still a hard and monotonous existence.

The Rousseau idyll that men are born good and happy and that society has made them wicked was simply a dialectic artifice, yet it has set the tone of the literature on the American Indian. It seems that, no matter how scientific the approach to the subject of the Incas, they still retain this romantic tinge.

Since then the theme of the Noble Savage has pursued us. When Jean Jacques Rousseau told women to copy nature and "nurse your children," a confused palingenesis of Madonnas took place; queens posed as shepherdesses, diplomats became natural philosophers, legislators proclaimed the natural rights of man—and the people, naturally "good" of course, took the bait and cut so many thousands of human heads that the sewers of Paris gagged on the viscous streams of blood. Fontenelle long ago observed, "All men are much alike so that there are no people whose foibles should make us tremble." The Incas were people—that is, they were good and bad, warlike and pacific, aggressive, cruel, revengeful, suspicious, libidinous, and generous. They lived out their lives within this human framework. To indulge in an idyllic representation of their society contradicts itself. To judge them by our form of history is equally illogical; history is *a priori* amoral. "Nature," as Remy de Gourmont wrote, "ignores the adjectives of 'good' and 'bad'; they are illusions, put up from time to time in a form of ironical antithesis or even in ignorance to explain away human actions." The flow that separates civilized man from uncivilized man is a rivulet that any child can, and does, step over.

 Crime and Punishment   19

T HE INCA EMPIRE was a functioning theocracy: the Inca was god and man, and any crime was at once disobedience and sacrilege.

The people of the Inca formed a very simple and sensible notion of evil—their functions and natural feelings were tied up with their prejudices. The moral base of Inca society was founded on ancient mores which had, since eternal time, ruled man in the Americas. Parental authority was strict, in fact severe. Parents had the respect of their children, and the daily round of the child and its education was by doing; a child had practically no life apart from his parents. In our society, in contrast, lives of parents and children are divided; there is the child's world of fantasy and reality, amusement and literature in which the parents enter albeit briefly and then almost as penitents. "Don't touch," "don't use," "don't drink," are the prime moral forces urged upon children, and the insistence on *meum et teum,* mine and thine, must be taught, enforced, disciplined. None of this existed in the Inca Empire; learning was by doing; education and "becoming-of-age" were by mimicry and seeing; there was no strong contrasting line of conduct between child and adult. Out of this continuity of parent and child grew the mores which formed the base of the Incas' justice, and out of it came a simple code of existence—and even this existed thousands of years before the Incas' advent.

Murder, violence, theft, lying, adultery, and laziness were, since they are human, motivations present in Inca society; all were punishable. Murder was punished by death: hanging, stoning, or merely pushing over a cliff was the method (there are several such execution places known, notably at the site of Ollantaytambo, near to Cuzco). Punishment, however, was mitigated if murder was done in self-defense or in a rage against an adulterous wife. Stealing carried with it its own prognosis—death. Since one pilfered from a god, taking anything from public property was the most heinous of crimes: breaking into the Inca's storage chambers, destroying bridges, and entering the precincts of the Chosen Women. Stealing was especially peccant since there was virtually no want and so there would normally be no temptation to steal. There was no incentive for the common Indian to accumulate possessions.

The basic honesty of the Indian under Inca rule is attested not alone by learned Spanish judges but by one of the conquistadors, the famous Mancio Sierra de Leguisamo, the one "who gambled away the sun."* In the preamble to his will, filed in Cuzco, he wrote: "The Incas governed in such a way that there was not a thief, not a criminal, not an idle man . . . the Indians left the doors of their houses open, a stick crosswise in front of the door was a sign that the owner was not in . . . and nobody would enter."

Theft was regarded as an aberration, and when theft did occur (the machinery of justice was administered merely by accused and accusers telling their sides of the story to a *curaca*) there was a dif-

---

* This conquistador received as his part of the Inca's golden hoard of Cuzco a huge golden image of the Sun. As soon as he had it, he, with the other soldiers, began to gamble throughout the night. In the process he lost it—from which rose the proverb "To play away the sun before the dawn."

ferentiation between robbery from malice and robbery through necessity; if the Indian did so through want, the official was punished for his lack of administration which brought about the crime.

Since laziness deprived the Inca of the Indian's services, this was punished first by public rebuke, then stoning, and, if continued, by liquidation. (A counterpart in our own country: one may murder and escape the consequences, but nonpayment of taxes brings inescapable punishment.)

Drunkenness was allowed, and was condemned only when occurring at the wrong time, i.e., when the Indian was supposed to be working; then drunkenness was a crime, since it encouraged laziness.

Conservation of animals, too, was in the Inca code of justice. The punishment for the unauthorized killing of a female llama, or the killing of a female vicuña when not part of a royal hunt, was death; as aristocrats everywhere regard it, poaching ranked as one of the cardinal crimes.

The administration of justice was *hiwaya;* in addition to the death penalty, which was usually rapid, ruthless, and impartial, there were other forms of punishment: exile to mines, a term spent in the moist jungles of the Montaña or on the coca plantations, or other forms of public rebuke, which, it was held, were almost as bad as death itself.

"For the Incas," said Garcilaso de la Vega, "never made laws to frighten their vassals, but always with the intention of enforcing them on those who ventured to transgress them. . . ."

There were, it appears, two forms of justice: Inca law distinguished crimes involving nobles from those concerning the common people (a concept dramatized by George Orwell in his *Animal Farm* wherein people are equal but some people are more equal than others). But here, under the Inca system, the people of the upper classes were given more severe punishments for infractions than the lower. What was mere public rebuke for the common people became for the noble, when involved, banishment; what was torture for the common Indian, such as having one of his eyes torn out, for the noble was—death.

The Incas codified and systematized the moral code of the Andean people, and since these codes of conduct were based on the collective conscience of the *ayllu,* therein lay its strength.

THE ANDEAN PEOPLE (and that is to say, everyone in pre-literate South America) were from birth to death tied to the supernatural; disease was superphysical, and as such had to be cured with both medicine and magic. If a harvest failed or an Indian fell ill from no apparently sufficient cause, this proceeded obviously from witchcraft, or perhaps the afflicted had somehow offended the unseen powers. The supernatural had made an intrusion into this life; magic and medicine were inextricably bound together.

There are no connected studies of Inca medicine, even though Peruvian botanists have identified numerous plants used by the Inca shaman; there were many plants, doubtless, that were efficacious in curing, but no matter what the disease it was bound up with magic.

Magic is the arrest of the intelligence, and while the "doctor" as well as the patient was aware of the connection between the related phenomena of illness and medicine, their minds were only slightly sensitive to the contradictions. "Magic," wrote Raoul Allier, "is a dream destined to act as a counterpoise to a state of unrest, an awakening dream obedient to rules, fantastic, indeed, but so methodical as at times to appear scientific."

When an Indian fell ill, a *hampi-camayoc,* literally a "remedy keeper," was called in. The usual beginning, after a display of the shaman's kit, was either a fast, a salt emetic, or a purgative root. Later, after a routine of enchantments, the *hampi-camayoc* acted as a masseur, rubbing the patient until he extracted by sleight of hand some foreign substance: a needle, a pin, a pebble. He had removed the "cause." After this, medicine was prescribed. This was not a fraud or chicanery. Patient and curer shared the illusion that was created; they both knew that the disease was caused by something lodged in the body, but to effect a final and permanent cure was something else. The "wild" Indians of the Upper Amazon used a brew made from a vine, *aya-huasca*—the vine of the souls—which both patient and medicine man drank; out of the visions brought on by this powerful alkaloid, "instructions" as to the cause and cure were given. Purging and bleeding were common medical practices among them; these techniques, it will be recalled, were also common medical practices in the Western world up to 1800.

The Indians had a wide knowledge of drug plants. Many have entered our own pharmacopoeia, such as quinine, cocaine (from the coca plant), ipecac (used as an emetic), belladonna (which yields a mild narcotic anodyne)—the list could be extended. The Inca medical practitioners had tobacco (*sayri*)—used as snuff to clear the nasal passages—the juice of the *matec-llu* (a water plant for the eyes), the resin of the *mulli* tree to help heal wounds, and so on to a very impressive number of plants which had real, not alone magical, power to effect cures. Yet despite the very *real* quality of the drug, the patient never escaped the power of magic; this application of magic, in the last analysis, was the final resort, needed to pass from illness (*oñ-qoy*) into the state of being *kamas-qa,* i.e., cured.

It was socially profitable to be a "remedy keeper"; a good one or fortunate one could acquire new tunics, gold and silver orna-ments as payment. But it was also dangerous. Since illness was caused by bewitchment, the medicine man could be, and often was, held accountable if the patient died; he was in fact held by the family to be the murderer. On the coast, the Mochicas would bury the patient tied to the trussed-up "doctor" and expose him to death in the desert.

What diseases afflicted the Indian? Again, this interesting ground has not been consistently explored. Of a certainty white man brought all the civilized diseases to the indigenous American; the introduction of smallpox, tuberculosis, measles, and mumps wrecked havoc upon the Indian. In turn, the American gave white man that best-known civilized disease—syphilis. Yellow fever and malaria presumably were present; they are tropicopolitan. Most of the lung diseases—pneumonia, bronchitis, and the common cold —were apparently present; infant mortality from this type of disease was, and still is, high. There were other endemic diseases which left dreadful marks. *Uta* is a destructive ulcerative disease, which begins about the nose, and the disease eats away the nose cartilage and the lips, leaving the face horribly mutilated; it appears pic-tured frequently on Mochica pottery, where, incidentally, all of the native indigenous diseases are depicted. It was called, in Quechua, *acapana ayapcha,* which merely means "red-fringed clouds," a reference to the bleeding red walls of the face ulcer. *Verruga* was another very feared disease; it occurs usually in valleys with an altitude of about 6,000 feet, and is transmitted by an insect (*titira*). It first manifests itself by a sore throat, pain in the bones, and then an eruption of red-colored pimples which increase in magnitude to the size of suppurating volcanoes. There is high fever and the warty, corrugated excrescences bleed until the sufferer is exhausted and dies from anemia. The disease is endemic. In 1869 it broke out so virulently that for months it stopped the building of the Peruvian railways. The natives treated it with an infusion of roots called *huayra-huayra*.

Scalpel

On the coast there were other subcutaneous diseases, one of which covered the arms, legs, and face with large pustules and, if an Indian survived it, left his body marked with indelible spots. This disease, immortalized by the Mochicas in their pottery, shows an Indian pocked with marks that have been mistaken by some archaeologists for smallpox.

There were other native and endemic diseases. Cretinism—physical deformity and degeneracy—appeared and was sufficiently common to be depicted, as were the other diseases, in the coastal pottery, among them *mal de pott,* another form of degeneracy appearing in the face. In the high Andes, in the snow regions, there was *surumpi,* a violent inflamation of the eyelids caused by looking at the dazzling light—a snow blindness—but which here was so acute that the eyes swelled and bled and if it was uncared for resulted in total blindness. Altitude sickness, *soroche,* affected all who ventured into the high altitudes without proper acclimatization. By studying the various diseases so accurately displayed on Mochica pottery, a physician trained in tropical medicine could obtain a very good idea of endemic diseases prevalent in pre-Hispanic America.

Bronze tumi for making incisions in bone

But this much is certain: like the cultivated plants of America, so with the American diseases; few are identical between the Old World and the New, with the exception of tropicopolitan yellow fever and malaria. Both of these facts are immutable evidence that there was no continuous contact between the two worlds until white men broke the cultural barrier in the year 1492.

Surgery, anesthetics, and other operative practices were considerably advanced in Peru. A blow on the head, a kick in the rump, a severed leg took the native out of the realm of metaphysics

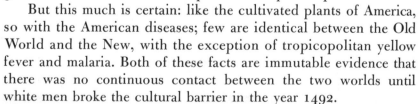

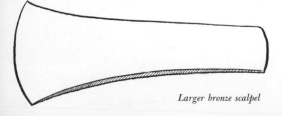

Larger bronze scalpel

and brought him to earth to seek a rational explanation of the pathological processes. The Peruvians, i.e., many of the cultures which preceded the Incas and the Incas themselves, performed the most delicate operations on the skull, trepanning heads of warriors wounded by a blow from a battle-ax and removing the pieces of skull that pressed on the brain and caused paralysis. Many patients, of course, died (as they do even now under such operations), but many lived, as is evidenced by the enormous number of skulls found in graves with the bone tissue renewed, showing the success of the operation.

Although the Incas seemed to have brought this type of surgery to perfection (they had to, since they were engaged in far-flung conquests involving much war), the technique of trepanning skulls was known two thousand years before them, for trepanned skulls are found in the graves of various pre-Inca cultures. Although there has been interest in trepanned skulls, and the techniques and speculations about them have appeared in literature for more than a century, it was not until two Peruvian surgeons, Francisco Graña and Esteban Rocca, undertook a serious study of ancient Peruvian surgical techniques that this interesting phase of Peruvian cultural development was fully appreciated. Now this profound study places the ancient Peruvians in an even higher category of advancement.

Bronze scalpel with wooden handle

One of the most common of military weapons was the *macana*, a weapon whose "business end" was rounded or star-shaped, cut in either heavy stone or cast in bronze. The best place of attack was the head, and the greatest number of casualties in battle were skull injuries. Sometime in their early history, the Peruvian Indians somehow raveled out the connection between the wound inflicted by the *macana* and pressure on the brain; out of this observation arose the technique of skull trepanning. Over ten thousand of such

139. *Inca and pre-Inca surgical instruments. These were found in graves with gauze bandages and a form of tourniquet which was primitive but very effective.*

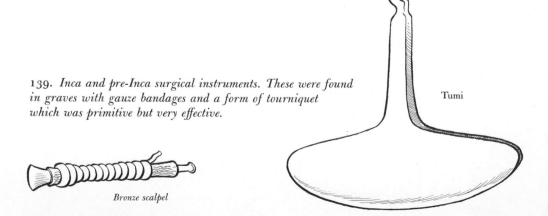

Tumi

Bronze scalpel

trepanned skulls have been found in graves throughout Peru, and in many tombs surgical instruments have been found: obsidian arrowheads shaped for trepanning, bronze *tumi* knives for cutting, scalpels, pincers, needles for sutures—in short, instruments which can be compared favorably with those known to the Romans. With these instruments Drs. Graña and Rocca actually performed trepanations of the skull on a living patient, using Inca operative techniques (except, of course, with a general anesthetic). They used the Inca form of tourniquet (applied about the whole of the round of the head), and proved the efficacy of the ancient operative techniques. The Indians had forms of gauze and cotton swabs, used a tourniquet, perfected local and perhaps general anesthesia. In addition to skull trepanning, many other forms of amputations were performed (archaeological evidence exists on Mochica pottery). In short, pre-Inca and Inca medicine and surgical practice seem to have been just as advanced, perhaps in many respects more so, than when the gifted Ambroise Paré of France was taking medicine out of its medieval doldrums in sixteenth-century Europe.

Little or nothing is known of the use of anesthetics and narcotics among Peruvians; about all that can be deduced is the types of narcotics that were available to them. Belladonna (*Datura ferox*) is well known; it yields atropine, and was once widely used as "twilight sleep" for childbirth. *Aya-huasca* ("vine of the souls"), a narcotic malpighiad (*Banisteria caapi*), grows in the Montaña on the lower slopes which lead to the Upper Amazon. The roots yield three forms of alkaloids, which were found to contain "a very active material producing effects on the central nervous system." [217] The *wil-ka* tree (identified botanically as *Piptadenia colubrina* and related to the acacias) produced a seed which, after being roasted and brayed, was used as a snuff. Little is known of it, although such Inca cities as Vilcapampa (i.e., *wil-ka*), and Vilcas-huamán, tell of the tree's presence and its presumed importance. It was a narcotic; whether it produced visions or anesthesia or was used as an emetic is not known.

Finally in the list of possible anesthetics is the well-known coca or *cuca*, which yields cocaine; there is no doubt about its efficacy as a narcotic. None of those aforementioned would seem, at least from here, to have been able to produce the general anesthesia which would be needed to prepare a patient with a battered skull to receive the assaults of a native "surgeon." In that case he would merely have to suffer through it as did Samuel Pepys when, without anesthesia, he had the "stones" removed from his gall bladder on March 26, 1658, "since it pleased God that I was cut of the stone at Mrs. Turner's in Salisbury Court." One just lay back and took it until merciful narcosis short-circuited the whole nervous system into temporary oblivion.

Coca, its use and disuse, has been a subject of debate—now more than ever—since white men came upon it in full use among the Incas. Coca is as old as Peru; of it Pedro de Cieza de León wrote: "If coca did not exist—neither would Peru." And not alone in Peru, but throughout all the Andes and into the Amazon; today there are over five million people addicted to it.

Coca (botanically it is *Erythroxylum coca*) is cultivated in the warm *yungas* and on the slopes of the eastern Andes. It is a low, thick bush, with glossy leaves not unlike tea leaves. The leaves are picked four times within fourteen months, very carefully sun-dried, then later shade-dried, so that the green of the leaf is retained. This leaf contains an alkaloid (chemically methyl-benzyl-ecogine) and has entered medicine as cocaine. It was once widely used for a local anesthetic, and up until 1900 was thought to be a wonderful nerve tonic. Coca wine was widely drunk until the Pure Foods and Drug Act prevented it. Sigmund Freud was an inveterate user of it.

Garcilaso "the Inca" wrote, "*Cuca* is a shrub the height and thickness of the vine; it has a few branches and on them many delicate leaves the width of the thumb and in length about half the length of the thumb—and of agreeable odor but not very sweet . . . so pleasant is *cuca* to the Indians that they prefer it to gold and silver and precious stones. . . . They chew them but do not swallow, they merely savour the fragrance and swallow the juice. *Cuca*," Garcilaso goes on, "preserves the body from many infirmities and our doctors [i.e., doctors in Spain] use it in powder form to arrest and placate the swelling of wounds. . . ." Coca was, as almost everything in Peru, pre-Inca; its presence is indicated by finding it in tombs and graves reaching far back into time in precisely the same form as it was used in the times of the Incas and is used today, small woolen bags were filled with coca leaves, and with them a small gourd holding the lime—lime which was made by burning seashells or limestone. Now as then, the method is to make a wad of coca leaves about the size of a brazil nut. The quid is stuffed into the side of the mouth, into which is placed a pinch of the lime, which helps to extract the juice. This when swallowed makes the chewer less susceptible to cold, thirst, hunger, and fatigue.

The Incas called it the "divine plant," and, as they did with all they touched, they extended and regulated the system of its agriculture. The plantations were vastly extended under Inca rule. Harvesting occurred three to four times a year, and the leaves were plucked when ripe, just before falling. The crop of leaves (*matu*) was kept covered overnight in a shed (*matuhuasi*), and sun-dried the following day. Drying was a delicate process. The vocabulary which grew up about the planting, harvesting, packing, and shipping shows to what extent the process entered the Inca world.

Mastication of the coca is called *coquear,* a word now half-Spanish, half-Quechua. The masticated leaves form a ball (*hacchu*), to which is added the lime-ash (*llucta*). Archaeologists are not agreed on the extent to which coca-chewing was general among the Incas. It was limited, it is believed, to the nobles and the soothsayers, i.e., the *amautas,* and to the *chasquis,* or couriers, who were forced to go at high speeds in high altitudes—and to the very old. Indubitably it was fully regulated, as was everything else in the Inca Empire. However, on the arrival of the Spaniards, with the Inca governing system thrown into complete chaos, the common Indians, the official restrictions lifted, turned wholesale to the use of the narcotic coca. The Spaniards enlarged the coca plantations; they controlled its sale (it *still* is a state monopoly under republican Peru), and within a few years many waxed rich upon it. As Pedro de Cieza de León avers: "There are some persons in Spain who are rich from the produce of this *cuca* [he was writing in 1550], having traded with it, sold and re-sold it in the Indian markets." And just as the pagan religion, the Sun, drew some of its sustenance from coca, so then did the church of the conquerors of the land. "It hath too yet another great profit, and this that the greater portion of the income of the bishop and canons and other clergy of the Cathedral Church of Cuzco derives *tithes* upon the *cuca* leaves."

What precisely the coca does to the human body is no longer in doubt: if one reads the evidence, it is there to see.[74] There is, among those long addicted to coca-chewing, a high frequency in the degeneration of sensory reception, disturbances of eyes, enlarged thyroid, and general physical breakdown; a list of the moral and physical breakdowns caused by this addiction is terrifying. Coca may well sustain the Indian at these high altitudes, but eventually it leaves him an addict, apathetic, abulic, and stupid. Although the Incas had it and used it primarily for religious ends, it had its uses among elders or *amautas,* and was also used for divination, when it was burned as frankincense (the sacred fumigant, which warded off ill-fortune or pacified the earth goddess).

 Death and the Little Gods   21

NO MATTER how organized the state—and here everything, as has been aforesaid, was prescribed from birth—nothing could prevent death, the final chapter of life. And with this there was much preoccupation. Death did not conform, it was unlike anything else, so when it came, as it had to come to all Indians, it imposed a strain on the living. The Indians were careful never to anger the undead, the recently dead. For the dead were in reality living, only they had become invisible, impalpable, and—for the discomfort of the living—invulnerable; hence the great preoccupation with the comforts for the dead.

"Indeed," said Pedro de Cieza de León, speaking of the immense monuments that surrounded Ayaviri, hard upon Lake Titicaca, "the place is . . . worthy of note, especially the great tombs, which are so numerous that they occupy more space than the habitations of the living. . . ."

Even death divided the common man from the higher. Death merely continued the dichotomy: the *puric* died almost as he had lived, communally; only for the great were reserved the enormous prestige burials. There has been described the ordinary Indian's way of life, his appearance, dress, language, marriage customs, birth, his round of daily life, his arts and crafts, his markets and his holidays, and the division between the worker and the Lord-Inca was sharply marked in all of these. Clothing (among the lower class) was worn until it became too old to retain; tunics of the Lord-Inca were never worn twice. The Indian had one wife; the

Inca had hundreds. The taxpayer had few privileges, the Inca created them. The Inca had considerable education; the Indian found his through the empiricism of his life.

In death, the little man had to be content with the little gods. His end, like his beginning, was a simple ritual. Although he had many gods, only one, the creator-god Tici Viracocha, was very real; Pachacamac led a pantheon of lesser gods, and these gods, like those of the older world, had special functions and powers. The Indian believed in immortality; in fact he believed one never died, for when shrived and flexed, the dead body merely became undead and it took on the influences of the unseen powers.

The *ayllu* was maimed by death; it undermined the clan, which was a mutual-aid society. At death, the survivors put on a sort of mourning. Women lopped off their long hair, shrouded their faces, and offered food to all who came to the rites. There was a slow dance performed near the body; the women beat on small drums and sang dirges. The body of the dead one was flexed, knees up to chin, and shrouded in his own tunic and wrapped in cloth. In the Andes his tomb was under rock eaves; the small catacombs—round, square, or oval—were made of field stone and cemented with adobe mud. Inside the tomb, the sitting body had placed about it food, bowls of *chicha*, and the many small things of his life—if a warrior, the instruments of his trade; if a weaver of note, those artifacts. A woman was given her loom, her color boxes, and wool to spin. All of this was of supreme importance, for the dead did not wish to go. They were hostile to the living, and they had to be made comfortable so that in their loneliness they would not carry off the living to comfort them. Death was contagious.

The dead now became *huaca*, i.e., godlike and mysterious; they exercised a charm so that one had to be careful that none of the *ayllu* offended the dead. The dead were numbered now among the unseen powers and had to be propitiated. Yet in time the dead died, and gradually, unless they were such as the Inca-God (who, even when dead, was surrounded by gaudy ritual) were forgotten. The ordinary Indian became absorbed in the trouble of living and one can speculate on the existence of his skepticism about the undead. Elsewhere, for example in the necropolis of ancient Myrina in Aeolis (now in Turkey), people buried the dead as the Incas did, with the things of their lives. They knew that the

XL. *The Sun Temple, Vilcas-huamán, 200 miles northwest of Cuzco. Composed of three tiers, a stone gate, and thirty-three stone steps (see plan, Figure 150), it is the only surviving sun temple in the Inca Empire.*
(Victor W. von Hagen)

XLI. *Detail of a doorway of the fortress of Sacashuamán. As the massive stones had to fit perfectly, the architectural features had to be worked out well in advance of construction.*
(Victor W. von Hagen)

XLII. *The Inca system of terracing in the Colca Valley, southern Peru. These terraces were so well made that they are still in constant use.* (Shippee-Johnson aerial photograph, courtesy Wenner-Gren Foundation)

XLIII. *A propitiatory cairn, called* apacheta, *found in all the high places of Peru on the ancient road. As heavily laden travelers passed along the road, they placed a stone on the* apacheta *as a symbol of burden, "and so left their tiredness behind." The Persians, the Chinese, and the Greeks adopted more or less the same custom.* (Charles Daugherty, Inca Highway Expedition photograph)

XLIV. *The ruins of Machu Picchu on the heights overlooking the Urubamba River. A daring example of city planning—a complex of terraces, gabled houses, temples, sacred palaces, and residential compounds. East of Machu Picchu is the jungle.* (Victor W. von Hagen, Inca Highway Expedition photograph)

XLV. *Architectural terracing is a feature of Machu Picchu that enabled the inhabitants of this fortified compound to be self-sufficient. The city was unmentioned in Inca annals until discovered in 1911 by the late Hiram Bingham.* (Charles Daugherty, Inca Highway Expedition photograph)

XLVI. *Road engineering within the Cuzco area. The Inca system of bridging culverts, a form of the corbeled arch, is shown. The road was later placed on top.* (Victor W. von Hagen, Inca Highway Expedition photograph)

XLVII. *A stone Inca bridge in the Carabaya area (east of Lake Titicaca). It shows an advanced use of the corbeled arch, over an actual distance of thirty feet. The whole is of stone, built about 1450.* (Charles Daugherty, Inca Highway Expedition photograph)

XLVIII. *The northern section of the long Inca coastal road running through Chiquitoy, Chicama Valley, near Trujillo. The Inca road, twenty-four feet wide, bordered by abode walls (to keep out sand drift), runs past a pre-Inca Mochica pyramid. The coastal road from Tumbes (Peru) to Santiago (Chile) was 2,520 miles long.* (Shippee-Johnson aerial photograph, courtesy Wenner-Gren Foundation)

XLIX. *"Tres Cruces" overlooking the Bay of Paracas near Pisco. Dug deep into the sandhill cliffs, 602 feet high, this "Tree of Life" motif occurs often in pre-Inca coastal textiles. Its precise function here is unknown.* (Victor W. von Hagen)

L. *Square and round built burial chulpas (pre-Inca) at Qutimbo, near Lake Titicaca. Chieftains were buried within; there were once so many that a Spaniard in 1547 wrote "... they outnumbered the houses of the living...."* (Silvia von Hagen, Inca Highway Expedition photograph)

LI. *Bath of the Chosen Women (Ñustas) at Ollantaytambo; an example of rock sculpture, cut from the living rock (in situ) and transformed into a fountain. This is a feature of Inca architectural planning.* (Victor W. von Hagen, Inca Highway Expedition photograph)

LII. *An example of pre-Inca tapestry. Three grades of wool cloth were woven and the dyes used yielded such brilliant colors that many articles have been recovered in perfect condition.* (Silvia von Hagen)

LIII. *A sculptural ceramic head of a blind man, of the Mochica tribe, Mochica culture,* 272 B.C.–A.D. 1000

LIV. *Man loading a llama. A ceramic from the Mochica culture who maintained llamas on the desert coast a thousand years before the advent of the Incas.* (Victor W. von Hagen)

dead were hard to please, but they also knew that they would *never* come back. They encircled the dead with diadems of gold, but so thin that a breath would reduce them to powder. They regulated their accounts with the dead as cheaply as possible; the obolus they put into the mouths of the dead to pay Charon to cross the river Styx was only a poor brass coin.

Yet the hold of religion on the Indian was enormous and very real, for life was practical and religion was life, and since all life was controlled by the all-pervading unseen powers, the Indian had to come to a tacit agreement with them for his own well-being. This, then, was the life of the Indian—typical of the unknown number who formed the base of the pyramid which was the Inca realm. At the summit was the Inca.

"At the base of the pyramid was the *puric*, an able-bodied male worker. Ten workers were controlled by a straw boss; ten straw bosses had a foreman; ten foremen in turn had a supervisor . . . The hierarchy continued in this fashion to the chief of a tribe, reportedly composed of ten thousand workers, to the governor of a province, to the ruler of one of the four quarters of the Inca empire, and finally to the emperor, the Sapa Inca . . ." [12]

The Inca and His City

 *The Inca*

Louis XIV, the Sun King of France, actually had to insist that *he* was the state: *"L'état c'est moi."* The Sun King of Peru, the Sapa Inca, never had to emphasize this—all which lay under the sun was his; it was known to everyone and accepted. He was divine, descended by direct line from the Sun, the creator-god; everything—the land, the earth, the people, gold (the sweat of the sun), silver (the tears of the moon)—belonged to him. He was absolute. He was God. His empire was no theoretical theocracy, it was an actual one.

The Lord-Incas were plenary rulers with their powers held in check only by the influence of ancient customs and the fear of revolt. Beyond his exalted position, there was no final court of appeal; the Inca had merely to lift a hand and with that gesture order death to a renowned general or even to a blood relative who had displeased him. The Inca's divinity was very real.

"I remember," said Pedro Pizarro, a cousin of *the* conquistador, "I remember the Lord of Huaylas once asked the Inca [for permission] to visit his estates and it was granted, the Inca giving him limited time in which to go and return. He took rather longer, and when he came back (I was present), brought a gift of fruit and arrived in the Inca's presence. The Lord of Huaylas began to tremble in such a manner before the Inca, that he was unable to remain on his feet. . . ."

If this emotional reaction occurred to one of the most powerful *curacas* of the land, what then must have been the effect of the Inca on mere men, on an Indian who was only a unit in the decimal classification of empire? Yet the concern of the Inca for his people, too, was very real; it was not, naturally, as benevolent as that Inca-descended historian, Garcilaso de la Vega, made it out to be when, with the pathos of distance, he wrote his *Royal Commentaries,* nor was it as tyrannical as the Spanish viceroys made it out to be in order to rationalize their destruction of the Inca Empire. The Inca's position and his wealth and his power came from the people and their well-being, for a country does not gain its wealth solely from the numerical quantity of its minerals but from the character and strength of its people. The people and their organization and development within the framework laid down for them were the primary concern of the Inca. All of his officials were held to account for maladministration. A French historian has written of *The Socialist Empire of the Incas,*[10] but this depends on the interpretation of socialism. The land was owned by the state, i.e., the Inca; the Indian, through his *ayllu,* which was a holding corporation, only had use of the land. Yet he owned his chattels, and while he could, theoretically, pile up personal luxury possessions, actually he did not.

An Indian's orbit was restricted; he traveled on the royal roads at the Inca's pleasure; he paid his taxes by labor; even his leisure was ritualistically regimented. Some scholars believe that the Inca, the religion, the state, actually created work artificially as a device of good government to keep the people constantly employed. The Inca, then, demanded *all* from his subjects; in turn he protected them from want, maintained storehouses for prevention of famine, conserved animals and soil. Produce was fairly divided, roads were maintained with superb communications, and the Inca kept the peace within the realm. But it would be a misconception to term this welfare state either socialistic or communistic: the empire was not for the people, and equality was not the ideal; on the contrary, the state existed alone for the Inca.

The Inca's head wife was a *coya* (queen). In the early beginnings of the Inca dynasty the ruler often married into families of other tribes for political alliances. Later, when the Inca was supreme over the land, he married his own sister as his principal wife. The right to marry within the clan belonged only to the Inca. Marriage within the totem group was strictly prohibited. There was an inviolable

140. *The litter was the principal transport for the nobility. The Inca and his* coya *(queen) being carried by Rucana tribesmen.*

custom—no one could marry within the first degree. The formal Inca statement was: "We, the Inca, order and decree that no one shall marry his sister or his mother, nor his first cousin, nor his aunt, nor his niece, nor his kinswoman, nor the godmother of his child, under penalty of being punished and of having his eyes pulled out ... because only the Inca is allowed to be married to his carnal sister. . . ." [144]

The meaning was obvious: the Incas wanted to insure that their divine descent remained unquestioned, and so from this purity of descent, from the male line of this marriage, came the successor to the "crown."

In addition to his *coya*, the Inca, being polygamous, had many subsidiary wives; the ménage of royal concubines (*pallas*) numbered into the hundreds, and so out of this fecundity flowed immense numbers of descendants of royal, "divine" blood. It is estimated that the last Inca before the conquest had in the male line alone five hundred living descendants; from these were formed the Lord-Inca's immediate family, his own royal *ayllu:* "a useful court circle of educated men trained in the imperial ideology and interested in its perpetuation. The [Lord-Incas] chose their top administrators from this group when possible." [155]

The Incas (like the Romans, in the last days of their empire), had no clear line of succession. The Roman Caesars invariably looked for a suitable successor, trained him for the throne and then adopted him; he became Caesar. The Lord-Incas were also without fixed rule; they named as their successor the most competent of those sons from the principal wife, the *coya.* In one sense this was politic, for the oldest son, as history has repeatedly shown, was not always the most competent, but when the supreme crisis occurred in the empire—the arrival of the Spaniards—a lack of a clear line of descent for an heir apparent laid the base, among other things, for eventual disaster.

Pomp and circumstance surrounded the sons of the Lord-Incas from birth. The smallest things, even such as a haircut, or putting on the breechclout at maturity, were clothed in ritual. Their education was first the study of *Quechua,* the official empire language, then the religion of the Sun (for the Inca was the Sun's vicar on earth, and they had to participate in all of the ritual attendant on it). They had to know the *quipus* so that they as Incas, and intended as administrators, could "read" what the string records said. And finally they learned from the wisemen—*amautas*—Inca history. Since they were expected to lead their people into battle and take active part, as they did, in the new conquests, they spent much time learning the use of arms—the sling, the *macana,* the spear thrower, the bola; they learned the arts of siege, envelop, and mass attack. The sons of the Incas and the nobility undoubtedly followed their elders as they made their rounds of the far-flung empire; this, coupled with the formal education, gave them the experience for governing. At fourteen years, the sons of the nobility assumed the breechclout; a llama was sacrificed, the blood of it smeared on the boy's face. An oath was sworn to the Inca, and the boy received his plaited wool sling, shield, and a silver-headed mace. At the end of the sixth day's ceremony, his ears were pierced, and he became officially a warrior in the Inca's elite guards.

The Inca history which was given out and absorbed by the nobility was the "official line"; it was selective and was no doubt the same as was told to young Garcilaso de la Vega, born in 1539 in Cuzco of a Spanish father and a noble Inca woman: ". . . as a boy . . . I took much delight to hear them tell [the old history] and my relations, being one day upon this conversation of the Inca-Kings and their ancient history, to the oldest of them . . . I asked: 'Inca, my uncle, since there is no writing with you . . . what intelligence have you of the origins and beginnings of our Inca-Kings? . . . You who have no books, what memory have you of our ancient history? Who was the first of the Incas?' " And so this royal person gave the youth, who later wrote the *Royal Commentaries,* the official list of the Inca rulers; since the nobility had a good reason for preserving this memory, those he gave young Garcilaso (and which have been affirmed from many other sources) can be taken as:

1.	Manco Capac	7.	Yahuar Huacac
2.	Sinchi Roca	8.	Viracocha Inca
3.	Lloque Yupanqui	9.	Pachacuti Inca Yupanqui
4.	Mayta Capac	10.	Topa Inca Yupanqui
5.	Capac Yupanqui	11.	Huayna Capac
6.	Inca Roca	12.	Huáscar

13. Atahualpa

Here is the chronology of the later Incas worked out by one of the leading scholars: [155]

1438—Pachacuti crowned
1463—Topa Inca takes command of army
1471—Topa Inca succeeds Pachacuti
1493—Huayna Capac succeeds Topa Inca
1527—Death of Huayna Capac; Huáscar succeeds him
1532—Coming of the Spaniards
1533—Huáscar killed by Atahualpa after long civil war

The Lord-Incas were of Andean origin, sprang from the people, and passed the succession in a continuous line without the introduction of any new aristocracy from the outside. This would not ordinarily have to be stressed, but in the last few years considerable literature has appeared (returning to an old, threadbare theme) suggesting that many of the indigenous American cultures owe their cultural origins to Old World migrations within historical

times. The voyage of the balsa raft *Kon-Tiki* from Peru's shores into
Polynesia has only exaggerated that which has been current in many
scientific circles for many years, i.e., that *all* can be explained by
migration. That there *were* sporadic, accidental contacts between
Melanesia and America (after the Paleo-Asiatic Mongoloid immigrants crossed to the continent more than twenty-five thousand years
ago) can be accepted, but since these contacts brought no exchange
of agricultural products, nor exchange of disease, and did not
influence either language or physical types, then . . . ! All this
"migratory fever" has been ebullient since 1492; the earlier chroniclers believed first that it was Shem, son of Noah, who arrived to
populate the land after the deluge; others gave Plato's mythical isle
of Atlantis as the source. The celebrated nineteenth-century historian John Ranking, without quitting England's shores, was positive
that Manco Capac was a son of Kublai Khan, the first Chinese
emperor of the Yuan dynasty, and that he had conquered Peru with
a brigade of elephants; this was strengthened by the fact that someone had found bones of the prehistoric mammoth elephants in
South America. Incas, it seemed, were of all races: Armenians,
Romans, Jews, English, and even Chinese; Arthur Posnansky's
monumental work on *Tiahuanacu* is weakened by his insistence
that the Chinese language could be understood in certain parts of
Bolivia, and that the Inca dynasty was based on the Chinese,
which, because of its advanced culture, imposed itself on the
politically undeveloped Indians of Peru.

Yet the Lord-Incas in their official history also denied that they
came from the people; natural enough, when Western civilization
only in the last century quitted the metaphysics of kings by divine
right. The history that young Garcilaso de la Vega heard from his
uncle, an Inca, is no doubt the official history which all the young
nobility learned:

"Cousin," said the old man, "I gladly will tell you, and it be-
hooves you to hear . . . ," and he heard how the Sun God, ". . .
seeing men as I have described them, commiserated with them and
took pity upon them and sent to earth a son and a daughter to instruct them . . . to give them law . . . and show them how to live
in houses and cities. . . ." These two were, of course, the first
Inca, Manco Capac, and his sister Mama Ocllo (pronounced "ok-
yo"). The Sun God went on in his briefing instructions: ". . . When

you have reduced these races [the other Indians, of course, living in the Andes] to your service, you shall maintain them in reason and justice, with benevolence, clemency and kindness. . . . And I therefore appoint and name you Kings, lords of all races. . . ."

There is not the slightest doubt that the Lord-Incas were Andean, were of the same people as they ruled, and were not imposed from without. They invented their own legend of their descent and their divinity, confirming what Anatole France himself wrote of it: ". . . History is not a science, it is an art, and man succeeds in it only by imagination."

The Incas and their "historians" suppressed all historical traditions anterior to their own, and soon the "rememberers," who with their *quipu* knot-string records counted and recounted the history, no longer spoke of anything before the divine Incas; so by a "selective manipulation of history," the Inca nobles grew up with only the knowledge derived from the official point of view. This made them, among other things, thoroughly convinced of their divinity; it was also accepted by the people.

By the time an Inca's descendant was ready to marry, he had as thorough an "education" as one could have in pre-Spanish America. He had accompanied the Inca on tours of the great empire; he had been with the governors who made their rounds; he had taken part in battles either to defend what the Incas had won by arms, or to suppress those who rebelled. He was soaked in ritual and immersed in Inca history; he had tasted love in various forms, and had no doubt served some sort of apprenticeship in government so as to gain experience in administration.

His dress, as well as that of the other nobles, was not different in style from the ordinary Indian's—only more sumptuous. His ears were pierced and extended with golden ornaments and jewels; his hair was cut in bangs. His tunic was of the finest alpaca, and often vicuña; his sandals were high and well made.

If the young noble in question was the eldest son of the reigning Inca, born of his first wife, the *coya,* and if it was finally decided by the Inca and his council ("twenty of his relatives," wrote a chronicler, "old and prudent men, full of experience in the government of the kingdom") that this son would be the Inca apparent, sometime toward the end of the Inca's life the son was so designated. The whole empire went into mourning at the Inca's

141. *The Inca's* coya *(queen). She was of royal blood, often his sister, and from among her issue the Inca and his council selected an heir. Redrawn from Felipe Guamán Poma de Ayala.*

death. His concubines and his personal servants, as in Egpyt, were expected, following good custom, to accompany him on his journey to the Sun; they were made drunk, danced, and then were strangled. The Inca's body was partially mummified; the entrails were removed and the vacuity stuffed with cloths. The technique used for mummification in Peru is little or imperfectly known; we have no Herodotus to describe for us the Peruvian system, as he personally observed, for example, the Egyptian. One thing notable is that the Greek word for mummification is *taricheuo*, which means pickling, salting, preserving—and embalming was consciously associated with the curing of fish. The fact that the Inca embalmers removed the viscera of the dead Lord-Inca, the first step toward successful mummification, does suggest the same techniques used for fish preservation.

Mummification was a magico-religious act, and its object in Egypt or in Peru was to keep the body as it was during life for the eventual return of the soul.[56] In the humid uplands of Peru mummification was a technical problem; on the desert Peruvian coast it was different, for the heat of the sun and the naturally sterile, porous sand made the conditions for desiccation and mummification of the dead bodies possible. The Egyptians removed, according to Herodotus, the brain, and viscera, and thoroughly cleaned the cavity with spices, wine, cassia, myrrh; rubbed the outward cadaver with oil, and wrapped it in swathes of cloth. As the Egyptians did, so the embalmers of the divine Inca; they also removed the viscera, which they put into canopic jars, and washed the body.

Nothing much else is known of the embalming, nor precisely how the royal mummies appeared, for they were the first things looted by the conquistadors. The mummy (*malquis*) of the dead Inca was placed in his house, and a life-size golden statue (*pucarina*) was made of him; it was served with food as though he still lived. He sat on his golden stool, which was the symbol for a throne. There are few descriptions of these mummies; some were carried away by Manco Capac II when the young Inca rose in revolt against the Spaniards in 1536 and fled into the vastness of Vilcapampa. In 1559 a Spanish official found the mummified bodies of three of the Incas. The Spanish viceroy ordered their removal from Cuzco to Lima, where they subsequently disappeared.*

The new Inca, after fasting for three days, was crowned. It was not really a "crown" but a fringe. There were, as on all occasions such as this, pomp, dancing, drinking; obeisance was made to the dead Inca, and the new Lord-Inca started, as was the custom, to build himself a new elaborate house in the center of Cuzco. (That of his predecessor, the deceased Inca, had become *huaca*, or shrine.)

---

* As related by Garcilaso de la Vega (Lib. v cxxix). The three bodies of Lord-Incas were Viracocha (d. 1400?); Topa Inca Yupanqui (d. 1493); and Huayna Capac (d. 1527). They were found with two of their wives in a perfect state of preservation. They were borne through the streets of Lima and interred in the courtyard of the hospital of San Andrés in the year 1562.

His principal wife, long acquired, now was his *coya*. Secondary wives were acquired, urged on him by other members of the select circle of nobility; concubines came to him from among the Chosen Women. He set the policy of his reign, and acquired many of the honorific titles of his father—Sapa Inca, "Shepherd of the Sun" (*Intip Curi*), "Lover of the Poor"—and he began to act like the divinity that he was.

The Inca "received" seated on a golden stool (*osño*); his visitors were barefooted and weighed down with a symbolic burden to suggest submission. All of his governing *curacas* prostrated themselves when they came before him.

As Inca, he was surrounded by a retinue of elaborate ritual. He ate from gold and silver services, placed upon finely woven mats; his Chosen Women held the plates as he ate. The uneaten food was put aside and stored to be burned later with ceremony, along with his clothes, which he never donned twice. He slept on a raised paillasse covered with colorfully woven woolens, and attended by numbers of his women. As befitted a god, he rarely walked for long distances: when he led a battle he was carried on the royal litter; when he made a tour of the empire, which could well occupy years, he was borne in his royal palanquin. "They traveled in great majesty," wrote Pedro de Cieza de León, ". . . seated in rich litters, fitted with loose poles of excellent wood, and enriched [i.e., covered by plate] with gold and silver. Over the litter there were two high arches of gold set with precious stones. . . ." Because of the precipitous terrain, despite the excellence of the roads, he traveled ponderously, no more than twelve miles the day. A large retinue of officials went with him and the people were gathered along the road to see him. There was always in attendance on him a company of litter-bearers, the Rucanas—a sturdy people who lived west of Cuzco—attired in a special blue livery; they changed in relays of eight. There is little doubt about the magnificence of these litters, for when Francisco Pizarro, *the* conquistador, entered Cuzco, he found one in the tombs of the mummified Incas; by his contract with the King of Spain he was allowed to select one of these for himself, which he considered the most precious object of his loot.

The Lord-Inca was accoutered as his people: tuniclike poncho, breechclout, sandals, all magnificently woven in vicuña wool by his

142. *An Inca general riding in a litter using the sling. This hurled an egg-sized stone fifty yards with accuracy.*

Chosen Women. His ear spools were immense, gold and jeweled; his hair was cut in bangs and he carried a golden-headed mace. There seems to have been an imperial standard, a pennant stiffened with dyestuff on which a symbol was painted. His crown was a royal fringe called *llautu* (pronounced "lyaw-to"), made of red wool and worn wrapped around the head. A fringe of red tassels lined with gold lamé hung down before the eyes. An eyewitness to the conquest saw the Inca wearing ". . . on his head a *'llautos,'* which are braids made of colored wools, half a finger thick and a finger in breadth, made in the form of a crown, rounded and without points, a hand's width, which fitted his head, the forehead a tassel called a borla . . . adorned very subtly with bangles of gold" [143]

The last Inca before the conquest, Atahualpa (apart from those puppet Incas placed on the royal throne-stool by their conquerors), is the only Lord-Inca whose personal description we have: "He was well set up for an Indian, of good presence, medium figure, not over stout, comely of countenance and serious withall, his eyes florid . . . much feared by his people . . ." [143] And fastidious: "One day as he was eating . . . while raising a piece of food to his mouth it dropped onto the robe he was wearing . . . he quickly rose and retired to the inner chamber and returned wearing an under-robe and a dark brown mantle," [143] made of bat skins. And of unchallenged power: "Nor have I seen in all this Peru an Indian like unto this Atahualpa either for this fierceness or for his air of authority." [143]

There is no doubt about the sumptuousness of the Inca's world; archaeology has confirmed it. The gold that did not disappear into the crucible of the conquistadors confirms all that had been first said about it. Tombs have yielded gold-spangled litters, superb

143. *A curaca or governor, learning from a* quipu *reader the amount of food stored in the stone storage bins.*

examples of feather weaving and woven tapestries which hang today in the world's most famous museums. The pottery from Peru is superior in form and variety to anything that the ancient world can offer. Those historians of the "natural school" who accused William Prescott, who worked from the original sources, of "romanticism," of painting too glamorous a picture of Inca ceremonial life, have been gainsaid; all has been affirmed by archaeology.

In his realm the Inca was absolute. As the Sapa Inca he ruled this immense land, which was called Tawantinsuyu, "Land of the Four Directions"; he used the nobility who were Incas by blood, or those Indians who had raised themselves by their qualities to become Incas by privilege (as England does by raising commoners of merit to the nobility).

The Incas, just as the common Indians, had their own royal *ayllus;* from them came the Incas by blood. They formed the ruling classes, and from them the Inca chose his administrators. They had their ears pierced. Pierced ears marked the nobility. The small hole in the ear lobe was gradually enlarged until an egg could pass through it; into this the Incas placed a rounded golden and jeweled disk. The Spaniards called this class "Big Ears," and as *Orejones* they have entered the literature. They went about their labors bejeweled and bedecked. They were polygamous, with many wives and concubines. They had other special privileges; they paid no taxes, yet they were a functional aristocracy. All their duties, which demanded much travel in this perpendicular world, were taken very seriously; there is no evidence in the chronicles of any sybaritic idleness. If they did not carry out the Inca's orders, they answered for it with their heads.

The second class of administrators were Incas by privilege, those called *curacas,* who were not necessarily born in the royal *ayllus* but whose ability pulled them upward. Because the Incas extended their empire so rapidly, they did not have the number of Incas by blood needed for administrative purposes; often a conquered land had its own chieftain confirmed in his rule, while his sons were whisked off to Cuzco for an orientation course and returned as *curacas.* All were exempt from taxation, i.e., the work tax: they drew their emoluments from the service (*mita*) of the common Indian. These Incas by privilege accoutered themselves in sumptuous feather tunics, the kind that are now unearthed from tombs; they had their ears pierced and decorated with golden spools; they selected their wives from the Chosen Women; they were bound by loyalty to the Inca because of his bestowal of office. And the capital, the heart of this empire which sent its life-streams pulsating in the four cardinal directions, the famous mecca of the entire realm was—Cuzco.

23   Cuzco

"THE FEELINGS of men have founded cities. Men have fallen on their knees when they came to a place where something within them came to rest; they have built a capital in a desert where it is not possible for a city to be; an emperor has *loved* a place of the earth and made it a great city." [89]

Cuzco was such a place. The founding of it by the legendary first Inca, Manco Capac, is placed circa A.D. 1100. Cuzco was, it will be recalled from Inca myths, the place where Manco Capac rested after his wanderings from the south and where the golden staff given to him by the Sun God disappeared when he threw it into the ground. Precisely whom the Incas displaced is not known; the pre-Inca cultures within Cuzco are referred to as merely "Chanapata." Yet there is no reason to doubt the history of the city as it is given by the Incas; archaeology is in agreement that its culture developed within its immediate valley.

Cuzco lies in the hollow of a valley at about 11,000 feet. On three of its sides the mountains rise precipitously, and at its southeast the valley yawns widely and stretches for miles between a double array of mountains, a succession of fertile plains and bog. Two small rivers flow down into it, and in Inca times these were canalized with finely worked stone; buildings were erected on the banks.

Cuzco was divided into two parts: Hanan, or Upper Cuzco, and Hurin, or Lower Cuzco. In the latter part, the capital center, the nobles had their houses. There were two main plazas from which narrow streets issued. "It was grand and stately," wrote one who

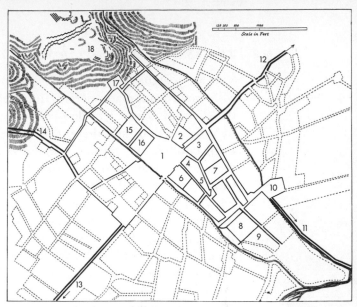

144. *Cuzco, the capital of the Inca realm as it probably appeared in* A.D. 1500.

1) In the center of the city, Huaycapata (Joy Square). 2) Palace of Viracocha Inca. 3) Hatuncancha. 4) Palace of Huscar. 5) Acclahuasi, Temple of the Virgins. 6) Amarucancha, Palace of Huayna Capac. 7) Palace of Topa Inca Yupanqui. 8) Temple of the Sun. 9) Curicancha ("Golden Enclosure"). 10) Rimacpampa. 11) Road to the south, the Collasuyu quarter. 12) Road to the east, the jungle or Antisuyu quarter. 13) Road to the west, the Cuntisuyu quarter. 14) Road to the north toward Quito, the Chinchasuyu quarter. 15) Yuchayhuasi, schools of the nobles. 16) Cora-Cora, Palace of Inca Roca. 17) Palace of Manco Capac. 18) Fortress of Sacsahuamán

saw it in its glory, "and must have been founded by a people of great intelligence. It has fine streets, except that they are narrow, and the houses are built of solid stones, beautifully joined. . . . [Cuzco] was richest of which we have any knowledge in all the Indies, for the great store of treasures was often brought to increase the grandeur of the nobles. . . ." [34]

Only five Europeans, one of whom was Hernando de Soto, saw Cuzco before it was raped of its gold and before it was partially destroyed by the wars, and they have left no report. Cuzco's archaeology is imperfectly known.

Cuzco, as a city, emerged in final form when it was rebuilt after A.D. 1400, and it showed good town planning. At this time the two rivers that entered from the north were canalized. There was a grid-iron scheme for streets, converging out of two central plazas. The houses of the meaner sort were one-storied, but others, the greater ones, were two-storied, and sometimes three stories in height. The principal buildings were located about the great plaza, and the towering Sun Temple occupied the most prominent part. To retain its purity, water was conveyed with great care through stone conduits laid in the middle of the street.

Out from the principal plaza, called Huaycapata ("Joy Square"), spread the twelve wards of the city, divided roughly into four sections—the four principal directions or quarters of the world which gave the empire its name, Tawantinsuyu.

Cuzco actually was a microcosm of empire; within it lived people drawn from many parts, all attired in traditional dress. "Each tribe," explained Cieza de León, who saw them, "is distinguished by differences in headdress; if they are *Yungas* from the coast, they went muffled like gypsies; the *Collas* [from around Lake Titicaca] wore caps in the shape of a plump box of wool; while the *Canas* [now the village of Tinta] wore another cap, larger and of greater width. The *Cañaris* [from the province of Cañar in faraway Ecuador] had crowns of thick lathes, like those used for a sieve. The *Huancas* [i.e., "Field Guardians" who were centered about Jauja, in mid-Peru] had short ropes which hung down as low as the chin, with the hair plaited. The *Canchis* [modern Sicuani was their center] had wide fillets of red or black passing over the forehead. All of these tribes were distinguished particularly by their form of headdress, so clear and distinct that when fifteen thousand men assembled, one tribe could be easily distinguished from another." In point of fact, the Inca ruled that all tribesmen should keep their distinctive headdress.

These were some of the inhabitants of Cuzco, all quartered in their local sections, occupying low houses of sun-baked mud, painted red or yellow and thatched with thick straw. The King of Spain's inspector said that there were 100,000 houses in the city— obviously an exaggeration—he perhaps meant the number of people—yet he affirmed that "in the eight days [that he was there], I have not been able to see everything." [54]

The Sun Temple, the edifices of the Lord-Incas, the Chosen Women, and others were constructed by professional architects and were the pride of the realm. They were defined by long reaches of stones elaborately cut and fitted with a precision which has never been duplicated anywhere in the world. The exteriors of the buildings (unlike the Maya or Aztec buildings, which were floriated with design) were seldom if ever decorated; the more important ones were sheathed with gold plate. The first Spaniard to see Cuzco— it seemed ablaze with gold—reported he saw a "quadrangular building . . . measuring three hundred and fifty paces from corner to corner, entirely plated with gold; of these gold plates they took down seven hundred which together weighed five hundred pesos of gold. . . ." [54] Much of the golden loot from Cuzco was plate torn from the walls: "These had been taken from the walls . . . they had holes in them showing that they had been secured by nails," showing that many of the royal edifices in Cuzco had been gold-plated.[34] At least enough to make the high sententious fantasy of the conquistador soar.

Cuzco, with all these gold-spangled walls, could not have been less spectacular than those cities which Marco Polo looked upon in Cathay, whose walls were covered with gold a good finger in thickness, and whose towers of silver and gold were girt about with bells.

Not only was Cuzco filled with tribesmen from all parts of the realm, each with their distinctive headgear, but here too resided the chieftains of other tribes which the Incas had absorbed, giving the city an Arabian Nights' unreality. The chieftains of the Chimús were here, with pierced nose septum from which jangled gold and emeralds, their heads wound high with plaited turbans. They were the Incas by privilege in enforced residence. Although treated royally, they were actually hostages to insure that their recently conquered territory allowed itself to be absorbed, and their sons were enrolled in the schools of the nobles to be reoriented in the new order of the Inca.

There were royal storehouses throughout the city, filled with tribute from all of the subject states: cotton was piled high from the coast; there were others with seashells and seaweed; some held arms for war. Cuzco was also an arsenal of quilted cotton armor, sharp-edged swords, star-shaped battle axes, slings, and javelins.

The royal artisans were located here too, the "professionals," nontaxpayers who worked for the Lord-Inca's pleasure by turning out fabulously cast gold and silver pieces, and, as averred by Pedro de Cieza de León: "There were a great many of gilders and workers in silver who understood how to work the things ordered by the Incas . . . and no gold nor silver might be taken out on the pain of death. . . ."

Cuzco was certainly a most magnificently planned city, of which there have been few counterparts in the world. The most fabulous edifice in Cuzco was the Curi-cancha, "Golden Enclosure," at the spot where legend said stood the first edifice erected by the first Inca. The conquistadors who saw it never tired of telling of what they saw, and after five hundred years archaeologists are still trying to piece together this most stupefying, ancient, and sacred of Inca shrines. The Temple of the Sun adjoined the Golden Enclosure. It was a shrine as well as a center for the priestly organization. It was presided over by the "chief priest *Huillac-Umu* who lived in the grand temple." This complex structure had six major buildings: sanctuaries to the Sun, Moon, Stars, Lightning, Rainbow, and a sort of chapter house for the priests of the Sun; all these various parts surrounded the Inti Pampa, "Field of the Sun." A fountain in its vast center was encased in gold on which was etched the image of the Sun, the same Sun which fell to the conquistador who gambled it away one night. The outside of the building (parts of which can now still be seen as part of the Church of Santo Domingo set on top of the Inca one) was covered with gold plate so massive that each sheet weighed from four to ten pounds. Although the roof was thickly thatched with grass, it also had, reportedly, golden straws among the others, which caught the rays of the sun's declension with each day.

To the utter amazement of the first Europeans to see it, the Curi-cancha had in its fields a golden mimicry of plants: maize, actual size, was "planted" and its stalks cunningly wrought in gold, and Cieza tells of the "garden where the clods [of earth] were pieces of fine gold, and it was artificially sown with cornfields which were of gold, as well as the stems of the leaves and the [corn] cobs. Besides all this they had more than twenty llamas of gold with their young, and the [Indian] shepherds life-size, with their slings and crooks to watch them . . . all made of gold." There is no doubting this report, for the King of Spain's inspector, Miguel de Estete, attached to the expedition to attest officially to the items of loot received, recorded that he saw "straws made of solid gold, with their spikes just as they grow in the fields. And if I was to recount all the different varieties in the shape of gold my story would never end. . . ."

Certainly the simulated vines with grapes or bunches of precious stones which were given to Darius the Persian by Pythias, and described so wonderfully by that wandering Greek, Herodotus, could not be compared to this whole Field of the Sun at Cuzco, planted with a golden garden; nor can the famous "Ram Caught in a Thicket" which was found in the royal tombs at Ur (dating from 2500 B.C.), a piece of polychrome statuary covered with thin gold foil nineteen inches high, even be compared to twenty life-size figures of llamas of cast gold, which grazed on golden stalks of grass in the Golden Enclosure of Cuzco.

It strains the imagination, at this distance in time, to accept all this as coming out of the indigenous American cultures, without contact with the old; but a visit to any of the museums which contain ancient Peruvian collections (bearing in mind that the best was melted down in the crucibles of the conquest) will convince even the most skeptical of the organization that this barbaric empire must have had.

But it must be repeated that the form of organization within the four quarters of the empire was only an *intensified* development of the original pre-Inca patterns. This specialization of Indian labor made possible the great achievements of the Inca Empire.

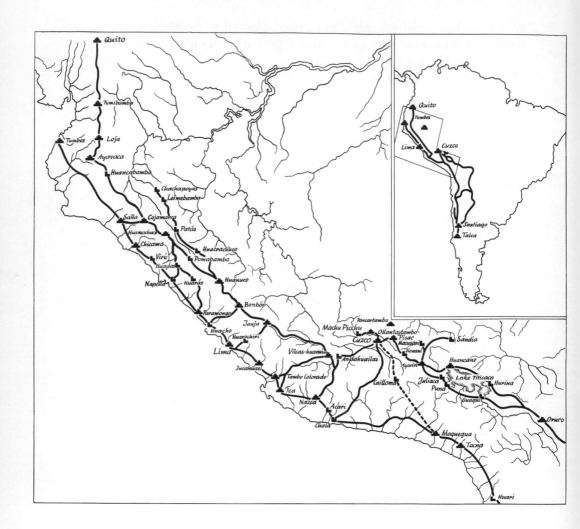

145. *Capacñan, the royal road of the Incas. The network of roads
as recorded by the von Hagen Expedition (1952–54). The series of
roads issuing from Cuzco ran more or less in the four cardinal
directions to the four quarters of the realm. Prepared from the
explorations of the author. Redrawn by Pablo Carrera.*

O O O O

The Achievements

 Inca Architecture 24

INCA ARCHITECTURE, as all great architectural styles, developed out of the rustic houses of the peasants. This was as true in Greece as it was in Peru. The most awe-inspiring of Inca structures—the cyclopean walls of polished stonework—are only a development of the one-room house of the common Indian, the kind which proliferated at random throughout the Andes at the beginning of the Inca realm.

These houses, placed in a square with a common yard (*cancha*), developed into the rectangular city plan of the Incas, and no matter how imposing the Inca building, it suggests always its humble origin. "For," writes Dr. John Rowe, developing this viewpoint, "even the most complex of Inca buildings in the finest masonry never became much more than a group of such houses [the native houses of field stone grouped to form a *cancha*], conveniently and usually rather regularly disposed within an enclosure wall. It is an architecture which like the Quechua language consists of irreducible units grouped together in complex but irregular patterns, but never quite losing their identity." [156]

The Incas are famed for the quantity and variety of their stone structures, but few have ever emphasized the sheer quantity of the mass of buildings that existed; it is true that much centers about Cuzco, yet much lies outside it.

At the height of the Inca Empire, say, A.D. 1500, Inca structures spread over an enormous distance—from the Sun temples and fortress of Purumauca on the north bank of the Maule River (35°

513

S. lat.) in southern Chile, north to the Ancasmayo River (approx-imately 1° N. lat.), which is now in Colombia—3,250 linear miles.

Along this route were large centers (*marcas*), replete with ad-ministrative centers and Sun temples; there were stone-laid palaces, temples for Sun Virgins, official storehouses, and fortresses. Along the entire web of roads, *tampu* way stations appeared every four to twelve miles, so that for the sheer mass of building, the empire almost equaled the Roman.

At the height of Egypt's Middle Kingdom, to give historical comparison, its structures covered a distance of only 625 miles, that is from Alexandria at the delta of the Nile to the rapids of Aswan, and then this land was only a narrow width within the same desert environment. So that the mass of Inca building, spread-ing over a diverse terrain, varying, as has been shown, from desert to high altitudes to jungle, is more than five times the distance of the Egyptian empire. Within this immense geographical span there was a uniformity of style and purpose of building marking it all "Inca." While it is true, and the theme has been constantly ham-mered home, that much of the Inca civilization was borrowed, nevertheless the Inca brought all the congeries of geography to-gether and gave its culture an architectonic unity.

The city—better, the idea of the city—is not much more than six thousand years old. Earthbound Neolithic man, then living in self-contained villages, formed an idea of the city. V. Gordon Childe has called this the "Urban Revolution." Though the American peo-ple were out of the broad stream of Eurasian evolution (a strong cur-rent from which all culture in the Old World drew), they none the less instinctively followed this selfsame pattern. The city every-where, whether it was in the valleys of the Nile, or in Greece, Egypt, in Sumeria, or even among the Incas exhibited the same dynamic features: specialized labor, intensified production, dis-ciplined organization, the construction of temples, palaces, pyramids, tombs, and other symbols of the collective imagination. The Inca city, of which Cuzco was the supreme example, had all these; one architectural writer thinks, "The Incas were the best planners South America ever knew . . . [After] four hundred years of Euro-pean domination . . . the urban spirit of the Incas still pervades Cuzco and many smaller towns in the region." [201] The form of Cuzco is more or less the city plan which the Inca's professionals imposed upon the realm: the gridiron scheme of streets converging on a central plaza with the principal buildings located about it; the large square; the truncated Sun Temple pyramid, with buildings around it housing the priests of the Sun; a palace for the visiting Inca; houses of the Virgins of the Sun; and an administration center. The houses of the people were arranged in the rectangular *cancha*-style.

There were no walled Inca cities. Each large city had, if it was built close to a hill, which it usually was, a fortress, called *pucara*, and within there was a miniature of the city it guarded. When attacked, the people were expected to go up to it with their weapons and from there defend themselves.

All this architecture came from central planning. In the extent of this type of realm, that is, in three thousand miles, there was, and still remains, a great variety of forms of architecture, and enough survives to gain a fair idea of what this civic-military planning appeared to be. To give some of these significant examples, one can begin at *Ayaviri,* around the northern end of Lake Titicaca at a place then, as now, of considerable importance.

"In ancient times," wrote Pedro de Cieza de León, "[Ayaviri] was a grand thing to see . . . and this place [in 1549] is still worthy of note . . . The Lord-Inca Yupanqui ordered that a great palace should be built there . . . together with many buildings where the tribute was stored up. A Temple of the Sun was also built. . . ."

Fifty miles north of this center, on the royal road (between the intervals of which were many smaller communities) was *Cacha,* "where there were great edifices . . . a temple built in memory of their god [Tici] Viracocha." [34] This city stands on the right bank of the Yucay River about forty-eight miles from Cuzco. The temple, one of the most unusual of Inca structures, was dominated by a row of round columns on its two sides. The structure, which has been in the most part destroyed, still has walls of beautifully worked stone at the base, adobe as it rises; it was straw-thatched and must have been equivalent to one of our buildings three stories in height. ("Within it there was a stone idol, the height of a man, with a robe and crown.") [34] Going out from this remarkable structure there are a series of formal streets with houses capped with gabled roofs. Beside it, and plainly to be seen still, runs the royal road, eighteen feet wide. Here appears the architectural impress of the Incas—the

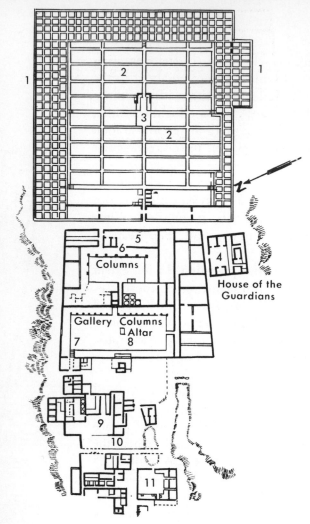

Columns

House of the
Guardians

Gallery Columns
□ Altar
7   8

146. Plan No. 1 *of the ruins of
Incahuasi (Runahuanac or
Lunahuaná), built circa* A.D. 1450
*in the Cañete Valley (Huarco).
Redrawn from Emilio Harth-
terré.*

1) *Granaries, for storing corn, beans, sea food.*
2) *Drying platforms for food.* 3) *Administration
center for food operations.* 4) *House of the
Guardians.* 5) *House complex, presumably for
chieftain.* 6) *Columns.* 7) *Gallery with ascending
steps.* 8) *Altar.* 9) *Habitations.* 10) *Street,
showing evidence of paving.* 11) *Habitations.*

trapezoidal niche—and it appears wherever they set foot; it is the dominant architectural decoration and is in effect the leitmotif of the Incas.

Urban centers of formal nature, plazas bordered with Sun temples and palaces (yet changing to fit the geography) are found all along the royal roadway toward Cuzco. There is a formal gateway at *Rumicolca*, twenty-one miles from the capital of Cuzco. The hills about are studded with ruins, Inca and pre-Inca; the sites keep to the plan. And in those intervening miles between the formal entrance to the valley and Cuzco itself there are, or were, many others.

Cuzco itself, as has already been said, was the focal point of the

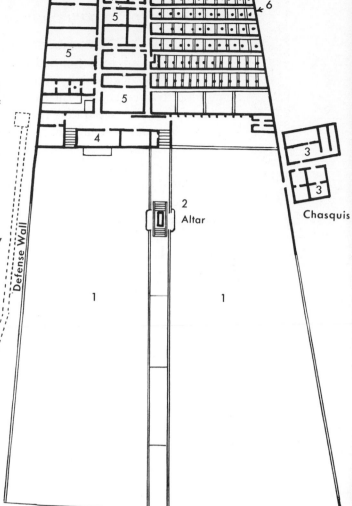

147. Plan No. 2 *of the ruins of Incahuasi. Redrawn from Emilio Harth-terré.*

(Note: *This section of the ruins lies one hundred yards west of Plan No. 1, across the canyon of a small dry river bed.*)

1) *Trapezoid-shaped plaza (typical in Inca town planning), site of religious pageants.* 2) *Altar (with steps), where high-priest conducted the "mysteries."* 3) *House of the* Chasquis *(road couriers).* 4) *Guards' house.* 5) *Habitations, possibly for chieftains.* 6) *Halls of the columns (an unusual feature in Inca architecture).* 7) *Wall, either for defense or against possible flash flood from dry river.*

empire, and within it are to be seen walls dating from the different epochs of its architectural history. The Incas emphasized that which Frank Lloyd Wright has termed "integral architecture"—the livable interior space of the room. In integral architecture, "the room space itself must come through, the room must be seen as architecture." This is fully apparent in Inca architecture.

They used no nails, no wood, except the poles held together with withes to serve as base for the thickly thatched roof. Although the corbeled arch was known and used in bridges, it was almost never used in the large buildings. The placing of the small niche window and the large stone door (see Plate XL) is a miracle of proportion and symmetry.

Next in the architectural parade in *Pisac,* twenty-one miles northeast of Cuzco; it guarded the upper Urubamba River. On the pinnacle of a rock massif stands, or better hangs, Pisac and its agricultural terraces. The Inca's engineers took advantage of this natural fortress, separated from the rest of the massif by deep gorges, to construct an amazing series of defensive forts, tunnels, walls, and gateways. Many of the important structures in the sacred part of the city of Pisac, i.e., the part built about the so-called sundial (*Inti-huatana,* "hitching place of the sun"), were built upon the outcrops of the living rock; the marvelously wrought stones fitted, in a perfect concourse, into this living rock, forming what Wright, that demiurge of modern building, called "organic architecture." It is the "nature of an organic architecture to grow from its site, come out of the ground into the light."

There is nothing quite like Pisac in the entire range of the Inca realm.

Yet, farther down this gorge, is *Ollantaytambo* ("Posthouse of Ollantay"), twenty-four miles northwest of Cuzco and set near to the upper Urubamba River. It was first a village; then in 1460 it was rebuilt as a fortress to protect against the incursions of tribes from the Antisuyu (northeastern quarter of the empire) advancing on Cuzco. There is a famous local legend which identifies Ollantay with the lover of an Inca princess, perhaps the best-known example of "Inca literature" (see page 569). Since the present-day village is set over the old one, it has been a favorite place for the study of Inca architecture, for the site still is one of the finest examples extant of Inca town planning.

The old part of the city is composed of a large plaza laid out like a gridiron, and rising above is an acropolis of rock with an enormous fortress (*pucara*) built on its sides; cut into the living rock itself are agricultural terraces. It was being built when the Spaniards arrived in 1536; work was stopped, and one can still see the immense stones lying where they were abandoned. The present-day village, dating from 1540, was built into and around Ollantay. The streets are narrow, the walls bounded by beautiful lines of masonry, so complete that one can form a fairly clear idea of this type of Inca town planning. Houses (*wasi*) constructed of stone foundations and adobe are built into a group and surrounded by a wall, the *cancha,* essential base of all complex Inca architecture. The fortress is built on top of the acropolis and frowns over the city; a massive stone stairway leads to the top. Here there are six

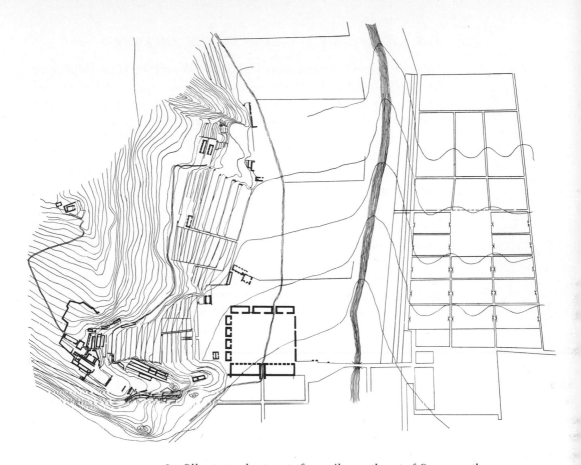

148. *Ollantaytambo, twenty-four miles northwest of Cuzco, on the upper Urubamba River. This typifies the "ideal" Inca urban planning: the self-contained city, formed of a series of* cancha *complexes, and above it, the* pucara *or fortress.*

famous megalithic stones which were to form the base of the Sun Temple, and a wall behind the fortress (which has a number of dwelling places and storage rooms) completes the fortress acropolis. On the other side of the Urubamba River are quarries; a road zigzags up the steep sides, and from here the Indian miners quarried the rock masses. Still to be seen are the rude houses of the workers, and the valley is full of half-worked stones.

Farther down this Urubamba gorge, high on the top of the V-shaped valley, are a series of stone-laid cities which constituted a veritable chain of fortress-sanctuaries, built, it is believed, to defend the empire from raids of the wilder tribes of the jungles. They are built about fifteen hundred feet above the gorge of the river and seem to be hanging. These fortress complexes, known in succession as Huamanmarca, Patallacta, Winay-whayna, Botamarca, Loyamarca, terminate in the most spectacular one of all—the well-known *Machu Picchu.*[55] All of these are bound together by a stone-laid road. They are approximately ten miles apart. At Machu Picchu the Urubamba River cascades onward and downward to the humid jungles.

Machu Picchu is so well known it hardly need be repeated that until its discovery in 1911 by the late Hiram Bingham, it was never mentioned by Inca or Spaniard. It was as if it had been left by its last inhabitants, so that here we have—almost without parallel in any other culture (if one excepts the ruins of Pompeii and Hercula-neum)—an undisturbed picture of what such a corporate village looked like before it was changed or "restored" by those who added their personal equation to history.

The ruins of Machu Picchu (no one knows what its original name was) lie in a topographical saddle between the peaks of Machu (Old) Picchu and Huayna (New) Picchu. In this "saddle is a complex of terraces, gabled houses, temples, sacred plazas and residential compounds." [207]

Machu Picchu is essentially a fortified city; its strongly con-structed houses were most probably defense units. Here there *was* a wall, one of the few walled places in Inca architecture. It had one stone entrance, with a massive wooden gate (an eye-bonder projected from the stone lintel to support it), and it had a small perpendicular stone pin to secure the hole to lock the gate. Machu Picchu was, like most *pucaras* (city defense units), a self-sustaining unit. There are here, as elsewhere in the Inca Empire, various styles of architecture: the royal palaces made of well-fitted granite ashlars, crude clan houses for the common people, barracks for soldiers. All houses were thatched with grass roofs, very thick and possibly of long duration; [15] the interiors of the houses were Spartan in their severity. Such is Machu Picchu, the terminus, it seems, of a constellation of hanging cities, joined by a stone-laid road (the best of the Roman imperial ways was laid no better) to the center of the empire—Cuzco.

Why were these cities built in the later days of the realm; what purpose this vast expenditure of labor? There was no shortage of land—the Inca conquests spread over a quarter of South America—but these hanging cities did not provide much in the matter of what

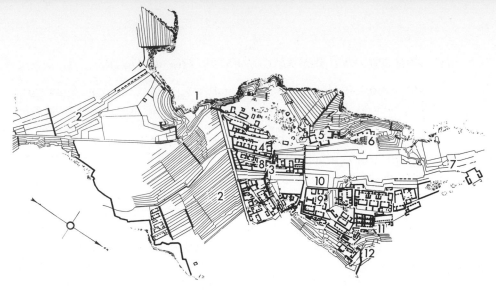

149. *Machu Picchu, lying in the saddle between two peaks, 2,000 feet above the rapids of the Urubamba River. This is essentially a fortified city:*

1) *The gateway to the city. This is the only formal entrance.* 2) *Terraces, agricultural* andenes. *These hanging gardens were banked with soil; crops were grown here and watered by aqueducts.* 3) *Stairway of the fountains; these supplied the city with water brought a mile to the city by aqueduct. It is composed of sixteen descending fountains (although often referred to as baths).* 4) *One of the residential sections of the clans.* 5) *The sacred plaza and the Temple of the Three Windows.* 6) *The* Intiahautana, *"hitching post of the sun."* 7) *Northern terraces and the road to Huayna Picchu.* 8) *The semicircular temple, the Palace of the Ñustas, the Chosen Women.* 9) *House of the clans.* 10) *A clan section of the "Three Doors."* 11) *The royal mausoleum, where gold-decked mummies were placed.* 12) *The place of the stairways and the cemeteries. Redrawn from Hiram Bingham's* Lost City of the Incas, *New York, 1951.*

the Germans would call *Lebensraum* (living space), for if the available space for crops is measured at Machu Picchu, it could not have supported much more than five hundred people! Yet if this question is not immediately answerable, the preconceived Inca concept of city planning is answered: all of these hanging cities over the gorge of the Urubamba show the same careful urban base plan.

Northwest of these, in a different valley and on a direct line to Cuzco, is *Limatambo* (actually in Incan times Rimactampu), lying in the frigid shadow of Mount Salcantay, 20,000 feet high. Limatambo was the way station before "the Great Speaker," the Apurimac River, one of the royal stations on the great 1,250-mile-long arterial road between Cuzco and Quito. Like the finest buildings of Cuzco, it is constructed in the polygonal style, large, irregularly shaped stones faced according to natural contours, and with such accuracy that the finest blade cannot be pushed between them. What remains of Limatambo again shows town planning.

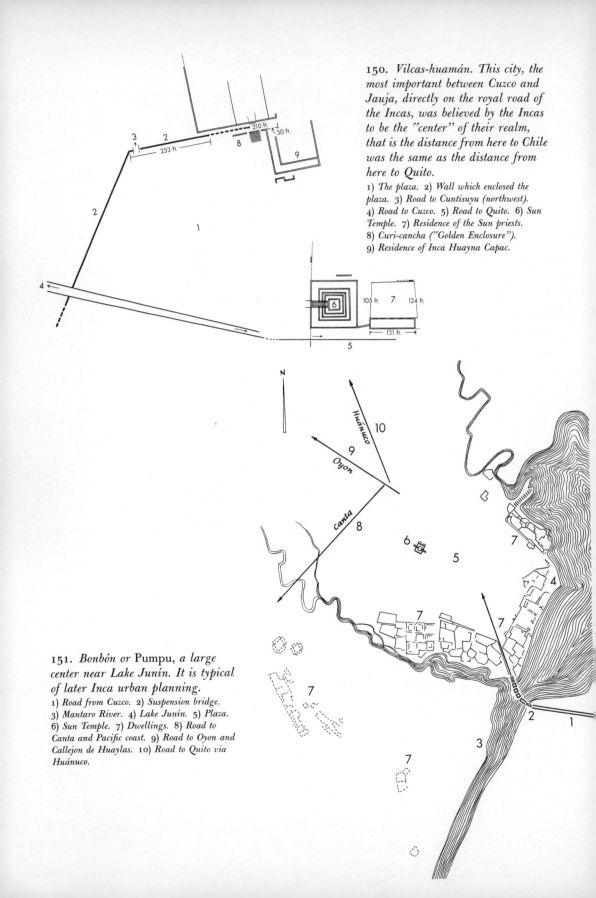

150. *Vilcas-huamán. This city, the most important between Cuzco and Jauja, directly on the royal road of the Incas, was believed by the Incas to be the "center" of their realm, that is the distance from here to Chile was the same as the distance from here to Quito.*

1) *The plaza.* 2) *Wall which enclosed the plaza.* 3) *Road to Cuntisuyu (northwest).* 4) *Road to Cuzco.* 5) *Road to Quito.* 6) *Sun Temple.* 7) *Residence of the Sun priests.* 8) *Curi-cancha ("Golden Enclosure").* 9) *Residence of Inca Huayna Capac.*

151. *Bonbón or Pumpu, a large center near Lake Junín. It is typical of later Inca urban planning.*

1) *Road from Cuzco.* 2) *Suspension bridge.* 3) *Mantaro River.* 4) *Lake Junín.* 5) *Plaza.* 6) *Sun Temple.* 7) *Dwellings.* 8) *Road to Canta and Pacific coast.* 9) *Road to Oyon and Callejon de Huaylas.* 10) *Road to Quito via Huánuco.*

Still continuing on the royal road and a hundred miles northward is *Vilcas-huamán,* at 11,000 feet altitude. "The Hawk's Sanctuary" lies on the high Vilcas plateau above the Vischongo River.
Here a stone-laid, truncated Sun Temple still stands, the only one
of those numbered in the thousands to survive. Vilcas-huamán,
although two hundred miles distant from Cuzco, has all of the
aspects of Inca architecture, and shows the striking uniformity
in Inca town planning. There is an immense plaza ("large enough
to hold," said Pedro de Cieza de León, who had apparently seen it
then, "fifty thousand people"). It is bordered to the west by the
Sun Temple, to the east by the palace of the Inca; the House of
the Virgins of the Sun occupied another corner, and in another
section were the royal storage chambers. The streets were narrow
and paved and were lined with houses.

Three roads of empire coming from different directions met in
the plaza. The Sun Temple (see Plate XL) is now as it was described
by Cieza de León: "made of very fine fitting stones with two large
doorways (on opposite sides), with two stairways leading up from
them with thirty-three steps . . . and on its truncated top one hundred feet above the plaza . . . a large stone seat [once gold-plated],
where the Lord-Inca sat to view the dances and festivals. . . ."

Inca architecture was functional. There were no structures in
the length of the realm that had the human uselessness of the pyramids, of the kind which gave Julian Huxley "no aesthetic pleasure," *
and which he thought to be the quintessential of conspicuous
waste.[87]

Once again northward, three hundred miles from the last mentioned Inca center, is little-known *Bonbón* at a land height of 12,500
feet. Here, as in Vilcas-huamán, three arterial roads met in a large
plaza. A suspension bridge spanned the river, the Mantaro, an approach road came through rows of houses—of the common sort
(field stone cemented together with adobe mud and thatched with
grass)—and the street debouched into an enormous trapezoid-
shaped plaza. In the center stood the Sun Temple; along three of
its sides were an impressive number of houses which were gabled
and grass-thatched. The roads of empire converged here, passed by
the Sun Temple, and went on into the void of the Andes.

On the same road, which goes between Cuzco and Quito, and

---

* Actually he was speaking here of Persia and its jewel-encrusted swords.

another hundred miles northward, is *Huánuco*. It is, or was, immense. Still to be seen is the outline of its square plaza, reached on all its four sides by a flight of stone steps. "Huánuco has a fine royal palace," said Pedro de Cieza, ". . . near it a Temple of the Sun with many virgins and priests. It was so grand a place in the time of the Incas that more than thirty thousand Indians were set apart solely for its service." The buildings that housed all these people, as well as the temples, are still to be seen. Again three roads of empire came into the plaza and left in different directions.

And still the architectural parade marches on. One would be bored with a repetition of it; how at *Cajamarca,* two hundred miles farther north (and where the last Lord-Inca Atahualpa was captured, held for ransom, and executed), there was yet another Inca center, planned as all the rest. Lying at 8,500 feet in altitude, halfway between Cuzco and Quito, it was small as Inca centers go; still the Spaniards who first saw it on Friday, November 15, 1532, found its plaza "larger than any in Spain," surrounded by a high wall and entered by two doorways which opened upon the streets of the town. The buildings were long, strongly built, "three times the height of a man and roofed with straw."

"They were," the king's inspector went on, "the finest we had seen." [54]

Continuing beyond the confines of what are now the political boundaries of Peru, and into Ecuador and along the royal road, the same careful urban planning of cities continued.

Tumipampa (now called Tumibamba), and the place that is now the city of Cuenca, was ". . . built much like all the others," wrote Cieza in 1550. "On a large plain . . . near two small rivers . . . The Temple of the Sun is built of stones very cunningly wrought, some of them being large, coarse and black, and others resembling jasper. Some of the Indians pretend that most of the stones of which these buildings and the Temple of the Sun are built had been brought from the great city of Cuzco . . . The doorways of many of the buildings were very handsome and brightly painted, with several precious gems and emeralds set into the stone, and the interior walls of the Temple of the Sun and of the palaces of the Incas were lined with plates of the finest gold stamped with many figures. The roofs were of straw so well put that no fire would consume it and it would endure for many ages. . . ."

The plan of the temple city included buildings with "more than two hundred virgins [who were very beautiful], dedicated to the service of the sun. Near the temples . . . were many buildings used as lodgings for the troops and as storehouses, which were always kept full." [197]

Quito, at the end of the Cuzco–Quito axis, three hundred miles from the Inca center at Tumibamba and 1,250 miles from Cuzco, was one of the large cities. Here, too—although Quito and its environs were not fully part of the empire until 1492—the Incas constructed their usual urban centers—and far in advance of anything Europe was doing at the same date. It was in full operation and "beautifully wrought" even within fifty years of its Inca conquest.

Architecturally we have now seen Inca centers picked at random and described along an approximate 2,000-mile-long stretch, from Lake Titicaca to Quito, at altitudes ranging between 8,500 and 13,000 feet. There are no other people in history who constructed and maintained such complex urban centers at such great heights.

As in the Andes, so with the coast: as they conquered the lands of the desert they modified the structures; when they had their victory, they leveled part of the old city and superimposed their plaza, Sun temples, and administrative center. When they built anew, they followed a formula almost exactly as had the Romans for their newly conquered territories. On the coast the Inca worked with adobe blocks; at important religious centers—such as the mecca of Pachacamac near Lima—stone was brought down and certain doorways and niches were constructed of it; adobe was used above the stone. At newly constructed sites such as Incahuasi in the Cañete Valley and Tambo Colorado in the adjoining valley of Pisco, the Inca masons worked only with adobe, but fashioned and shaped it as they would stone.

As the Greeks had their "key," and the Romans their eagle, so the Incas had their niche. The trapezoidal window (false or real) was the mark of the Inca; whenever an existing structure was modified, the architect added the niche. Nothing is so indicative as this; wherever it appears it marks the presence of these people.

Enough, then, has been shown of Inca structures along a wide and lengthy geography to show that we are dealing with a *master plan;* the sheer quantity of extant Inca structures, in whole or in part, is so utterly astonishing that no one has ever attempted to make a detailed account of the whole of it. However, the persistence of design throughout thousands of miles of varied terrain proves the point long insisted upon by an old Inca hand: "All the best-known monuments of *Inca* architecture were constructed not by individuals but by the government, according to careful plans." [155]

It is now time to see how the builders worked.

Many writers on these problems—and included therein are many archaeologists—take this position, that the cyclopean stonework which one sees in Cuzco and especially in the fortress of Sacsahuamán (one of tne greatest single structures ever reared by ancient man) was pre-Inca, and all this stonework is attributed to some vague and shadowy anterior civilization called by them the "Megalithic empire." This position has little archaeological support. The varying styles, it has been abundantly shown by excavation and restoration, are only the evolution of Inca styles themselves, or what is more likely, the difference in building materials and the plasticity of the Inca craftsmen.

And of stone. When the gigantic size of the stones that form these structures is viewed for the first time, the utter enormity of the task of shaping, transporting them, and putting them into place —the edges so chamfered as to join without even a semblance of joining—is such that the viewer refuses to submit to the inescapable conclusion that the stone was quarried, pulled into place without draft animals, fashioned by stone instruments, and raised by crude leverage. Although such monoliths weighed as much as sixty tons and were variously shaped, they were made and fitted easily without cement, seemingly as a Chinese craftsman handles a piece of ivory. Such structures, except where destroyed by man, have resisted the insults of time for hundreds of years.

While working stone with stone celts seems to hinge on the marvelous, it is scarcely unique in history. Polished stone-celt instruments had a great significance for Neolithic man—before the introduction of metal—and great care was given to the making of stone instruments; axes, adzes, chisels, hammers, all appear in stone, and later metal ones are only a counterpart of stone instruments. The Incas, as well as the other cultures before them, had metal, even a hard bronze, but the stone celt remained their tool. The early Egyptians worked stone similarly. Metal, although it appeared in the Near East as early as 4000 B.C., *did not wholly replace stone celts until after 2000 B.C.* The sculptures in low relief that adorn the temples of Thebes in Egypt (dating circa 1500 B.C.) show Egyptian masons using stone implements almost identical in form and method of handling to the stone celt used by the Incas. Shaping stone with stone was universal and should occasion no surprise, nor is there the need of a fantastic explanation of how the Inca craftsman worked large rock masses.

Metal replaced stone celts very slowly in Eurasia, and it shows the slowness of the acceptance of new ideas that it took man (even when he had metal) two thousand years to replace stone instruments. It is not surprising, then, that the Incas, even with good bronze instruments, should continue to use stone celts. The advantages of metal should not be exaggerated in stoneworking; the Neolithic cultures showed clearly that trees could be felled, canoes shaped, posts made, and stone walls carved with stone instruments. Stone hammers were made from fine-grained heavier stone: hematite, basalt, or epidiorite. Stone chisels made of these materials are found abundantly in many Inca sites.

Quarrying of stone was done in America as the Egyptians and all other earlier cultures did it. Rock was searched for natural faults; after boring, the holes were filled with wooden wedges, swollen with water, and in time this swelling action cracked the huge rock masses. (The Romans, even with the most advanced technology of the ancient world, did it no differently.) Inca quarries are still to be seen on the mountain slopes opposite Ollantaytambo. There, at 1,500 feet above the river, are the quarries; stone, half-shaped, is still there. Rock shapes are partially formed out of the porphyritic rock, and the place is piled with rock chips. Quarries are also found at Huaccoto (black andesite), eight miles from Cuzco, and others at Rumicolca (*rumi*, "stone"), twenty-one miles from Cuzco, which yielded the fine rock reserved for the best of Inca structures. Limestone was used for the great fortress of Sacsahuamán, and it was fashioned into the enormous polygonal megaliths that form the base of the fortress. A study of the quarrying techniques of the Egyptians shows that they were almost identical with the techniques of the Incas.[173]

Transport of stone was by manpower. We can only deduce the transport techniques. Although the Indian did not have the wheel, he used wood and stone rollers, and the rock in the rough was pulled by ropes with manpower. He used levers operating on bosses, perhaps sledges for dragging, but had only the most elementary knowledge of dynamics and of methods for handling mass weight.

How were the buildings constructed? How was such intricate stonework (admittedly the finest ever done) worked without the tools we think necessary for such an operation? How the plans, the Incas having neither paper nor writing?

The Incas used clay models for buildings and terraces, even for town planning; some of these have survived in clay and stone. We have no knowledge of how the architect or mason measured. They had a crude slide rule and used a plumb bob (*wipayci*). Their standard for measurement is unknown. Doubtless, like the Egyptians, they used hands, feet, and other parts of the body for the basic measurements (the ancient Egyptian hieroglyph for the cubit was a forearm). We know that the spread of the human body became the measurement for the fathom. The Incas had a standard measurement for land. The standard width of a typical Inca road was about twenty-four feet, the spread of about five human Indian bodies; we know nothing beyond this.

This is admittedly not a wholly adequate explanation of how they attained the precision which they did. A study of the various stone styles displays their plasticity with stone, for the Inca craftsman had a long heritage in stoneworking. Some of the pre-Inca cultures, notably Tiahuanaco and those who built the beautiful round burial *chullpas* about Lake Titicaca five hundred years before the advent of the Incas, suggest this long inheritance. They had an aesthetic feeling for the *quality* of stone; this is only acquired after generations.

Stonework differed markedly in each structure according to its importance. The stones of the Temple of the Sun in Cuzco were squared and set with precision and made as smooth as marble; larger stones, on the temple of Inca Roca, were polygonal in style, showing a knowledge of thrust and strength by interlocking. How the Inca mason obtained this minute precision, in which the enormous stone had to be lifted and set down a hundred times before the massive rock fitted perfectly on all its sides like a bottle stopper, still cannot be satisfactorily explained.

Sacsahuamán was the great fortress, the *pucara* of Cuzco. It is without doubt one of the greatest structures ever erected by man. It was begun by Pachacuti ("Earthshaker") after A.D. 1438, and it employed thirty thousand Indians for the seventy years of its construction.[208] It was completed circa 1500; its fate was not unlike that of the Maginot line—it fell quickly. The principal fortifications face north; along this side is an unbroken wall over fifteen hundred feet in length. The cyclopean wall is composed of three massive tiers of stone walls, broken into forty-six parts, each supporting a terrace; the three parapets rising to a combined height of sixty feet are constructed of salients, retiring angles, and buttresses. There were only three doors—three entrances—and one of these still retains the name of the principal architect. There were two square military towers (*mayumarcas*) at either end of the front underground passages, an enormous water reservoir with stone-laid conduits in which the water passed from one place to another, a beautifully wrought palace for the Inca, storage places for food and arms, habitations for soldiers and people who would maintain the defense. The first Spaniards who saw it were speechless with astonishment ". . . neither the stone aqueduct of Segovia nor the buildings of Hercules nor the work of the Romans had the dignity of this fortress. . . ."[34]

How did they move the massive stones—some weighing as much as twenty tons—into place and, even more, set these giant megaliths into place in such a way that the edges were chamfered where they joined and yet left the outer faces rough and even extended? First, the quarried stones were pulled on rollers. A pit was dug and the first stone was placed in it. The next stone, to be laid on top, was brought up by a ramp of pounded earth and stones (this method was seen by a Jesuit chronicler in the seventeenth century, and ramps are still found at the sites of some of the ruins). The protuberances one sees on the stones at Sacsahuamán were actually left there by the stonemason, to serve as a fulcrum to push the stone into place. As is obvious, the stone was brought unfinished; then it was cut so accurately it is impossible to push a knife blade between the stones. The immense rock masses remain to amaze us; Stonehenge pales beside it, the tomb of Agamemnon at Argos is as nothing alongside it; even the cyclopean walls of Agrigentum fall far short in comparison with the fortress of Sacsahuamán.

Aᴌᴛʜᴏᴜɢʜ ɢᴏʟᴅ, the old successful metal, was found in great quantities, the Incas in fact mined a considerable variety of other metals. Since copper, when mixed with tin, gave them bronze, it was the most important and was the only metal allowed to be used decoratively by the ordinary Indian.

The technology of metals was known, it seemed, to all the world's peoples. Historically the first metal to be mined was gold, for it made life sumptuous. Iron rusted, silver tarnished; gold was the metal of great ductility. Copper came next in man's metal age, then tin. Man's pattern in the New World was the same as in the Old.

Copper was mined in Mesopotamia as early as 3500 B.C., and it appears first in Peruvian graves sometime after 2000 B.C. The Incas, when they appeared, brought no new techniques, but they did organize the method of obtaining it. First, all the gold and silver mined and in mines belonged to the Inca. All bullion had to come to Cuzco; no Indian was allowed to leave the city with any of it on his person.

Mining, then as now, was disliked by the Indian. It took him from his land and, while gold might have its value, land was forever. Since gold and copper and silver came from the Andes, the metal-bearing hills were sacred. They were considered *huacas,* and the Indians prayed while they dug that the gods would yield the metal from the hills.

The Incas had precise laws for mining and miners. The mines were only allowed to be worked in the Andes during the four warmest months. Miners were rotated; no miner could go into the mining districts without his woman. In the perpendicular hills that surrounded the terribly humid lands of the Carabaya (east of Lake Titicaca in the Montaña), where the Inca got much of his gold, the hills are terraced for crops and the remains of gold-mining villages are still found there. Gold was mostly secured by panning; another method was to build a series of stone riffles across the bed of a river, and stones which held gold particles were collected after the rains. Smelting of the gold into ingots was done by bringing the gold to the furnaces atop lofty hills, called *huayras;* these furnaces, operated with charcoal and bellows, faced east into the wind of the trades and gave sufficient draft to obtain the high temperatures needed for melting.

The Inca metallurgists used all the techniques known to metal-working: casting, hammering, soldering, riveting, and *repoussé*. The goldsmiths (who were stationed within Cuzco itself and were exempt from taxes) used the techniques described by Garcilaso de la Vega, "the Inca," who was born in Cuzco in 1539 and no doubt saw them at their bellows and blast furnaces: "they went round the fire blowing with the tubes."

This technique is no different from that depicted on an Egyptian tomb at Saqqara (dating back to 2400 B.C.), where goldsmiths can be seen blowing into a fire to create the heat needed to melt gold. From this relatively crude method came the Inca gold pieces which so astonished the Spaniards, such a golden torrent that the captured Lord-Inca Atahualpa could fill a vast room twice with silver and once with gold images torn from the walls and interiors of his empire; and all within the space of six months. From these crude methods they were able to cast life-size figures of Incas, and the golden mimicry of plant life found in the Golden Enclosure at Cuzco.

Gold, of course, is highly ductile; it is softer than silver—a single grain of it can be drawn into a wire a hundred feet long—and it is universal in appeal. Gold roads are found in many parts of the ancient world, and ancient peoples knew more about gold than any other metal. The Egyptians had a papyrus map dated 1300 B.C. which showed where gold mines were located. The Incas, too, had detailed statistics on gold. There were officials at the mines to check on production and miners, but whereas in other lands miners were usually criminals, among the Incas it was carried on by the people as part of their work tax.

Gold belonged to the Inca. No one knows how much gold the empire produced, yet from the accurate *quipu* records which were interpreted to the Spaniards it was believed that gold came into Cuzco at the rate of seven million ounces annually.

After his death, each of the Lord-Incas had a life-sized gold statue (*pucarina*) made of him, and his palace, which became his tomb, was ornamented with gold.

Silver, too, was the Inca's divine property. Silver was a quality rather than a substance, and the tender moonlight luster of its bril-

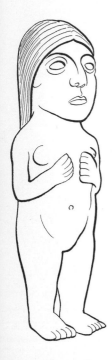

152. *Figure of a woman cast in silver. Although this is only eight inches in height, the conquistadors reported they found life-sized figures of cast gold and silver.*

liance caused the Indians to regard it as the tears of the moon. It was plenteous in Peru. All people at all times have loved the elegance, the elegy of silver; Sanskrit poems are full of images of silver bells; the Greeks who went as far as the Volga River for trade, found silver mines being worked there by the primitive Scythians. And even though silver tarnished easily in the humidity of the Andes, the Incas regarded it highly; much of the metalwork in Cuzco was of silver. Quicksilver, too, was known to the Incas; there is a large mine at Huancavelica, worked by the Spaniards for centuries; it was no doubt used in the gold- and silver-plating of bronze, a technique used by the Inca smiths to "extend" the quantity of gold. The techniques of Peruvian metallurgy have not been extensively studied. However, we know they used tin alloys, and tin is found in much of what appears at first sight to be pure gold; they employed a formula for combining copper and tin to produce bronze, casting them in one piece and hammering it cold. With such casting techniques they produced maceheads for war clubs, hard bronze levers (*chumpis*), knives (*tumis*), a fairly diverse list of surgical instruments, bolas used for the ensnaring of birds and animals, pins (*topos*) to hold the women's garments together, ear spoons and hair tweezers; the list could be extended, yet it is enough to display the wide application of metallurgy. All of it was overshadowed, of course, by the immense amount of gold and silver ornaments.

What this golden flow amounted to in terms of bullion value and purchase value has been shown by Dr. Samuel K. Lothrop.[110] The gold and silver which was collected at Cajamarca, brought there by the orders of the Lord-Inca Atahualpa who was held captive by the Spaniards and who agreed to ransom himself by filling a room twenty-five feet long and fifteen feet wide "as high as a white line which a tall man could not reach,"[259] amounted to 1,326,539 pesos of pure gold and 51,610 marks of silver.* This amounted, in terms of actual value of bullion (at $35.02 the ounce), to $19,851,642.00. In purchasing value this sum would be at present worth ten times that amount. The Inca hoard of gold and silver is put forward in terms of bullion value only to give some idea of the enormous amount of it; in terms of art, the value of these objects is incalculable. Naturally, to be transportable and divisible among the

* Lothrop gives the complicated methods of determining gold and silver weights in the sixteenth century, mark = 230.675 grams; peso de oro = 4.18 grams.

conquistadors, these art objects had to be melted down and put into ingots. Although some of the remarkable pieces of goldwork were set aside for the Emperor Charles V of Spain, *not a single object of art survived;* all of it went into the crucibles by reason of a royal edict (February 13, 1535): "All gold and silver from Peru shall be melted in the royal mints at Sevilla, Toledo and Segovia."

All we know of this lost art is what the common soldier, touched by what he saw, wrote about these fantastic pieces of goldsmithery, many worthy of a Benvenuto Cellini. "In Cuzco . . . they found many statues and images entirely of gold and silver, complete shape of a woman *in natural size* very well wrought, well shaped and hollow; these I believe were the finest that could be made anywhere. . . ." Another conquistador wrote of seeing "many vessels of gold, lobsters of the sort that grow in the sea and on other gold vessels were sculptured with all birds and serpents, even spiders, lizards and sort of beetles . . . carved on the body of gold." And the conquistador's secretary, who recorded all of the booty before it was consigned to the goldsmiths who melted it down into ingots, saw it all piled high: "Truly it was a thing worthy to be seen . . . vessels, vases and pieces of various forms in which the [Inca] lords of the land were served . . . there were four llamas in fine gold and very large, ten or twelve figures of women, natural size, all of fine gold and as beautiful and well made it seemed as if they were alive. . . ."

 Tawantinsuyu: The Four Quarters of the World 26

FROM CUZCO (as from Rome, with its imperial ways) issued the great roads which ran the length and breadth of the empire. The center point from which all the roads issued was the great square of Cuzco, Huaycapata, around which stood the principal buildings of the realm. Here the people met, their voices in jarring contention, and had their fetes, days of merrymaking that broke the monotony of their lives.

The great square was also the demarcation for the four great quarters, or *suyus*, of the world into which the Inca realm was divided. The sum of those parts made up Tawantinsuyu, the official name of the empire.

Neither the four quarters nor the roads conformed exactly to the direction of the four cardinal points of the compass. Rather the boundaries were fixed by the conformation of the geography of the land. Each *suyu* was ruled by a governor (*apo*), of royal lineage and related by blood ties to the Inca; he was answerable only to the Inca.

Cuzco, although in the heartland of the Andes, actually lies very close to the jungles of the Upper Amazon. It is only scant miles from the upper Urubamba River; four days of an Indian's walk northeast would carry him into the jungles. And directly east, two days' walk would bring an Indian to the Paucartambo, a gigantic river which cascades mile upon mile down into a jungle of towering trees and constant rainfall. Here a bewildering number of fierce tribesmen, "untamed" Indians, who, with the consistency of ants, were never discouraged by devastating setbacks, kept hacking at the outposts of the Inca's realm. Three of the empire's most gigantic fortresses— Sacsahuamán, which guarded holy Cuzco itself, Ollantaytambo, twenty-four miles northwest of Cuzco (which defended the upper Urubamba River, a natural gateway to Cuzco), and Pisac, another gigantic fortress, which guarded the upper reaches of the same river as well as the pass which led east to Paucartambo—were erected to guard against the incursions of the jungle tribes into the environs of Cuzco.

The whole of this quarter was the Antisuyu. It is difficult to be precise about what the quarter covered. Presumably all land east of the Andes, where the trees began—the eyebrows of the forest, as the Spaniards had it—fell under the administration of the governor of the Antisuyu. It was immense. The Inca seemed to lump all the people under the name of *yungas* or hotland people; actually they were very diverse, and ranged from those who wore woolen ponchos and lived mostly off a tuber called manioc, to the half-naked Indians in the hotlands of the Amazon. Stone-paved roads were pushed into the very jungle itself, garrisons were kept up at full war strength, and the Inca himself, in the later days of the reign, was engaged constantly in repulsing attacks from that quarter.

The Incas were able, in some instances, to win over the tribes here, and they yielded tribute in the form of gold, bird feathers, *chonta* wood, dyes, fruits, animal skins, wood fibers, and jungle-reared cotton. Other tribes, notably the Aguarunas ("water people"), a subtribe of the head-hunting Shuaras, never yielded, and the Inca's troops were decimated in the humid jungles where the tactics of mass attack and envelopment were of little value. Most of these jungle Indians knew of copper and bronze instruments, which they had through trade with the Incas. Each quarter had its official royal *tampu,* or way station, approximately thirty miles from Cuzco; the administrative post of the Antisuyu quarter was Paucartambo.

The next quarter, in the exact opposite direction from Cuzco, was the Cuntisuyu. It lay southwest of Cuzco, and was reached by a road (still to be seen in parts) which led over the Andes. The administrative *tampu,* approximately twenty-one miles from Cuzco, was Paccari-tampu (called "Origin Tampu," and believed to have been one of the places where the first Incas emerged to begin the wars that led to their capture of the Cuzco Valley).

Cuntisuyu is not clearly defined, but conforming to the Inca concepts of geography it embraced all the land lying between Cuzco and the Pacific Ocean and south as far as what is now the Peru-Chile border, and north to, and perhaps beyond, where modern Lima now stands. It took in the high bleak Andean lands, and also the great tribal cultures that lived on the Peruvian desert littoral, those which we now call the Nazca, Ica, Chanca, etc., as well as the famous shrine of Pachacamac, the mecca of the creator-god.

For one hundred years the Incas made war upon the coastal tribes who lived in this quarter, and lateral roads, wonderfully built, were made to cling to the sides of the gorges of the rivers which ran west; almost every valley had such roads. War occupied the affairs of the *apo* or governor of this quarter until about 1466, when the Incas finally conquered the Chimú Empire. This effectively ended all opposition on the coast.

This administrative post was very important. It involved winning the conquered people over to the Inca system and organizing their tribute, resettling "safe populations" (referred to as *mitimaes*) among them, and setting up the royal *tampus* along the roads so as to bring to Cuzco the coastal products: cotton, dyestuffs, food (peanuts, manioc, sweet potatoes, squash, etc.), and especially fresh fish and seaweed (of considerable importance to the Inca diet), which had to be brought by running relays.

The third quarter was the Collasuyu. In size of territory it was the largest of the four, and lay to the southeast. The road to it went out from the small plaza in Cuzco still known by its Quechua name Rimacpampa. This quarter embraced all the land southeast of Cuzco, including Lake Titicaca, what is now Bolivia, Chile (except its very humid tip), and the whole of mountainous Argentina. The governor of this *suyu,* after the conquests won it for the Inca realm, had to balance his administration between severe reprisals and the winning arts of diplomacy, for here were the Aymara-speaking peoples, once as great in numbers as the Quechua-speaking peoples. They still lived in the aura of the past greatness of Tiahuanaco, whose ruins, lying at the edge of Lake Titicaca, were always there to give evidence that the Incas had arrived late and were not the Sun God-inspired people that they claimed to be. There was gold from the Carabaya, vicuña and alpaca wool from the high places, tin and copper from Bolivia to make bronze, and ostrich feathers from the pampas.

The fourth and last quarter was Chinchasuyu. Its royal *tampu* and administrative center was Rimacpampa, some thirty-six miles from Cuzco near the banks of the Apurimac River. Its direction was northwest and its administration included all the Andean area between Cuzco and Quito, a distance of 1,250 miles. The immense quarter was named after a lake, Chinchaycocha (now Junín) the second largest in South America after Titicaca, which lies more or less in the geographical center of Peru. The Chinchay had tribes who fought long and valiantly against the Inca, but when finally subdued they became loyal vassals.

All of the important later conquests of the Incas took place within this last section, and from it many of the great arterial roads struck off for conquests of the desert coast and the Upper Amazon. As a symbol of this great quarter the Inca selected tribes, keeping them to their dress and customs, and set them at Karmenka, at the "gateway" to Cuzco on the road to Chinchasuyu. Here lived the Cañari and the Chachapoya tribesmen.

The posts of governors (*apos*)—Incas of royal blood—were hereditary; they ruled their quarters from Cuzco or from the administration center of each royal *tampu* located thirty miles from Cuzco in each direction. Statistical records were kept in each quarter by means of the *quipu* knot-string records. These arrived with each post by *chasquis* (couriers) who came bearing messages in this form; they

153. *The* quipu, *as redrawn from the Inca-Spanish chronicler, Poma de Ayala. The domino-like figure to the left suggests the manner in which its decimal system of counting should be understood.*

were then translated into decimal figures by the *quipu* readers (*quipu-camayoc*) and transmitted to the governor. Thus he would know how many taxpayers (able-bodied Indians) lived in his quarter, the number of llamas in the herds, the exact number of soldiers he could call at a moment's notice, the cities, and the royal stopping places that lay within his jurisdiction. At any imperial council, also a hereditary post, he could give this information to the Inca. Since we do not have any exact figures of the number of Indians in the Inca realm at the time of the Spanish conquest, we do not know how many people each governor of a given *suyu* controlled. Various population figures have been given—six million, one of the "accepted" numbers, seems far too large; two million is perhaps more in line. With this as a hypothetical figure then, each governor would control 500,000 people. The next chieftain was a *hono-curaca*, who controlled 10,000 people; under him, a *pica-waranka-curaca*, who controlled 5,000 Indians, and so it went down the line until the very last, the "straw boss," a *cancha-camayoc,* responsible for ten Indians. For every 10,000 Indians there were 1,331 officials. Everything was based on head count; all was decimally organized.

The Inca's orders, as Dr. Wendell Bennett sagely observed, "flowed up and orders flowed down, but there was little communication between officers of the same rank." This was to cause problems later.

Certain of the quarters provided their specialists; from the Cuntisuyu quarter came the Rucana tribe, a rugged high-dwelling people who were used to the perpendicular world. They were the official litter-bearers; eighty of them, in a special blue livery, were assigned to each royal litter. The Chumpivilcas tribesmen from another quarter were the dancers, and the Chichas supplied the incense for the religion of the Sun. There were others who were distinctly professionals: architects, professional soldiers, accountants (*quipu-camayoc*), silversmiths (*kolki-camayoc*), tapestry weavers (*kumpi-camayoc*), and this again suggests how well defined was the organization.

Women within the four quarters were, as were their menfolk, fully controlled. They were subject to a head count, and all girls above ten years of age were classified. Young girls who possessed beauty, grace, or talent were brought to the attention of the visiting *curacas,* signaled out, and brought to Cuzco to become Chosen Women. Those not selected were known as "left-out girls." The Chosen Women were placed under supervision (they might be likened to nuns), trained to weave, and were attached to the rituals attending the religion of the Sun. Those so trained were "Handmaidens of the Sun," and were established throughout the empire wherever there were Sun temples. Their dwelling places, out of reach of ordinary men, were placed high in some inaccessible spot, such as one can still see at the ruins of Ollantaytambo or at Incahuasi (New Cuzco) in the Cañete Valley.

There were as many as fifteen thousand such Chosen Women, and those who were not connected with the rituals pertaining to the Sun were either taken in royal concubinage or else as wives by famous generals. Later, if unmarried, the Chosen Women assumed the titles of *mamacuna* and became the instructresses of the newly arrived Chosen Women. They wove garments exclusively for the use of the Lord-Inca and his *coya.*

It was these women, quartered at Caxas in the Sun Temple in northern Peru, that the Spanish soldiers raped in the first five days of the conquest. This so enraged the Inca that he planned their annihilation, which only his capture prevented.*

The four quarters of the Inca realm were constantly being enlarged, and territorial expansion gave the Incas a new social world with an "intensified horizontal and vertical social mobility. The need for administrators was so urgent that any man, no matter how humble his origin, who showed the slightest spark of administrative ability might find himself set down in a strange village miles from his home and told to enforce the emperor's law." [155]

The *apo* governors knew no rest from their labors. Since conquest with the Incas constituted the growth of empire, administration was bound up with colonization. Upon conquering a new area, perhaps an alien tribe, the governor of the quarter in which the conquest took place had one of several policies to follow. If the tribe had yielded gracefully, even after furious battle, the conquered chiefs were allowed to retain their titles (although they remained under the dominance of the Inca governor), and their sons, as aforementioned, were sent to Cuzco for training and held as hostages for the good behavior of the chieftains. Conquered peoples were allowed their local dress; in fact this was insisted upon, and up to a certain point they retained their own speech, although all the officials had to learn Quechua if they did not know it already. All had to observe the religion of the Sun. If their local gods were efficacious, if they had a well-known *huaca* within their territory, the gods were adopted into the Inca pantheon.

However, if the conquered tribe was recalcitrant and refused to accept the Inca's ways, they were decimated, or if too large, they were moved out of their own lands and a reliable, "safe" Quechua-speaking people were put into the voided land. These *mitimaes* played the same role in the newly conquered quarter as the Roman soldier had played in his conquests. Their mission was to teach Inca cultural ways, so they were in their way the "civilizers."

---

* These were the Chosen Women that the first Spaniards mass-raped at the mountain village of Caxas. They forced five hundred Virgins of the Sun out into the plaza, and while crossbowmen kept off any Indians, the soldiers had their way with them until worn out and spent; they went off then and continued the conquest. Later, when he met them at Cajamarca, the Inca charged the Spaniards with this as a heinous crime.

The administration of so far-flung an empire depended on its communications, and as the great plaza of Cuzco was the demarcation of its four sections, so too was the plaza the starting point of its roads—the web of communications which bound the realm together.

27   *The Royal Roads of the Incas*

THERE WERE historically only two road systems: the Roman roads, which covered fifty-six thousand linear miles through Europe, the Near East, and Africa, and that of the Incas, which moved across the surface of the Andes from Argentina to Colombia and along the entire length of desert coast, amounting to more than ten thousand miles of all-weather highways.

In order to hold the Inca realm together and to convert these congeries of geography—desert, mountain, and jungle—into a close-knit empire, the best of communications was needed; the result was the Inca road, a system only comparable to the Roman roads, an American labor which Alexander von Humboldt (who knew both) characterized as "the most useful and stupendous works ever executed by man."

In the main there were two sections of roads; the royal road (*Capacñan*), which moved through the Andes from the border of the empire at the Ancasmayo River (1° N. lat.), down through Ecuador, Peru, Bolivia, and thereafter into Argentina (coming to an end at Tucumán), and then into Chile, where it ended at the Rio Maule (35° S. lat.). There the Incas built a fortress and their most southern station at Purumauca. The coastal road, beginning at Tumbes (3° S. lat.), the frontier city which marked the coastal end of the Inca realm, ran southward through the brazen desert, the entire length of Peru; thence down deep into Chile, connecting at Copiapó with the road coming over from Argentina and continuing down to the Maule in Chile, which marked its end.

The Andean royal road was 3,250 miles in length (making it longer than the longest Roman road—from Hadrian's Wall in Scotland to Jerusalem); the coastal road was 2,520 miles in length.

In addition to these arterial roads, there were numerous laterals, careening down the sides of the V-shaped valleys and connecting the mountain roads with the coastal one; there were special gold roads, such as those which moved into the rich gold areas of Carabaya, east of Lake Titicaca, and there were especially wide military roads such as the one built from Huánuco to Chachapoyas, stonelaid in its entire length of four hundred miles in order to undertake the conquest of an escaped tribe of Chanca Indians. Roads also pervaded the jungle. They were built at the highest altitudes ever used by man in constant travel; the highest Inca road recorded (17,160 feet) is the one behind Mount Salcantay.

The standard width of the Inca coastal road was twenty-four feet. It is not known, as yet, why so wide a standard was set or what precise measurement determined it, but from hundreds of measurements made upon the road by the von Hagen Expedition along one thousand miles, this was the standard gauge; [209] it only departed from it when some immovable obstacle prevented this "official" width from being obtained. Considerable nonsense has been written about the roads: to some they were mere footpaths, and to others stone roads laid with porphyry; neither extreme is true. The Incas had no wheel and no draft animals; the common denominators were the foot of the Indian and the hoof of the llama. There was no need for the deep roadbed of the Roman roads which were solidly constructed to accommodate vehicular traffic. And it is known historically that *nowhere did prepared surfaces appear on ancient roads* until wheeled transport came into general use.

On the coast the natural hard-packed surfaces of the coastal llanos were sufficiently hard to support traffic without a surface. When the road passed over a bog it was raised high like a causeway; when it moved down steep inclines it became a step road. When the roads entered the larger coastal cities and their environs, they were often paved for short distances.

The consistent twenty-four-foot width is the architectural feature which distinguishes the Inca roads from those built by anterior civilizations. Another feature of the Inca road is the side wall to keep out the sand drift, to mark the road, and to keep the soldiers, who mostly used it, within the bounds of the road. This was one of the first things noted by the Spaniards. "Along this coast and vales the Caciques and prime men made a road . . . with strong Walls on both sides. . . ." [34] These walls can still be seen in many places marching across the naked desert, which is devoid of everything else save this remarkable road.

The road was marked along its entire length by *topos* (road markers), "with the distance between them," said Cieza de León, who interested himself in such things, "a Castillian league and a half," i.e., 4½ miles. (The Romans, it will be recalled, put up road markers computing the distances in number of miles from the Forum in Rome; more than four thousand have been found.)

There is always a reason behind communications; the Assyrians had roads for conquest, and they built one "making it shine like the light of day"; Darius the Persian built a royal road of stone between Susa and Babylonia, which Herodotus knew; it, too, had stone mile-markers. All roads of any length have always been royal roads and have always had distances marked. There is a line of logic which appears in the road story: all land armies, bound on conquest, had to have roads. Rome was such a state, the Incas were such a people; both had good roads.

The coastal road, twenty-four feet wide along its length of 2,520 miles, was connected by lateral roads with the royal road in the Andes. Eleven such laterals have been explored, but there are doubtless many more. Every valley of consequence had these lateral communications. Many were pre-Inca roads (not as well engineered and lacking the overall master plan of width and construction) and these the Inca engineers either disregarded or else in time-honored fashion built theirs on top of the older ones. At first these were Inca conquest roads, brought down from the Andes into various valleys to overwhelm the enemy by mass attack. One lateral, typical of all of them and the best preserved, is that road which connects the two arterial roads through the valley of Cañete. The Incas had built New Cuzco (now called Incahuasi), the largest coastal structure there, and their road alongside it. They preferred to build their road against the canyon walls; it was chipped away, terraced, and the sides built up with dry-laid stone. Drainage, when the roads reached the wet zone, was important, and it was provided for every rivulet, for here streams and rivers shift their banks with callous ease. They excluded water, that wanton destroyer of communications, completely from their roads. They dealt with water as the Romans did: they outwitted it by making sure that it was not there. This particular Cañete Valley lateral moved up from sea level across and up over a land height of 15,600 feet, stone-paved a good portion of the way, to emerge 125 miles beyond in the valley of Jauja (a great Inca center in the later days of the realm); there it became connected with the royal road of the Andes.

The 3,250-mile-long road commenced beyond Quito, close to the natural bridge across the Ancasmayo river (now Colombia), made its way down the Andean valleys, then over the treeless *puna*, and, as has already been described, moved down toward South America's southern tip. This was, until the nineteenth century, the longest arterial road of history. Its width varies between fifteen and eighteen feet, suggesting that either the coastal twenty-four-foot road was a later development or that the Andean road was a compromise with geography; it was difficult to maintain so wide a road except under unusual circumstances in this perpendicular land. Like its coastal counterpart, it was unpaved except where there was unavoidable water; then it was made into a causeway as at Anta, near to Cuzco, built circa A.D. 1300. It is twenty-four feet wide and *eight miles long* and stands eight feet above the wide-spreading quagmire; it is more or less as Pedro de Cieza de León saw it in 1549, a "great swamp which could only be crossed with difficulty, had the Inca not built a wide-paved causeway."

There are other engineering feats to be seen elsewhere on this long road.

It is not possible to give an exact date for the construction of these roads. All anterior Peruvian cultures had roads. There were those built by the Mochicas, Tiahuanacans, and Chimús, the techniques of which were taken over by the Incas. But as the Romans, so the Incas. In Rome it was the highest honor to build a road and have it carry one's name; Gaius Caesar personally laid down stretches of Roman road, and the Claudian family defrayed expenses for the roads when public funds were not available. The Incas were justly proud of their *Capac-ñan;* many of the names of the reigning Incas are connected with a particular road.

In Peru, to show the logic behind the road of any imperial people (who, landbound, acted similarly), the 2,500-mile road that joined Cuzco to Chile was known as the *Huayna Capacñan,* named after one of the last Incas (died 1527). Often an Inca would build a road wider and longer than his predecessors.

And how were they built? "I will explain," wrote Cieza de León in 1550, "the ease with which they were constructed by the Indians without increasing the death rate or causing excessive labor. When the Inca decided to have one of these famous roads constructed much preparation was unnecessary; it remained but for the Inca to give orders. For then the overseers [i.e., professional roadbuilders] went over the ground, made the trace of the road, and the Indians received instructions to construct the road using local labor. Each province completed the section of the road within its own limits; when it reached the end of their boundary [*ayllu*], it was taken up by others; when it was urgent, all worked at the same time."

It was evident that the builders were instructed from a master plan; the engineering of the bridges, the step road, constructed when perpendicular mountains were to be crossed, drainage, and terracing show general uniformity throughout this long stretch of road.

Although the road was wide, it was not designed for vehicular traffic, and it is very doubtful that, without draft animals, and in this upside-down land, it would have done them much good, even if they had had the wheel. This type of terrain was not fitted, in the mountains at least, for wheeled traffic. Then, why so wide a road?

The empire, for economical reasons, did not need so elaborate a network of roads since most of the provinces had considerable economic independence; for the north-south axis such a road designed for pure commerce was superfluous. In the main they were roads of conquest. Once a territory was conquered, the roads were important for control over the newly annexed territory. Prescott was correct when he wrote: "Not an insurrectionary movement could occur, not an invasion on the remotest frontier, before the tidings were conveyed to the capital and the imperial armies were on the march across the magnificent roads to suppress it. . . ."

Since the object of battle was to win, roads were built to get the warriors into battle in the fastest possible time. This was the *reason* for the Inca's roads.

On the high places along the road, the Incas, following ancient customs, placed *apachetas* (*apa*, "burden," *cheta*, "depositor"). Still to be seen in some places, they were propitiatory cairns formed of small rocks of about hand size. As travelers passed along the road, heavily laden, they placed a stone on the *apacheta* as a symbol of the burden, "and so they left their tiredness behind." [66] This road feature, which has nothing to do with engineering, is mentioned be-

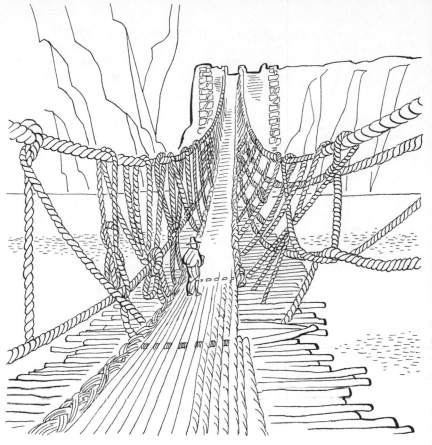

154. *The Apurimac chaca—the bridge that crossed the Apurimac River. Known in literature as* The Bridge of San Luis Rey. *It was one of the greatest engineering feats of the Incas. Although the fiber cables had to be changed every two years, the bridge survived from 1350 until 1890. Drawn from a daguerrotype taken by E. George Squier in 1865.*

cause the Persians did the same along their roads: ". . . Darius came to another river, the Artiscus . . . here he indicated a certain spot where every man in the army was ordered to deposit a stone as he passed by. This was done with the result that when Darius moved on he left great hills of stones behind him." Thus Herodotus.

 Bridges 28

T HE BRIDGE, an integral development of the road, and the little brother of the road, was one of the proudest of Inca achievements. So sacred the bridge that death was decreed for any who tampered with one.

There were many types of bridges: suspension, pontoon, canti-

155. *Hanging bridge over the Rio Pampas. Redrawn from E. George Squier, Peru, 1877.*

lever; clapper types (for crossing small streams), permanent and of stone slabs. All had their special names, but the generic name for bridge was *chaca*. The greatest of these *chacas* was the one that crossed the formidable gorge and river of the Apurimac. It has entered literary immortality as *The Bridge of San Luis Rey;* it was the greatest and without doubt the most outstanding example of native engineering known in the Americas.

When the Incas broke out of the traditional territory that was Inca, they first had to bridge the Apurimac River in order to be able to move northward. This occurred circa A.D. 1350 and the bridge was built by the Lord-Inca Roca.

To describe it (since it was carefully studied by the von Hagen Expedition) [209] is to describe most of the bridges of this type (of which more than forty large ones, and no less than a hundred smaller ones, bridged the chasms along the route of the royal roads of the Incas).

The limitations: the Andean Indians had no wood readily available; they did not know the arch; they knew and often used the cantilever type of bridge, as for the stone bridge of Carabaya (see Plate XLVII), but this could only be used to bridge rivers not much more than forty feet in width; so without arch or wood, they perfected the suspension bridge. They reversed the arch through suspension cables, for depending as it does on the principles of gravity, pressure, and weight, the arch is earthbound and passive. The Incas reversed the arch curve and gave it wings—and it became the hanging bridge. First in construction—the cables; those of this particular bridge were accurately measured by an American in 1864; they were 148 feet long (add an additional forty feet for imbedding). They were as thick as a man's body, plaited and twisted as rope cables are, made in fact from the same material as modern rope is—the *cabuya* (a plant related to the *agave*, the fleshy-leaved century plant). The cables were spun at the edge of the river to be bridged (it was the technique of spinning steel cables at the place of construction that

156. *The overseer of the bridges, as redrawn from Felipe Guamán Poma de Ayala circa 1565. The first illustration ever made of an Inca bridge. It is a good representation of the stone structures built to hold the fiber suspension cables.*

John Roebling introduced for the first time in the building of the Brooklyn Bridge), and then the cables were brought across to the other side. They were then buried deep in the earth and held by six wooden beams ("as thick as oxen" says Garcilaso "the Inca"), then raised onto tall stone pillars which supported the cables. The action was repeated on the other side. Three other cables, tied to the base of the stone towers, formed the "floor" of the bridge; the suspension cables and the floor cables were then held together by additional cables and the floor of the bridge had wooden supports (see Figures 154 and 155). The middle of the bridge sagged from its own weight, and there were no guy ropes added to steady the bridge so that in the high winds it swayed dangerously.

The Apurimac bridge was known as the *huaca chaca*. The early Spaniards crossed it with fright and terror, and their letters are filled with their plaints about it. Yet to the Incas crossing it was no problem. They were not mounted and their llamas did not seem to share the fright of white man's mules.

This bridge, built circa A.D. 1350, endured for over five hundred years; it lasted through the entire Inca regime, was kept up by the Spaniards during the entire colonial epoch (ended 1824), and it continued in use during the republican government. The bridge was finally abandoned about 1890.

Suspension cables were renewed every year. The village of Curahuasi, eighteen miles north, had as part of its *mita* the job of upkeep of the bridge (and it was so traditional that the villagers kept this up until the bridge fell into disuse). This was equally true of all bridges of this type in the Inca realm; the village closest to it was expected to keep it up. At many places along the road there were two suspension bridges, hanging side by side—one for the higher men, the other for the lower, who paid tolls to cross it. Hernando Pizarro, on his march to the coast from the Andes to hurry up the flow of gold for the Inca's ransom, first described an Inca bridge on January 14, 1533, after coming down the step road to Piga, where they came to a canyon (Santa River): "It was spanned by two bridges close together made of network . . . They build a foundation near the water and raise it to a great height, and from one side of the river to the other there are cables . . . thick as a man's thigh. By one of these bridges the common people cross over and a guard *is stationed to receive transit dues* [italics added]." Later on, during

157. *Totora balsa bridge over the outlet of Lake Titicaca. Redrawn from E. George Squier, Peru, 1877.*

their return over another road, at the great city of Huánuco they crossed another bridge, "over a torrential river [the Vizcarro] made of three thick logs and where *there are guards who collect a toll as is customary among these Indians* [italics added]."

Permanent bridges of stone or of wood were used over small streams (many are still to be seen), and where minor traffic did not justify labor expenditure, there was another type, called *oroya*, two cables stretched between stone towers, with a basket attached to one of the cables and drawn to either side by means of additional ropes.

The final bridge type, which also struck the first Spaniards as ingenious, was the balsa pontoon bridge. The most notable was the one that crossed the only river that drains Lake Titicaca. These were built as all pontoon bridges, except that here the pontoons were balsas, straw boats made of *totora* grass. These craft (see Transport, page 553) were placed side by side, linked by a thick cable, which in turn was held by stone towers on the opposite shore; a grass floor was laid over the grass balsa boats. As this type of grass boat becomes water-logged, the pontoons were replaced every two years; it was the duty of the village of Chacamarca ("Bridge Village") to replace these as part of their *mita* (labor tax). This bridge endured for over eight hundred years; it was used until 1875.

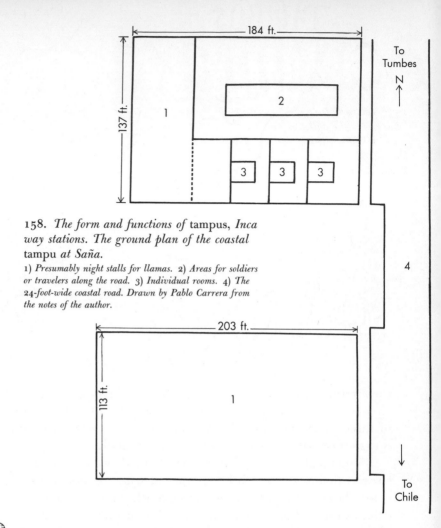

158. *The form and functions of* tampus, *Inca way stations. The ground plan of the coastal tampu at Saña.*

1) *Presumably night stalls for llamas.* 2) *Areas for soldiers or travelers along the road.* 3) *Individual rooms.* 4) *The 24-foot-wide coastal road. Drawn by Pablo Carrera from the notes of the author.*

29 *The* Tampu *Stations*

Two necessary functions *make* a road: one is maintenance (for without it, as the African natives say, "the road dies"); the other is accommodation. All of those historical empires that built roads, Persian, Chinese, or Roman, had a system of post-houses for the accommodation of travelers. The Persians maintained theirs approximately eighteen miles apart, Herodotus affirms, ". . . at intervals along the road are recognized stations with excellent inns . . . over a distance of 94½ *parsangs* [about 330 miles] there are twenty stations . . . and the total of stations or post-houses on the road from Sardis to Susa is 111 . . ."

Along the sides of the Chinese roads, built by the Chou Dynasty

TAMBOS

ᚯCAXAMARCA

ciudad ymezon rreal adonde estagua atagual pay
gaa donde le prendierõ y amatarõ donfrãçisco pizarro —
san migel pueblo tanbo rreal ———
caxapampa pueblo tanbo rreal ———
guamachuco pueblo tanbo rreal ycasas deguaynaca
pac ynga ———
tanbillo ———
tanbo nuebo pueblo tanbo rreal ———

concho couillatanborre

al yminas de plata mezon rreal ———
ciudas pueblo tanbo rreal ———
quiropampa tanbillo ———
pisco pampa pueblo tanbo rreal ———
guancabamba pueblo tanbo rreal ———
guari pueblo tanbo rreal ycasas deguay na capaynga
pincos tanbo rreal ———
quinua tanbillo ———
toparaco tanbo rreal ———
guanoco biejo ylos banos tanbillo casas de topayn
ga yupanqui p deguaynacapacynga ———
runsucancha tanbo rreal ———
ancas mayo tanbo rreal ———
uorau tanbo rreal ———
bombom tanbo rreal puente de cris nexas delyn
ga topaynga yupanqui ———
ninacaca pueblo tanborreal ———
chinchaycocha pueblo tanbo rreal ———
tarma pueblo tanbo rreal ———

desde

159. *List of tambos (tampus)* along the entire Inca highway as given by Felipe Guamán Poma de Ayala. The orthography is Spanish, but the text is Quechua mixed with Spanish. The symbols indicate the type of *tampu* at each stopping place.

(circa 1150 B.C.), the way was spotted with khans along the desert, mountain, and plain; along the imperial highways of the Romans there were *mansiones,* night quarters. One traveled this road without prerogatives or penalties, and one could even purchase an *Itinerari Maritimi* which gave the distances between way stations and the positions of posthouses.

The Inca was also such an empire. They had a system of posthouses, and they were called *tampus:* ". . . there were buildings and storehouses," wrote Pedro de Cieza de León who traveled between 1547 and 1550 along the entire royal road, "at every four-six leagues [twelve to eighteen miles], with great abundance of all provisions that the surrounding districts could supply . . . the overseers [*curacas*] who resided at the chief stations in the provinces took special care that the natives kept these *tampus* well provisioned."

551

Tampus were official. Since no one moved on the roads without permission, it follows that they could only use the way stations as part of their official journey. The distances between them depended on the terrain; in the mountains, if the going was perpendicular, they were twelve miles apart, a convenient day's journey upward; if on level ground, eighteen miles apart; if in the desert, the distance between water (for here water decides everything).

They were utilitarian, and so were built of rough field stone or adobe. Some of them consisted of a single large structure, 100 by 300 feet, others had a series of smaller rooms opening on a larger corral where the llamas were kept. On the coast, particularly at Chala in southern Peru in the midst of the sun-drenched desert, there

160. *The symbols of the three different types of* tampus *as listed by Felipe Guamán Poma de Ayala (see Figure 159).* A) *Royal* tampus *represented by a house.* B) *Lesser* tampus *for ordinary Indians.* C) *Auxiliary halting places represented by a circle.*

were a series of small rooms with stone-lined underground storage chambers.

Tampus were kept up by the local *ayllu* as part of its labor tax; each community was expected to see that the road approaching its section was in constant repair (women spun their wool as they walked so the roads had to be well metaled), and that the *tampus* were in order and the storage bins filled. Dried corn, potatoes, sun-dried llama meat, and dehydrated potatoes keep indefinitely. In time of war, when fifty thousand or more warriors might move along the road at one time, advance notice was given and abundant food stores were placed at the military's disposal—a far better commissary than that which faced the revolutionary forces of Simón Bolívar when in 1824 he made his passage of the Andes to attack the forces of imperial Spain. Then six thousand live steers for nine thousand soldiers had to be sent ahead by the Spaniards; for every hundred men, one bullock per day.[204]

There were various types of these *tampus:* those called "royal," to distinguish them from those of the ordinary kind, were reserved for the Lord-Inca or his governors when they made their inspection tours of the empire. In a list of such way stations made by the half-caste Felipe Guamán Poma de Ayala, the Ayacucho-born (1534?) chronicler of things Inca, one can see how he has distinguished them: the royal *tampus* are indicated by a building, others of less conse-quence by a cross, while the auxiliary, those placed in the intervals of long distance, he has marked with a circle, and he calls these by the diminutive *tambillos*. We also know much about their operation because the Spanish officials in 1543, only ten years after the con-quest, had a group of Spanish officers make an inspection tour over a great part of the ancient road. Out of this came a report entitled "The Ordering of the Halting Stations [*Tampus*], the Distance of One to the Other, the Methods of the Native Cargo-bearers, and the Obligations of the Respective Spanish Overloads of Said Tambos," done in Cuzco on May 31, 1543; it reads something like ancient Greece's *Manual of Road Repairs*. It was the first of its kind in the Americas.

 Transport   *30*

WOMAN was man's oldest beast of burden.
She was the carrier, allowing the man to be free to fight. This was true in the beginnings of every old culture. The Peruvians, the Indians Inca or pre-Inca who lived within the orbit of geographical Peru, were the only primitive Americans to develop an auxiliary to women or man for transport; this was the domesti-cated llama.

The llama was principally employed to transport cargo, either for war or commerce; as many as twenty-five thousand might be sent on a single convoy. Averaging eighty pounds of cargo each, they could travel about twelve miles a day. Man can outlast any animal, including the horse, especially in this up-and-down world of Peru, and can carry more than a llama and go longer distances; thus transport on the roads was shared between man and llama. The llama was not a draft animal. There is no record of it having been so used, although it can be mounted and there are many pre-Inca vases showing crippled Indians riding llamas; riding, however, was not general. Since they had no draft animals they also had no wheel, and moreover no American Indian (no matter where) had even the idea of the wheel in any of its forms (the architectural arch, the potter's wheel, or the rotary quern), and for good reason: early man migrated in a series of long-drawn waves into the Americas at the Neolithic period, before the invention of the wheel. The wheel seems to have evolved and then spread from one source within the rim of the Fertile Crescent, that section of the Middle East from which so many "new" things came. The wheel was present in India as early as 3000 B.C. The caravans which arrived there found roads already built for them; Alexander the Great was amazed at brick-laid roads made for cargo and shaded by all manner of fruit-bearing trees. Yet the idea of the wheel took a thousand years to penetrate the regions beyond. Man living out the Iron Age in Britain did not use the wheel until 2000 B.C.

It is, then, quite understandable why the American cultures never had it. First, they had no draft animals, and then they had migrated into the vacuum of the New World at a time when man, in general, still relied on his own back, or better, that of his woman, for carrying. The foot was the denominator of travel.

The litter as a means of transport seems to be world-wide. Some of the oldest illustrations of Mesopotamia, for example a relief from Ur dated 2500 B.C., shows bearers carrying a litter. Models of palanquins from Crete are dated 1600 B.C., so it is not surprising to find that the Incas were carried along their royal roads in litters. The use of litters was confined, however, to the highest nobility.

"When the Incas visited the provinces of their empire . . . they traveled in great majesty," says Cieza de León, "seated in rich litters . . . enriched with gold and silver." There were curtains to be drawn during long journeys or to protect against sun or rain, ". . . round the litter marched the Lord-Inca's guard . . . in front went five thousand slingers." There were eighty litter-bearers, men

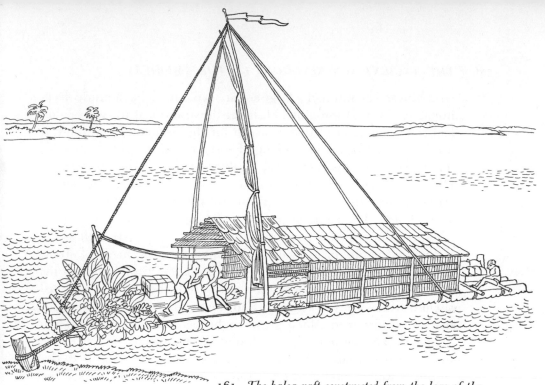

161. *The balsa raft constructed from the logs of the genus Ochroma found outside of Peru. This was the largest type of vessel known to the Peruvians. It is pre-Inca. From a drawing by Alexander von Humboldt made in 1803. Redrawn by Alberto Beltrán.*

drawn from the rugged Rucana peoples, clothed in special blue livery; they ran beside the litter in teams and took turns carrying. The royal road even had resting platforms where litter-bearers could pause on steep ascents.

Water transport was minor for such a thoroughly land-based people. The Incas had no concept of the sea, it was a *hatun-cocha,* a "great lake." This was one of the fundamental errors of Inca psychology in their war with the Spaniard: the Incas could not even conceive of anyone getting reinforcements from the sea. They did not fear the sea; they ignored it. It is this basic and fundamental mental block that makes historically untenable the specious arguments of those who took the *Kon-Tiki* voyage. The Incas were, in the words of Philip Ainsworth Means, "utter landlubbers."

The largest vessel known in the Americas was the Peruvian balsa raft. The logs of the balsa tree (*Ochroma*), which grows in humid Ecuador beyond the confines of the Inca realm, formed the raft. These logs, sun-dried and naturally buoyant, were lashed together with vines. The raft had a large square sail, aft of that a crude deck-house (see von Humboldt's classical illustration of it), with palm-leaf roof, and abaft of that a hearth for the preparation of food. It used the centerboard for tacking of sorts; it had no pseudo bow.[127] There is, as Means remarked, "a conspicuous lexical poverty in Quechua or any other pre-Inca coastal language on sailing, and is a reflection of the general ineptitude of the people for seamanship as a whole." The name for rafts was *huampus*.

In addition to this large raft, the coastal people (as well as the mountain people on navigable lakes) had a vessel, made of straw, called by the Spaniards (with no little humor) "little horses of the sea" in reference to the way they were used: the Indians mounted them astride. These *huampus* (also now called balsas) were made from a tubular reed which grows eight feet tall and a half inch in diameter. This swamp sedge is found at sea level as well as in the higher Andean lakes. To describe the coastal rush boat is to de-scribe as well its highland imitation. The reed, which grows in the shore swamps, is dried and fashioned into four cigar-shaped bundles. Two of these bundles, tied with grass rope, form the prow. The other two, laid on top and off center, form its sides, and it is thus a vessel with tapering prow and square-cut stern. The sail, operating like a venetian blind, propels the boat; when there is no wind, the paddle or punt is used. Generally these boats, as shown by the old illus-trations taken from Chimú or Mochica pottery, showed one, or at most three, fishermen in the boat, but on the surface of Lake Titi-caca rush boats were made sufficiently large to hold forty people. These boats were also used for the floats of the Inca pontoon bridges.

Now, while rush boats are ingenious, they were by no means unique. Peoples of other cultures who lived in treeless lands, or wherever wood was not readily available, made more or less the same type of boat. The Egyptians, as one can see from the relief on the tomb of Saqqara (dated 2500 B.C.), depict workmen making a rush boat from the stems of the papyrus. Another sculpture from the tomb of Deir el-Bahri of the same epoch shows another papyrus reed boat under sail using a bipod mast (a type still used by the people of Lake Titicaca). Moreover, present-day tribes, the Dinka on the White Nile, for example, use boats made from the stems of the ambatch reeds. All these similar cultural traits, as has been consistently shown in this book, are chance parallels reached inde-

pendently by people who live under similar geographical conditions; it shows how limited in imagination the human animal really is.[267]

Ne plus ultra—go no farther—was the psychological barrier that stood at the entrance of the Mediterranean into the Atlantic, and for a thousand years it kept man from venturing beyond the confines of that continent. The sea was far more of a barrier to the natives in America than to Eurasians. So fundamental was this ingrained concept that the Inca could not even conceive an invasion from the sea. Dr. George Kubler put it this way: "That which Atahualpa [the Inca captured by the Spaniards in the heart of his realm by only 130 foot soldiers and 40 mounted men] fatally misunderstood was the ability of the Spaniards to receive sea-borne reinforcements. In his experience and that of his dynastic predecessors no coastal society or state could expand beyond the wishes of a unified and powerful highland group since the ocean at their backs constituted an impassable barrier *from which no aid could come* [italics added]." [99]

It was the Inca's fatal mistake.

 CHASQUI: *The Courier*   *31*

SINCE MAN'S earliest beginnings he has attempted communications; he has shouted from hill to hill, sent smoke signals, beaten drums, tried relays of men, of horses, and carrier pigeons; he has fired cannons, but until the telegraph was invented no system of communication was as rapid as the *chasqui* courier system perfected by the Incas. It is true that other cultures had developed the relay system. That of the Persians is best known, for Herodotus himself wrote: "There is nothing in the world which travels faster than these Persian couriers, the whole idea is a Persian invention . . ."; he explains how the mounted riders were stationed along the road at intervals in posthouses and then messages passed in relays from rider to rider.

The Romans, more systematized in their communication system,

relied on relays (similar to the pony-express rider of the western United States), yet even then at Rome's height (and over finely laid roads), one hundred miles a day was considered very good time. A letter traveling a thousand miles from Rome reached its designation in forty-seven days; this was considered fair time. That was the fastest communication man had ever enjoyed. With the decline of Rome such speed was never again reached until relatively recent times. That is, with the exception of the Incas.

"The Incas [again Pedro de Cieza de León is writing] invented a system of posts which was the best that could be thought of or imagined . . . and so well was this running performed that in a short time they [the Lord-Incas] knew at a distance of three hundred, five hundred or even eight hundred leagues [1 Spanish league = 2½ to 3 miles] what occurred . . . it may be certain that the news could not have been conveyed with greater speed on swift horses."

These distances seemed incredible. Yet almost all early chroniclers agree that the *chasquis* could run in relays between Quito and Cuzco, a distance of 1,250 miles, in five days—and this at an altitude ranging between 6,000 to 17,000 feet! This means that the runners had to run an average of some 250 miles a day, two and a half times faster than the Roman couriers on their metaled roads. Even fresh sea fish was said to have been relayed daily to the Lord-Inca, and the shortest distance to Cuzco from the sea was 130 miles. These statements have been alternately quoted and questioned. And with good reason, for it seemed incredible that men could run in such high altitudes without collapsing from anoxia—shortness of breath. However, the work of the von Hagen Expedition, experimenting with known and marked distances along the still extant highway, proved that the Indians could run a 6½-minute mile, and in a relay system cover this distance in the stated time.[209]

Speed was essential to the Incas. The distances were so enormous that uprisings could only be curbed by the swift marching of warriors to the center of infection. Speed, naturally, is not civilization, but speed does cancel space, and the abilities of the *chasquis* to bring notice of any invasion or uprising was the prime factor in keeping the empire intact. The much quoted comment of the Confederate General Forrest, "I git thar fustest with the mostest," was precisely an Inca point of view. The time-space equation added up to the *chasqui* system; the Inca conquered space by eliminating it.

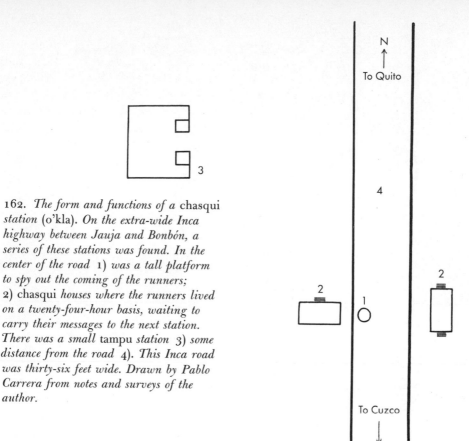

162. *The form and functions of a* chasqui *station* (o'kla). *On the extra-wide Inca highway between Jauja and Bonbón, a series of these stations was found. In the center of the road* 1) *was a tall platform to spy out the coming of the runners;* 2) chasqui *houses where the runners lived on a twenty-four-hour basis, waiting to carry their messages to the next station. There was a small* tampu *station* 3) *some distance from the road* 4). *This Inca road was thirty-six feet wide. Drawn by Pablo Carrera from notes and surveys of the author.*

In addition to the *tampus* built along the highway there were the huts (*o'kla*) for the *chasquis* (pronounced "chas-ki"); rudely made and large enough to hold two men, with bed and hearth, they were placed approximately one and a half miles apart. Trained runners, with a special badge of office, waited the coming of the runners from the next station. These couriers were furnished by the village through which a particular section of the Inca road passed. They were trained from earliest youth to run at these high altitudes; games that involved racing and running were part of their pageantry. "The young sons of the nobility," said an observant Jesuit of the sixteenth century, "used to race one another up Huanacauri hill and to practice running; this has been and still is [he was writing in 1570] a widely used custom among the Indians." With his abnormally developed lungs, the result of living in the high altitudes, the *chasqui* fitted all the requirements of a true athlete and could run at full speed at heights where other unacclimatized runners could not.

163. *The* chasqui, *drawn from life. This is a post-conquest drawing. He blows a conch shell to announce his arrival. In his hand he carries a mace and a slingshot for defense. Redrawn from Felipe Guamán Poma de Ayala.*

It is essential to know that these courier stations were erected within one or one and a half miles of each other, and that the *chasqui* ran only between these points. "In each house," said Cieza, who actually saw hundreds of such places, "there were two Indians stationed [on a twenty-four-hour service] with provisions. The *chasqui* then ran with great speed without stopping, *each one for his half league* [italics added] or mile and a half." Tests made by the von Hagen Expedition, with natives running between those courier stations still standing, determined that they ran on average a 6½-minute mile (present record for the mile at writing is 3:54.5). It has been proven fully that the *chasquis* could run some 250 miles a day using these relays. They could and did cover the distance of 1,250 miles, that is from Quito to Cuzco, in five days. The system of *chasqui* runners was so efficient that the Spanish colonial governments retained it until 1800. There are many Spanish records in the National Archives of Peru which prove this in detail.

The *chasquis* worked on fifteen-day shifts. Their duty was to watch the road for the arrival of runners coming from either direction. When the runner arrived he gave a verbal message, along with the knot-string recordkeeper, and then with this in hand the next courier made the run to the next station at top speed. He was punished with death if he did not transmit the message or divulged it to any other than the next *chasqui*.

"With such secrecy did the runners keep their messages," writes Cieza, who no doubt witnessed many times the attempt to force out of them the contents of their messages, "that neither entreaty nor menace could extort it from them."

 QUIPU: *The Knot-String Record—* *Inca Literature*

32

THE *quipu* (pronounced "kee-poo"), which means simply "knot," and which the couriers passed from hand to hand, was as close to writing as man got in South America; still no matter how much writers have strained their imagination, the *quipu is not writing,* and, moreover, the device is not even an Inca invention. It is simply a mnemonic device to aid the memory and its knotted strings are based on a decimal count. Too, all *quipus* had to be *accompanied by a verbal comment,* without which the meaning would have been unintelligible.

The *quipus* have been thoroughly studied and described.[108] The *quipu* was a simple and ingenious device; it consisted of a main cord (ranging from a foot to many feet in length) and from this cord dangled smaller colored strings which had at intervals knots (*quipus*) tied into them. It has been shown most conclusively by those who have studied them that the strings were used to record numbers in a decimal system, and that there was a symbol for zero, that is, a string with an "empty space"; this allowed them to count to over ten thousand. Knots were tied into the string to represent numbers; if a governor was visiting a newly conquered tribe and the Inca wanted to know how many able-bodied Indians there were, these were counted and the number tied into the *quipu*. It may be that there was a certain symbol or heraldic device for "men," but if there was one it is not known. There was attached to the governor an official knot-string-record interpreter known as a *quipu-camayoc,* whose duty it was to tie in the records. He then had to remember which *quipu* recorded what; numbers of men, women, llamas, etc., in the newly conquered lands. When a governor had an audience with the Inca he could, with this knot-string record plus the "rememberer," recite the facts as gathered. It was a surprisingly efficacious method of counting and one that their Spanish conquerors much admired.[138]

The different colors of the wool threads apparently had meaning; the mode of intertwining the knot or twisting the thread or the distance of the knots from each other gave nuance. With these *quipus* the Inca had the numbers of tribes, llamas, women, old people.[4] Beyond mere numbers the colors, the smaller threads, the green, blue, white, black and red colors, could, it is believed, express meanings and even, it is asserted, abstract ideas. When Pedro de Cieza de León in 1549 talked to some of the old "rememberers" they explained that these "knots counted from one to ten and ten to a hundred, and from a hundred to a thousand. Each ruler of a province was provided with accountants, and by these knots they kept account of what tribute was to be paid . . . and with such accuracy that not so much as a pair of sandals would be missing.

"I was incredulous respecting this system of counting and although I heard it described, I held the greater part of the story to be fabulous. But when I was in Marca-vilca, in the province of Xauxa [i.e., central Peru near to present-day Huancayo] I asked one of them to explain the *quipu* in such a way that my curiosity would be satisfied . . . the *quipu-camayoc* proceeded to make the thing clear to me . . . he knew all that had been delivered to Francisco Pizarro, without fault or omission, since his arrival in Peru. Thus I saw all the accounts for the gold, the silver, the clothes, the corn, the llamas and other things, so that in truth I was astonished."

Like all preliterate peoples, they had good memories. While the *quipu* itself could not be read without verbal comment to make all the entanglements and knots understandable, it did (this much is certain) go beyond mere compilation of statistics; it was used as a supplement for the memory of historical events.

When a Lord-Inca died and his burial ceremonies were over, a council of *amautas* was called into session to decide "what of his memory should be forever preserved."[34] Having decided this among themselves, they composed their history and then called in the *quipu-camayocs* and gave them the official history; then those skilled in rhetoric and the use of words—and they knew how to narrate the event in regular order like ballad singers—were brought in, and *thus they were instructed* what to say concerning the deceased Inca, and if they treated of wars, they sang in proper order of the many battles he had fought.

The wholesale destruction of the "archives" of *quipus* by the crusading padres in the seventeenth century (in their zeal to stamp out idolatry, believing naively that the *quipus* "were books of the devil" [167]) and the gradual dying out of the "rememberers," the interpreters of the *quipus,* were the twin disasters to Andean history. With the destruction of one and the passing of the other there was lost that history of the whole Andean area which now can be bridged only by archaeology. The *quipus* now found in graves tell us nothing; they are only lifeless strings.

They were obviously neither alphabet nor hieroglyphs, though the amusing book written by a baroque Italian, Prince Sansevero, of Naples, [165] in the eighteenth century, in which he illustrated Peruvian *quipus* with all forms of glyphs attached to them, claimed for the *quipu* an "alphabet" and even claimed that he was able to read them. Obviously faked, as Johann Wincklemann, the famous German art historian, well knew, such an interpretation is impossible except for the lunatic fringe of archaeologic enthusiasts who read about the lost continent of Mu and its minor appendages. It is now fully established, as it has long been surmised, that *no South American people possessed writing*.

Yet history was transmitted with their aid. "Suppose," wrote Padre Calancha in 1638, "that a functionary wishes to express that before Manco Capac, the *first Inca,* there was neither king, chief, cult or religion; that in the *fourth* year of his reign this emperor subdued *ten* provinces, whose conquest cost him a certain number of men; that in one of them he took a *thousand* units of gold, and *three thousand* units of silver, and that in thanksgiving for the victory he had celebrated a festival in honor of the god, Sun." [27] All this, then, would be done on a *quipu,* tying knots in the decimal divisions, using certain colored knots symbolizing "gold," "Inca," or "Sun."

There is no lack of confirmation from contemporary sources of the ability of the professional knot-string readers to interpret them, "with as much ease," said Cieza de León, "as we in our language understood from paper and ink." An intriguing fellow, Pedro Sarmiento de Gamboa, navigator, warrior, and executioner (he exterminated the surviving members of the royal Inca line), confirmed the use of the *quipus* as histories. He was asked by his viceroy to write an official history of the Incas, which was to be an apologia for the Spanish conquest. He started in 1569 by assembling all those chieftains who knew of the past Inca history and took down what they told him. He explained in the beginning of his own history how the "barbarians of this Land" transmitted history one to another, from fathers to sons, "persisting in the repetition until it was fixed in the memory—history, exploits, antiquities, the number of tribes, towns and provinces, days, months, years, deaths, destructions, fortresses and leaders, the number of cords which they called *quipus*. . . ."

In this way and manner Inca history was conveyed. First it was selected, then memorized by means of the *quipus,* then given to the troubadours to chant, as Pedro de Cieza de León noted: ". . . they used a kind of folk-poems and romances by means of which they would retain a memory of events and without forgetting them."

This was the manner in which the Incas made a "selective manipulation of history," as discussed earlier in this book. They blotted out whole generations of racial memory of the tribes which had preceded them so that they could pose as *the* culture bearers. This system began with the Lord-Inca called Pachacuti ("crowned" Inca in 1438). After he had rebuilt Cuzco he called together the professional *quipu-camayocs.* He had them tell him their histories. Then he had these painted on the wall in chronological order, ". . . and into this room no one could enter except the Lord-Inca." That which was distasteful to the Inca was eliminated from official memory—the *quipu* did not speak of it, the romancers did not sing of it; in this way much of pre-Inca history was eliminated. Such a performance is not wholly incredible. The Soviet Encyclopedia today can eliminate well-known personalities by sending to its subscribers new pages to replace its censored pages. People disappear from life and become, in the Orwellian phrase, "unpersons." During World War II, 100,000 Caucasians of the Kabard and Balkar mountain-dwelling tribesmen were deported as alleged "collaborators." Their names were dropped, their literature suppressed,

164. *A woman of the Quechua tribe in her dress of the Inca period. She beats a drum. Redrawn from Felipe Guamán Poma de Ayala.*

their whereabouts kept secret; only recently have they emerged.

The lack of writing in any form among the South Americans is at once a puzzle and a problem; it renders the chronology of the cultures exceedingly difficult and makes us fall back on an oral history and archaeology. It is a cultural hiatus, almost without parallel. The Aztecs had pictographic writing and were arriving at the stage of syllabic phonetics when the Spaniards arrived. The Maya glyphic writing, far earlier than the Aztec, and far more advanced, was sufficiently perfected as to work out a very involved calendar; they have left behind a corpus of glyphic inscriptions which will occupy Maya scholars for many years to come. Even the North American Plains Indians had a form of rebus writing which by puns, positions, color, and crude drawings conveyed ideas. There was no such thing in South America; and unbelievably no writing among the Incas, who needed it most of all. There has been an attempt by Señor Rafael Larco of Trujillo, Peru, to interpret the "beans" painted on Mochica pottery as a glyphic language. This study, more extensive than any published, has been given short shrift by the professionals. It needs to be carried further; beyond this we are in the same position as the first Spaniards who said *the Incas had no form of writing.*

One scholar dismisses the need for writing, saying, "The fact is that the Andean peoples possessed substitutes for writing which were so satisfactory that they probably never felt the need for anything more elaborate." [155] Such a conclusion is praise of intellectual castration; it belies the whole of cultural history. For of all discoveries and inventions, writing gave us the continuity of what we are pleased to call civilization; even the cave man used pictographs, the first writing forms, and as man became Man and formed himself into societies with cities, tribute, and trade, writing became part of life. The need forced the invention; writing was a *must* if only for economic reasons.

The Sumerians, who lived in that Fertile Crescent of the Middle East, seemed to have invented it circa 4000 B.C., and it then spread. The Phoenicians developed the alphabet sometime before 1000 B.C., and it became a cultural lever. "Give me but a place to stand and I can move the world," said Archimedes. Writing did just that. Our knowledge of the Romans would be very vague if they, like the Incas, had had no form of writing. Dated Roman coins found in India suggest their presence there; outside the purlieus of the Roman frontier, in northern Germany or Denmark, the presence of dated coins tells the approximate date of Roman conquests; their literature supplies the details. Literature *fixed* historical traditions; it strengthened social cohesion. Would it not be impossible to know the Greeks without their literature, or the Romans without their interminable reports, or the Egyptians without their long and involved personal histories as told in the hieratic glyphs?

Still if the Incas had no writing, they had a form of literature, which has come down to us by oral tradition. Yet it soon becomes obvious that since there was no writing, there is no "pure" literature; the literature has undergone the alchemy of change, in translation, in meter, even in idea and symbol. It is, however, quite obvious that a people who were so saturated with symbol and pageantry would have lyrical verse, and although unrhymed it at least was cadenced, for it is in rhythm that one remembers best. Those fragments of Inca "literature" that have come down to us were gathered by some of the earlier writers, notably Inca-Spaniard Garcilaso de la Vega (who affected the verse and ideas of seventeenth-century Spain) as well as others. These cadences were remembered from the professional bards (*haravecs*), who chanted them at festivals or before the court. This particular verse, said Garcilaso, surnamed "the Inca," was preserved by the *quipu*. (He does not say how, and this is not surprising in view of the limitations.)

> *Beautiful Princess,*
> *thy dear brother*
> *thy cup*
> *is now breaking.*
> *So for this there is thunder,*
> *lightning, lightning*
> *thunderbolts falling.*
> *But Princess,*
> *thy water*
> *dropping, rains*
> *where sometimes also*
> *there will be hail,*
> *there will be snow.*
> *The maker of the earth,*
> *Pachacamac*
> *Viracocha,*
> *for this duty*
> *has placed thee,*
> *has created thee.*

The ideas, the cadence, the repetition, the imagery, is decidedly Inca. And from Felipe Guamán Poma de Ayala, an Inca-Spaniard of the same epoch as Garcilaso, comes this cadenced prose. He did not see the courts of Spain, and was not seduced by the gilded ennui of Spanish poets: what he gives here would seem reasonably pure, reasonably Inca. As an Indian woman plants her corn she chants:

> *Pity my tears,*
> *Pity my anguish.*
> *The most distressed*
> *Of your children,*
> *The most distressed*
> *Of your servants*
> *Implores you with tears,*

> *Grant the miracle*
> *Of water, your own,*
> *Grant the gift of rain*
> *To this unfortunate*
> *Person,*
> *To this creature*
> *You have created.*

Another from the same source—a touching love song:

> *To this my song,*
> *You shall sleep,*
> *In the dead of night*
> *I shall come.*

There are others, which the late Philip Ainsworth Means selected as undoubtedly coming from the official festivals. This has all the majesty of ritual:

> *Viracocha, Lord of the Universe.*
> *Whether male or female*
> *Anyway, commander of warmth and generation*
> *Being one who*
> *Even with his spittle can work magic.*
> *Where are you?*
> *Would that you would not hide from this your son,*
> *He may be above,*
> *He may be below,*
> *Or alight in the sky,*
> *Where is his council seat,*
> *Hear me!*

There were many others, and many of them have been collected and published as "Quechua poetry,"[102] but all are suspect for the very reason that without written literature no one is in a position to challenge the translator as to the source. So when a verse begins as though an Indian is weeping for his dead wife:

> *What cruel land has buried*
> *Her who was my only joy?*

and continues in such lyrical sentiments as:

> *I scrabble the tomb where she sleeps*
> *While my tears flow like rain, endlessly,*
> *Thus should the earth be softened,*

you may be instantly aware that this is not Quechua poetry; it is modern contrivance.

The best known Inca dramatic piece—the drama of *Ollantay*—was long thought to have been "pure Inca" and was acted in some of the semicircular arenas thought to have been Inca theaters.* The place itself is historic; Ollantaytambo (see Figure 148) lies twenty-four miles from Cuzco in the valley of Yucay on the upper Urubamba River. Early in the fifteenth century Ollantaytambo was ruled by semi-independent chieftains. They disputed with the Inca, who sacked and destroyed the original site and rebuilt the formidable place—still to be seen. The Incas were still building it when the Spaniards arrived in 1536 and continued to build it even after their revolt and the siege of Cuzco later that year. The name Ollantaytambo means "posthouse of Ollantay," and there is a famous local legend which identifies Ollantay as a hero of ancient days who had a tragic love affair with an Inca princess. According to the story, Ollantay was a feudal noble in the days of the empire who asked for the hand of an Inca princess. The emperor was angered by such presumption and put his daughter in a house of Chosen Women (convent). Ollantay violated the convent to visit her, was caught, fled for his life, and raised a revolt against the emperor. After a frontal attack failed, his fortress was taken by treachery. We do not know whether this story was already being told before the Spanish conquest or not; others like it probably were, however.

When, in the middle of the eighteenth century, the last of the Inca nobility were preparing the great national revolt of 1780, the story of Ollantay was made into a play written in the Inca language by a sympathizer with the Inca cause—probably Antonio Valdez of Tinta, Peru.

The play treats the old legend somewhat freely, amplifying the

---

* A number of older writers believed that *Ollantay* was a pre-conquest composition, but this view is now thoroughly discredited. The English translation of 1871 was made by Sir Clements Markham; it was reissued as an appendix to his work *The Incas of Peru* in 1910. This play is perhaps the best-known example of Inca literature; it has been translated into Spanish (1868), English (1871), German (1875), French (1878), and Czech (1917–18). In 1941 the Argentine writer Ricardo Rojas published a modified version of it which was a notable stage success in Buenos Aires.

love story and providing it with a happy ending. It is not a particularly good play, but certainly no worse than most of its European contemporaries, and it contains a few very fine dramatic passages and some traditional songs. The dramatic style follows the Spanish cloak-and-dagger comedy pattern, as Ricardo Palma, the famed Peruvian writer of the *tradiciones* of Peru, has pointed out.

The drama opens with a colloquy between Ollantay and his servant, Piqui Chaqui ("Flea Foot"), who are walking in the narrow streets of Cuzco:

> OLLANTAY: *Flea Foot, from her house thou comest;*
> *Hast thou seen my Cusi Coyllur?*

> PIQUI CHAQUI: *Now may our lord the Sun protect me!*
> *Knowest thou not it is forbidden?*
> *Hast thou no fear of royal justice*
> *Since she is the Inca's daughter?*

So it transpires that Ollantay, the military hero of the hour, is in love with the favorite daughter of the Inca. The introduction prepares the listener to understand the punishment that Ollantay must face if he insists upon making love to Cusi Coyllur ("Happy Star").

The Inca brushes aside Ollantay's lovesickness and insists that he follow the laws of the Incas; he puts Happy Star in the house of the Chosen Women (a bit too late as the rest of the story reveals); he rebukes Ollantay. The hero, angered at this, retires to his fortress at Ollantaytambo, pours out his grievance to his followers, and raises the whole province in rebellion against the Inca:

> OLLANTAY: *From this day, beloved Cuzco,*
> *As thy foe I must be counted.*
> *Thy warm breast will feel my talons*
> *And I'll tear thy heart and feed it*
> *To the vultures and the condors.*
> *Thy great Inca is a liar,*
> *Is a traitor and deceiver,*
> *Heaping shame upon my Antis.*
> *On the hill of Sacsahuamán*
> *Thou shalt see the cloud assemble:*
> *Thousands upon tens of thousands*
> *Of my spearmen stoutly shielded.*

> *Then the fire will lick thy rooftops,*
> *In thy blood thou'lt find thy slumber.*

And so to war.

The old Inca, who bears the scars of a thousand battles, smiles at this minor rebellion until he hears that his daughter Happy Star, while in the house of the Chosen Women, has given birth to a daughter called Ima Sumac ("How Beautiful"). With that, the Inca tosses his daughter into an underground cave and sends his general Rumiñaui ("Stony Eye") off to do battle with Ollantay.

However, Ollantay prepares an ambush and Rumiñaui is lucky to escape to Cuzco with his life. He arrives at the capital to find Pachacuti dead and his son Topa Inca Yupanqui on the throne. To redeem his lost honor, Rumiñaui volunteers to capture Ollantay by treachery. He mutilates his own face and presents himself to Ollantay as a fugitive. The hero, overgenerous, receives him with open arms, and Rumiñaui persuades him to hold a great feast. When the whole army is properly drunk, Rumiñaui ties up Ollantay and betrays the fortress to the Inca's men.

The newly "crowned" Lord-Inca, however, does not feel his father's enmity toward the lovers. He pardons Ollantay and frees Happy Star and How Beautiful to join him in romantic embrace. The drama closes as the Inca faces the audience and declaims:

> *I decree an end to sorrow,*
> *To your joy I add my blessing.*
> *In thine arms thy wife is folded,*
> *From death's shadow thou art free.**

Ollantay cannot be regarded as Inca except in its theme, yet the Incas did perform dramatic presentations of sorts, with mimes, dancers, hunchbacks, and bards, followed by chanting recitations of dramatic history by the *amauta* wisemen. Padre José de Acosta, who traveled in the realm of the Incas when traditions were still alive, tells of seeing "plaies in the manner of combats . . . I have also seene divers sortes of dancers wherein they did counterfait and represent certaine trades and offices, as sheepsheards [llama-watchers], fishers and hunters . . . In these dances they use sundry

---

* The translation from *Ollantay*, in the meter of the original, is by Dr. John H. Rowe, and is here reproduced by his permission.

sortes of instruments . . . they sing all with the voyce and first one or two sing . . . then all the rest; some of these songs were very wittyily composed, contayning historyes . . . some were meere follies. . . ."

All that is given here of this is only a lugubrious fragment. The Incas would have saved us a good deal of speculation (for a good part of the archaeological literature is taken up with attempts at an exact chronology, with speculation of time-space relationships), if they would have taken less time working out their mythical genealogy with the Sun and concentrated on elaborating, like other cultures, some form of written language.

33 Military Conquests

ALTHOUGH the Incas lacked writing, the idea of the wheel, iron, and many other civilized attributes, they possessed one thing in common with all of the most advanced civilizations: *war and conquest.* In fact the Inca state was based on the supposition that war is the natural state of man; it owed its aggrandizement to war, developing its empire (as all empires do) at the expense of its neighbors.

The army of the Incas was actually an agrarian militia. Every able-bodied Indian was liable for military service, trained in the use of such arms as were used in battles. The only professional army was the Inca's bodyguard, an unknown number but thought not to have been many more than ten thousand; these served as a sort of cadre for the militia.

Arms were supplied by the state, and there were depositories for this equipment which were seen by the Spaniards at strategic places in the realm.

When he became a warrior, the *puric,* called from his farm, kept his regular clothing except that he put on a distinctive helmet made either of wood or plaited cane and painted with a totemic device; it had red wool fringes, and the same type of red wool fringe was put about the ankle. He wore a quilted cotton jacket for body armor (similar to that worn by the Aztecs). And around the back of his

Ceremonial Mace

neck, slats of iron-hard *chonta* wood were hung, covering the spine, to protect him from attack. The soldiers carried shields (*walkanqas*), round or square, made from wood or toughened tapir or deer hide. These were painted with geometric devices which marked their war grouping.

Shield

The soldier's primary weapon was the sling for long distance, and the star-headed mace for close infighting. They were not bowmen. It is a curious parallel between the Roman and Inca fighting men that both of these land armies fought the same way: the Romans did not have the bow, but they had the pilum, a spear six feet long, hurled at the enemy when ten paces away; then they closed in with the short sword.

The Inca spear was six feet long with either metal-tipped or fire-hardened point. The long-range weapon was the sling. Made from plaited llama wool, measuring from fourteen to twenty-eight inches when doubled, it was fearfully and simply made; it had a sort of egg-size cradle for the stone. The sling was whirled about the head, an end released, and the stone shot forward to its mark with great accuracy; it could dent a steel helmet at fifteen yards, stunning the man in it (as the Spaniards could testify); without the protection of a helmet, the injury inflicted by the sling-tossed stone was fatal. The closing-in weapon was the mace, a three-foot-long wooden shaft, topped with a heavy bronze or stone star-shaped piece at its "business end." Its effectiveness is borne out by the number of crushed skulls found which had been operated on to relieve the pressure on the brain from such blows. In addition, the Incas used a sort of double-edged sword made from *chonta* wood and used like the two-handed broadsword of the sixteenth century. These were their weapons.

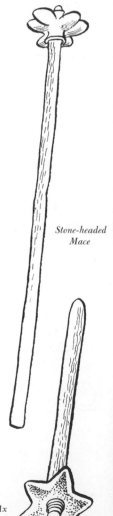

Stone-headed Mace

Since man *is* war, it is useless to discuss causes; they arose among the Incas as they do among us: survival, aggrandizement, pressure, caprice, necessary and unnecessary reasons, but since the Incas were dedicated to bring the religion of the Sun as well as "Inca civilization" to all people (with that fearful dedication so well known to militant Christianity), war was almost constant. Either the Incas were conquering new peoples, or defending what they had taken. Many were preventive wars; others were undertaken to keep the professional army occupied, says John H. Rowe, "to prevent generals plotting against the Inca's succession."

War Ax

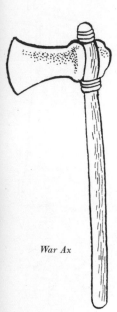

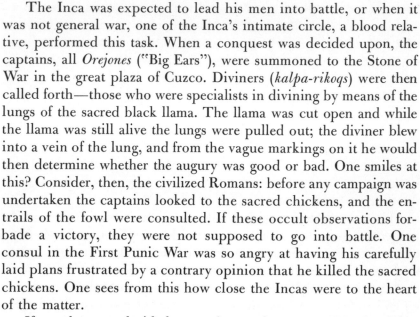

The Inca was expected to lead his men into battle, or when it was not general war, one of the Inca's intimate circle, a blood relative, performed this task. When a conquest was decided upon, the captains, all *Orejones* ("Big Ears"), were summoned to the Stone of War in the great plaza of Cuzco. Diviners (*kalpa-rikoqs*) were then called forth—those who were specialists in divining by means of the lungs of the sacred black llama. The llama was cut open and while the llama was still alive the lungs were pulled out; the diviner blew into a vein of the lung, and from the vague markings on it he would then determine whether the augury was good or bad. One smiles at this? Consider, then, the civilized Romans: before any campaign was undertaken the captains looked to the sacred chickens, and the entrails of the fowl were consulted. If these occult observations forbade a victory, they were not supposed to go into battle. One consul in the First Punic War was so angry at having his carefully laid plans frustrated by a contrary opinion that he killed the sacred chickens. One sees from this how close the Incas were to the heart of the matter.

War Ax

If war then was decided upon, the word went out. Warriors were summoned and, on arrival, placed in companies corresponding to their *ayllus*. Each wore the totemic device of his clan. All warriors were, of course, classified by the decimal system. It is related how the Lord-Inca Huayna Capac (died 1527) made war. He was "a man of few words but many deeds, a severe judge who punished without mercy. He wished to be so feared that his Indians would dream of him at night." He set out for the conquest of Quito with 300,000 soldiers; roads were made ready, the enemy ahead was scouted, the *tampus* along the roads filled with food, the llamas assembled to carry, supplemented by thousands of human carriers. The army on the march was severely disciplined. No warrior was allowed off the road to steal or bother the civilians; penalty, death.

Now the reason for the wide, well-kept roads is fully apparent—conquest.

When the enemy was sighted, the Incas's troops did what all their enemies did, they blew their horns, shouted insults, trying to overwhelm them in a chaos of sound; for this reason their Spanish enemy characterized them all as "brown and noisy." But with the Incas the object of the battle was to win it; war for them was not, as it had been with pre-Incans, ritualistic promenades, elaborate

Sling

panoplies to overawe an enemy; they had but a single object—victory. They had neither superior weapons nor superior tactics, but they had discipline, and a good system of supply and roads; roads decided it. The object of these roads, then, was not economic but military, to get their warriors there and in mass.

Battle began with the slingers tossing their hail of stones, while those armed with the *macanas* advanced. Spears were thrown at short distances; then the warriors closed in with the mace. Once battle was joined, it was a formless melee. They used ambush and the burning of grass to force the enemy into positions to be attacked by mass. If they attacked hilltop fortresses, they advanced under a canopy of hides shaped into shields to protect them from the slingshot missiles. If the enemy took refuge in a building, fire-hot stones were hurled to burn the grass thatch and force them out into the open. The formlessness of Inca battle, once it was joined, was a tactical error that the Spaniards exploited to the full, and that is why a Spanish *capitán* could boast: "I took no more notice of a hundred armed Indians than I would have of a handful of flies." [142]

Mace

There was another traditional weakness in Inca warfare which, they practiced, like all Andean people. They launched most of their attacks on the advent of the full moon and they kept to a twenty-day rhythm of battle. They rarely fought in mass at night. All these ritual tactics, when understood by their Spanish enemy, were used with marked effect against them.

Yet the Incas learned quickly. After their swift initial defeat by the Spaniards in 1532, they made defense against the horses, they learned to fire the arquebus, they put captured Spanish munitions makers to work; some of them learned to ride horses. In the neo-Inca state (1537–72), operating out of the sanctuary of Vilcapampa, the surviving Lord-Incas and their warriors waged a guerrilla warfare for thirty-five years, and had not the last Inca, Tupac Amaru, been seduced by "honied words" they might have prevailed.

Once the Incas decided on the conquest of a given territory, no force in the Andes could stem the tide of their wave of the future; the Incas never lost a battle of importance after 1437, and the violence, from all surviving accounts, was sufficiently awesome. There was a wholesale slaughter of the defeated in the field and a ceremonial slaughter later. A warrior was decorated for killing (one man killed, one of the warrior's arms was painted black; two killed,

War Ax

his chest was painted; three killed, a black mark was painted across the face between both ears, etc.). The Incas were not as blood-thirsty as were the Aztecs, but captives were taken, led in triumph through Cuzco, and forced to lie prone in front of the Sun Temple as the Inca trod upon their necks, symbolizing the victory. Heads were taken from the more ferocious of the enemy and made into drinking cups (as with the Vikings). If the enemy was especially hated, they flayed the captives alive, then stuffed their skins in a ri-diculous mimicry of life, making the stomachs into drums which they beat when warming themselves up for battle. A sort of museum of these stuffed skins of the Chanca tribe—hereditary enemies of the Inca who had the temerity to attack sacred Cuzco in 1437—was seen by the Spaniards when they entered Peru. Yet the Inca policy generally was: conquer by arms, reconcile by kindness.

34 *The Organization and Assimilation of Conquered Lands*

T HE INCAS organized their conquests as they organized everything else in their world. The methods of other South American tribes before their coming had been to raid, loot, take slaves, levy tribute, and return to their tribal lands; only the religio-military conquest of Tiahuanaco (circa A.D. 1000–1300) had attempted to assimilate all Peru, but this failed and they left be-hind (see page 410) only vague memories of their cult of the Weep-ing God.

The Incas were masters of organization. They turned conquest into empire. They began their political life, circa A.D. 1100, in the limited orbit of the Cuzco Valley. At this time the whole of the Andean and coastal areas of the land which one day was to be Inca were broken into an almost unbelievable number of small and great tribes of different tongues and customs. By 1500, the Incas had absorbed every one of these tribes—conservatively estimated at over five hundred—into their empire which stretched all the way from Argentina to Colombia, from the shores of the Pacific into the Upper Amazon. It was one of the great empires of all time, totaling

350,000 square miles, equivalent to the land mass comprehended in the Atlantic seaboard states of North America. The conquests were gradual: first the immediate territory was taken around Cuzco, then beyond to the south, then to the west, then to the north; only when they were fully tested did the Inca's armies try to come to grips with the people of the jungle to the east.

No sooner had the new territory fallen into their conquering maw than a census of all the people was taken by means of the *quipus*. If the conquered were still belligerent, they were liquidated; if they were a valiant foe they were treated with considerable kindness. Local customs and dress and language were respected; the local language was allowed, but officials had to learn Quechua.

The Sun replaced all other religions, yet if their local gods were efficacious they were adopted into the Inca pantheon. Local chieftains either were put to death, or sent to Cuzco as hostages and trained to the "new order," then sent back and allowed to keep their titles. A relief model, clay or stone, was made of the territory and taken to Cuzco along with a census of people, animals, agriculture. If the principle of the *ayllu*, the earth cell, was not already in operation, it was established on Inca lines. The roads which had been built up to the border of the territory to be seized were now extended through the conquered lands, which were integrated into the empire. Professional architects were sent out from Cuzco and directed the building of a new urban center, and especially the Temple of the Sun. If the whole population was irreconcilable, then they were moved out bodily—as the Soviets do today—and the vacuum filled by *mitimaes*, Quechua-speaking peoples loyal to the Inca. They were moved into the conquered lands, often many hundreds of miles from their original homes; population transference was an important part of Inca policy. The *mitimaes* were of three orders: military, political, and economic. Quechua-speaking soldiers were quartered in frontier stations, some as far away as the Paraguayan *chaco*, or at the bridgeheads in the Amazon, to prevent incursions of wild tribes. Political *mitimaes* were settled, for example, in the Chachapoyas region won to the empire circa A.D. 1480. Economic *mitimaes* were settled in humid areas of the Montaña east of Cuzco to raise the coca leaf, to name one instance. There were innumerable other population transfers into regions which were uninhabited. Where there was a bridge to be guarded as at

Uranmarca, to give but one example, they erected a *marca* above it with the sole object of keeping in repair the second largest suspension bridge in all Peru, that which crossed the Vilcas (now Pampas) River, which lay beyond the great Inca center of Vilcas-huamán.

By peopling thinly populated regions, by placing *mitimaes* in regions devoid of population so that the roads would be kept open, the bridges repaired, etc., the Incas welded the land into empire.

"One of the things for which one feels envious of these Lords-Incas," wrote that wonderful observer Pedro de Cieza de León, "is their knowledge of the way to conquer . . . and to bring them by good management into empire. I often remember when in some wild and barren province outside of these kingdoms [of the Incas] hearing Spaniards themselves say, 'I am certain that if the Incas had been here the state of things would be different' . . .

"In all things the *system* [i.e., replacing buildings damaged by war, bringing in llamas where needed, sending in official builders, instructing the newly conquered how to cultivate their fields better] was so well regulated that when one of the Incas entered into a new province . . . in a very short time it looked like another place . . . In other words, those who conquered by force of arms were given an order that as little harm should be done to property and houses of the vanquished as was possible; for the Lord-Inca said:

" 'These will soon be our people as much as others.' "

So then these *mitimaes* were civilizers as the Roman soldiers were civilizers; each group was a representative of order—soldier and agriculturist, road builder and bringer of civilization.

So complete was this integration of the Andes and the coast of that part which lay in the Inca realm, that the Inca style was etched indelibly in the land. "One short century of Inca rule [1400–1500]," writes Dr. John Rowe,[155] "completely altered the course of Andean cultural history." To this day Inca provincial boundaries and names are widely used and the Inca language flourishes (spoken by upwards of five million people), while even the memory of the older states and languages has vanished. And so the whole Andean area is colored indelibly with the Inca dye.

And to this day, in every part of the territory ruled by the Incas, one is hourly conscious of the ghost of the Incas' supremacy manifesting itself in a score of ways: through speech, customs, and material culture.

Thus stood the realm of the Incas on that fatal day of 1527, when a small Spanish caravel, no more than ten tons burthen, sailed into Tumbes.

 Decline and Fall   *35*

W HY AND HOW did such a benevolent despotism fall so quickly? How was it possible for only 130 foot soldiers and 40 cavalry with but one small falconet-cannon able to penetrate the Andes, seek out the Lord-Inca surrounded by fifty thousand warriors, and then in one skirmish—which lasted precisely 33 minutes—psychologically reduce by that bold action this great realm of the Incas? The question has been asked over and over again through these centuries, and no one has yet come up with a satisfactory answer, just as there have been thousands of books to attempt to explain the decline and fall of Rome. There are, however, some historical details which might help explain this decline and fall of the Inca Empire.

By 1493, when Huayna Capac was "crowned" Lord-Inca, the Inca Empire had almost reached its greatest heights. After a series of setbacks in his attempt to bring some of the jungle Indians in northern Ecuador and Colombia under control, he finally set the limits to the most northern realm at the Ancasmayo River (1° N. lat.) in the mountains, and Tumbes (3° S. lat.) on the coast. Like the Roman Emperor Hadrian, this last great Inca attempted to set limits to his realm.

There is a natural limit to conquest, and that is the power of assimilation. Time gnawed at the bones of the old Inca, who had to consider whom among all his hundreds of male heirs would be named Inca. The first years of this "setting bounds to the fields" were ones of inward peace within the Inca realm, but in the later years of the reign of Huayna Capac there was disquieting news from without. The later years were full of gloom and evil portent.* In defeating a tribe in the Chaco region there had been reported

* For a detailed discussion of this see Philip Ainsworth Means, *Ancient Civilizations of the Andes.*

the presence of a strange man, white and bearded, among the enemy. There were further reports, vague and contradictory yet persistent, of other white men sailing in large ships down the Pacific coast.

The Peruvians had little concept of humanity beyond their own sphere, nor of geography beyond the immediate; they had no direct contact with either the Mayas or the Aztecs. They were completely unaware of their existence. The Aztecs were conquered in 1521 and the Mayas set upon in 1527; this must have produced shock waves (since the Mayas traded as far south as Panama) which were felt in Peru even though uncomprehended. All contact with these other civilizations was only by geographical filtration. The Incas had emeralds, for instance, which occur in the Americas only in the mines in Colombia, but they had them not by direct contact; they filtered down to them from tribe to tribe.

The people of Panama had known white man since the time that Columbus in 1502 had set up a colony near to the isthmus. Nuñez de Balboa had wandered to the Pacific as early as 1513, yet none of this information came down in tangible pattern to the Incas. For the Indians of Panama, too, had only the vaguest idea of this great realm to the south; it came to their common ken by means of a multiple cascade of interpretations, so that all an Indian chieftain could do when pressed by the conquest-hungry Spaniards for news of other lands, was to model in clay for Capitán Pascal de Andogoya in 1522 on some muddied shore of Darien, an animal, which the Indian meant to be a llama (but which the Spaniards mistook for a sheep), saying that the people who had such "sheep" were those of the Kingdom of Gold.

It is important that this lack of direct contact between the great American civilizations be stressed; they were, so far as we know now, in complete unawareness of each other's existence. If there had been such contact, then that terrible catastrophe of the Conquest of Mexico in 1521 would have been transmitted to the Incas, and they would have put themselves into a state of defense for a doom which could have been deduced. Yet they must have received vague rumors, through trade that passed from hand to hand coming down from Mexico to Panama, Colombia to Peru, of something that was occurring, and vague foreboding settled over the land. A pestilence at this time came to Peru, and although it cannot be positively identified, it was new in their experience and could have been one of the diseases, perhaps smallpox, brought by the Spaniard.

Then, toward the end of Huayna Capac's reign, an Inca outpost in the Chaco was attacked by Chiriguano Indians led by a white man. That man we now know was a Spaniard named Alejo García, who, captured by Indians in Brazil, had become their captain. The time was 1525.

Two years later, Francisco Pizarro arrived at Tumbes with his famous "thirteen men of Gallo"; they embraced the natives, traded gewgaws, shot off guns, skirted the Peruvian coast, and then took Indians aboard to train them as interpreters for their contemplated return. Pizarro left behind for future use two Spaniards, one named Alonso de Molina, and a Negro, Gines. All these strange marvels were transmitted to the Inca, who in 1527 lay on his death bed.

Huayna Capac then died without naming his successor. As will be recalled, when discussing the Inca as state (see page 496), there was no fixed rule of descent; the Inca chose with advice from his council the most competent of his sons born of his principal queen, the *coya*. Now that son whom most considered would be made Inca was Huáscar, who resided in Cuzco, and in default of a clear line of descent he was proclaimed Inca, but the deceased Inca had among his numerous subsidiary offspring one named Atahualpa, who was born in the region which is now Ecuador and who traveled much with Huayna Capac in his later years, and was personally known and much liked by the principal generals of the army.

The result of this dispute for Inca-ship was a devastating civil war between the two brothers which lasted five years, corresponding precisely with the intervening years when Francisco Pizarro was in Spain organizing for his conquest of the Kingdom of Gold.

In the final battle Huáscar was captured, his generals killed, thousands of Indians slaughtered, and Atahualpa's generals were sent to Cuzco to put to death as many of Huáscar's family as they could apprehend, and also to prepare the capital for Atahualpa's entry into Cuzco to be proclaimed Inca.

At this precise moment Francisco Pizarro arrived with his small army at Tumbes; the date: May 13, 1532.

Atahualpa (who was to be proclaimed Inca) was at this time taking the hot sulphur baths at Cajamarca, a place then of no great importance in the Inca realm. He was awaiting the reports from his *chasquis* from Cuzco about the preparations for his triumphant entry. He was surrounded by his battle-tried warriors, men who had fought this terrible fratricidal war for five years. He was the master now of everything, everyone in the domain; he could lop off the head of his most famous general merely by raising his hand; he could do it even by long distance via a messenger. It was then at this moment that he received messages from the coast of the arrival of the Spaniards.

His intelligence was exact; the *quipus* counted out the number of men and animals (so strange that no one could give them a name except that they thought man and beast were one). It was the *interpretation* of this intelligence that was faulty: The animals had feet of silver (the horseshoes gave that effect), they were impotent at night; if the rider fell off the animal that ended both. As for the guns which spouted fire, they were only thunderbolts and could only be fired twice. One of the coastal chieftains, so the report said, poured a libation of corn *chicha* into a barrel of one of the guns so as to solace the thunder god. Moreover, the steel swords of these bearded men were as ineffectual as women's weaving battens. From all this it shows that the Inca had absolutely no advance notice of the white man. It is true that at first Atahualpa thought that they were returning gods, for it was legend that the Inca's creator-god, Tici Viracocha, who had helped bring civilization to them, had been dissatisfied with his handiwork and sailed away and would someday return (this is a persistent legend throughout the Americas about ships returning over the ocean sea, and must somewhere have substance).

For when a chieftain himself puffed up the Andes to report: "People have arrived by a big ship from out of the *hatun-cocha* [sea], with different clothing, beards and animals like llamas, only larger," Atahualpa thought that the gods themselves were coming to conduct him to Cuzco to his rightful heritage as Inca. Still he was no fool. After he had reports on the Spaniards' progress and heard how they raped his Virgins of the Sun at the village of Caxas, he knew by then that he dealt with no gods.

His strategy, supposedly, *since he believed as all other Indians*

did that no one could get reinforcements from the sea, was to offer no
resistance, draw them in, set them down neatly in one of the towns,
perhaps at Cajamarca itself, give the signal, and that would be finis
to this little episode which delayed his trip to Cuzco. For what had
Atahualpa to fear? He was god. He was surrounded by thousands
of warriors, and against so small a number . . . So then he accepted
—we believe naively, but to him it was doubtless a whim of those
about to die—an invitation from the Spaniards to visit their chieftain Francisco Pizarro in the plaza at Cajamarca. His warriors were
to come unarmed "so as not to give offense."

It was at vespers during the early evening of November 16,
1532,[54] when the Inca, carried in his litter and surrounded by an
unarmed bodyguard, moved into the plaza of Cajamarca. There
was, if one will recall reading Prescott's *Conquest of Peru,* an unintelligible parley between Christian priest and Inca god, then that
one cannon belched out its thunder into the ranks of brown bodies,
and with the cry of "Santiago!" and "At them!" the Spaniards
ambushed the hapless Inca.

The rest is history.

BIBLIOGRAPHY

1. Acosta, José de, *The Naturall and Morall Historie of the East and West Indies.* London, 1604.
   A very learned and balanced Jesuit, whose intellectual love of God did not blind him to the good qualities of the Indian; this book is notable since it deals with Acosta's travels in Mexico and Peru as early as 1565. He compares the cultures, he is colorful and accurate. When obtained (which will be difficult) the work should be read.

2. Adam, Leonhard, *Primitive Art,* 3rd rev. ed. Harmondsworth, England, 1954.

3. Allier, Raoul, *The Mind of the Savage,* trans. by Fred Rothwell. New York, 1929.

4. Altieri, Radamés A., "Sobre II Antiguos Kipu Peruanos," *Revista del Instituto de Antropológia de la Universidad Nacional de Tucumán,* vol. II (1941), 177–211.

5. Alzate y Ramírez, José Antonio, *Descripcion de las antiguedades de Xochicalco.* Mexico, 1791.
   Xochicalco was one of the first Mexican sites to enter the literature. Although Humboldt did not visit it, he gathered the description made by Señor Alzate with a drawing (something less than accurate) by F. Aguera done in 1791. This he published in his famous *Atlas Pittoresque* (Paris, 1810).

6. Anonymous Conqueror, *Anonymous La Conquista del Peru,* Seville, April, 1534.
   (See a critical reprint, edited by Dr. A. Pogo, in Proc. Am. Acad. of Arts and Scs., vol. 64, No. 8, July, 1930.)

7. Anonymous Conqueror, *Narrative of Some Things of New Spain and of the Great City of Temestitan,* trans. by Marshall H. Saville. New York, 1917.
   Not easily available, since it has been reprinted in only limited editions, this short work by one who was anonymous and communal should be read alongside that of Bernal Díaz del Castillo and the letters of Cortés, to gain a full-sided picture of the impact of the Conquest on Aztec—and Spaniard.

8. Avendaño y Loyola, Fray Andrés de, *Relacion de las dos entradas que hize a la conversion de los gentiles Itzaes y Cehaches,* dated Merida 6, de abril 1696. Manuscript, Newberry Library, Chicago. (See No. 126 below.)

9. Barrow, R. H., *The Romans.* Harmondsworth, England, 1949.

10. Baudin, Louis, *L'Empire Socialiste des Inka.* Paris, 1928.

11. Benedict, Francis G., and Steggerda, Morris, *The Food of the Present-Day Maya Indians of Yucatan.* Contributions to American Archaeology, vol. III, no. 18, Carnegie Institution of Washington, Pub. 456. Washington, D. C., 1937.

12. Bennett, Wendell, *Ancient Arts of the Andes.* New York, 1954.

13. ———, and Bird, Junius B., *Andean Culture History.* American Museum of Natural History, Handbook Series, no. 15. New York, 1949.

14. Beyer, Hermann, *Studies on the Inscriptions of Chichen Itza.* Carnegie Institution of Washington, Pub. 483. Washington, 1937.
    Beyer was a tireless worker until he was betrayed by some of his American colleagues and died in a Texas concentration camp during World War II.

15. Bingham, Hiram, *Lost City of the Incas: the Story of Machu Picchu and its Builders.* New York, 1948.

16. Blom, Frans, *The Maya Game pok-a-tok.* Middle American Research Series of Tulane University, Pub. 4. New Orleans, 1932.

17. ———, et al., *Tribes and Temples,* 2 vols. Middle American Research Series of Tulane University, Pub. 1. New Orleans, 1926–27.

18. Boas, Franz (ed.), *General Anthropology.* Boston, 1938.

19. *The Book of Chilam Balam of Chumayel,* trans. by R. L. Roys. Carnegie Institution of Washington, Pub. 438. Washington, D. C., 1933.

20. Borah, Woodrow, *Early Colonial Trade and Navigation Between Mexico and Peru.* Berkeley, Calif., 1954.

21. Brainerd, G. W., *The Maya Civilization.* Los Angeles, 1954.

22. Brasseur de Bourbourg, C. E., *Histoire des Nations Civilisées du Mexique et de l'Amérique Centrale,* 4 vols. Paris, 1857.

23. ———, *Popol Vuh. Le Livre Sacré et les Mythes de l'Antiquité Americaine.* Paris, 1861.

24. Brinton, D. G., *The Maya Chronicles.* Philadelphia, 1882.

25. Burland, C. A., *Magic Books from Mexico.* London, 1953.

26. Caddy, Herbert, *City of Palenque.*
    This manuscript, illustrated with twenty-four sepia drawings, is unpublished. Caddy preceded Frederick Catherwood.

27. Calancha, Antonio de la, *Cronica moralizada del orden de San Augustin en el Perú . . .* Barcelona, 1638.

28. Caso, Alfonso, *Las Exploraciones en Monte Albán, Temporada 1934–35.* Instituto Panamericano de Geografía é Historia, no. 18. Mexico, 1935.
    One of the great figures in Mexican archaeology. His explorations into Monte Albán,

an Olmec-Zapotec-Mixtec religious site in Oaxaca, and its restoration gave us more than fifteen hundred years of chronology. His discovery of the famous golden jewels at Monte Albán, in an untouched, unrifled tomb, gave the physical evidence of the excellence of Mexican goldsmithery.

29. ———, *El Pueblo del Sol.* Mexico, 1953.

30. Castañeda, Paganini Ricardo, *Las Ruinas de Palenque.* Guatemala, 1946.

31. Catherwood, Frederick, *Views of Ancient Monuments in Central America, Chiapas and Yucatan.* New York, 1844.

32. Chamberlain, Robert S., *Francisco de Montejo and the Conquest of Yucatán,* Ph.D. dissertation, Harvard University, 1936.

33. Childe, V. Gordon, "Early Forms of Society," in Singer, et al. (eds.), *A History of Technology,* vol. 1.

34. Cieza de León, Pedro de, *The Travels of Pedro de Cieza de León,* trans. and ed. by Clements R. Markham. London, 1864.
But see a new edition of these famous chronicles, translated by Harriet de Onis, edited by Victor Wolfgang von Hagen, published by the University of Oklahoma Press, Norman, 1959.

35. Ciudad-Real, Antonio de, and San Juan, Alonso de, *Relación Breve y Verdadera de Algunas Cosas de las Muchas que Sucedieron al Padre Fray Alonso Ponce en las Provincias de la Nueva España . . .* Colección de Documents Ineditos para la Historia de España, vols. LVII–LVIII. Madrid, 1872.
Ciudad-Real was a famous Maya scholar of the late sixteenth century who wrote an account of a journey of inspection as secretary-general of the Franciscan Order.

36. Cline, Howard F., "The Apocryphal Early Career of J. F. de Waldeck," *Acta Americana,* vol. 4, no. 4 (1947).

37. Cobo, Bernabé, *Historia del Nuevo Mundo,* 4 vols. Seville, 1890–93.

38. *Codex Florentino,* ed. Francisco del Paso y Troncoso, Madrid, 1905.

39. *Codex Mendoza,* 2 vols. Mexico, 1925.

40. *Codex Tro-Cortesianus,* 2 parts: Madrid, 1892, Paris, 1869–70.

41. Collis, Maurice, *Cortés and Montezuma.* London, 1954.
A recent interpretation, by a well-known English writer, of the strange relationship between Moctezuma and Hernán Cortés. Well guided by Aztec specialists, the author has given a new twist to the old facts.

42. Cornyn, John H. (trans. and ed.), "Aztec Literature," in *The Song of Quetzalcoatl.* Yellow Springs, Ohio, 1930.

43. Cortés, Hernán, *Five Letters, 1519–1526,* trans. by J. Bayard Morris. London, 1928; New York, 1929.
The five letters were written between 1519 and 1526. In Spanish they were termed *Cartas-Relaciones,* half letters, half dispatches. These could not be called literary

masterpieces; still, many were penned in the heat of battle—and bear this imprint. Two of them were published in 1524 in Nuremberg with the only plan of the city of Tenochtitlán as it was in 1519.

44. ———, *Letters of Cortes,* trans. and ed. by F. A. MacNutt. New York, 1908.
The originals of these letters are in the Nationalbibliothek in Vienna.

45. Covarrubias, Miguel, *Indian Art of Mexico and Central America.* New York, 1957.

46. ———, *Mexico South: The Isthmus of Tehuantepec.* New York, 1946.
The late Miguel Covarrubias was by far and large more than a clever illustrator, he was an imaginative archaeologist. He wandered much over the Mexican scene and pursued archaeology; his belief that the Olmec would emerge as one of the earliest of the Mexican tribes has been borne out by radiocarbon dating.

47. Díaz, Juan, *Itinerario de Grijalva.*
The original is lost, but the narrative has come down to us through an Italian translation. Lothrop, *Tulum* (pp. 14, 15), quotes Juan Díaz but does not mention the exact source in either that text page or in the bibliography.

48. Díaz del Castillo, Bernal, *The Discovery and Conquest of Mexico, 1517–1521,* trans. by A. P. Maudslay. New York, 1956.
Since it is an honest work and deals with people—the basic foundation of history —Bernal Díaz's book is a rich tapestry of human events. Its vitality is attested to by the continuously new editions that appear. Of the numerous editions, the one published recently in Mexico (1955) is the most complete and gives the whole of Díaz's travels with Cortés in the Maya country. I have used this edition as well as the Maudslay translation cited above.

49. Doughty, Charles, *Travels in Arabia Deserta.* New York, 1923.

50. *Dresden Codex,* reproduced by William Gates. Baltimore, 1932.

51. Drucker, Philip, "Radiocarbon Dates from La Venta, Tabasco," *Science,* vol. 126, no. 3263 (July 12, 1957), 72–3.

52. Durán, Fray Diego, *Historia de las Indias de Nueva-España . . .* 2 vols. and atlas. Mexico, 1867–80.
Written in the sixteenth century.

53. Ekholm, Gordon F., *Excavations at Tampico and Panuco in the Huasteca, Mexico.* Anthropological Papers of the American Museum of Natural History, vol. 38, pt. 5. New York, 1944.

54. Estete, Miguel de, *Noticias del Peru,* Col. Libr. Documentos, Ref. de Historia del Peru, vol. 8, Lima, Peru, 1924.

55. Fejos, Pál, *Archeological Explorations in the Cordillera Vilcabamba, South-eastern Peru.* New York, 1944.

56. Forbes, R. J., "Chemical, Culinary and Cosmetic Arts," in Singer, et al. (eds.), *A History of Technology,* vol. 1.

57. Ford, James A., "The History of a Peruvian Valley," *Scientific American,* vol. 191, no. 12 (August, 1954), 28–34.

58. Frank, Waldo, *America Hispaña: A Portrait and a Prospect,* New York, 1931.

59. Gage, Thomas, *Travels in the New World,* ed. by J. E. S. Thompson. Norman, Okla., 1958.

60. Galindo, Juan, *The Ruins of Copán.* 1835.
    Juan Galindo was the pseudonym of an Irish soldier of fortune.

61. Gamio, Lorenzo, *Archaeological Guide of Monte Albán.* Mexico, n.d.

62. Gamio, Manuel, *La Población del Valle de Teotihuacán,* 3 vols. Mexico, 1922.

63. Gann, Thomas, *Maya Cities.* London, 1927; New York, 1928.
    Gann, a medico who lived in British Honduras, made known, through his explorations and publications, a new area of the Mayas.

64. García, Gregorio, *Origen de los Indios . . .* Madrid, 1732.
    This, written in 1607, is one of the many, albeit better-known, theological proofs offered as to why the American "Indians are Jewes." Gracía identifies the Biblical Ophir with Peru; Joktan of Genesis becomes Yucatán.

65. García Payón, "Malinalco," *Revista Mexicana de Estudios Antropologicos,* vol. VIII (1946).

66. Garcilaso de la Vega, *Primera Parte de los Commentarios reales . . . ,* Lisboa, 1609.
    (There is an English edition of Garcilaso translated by Sir Clements Markham and published by the Haykluyt Society, London, 1869.)

67. Garibay, Kintana, Angel María, *Historia de la Literatura Nahuatl.* Mexico, 1953.
    A fascinating inquiry into the nature of Aztec literature, this book shows the sensitive nature of a people renowned mostly in human memory for their massive human sacrificial rituals. Sections appear in translation for the first time in the Aztec part of the present volume.

68. Gates, William (trans.), *The de la Cruz-Badiano Aztec Herbal of 1552.* Baltimore, 1939.

69. ———, *An Outline Dictionary of Maya Glyphs.* Baltimore, 1931.

70. Gazin, C. Lewis, *Review of the Upper Eocene Artiodactyla of North America.* Smithsonian Miscellaneous Collection, vol. 128, no. 8. Washington, D. C., 1955.

71. Genêt, Jean, and Chelbatz, Pierre, *Histoire des Peuples Maya-Quichés (Mexique, Guatemala, Honduras).* Paris, 1927.

72. Goodman, J. T., "The Archaic Maya Inscriptions," in *Biologia Centrali-Americana,* section on Archaeology. London, 1897.

73. Graña, Francisco, Rocca, Esteban R., and Graña R., Luis, *Las Trepana-ciones Craneanas en el Perú en la Epoca pre-Hispanica.* Lima, 1954.

74. Gutuérrez Noriega, Carlos, and von Hagen, V. W., "The Strange Case of the Coca Leaf," *Scientific Monthly,* vol. 70, no. 2 (February, 1950), 81–9.

75. Harcourt, Raoul and Marie d', *La Musique des Incas et ses Survivances.* Paris, 1925.

76. Harth-terré, Emilio, Drawings in Means, *Ancient Civilization of the Andes,* N. Y., 1931.

77. Healey, Giles G., "Maya Murals: Great Discovery Sheds Light on Cul-ture of Ancient Race," *Life* (April, 1947).

78. Hernández, Francisco, *Rerum Medicarum Novae Hispaniae Thesaurus seu Plantarum.* Rome, 1649.
The work of the great Spanish proto-medico Francisco Hernández, who came to Mexico during the years 1570–75. With his Aztec assistants, he filled sixteen folio volumes with drawings of three thousand plants and descriptions in Spanish, Nahuatl, and Latin. Reduced to one thousand species, the book was a gigantic her-bal on Dioscoridean lines. Unpublished in his lifetime, this badly edited thesaurus of 951 pages was printed in Rome.
See also: von Hagen, "Francisco Hernández: Naturalist, 1515–1578."

79. Heyerdahl, Thor, *Kon-Tiki: Across the Pacific by Raft,* trans. by F. H. Lyon. Chicago, 1951.

80. Holmes, William H., *Archaeological Studies Among the Ancient Cities of Mexico.* Field Columbian Museum, Pubs. 8, 16. Chicago, 1895–97.

81. Hooke, H. S., "Recording and Writing," in Singer, et al. (eds.), *A His-tory of Technology,* vol. 1.

82. Hornell, J., "South American Balsas; The Problem of Their Origin," *The Mariners' Mirror,* vol. XVII, 347–55.

83. Humboldt, Alexander von, *Vues des Cordillères et Monuments des Peuples Indigènes de l'Amérique,* Paris, 1810.
Humboldt was the great figure of the opening of the nineteenth century. After explor-ations in South America, Cuba, and Mexico, he compiled a vast amount of data extraordinary in both its range and its accuracy. This work is a landmark in American archaeology but now little used since the volume is in folio and is expensive. Yet it deserves to be reconsidered. His attitude toward archaeological remains as fragments of history laid the solid base of American scholarship. He was the first to stress the oneness of indigenous culture.

84. Hunter, Dard, *Chinese Ceremonial Paper,* Chillicothe, Ohio, 1937.

85. ———, *Papermaking: The History and Technique of an Ancient Craft,* 2nd ed. rev. and enl. New York, 1947.

86. Huxley, Aldous, *Beyond the Mexique Bay.* New York, 1934.
A charming small book on the effect of Middle America and Mexico on Aldous Hux-

ley. All of the conclusions are Huxleian, always stimulating and with a slant which the professional scholar has not seen or does not see.

87. Huxley, Julian, *From an Antique Land.* London and New York, 1954.

88. Ixtililoxochitl, Fernando de Alva, *Obras Históricas . . .* , 2 vols. Mexico, 1891–92.
    Written in the seventeenth century.

89. Jenison, Madge, *Roads.* New York, 1948.

90. Jimenez, Arturo, *Instrumentos Musicales del Perú.* Lima, 1951.

91. Jones, Sir Harold Spencer, "The Calendar," in Singer, et al. (eds.), *A History of Technology,* vol. 3.

92. Joyce, T. A., *Mexican Archaeology.* London and New York, 1914.
    A very successful attempt to portray the whole of the field of Mexican archaeology. A rare book when obtainable, and expensive.

93. Kelemen, Pál, *Medieval American Art,* 2 vols. New York, 1943.
    This, the mature work of a Hungarian-born and -educated art historian, has a freshness and directness not always found in literature on the Maya and Aztec. He treats the objects as art, not as potsherds; his observations, since they are neither hipped nor dulled by the standard archaeological vocabulary, are thought-evoking. It should be read by any who wish to push their interest in American cultures beyond the dim outline of general books.

94. Kidder, A. V., *Excavations at Kaminaljuyu, Guatemala.* Carnegie Institution of Washington, Pub. 561. Washington, D. C., 1946.

95. King, Edward, Viscount Kingsborough, *Antiquities of Mexico,* 9 vols. London, 1831–48.
    Lord Kingsborough would have been sunk in the stream of time except that he published, at the cost of both life and fortune, this folio collection of nine volumes at $150 a copy. The set is now eagerly sought by collectors and scholars since Lord Kingsborough reproduced many of the heretofore unpublished Mixtec, Aztec, and Maya codices. The text, which is a ragbag of every unconsidered theory, attempts to prove in short that the American Indian descended from one of the Lost Tribes of Israel. He belonged to the lunatic fringe of archaeological enthusiasts. He died, quite undeservedly, in debtors' prison, because of his failure to pay for the paper that was used in this publication. Kingsborough belongs to history, but his history scarcely belongs to him.

96. Kirchhoff, "Mesoamerica," *Acta Americana,* vol. 1 (1943).

97. Kitto, H. D. F., *The Greeks.* Harmondsworth, England, 1951.

98. Knorosow, Yuri, USSR Academy of Sciences, Moscow, 1955.
    A brief summary of the studies done in the Soviet Union on the ancient Maya hieroglyphic writing.

99. Kubler, George, "The Quechua in the Colonial World," in Steward (ed.), *Handbook of South American Indians,* vol. 2.

100. Landa, Diego de, *Relación de las Cosas de Yucatán,* ed. with notes by Alfred M. Tozzer. Papers of the Peabody Museum of American Archaeology and Ethnology, vol. XVIII. Cambridge, Mass., 1941.
Landa wrote his *Relación* in Spain in 1566, and took the manuscript back to Yucatán in 1573. After his death the work was kept in the convent at Mérida. It was first published by Brasseur de Bourbourg (Paris, 1864). There were later editions by Jean Genêt and William Gates. Alfred M. Tozzer's is the sixth edition and the most authoritative to date.

101. Larco Hoyle, Rafael, "La Escritura Peruana Sobre Pallares," *Revista Geográfica Americana,* Año 11, vol. 20, nos. 122–3 (1943), 93–103.

102. Lata, Jesús, *La Poesía Quechua.* La Paz, 1949.

103. Lehmann, Walter, *Zentral-Amerika,* 2 vols. Berlin, 1920.
Lehmann's work on Maya-Mexican languages has never been supplanted.

104. León Portilla, Miguel, *La Filosofía Nahuatl.* Mexico, 1956.
An unusually profound and thoroughly documented work using the remains of the Aztec literature to suggest the complex Aztec interest in the world about him. The selection of the material, its elucidation through actual Aztec texts, provides another aspect of Aztec life, otherwise missing in the literature about them.

105. L'Éstrange, Hamon, *Americans no Iewes . . .* London, 1652.

106. Lévy-Bruhl, Lucien, *Primitives and the Supernatural,* trans. by Lilian A. Clare. New York, 1935.

107. Linné, Sigvald, *Archaeological Researches at Teotihuacán, Mexico.* New York and London, 1934.

108. Locke, L. Leland, *The Ancient Quipu or Peruvian Knot Record.* New York, 1923.

109. López de Gómara, Francisco; *Crónica de la Nueva-España, con la Conquista de Mexica . . . hechos por el valeroso Hernando Cortés, Marqués del Valle.* Zaragoza, 1552.

110. Lothrop, Samuel K., *Inca Treasure as Depicted by Spanish Historians.* Los Angeles, 1938.

111. ———, *Metals from the Cenote of Sacrifice: Chichen Itza, Yucatan.* Memoirs of the Peabody Museum of American Archaeology and Ethnology, vol. X, no. 2. Cambridge, Mass., 1952.
This study, done by *the* expert on indigenous American goldwork, is the belated report on Thompson's dredgings.

112. ———, "South America as Seen from Middle America," in *The Maya and Their Neighbors.*

113. ———, *Tulum, an Archaeological Study of the East Coast of Yucatan.* Carnegie Institution of Washington, Pub. 335. Washington, D. C., 1924.

114. Madariaga, Salvador de, *Hernán Cortés, Conqueror of Mexico.* New York, 1941.

115. Maler, Teobert, *Researches in the Central Portion of the Usumatsintla Valley* . . . Memoirs of the Peabody Museum of American Archaeology and Ethnology, vol. II, no. 2. Cambridge, Mass., 1901.

116. Mangelsdorf, Paul, *Races of Maize in Mexico.* Cambridge, 1956.

117. ———, and Reeves, Robert G., *The Origin of Indian Corn and Its Relatives.* Texas Agricultural Experiment Station, Bulletin 574. College Station, Texas, 1939.

118. Markham, Sir Clements R., *Cuzco: A Journey to the Ancient Capital of Peru; and Lima: A Visit to the Capital and Province of Modern Peru.* London, 1856.

119. Marquina, Ignacio, *Arquitectura Prehispánica.* Mexico, 1951.

120. Martinez, Perez (ed.), *Información de Servicios y Meterios de Gerónimo de Aguilar* . . . Archivos de las Indies. Mexico, 1938.

121. Mason, John Alden, "Native Languages of Middle America," in *The Maya and Their Neighbors.*

122. Maudslay, Anne Cary and A. P., *A Glimpse at Guatemala.* London, 1899.

123. *The Maya and Their Neighbors.* New York, 1941.

124. Means, Philip Ainsworth, *Ancient Civilizations of the Andes.* New York, 1931.

125. ———, *Fall of the Inca Empire and the Spanish Rule in Peru: 1530–1780.* New York, 1932.

126. ———, *History of the Spanish Conquest of Yucatán and of the Itzás.* Papers of the Peabody Museum of American Archaeology and Ethnology, vol. VII. Cambridge, Mass., 1917.
This study gives full details of the final throes of the Itzá-Maya struggle.

127. ———, "Pre-Spanish Navigation on the Andean Coast," *American Neptune,* vol. II, no. 2 (1942).

128. Monge, Carlos, *Acclimatization in the Andes,* trans. by Donald F. Brown. Baltimore, 1948.

129. Morison, S. E., *Admiral of the Ocean Sea.* Boston, 1942.

130. Morley, Sylvanus G., *The Ancient Maya.* Palo Alto, Calif., 1946.

131. ———, *Guide Book to the Ruins of Quirigua.* Carnegie Institution of Washington, Supplementary Pub. 16. Washington, D. C., 1935.

132. ———, *The Inscriptions at Copan.* Carnegie Institution of Washington, Pub. 219. Washington, D. C., 1920.

133. Morris, Earl H., Charlot, Jean, and Morris, A.A., *The Temple of the Warriors at Chichén Itzá, Yucatán.* Carnegie Institution of Washington, Pub. 406. Washington, D. C., 1931.

134. Motolinía, Toribio de Benavente o, *Historia de los Indios de la Nueva España.* Barcelona, 1914.
     Written in the sixteenth century.

135. ———, *Vocabulario.* Mexico, 1555.

136. Neugebauer, O. "Ancient Mathematics and Astronomy," in Singer, et al. (eds.), *A History of Technology,* vol. 1.

137. Noguera, Eduardo, *Cerámica de México.* Mexico, 1932.

138. Nordenskiöld, Baron Erland, *The Secret of the Peruvian Quipus.* Comparative Ethnographical Studies, no. 6. Göteborg, 1925.

139. Nuttall, Zelia (trans. and ed.), *Codex Magliabecchi: The Book of Life of the Ancient Mexicans, Containing an Account of Their Rites and Superstitions.* Berkeley, Calif., 1903.

140. Osborne, Harold, *Indians of the Andes: Aymaras and Quechuas.* London and Cambridge, Mass., 1952.

141. Paulsson, Gregor, *The Study of Cities.* Copenhagen, 1959.

142. Pizarro, Pedro, *Relacion del Descubrimiento y Conquista de los Reinos del Perú* (written in 1570–1) in Col. Docs. ineds. Historia de Espana, vol. V: 201–388, Madrid, 1844.

143. ———, *Relation of the Discovery and Conquest of the Kingdoms of Perú,* trans. and ed. by P. A. Means, 2 vols. Cortez Society, New York, 1921.

144. Poma de Ayala, Felipe Guamán, *Nueva Cronica y Buen Gobierno.* Paris, 1936.

145. *Popol Vuh: The Sacred Book of the Ancient Quiché Maya,* ed. by Delia Goetz and Sylvanus G. Morley. Norman, Okla., 1950.

146. Posnansky, Arthur, *Tihuanacu, the Cradle of American Man,* trans. by James F. Shearer. New York, 1945–57.

147. Prescott, William H., *History of the Conquest of Mexico.* New York, 1843.
     This work has withstood a century of siege, from all quarters. It still remains, since Prescott worked from original sources and knew how to thread his way between fact and fiction, the best over-all history of the Conquest of Mexico. New material has altered it, new evidence and discoveries have augmented it, but it remains the master work.

148. ———, *History of the Conquest of Peru.* New York, 1847.

149. Proskouriakoff, T. A., *An Album of Maya Architecture.* Carnegie Institution of Washington, Pub. 558. Washington, D. C., 1946.

150. ———, "The Death of a Civilization," *Scientific Monthly* (December, 1946), 82–7.

151. ———, *A Study of Classic Maya Sculpture.* Carnegie Institution of Washington, Pub. 593. Washington, D. C., 1950.

152. Redfield, Robert, *The Folk Culture of Yucatan.* Chicago, 1941.

153. ———, and Villa, A., *Chan Kom, a Maya Village.* Carnegie Institution of Washington, Pub. 448. Washington, D. C., 1934.

154. Ricketson, O. G., Jr., *Uaxactun, Guatemala.* Carnegie Institution of Washington, Pub. 477. Washington, D. C., 1937.

155. Rowe, John H., "Inca Culture at the Time of the Spanish Conquest," in Steward (ed.), *Handbook of South American Indians,* vol. 2.

156. ———, *An Introduction to the Archaeology of Cuzco.* Papers of the Peabody Museum of American Archaeology and Ethnology, vol. XXVII, no. 2. Cambridge, Mass., 1944.

157. Roys, R. L., *The Ethno-botany of the Maya.* Middle American Research Series of Tulane University, Pub. 2. New Orleans, 1931.

158. ———, *The Indian Background of Colonial Yucatan.* Carnegie Institution of Washington, Pub. 548. Washington, D. C., 1943.

159. Ruppert, K., *The Caracol at Chichen Itza, Yucatan, Mexico.* Carnegie Institution of Washington, Pub. 454. Washington, D. C., 1935.

160. ———, Thompson, J. E. S., and Proskouriakoff, R., *Bonampak, Chiapas, Mexicao.* Carnegie Institution of Washington, Pub. 602. Washington, D. C., 1955.

161. Ruz Lhuillier, Alberto, "The Mystery of the Temple of the Inscriptions," *Archaeology,* vol. 6 (March, 1953), 3–11.

162. Sahagún, Bernardino de, *A History of Ancient Mexico,* trans. by Fanny R. Bandelier. Nashville, Tenn., 1932.
Sahagún came early to Mexico (1595) while the Aztec traditions were still alive. The work is wonderfully detailed (there are accompanying illustrations which do not appear in all the publications) and it is an honest attempt at reportage. The edition in English was prepared by Fanny Bandelier, the widow of Adolph Bandelier, one of the pioneers in American Indian studies.

163. ———, *Historia General de las Cosas de Nueva España,* 3 vols. Mexico, 1938.

164. Salaman, Redcliffe N., *The History and Social Influence of the Potato.* Cambridge, England, 1949.

165. Sansevero, Raimondo di Saugro, *Lettera Apologetica* . . . Naples, 1750.

166. Sapper, Karl Theodor, *Das Nördliche Mittel-Amerika.* Braunschweig, 1897.

167. Sarmiento de Gamboa, Pedro, *History of the Incas,* trans. and ed. by Sir Clements Markham. Cambridge, England, 1907.

168. Satterthwaite, Linton, Jr., "Thrones at Piedras Negras," *University Museum Bulletin* (University of Pennsylvania), vol. VII, no. 1 (1937), 18–23.

169. Sauer, Carl O., "Cultivated Plants of South and Central America," in Steward (ed.), *Handbook of South American Indians,* vol. 6.

170. Saville, Marshall H., *Bibliographic Notes on Palenque, Chiapas.* Indian Notes and Monographs of the Museum of the American Indian, Heye Foundation, vol. VI, no. 5. New York, 1928.

171. ————, *Tizoc, Great Lord of the Aztecs, 1481–1486.* Museum of the American Indian, Contributions from the Heye Museum, vol. 7. New York, 1929.

172. Seler, Eduard, *Antiquities of Guatemala.* Bureau of American Ethnology, Bulletin 28, vol. III. Washington, D. C., 1904.
One of many important contributions.

173. Seton, Lloyd, "Building in Stone and Brick," in Singer, et al. (eds.) *A History of Technology,* vol. 1.

174. Shepard, Anna Osler, *Ceramics for the Archaeologist.* Carnegie Institution of Washington, Pub. 609. Washington, D. C., 1956.

175. Singer, Charles, Holonyard, E. J., and Hall, A. R. (eds.), *A History of Technology,* vols. 1, 3. New York and London, 1954, 1957.
Volume 1 of this work is a magnificent encyclopedic volume (827 pages) providing students of technology, science, and archaeology with some human and historical background for studies of preliterate societies. A pioneer work, each part written by a specialist in its field, this volume deals mostly with the Near East and the civilizations around the Fertile Crescent. It seldom enters the American area, and when it does, it is usually wrong, e.g., the Chimú culture of Peru is dated 1200 B.C. (actually A.D. 1000) on p. 731; its information on Peru's roads is hopelessly entangled.

176. Smith, A. Ledyard, *Archaeological Reconnaissance in Central Guatemala.* Carnegie Institution of Washington, Pub. 608. Washington, D. C., 1955.

177. Smith, R. E., *Ceramics of Uaxactun: A Preliminary Analysis.* Guatemala, 1936.

178. Sorensen, John L., "Some Mesoamerican Traditions of Immigration," *El México Antiguo,* vol. VIII (1955), 425–39.

179. Soustelle, Jacques, "La Culture Matérielle des Indiens Lacandons," *Journal de la Société des Américanistes,* N.S., vol. XXIX (1937), 1–95.

180. ————, "Notes sur les Lacandon du Lac Peljá et du Río Jetjá Chiapas)," *Journal de la Société des Américanistes,* N.S., vol. XXV (1933), 153–80.

181. ————, "Le Totemisme des Lacandons," *Maya Research,* vol. II (1935), 325–44.

182. ————, *La Vida Cotidiana de los Aztecas.* Mexico, 1955. *La Vie Quotidienne des Aztèques à la Veille de la Conquête Espagnole.* Paris, 1955.
Pre-Conquest and later post-Conquest reportorial drawings of the Aztecs tell their

own story. Written by a Frenchman, very expert in his field, with a new presentation, the book is available in French and Spanish, not yet in English.

183. Spengler, Oswald, *The Decline of the West*, 2 vols., trans. by Charles F. Atkinson. New York, 1927–28.

184. Spinden, H. J., *A Study of Maya Art*. Memoirs of the Peabody Museum of American Archaeology and Ethnology, vol. VI. Cambridge, Mass., 1913.

185. Squier, E. George, *Peru: Incidents of Travel and Exploration in the Land of the Incas*. New York, 1877.

186. Stephens, John Lloyd, *Incidents of Travel in Central America, Chiapas, and Yucatan*, 2 vols. New York, 1841.
    This work is to all intents and purposes the first recording of the discovery of the great extent of the Mayas. With its accurate yet dramatic drawings by Frederick Catherwood, it was a pioneering work. A reprint is now available (1 vol., ed. by Richard L. Predmore, New Brunswick, N. J., 1949) and a two-volume edition is shortly to appear (ed. with notes by von Hagen, Norman, Okla.).
      See also: von Hagen, *Maya Explorer* and *Frederick Catherwood, Architect*.

187. Steward, Julian H. (ed.), *Handbook of South American Indians*, 6 vols. Washington, D. C., 1946–50.

188. Stirling, Matthew W., "La Venta" in *An Initial Series from Tres Zapotes, Vera Cruz, Mexico*. Contributed Technical Papers of the National Geographic Society, Mexican Archaeology Series, vol. 1, no. 1. Washington, D. C., 1940.

189. Tapia, Andres de, *Relación hecha por Andres de Tapia sobre la Conquista de México*. Colección de Documentos para la Historia de México, vol. 11. Mexico, 1866.

190. Teeple, J. E., *Maya Astronomy*. Contributions to American Archaeology, vol. I, no. 2, Carnegie Institution of Washington, Pub. 403. Washington, D. C. 1937.

191. *Tenayuca Official Guide*. Mexico, n.d.

192. Thompson, J. Eric S., *Maya Hieroglyphic Writing*. Carnegie Institution of Washington, Pub. 589. Washington, D. C., 1950.

193. ———, *Mexico Before Cortez*. New York, 1933.

194. ———, *The Rise and Fall of Maya Civilization*. Norman, Okla., 1954.

195. ———, Pollock, H. E. D., and Charlot, Jean, *A Preliminary Study of the Ruins of Cobá* ... Carnegie Institution of Washington, Pub. 424. Washington, D. C., 1932.

196. Torquemada, Juan de, *Los Veinte y un Libros Rituales y Monarquia Indiana*, 3 vols. Madrid, 1723.

197. Uhle, Max, *Las Ruinas de Tomebamba*. Quito, 1923.

198. Vaillant, George C., *The Aztecs of Mexico*. New York, 1941.
     One of the first archaeological histories of the Aztec, and still the most complete. It was written by the best-grounded of all the present-day scholars and although written for the general reader, it suggests the method of Vaillant's thinking.

199. Valcárel, Luis E., "The Andean Calendar," in Steward (ed.), *Handbook of South American Indians*, vol. 2.

200. Villa Rojas, Alfonso, *The Yaxuna-Cobá Causeway*. Carnegie Institution of Washington, Pub. 436. Washington, D. C., 1934.

201. Violich, Francis, *Cities of Latin America*. New York, 1944.

202. Volney, Constantin, *Les Ruines: ou Méditation sur les Révolutions des Empires*. Paris, 1791.
     There is an edition in English of *The Ruins* which was prepared by Count Volney himself. Although the book is rhapsodic and, as archaeology, inaccurate, still it had great influence in France, England, and the United States. It provided at this early date (1791) much stimulus toward interest in man's past.

203. von Hagen, Victor Wolfgang, *The Aztec and Maya Papermakers*. New York, 1943.
     There are three editions of this work, the first book on the subject. The 1943 edition was limited to 220 copies and contained actual samples of bark paper. Another edition published the following year from the same type has been better proofread, but lacks the paper samples. A superb edition, limited to 750 copies, was issued in Mexico (*La Fabricación del Papel entre los Aztecas y los Mayas*, 1945).
         See also: von Hagen, "Mexican Papermaking Plants" and "Paper and Civilization."

204. ———, *The Four Seasons of Manuela*. New York, 1952.

205. ———, "Francisco Hernández: Naturalist, 1515–1578," *Scientific Monthly*, vol. 58 (May, 1944), 383–5.

206. ———, *Frederick Catherwood, Architect*. New York, 1950.

207. ———, *Guide to Machu Picchu*. New York, 1945.

208. ———, *A Guide to Sacsahuaman, the Fortress of Cusco*. New York, 1949.

209. ———, *Highway of the Sun*. New York, 1955.

210. ———, *The Jicaque Indians of Honduras*. Indian Notes and Monographs of the Museum of the American Indian, Heye Foundation, Misc. no. 53. New York, 1943.

211. ———, *Jungle in the Clouds*. New York, 1940.

212. ———, *Maya Explorer: John Lloyd Stephens and the Lost Cities of Central America and Yucatán*. Norman, Okla., 1947.

213. ———, "Mexican Papermaking Plants," *Journal of the New York Botanical Gardens*, vol. 44, 1943.

214. ———, "Paper and Civilization," *Scientific Monthly*, vol. 57 (October, 1943), 301–14.

215. ———, "The Search for the Gilded Man," *Natural History*, vol. 61 (September, 1952), 312–21.

216. ———, *South America Called Them: Explorations of the Great Naturalists: La Condamine, Humboldt, Darwin, Spruce.* New York, 1945.

217. ———, *The Tsátchela Indians of Western Ecuador.* Indian Notes and Monographs of the Museum of the American Indian, Misc. no. 51. New York, 1939.

218. ———, "Waldeck," *Natural History*, vol. 55 (December, 1946), 450–6.

219. Wagner, Henry R., *The Rise of Fernando Cortés.* Berkeley, Calif., 1944.

220. Waldeck, J. F. de, *Voyage Pittoresque et Archéologue, dans la Province d'Yucatán* . . . Paris, 1838.
That which Humboldt put forward, Waldeck retarded. Humboldt compiled evidence as to the American origin of the Indian; Waldeck, a brilliant draftsman, falsified Maya figures and hieroglyphics and gave "substance" to the vague theory of the Jewish origin of the American Indian. His title of "Count" was bogus, his personal history in great part an invention. We know that he lived in Paris, managed a silver mine at Tlalpujahna and painted backdrops for the stage in Mexico, traveled in Yucatán and visited Palenque. The book is beautiful, facile, and contrived.
For critical appraisal of Waldeck, see also: von Hagen, "Waldeck"; and Cline, "The Apocryphal Early Career of J. F. de Waldeck."

221. Wauchope, Robert, *House Mounds of Uaxactun, Guatemala.* Carnegie Institution of Washington, Pub. 436. Washington, D. C., 1934.

222. ———, *Modern Maya Houses.* Carnegie Institution of Washington, Pub. 502. Washington, D. C., 1938.

223. Xerez, Francisco de, *Verdadera relacion de la conquista del Peru,* Seville, 1534.
(There is an English translation by Sir Clements Markham. Pub. by the Hakluyt Society, London, 1872.)

224. Zeuner, F. E., "Cultivation of Plants," in Singer, et al. (eds.), *A History of Technology,* vol 1.

Europe and North America	AZTEC	MAYA	INCA
c. 2000 B.C. *Greeks active in Troy.*	c. 2000 B.C. "Tepexpan Man" valley of Mexico; bones associated with mammoth elephants.	c. 2000 B.C. Proto-Maya. Widely scattered settlements of people of Maya speech.	c. 2500 B.C. Coastal Indians at Chicama engaged in agriculture.
		c. 2000 B.C. Huastecs, a tribe of Maya speech separated from main body of Maya. They carry on different form of culture, about Rio Panico in Tampico, but retain related Maya speech and physical characteristics.	
850 B.C. *Age of Homer.* 776 B.C. *First Olympiad held in Greece.* 753 B.C. *Legendary founding of Rome.*	800 B.C.–A.D. c. 600 Olmecs. La Venta culture in Mexico hotlands.	2000–500 B.C. *Mamom* ("Grandmother") stage of Maya development. Early pottery, strictly utilitarian, widely scattered. Figurines molded by hand.	1200–400 B.C. Chavín de Huantar culture, central Andes. 750 B.C. Coastal cultures: Virú, Cupisnique, Gallinazo. Formative period in many Peruvian coastal cultures.
	500 B.C.–A.D. 1469 Monte Albán. Large stone temple-city in Oaxaca. Goes through five stages of culture and growth over two-thousand-year period.		
431–404 B.C. *Peloponnesian Wars.* 331 B.C. *Alexander the Great defeats Darius at Arbela.*	c. 500 B.C. The formative period of many highland and lowland cultures: Teotihaucán, Olmec, Huastec, Monte Albán, early Totonac. c. 500 B.C. *Tlachtli* (a form of basketball) invented by Olmecs. *Tlachtli* spreads to tribes from Arizona to Nicaragua.	500 B.C. – A.D. 300 *Chichanel* ("Concealer"). Transitional period in Maya culture. Polychromic pottery appears; human form is painted realistically. Pottery is often glyph dated.	400 B.C. – A.D. 400 Paracas (Caverna) I. Peru, south coast on dry shores of Paracas Peninsula (Pisco). 400 B.C. – A.D. 1000 Nazca, south coastal culture.
c. 240 B.C. *Eratosthenes computes the size of the earth.*			272 B.C. Carbon-14-dated appearance of Mochica culture.

272 B.C. – A.D. 1000 Mochica coastal empire.

200 B.C. First evidence of Toltec culture in the valley of Anáhuac.

c. 200 B.C. Dzibichaltún in northern Yucatán functioning as city. Endures to A.D. 1500.

146 B.C. *Romans capture and destroy Carthage.*

44 B.C. *Assassination of Julius Caesar.*

31 B.C. First known dated Olmec monument. Inventors of glyph writing, which spreads throughout Mexico and Maya country.

A.D. 79 *Volcanic Destruction of Herculaneum and Pompeii.*

c. A.D. 100 Sun Temple at Teotihuacán is built (Chimalhuacan phase).

c. 117 *Roman Empire at its greatest extent.*

c. A.D. 150 Maya ceremonial centers spring up in various regions.

162 The Tuxtla jade piece. The earliest known authentically dated Maya inscription.

c. 200 Monte Albán (Period 1) in Oaxaca.

235 *Disintegration of Roman Empire.*

337 *Death of Constantine.*

317–650 *Tzakol* ("The Builders"). Maya classical period. The rise and florescence of the great Maya ceremonial centers and temple-cities. Dated monuments (the stelae cult) and the culture of cities. Uaxactún (328), Cobá (361), Tikal (416), Chichén Itzá (432), Copán (460), and Tulum (564) founded.

400–800 *The Mound Builders: Wisconsin to Gulf of Mexico.*

c. 400 Monte Albán rebuilt, extended (Zapotec period).

A.D. 400–800 Paracas (Necropolis) II.

400–1000 Tiahuanaco Empire (Andean).

410 *Alaric sacks Rome.*

500 *Pueblo Indian culture begins in Utah, Colorado, Arizona.*

510 Toltecs, under "king" Chalciuh Tlanetzin begin to build temples of the Sun and Moon at Teotihuacán.

529 *Publication of the Justinian Code.*

Europe and North America	AZTEC	MAYA	INCA
632 Death of Mohammed.		642 Palenque, in Chiapis, is built in a rain forest.	700 Gate of the Sun, Tiahuanaco, carved. Erected from a single piece of immense stone. The symbol of the "Weeping God" influences much of latter-day Peruvian fabric and ceramic motifs.
		765 Copán holds "astronomical congress" to adjust Maya calendar.	
	770 Teotihuacán Period II. Mitl-Tlacomihua, chief of Toltecs, builds temple to Quetzalcoatl.		
800 Imperial Coronation of Charlemagne at Rome.		800 The murals of Bonampak (founded 540) are painted.	800 Huari–Tiahuanaco. An offshoot of the ceremonial center about Lake Titicaca. Province of Huanta near to Ayacucho, 8,000 feet altitude.
		879 Kabah founded. Triumphal arch now restored.	
871–899 Alfred, king of Wessex and of England.		889 The Maya cities of Uaxactún, Xultun, and Xamantun erect dated stelae; last dated monuments.	
	c. 890 Great drought. Period of decline of Teotihuacán.	890 First American book. Mayas produce a 72-page illustrated book (The Dresden Codex), a copy of an earlier document.	
900 Golden Age of Arabian power in Spain.	900 Xochicalco, a temple-city (south of Cuernavaca), built by the Toltecs. Tula, new center of Toltecs, is built.		900 Chanapata period in Cuzco. Pre-Inca occupation of valley of Cuzco.
	967 Ce Acatl Topiltzin takes name of the god Quetzalcoatl, rules Tula for 20 years.	987 Chichén Itzá refounded. Occupied by Maya-Itzás and Quetzalcoatl with Toltec warriors.	
c. 985 Vikings settle Greenland.	987 Quetzalcoatl, exiled from Tula, moves southwest toward Yucatán with large body of warriors.	987 Maya renaissance: Uxmal and Mayapán founded; League of Mayapán begun.	
		1000 Tepeuh ("Conqueror") period ends. Interior cities of Mayas culturally dead. All Maya activity now concentrated in Yucatán and adjacent territories.	1000 Tiahuanaco Empire, either from regions about Titicaca or Huari, sweeps down upon the coast in religio-military conquest.
1066–87 William I (the conqueror), king of England.			

| | 1156 Tula destroyed by Chichimecs. Another migration of Toltecs results. They settle at Xicalango. | | c. 1100 Cuzco founded by legendary historical figure of Manco Capac. First Lord-Inca. |

1189–92 *Third Crusade, Frederick Barbarossa, Richard the Lion-Hearted, and Philip II.*

1168 Aztec history begins. Migratory tribes enter valley of Anáhuac.

1194 Cocoms headed by Huanc Ceel, expel other Mayas from Chichén Itzá with aid of Toltec mercenaries. Mayapán becomes dominant capital from 1200–1441.

1227 *Death of Genghis Khan.*

1275 *Five-year drought in American Southwest. Raid by Navaho brings end to Cliff Dweller culture.*

1250 Aztecs, called Tenochas, living in area about Chapultepec close to Lake Texcoco.

1250 Mayas spread into Mexico. Their canoes trade from Tampico to Panama. Age of metals, gold, copper, silver.

1250 Ica culture in and about Cuzco Valley.

1300 Cocoms and Tutul Xius jointly ruling Mayapán compel all local chieftains to reside in the capital of Mayapán.

1300–1400 Period of Maya trade expansion. Seagoing canoes sail southward to Nicaragua, Panama.

Gold, silver, copper appear in Maya culture.

1300 Tiahuanaco coast invasion collapses. Many other cultures spring out of its ruin. Chimú, Mochic-speaking people as were the Mochicas, rise and form an immense empire; rivals of Incas.

c. 1325 Aztecs occupy two islets in Lake Texcoco. Tenochtitlán, "Place of the Tenocha," is founded.

1347 *Black Death spreads through Europe.*

1386 *Chaucer composes the Canterbury Tales.*

1375 Acamapichtli, first historical "king," or Chief Speaker, of the Tenochas.

1350 Incas begin expansion. Inca Roca, 6th Inca, builds bridge across the Apurimac. Quechua becomes official language.

1395 Huitzilhuitl, second in line, begins to enlarge his capital.

1390 Chimú, kingdom of Chimor, rules 600 miles of land, completes capital Chan-Chan.

1400 Mayas expand trade with Mexico through trading center of Xicalango located in Laguna de Términos "the land where the language changes."

1415 *Henry V defeats French at Agincourt.*

1414 Chimalpopoca elected Chief Speaker by the noble *tlatoani,* the electors of Aztec rulers.

1431 *Joan of Arc burned at the stake.*

1428 Izcoatl, born a slave, rises to leadership. Tenochas assume Aztec

(1428) civilization. Izcoatl orders all previous historical picture paintings to be destroyed. Begins systematic wars on all neighboring tribes.

1440 Moctezuma I elected Chief Speaker.

1441–56 Drought. Crop failures, snow, frost.

1450–55 The Gutenberg Bible.

1453 Fall of Constantinople.

1441 Fall of Mayapán. Tutul Xiu clan murder leaders of their rivals the Cocoms. First and only known central capital of the Mayas disintegrates. Itzás make mass migration to El Petén, set up independent kingdom.

1437 Viracocha, 8th Inca. Cuzco is besieged by Chanca tribe.

1438 Inca troops under Yupanqui, son of Viracocha, defeat Chancas. Proclaimed 9th Inca, he takes name of Pachacuti.

1450 Chimú influence felt from Lima to Tumbes.

1450 Pachacuti enlarges Inca Empire by series of local wars.

1463 Pachacuti directs war of extermination against Lupaca and Colla tribes centered about Lake Titicaca in the ruins of Tiahuanaco Empire.

1469 Union of ruling houses of Castile and Aragon through marriage of Ferdinand and Isabella.

1469 Axayacatl succeeds his father Moctezuma I. Extends conquest to Isthmus of Tehuantepec. Campaigns into Tarascan territory, suffers sharp defeat.

1481 Tizoc succeeds his brother Axayacatl. Begins construction of great temple to Huitzilopochtli, the Aztec War God.

1467 Great hurricane. Destroys cities, houses, people.

1466 Chimú Empire is overrun by troops of Incas. Incas control all of Peru.

1471 Topa Inca, 10th Lord-Inca. State reorganized. Era of road-building.

1480 Inca army under Topa Inca builds roads leading into Chile, preparatory to Conquest.

1483 Richard III, last of Plantagenet kings of England, begins reign.

1482 Pestilence (yellow fever) decimates cities of the Mayas. Abandonment of whole areas.

1485 Topa Inca is supposed to have marshaled a fleet of balsa rafts and sailed to the Galápagos Islands. (No scientific collaboration.) '

1481 Great sacrificial stone carved. Calendar stone set up. Recovered in 1790.

1492 Columbus discovers America.

1486 Ahuitzotl succeeds his brother Tizoc. Dedicates temple to Huitzilopochtli by immolating 20,000 sacrificial victims. Extends conquests down into Pacific side of Guatemala. *Pochteca* merchants in Honduras, Nicaragua.

1492 Topa Inca conquers all of Chile to the Maule River. Establishes Inca fortress called Purumaucu.

1493 Huayna Capac, 11th Lord-Inca. Completes coastal road from Chile to Tumbes.

605

1497 North America discovered by John Cabot.

1498 Columbus discovers mainland of South America.

1498 Huayna Capac extends conquest beyond Quito into Colombia. Completes Andean highway, Quito to Talca (Chili), 3,250 miles.

1500 Birth of Benvenuto Cellini.

1503 Moctezuma II, grandson of other of same name, elected Chief Speaker.

1507 New Fire ceremony. Columbus' presence in 1503 reported. Priests believe end of world is near.

1502 Christopher Columbus on his fourth voyage makes first European contact with Mayas at Guanaja, one of Bay Islands off Honduras.

1500 Huayna Capac undertakes final conquest of Chachapoyas.

1513 Juan Ponce de León discovers Florida.

1511 Gerónimo de Aguilar and Gonzalo Guerrero are captured on Cozumel Island, kept as slaves.

1513 Vasco Nuñez de Balboa discovers the Pacific. The Incas become aware of white man's presence in South America.

1518 Juan de Grijalva explores coast with flotilla of ships. Discovers all the coastal towns including Tulum.

1519 Magellan begins circumnavigation of the globe.

1519 Cortés enters Tenochtitlán. Captures Moctezuma.

1520 Moctezuma stoned and killed by own people.

1520 Cuitlahuac is made Leader, dies in melee as Spaniards fight their way out of Tenochtitlán.

1521 Cuauhtémoc is named last Chief Speaker. Defends Mexico against Cortés. Tenochtitlán falls to conquistadors.

1519 Hernándo Cortés arrives at Cozumel. Sails to Vera Cruz and thence to Mexico.

1519 Atahualpa (age 19) destined to be last Inca, takes part in military campaigns.

1522 Pascal de Andogoya on an expedition of small ships down toward Darien is made aware of the Kingdom of Gold (Peru).

1524 Cortés marches through Tabasco, Campeche, into El Petén in order to subdue an unau-

1524 Cortés marches through El Petén.

1525 Alejo Garcia, leading an attack of Chiriguanos on an Inca

(1524) thorized Spanish colony in Honduras.

1525 Cuauhtémoc taken as hostage. He is hanged in the Maya province of Acalán.

1525 End of Aztec Empire.

(1525) outpost in the Gran Chaco, is killed. Incas are made aware of "white men."

1527 Francisco de Montejo arrives in Yucatán. Occupies walled city of Xelha and Tulum.

1527 Francisco Pizarro makes first landing.

1527 Death of Huayna Capac.

1527 Civil war between Huáscar, crowned 12th Inca, and Atahualpa, who dominates the north. Huáscar defeated in 1532.

1529 First siege of Vienna by the Turks.

1532 (May 13) Francisco Pizarro returns to Tumbes.

1532 (Nov. 16) Atahualpa captured by Pizarro in Cajamarca, held captive, agrees to ransom himself.

1533 (Aug. 29) His ransom completed, Atahualpa is executed for crimes against the Spaniards.

1534 Church of England established.

1535 Montejo defeated by the Mayas, sails to the south. Not a single white man remains in Yucatán.

1535 Inca Empire completely subjugated. Manco II crowned "Inca" by the Spaniards.

1536 Manco II leads revolt, Cuzco under siege.

1537 Siege of Cuzco lifted. Manco II retires with large force into sanctuary of Vilcapampa. Establishes Neo-Inca state.

1538 Civil war between conquistadors. Battle of Salinas. Almagro captured, executed.

1539–42 Hernando De Soto explores the Mississippi.

1541 Francisco Pizarro assassinated by men of Almagro.

Europe and North America	Aztec	Maya	Inca
		1542 Montejo the Younger renews conquest. Spaniards destroy inland town of Tiho, build their own capital of Mérida.	1542 Battle of Chupas between Almagro the Younger and royal Spanish forces. Almagro defeated.
			1542 "New Laws for the Indies" protects Indians. Spanish conquistadors revolt led by Gonzalo Pizarro.
1547 *Death of Henry VIII.*		1546 Maya rising against the Spaniards marks the end of resistance in Yucatán.	
			1548 La Gasca leading royal forces defeats Gonzalo Pizarro at battle of Sacsahuamán.
			1551 Antonio de Mendoza named first Viceroy to Peru.
1565 *Ivan the Terrible of Russia initiates reign of terror.*		1566 Diego de Landa finishes his "Account of the Things of Yucatán."	1553 Pedro de Cieza de León publishes (Seville) epoch-making *First Part of the Chronicles of Peru.*
1579 *Francis Drake explores California coast.*		1576 Diego García de Palacio discovers the ruins of Copán.	1572 End of the Neo-Inca state. Tupac Amaru executed.
1588 *Defeat of Spanish Armada.*			1595 Sir Walter Raleigh explores lower part of Orinoco River in search of El Dorado.
1620 *Plymouth Colony established in Massachusetts.*		1622 Failure of the first Spanish attempt to conquer the Itzá-Mayas living in El Petén.	1601 Garcilaso de la Vega, surnamed "The Inca," born in Cuzco of a Spanish father and an Inca princess, publishes *The Royal Commentaries of the Incas.*
1675–76 *King Philip's War in New England.*			1691 Father Fritz, after years of exploration, publishes the first detailed map of the Amazon River.
1680 *Pueblo revolt in Nuevo Mexico.*		1697 Martin de Ursua takes Tayasal, the Itzá-Maya capital, puts chiefs to death.	
1733 *Molasses Act stirs up English colonies.*		1697 End of Maya Empire.	1767 Jesuits expelled from all the Americas by order of Charles III of Spain.
1748 *Excavations at Pompeii begin.*			1780–1 Revolt of Andean Indians lead by José Gabriel Condorcanqui, styled Tupac Amaru II. Tupac Amaru II is defeated and executed.
1776 *Declaration of Independence by the Thirteen Colonies.*			1781 End of Inca Empire.

608

A Selection of Books
by Victor Wolfgang von Hagen

Exploration

Off with Their Heads	*Macmillan*	1937
Ecuador the Unknown	*Oxford University Press*	1938
Jungle in the Clouds	*Duell, Sloan & Pearce*	1940
Ecuador & the Galápagos Islands	*University of Oklahoma Press*	1956
Highway of the Sun	*Duell, Sloan & Pearce*	1956
The Royal Road of the Incas: a Pictorial History	*in preparation*	1962

Archaeology-Anthropology

The Tsatchela Indians of Western Ecuador	*Museum of the American Indian*	1939
The Jicaque Indians of Honduras	*Museum of the American Indian*	1942
The Maya & the Aztec Papermakers	*J. J. Augustín*	1943
The Realm of the Incas	*New American Library*	1957
The Aztec: Man & Tribe	*New American Library*	1958
The World of the Maya	*New American Library*	1960
The Ancient Sun Kingdoms of the Americas	*The World Publishing Company*	1961

Biography

South America Called Them (La Condamine, Humboldt, Darwin, Spruce)	*A. A. Knopf*	1943
Maya Explorer: The Life of John L. Stephens	*University of Oklahoma Press*	1947
Frederick Catherwood: Architect	*Oxford University Press*	1950
The Four Seasons of Manuela	*Duell, Sloan & Pearce*	1952

Editor

Maeterlinck: The Life of the White Ant	*Dodd, Mead & Company*	1939
Herman Melville's Las Encantadas, or The Enchanted Islands	*Grabhorn Press, San Francisco*	1939
South America: The Green World of the Naturalist (an anthology)	*Eyre & Spottiswoode*	1950
The Incas of Pedro de Cieza de León	*University of Oklahoma Press*	1959
Prescott's "Conquest of Peru" (abridged)	*New American Library*	1961
John Lloyd Stephens' "Incidents of Travel in Yucatán"	*University of Oklahoma Press*	1961
Prescott's "Conquest of Peru" 2 vols.	*University of Oklahoma Press*	1962

About the Author

VICTOR WOLFGANG VON HAGEN was born in St. Louis, Missouri, in 1908. Although he attended schools in the United States, England, and South America, his real education began with his first expedition to Mexico when he was twenty-three. Since then he has done his basic research—often over long periods of time—in the raw earth of the three Americas, in such far-ranging places as the Galápagos Islands, the Amazon, the rain forests of Central America. He has augmented his field work with research in the archives of the United States, England, France, Spain, Austria, and Peru. The result has been a series of books on Man in the Americas. He depicted the great naturalists in *South America Called Them;* his biographies of John Lloyd Stephens and Frederick Catherwood, all from original source material, revived interest in these pioneers of Maya archaeology. His biography of Pedro de Cieza de León, the great historian of the Peruvian Conquest, provided material about a man who had been a mystery for four hundred years. He draws upon his research in botany, zoology, geography, ethnology, and history to make primitive man understandable in the Americas. Since 1952, Victor von Hagen has devoted himself to the study of the Inca Highways, a work only partially told in *Highway of the Sun.* For this work, and for much of the work contained in his forty publications, he was decorated by Peru this year with its highest award, the "Orden al Merito." Now, after ten years in Peru his work on the Inca Highways is completed, and he leaves for Italy with his family to undertake an even greater task—a study of the Roman Highway system of the Imperial Caesars.

This book was set in Bulmer and Albertus

types by Graphic Services.

It was printed by Colorgraphic Offset Company

and bound at The Haddon Craftsmen.

Typography and design by Andor Braun

65 64 63 62 61 5 4 3 2 1